THE
SOCIAL IMPACT
OF
COMPUTERS

SECOND EDITION

The
Social Impact
of
Computers

SECOND EDITION

Richard S. Rosenberg

Associate Professor
Department of Computer Science
University of British Columbia
Vancouver, British Columbia

ACADEMIC PRESS, INC.

San Diego   London   Boston   New York   Sydney   Tokyo   Toronto

ACADEMIC PRESS
525 B. St. Suite 1900, San Diego, California 92101-4495, USA
1300 Boylston Street, Chestnut Hill, MA 02167, USA
http://www.apnet.com

Academic Press Limited
24–28 Oval Road, London NW1 7DX, UK
http://www.hbuk.co.uk/ap/

Library of Congress Cataloging-in-Publication Data

Rosenberg, Richard S.
    The social impact of computers / Richard S. Rosenberg.—2nd ed.
        p.   cm.
    Includes bibliographical references and index.
    ISBN 0-12-597131-1 (alk. paper)
    1. Computers—Social aspects.   I. Title.
QA76.9.C66R64   1997
303.48′34—dc21   97-8076
                                                                         CIP

Printed in the United States of America

97 98 99 00 01 IP 9 8 7 6 5 4 3 2 1

. . . But not because I am out of sympathy with their feelings about technology. I just think that their flight from and hatred of technology is self-defeating. The Buddah, the Godhead, resides quite as comfortably in the circuits of a digital computer or the gears of a cycle transmission as he does at the top of a mountain or in the petals of a flower.

In memory of my parents, Leibel and Malka, who planted the seed of social concern, helped it grow, but could not see it flower.

CONTENTS

3

CRITICISM AND HISTORY   55

4

THE BUSINESS WORLD   91

5

MEDICINE AND COMPUTERS   141

6

COMPUTERS AND EDUCATION   171

9

PRIVACY AND FREEDOM OF INFORMATION 273

10

EMPLOYMENT AND UNEMPLOYMENT 317

11

BUSINESS AND GOVERNMENT   367

12

THE INFORMATION SOCIETY   413

13

ETHICS AND PROFESSIONALISM   465

PREFACE

The first edition of this book was published in 1992. It contained two references to the Internet. One was the infamous INTERNET worm of Robert Morris; the other referred briefly to the uses of the Internet as a tool to facilitate research among geographically distant collaborators. That's all. It hardly seems possible that in the past few years, the Internet has literally become a household term and the World Wide Web is now commonly referred to on many television shows and just about everyone has a Web page.

In response to these technological innovations and for other reasons as well, a second edition was necessary and appropriate. The necessity arises from the need to respond to a host of social issues that have appeared suddenly and seem to require immediate attention. In addition to the Internet, there is the Information (Super) Highway, the National Information Infrastructure, the Clipper Chip, Netscape, Yahoo, Virtual Communities, MUDs, Cookies, Jake Baker, Kevin Mitnick (again), the Communications Decency Act, and more. New urgency has been attached to such concerns as privacy, free speech, security, risks, access to information, personal responsibility, and national interests. Though the treatment of these and other social issues is still basic and relevant, new domains of applications require a wider view and a more extended analysis. The Internet and the Web qualify as powerful and wide-ranging applications and their popularity certainly has created a wealth of opportunities accompanied by the social problems just mentioned.

The structure of this book is very similar to the previous edition, and although the number of chapters is one fewer, it is longer. The chapter on robots has been removed and some of the material folded into Chapter 10. Given the wealth of material to be covered, robotics and industrial automation seemed to require less space than in the first edition. Otherwise, the superficial resemblance between the two editions is misleading. Although much of the early history of computers and the discussion of the technological imperative remains, much more is new, especially the issues accompanying the Internet and the Web. It is difficult to imagine that a course using this book will not also require that students get on the Internet and explore the chaotic new world of online information.

The Appendix contains a long list of organizations that are concerned with many of the social issues addressed in the book. These can be accessed over the Internet and many provide extensive archives of information on privacy, freedom of speech, access, and government policies. Take advantage of these sources but remember that the sheer quantity of information available at Web sites is no substitute for careful choice, careful reading, and careful thought.

ACKNOWLEDGMENTS

Many people have helped in the writing of this book, either directly or indirectly: I therefore apologize in advance to anyone I may have omitted. Let me mention, in no particular order, Alan Mackworth, Ron Anderson, C. Dianne Martin, Mary Culnan, Marc Rotenberg, Colin Bennett, Joe Smith, Cal Deedman, Cynthia Alexander, Kelly Gotlieb, David Flaherty, Gale Arndt, Monika Silbermayr, Jean Forsythe, Sunnie Khuman, Deborah Wilson, Abbe Mowshowitz, Rob Kling, Robert Ellis Smith, Janlori Goldman, Arek Shakarian, Harriet Rosenberg, Richard Lee, Carol Whitehead, Tara Ehrcke, Daniel Poulin, David Jones, Jeff Shallit, Brian Fuller, Orvin Lau, Ian Cavén, Steven Page, Bradley Harrison, Allan Rempel, Elisa Baniassad, Paul Jubenvill, and Nou Dadoun. The comments of anonymous reviewers were welcome and helpful. I also acknowledge the many students at the University of British Columbia, who have asked many of the right questions.

Of course, I take sole responsibility for the final version of this book. Nothing would have been possible without the constant support and encouragement of my wife Sheryl and my children Rebecca, Hannah, and Aryeh, who scanned and scanned.

1

COMPUTERS ARE EVERYWHERE

The empires of the future are the empires of the mind.
Winston Churchill (1874–1965)[1]

INTRODUCTION

You are about to begin the study of how computers and associated technologies have affected and will continue to affect societies around the world. In the long history of technological innovation, the computer in some sense is no more notable than such major inventions as the steam engine, the train, electricity and electronics, the telegraph and the telephone, the automobile, the airplane, radio, motion pictures, and television. Yet there is something special about the computer that makes it more than just another machine. Its ability to be programmed to perform an incredible variety of tasks distinguishes it from all others.

The first electronic computers filled large rooms, weighed many tons, and generated vast quantities of heat. Now computers of equal or far greater power sit comfortably on the tops of desks. Within the last few years, electronics engineers, physicists, and computer specialists have produced powerful microprocessors that can slide easily through a paper clip. Such microprocessors are used in watches, cameras, microwave ovens, portable computers, automobiles, and assembly line robots. Other applications continue to appear at an ever accelerating rate. Computers are now commonplace in schools, offices, and the home. They generate our checks, our bills, and our receipts. They are used to store and retrieve enormous quantities of information for a wide variety of purposes. They underlie that worldwide network known as the Internet. Work and play are equally affected as the following examples show:

• In a front-page story in *The New York Times*, John Cardinal O'Connor is shown sitting next to a woman operating a portable computer:

New York–Give them that on-line religion. In a computerized session of give-and-take, John Cardinal O'Connor took his message today to one of the few forums he had yet to address during his tenure as Archbishop of New York: Cyberspace. The Cardinal fielded questions put to him by a nationwide audience of nearly 100 people who logged on to Prodigy, the computer information service, to solicit his opinion on topics from abortion and prayer to his opinion of New York and his favorite author. [2]

• Not to be outdone, New York's Temple Emanu-El advertised a new service (no pun intended). "It's the High Holidays, Can't Get to the Temple? Get to the Computer." In more detail:

It is unlikely that many Jewish worshippers among us will indeed sit in front of their screens, but that is close to what the World Wide Web site of New York's Temple Emanu-El has in mind. Over the weekend, for the holiday of Rosh ha-Shanah, the synagogue broadcast a taped audio portion of a service every half-hour over the Internet . . . This is, obviously, not quite what Jewish rabbinic law had in mind: not only would computer use be anathema to those strictly observing the holiday, but the solitary screen watcher would be also missing the explicitly communal nature of the prayers. What does the "we" refer to in the holy day's declarations of repentance when the word emerges from a pair of multimedia loudspeakers? [3]

• Reporting of the O. J. Simpson murder-trial-of-the-century saturated the media as the public's appetite seemed to be unbounded. It is not surprising, therefore, that additional sources of information soon became available:

The Internet and other computer-based on-line services are emerging as global repositories of trial news and trivia:

Is there a conspiracy in the news media to frame O. J.?

Does CNN offer gavel-to-gavel coverage of the trial for a businessman traveling in Europe? ("What's with you?" an unsympathetic reader responded. "C'mon, get a life!") [4]

• Technology changes but attitudes and traditions may not, as the following article demonstrates:

Phoenix, Aug. 27 (AP)–The parents of an 11-year-old black student have sued his school district for classroom use of a computer game in which players take on the role of enslaved Southern blacks trying to escape. In the game, called "Freedom!" players start off as illiterate and are referred to as "boy" as they try to gain the educational skills necessary to head to the North, said the Federal lawsuit filed by the parents, . . . [5]

• Computers have affected the work of historians and archivists as the following story reveals:

It seems like a simple idea: Make bureaucrats save their E-mail in case historians—or law enforcement officials—want to trace the background of some action. The hitch: Proposed new rules set to take effect next year [1995], allow federal agencies themselves to decide what will be saved and sent to the National Archives, the repository for all government records . . . Defenders of the rules note that they at least make deleting crucial E-mail illegal. [6]

• Pop music icons have their own Web page (to say nothing of millions of lesser fame) and the death of Grateful Dead leader Jerry Garcia produced a flood of condolence messages:

> The Dead Web, the interlocking Web pages dedicated to the Grateful Dead, was a very busy place last week. The speed at which Dead Web pages were transformed into memorials after the death of the band's leader, Jerry Garcia, is a testament to the passion of the Grateful Dead's fans, who call themselves Deadheads, and the ease with which World Wide Web pages can be kept current . . . An astonishing amount of detailed Grateful Dead material is available on the Web: Sites include annotated lyrics, movie clips of Mr. Garcia, digitized sound clips of unofficial recordings made at Grateful Dead concerts, and an exhaustive list of Grateful Dead concerts. [7]

• Computer access to the Web usually takes place at home, at work, or at school, but a growing number of public sites have installed computers to attract customers:

> Cyber geeks now have a place to meet for Internet access, sit in virtual reality pods, play video games, and slurp cappuccino—all under one roof. **Cybersmith**, a Boston-area retailer, has opened a 48-station electronic environment in Harvard Square. For 17.5 cents a minute, users can browse the Web, tap into on-line-services, sort through more than 100 CD-ROM titles, play video games, and morph their faces. Patrons also can order fresh-squeezed carrot juice ($1.75); foccacia ($2.00); or goat cheese, tomato, fresh basil, and olive oil on ficelle ($4.95) from Smitty's On-line Cafe, via the Internet, even though it's in the same room. [8]

• The Internet, long hailed as a bastion of free speech and anything goes, is frequently the target of aroused public and private critics, as the next two pieces illustrate:

> The battle over on-line pornography, which had been tilting toward free speech and free market forces, veered sharply in the other direction last week. An Internet porno ban is now likely to become law as part of the huge telecommunications reform package pending in Congress. A House committee kept in a Senate bill most of the provisions that would impose fines and prison sentences on those who knowingly transmit pornography viewed by children on the Internet. "There is no way [Internet service providers] can filter and investigate everything they are passing on," said Raymond H. Hoving, vice president for issues advocacy at the Society for Information Management. "This will put some of them out of business for liability reasons and hurt the ability to have electronic commerce." [9]

> In the most far-reaching example yet of Internet censorship, CompuServe Inc. has blocked access by its subscribers in the United States and around the world to more than 200 sexually explicit computer discussion groups and picture databases, after a federal prosecutor in Munich said the material violated German pornography laws. The action which CompuServe described as a temporary move while it studies its legal options, underscores the extent to which diverse national, cultural and political values are coming into conflict with the essentially borderless technology of the global Internet computer network. [10]

• The Atlanta Olympics of the summer of 1996 were advertised as the high-technology gateway to year 2000; assuming the major responsibility for the do-everything computer network was IBM. But there were some problems . . .

> From the beginning it looked like an impossible mission . . . The risk became a reality from the first moments of the Games, when one of the seven major systems that IBM created—one that was to have distributed sporting results to the major international news organizations—went haywire. There were frequent system crashes, agonizingly slow response times and missing, incomplete, delayed or even inaccurate results. [11]

• We might wish that our memories could be saved and made available to others after we have died. Well, technology once again may come to the rescue.

> Last week a team of BT [British Telecom] researchers announced plans to develop new technology that may offer, in a limited form, immortality. Conceived by BT's Artificial Life Program, the solution involves a yet to be fashioned generation of computer chips that will work inside the brain, saving memories to be transferred onto a computer. BT is investing $50 million in order to create, in the words of researcher Chris Winter, "immortality in the truest sense." [12]

• Is too much computer use a bad thing? Can we be online too much and thereby jeopardize direct human relationships? Not surprisingly, the answer is yes.

> What would you say about someone who spent 18 hours a day online? Not a research scientist, mind you, but a stay-at-home mom from Texas . . . Some experts estimate that 2 to 3 percent of the online community—about 200,000 of the estimated 8.6 million consumer users—have serious "Internet addictions." . . . Steve Jones, chair of the University of Tulsa's communications department, says worry is overblown but to be expected. "Just about every medium can't achieve widespread use without making us fearful that it's going to become addictive." [13]

The range of concerns in this limited group of selections is indicative of the degree to which computers have made a major inroad into the national consciousness. It is difficult to avoid either reading about computers and computer networks such as the Internet, encountering them directly, or having someone tell you about his or her most recent experience with them. Furthermore, we can appreciate their impact without knowing how they work or how to program them, just as we may be able to appreciate the effects of traffic jams or automobile pollution without understanding the principles of the internal combustion engine, or even how to operate a motor vehicle.

A VARIETY OF APPLICATIONS

> It troubles me that we are so easily pressured by purveyors of technology into permitting so-called "progress" to alter our lives without attempting to control it—as if technology were an irrepressible force of nature to which we must meekly submit. (Admiral Hyman G. Rickover)

Even the relatively few applications presented here are indicative of how pervasive computers have become. Many of these applications incorporate microprocessors, tiny computing elements that perform a decision-making function when supplied with information from a variety of sensors—voltage, heat, light, and pressure. As such, much computer-governed behavior is hidden from view, and thus the true extent of computer penetration into contemporary technology is probably unappreciated. It is important to recognize that although computers have opened up many new possibilities, for the most part society functioned in much the same way prior to the onset of the "computer age," except for a few major exceptions. Checks were processed, taxes collected, students educated, products manufactured, airplanes flown, medicine practiced, people entertained, and wars fought, all without the benefit of computers. Not to deny the many advantages that have accrued from the introduction of computers into all areas of life, some balanced perspective should be maintained. Computers are indeed marvelous inventions that are transforming the workings of society, but their diffusion is accompanied by a variety of real and potential problems. The following applications, chosen from disparate areas, illustrate the flexibility and versatility of computer-mediated equipment. In some instances computers improve the efficiency of existing processes; in others, they make possible new and innovative ones. New industries have been created—home computers, for example—and others have disappeared—for example, slide rules.

Smart Vehicles

A major effort is underway to increase automobile performance and safety in the areas of handling, fuel efficiency, riding comfort, informational aids, and entertainment. Microprocessors have been used for several years to control engine functions in order to improve fuel economy. New systems, control displays, and monitors continue to be introduced. Some questions have arisen about whether or not the average driver really benefits from a growing array of dashboard gadgets. Voice systems have largely disappeared because of driver irritation, as have CRT (cathode-ray tube) displays. Nevertheless, automobile designers foresee an accelerating growth in the incorporation of microprocessors and sensors in automobiles. For example, Philips Semiconductors predicts "that in the year 2002 the world-wide demand for semiconductor technology used in automobiles will be on the order of $10 billion."[14] Although another forecast claims that "Revenues worldwide could reach US $20 billion by 2000, and $28 billion by 2005."[15] At present most cars employ microprocessors to perform the following control functions:[16]

- power train management;
- anti-lock braking;
- onboard diagnostics;
- cruise control;
- automatic climate control;
- "memory" power seats;
- headlights turn on by themselves when needed, windshield wipers sense moisture on the windshield glass, then automatically adapt to existing weather conditions on their own;

- computer-controlled fuzzy-logic that 'learns' a motorist's driving habits and preferences, then sets an automatic transmission's shift points to fit a driver's needs based on past driving performance.

In somewhat more detail, the current state of the art is represented in Ford Motor Company's luxury car, the Lincoln Continental. Consider the following features:[17]

- An optional satellite location system allows motorists to signal a rescue center [by pressing a button that causes the car's cellular phone to automatically dial the center] when the car breaks down. The center uses satellite technology to direct the repair vehicle.
- Ride control controls the car's air suspension system and shock absorbers and variably alters the power-steering system through altering sensors and controls at each wheel. The driver can select "plush" for a floating-on-air, no-handling type of drive, or "firm" for something more solid.
- Cell phone control controls calls including whether or not conversation takes place on handset or through stereo system.
- The speedometer, odometer and gas gauge have a three-dimensional look to them.
- A set of twisted pair wires form a sort of local-area computer network for the car. The car uses multiplexing technology so that sensors scattered throughout the car can send information to different control centers.

A number of developments are either just coming online or on the horizon. These include a variety of navigation systems such as Sony Electronics' NVX-F160 mobile navigation system that uses a combination of the global positioning system and maps on CD-ROM discs, the Bosch-Blaupunkt vehicle navigation system that prompts drivers with voice and visual aids, and the Oldsmobile Guidestar navigation system that provides a "destination menu," and "turn-by-turn route guidance."[18] Other aspects of vehicle handling and ownership that are being improved by technological advances are security and antitheft devices that use engine immobilizers initiated by complex codes, automated collision alert based on radar, improved air bag systems, and aids to night driving employing infrared cameras and thermal imaging.

One final area of development is a technology for both smart cars and smart roads, called IVHS (Intelligent Vehicle/Highway Systems) or ITS (Intelligent Transportation Systems). These terms apply to systems that include such features as providing current information on accidents, detours, congestion, and services to central controllers and drivers. More advanced features would be systems to avoid collisions by warning drivers, or even assuming direct control of the vehicle. In 1991, the US Congress passed the Intermodal Surface Transportation Efficiency Act (ISTEA), with its purpose stated in its statement of policy: ". . . to develop a National Intermodal Transportation System that is economically efficient and environmentally sound, provides the foundation for the Nation to compete in the global economy, and will move people and goods in an energy efficient manner." Thus the goals for ITS in the US are given as follows: improved safety design, reduced congestion, increased and higher mobility, reduced environmental impact, improved energy efficiency, improved economic productivity, and a viable US ITS industry.[19] In somewhat more detail, 29 user services have been identified that fall into seven general categories. These are worth listing because of the scope of the program and its considerable potential impact on society at large. Thus the following is a list of ITS User Services:[20]

- Travel and Transportation Management
  — En-Route Driver Information
  — Route Guidance
  — Traveler Services Information
  — Traffic Control
  — Incident management
  — Emissions Testing and Migration

- Travel Demand Management
  — Pre-Trip Travel Information
  — Ride Matching and Reservation
  — Demand Management and Operations

- Public Transportation Operations
  — Public Transportation Management
  — En-Route Transit Information
  — Personalized Public Transit
  — Public Travel Security

- Electronic Payment
  — Electronic Payment Services

- Commercial Vehicle Operations
  — Commercial Vehicle Electronic Clearance
  — Automated Roadside Safety Inspection
  — On-Board Safety Monitoring
  — Commercial Vehicle Administrative Processes
  — Hazardous Materials Incident Response
  — Commercial Fleet management

- Emergency Management
  — Emergency Notification and Personal Security
  — Emergency Vehicle Management

- Advanced Vehicle Control and Safety Systems
  — Longitudinal Collision Avoidance
  — Lateral Collision Avoidance
  — Intersection Collision Avoidance
  — Vision Enhancement for Crash Avoidance
  — Safety Readiness
  — Pre-Crash Restraint Deployment
  — Automated Highway Systems

A Sampler of Scientific Applications

The first applications requiring considerable computational speed arose from scientific questions, albeit mediated by military exigencies, namely computations associated with ballistic requirements as well as the much more important Manhattan project, to produce nuclear weapons. It is not surprising therefore that computers, from supercomputers to personal computers, have become an integral component of scientific investigation whether monitoring laboratory experiments, directing telescopes, counting particles, simulating complex ecological systems, or solving large systems of equations for weather prediction. We briefly describe a few applications in the following scientific areas.

Biology

Whereas medical research has developed many antibiotics that combat a wide variety of bacterial diseases, successes have been quite limited with respect to viruses. Although vaccines exist for polio and smallpox, influenza (because of the large number of strains), HIV (because of its complexity), and others (such as hepatitis and viral pneumonia) have proven resistant. One promising approach, in what has been called computer-aided drug design, is the use of high-powered workstations and computer-aided design (CAD) systems to produce models of viruses based on current theories in chemistry, crystallography, and molecular biology. Then models of candidate antiviral agents can be constructed, studied, and modified in hopes of obtaining effective drugs. Although success has been limited, increased computational power offers hope for the future.[21]

Other current efforts include simulated experiments that help "amplify intuition and creativity" in the words of biologist Robert Langridge.[22] Two researchers at New York University have developed a three-dimensional model of the human heart that, even running on a Cray C90 Supercomputer, requires hours to simulate each heartbeat. In the area of computer-designed molecules, researchers at Monash University in Australia are working on molecules to disable flu viruses permanently, a difficult problem because of their ability to mutate so rapidly. The molecular biology program at the University of Washington, financially supported by Bill Gates, seeks to increase understanding of the human genome as well as the functioning of the many billions of neurons in the human brain.[23]

On a larger scale, computer models are in use to help forest companies plan their logging policies. In British Columbia, Canada, models have been developed to simulate second-growth tree stands, so that managers can "measure the economic effect of silvicultural practices on second-growth forests. Silviculture is a catch-all term for pruning, thinning and spacing of seedlings, practices used by managers who seek to grow the best possible trees in the shortest possible time."[24]

Astronomy

In April 1990, the $2 billion Hubble space telescope was launched after many years of delay. Its purpose is to provide astronomers with much clearer pictures than those currently available on earth because of atmospheric interference. Although flaws in the quality of the mirror were only discovered after launch, corrections were possible so that useful images could be recovered. Images sent back by the telescope will be processed by a computer program developed by Alias Research Inc. of Toronto. This program will produce three-dimensional color pictures, which NASA (National Aeronautics and Space Administration) expects to use as a means of informing and educating the public about the findings of this project.[25]

The search for interesting and important cosmic events has been largely dependent on direct human observation, but with the vastness of the universe and the faintness of light arriving from enormous distances, it has been necessary to develop tools to increase the probability of detecting rare events. Berkeley's Lawrence Laboratory has developed a computer program to guide a telescope autonomously all night long searching for one of 1,300 preprogrammed galaxies. It then compares any new image discovered with the previously saved ones to detect any differences, which if discovered will serve to warn astronomers that this galaxy may have undergone a supernova.[26]

Physics

For many phenomena, the computer has come to serve as an experimental testbed with computational power being used to simulate the real world. In fact, the needs of scientific computing have been a major motivating force in the development of larger and faster computers including, of course, supercomputers. However, the simulation of a complex physical phenomenon produces vast quantities of data, which necessitates the development of presentation methodologies such as high resolution graphics. More recently, with increased computing power, resulting from networks of workstations linked to a supercomputer, a new field has emerged—Visualization in Scientific Computing (ViSC), or simply, Scientific Visualization. For example, to study matter under extreme circumstances such as during a supernova or at the Big Bang, computer models can be important. Almost as important is the means by which the results are presented. At the Cornell Theory Center, supercomputers are so employed to study a host of scientific questions and many benefit from visualization presentations.

The requirements of large-scale physics have also been an impetus to the development of larger and faster computers. For example, calculations in computational cosmology have required speeds of 30 gigaflops per second; that is, one thousand million floating point operations per second. According to data provided by the US National Science Foundation, by the year 2000 speeds of 200 gigaflops will be needed, and long-range needs will be 10 exaflops, where "one exaflop is 1 quintillion calculations per second—a 1 followed by 18 zeroes."[27] Of course, the principles of quantum physics, long of theoretical interest only, will shortly, by the year 2010 perhaps, have an important role to play in the development of computers based on semiconductors that depend on quantum effects. It will be necessary to understand quantum phenomena that depend on the activities of individual electrons, and so in a neat reciprocal arrangement, supercomputers will be used to study experimentally the phenomena that may well be required in the construction of a future generation of supercomputers.[28]

Mathematics

Traditionally, mathematicians have required only a pencil and paper, or chalk and a blackboard to do their work, but more recently, the computer has assumed an important role and thereby changed the way mathematics is done. Consider the following:

• In 1976, Wolfgang Haken and Kenneth Appel used a computer to prove the Four Color Conjecture, that any map can be colored with at most four colors such that no two adjacent regions have the same color. They managed to "reduce" the problem to a large number of cases (1,482), each one of which could be examined by the computer program.[29]

• Late in 1988, a team of researchers lead by Clement Lam of Concordia University in Montreal announced the proof of one example of a conjecture made almost 200 years ago by Carl Friedrich Gauss. The formal statement of this conjecture is that there are no finite projective planes of order 10, which in somewhat simpler terms corresponds to the impossibility of constructing a matrix with 111 rows and columns such that each row has exactly 11 positions filled with ones, and any two rows have only one filled position in common. This result required 3,000 hours of computation on a Cray-1, carried out over a two-year period, during idle time. Note that checking such a result by hand is obviously impossible. [30]

- In many cases, mathematical results are implemented in a computer program to improve the efficiency of existing algorithms or to make possible previously intractable processes. One very famous example is the result achieved by Narendra K. Karmarkar, a mathematician at AT&T Bell Laboratories, in 1984. Without going into any details, we note that in the area of linear programming, a mathematical technique used to solve very large problems in scheduling, Karmarkar's result improves speeds by a factor of 50 to 100, so that for a difficult problem for which traditional methods would require weeks to solve, a solution can be obtained in less than an hour, resulting in considerable financial savings. It is interesting that a program incorporating Karmarkar's method was patented by AT&T. [31]

- Current methods in cryptography to ensure the security of transmissions by governments, financial institutions, and others, depend on the expectation that very large numbers, used for encoding and decoding keys, are extremely difficult to factor—that is, to determine numbers whose product yields the original number. However, recent results suggest that the optimistic expectation is not warranted. For example, in 1971 a 40-digit number was factored to considerable acclaim. In October, 1988, almost unbelievably, a 100-digit number was factored and most recently, barely a year and a half later, in an extraordinary achievement by several hundred researchers and about one thousand computers, a 150-digit number was factored into three irreducible factors. To indicate the magnitude of the computations required, consider that a brute-force method that attempted to factor the number by trying to divide it by every smaller number would take 1,060 years even if each division could be performed in one billionth of a second. A new factoring method was developed and the problem was subdivided into many smaller pieces to achieve the final answer. [32]

- Some four years later, in 1994, yet another large number, a famous one at that, RSA 129, was on the verge of being factored. It had been proposed in 1977 as an example of the security of the RSA encryption scheme, named after its inventors, Dr. Ronald Rivest of MIT, Dr. Adi Shamir of the Weizmann Institute, and Dr. Leonard Adelman of UCLA. The historical importance of this 129-digit number had stimulated many to attempt its factoring. [33]

High Definition Television (HDTV)

If ever a technology has been promoted as a test of a nation's determination to maintain economic dominance in the face of repeated and growing challenges, it is high definition television (HDTV). However, the term is rife with political, economic, and engineering overtones and for a variety of reasons represents perhaps the most anticipated technology since the personal computer itself. In brief, HDTV would have about twice the horizontal and vertical resolution of current television, a significant increase in picture quality, achieved by a doubling of the number of lines transmitted as well as an increase in the ratio of horizontal to vertical picture size, from 4:3 to 16:9, approximating a film screen.

HDTV is viewed by many legislators as a last-ditch effort to resume a previously dominant presence in this most important consumer industry, especially given the prediction "that the television receiver of the year 2000 will contain a greater number and more sophisticated microchips than the personal computer of the year 1990."[34] Estimates vary but in the most optimistic scenario, presented in a report by the American Electronics Association, world semiconductor sales for US firms would be $124 billion with a strong US presence in HDTV (50% of the US market controlled by US firms), compared to $62 billion for a weak US presence (only 10%).[35] The stakes are obviously high, so high indeed that considerable pressure has been generated by politicians, trade associations, and professional societies to encourage government spending to support research and development in the private sector.

There is, however, a lack of consensus on whether or not HDTV represents the true wave of the future or merely a consolidation of the past. Although, as previously noted, television receivers will have many microprocessors, the basic transmitted signal is still expected to be analog. Thus some critics of HDTV have argued that the US should skip this technology altogether because of the lead currently held by Japan and Europe and move vigorously towards blanketing the country with a fiber-optic network over which signals can be transmitted digitally. As author George Gilder notes, "Replacing moribund TV technology will be digital telecomputers, connected to the world through a network of fiber optics. Telecomputer users will be able to dial up digital databases, programs, movies, classrooms, or news coverage anywhere on the continent, ultimately, all over the world."[36] Furthermore, then Senator Al Gore, chairman of the Subcommittee on Science, Technology, and Space made the following statement:[37]

> We can't just worry about HDTV, we need to pay attention to the next revolution in TV technology—digital TV. The technology being developed for visualization can be used to develop super-high-resolution digital television and the same fiber-optic network that links computers today could be used to carry digital TV signals in the future. The US has a lead in visualization and networking, but we need to redouble our efforts in order to keep that lead and to leapfrog the Japanese. We can lead the digital TV revolution.

Two years later, in 1991, Senator Gore coined the by-now famous term, "The Information Superhighway." Movies on demand are intended to be a major component of this highway and presumably digital transmission will be the basic mode of distribution. In the next section, we will introduce the Internet and the Information Highway vision, as they will play an important role in the discussion to follow. We should note that although digital transmission will necessarily underlie the Information Highway, it does not follow that high-definition digital TV is part of the picture.

After many years, a Grand Alliance of companies is proposing standards for digital television transmission in the US. These consist of AT&T, General Instruments, the Massachusetts Institute of Technology, Philips Electronics North America, the David Sarnoff Research Center, Thomson Consumer Electronics, and Zenith (the last US manufacturer of television sets). Standards in this area have implications beyond the shape of the television signal, as digital transmission opens up such interactive services as movies on demand and home shopping. Thus, "It requires new architectures for networks, network servers, new set-top boxes, and even new videocassette recorders."[38] Experiments in HDTV in Europe and Japan are also in progress and perhaps more advanced than in the US. Indeed, Japan is actually transmitting high-definition services via satellite. In March 1997, the Federal Communications Commission approved conversion to digital TV by the year 2001.

Video Games

There is certainly little need to describe video games to anyone living during the early 1980s, when they suddenly captured a large share of the entertainment market, and the late 1980s, when they made a successful comeback after a difficult period. Teenagers were the prime group to whom advertisers devoted their attention. A number of companies—Atari, Mattel, and Coleco in the early days, and Nintendo, Sega, and NEC more recently, and a newly arisen Atari—suddenly achieved prominence, attracting considerable attention on the stock market as well. As their popularity mounted, so did public criticism. Children seemed to be so mesmerized that they would use their food allowance on video games and even steal money to play. Very little sustained criticism has continued to the present day other than a general concern with the mounting costs of both players and game cartridges.

In 1990 with sales of about $2.5 billion, making it the best selling toy in the United States, Nintendo controlled about 90% of the home video-game market.[39] Its sales peaked at almost $6 billion in 1993 before falling to about $3.5 billion by the end of its fiscal year in March 1996.[40] By 1995, the videogame market had reached about $10 billion[41] with such expensive machines as the 3DO Interactive Multiplayer at $399, the Sega Saturn, $525 in Japan, the Sony Playstation, $470 in Japan, and the leader Nintendo with the Nintendo Ultra 64, expected to sell for $250. These are serious 32-bit machines with very powerful processors necessary to support ever more complex 3D graphics and faster action.[42] In an interesting development, several movie studios have either entered the video game market or are on the verge of doing so, presumably to take advantage of their hit movies by producing related video games. For example, Disney Interactive has released games based on "The Lion King" and "Pocahontas" and Universal Interactive Studios has a "Jurassic Park" game. The studios do not manufacture game players but produce games in CD-ROM format or in cartridges for such platforms as the Sega Genesis and Saturn, Sony Playstation, and Super Nintendo.[43]

Social Sciences

Statistical analysis of large data sets, the creation and distribution of linguistic and literary corpi, the modeling of political, historical, economic, and social phenomena, and the collection of historical, archeological, and fine arts image databases are all part of the applications of computers in the social sciences. For example, in the area of historical linguistics, attempts have been made to account for the relationship among modern European and Indian languages by proposing an ancient language from which most evolved. But the nature of this evolutionary process is very difficult to explore because of the sparseness of data on the one hand and the very large number of possible evolutionary paths; by one estimate, more than 34 million.[44] As an exploratory and hypothesis-testing tool, a computer program has been developed by two linguists and a computer scientist at the University of Pennsylvania. As one of the linguists notes, in defense of this approach:[45]

> We've shown what we principally set out to show, that this new computational method for evolutionary tree construction is more powerful and more reliable than any in existence, and that it is especially apt for the testing of hypotheses about the subgroupings of languages. We're hoping this will help lead to new directions of research in historical linguistics.

Other social sciences have benefited as well. The use of networks for communications of all kinds, including the publication of electronic journals has flourished and of course for many disciplines such as anthropology, sociology, psychology, and English, the Internet has provided an experimental testbed and the source of many interesting social phenomena. Such issues as the formation of virtual communities, the presentation of self, the use of anonymity, gender switching, and the organization of political, social, religious, and other online global groups have stimulated considerable research efforts. Pathological behaviors such as so-called Internet addiction, the utterance of threats and sexual harassment, flaming, racism, and more have found a home on the Internet and become grist for the research mill. See Chapter 12 for more discussion of some of these topics.

THE INTERNET AND INFORMATION HIGHWAY

> Describing the Internet as the Network of Networks is like calling the Space Shuttle, a thing that flies.[46]

In the last few years, the Internet has become a commonplace term in the media. If you are not on the Net you must be missing out on something exciting, interesting, and trendy. Providing Internet access is a growth industry. The Internet is yet another interesting example of a technology evolving from rather humble origins to encompass a realm of experience in a manner beyond the expectations of its originators. It is an American creation and its growth is witness to the vigor and vision of a free and open society, but by the same token its future is dependent on political and economic forces beyond the control of its many millions of users worldwide.

Internet Services

The range of Internet activities almost beggars description, but a brief overview is necessary to appreciate the fervor of its supporters, especially the veterans. The earliest applications and the basic ones today are the transfer of files, in one form or another, and remote computing. In fact, the success of the Internet is based on the development of protocols, or rules of the road, for transferring files over distributed networks and maintaining the integrity of the files while ensuring their delivery over member systems without planning the route in advance. This means that messages will be rerouted automatically around nonfunctioning subsystems on a regular basis. Messages can be thought of as packets of information with a destination address and a return address. Thus for personal messages, file transfer may be referred to as e-mail, that is, electronic mail. (Note that e-mail users typically refer to traditional mail as snail-mail.) In its simplest form, e-mail has a single sender and a single recipient, similar to ordinary mail. There is also a form of broadcast mail, or one-to-many messaging, typically used by a group of individuals to inform one another, but no others. The almost instantaneous transmission times, even worldwide, make e-mail a powerful communication tool.

Remote computing—that is, the ability to access a computer over the Internet, on which you have an account—is certainly important, but not as much to the general public. However, accessing files remotely and transferring them to a home computer is as important and considerably more widespread. Vast quantities of information, including software, government publications, books in the public domain, pictures, magazine articles, legislation in progress, and much more is available. A variety of search and access tools such as Archie, Gopher, and WAIS have been developed, and more recently, Web browsers such as Netscape and Internet Explorer and search engines such as Alta Vista and Yahoo. Files can be downloaded using ftp (file transfer protocol) in an anonymous fashion; that is, no information is maintained at the site of the documents about who did the downloading. Probably the most publicized, the most controversial, and the most interesting of the Internet uses is the collection of discussion groups, known as newsgroups or bulletin boards. The term USENET usually is applied to this Internet application and frequently is confused with the Internet itself.

The number of newsgroups varies over time, but there are probably more than 20,000 devoted to an extraordinarily broad range of topics. A newsgroup can be considered as an electronic forum to which USENET readers can send messages, or postings, on an existing topic, the current thread, or initiate a new topic. The newsgroups form a hierarchy based on their subject areas with the following seven major categories:[47]

CATEGORY	TOPICS
comp	Computer science, hardware, software, hobbyists
misc	Miscellaneous: law, jobs, investments, sales
sci	Sciences, research
soc	Social issues, socializing, cultures
talk	Debates, open-ended topics, endless talk
news	Network information, maintenance, software
rec	Hobbies, recreational information

Alternative hierarchies include alt (sex, privacy, Simpsons, and just about anything else that doesn't fit in elsewhere), gnu (groups related to the Free Software Foundation), and biz (business-related groups). Individual newsgroups are named by a sequence of terms indicating a descent through the hierarchy; so for example, comp.admin.policy, which falls within the comp major category, is of concern to administrators, and deals with policy issues. Some groups are moderated, which means that they have a moderator who must review every posting before distributing it over the network, whereas in the unmoderated ones individual postings are immediately distributed. Thus moderated groups tend to be more focused and less controversial. Unmoderated groups are more chaotic, eclectic, wild, outrageous, with large numbers of postings and readers.

One way to get a quick feeling for the nature of the USENET is to review some online comments made by experts. Every month, for the benefit of new users, a series of announcements are posted on news.announce.newusers. The following is a selection from such a posting, originally written by Chip Salzenberg to provide a snapshot of USENET's history, organization, and structure.[48]

What Usenet is Not
(1) Usenet is not an organization. No person or group has authority over Usenet as a whole. No one controls who gets a news feed, which articles are propagated where, who can post articles, or anything else. There is no "Usenet Incorporated," nor is there a "Usenet User's [sic] Group." You're on your own.

(2) Usenet is not a right. Some people misunderstand their local right of "freedom of speech" to mean that they have a legal right to use others' computers to say what they wish in whatever way they wish, and the owners of said computers have no right to stop them. Those people are wrong. Freedom of speech also means freedom not to speak. If I choose not to use my computer to aid your speech, that is my right. Freedom of the press belongs to those who own one.

(6) Usenet is not an academic network. It is no surprise that many Usenet sites are universities, research labs or other academic institutions. Usenet originated with a link between two universities, and the exchange of ideas and information is what such institutions are all about. But the passage of years has changed Usenet's character. Today, by plain count, most Usenet sites are commercial entities.

(8) Usenet is not the Internet. The Internet is a wide-ranging network, parts of which are organized by various governments. It carries many kinds of traffic, of which Usenet is only one. And the Internet is only one of the various networks carrying Usenet traffic.

(10) Usenet is not a United States network. It is true that Usenet originated in the United States, and the fastest growth in Usenet sites has been there. Nowadays, however, Usenet extends worldwide.

What Usenet Is
Usenet is the set of people who exchange articles tagged with one or more universally-recognized labels, called "newsgroups" (or "groups" for short).

Control
Every administrator controls his own site. No one has any real control over any site but his own.

If You are Unhappy . . .
Property rights being what they are, there is no higher authority on Usenet than the people who own the machines on which Usenet traffic is carried. If the owner of the machine you use says, "We will not carry alt.sex on this machine," and you are not happy with that order, you have no Usenet recourse. What can we outsiders do, after all?

More recently, during 1993, a new application seemed to appear out of nowhere and transformed the Internet into a topic of everyday discourse as well as representing the breakthrough that business seemed to require to take the Internet seriously. The World Wide Web, or the Web for short, was first implemented in 1990 by researchers at CERN (actually the European Laboratory for Particle Physics) to aid fellow physicists to share data and results. In the words of Wayne Roush:[49]

> The idea was that one physics team might create a Web document, or "page," of text using an article or set of data, noting somewhere within the text the existence of, say, a corresponding graphic set up as a separate page in the system. After starting up a program to browse for Web pages, a user could find and read the text and then retrieve the graphic by clicking on the "link" to it (the link, in the form of a word, phrase, or icon, would be highlighted). The user might wish to correspond about the information by electronic mail with the original team, or might develop additional Web documents which could also take the form of color photographs, sound, and animation that perhaps could be linked to the original text page by the same highlighting process.

The net result is a highly structured document consisting of text and pictures with links to other documents similarly structured. Clicking on a link activates another page at some other site, itself containing links. Thus the worldwide collection of Web pages represents a massive collection of information linked in many ways, creating a global instance of hypertext.

There is more. The Internet provides MUDs (Multi-User Dungeons), online role-playing games; IRC (Inter Relay Chat), online written conversions, a precursor of chat rooms available on America Online; and phone calls between any two Net users without surcharge, although somewhat lacking in quality and intimacy. The astronomical growth of the Web in terms of numbers of sites and volume of pages has necessarily been accompanied by browsers such as Netscape and earlier, Mosaic, tools to access and explore the wealth of information. In addition, search tools such as Yahoo, Webcrawler, and Lycos have been developed to facilitate effective searches for specific information. Finally, the Web has grown so fast largely because of the forum it provides for businesses, large and small, organizations of all kinds, government departments of all sizes, and of course multitudes of individuals, to display their wares in a colorful and occasionally interesting manner. One last application is multicasting, which uses the M-bone (multicast backbone) and "enables groups of specially equipped computers to share text, audio and video. A multicast differs from a unicast, in which one computer communicates with one other, and a broadcast, in which one computer communicates with many. In multicasting, many computers can communicate among themselves simultaneously."[50]

The Information Highway: What Is It?

Because both the Internet and the Information Highway, in the US usually referred to as the National Information Infrastructure (NII), will be the subject of considerable discussion and analysis, it is important that the stage be set appropriately by presenting the visions of the US administration as articulated in an early White House document, "The National Information Infrastructure: Agenda for Action." At the beginning of the document, in response to the question, "What Is the NII?" the following answer is supplied.[51]

The phrase "information infrastructure" has an expansive meaning. The NII includes more than just the physical facilities used to transmit, store, process, and display voice, data, and images. It encompasses:

- A wide range and ever-expanding range of equipment including cameras, scanners, keyboards, telephones, fax machines, computers, switches, compact disks, video and audio tape, cable, wire, satellites, optical fiber transmission lines, microwave nets, switches, televisions, monitors, printers, and much more.

The NII will integrate and interconnect these physical components in a technologically neutral manner so that no one industry will be favored over any other. Most importantly, the NII requires building foundations for living in the Information Age and for making these technological advances useful to the public, business, libraries, and other non governmental entities. That is why, beyond the physical components of the infrastructure, the value of the National Information Infrastructure to users and the nation will depend in large part on the quality of its other elements:

- The information itself, which may be in the form of video programming, scientific or business databases, images, sound recordings, library archives, and other media. Vast quantities of that information exist today in government agencies and even more valuable information produced every day in our laboratories, studios, publishing houses, and elsewhere.

- Applications and software that allow users to access, manipulate, organize, and digest the profilerating mass of information that the NII's facilities will put at their fingertips.

- The network standards and tranmission codes that facilitate interconnection and interoperation between networks, and ensure the privacy of persons and the security of the information carried, as well as the security and reliability of the networks.

- The people—largely in the private sector—who create the information, develop applications and services, construct the facilities, and train others to tap its potential. Many of these people will be vendors, operators, and service providers working for private industry.

Every component of the information infrastructure must be developed and integrated if America is to capture the promise of the Information Age.

For a slightly different perspective, it may be helpful to compare this statement with similar proposals for a "Canadian Vision for the Information Highway." Consider the following. [52]

The goal for Canada is to build the highest-quality, lowest-cost information network in the world, in order to give all Canadians access to the employment, educational, investment, entertainment, health care and wealth-creating opportunities of the Information Age. In short, the vision is to make Canada number one in the world in the provision and utilization of the Information Highway, creating substantial economic, social and cultural advantage for all Canadians.

Canada's information and communications infrastructure will be a "network of networks," creating vital communications links among Canadian businesses and their clients; among industry, government and universities; among artists, cultural organizations and their audiences; among hospitals, clinics and patients; among schools; and among communities, large and small, from one end of the country to the other. It will accelerate the pace at which we exchange ideas, and will revolutionize our way of doing business. It will act as the catalyst for Canada as a vital and competitive knowledge-based society.

Keep in mind a couple of points. The NII is not here yet although many necessary components are in place; as such, much of the commentary directed towards its promise and potential problems is highly speculative, however well-intentioned. Furthermore, the Internet is not the NII, although many of its applications should be available on the NII when it is realized. However, we may be able to anticipate some of the features of the NII by studying the ongoing development of the Internet.

SOCIETAL ISSUES

For a list of all the ways technology has failed to improve the quality of life, please press three. (Alice Kahn)

Technology makes it possible for people to gain control over everything, except over technology. (John Tudor)

All technology should be assumed guilty until proven innocent. (David Brower)

Issues and Problems

There are many ways to present and discuss social issues arising from the increasing use of computers and computer-based electronic networks such as the Internet. One method is by category; that is, each major application area is studied and the particular problems identified and characterized. Another is to propose a list of areas of social concern, or potential problems, and then to explore each application to determine whether or not it exemplifies one or more of these problems. The results of both approaches could be combined by representing them in a simple diagram that depicts which social issues are of particular concern to which applications or technological innovations. The simple metaphor is to view society as a fabric woven with warp and woof threads. The warp consists of the lengthwise threads of a woven cloth through which woof threads are woven, and the woof consists of the crosswise threads carried back and forth by the shuttle and interwoven with the lengthwise threads of the warp. These definitions are obviously interdependent just as the social issues and applications are. For the purposes of this metaphor, societal issues are the warp, and computers, technology, and applications are the woof. The dividing lines are not always sharp, however.

Application areas and technological developments include the following.

Robotics and Industrial Automation. The integration of computers and movable electro-mechanical arms—to perform such tasks as assembling parts, welding, and spray painting—define industrial automation. Robots also may be used for jobs dangerous to humans in hazardous environments such as under the sea, mines, space, and nuclear reactors. Flexible manufacturing systems represent newer ways of organizing production.

Office Automation. The integration of computers, large and small, local and long-distance networks, fax, and printers is transforming the office. Sophisticated word processing, database systems, e-mail (electronic mail), automatic meeting schedulers, management information systems, telecommuting, and portable computing are among the components of what has been called "The Office of the Future."

Telecommunications. The interconnection of computers with communication networks opens up a wide range of possibilities for distributed computing, distributed work, and worldwide information networks for business and government use.

Electronic Financial Transactions. The use of ATMs (Automatic Teller machines), POSs (Point-of-Sales Terminals), and computer communication systems, results in electronic financial transactions and may at some point produce the so-called "cashless" society. A dense network linking financial institutions, retailers, wholesalers, and the public is continually changing shopping and banking habits. Commercial transactions on the Internet present special security problems.

Personal Computers. The explosion of computers available for use in the office, school, and home has brought computers from the hands of professionals into the homes of the general public. Marketed as just another consumer item, granted an expensive one, they may have been oversold, but do provide an ever-expanding range of possibilities for the family including games, financial programs, educational programs, and a means to access the Internet and commercial networks.

Microprocessors. The miniaturization of computing power in the form of microprocessors has enabled the computer to be incorporated into an ever-increasing variety of consumer products. Among these are cameras, automobiles, television sets, microwave ovens, fax machines, stereo systems, etc. Improvements in efficiency and repair procedures are changing production practices and servicing strategies. Consumer products can be more energy-efficient and more flexible; that is, more bells and whistles.

E-mail and Teleconferencing. The use of computer terminals and communication networks permits messages to be sent across the office or across the country and stored in computers or printed and delivered locally as ordinary mail. Combined with fax and teleconferencing, these new communication modes are changing the way companies do business.

AI (Artificial Intelligence). Developments in AI are continually expanding the role computers play in our lives, especially in areas that directly challenge human uniqueness. Once an academic pursuit, AI is achieving varying degrees of economic impact in such areas as expert systems, intelligent robots, and sophisticated diagnostic systems.

Virtual Reality. Recent developments in computer graphics, interfaces, and hardware have opened up the possibilities of real-time interactions in simulated worlds. The proponents claim that shaking off physical limitations will liberate the mind, initiate unpredictable relationships, and usher in an age of unlimited potential, but there are dangers including threats to self and loss of community.

Internet. The Internet is the current worldwide network linking millions of people and permitting the rapid distribution of text, images, and sounds at low costs. It may be superseded by the Information Highway, that much-advertised broadband entertainment network, combining cable, telephone, and broadcasting systems. Such networks are hallmarks of the Information Age.

This list provides a sense of how important computers have become to the functioning of modern society, if any such message is necessary. It now remains to outline an accompanying list of relevant social issues. For some of these, computers are only the current stage in technological development, and so the problems are only existing ones exacerbated. Others are unique to the computer and must be treated as directly associated phenomena. The issues will be characterized by a series of crucial questions highlighting the areas of concern. Among the social issues are the following.

Work. How do all these computer-related developments affect the employment of people? Will the number of available jobs that can sustain both body and mind increase or decrease? How will the skill requirements of jobs change? How well will people accommodate to the increased automation of the workplace? What will happen to the traditional social organization of the office under office automation?

Health. Is long-term health affected by lengthy exposure to VDTs (Video Display terminals)? Are other computer-related activities problematic? What about the effects of repetitive actions on hand and wrist muscles and nerves? Are there psychological effects associated with "excessive" computer use?

Privacy. Computers permit, indeed encourage, enormous amounts of information to be gathered, stored, processed, linked, and distributed. There is a general concern about how these records are used, about the proliferation of incorrect information, and about access to individual records. Can a claim be made to treat personal information as property, which would require traffickers in personal data to pay for use? Can or should North American governments regulate the handling of personal information in the private sector as is done in the province of Quebec and in many countries in Western Europe?

Centralization of Control. Will computers be used to extend the power of management over employees? Is it inevitable that increased amounts of more accurate information will shift more power to the top of organizations, or will distributed computing lead to distributed responsibility and control? Will governments, even democratic ones, become more powerful and centralized as in Orwell's *1984*, in spite of efforts to minimize their "intrusion into the lives of ordinary citizens?"

Responsibility. Will the widespread use of computers and communication systems fragment society? Will families cluster around their home information systems for entertainment, shopping, education, and even work? In large organizations that are heavily dependent on information technology, will responsibility devolve from people to machines?

The Information Society. How will society change as fewer and fewer people actually produce things and more and more people engage in service activities and information processing? Are we heading to a modern version of "bread and circuses?" Will the home become central to life as information in its broadest interpretation becomes the leading economic commodity? How will access to information be made available?

Human Dignity or Self-Image. How does the computer affect our self-image? Is there a threat to human dignity as machines continue to perform more activities formerly the sole province of people? Is technology an irresistible and autonomous force? Can we maintain human(e) qualities in a computer age?

Ethics and Professionalism. How responsible are computer professionals for their actions? Should they adopt codes of behavior similar to those of doctors and even lawyers? Do computer-mediated situations present new problems for ethical behavior?

National Interests. Does the future economic well-being of a country depend on its achievements in high technology? Should governments play an active role in the marketplace to ensure that technological leadership is maintained? Will success for some countries mean failure for others?

Meritocracy. Will the use of computers accentuate the tensions between the educated and the untrained? Will the work of society be divided between challenging and interesting jobs and routine and boring ones? Will the poor and uneducated view computers as yet another powerful tool for the rich to maintain their status, and will they be right?

Freedom of Expression. In the US the First Amendment guarantees the right of all citizens to say and write what they wish with very few restrictions, but the battle to exercise this right is a never-ending one. The Internet and commercial networks such as Prodigy and CompuServe currently form one such battleground. The ease with which all kinds of information can be transmitted on networks immediately raises questions of responsibility and liability. Will content be regulated and how might this work over a global network? (This last question has an answer—yes—The Communications Decency Act of 1996.)

Intellectual Property. In the age of information, the ownership of information assumes major importance. An emerging battleground is the electronic rights for text, images, sounds, hypertext, and multimedia. Will existing information conglomerates reinforce their control or will an emerging grass roots constituency begin to distribute information free of traditional ownership patterns?

Which issues apply to which technological areas? Figure 1.1 is clearly not a precise formulation for many reasons, a primary one being that the definitions are not very precise. It should suggest the general patterns of interaction of social issues and technological innovations. As time goes on, the number of rows and columns as well as the contents will vary as new concerns emerge in response to new applications. Thus treat this formulation as suggestive and in no way definitive. It is important to be aware of the possible conse-

	Work	Health	Privacy	Centralization of Authority	Responsibility	Information Society	Human Dignity	Ethics and Professionalism	National Interests	Meritocracy	Freedom of Expression	Intellectual Property
Robotics	X	X					X		X	X		
Office Automation	X	X	X	X	X	X	X	X		X		
Telecommunication	X		X	X		X		X	X		X	
Electronic Financial Transactions	X		X	X	X			X				
Personal Computers	X	X				X			X	X	X	
Microprocessors	X					X				X		X
E-mail	X	X				X			X			
AI	X					X	X		X			
Virtual Reality		X					X	X				
Internet	X		X		X	X			X		X	X

FIGURE 1.1 Social Issues and Computers.

quences of technological developments, but this awareness requires a familiarity with the technology itself as well as with the economic, political, social, and legal structures of society. Only a beginning is attempted here, but an old Chinese saying is appropriate: "A journey of a thousand miles begins with one step."

Public Opinion

We have presented a selection of possible problems associated with computer use in today's society. Their severity is a matter of debate among computer professionals and social scientists—but how do nonexperts, ordinary people, feel about computers? It was not until the late 1950s that the computer emerged as an object of praise and fear. Cartoonists of the period depicted computers or robots as challenging the ability of humans at work and at play. Operators at consoles in front of floor-to-ceiling computers typed in queries that elicited humorous responses. The cartoons reflected such concerns as possible loss of jobs, threats to human problem-solving skills, personal liberty, and an increasing intrusion into all aspects of human life. Did the cartoonists and editorial writers truly capture the hopes and fears of the general population or did they exacerbate them?

In 1971, *Time* magazine and the American Federation of Information Processing Societies, Inc. (AFIPS) conducted a major survey to determine the public's attitudes towards computers.[53] Over 1,000 adults from a representative sample of the US population were interviewed on a wide range of topics. The survey results are extensive and lengthy, but a few observations are revealing.

- Almost half of the working public has had some contact with computers.
- About 90% felt that computers will provide much useful information and many kinds of services.
- 36% felt computers actually create more jobs than they eliminate; 51% believed the opposite.
- 84% wanted the government to regulate the use of computers.
- With respect to privacy, 58% were concerned that computers will be used in the future for surveillance and 38% believed that they were a threat to privacy (but 54% disagreed).
- Only 12% believed that computers could think for themselves but 23% expected that they might disobey their programmers in the future.
- 54% thought that computers were dehumanizing people and 33% believed that they were decreasing freedom; 59% disagreed.

On the whole, the general public displayed a reasonable attitude to the ability of computers and the potential threats they posed.

Some 12 years later (September 1983) Lou Harris and Associates, Inc. conducted a study for Southern New England Telephone entitled *The Road After 1984: The Impact of Technology on Society*.[54] Conducted well into the age of the home computer, this survey should have revealed the opinions of a more sophisticated public. Some highlights are:

- Some 67% of the general public believed that personal information was being kept in files, somewhere, for purposes unknown to them.
- 45% acknowledged that they knew how to use a computer, most at the beginner level.
- 88% believed that the computer would make the quality of life somewhat or a lot better.
- 85% agreed that computers could free up time for individuals to do creative and highly productive work.
- 55% felt that computers could make human robots out of workers by controlling every minute of their day.

In 1994, the Times Mirror Company conducted a broad survey on attitudes towards technology, including computers and online systems, as well as attitudes with respect to the impact of computer-based technologies on social issues. Once again here are a few findings: [55]

- 31% of all American households have a personal computer and one in three of these have a modem, permitting communication with an online information system.
- 65% like computers and technology and 42% think that they give people more control over their lives; 17% say less control.
- 55% worry some or a lot that computers and technology are being used to invade their privacy; 42% say not much or not at all.

There is much more in this survey about uses of computers, working at home, gender differences, children's interests, and detailed profiles of technology users. More information gathered from privacy surveys is reported in Chapter 9, but suffice it to say at this point that most surveys have consistently shown over the past few years that the general public is much more concerned than the 55% figure given previously. In fact, about 77% to 80% of respondents have indicated over the past few years that they were very concerned or somewhat concerned about threats to personal privacy.

One area of considerable current interest is the number of regular Internet users and Web browsers (people, not software, that is). Individual Web sites can keep track of the number of visits made but not the number of independent ones, an important measure of how popular the site is. One estimate of Internet users was about 40 million in 1995 worldwide, but this number is suspect. In October 1995, A. C. Nielsen, well known for its extensive measurements of television viewing habits, reported that 24 million people in Canada and the US had used the Internet between August and October, and of these, 18 million had accessed Web sites.[56] These numbers were challenged by some and in January 1996, it was reported that "A new survey by New York-based Find/SVP pegs the number of US Internet users at 9.5 million, far below the findings of a disputed Nielsen Media Research survey a couple of months ago, which had reported 24 million North American users. The Find/SVP study also estimated the number of US Web users at about 7.5 million."[57]

Survey results reported from MCI Communications and Network Wizards in July 1996 provide the following information: 35 million users worldwide, 186 countries connected, 10 million host computers, 76,000 Web servers, 300% growth in annual traffic, and 2,400% growth in Web servers.[58] And finally, results of a Nielsen poll reported in August 1996, revealed that "the number of North Americans with Internet access jumped from 37 million last August to 55.5 million six months later . . ."[59] Having Internet access is not equivalent to being an Internet user, but this survey does indicate that basic exposure to the Internet, probably the Web, is increasing at a significant rate. The survey also produced some demographic results that revealed a few interesting findings. Among longtime users, 67% are men, 88% own their own computer, 56% have college degrees, and 27% have a household income of at least $80,000.[60] More recent users are less affluent, own fewer computers, have less education, and have a higher representation of women (60% are men).

These and other surveys are intended to answer other questions such as age, frequency of use, type of use, impact on leisure time, and of course how much money has been spent both to access Web sites and make purchases. Why all the concern about these numbers? The answer is simple. Money. Not yet but soon as companies, large and small, position themselves in this new highly-competitive environment.

SUMMARY

Computers have become pervasive in contemporary society. They have been used to distribute religious services over networks, provide a site for condolences over the death of rock star Jerry Garcia, permit people to drink coffee and exchange messages over the Internet at a cafe. There are also problems such as IBM's failure to provide a working system at the Atlanta Olympics. Designers of some game-playing programs seem to be unable to avoid the use of racism as a feature. The issue of free speech on the Internet has become an ongoing battleground as not unexpectedly this new media has attracted the attention of many interested in material with sexual themes. Major applications also include improved automobile performance, the use of computers to explore the evolution of human language groups, the computer visualization of scientific phenomena, the proof of difficult mathematical theorems, the development of high-definition television, and of course, videogames.

In recent years, the Internet and the World Wide Web have become extremely popular as the number of hosts and users has grown very rapidly. From its humble beginnings as a research-oriented computer network funded by the US Department of Defense and later by the National Science Foundation, the Internet has become a global network and a worldwide phenomenon. Advances in telecommunications technology and applications software, as well as US government deregulation legislation has prepared the groundwork for the much-advertised Information Highway.

Associated with the benefits of computers are a number of real and potential problems. The many and varied applications of computers, including robotics, office automation, electronic money systems, personal computers, home information systems, and artificial intelligence, have given rise to social problems. Relevant issues include work, health, privacy, responsibility, self-image, and national interests.

From their earliest appearance, computers have aroused feelings of fear, awe, and concern, as revealed in public opinion surveys. Despite increased familiarity, the general public's perception of computers seems still to be conditioned more by media exaggerations than by reality. Recent surveys have shown conflicting estimates in the number of Internet users, but all agree on significant growth rates.

NOTES

1. Collected in online quotation list. Copyright: Kevin Harris 1995.
2. David Gonzalez. "Cardinal Takes His Message to Cyberspace," *The New York Times,* January 4, 1995, p. A 1.
3. Edward Rothstein. "Temple Emanu-El Broadcasts High Holiday Services on the Internet," *The New York Times,* September 16, 1996, p. C 4.
4. Peter Lewis. "Discussion of the O. J. Simpson Murder Trial is On-Line as Well as on the Air," *The New York Times,* February 14, 1995, p. C 19.
5. "School's Computer Game on Slavery Prompts Suit," *The New York Times,* August 28, 1995, p. A 6.

6. Mark Lewyn. "Making a Federal Case out of E-mail," *Business Week,* December 19, 1994, p. 4.

7. Walter R. Baranger. "Grateful Dead Fans Mourn Garcia on Net," *The New York Times,* August 14, 1995, p. C 6. (See the Grateful Dead Web site with URL: <http://sinclair.mathcs.duq.edu:80/~wiegand/SYF/dead.html>.

8. KT. "Cambridge Cyber Cafe," *Datamation,* April 15, 1995, p. 15.

9. Gary H. Anthes. "High-tech roundup on Capital Hill," *Computerworld,* December 11, 1995, p. 15.

10. John Markoff. "On-Line Service Blocks Access to Topics Called Pornographic," *The New York Times,* December 29, 1995, pp. A 1, C 4.

11. Peter H. Lewis. "A Computer System Buckled Under Pressure," *The New York Times,* July 29, 1996, C 5.

12. "The Catcher in the Eye," *Time,* July 29, 1996, p. 11.

13. Kendall Hamilton and Claudia Kalb. "They Log On, But They Can't Log Off," *Newsweek,* December 18, 1995, pp. 60–61.

14. Leonard Arguello, international product marketing manager at Philips Semiconductors. "Smart Cars," Special Advertising Section, *Fortune,* December 11, 1995. But note that in 1988, Motorola anticipated a market of $10 billion in computer chips by 1993. William J. Hampton, Neil Gross, Deborah C. Wise, and Otis Port. "Smart Cars," *Business Week,* June 13, 1988, pp. 68–71, 74.

15. A study released in October 1994 by Siemens Automotive Corp. and *Ward's Auto World* as reported in Ronald K. Jurgen, "The Electronic Motorist," *IEEE Spectrum,* March 1995, p. 37.

16. *Ibid.*

17. "Highway Information," *The New York Times,* November 6, 1996, p. C 3.

18. *Ibid.,* Jurgen, p. 39.

19. "ITS Architecture Development Program, Phase I, Summary Report," US Department of Transportation and ITS America, November 1994.

20. *Ibid.,* p. 3.

21. Joseph Alper. "The Microchip Microbe Hunters," *Science* **247,** February 16, 1990, pp. 804–806.

22. Russell Mitchell and Otis Port. "Fantastic Journeys in Virtual Labs," *Business Week,* September 19, 1994, p. 76.

23. *Ibid.*

24. Bill Atkinson. "The Virtual Forest," *The Globe and Mail* (Toronto, Canada), January 6, 1996, D 8.

25. Geoffrey Rowan, "Canadian Computer Program to Shape Space Pictures," *The Globe and Mail* (Toronto, Canada), April 30, 1990, p. B 6.

26. Malcolm W. Browne. "Devices Help Scientists Find Supernovas," *The New York Times,* April 3, 1990, p. B 5.

27. Otis Port. "Speed Gets a Whole New Meaning," *Business Week,* April 29, 1996, pp. 90–91.

28. John Carey and Heidi Dawley. "Science's New Nano Frontier," *Business Week,* July 1, 1996, pp. 101–102.

29. Paul Wallich. "Beyond Understanding," *Scientific American,* March 1989, p. 24.

30. *Ibid.*

31. William G. Wild Jr. and Otis Port. "The Startling Discovery Bell Labs Kept in the Shadows," *Business Week,* September 21, 1987, pp. 69, 72, 76.

32. Gina Kolata. "Giant Leap in Math: 155 Divided to 0," *The New York Times,* June 20, 1990, p. A 8.

33. Gina Kolata. "The assault on 114, 381, 625, 757, 888, 669, 235, 779, 976, 146, 612, 010, 218, 296,

721, 242, 362, 562, 561, 842, 935, 706, 935, 245, 733, 897, 830, 597, 123, 563, 958, 705, 058, 989, 075, 147, 599, 290, 026, 879, 543, 541," *The New York Times,* March 22, 1994, pp. B 5, B6.

34. Karen A. Frenkel. "HDTV and the Computer Industry." *Communications of the ACM* **32** (11), November 1989, pp. 1300–1312.

35. *Ibid.,* p. 1303.

36. George Gilder. *Microcosm: The Quantum Revolution in Economics and Technology.* (New York: Simon & Schuster, 1989).

37. *Ibid.,* Frenkel, p. 1307.

38. Tekla S. Perry. "HDTV and the New Digital Television," *IEEE Spectrum,* April 1995, p. 35.

39. Thane Patterson and Maria Shao. " 'But I Don't Wanna Play Nintendo Anymore!'," *Business Week,* November 19, 1990, pp. 52, 54.

40. Andrew Pollack. "Nintendo Chief Is All Work, No Play," *The New York Times,* August 26, 1996, pp. C 1–C 2.

41. Ty Ahmad-Taylor. "Studios Look to Interactive Games," *The New York Times,* August 28, 1995, p. C 7.

42. Lawrence M. Fisher. "Battle in the Big Video Game Market," *The New York Times,* May 8, 1995, p. C 7.

43. *Ibid.,* Ahmad-Taylor.

44. George Johnson. "A New Family Tree Is Constructed for Indo-European," *The New York Times,* January 2, 1996, pp. B 5, B 7.

45. *Ibid.,* p. B 7.

46. John Lester. E-mail signature file, Massachusetts General Hospital. Available in EFF Quotes Collection 9.0 at Web site with URL: <http://www.eff.org/pub/EFF/quotes.eff>.

47. Brendan P. Kehoe. *Zen and the Art of the Internet: A Beginner's Guide.* (Englewood Cliffs, NJ: Prentice-Hall, 1991).

48. Gene Spafford. "What Is Usenet?" Posted on *news.announce.newusers,* April 26, 1993. Message-ID: <spaf-whatis_735800479@cs.purdue.edu>.

49. Wade Roush. "Spinning a Better Web," *Technology Review,* April 1995. Available at the Web site with URL: <http://www.mit.edu/techreview/www/>.

50. Peter H. Lewis. "Peering Out a 'Real Time' Window," *The New York Times,* February 8, 1995, p. C 1, C 5.

51. "The National Information Infrastructure: Agenda for Action," NTIA NII Office, September 15, 1993. Available at the NTIA Web site with URL: <gopher://ntiant.ntia.doc.gov:70/00/papers/documents/files/nii_agenda_for_action.txt>.

52. "The Canadian Information Highway," Spectrum, Information Technologies and Telecommunications Sector, Industry Canada, April 1994, p. 8. Also available at Industry Canada Web site with URL: <http://info.ic.gc.ca/info-highway/reports/building/rpt-fnl.txt>.

53. *A National Survey of the Public's Attitudes Toward Computers.* (New York: *Time,* 1971).

54. Louis Harris and Associates. *The Road After 1984: The Impact of Technology on Society* (for Southern New England Telephone, 1983).

55. *The Role of Technology in American Life.* The Times Mirror Center for the People & the Press, May 1994.

56. Peter H. Lewis. "Technology: Another survey of Internet users is out, and this one has statistical credibility," *The New York Times,* October 30, 1995, p. C 3.

57. "New Survey Lowers Internet User Estimates," *The Wall Street Journal,* January 12, 1996, p. B 2. For more detail, see Find/SVP, Inc., at the Web site with URL: <http://etrg.findsvp.com/>.

58. Gary H. Anthes. "ISP = Internet Service Problems?" *Computerworld,* July 8, 1996, pp. 53–54.

59. Justin Hibbard. "Net Snares Mainstream," *Computerworld,* August 19, 1996, p. 6.

60. *Ibid.*

ADDITIONAL READINGS

A Variety of Applications

Advanced Automotive Technology: Visions of a Super-Efficient Family Car. U.S. Congress, Office of Technology Assessment, OTA-ETI-638. (Washington, DC: US Government Printing Office, September 1995).

Brahm, Robert. "Math & Visualization: New Tools, New Frontiers." *IEEE Spectrum,* November 1995, pp. 19–21.

Del Valle, Christina. "Smart Highways, Foolish Choices?" *Business Week,* November 28, 1994, pp. 143–144.

"Digital Television." Special Issue, *IEEE Spectrum,* April 1995, pp. 34–80.

Forefronts. Cornell Theory Center, Cornell University, Ithaca, NY. Also available at the Web site with URL: <http://www.tc.cornell.edu/>.

"Key Technologies for the 21st Century," *Scientific American,* September 1995, 150th Anniversary Issue.

Port, Otis. "Look Ma, No Hands," *Business Week,* August 14, 1995, pp. 80–81.

Robinson, Edward A. "Soon Your Dashboard Will Do Everything (Except Steer)," *Fortune,* July 22, 1996, pp. 76–78.

Stix, Gary. "Waiting for Breakthroughs," *Scientific American,* April 1996, pp. 94–99.

Sweet, William. "The Glass Cockpit," *IEEE Spectrum,* September 1995, pp. 30–38.

Taylor III, Alex. "Cars That Beat Traffic," *Fortune,* February 20, 1995, pp. 64–66, 68, 70, 72.

Wouk, Victor. "Hybrids: Then and Now," *IEEE Spectrum,* July 1995, pp. 16–21.

The Internet and Information Highway

"The Accidental Superhighway: A Survey of the Internet," *The Economist,* July 1, 1995. Available at the Web page with URL: <http://www.economist.com/surveys/internet/index.html>.

The Challenge of the Information Highway: Final Report of the Information Highway Advisory Council, Industry Canada, 1995. (Ottawa, Ontario: Distribution Services, Industry Canada). Available at the Web page with URL: <http://info.ic.gc.ca/info-highway/ih.html>.

Realizing the Information Future: The Internet and Beyond. Computer Science and Telecommunications Board, National Research Council. (Washington, DC: National Academy Press, 1994). Available at the Web page with URL: <http://www.nap.edu/readingroom/books/rtif>.

The Unpredictable Century: Information Infrastructure Through 2000. NII Steering Committee, National Research Council. (Washington, DC: National Academy Press, 1996). Available at the Web page with URL: <http://www.nap.edu/readingroom/books/unpredictable>.

Societal Issues

Johnson, Deborah G. and Nissenbaum, Helen. *Computers, Ethics & Social Values.* (Englewood Cliffs, NJ: Prentice-Hall, 1995).

Miller, Steven E. *Civilizing Cyberspace: Policy, Power, and the Information Superhighway.* (New York: ACM Press and Addison-Wesley Publishing Company, 1996).

2

COMPUTERS AND THE HUMAN IMAGINATION

Some men see things as they are and ask why. Others dream things that never were and ask why not.
George Bernard Shaw (1856–1950)[1]

INTRODUCTION

Machines that can move, talk, play games, or mimic human behavior in some other way have held a considerable fascination for people in every era. It is not surprising these days to encounter at the newsstand one or more magazines that report yet another human ability recently achieved by a computer. The mechanisms used to produce such interesting behavior have ranged from steam, clockwork devices, and electromechanical systems to today's mainframes and workstations.

Contemporary depiction of robots is generally favorable—witness the lovable robots of the *Star Wars* movies and their part in the series' phenomenal success. Only a few years earlier, however, one of the main protagonists in *2001: A Space Odyssey* was a malevolent computer called HAL. Robotic machines, such as those in *Terminator* (I and II) and *Robocop* (I and II), have been perceived as threats to both society in general and humans in particular and as tools or even partners in the process of civilization.

Contemporary artists in many fields have been eager to use computers as partners in the process of creating imaginative works. Music and the visual arts have been the primary beneficiaries (perhaps too strong a term in the opinion of many) of the advances in computer technology. Recently, computers and sophisticated graphics terminals have been used in movie animation to produce extraordinarily complex images. This development will permit directors to combine humans and computer-generated images without recourse to the construction of physical sets or even to produce animated movies entirely by computer. Less interesting results have been achieved in the application of computers to the written or spoken arts. Except perhaps for free verse, where much of the art is in the ear and mind of the beholder, computers and language have not meshed successfully.

As a medium for artistic endeavor, the Internet is being employed in a number of interesting ways to extend the scope of creativity instantaneously worldwide. Music can be downloaded, world-famous museums visited, and famous archeological sites explored, all from one's computer. The possibility of assuming arbitrary identities, including gender switching, may initiate global communities of active participants creating drama without boundaries. Virtual reality (the simulation of artificial worlds) which permits people to role-play is gaining in popularity and will continue to do so as the necessary technology becomes increasingly affordable. On a more mundane level, the explosion of Web pages has stimulated employment for many graphic artists. Terms such as multimedia and electronic art conjure up some of the excitement of the new media. Of course, technology in the employment of mediocre artists will result in mediocre art, but the possibilities of wonderful art available on demand for everyone continue to exist.

There has always been (or so it seems) a curious attraction to artifacts that resemble humans. In our own time, the digital computer has become the test bed for exploring the possibility of artificial intelligence (AI), that branch of computer science concerned with the attempt to develop programs and programmed machines, that exhibit intelligent behavior. Indeed, AI has become not only a major branch of computer science but also a growing presence in the marketplace. Where relevant, applications involving AI will be discussed.

THE INTELLIGENT MACHINE IN FACT AND FICTION

Charlie had his way, and I was soon on the show. Charlie was right: Abdullah [a mechanical figure controlled internally by a hidden person] pulled them in because people cannot resist automata. There is something in humanity that is repelled and entranced by a machine that seems to have more than human powers. People love to frighten themselves. Look at the fuss nowadays about computers; however deft they may be they can't do anything a man isn't doing, through them; but you hear people giving themselves delicious shivers about a computer-dominated world. I've often thought of working up an illusion, using a computer, but it would be prohibitively expensive, and I can do anything the public would find amusing better and cheaper with clockwork and bits of string. But if I invented a computer-illusion I would take care to dress the computer up to look like a living creature of some sort—a Moon Man or a Venusian—because the public cannot resist clever dollies. Abdullah was a clever dolly of a simple kind and the Rubes couldn't get enough of him. [2]

Automata and Androids

In his interesting and informative book, *Human Robots in Myth and Science,* John Cohen has traced the human fascination with the possibility of living and thinking artifacts. [3] He describes a variety of instances in antiquity of statues that were supposed to speak and offer advice and prophecies. Hephaestus, also known as Vulcan, god of fire, was accompanied by two female statues of pure gold that assisted him in his activities. In the fifteenth century B.C., the statue of King Memnon near Thebes, supposedly emitted a variety of sounds depending on the time of day. Hero of Alexandria (285–222 B.C.) built mechanical birds that apparently flew and sang.

There are many stories of devices originating in the East that moved and talked. Consider this tale of a robot of the third century B.C. in China.

> King Mu of Chou made a tour of inspection in the west . . . and on his return journey, before reaching China, a certain artificer, Yen Shih by name, was presented to him. The king received him and asked him what he could do. He replied that he would do anything which the king commanded, but that he had a piece of work already finished which he would like to show him. "Bring it with you tomorrow," said the king, "and we will look at it together." So next day Yen Shih appeared again and was admitted into the presence. "Who is that man accompanying you?" asked the king. "That, Sir," replied Yen Shih, "is my own handiwork. He can sing and he can act." The king stared at the figure in astonishment. It walked with rapid strides, moving its head up and down, so that anyone would have taken it for a live human being. The artificer touched its chin, and it began singing, perfectly in tune. He touched its hands, and it began posturing, keeping perfect time. It went through any number of movements that fancy might happen to dictate. The king, looking on with his favourite concubine and other beauties, could hardly persuade himself that it was not real. As the performance was drawing to an end, the robot winked its eye and made advances to the ladies in attendance, whereupon the king became incensed and would have had Yen Shih executed on the spot had not the latter, in mortal fear, instantly taken the robot to pieces to let him see what it really was. And, indeed, it turned out to be only a construction of leather, wood, glue and lacquer, variously coloured white, black, red and blue. [4]

The willingness of people to accept life in objects of stone, metal, or wood seems evidence of some deeply embedded need to believe in the power of either the gods or their specially chosen servants to create life in any form. The effect is even stronger if the things that move or talk resemble humans. This need has not diminished over the centuries.

The illustrious figures Albertus Magnus (1204–1272) and Roger Bacon (1214–1294) are supposed to have created, respectively, a life-size automaton servant and a speaking head. At the end of the sixteenth century in Prague, Rabbi Loew produced a living being—the legendary Golem—out of a clay figure by inserting into its mouth a strip of paper with a magical formula. The creation of life from earth or other inanimate substances is a common theme in both history and literature that reached its apogee, in fiction at least, with Baron Frankenstein's monster some two centuries later.

The golden age of automata perhaps was in Europe in the eighteenth century. Skilled craftsmen built incredibly lifelike mechanisms that were exhibited to enormous crowds. The more lifelike the appearance, the greater the acclaim. Apparently the most impressive of these automata was a duck built by Jacques de Vaucanson (1709–1782) and exhibited in 1738. A rebuilt version of this automaton was displayed in Milan at La Scala in 1844 amid great excitement. A member of the audience wrote the following:

> It is the most admirable thing imaginable, an almost inexplicable human achievement. Each feather of the wings is mobile. . . . The artist touches a feather on the upper portion of the body, and the bird lifts its head, glances about, shakes its tail feathers, stretches itself, unfolds its wings, ruffles them and lets out a cry, absolutely natural, as if it were about

to take flight. The effect is still more astonishing when the bird, leaning over its dish, begins to swallow the grain with incredibly realistic movement. As for its method of digestion, nobody can explain it.[5]

There is no question of such devices exhibiting free will or initiating independent action. However lifelike, the duck was no more than a complex clock mechanism of approximately 4,000 parts, and from the moment it began to move, its actions were completely predetermined. We marvel at the incredible ingenuity of the inventor but at the same time we are aware of the limitations of the invention. Still, the skill of these inventors was mind boggling. Especially impressive are the life-size androids built by Pierre Jacquet-Droz and his two sons near Neufchatel, Switzerland between 1768 and 1774. One, a "child" android called the Writer, can be mechanically programmed to write any 40 characters of text. Another, the Musician, which has the form of a woman, moved with a marvelous grace replete with subtle gestures that included head motions and a curtsy.

The so-called Chess Player of 1769, built by Baron Wolfgang von Kempelen (1734–1809) was a famous fraud. Costumed as a Turk, the automaton appeared to move the pieces on a chess board and to play quite a good game of chess. It is believed that, unknown to the audience, a person was concealed under the board, though this fact was not actually established during the automaton's lifetime. Edgar Allan Poe, one of those who argued for the hidden person hypothesis, exploited this theme when he wrote the short story called "Maelzel's Chess-Player" in 1838.

The Theme of the Robot

> It is unreasonable . . . to think machines could become *nearly* as intelligent as we are and then stop, or to suppose we will always be able to compete with them in wit or wisdom. Whether or not we could retain some sort of control of the machines, assuming that we would want to, the nature of our activities and aspirations would be changed utterly by the presence on earth of intellectually superior beings.[6]

A robot can be thought of as a mobile computer with sensory, tactile, and motor abilities. Furthermore, it is typically an artifact made in the image of its human creator, who has endowed it with some form of lifelike behavior. It need not, at least in principle, be machine-like. We might argue that Frankenstein's monster was a robot created from a human corpse and given the spark of "life" by the power of lightning.

The relationship between the scientist or inventor and his or her creation has inspired many tales. Two basic plots have emerged. In one, the robot is a subordinate, a servant quick to obey but unable to initiate independent action. The other is concerned with self-motivated behavior, with the robot (or creation) as potential adversary or potential master. Creations of this type have caused trouble through willful disobedience, as exemplified by Frankenstein's monster, and by carrying out a request too zealously and too literally, as shown in the story of the sorcerer's apprentice and in *The Monkey's Paw* by W. W. Jacobs.[7]

Much of the literature in this area relates to the Greek myth of Prometheus, the hero who disobeyed Zeus, stole fire from heaven, and gave it to humankind. This gift permitted people to keep themselves warm, to illuminate the night, and to create tools and other objects, presumably without either the help or permission of the gods. As punishment for this outrageous theft, Prometheus was chained to a mountain top and plagued for eternity by vultures picking at his liver—a torment one might recommend today for the designers of some particularly terrible computer programs. It is often forgotten that the full title of Mary Shelley's *Frankenstein*, published in 1818, is *Frankenstein: or, the Modern Prometheus*. (Remember also that Baron Frankenstein's monster has no name of its own. Thanks to Hollywood, it has become known simply as Frankenstein.)

In her study of robots and androids in science fiction, Patricia Warrick isolates four themes that emerge from Shelley's novel and recur in modern science fiction.

1. The Promethean theme: the acquisition of a hitherto forbidden skill that is now put to the supposed benefit of humankind.
2. The two-edged nature of technology: benefits are frequently offset by unanticipated problems.
3. The precipitous rejection of technology: the monster launches a campaign of terror only after Dr. Frankenstein abandons him.
4. The uneasy relation between master and servant: what is created sometimes turns against the creator and becomes the master.[8]

This last point is perhaps best exemplified in *Erewhon* (1872), by Samuel Butler, which explores the relationship between humans and their machines. The narrator, discussing the reasons given by the society of Erewhon for banishing machines, notes that it is not existing machines that are to be feared, but the fact that they evolve so rapidly and in such unpredictable directions that they must be controlled, limited, and destroyed while they are still in a primitive form. Compare this fear with the sentiment expressed nearly a century later by one of the founders of artificial intelligence in the quotation that began this section. The following quotation from *Erewhon* may serve as a grim commentary on our age:

> True, from a low materialistic point of view it would seem that those thrive best who use machinery wherever its use is possible with profit; but this is the art of the machines: they serve that they may rule. . . . How many men at this hour are living in a state of bondage to the machines? How many spend their whole lives, from the cradle to the grave, in tending them by night and day? Is it not plain that the machines are gaining ground upon us . . . [9]

Other Utopian, or perhaps more precisely dystopian, novels, such as Aldous Huxley's *Brave New World*—written about 50 years later—and George Orwell's *1984,* are more concerned with general issues surrounding the organization of a future society. Nevertheless, the all-powerful computer plays an integral role in these societies, whether it regulates the birth process, as in *Brave New World*, or controls a vast two-way communications network by which Big Brother has access to every person, as in *1984*. The title *1984* has itself become the shorthand term for the perfectly totalitarian society in which all efforts are devoted to maintaining the state against its enemies, both internal and external, real and imagined. "Big Brother is watching you" is the ultimate warning for a society in which there is complete absence of privacy and individual freedom.

In the twentieth century, perhaps *the* work of art that most successfully addresses the problem of people and their people-like machines is the play *R.U.R.* (1921) by Karel Capek.[10] In fact the word "robot" made its first appearance in this play, whose title is an abbreviation for "Rossum's Universal Robots." In *R.U.R.* humankind has become so dependent on robots that when the robots revolt, there is no hope. However, the robots do not know how to reproduce themselves, the formula having been lost in the general destruction accompanying their takeover. Thus, the people are ultimately destroyed by their creations, a bitter example of the fourth theme mentioned above.

At variance with the almost universal pessimism expressed so far has been the impact on science fiction of Isaac Asimov's robot stories. Asimov, one of the most prolific writers of our time, wrote a series of short stories dealing with robots and in the process introduced a substantial realignment into the imagined human-robot relationship. In his 1942 story "Runaround," Asimov described "the three fundamental Rules of Robotics—the three rules that are built most deeply into a robot's positronic brain." These govern robot behavior with respect to humans to prevent any harm coming to a human either through an action or lack of action by a robot. The three laws are as follows:

> First Law: A robot may not injure a human being, or, through inaction, allow a human being to come to harm. Second Law: A robot must obey the orders given it by human beings except where such orders would conflict with the First Law. Third Law: A robot must protect its own existence as long as such protection does not conflict with the First or Second Laws.[11]

The working out of implications inherent in these three laws informs the plots of many of the subsequent stories in Asimov's robot series.

The trend of reforming robots has probably reached its peak in the *Star Wars* movies, in which the two robots—R2D2, the chirpy fire hydrant, and C3PO, the prissy, gold-encased English butler—do not appear to have even one malevolent transistor between them. They exist only to serve their masters—humans. In real life another race of robots has appeared in the last few years: those indefatigable workers on the assembly line, the industrial robots. We can conclude with the observation that intelligent artifacts, whether in the form of humans or not, continue to exert a powerful influence on the human imagination. In many ways technology, the product of our minds and hands, is a mixed blessing. Writers have explored this ambivalence for many years, but the issues have sharpened with the appearance of that most marvelous of all inventions, the computer.

COMPUTERS AS A CREATIVE MEDIUM

"The Eureka"
Such is the name of a machine for composing hexameter Latin verses which is now exhibited at the Egyptian Hall, in Piccadilly. It was designed and constructed at Bridgewater, in Somersetshire; was begun in 1830, and completed in 1843; and it has lately been brought to the metropolis, to contribute to the "sights of the season. . . ."

The rate of composition is about one verse per minute, or sixty an hour. Each verse remains stationary and visible a sufficient time for a copy of it to be taken; after which the machine gives an audible notice that the Line is about to be decomposed. Each Letter of the verse is then slowly and separately removed into its former alphabetical arrangement; on which the machine stops, until another verse be required. Or, by withdrawing the stop, it may be made to go on continually, producing in one day and night, or twenty-four hours, about 1440 Latin verses; or, in a whole week (Sundays included) about 10,000. During the composition of each line, a cylinder in the interior of the machine performs the National Anthem. (Anonymous, Illustrated London News, 1895.)

What effects has the computer had either directly or indirectly on the arts? "Arts" here means music, drawing and graphics, film, literature, multimedia, and virtual reality. We are concerned with the use of computers in the creative process as a tool or aid or as the very medium for artistic creation, rather than as the subject matter of the work itself. In the best of all possible worlds you would have access to a computer and be able to use it to produce music (with a synthesizer), art (with a graphics system), and perhaps poetry. Second best would be a tape of music, a portfolio of drawings, and a slim volume of computer-generated poetry. Unfortunately, we are in a position only to describe and comment, not to present and demonstrate, but you are encouraged to access the Internet, to search out Web sites that make music, art, film, and literature instantaneously available.

There are a number of issues to keep in mind as we proceed. To what degree is the computer itself creative? This seems to be a question with which the artists themselves have little concern. For those interested in the computer as a tool, there is hardly any reason to attribute special powers of creativity to it. The artist wants to explore ways of creating under his or her initiative. The computer can give the artist a variety of means to extend and augment his or her abilities. Will anything significant emerge from the application of computers to art? The simple answer is "only time will tell." There may not appear to be any great artistic accomplishments up to now, although a recent computer-animated film seems to be close. The computer is a relatively new invention, and artists will take time to learn how to use it.

Music

Music has probably been that art form most amenable to computer experimentation and the history of computer music is almost as old as that of the first electronic computer. This is not very surprising, because even before computers were invented, music could be represented by means of an electronic signal that is readily available for a computer to modify. The original signal itself can be generated by electronic equipment. That is, a complex piece of equipment incorporating signal generators, synthesizers, and microprocessors is like a giant "intelligent" organ that can be used by the contemporary composer.

In the 1950s, electronic music meant tape splicing and other manual rearrangements of sound. It was not until the 1960s that sound synthesizers, high-speed digital-to-analog converters, and sound generation programs appeared. One of the most famous early works was the "Illiac Suite for String Quartet" by Lejaren Hiller of the University of Illinois. This composition relied on the computer for the generation of random numbers. Music with a strong random component in its performance or composition is called aleatory music. For purposes of composition, computers have proven invaluable because the composer is able to set the parameters of permissible variation, and the computer can select the actual path to be followed. Once the program has been designed the role of the composer is to modify, shape, and select.

However, quite a few discordant sounds have been made as well by critics and the general public. For example, Lars Gunnar Bodin of the Electronic Music Studio of Stockholm has written, albeit more than 15 years ago, "in spite of great efforts in time and money, relatively little of artistic significance has been produced in computer music."[12] The composition of music using mechanical and electronic aids has been subject to criticism similar to that once directed at the mechanical reproduction of music. The German writer E. T. A. Hoffman (about whose life and stories Jacques Offenbach composed the opera *Tales of Hoffmann*) wrote the following in 1816:

> To set to work to make music by means of valves, springs, levers, cylinders, or whatever other apparatus you choose to employ, is a senseless attempt to make the means to an end accomplish what can result only when those means are animated and, in their minutest movements, controlled by the mind, the soul, and the heart. The gravest reproach you can make to a musician is that he plays without expression; because, by so doing, he is marring the whole essence of the matter. For it is impossible that any impulse whatever from the inner man shall not, even for a moment, animate his rendering; whereas, in the case of a machine, no such impulse can ever do so. The attempts of mechanicians to imitate, with more or less approximation to accuracy, the human organs in the production of musical sounds, or to substitute mechanical appliances for those organs, I consider tantamount to a declaration of war against the spiritual element in music; but the greater the forces they array against it, the more victorious it is. For this very reason, the more perfect that this sort of machinery is, the more I disapprove of it; and I infinitely prefer the commonest barrel-organ, in which the mechanism attempts nothing but to be mechanical, to Vaucanson's flute player, or the harmonica girl.[13]

An important aspect of the creation of computer-related art is the availability of the necessary hardware, typically a specially equipped workstation, and the appropriate software. For music, the Musical Instrument Digital Interface (M.I.D.I.) sound synthesis system has been the relatively low-cost system of choice for many musicians. A typical M.I.D.I. system consists of a method for generating signals at given frequencies, a process to shape and modify these signals and finally a sound chip to create the synthesized music that can be converted to analog form and played back through a speaker.[14] Apparently, using M.I.D.I. is not straightforward and has been difficult for many musicians to learn. A new technology, called Wave-Table sound synthesis, is now available. It provides a bank of digitally compressed sounds originally recorded from a wide variety of musical instruments. Although not every note from every instrument is directly available, missing notes can be interpolated from the existing ones. Thus sounds are more realistic, in that actual physical processes that produced the sound can be captured. Faster microprocessors and more powerful sound chips, including better digital-to-analog converters and improved amplifiers, have led to this new system.

As mentioned previously, once created, musical compositions can be made instantaneously available worldwide over the Internet. In fact, a number of Web sites exist that provide music for every possible taste. Samples can be downloaded and played on demand

and even online concerts have become a fairly frequent occurrence on the Internet. The future holds such possibilities as the ability to purchase music directly from home by downloading it to a computer. This development is consistent with the improvement in the sound quality of computers and their evolution into a major component of distributed home entertainment centers. However, as technology improves it is good to keep in mind the message contained in the following quotation by the composer John Melby:[15]

> [T]he aim of computer music is (or, at least, should be) the enhancement of the capability to produce significant works of music utilizing the digital computer as a medium. The production of sound per se is, of course, a part of the whole process, but it is a means to an end and not the end in itself.

Visual Arts

Turning to drawing, graphics, and video art, we find, up to fairly recently, considerable inventiveness but a certain sameness of technique. Facile use of a new and powerful tool may be the problem. As in music, we may have to look to the future for the emergence of real art and not just the obvious exploitation of an available technology. One of the early and important artists to use computers was A. Michael Noll. In an article written in 1967, he makes the point that even though the computer must be programmed to perform each action, its speed, decision-making ability, and large memory give it great power even to the point of appearing to produce the unexpected.[16] The computer permits the artist to explore many possibilities and, in some sense, demonstrates a measure of creativity.

In the interest of exploring this notion, Noll programmed a computer to generate a picture composed of pseudo-random elements resembling paintings done by Piet Mondrian, a well-known twentieth-century artist. The computer-generated picture was displayed, along with a Mondrian painting for the benefit of one hundred subjects, who were asked which they preferred and which was in fact the Mondrian. Fifty-nine percent preferred the computer picture and only 28% could identify the Mondrian picture. An interesting fact is that people found the Mondrian too precise and machine-like in its placement of the picture elements, whereas the randomness in the placement of the corresponding picture elements in the computer picture was found pleasing.[17]

Another early computer artist is Charles Csuri at Ohio State University. He began in 1964 to use a mainframe computer and has continued to the present day, but he is not interested in using paint programs. He "wants the full power of a sophisticated computer at his fingertips, which lets him sculpt images in three dimensions, view them from any angle, set them in motion, and alter them in ways that often blur the distinction between special effects and art."[18] Csuri's view on the role of the computer in the creation of art is interesting and valuable, given his experiences over many years. He insists that, "Just because the computer can do perspective and beautiful shadows and shininess, or make things look like glass, you still need to have an esthetic sensibility, you need a sense of culture and history. That has not changed."[19]

The relationship between art and technology has always been uneasy. It has taken many years for photography to be recognized as art and the suspicion remains that the photographer achieves most by selection rather than by creation, since the camera seems to do most of the work. Thus, it is not surprising that acceptance of such a marvelous piece of equipment as a computer should be resisted by both the public at large and the artist as well. But change is inevitable, given the nature of our times. Too frequently the computer is used as an overpriced electronic paintbrush. Most of the results could hardly be termed "fine art": repetitious patterns, distorted images of human forms, and randomly placed patches of randomly generated lines. However, many artists have used the computer in a creative and exciting way. One of these is Harold Cohen, who more than 25 years ago, designed a program called AARON in order to study the way people both produce and understand drawings. Not surprisingly, Cohen has discovered that much of the enjoyment and appreciation of a work of art is brought by the viewer. Many times he has been asked if what is being displayed is indeed art. What may be surprising is that AARON itself has "advanced from drawing squiggly lines to painting portraits that look handmade and are hung in major art museums." [20]

The critic Cynthia Goodman, writing in the catalog accompanying the show of computer art, *Digital Visions*, [21] points out that artists have resisted computer technology because of "their fear that the computer would usurp artistic creativity and control." [22] On the other hand, the artist Lillian Schwartz, reflecting the opinion of many, was concerned "that remarkably repetitive images were being produced by those with access to the same program and equipment." [23] Artist Colette Bangert, who works with her husband, has expressed her relationship with the computer in the following way: [24]

> I now think much more clearly about my handmade work and have much more control as a result of having made computer drawings. In addition, I recognize that our computer efforts have led to unique and unfamiliar images, which I might never have considered introducing into my drawings. On the other hand, I consider that our computer drawings are extensions of my handmade drawings.

Another artist, Hubert Hohn, [25] in reaction to the idea of the computer as a sophisticated tool, has decided to "try to define a computer aesthetic based on the unique properties of the machine. . . . I want to see what happens when a computer is allowed to be itself—not forced to function as a paintbrush or a camera or a lump of charcoal." [26] Letting the computer be itself in this case involved writing a simple program to print out the current state of memory as a structured array of 0s and 1s and attaching titles such as "SELF POR-TRAIT, or THE MACHINE EXAMINES THE STATE OF ITS MEMORY IN THE ACT OF EXAMINING THE STATE OF ITS MEMORY, or THE MACHINE SEEKS THE ORIGIN OF ITS CONSCIOUSNESS." In some sense the titles have assumed an importance far beyond the work itself.

In the last few years, the technology and software have improved so dramatically that the computer has become a major factor in the production of graphic art. Traditional art making has also taken account of the computer in a number of ways. Consider the following examples: [27]

- Portraits by Montreal artist Luc Courchesne do not hang quietly on a gallery wall. They chat and, occasionally, argue with each other. They talk to viewers and, if they like someone, will share their feelings and perhaps even confide a secret. If not, they become moody, abruptly ending the dialogue . . . They appear suspended in space, as if separate from the computer, video monitors and laser discs that generate them.

- Some [artists] deal with issue of privacy, notably American Jim Campbell's *Untitled (for Heisenberg),* in which, through an ingenious use of computers and video, the viewer's image pops up in bed with a naked couple.
- Others, such as German artist Christian Möller's *Electronic Mirror,* which unexpectedly erases a visitor's reflection, illustrate a lack of control over technology.
- In the installation [of *Silicon Remembers Carbon*], [David] Rokeby's "canvas" is a bed of sand enclosed by a narrow walkway, on the floor of a darkened room. Sounds and images of flowing water, blowing winds, fire and shadow are projected onto the sand in ever changing patterns . . . If visitors, for instance, dip their hands into the convincing video "pools of water," they will feel dry sand.

Themes in this new art are a mixture of exploring general fears of technology in today's society, provoking such fears, exploitation of the technology itself as a window and even a door into alternative domains of experience, and playing with images, sounds, and textures in unpredictable ways. Some of the earliest applications appeared in advertising and this trend has continued in the relatively new area of Web pages. Thousands of Web sites are in active competition to attract first-time viewers and to maintain their interests. One method is to design flashy graphics, but unless the content is equally compelling, first-time viewers may well not return. In any case, a lucrative application area has appeared for graphic artists to practice their craft and many talented designers have been attracted. [28]

An interesting exhibition was held at the Parsons School of Design in New York in 1994 with the title, "From Drawing to Montage: Computers in Art." The curator, Michael Dashkin, raised some very interesting questions about the role of computers, and technology in general, in art. Dashkin states his aims in presenting this exhibition: "I have chosen work in which it is not always immediately evident that a computer was part of the process. One of the reasons for this is that the artists in this exhibition are not primarily interested in foregrounding the technologies they employ . . . but a work that is informed by its methods of production differs markedly from one that is manifestly centered on them." [29] It is also not clear to him that there is such a field as computer art, that the computer is more than a tool. This comment is revealing because it indicates that as recently as 1994, after at least 25 years of involvement in the visual arts, the computer has not assured itself a place as an esthetically defining force. Nevertheless, Dashkin does not minimize its importance: "In seeking a new paradigm for artists' use of computers, we avoid assigning a reductive role to the technologies used and instead locate their use within a century-long tradition of artists' use of new technologies, a tradition that has enriched the language of the visual arts, and at the same time, posed a challenge to older art practices." [30]

As with so much of the material in this book, much more could be said, but because of space limitations, only three more issues will be raised. Fast becoming an important factor in picture-making is three-dimensional imagery. Increased computing power has enabled software to be created to present 3D pictures in such areas as medicine, advertising, games, engineering, military, and science. [31] One possibly dangerous application of this technology is that the ability to manipulate digital images can destroy all confidence in the fidelity of photographic evidence. Obviously, altering photographs or creating photographs that depict events that did not occur can have devastating impact for historical research, news reporting, and of course in the courts. At the very least, a healthy skepticism must now be maintained: [32]

> Photographs appeared to be reliably manufactured commodities, readily distinguishable from other types of depictions. They were generally regarded as causally generated, truthful reports about things in the real world, unlike more traditionally handicrafted images, which seemed notoriously ambiguous and uncertain human constructions. The emergence of digital imaging has irrevocably subverted these certainties, forcing us all to adopt a far more wary and vigilant interpretive stance. The information superhighway will bring us a growing flood of visual information in digital format, but we will have to take great care to sift facts from the fictions and the falsehoods.

The reference to the information superhighway is well-taken, but from another point of view the ability to visit the world's museums remotely via the Internet provides heretofore unavailable opportunities.

Film

Some would say that movies are *the* exciting domain of contemporary arts. They are another fairly recent art form. In their early years, movies were seen mainly as popular entertainment, and profits were the main motive for their production. Almost inadvertently, artists were attracted to this new medium and succeeded over time in producing important and serious artistic endeavors. However, there has always been an uneasy peace between the goals of profit and art. Many of the experimental efforts in film have emerged from a stream outside the commercial film industry.

One of the earliest and most important filmmakers to use the computer as an integral part of the creative process is John Whitney. Fully aware of the potential of computers as early as the 1940s, Whitney observed that

> the best computer art did not compare well with lacework from Belgium made a century ago. But the computer possessed a unique capability of making very complex pattern flow. One could plan exacting and explicit patterns of action and distinctive motions as intricate as lace, but in a way no Belgian lacemaker would ever have imagined. [33]

Whitney created a number of films, with music, generated by computer. They are characterized by the complex development of geometric themes in a rhythmic pattern accompanied by an original musical score. He had no illusions about the role of computers in the creation of art and very bluntly stated his beliefs that computers would never create "meaningful" art. The crucial issue in creativity is judgment, not calculation.

It is altogether fitting that the real breakthrough in the application of computers to the making of films was made by Walt Disney Studios in *TRON* (1982). Long the world leader in animated feature films, Disney Studios recognized that the state of the art in computer animation was sufficiently well developed for computers to make a major contribution to filmmaking. The traditional Disney animation system required that many people work over long periods of time to produce thousands upon thousands of drawings. Developments in graphics, however, both in hardware and software, have permitted generation by computer of representational three-dimensional scenes. In all previous movies based on fantasy or science fiction, very complex models—usually quite small—were designed and built. Actors were positioned and cleverly photographed against these models to give the illusion of vast reaches of space, giant castles, enormous space ships and other constructs of the projected future or distant past. Of course many other techniques have been employed in the composition, photography, and editing of films, and computers have played an important role in these phases as well. As for *TRON*, although in its time it was a technological success, its artistic failure limited its influence.

In July 1984, *The Last Starfighter* was released. It included about 25 minutes of computer-generated film, compared to about 5 minutes in *TRON*. The computer scenes were generated by Digital Productions, using a Cray X-MP. This machine replaced the earlier Cray-1 (used in the making of TRON) and was needed in such prodigious computations as those for the hero's space ship *Gunstar,* which required 750,000 polygons and achieved an extraordinarily realistic effect. Interestingly enough, it is a more difficult challenge to represent soft objects such as flowers and people than spaceships and robots.

A Lucasfilm division called Pixar (founded by George Lucas, the creator of the enormously popular and successful *Star Wars* series), set up to carry out research and development in advanced computer graphics, was purchased in 1986 by Steven Jobs and is now an independent company. It has made a number of important contributions to such movies as *Star Trek II: The Wrath of Khan* and *Return of the Jedi,* as well as producing award winning animated shorts such as *The Adventures of Andre and Wally B.,* and culminating with the five-minute *Tin Toy,* the first computer-generated film to win an Academy Award. Although the computational efforts to create even short films are prodigious, the fundamental creative act still resides in the human animators, who must design the original figures, environment, and of course, story line. The appearance of the very successful film *Roger Rabbit,* a full-length movie integrating hand-drawn animated characters with humans, serves as a reminder of how much is yet to be achieved by computer animation systems. The long period of time involved in producing traditional animated movies, however, to say nothing of the associated high costs, certainly provides impetus for further research.

The past few years have seen this challenge being met. The production of such successful films as *Casper, Terminator 2, Jurassic Park, The Mask, Forest Gump, Toy Story,* and *Jumanji* has finally indicated that completely automated animation is possible and that an entire film of high quality is well within reach; in fact *Toy Story* may very well be that film. One technique that has been employed successfully is called morphing, the continuous deformation of one image into another. It was an integral part of the treatment of the android in *Terminator 2* that repeatedly reconstructed itself from the results of episodes of drastic dismemberment, and permitted Jim Carey's face to undergo the most startling transformations in *The Mask,* but that old question remains:[34]

> *The Mask* is not so much a movie, more a feature-length demo reel for the wonders of digital conjuring on screen . . . You end up enthused by the product but wondering, before you take out your cheque book, whether you should not wait a little longer while they improve the story-packaging.

Toy Story is 77 minutes long and every frame was computer generated:[35]

> Each one of its 1,560 shots was created on Silicon Graphics and Sun workstations by artists working from some 400 computer-generated mathematical models and backgrounds. The shots were then edited using Avid editing systems and painstakingly rendered by powerful Pixar-developed RenderMan software. (That software consumed 300 Mbytes per frame, provided by 117 Sun SPARC 20s. Four years in the making, the 77-minute film required 800,000 machine-hours just to produce a final cut.)

Interestingly enough, this enormous expenditure in computer resources was produced by Disney, the world leader in traditional animation methods. And even more surprising, the film is an artistic success, with many critics rating it as one of the best of 1995. The success is a result of a good story with funny dialogue and excellent characters, well-served by the exciting and surprisingly effective animation. The future looks more than promising in the application of technology to the making of movies.

However, there is an area in which the application of current computer technology to films has aroused some controversy, namely the colorization of black and white movies. For a generation raised with color television and primarily color movies, black and white images do not seem to be attractive, or at least this is what Turner Entertainment, the current owner of such classic movies as *The Maltese Falcon, Casablanca, Miracle on 34th Street,* and *It's a Wonderful Life,* maintains.[36] Consider the following summary of two positions, keeping in mind that the owner of a work of art, or any property for that matter, has complete control over his or her possession:[37]

> The Directors Guild of America has protested colorization on the grounds that its members' works of art are being tampered with. [They] defended black-and-white films as an art form, meriting the preservation granted to historical films or national landmarks. The colorists' position is that they are simply offering the public an option; those who prefer the black-and-white can simply turn down the color control on their television set.

Not only is computer technology the tool of film production, it has also become the subject of films, with such 1995 releases as *Hackers* and *The Net*. A quick summation of the plots suggests reasons for the failure of both films. *Hackers:* "Stringy-haired youths compete to obtain secret virus information;" *The Net:* "Assassin seeks to obtain secret virus information on floppy disk. In the process, he wipes out the main character's credit card history, driver's license and passport information."[38]

Multimedia and Virtual Reality

Whatever role the computer plays in traditional art forms and whatever contributions it makes, it will generally be viewed as a tool, albeit a sophisticated one. Recent technological developments combining video cassette recorders (VCRs), TVs, computers, and compact disk (CD) players suggest the possibility of a new art form, usually referred to as multimedia. The ability to represent digitally both sounds and images permits their manipulation by computer programs and their display using high resolution television and high fidelity amplifiers and loudspeakers. As with many other innovations in their early stages, there seems to be a lack of agreement on what multimedia actually is. Witness the following: [39]

> For some, it means simply choreographing text, sound, and animated graphics to create relatively crude cinematic effects. Others reserve the terms for PCs that also can control laser-disk players and VCRs and perhaps even display the contents on a PC screen. Still others look forward to sophisticated and expensive systems that would treat video information as just another type of digital data, thus permitting enormous flexibility in how it can be edited, manipulated, and displayed.

Given that some of the major players in computers and software such as IBM, Apple, Intel, Microsoft, NeXT, Fujitsu, and NEC are involved, one can expect a stream of products, advertisements, and testimonials to the virtues of multimedia. The terms hypermedia and multimedia are frequently used interchangeably to suggest this mixing of electronic media to achieve new and startling effects. Currently multimedia exists primarily in educational software and in-house training programs available via CD-ROMs. Story-telling CD-ROMs have been produced that permit a variety of options, such as multiple story lines with appropriate sound and images. The best example of hypermedia is probably the Web with its worldwide digital information sources—text, sound, images—accessible by the mere clicking on a highlighted link. One interesting area is electronic magazines that have appeared with some regularity. For example, C/net is an online computer magazine that first appeared in June 1995. Apparently, the C/net management has ambitious plans: ". . . the Web site is the leading edge of Mr. Minor's [chief executive of C/net] multimedia assault, a business strategy that he hopes will outflank rivals whose roots are in the print-and-ink world. Calling his computer information service a "network" (perhaps a bit prematurely), Mr. Minor is also offering a half-hour cable television show, 'C/net Central,' that runs several times a week . . ." [40]

Virtual reality has been hailed by some and condemned by others. The creation of disembodied simulated worlds with computer-generated human simulacra that see, hear, and touch has many applications including games, advertising, industrial product testing, and of course new forms of art. By wearing suitably designed gloves, a helmet, and body suit, it is possible to plunge into an artificial world in which the laws of physics have been suspended and everything is possible, even virtual sex. At a more mundane level, products can be tested by simulating them and having a person use them in a virtual world. Architectural models can be more realistically evaluated by embedding them in artificial environments. With the simulation of touch, positive feedback is available and more realistic simulations can be used. Early virtual reality implementations were criticized because of the frequent occurrence of vertigo-like reactions to the point that some people became physically sick. Better systems with more computational power provide smoother motions and thereby reduce the more extreme unpleasant sensations.

CONTEMPORARY VIEWS OF THE MACHINE

All life is an experiment. The more experiments you make the better. (Ralph Waldo Emerson [1803–1882]) [41]

We are living in an age of science and technology. The newsstand has exploded with computer and technology magazines such as *MacWorld*, *PC World*, *Wired*, *Internet World*, *Virtual Reality*, and others, whose covers advertise stories on biotechnology, artificial life, new theories of the universe, and, inevitably, computers. In addition to the purely technological articles on how microprocessors will revolutionize our lives, stories on intelligent machines appear with regularity. We are told how computers will do the work of doctors, lawyers, and other professionals and that robots will soon be making regular appearances in our homes and in our places of work and play.

The public at large is infatuated with the robot. The immensely popular R2D2 and C3PO of the by-now classical *Star Wars* series, are totally dedicated to the well-being of their human masters. They are the complete antithesis, of, say, Frankenstein's monster and are, in fact, a realization of the kind of robot proposed by Isaac Asimov. We are now in the era of the robot as friend and servant. Some voices have been raised in warning about the possibility of massive unemployment resulting from the introduction of robots into the assembly line. The counter-argument is that robots will be engaged in boring and dangerous activities and thus free people to realize their full potential in other areas of life. In any case, robots are on the way. We are even being encouraged to attribute robotic qualities to household devices that incorporate microprocessors, sensors, and actuators—manufacturers inform us in their advertisements that our televisions, microwave ovens, cameras, and other pieces of everyday equipment have an "electronic brain" that can think (for us) and therefore act for us.

Intelligent machines may not be an entirely unmixed blessing, as you will recall from that powerful motion picture, *2001: A Space Odyssey*. A computer called HAL (a name only one letter removed from IBM) begins acting unpredictably as it tries to ensure the success of the space mission, believing that it is in jeopardy because of the actions of the human crew. It causes the death of four men before it is dismantled by the one remaining human. As its circuits are progressively disconnected it appeals piteously to be allowed to continue functioning. It even promises to be good in the future. All this is to no avail, as it has in fact violated Asimov's First Law and must be punished.

This impressive film leaves us with the assured feeling that we humans will retain ultimate control because we can "pull the plug." The popular media generally present a favorable viewpoint toward robots or intelligent machines: They will secure more leisure time for everyone and liberate people from dangerous work; they will mine the seas, explore space, and bring prosperity to all. However, some nonscientific observers think that if machines become intelligent enough they will develop a sense (a strategy) of self-preservation that will cause them to defend their existence. From Hollywood, the frequent creator and arbiter of mass taste have come a series of beings illustrating such diverse themes as the destruction of humans (*Terminator*, played by Arnold Schwarzeneger) and their protector (*Terminator II*, with the protecting android played by Arnold confronting a more advanced killing model). More recently, *Screamers* shows what happens when robots designed for special tasks of directed destruction somehow mutate and destroy humans indiscriminately, yet another instance of the slave turning on the master. These movies and many others are all products of the human imagination as typically revealed in science fiction, and while the vision of the future they present is possible, at root it is clearly more fiction than science. However, there is a scientific discipline concerned with the development of intelligent machines, namely, artificial intelligence or AI.

ARTIFICIAL INTELLIGENCE: A BRIEF INTRODUCTION

All great ideas are dangerous. (Oscar Wilde [1854–1900])[42]

Machines and Living Things Compared

In a paper written in 1955, Anatol Rapoport points out the strong relationship between the level of technology and contemporaneous mechanical models of living things.[43] He first defines a technological "phylum," in comparison with a biological phylum, as characterized by a principle of operation. He then goes on to distinguish four technological phyla that came into being successively. The first phylum is the tool that serves primarily to transmit muscular forces; the second is clockworks that operate under the principle of stored mechanical energy, released subsequently and perhaps gradually; the third is heat engines that operate on supplied fuels; the fourth is machines that operate on the principle of storing and transmitting information.

Because tools do not operate independently, they have rarely been compared to living things, although weapons are often personified in mythology, for example, King Arthur's Excalibur and Siegfried's Nothung. The second phylum, however, has suggested living things, especially in such complex realizations as mechanical dolls and animals. (In fact, for Descartes, animals were equivalent to highly complicated automata that lacked only souls to differentiate them from humans). The main difficulty with clockworks is that their source of energy is too much unlike the source of energy of living things to allow for a strong comparison. The analogy to living things becomes much stronger when we turn to heat engines powered by such fuels as coal and oil. "It became apparent that machines could be constructed which did not need to be 'pushed' but only 'fed' in order to do work."

In the early twentieth century, the development of the telephone switchboard served as a technological model for the central nervous system. This model, together with the physiological research on the reflex arc, suggested—mainly to the early behaviorists—that "behavior was . . . a grand collection of units called reflexes," to use Rapoport's words.

It was with the arrival of the fourth phylum, however, best represented by the general purpose digital computer, that the possibilities of "thinking machines" became most likely, at least in the opinion of the most devoted practitioners of artificial intelligence (AI). Here is a machine of such structural and behavioral complexity that comparisons to the human brain invite serious analysis. Computers are applied to an incredibly wide variety of tasks including many that were formerly the sole province of humans. This gradual encroachment on a private domain has undoubtedly indicated to many people that it is only a matter of time until no exclusively human activities or skills remain. As has often been pointed out, whereas the first industrial revolution replaced man's muscle, the second is replacing his hand and brain.

Few disciplines can have their historical beginnings precisely determined as AI can. In the summer of 1956, a number of researchers met at Dartmouth College to discuss issues of mutual concern focused on the central question of how to program machines (digital computers) to exhibit intelligent behavior. Among the attendees were Marvin Minsky, John McCarthy (who is said to have suggested the term artificial intelligence), Allen Newell, and Herbert Simon (subsequently a Nobel laureate in economics). They gave impetus to, and shaped the direction of, research for years to come. The story of their motivations, how they attempted to realize them, and the major developments—a tale of almost epic dimensions—is recounted by Pamela McCorduck in her book *Machines Who Think*.[44] A shorter version is presented here.

There are a number of reasons to introduce AI at this point. First, it represents the current best attempt, together with cognitive science, to understand the nature of intelligent behavior. Second, the computational models it has developed have had an impact on a variety of disciplines such as linguistics, psychology, education, and philosophy. Third, and probably most important, is its current visibility in the public eye as a developer of systems for providing "senses" for industrial robots, natural language interfaces for databases, expert systems for chemistry, medicine, financial planning, and so forth. Aside from the typical, sensational claims made for AI in the public media, there are some solid achievements and, more importantly, some hope for significant accomplishments in the future.

A Short History of Artificial Intelligence

A number of events coincided after the Second World War to give rise to the new discipline called AI. Most important, of course, was development of the digital computer, significantly accelerated by the needs of war research. A significant paper written in 1943 by Warren McCulloch and Walter Pitts, called "A Logical Calculus of the Ideas Immanent in Nervous Activity,"[45] stimulated a number of people to explore the possibilities of achieving intelligent behavior from a machine. In 1948 Norbert Wiener's *Cybernetics* appeared. This book was subtitled *Control and Communication in the Animal and the Machine* and arose from Wiener's wartime research for designing mechanisms to control antiaircraft guns.[46] Researchers interested in intelligent behavior were stimulated to apply the principles of feedback, whereby a system's desired goals are compared to its current situation in order to drive the system closer to where it should be.

Much of the early research could be characterized by its reference to such terms as *adaptive, learning,* or *self-organizing.* That is, what seemed to be required was the application of powerful and general learning principles to a system with very little built-in knowledge. There were hopes of simulating certain aspects of the neuronal structure of the brain, based both on the McCulloch and Pitts work and that of the psychologist Donald Hebb. However, by the early 1960s the directions for the next 20 years were firmly in place. Basically, work on learning systems was abandoned, especially in North America, and the effort turned toward determining how knowledge could be represented in a computer and furthermore how it could be used to solve problems, play games, "see" the world, communicate in natural language, and even infer new knowledge.

Right from the outset of this new direction two streams developed that were sometimes complementary and sometimes antagonistic. One arose from parallel developments in psychology that signaled a movement away from the then dominant theoretical position of behaviorism toward the newly emerging field of information processing or cognitive psychology. Here the metaphor of information processing by computer was applied to the human system and the heretofore restricted domain of the human mind. Practitioners design models, construct programs, and carry out experiments in an attempt to answer questions about how humans think, solve problems, use language, and see the world.

The second stream is concerned with the building of computer programs to exhibit various aspects of human behavior. That is, to program a computer to solve problems, it is not obviously necessary that the methods used have anything, or much, in common with how people do it. Researchers in AI may be influenced in designing their programs by a variety of sources, of which perceived human methods is one and introspection, hardware architecture, available software, and computational limitations are others. It may turn out that the programs developed are suggestive of mechanisms underlying human performance, but this result is not the primary aim of the researchers.

In the early 1960s, programs were developed to play games such as checkers and chess, communicate in English, prove theorems in logic and geometry, and recognize simple patterns. Their level of performance was not very high in general but there were indications that a new enterprise had been launched that promised to make a major contribution to the study of intelligent behavior. In these early years, AI was sometimes viewed as a somewhat less than respectable branch of computer science. Since then, however, the founding fathers, as they are sometimes called—John McCarthy, Marvin Minsky, Allen Newell, and Herbert Simon—have all been awarded Turing Awards. The Turing Award is given annually to outstanding figures in computer science by the Association for Computing Machinery (ACM), the major association of computer scientists in the United States.

In the mid-1960s much of the research effort was devoted to robotics or integrated artificial intelligence. We can mention here that a number of hand-eye systems were built consisting of a computer-controlled mechanical arm and television camera, as well as one mobile robot called Shaky. Out of this period came a renewed interest in the major components of intelligent behavior, namely vision or image understanding, natural language understanding, problem solving, game-playing, and so forth. It became quite clear that the major issues underlying much of the research in AI could be characterized—but not solved, of course—by two words: representation and control. That is, it will be necessary to represent vast amounts of knowledge in the computer even to carry out rather simple tasks. Of course, knowledge is not enough; how and when to use it—control—is of paramount importance.

In pursuit of these goals, new programming languages have been developed. LISP, designed by John McCarthy, was among the earliest and clearly the most important. More recently, the language Prolog (Programmation en Logique), primarily developed by Alain Colmerauer and his group in France and building on seminal work by Robert Kowalski in London, has also achieved worldwide support. Some of the principles incorporated in these languages have been adopted by other language designers. A history of ideas for AI would show that many formerly esoteric notions arising from AI research have become commonplace in other fields. This has become a major side effect of the research.

During the 1970s the earlier research areas continued to develop, with new branches emerging. Among the latter are expert systems, knowledge engineering, advanced question-answering interfaces to databases, and a variety of new applications. The work in expert systems involves the design and building of large programs to incorporate specialized knowledge and inference mechanisms to advise and assist users of the system. Thousands of such systems have been developed, primarily for business applications, such as diagnosis, maintenance, fault determination, financial prediction, design, and process monitoring. There are also applications in medicine, geology, physics, and many other scientific disciplines. Typically, teams of researchers, both computer scientists and domain experts, work together to extract and reformulate the specialized knowledge. Programs are written, tested, and modified until they achieve a satisfactory level of performance. For example, one of the most successful systems, R1/XCON, was developed by Digital Equipment Corp. to configure complex computer systems.

Artificial Intelligence Now

During the 1980s, AI evolved in several interesting directions. Expert systems (ES) have continued their diffusion into the business sector as the most visible evidence of the AI enterprise. Companies large and small set up groups to design and implement ES in the hopes of improving performance and maintaining corporate knowledge beyond the work life of individual employees. Most companies have used special high-level programming languages called shells for the implementation of ES and many seemed to be satisfied with the results.[47] Other approaches and applications include fuzzy logic, favored by some Japanese manufacturers as a way to improve washing machine performance; data mining or data discovery, "Extracting previously unknown information from existing data, often with the help of another AI program, using statistical and visualization techniques to discover and present knowledge in a form that is easily comprehensible to humans;"[48] genetic algorithms that use evolutionary strategies to solve problems; and intelligent agents, programs that cooperate to solve a variety of real-world problems such as intelligently exploring the Web to discover resources that satisfy the needs of individual users.

With respect to more technical aspects, a greater emphasis has been placed on putting AI on a firmer theoretical foundation through the increasing use of logic as both a representational language and a computational one. A range of human activities, such as common sense reasoning, reasoning in the face of uncertainty, diagnosis of faulty systems, and learning under a variety of conditions has been formalized and modeled using a variety of different logics and statistical theories. That favored language for implementing AI programs, LISP, has been superseded in many parts of the world by Prolog, a language with a built-in problem solver, based on formal theorem-proving in logic. Prolog is the most popular example of a programming approach called logic programming, an attempt to take traditional logic, a passive descriptive language, and to add a control structure to transform it into a problem-solving language. Current research is focused on developing distributed, or parallel, implementations as well as incorporating a system of constraints to increase problem-solving efficiency.

The 1980s and 1990s have also witnessed a return, albeit in a modified form, to the neural networks of the 1950s and 1960s. In their current incarnation, such terms as connectionism and parallel distributed processing have also been applied to research in this area. Once again the goal is to design individual neurons, geometries, learning rules, and training procedures to construct large networks to learn interesting and complex behaviors. The primary emphasis is on learning and the motivation derives in part from the availability of cheap microprocessors, which permit the construction of relatively large, fast networks. In addition, the behavior of such networks has attracted the attention of researchers from such disciplines as physics, mathematics, and psychology, in addition to AI. Some interesting results have been reported but connectionism remains controversial as some of these results have not been adequately explained. Furthermore, many in the AI community are familiar with the devastating criticism launched against the previous generation of neural networks, known as perceptrons, by the distinguished AI researchers Marvin Minsky and Seymour Papert.[49]

In a somewhat lighter vein, but probably more accessible to the public, have been reports of the remarkable progress in chess-playing programs. Particularly noteworthy is a program called Deep Thought, which, in late 1988, achieved the distinction of being the first program to defeat a grandmaster, Bent Larsen of Denmark. Subsequently it was defeated by current world champion Gary Kasparov and former world champion Anatoly Karpov. Nevertheless, its overall level of performance is now world caliber and improving. Deep Thought was developed at Carnegie-Mellon University by five graduate students and employs a special-purpose chip that permits it to examine about 750,000 moves per second. Thus success has been achieved not through the incorporation of explicit, deep chess knowledge, but rather because of increases in brute-force speed made possible by advances in computing technology. By 1996, Deep Thought, now supported by IBM, and referred to as Deep Blue, could look at more than 100 million moves per second and engaged Gary Kasparov in a series of heavily publicized matches. In a stunning victory, reported and debated worldwide, Deep Blue won the first match decisively on February 10. After some reflection about what had happened, Kasparov recovered quickly, won the next game, drew two, and won the final two decisively, taking the match four points to two.

This match aroused considerable attention and focused world attention, for a brief time, on the issue of machine versus human intelligence. Within days after the match had concluded, *Time*'s cover story asked the hoary question, "Can Machines Think?"[50] Kasparov, in discussing his opening game loss, reports that when Deep Blue made its pawn sacrifice, he was stunned; "What could it mean? I had played a lot of computers but had never experienced anything like this. I could feel—I could *smell*—a new kind of intelligence across the table."[51] This sense of awe did not last once he realized that this "surprising" move was just the product of Deep Blue's remarkable computational speed. Thus it was necessary to "confuse" the program by presenting it with situations without any "concrete goals to calculate towards." If it can't find a way to win material, attack the king, or fulfill one of its other programmed priorities, the computer drifts planlessly and gets into trouble." Thus the answer to *Time*'s question, at least for now is, no.

There are critics of the AI enterprise, and their arguments range from questioning the morality of doing research that can be used by government in surveillance activities to concern about the possibly false philosophical principles that underlie AI. The former position is held by Joseph Weizenbaum of the Massachusetts Institute of Technology. Much of the early research in AI, well into the 1970s in the US, was in fact funded by the Advanced Research Projects Agency (ARPA) of the Air Force, and through the 1980s by its successor, DARPA (Defense ARPA). Additional funding came from the Strategic Defense Initiative (SDI, popularly known as "Stars Wars") as well as more traditional sources such as the National Science Foundation (NSF) and the National Aeronautics and Space Administration (NASA). This heavily defense-oriented association led some critics to suggest that the major beneficiary of the research would be the defense establishment. For example, an important research area in the early 1970s was speech recognition. In this process a computer, programmed to receive the electrical signal resulting from the transformation of the acoustic speech wave, produced first a representation in words and second a representation of the underlying meaning. It was Weizenbaum's claim that one of the goals of this research was to enable US security agencies to monitor conversations automatically and determine whether or not they posed a risk to government. His argument was also broader, in that he criticized the entire AI enterprise for attempting to produce what he called an "alien intelligence." That is, although programs that could engage in a broad range of behavior might be possible, they would not be desirable because they would be fundamentally at odds with the human experience and spirit. Not surprisingly, this opinion was immediately and vigorously challenged by leading researchers in the field.

Criticism on the basis of philosophical principles was launched by Hubert Dreyfus, a philosopher at the University of California at Berkeley. He argued that the goals of AI were impossible in principle and that researchers were either misguided or were misleading the community at large. He and his brother Stuart, a distinguished applied mathematician, have criticized the extravagant claims made for expert systems, countering them with the contention that human expertise is too deep, too intuitive, too broad, and too open-ended to be captured by a computer program. The Dreyfusses (mainly Hubert) argue that because the dominant stream of Western philosophy, analytic philosophy, is bankrupt, any applied research based on it, such as AI, will not succeed. These criticisms are considerably weakened when applied to neural networks, about which the Dreyfusses have reserved judgment.

Another philosopher, John Searle, has long criticized AI researchers for what he calls their commitment to "strong AI," the belief that computers can be programmed to exhibit intelligent behavior equivalent to that of humans, or in Searle's words:

> Many people still think that the brain is a digital computer and that the conscious mind is a computer program, though mercifully this view is much less widespread than it was a decade ago. On this view, the mind is to the brain as the software is to the hardware. There are different versions of the computational theory of mind. The strongest is the one I have just stated: the Mind is just a computer program. There is nothing else there. This view I call Strong Artificial Intelligence (Strong AI, for short) to distinguish it from the view that the computer is a useful tool in doing simple simulations of the mind, as it is useful in doing simulations of just about anything we can describe precisely, such as weather patterns or the flow of money in the economy. This more cautious view I call Weak AI. [52]

The charges have largely been ignored within the AI community and occasionally angrily denounced as being ill-informed. Other philosophers, however, such as Daniel Dennett[53] and John Haugeland[54] have found useful ideas in AI.

When all is said and done, AI has become an important factor both in computer science and in society at large. Clearly the development of intelligent or even pseudo-intelligent machines will have a significant impact on our future. The role of AI in the various areas investigated in this book will be assessed, for it has become much more than an academic discipline. Furthermore, note that it will not be necessary for sophisticated systems to be developed before their impact is felt. The premature use of pseudo-intelligent machines may introduce the unfortunate possibility of people being forced to adapt to machines that are not really very smart at all.

SUMMARY

The human fascination with artifacts that mimic human behavior is long-standing and has inspired tales and legends from many cultures. Particular noteworthy are the automata built by the Jacquet-Droz family of Switzerland between 1768 and 1774. The theme of robots and their ambiguous relation to their human creators has been expressed in such works as *Frankenstein, R.U.R.,* and *2001: A Space Odyssey*. In the twentieth century Isaac Asimov, in his robot stories, and George Lucas, in his *Star Wars* series of movies, have presented robots whose sole purpose has been to serve their human masters.

Many artists, musicians, and film makers consider the computer to be a new and powerful tool for the creation of art. Supercomputers are being used to generate extraordinarily realistic film images, doing away with the need for special models and special photographic effects.

In the mid-1950s a new scientific discipline made its appearance. Its goal was to develop computer programs to exhibit intelligent behavior. Its name is artificial intelligence and its contributions to technology will be significant. AI techniques are currently being used in vision systems for robots, natural language interfaces for databases, and expert systems for many applications. A match pitting world chess champion Gary Kasparov against IBM's computer program Deep Blue ended with a decisive win by Kasparov, after he had lost the first game. Once again, debate raged among the general population as well as philosophers and computer scientists about whether or not computers can or could think.

NOTES

1. Collected in online quotation list. Copyright: Kevin Harris 1995.
2. From *World of Wonders* by Robertson Davies. © 1975. Reprinted by permission of Macmillan of Canada.
3. John Cohen. *Human Robots in Myth and Science*. (London: Allen & Unwin, 1977).
4. Joseph Needham. *Science and Civilization in China. History of Scientific Thought, Vol. 2.* (Cambridge, United Kingdom: Cambridge University Press, 1956), p. 53.
5. John Kobler. "The Strange World of M. Charliat," *Saturday Evening Post,* March 25, 1955, p. 70.
6. Marvin Minsky. *Information.* (San Francisco, CA: Scientific American, 1966), p. 210.
7. W. W. Jacobs. The Monkey's Paw. (New Rochelle, NY: Spoken Arts *Records*, SA1090, 1970).

8. Patricia S. Warrick. *The Cybernetic Imagination in Science Fiction.* (Cambridge, MA: MIT Press, 1980).

9. Samuel Butler. *Erewhon.* (New York: New American Library, 1960), p. 180.

10. Karel Capek. *R.U.R.* (London: Oxford Universe Press, 1923).

11. Isaac Asimov. "Runaround," in I, *Robot.* (London: Granada, 1968), pp. 33–51.

12. Lars Gunnar Boden, in Leopold Froehlich. "Give Tchaikovsky the News," *Datamation,* October 1981, p. 136.

13. E. T. A. Hoffman. "Automata," in E. F. Bleiler (ed.), *The Best Tales of Hoffman.* (New York: Dover, 1967).

14. Lawrence B. Johnson. "PC Makers Are Focusing on Fine-Tuning the Sound," *The New York Times,* December 11, 1995, p. C 3.

15. John Melby. "Computer *Music* or *Computer* Music?" in Robin Julian Heifetz (ed.), *On the Wires of Our Nerves.* (London and Toronto: Associated University Presses, 1989), pp. 95–96.

16. A. Michael Noll. "The Digital Computer as a Creative Medium," *IEEE Spectrum,* October 1967. Reprinted in Zenon W. Pylyshyn (ed.), *Perspectives on the Computer Revolution.* (Englewood Cliffs, NJ: Prentice-Hall, 1970), pp. 349–358.

17. *Ibid.,* pp. 354–355.

18. Paul Trachtman. "Charles Csuri is an 'Old Master' in a New Medium," *Smithsonian,* February 1996, pp. 56–60.

19. *Ibid.,* p. 57.

20. Steven R. Holtzman. "Painting by Number," *Technology Review,* May/June 1995, p. 60.

21. Cynthia Goodman. *Digital Visions: Computers and Art.* (New York: Henry N. Abrams, Inc. and Everson Museum of Art, Syracuse, 1987).

22. *Ibid.,* p. 46.

23. *Ibid.,* p. 47.

24. *Ibid.,* p. 56.

25. Hubert Hohn, "The Art of a New Machine or Confessions of a Computer Artist," *Technology Review,* November–December 1988, pp. 64–73.

26. *Ibid.,* p. 67.

27. Sharon Doyle Driedger. "Hi-tech Art That Talks Back," *Maclean's,* April 24, 1995, pp. 60–61.

28. Glen Rifkin. "Increasingly, Top Designers Are Drawn to the Web," *The New York Times,* November 27, 1995, p. C 7.

29. Michael Dashkin. "From Drawing to Montage," *Leonardo* 28 (1), 1995, pp. 3–5.

30. *Ibid.,* p. 4.

31. Peter Coy with Robert D. Hof. "3-D Computing," *Business Week,* September 4, 1995, pp. 70–73, 76–77.

32. William J. Mitchell. "When Is Seeing Believing?" *Scientific American,* February 1994, p. 73.

33. John Whitney. *Digital Harmony.* (New York: McGraw-Hill/Byte Books, 1980), p. 30.

34. Nigel Andrews in *The Financial Times,* as quoted in Glenn Zorpette. "An Eye-popping Summer," *IEEE Spectrum,* October 1994, p. 19.

35. Burr Snyder. "The Toy Story," *Wired,* December 1995, p. 147.

36. Mark A. Fischetti. "The Silver Screen Blossoms into Color," *IEEE Spectrum,* August 1987, pp. 50–55.

37. *Ibid.,* p. 50.

38. Ty Ahmad-Taylor. "Using Some of that Crazy Internet-Type Stuff in Films," *The New York Times,* October 9, 1995, p. C 5.

39. Maria Shao, Richard Brandt, Neil Gross, and John Verity. "It's a PC, It's a TV—Multimedia," *Business Week,* October 9, 1989, pp. 152–155, 158, 162, 166.

40. Laurie Flynn. "A Multimedia Assault Takes Shape," *The New York Times,* November 27, 1995, p. C 5.
41. Collected in online quotation list. Copyright: Kevin Harris 1995.
42. *Ibid.*
43. Anatol Rapoport. "Technological Models of the Nervous System." Reprinted in K. M. Sayre and F. J. Crosson (eds.), *The Modeling of Mind.* (New York: Simon & Schuster, 1968), pp. 25–38.
44. Pamela McCorduck. *Machines Who Think.* (San Francisco, CA: Freeman, 1979).
45. Warren McCulloch and Walter Pitts. "A Logical Calculus of the Ideas Immanent in Nervous Activity," *Bulletin of Mathematical Biophysics,* 5, 1943, pp. 115–133.
46. Norbert Wiener. *Cybernetics: Control and Communication in the Animal and the Machine, Second Edition.* (New York: Wiley, 1961).
47. Edward Feigenbaum, Pamela McCorduck, and H. Penny Nii. *The Rise of the Expert Company.* (New York: Times Books, 1988).
48. Otis Port. "Computers that Think Are Almost Here," *Business Week,* July 17, 1995, p. 69.
49. Marvin Minsky and Seymour Papert. *Perceptrons: An Introduction to Computational Geometry, (First Edition, 1969) Second Edition.* (Cambridge, MA: MIT Press, 1988).
50. Robert Wright. "Can Machines Think?" *Time,* April 1, 1996, pp. 50–53, 56–60.
51. *Ibid.,* p. 57.
52. John R. Searle. "The Mystery of Consciousness," *The New York Review of Books,* November 2, 1995, p. 60.
53. Daniel Dennett. *Brainstorms.* (Montgomery, VT: Bradford Books, 1978).
54. John Haugeland. *Artificial Intelligence: The Very Idea.* (Cambridge, MA: MIT Press [A Bradford Book], 1985).

ADDITIONAL READINGS

Computers as a Creative Medium

Anderson, J. "Multimedia: About Interface," *MacUser,* March 1990, pp. 89–93, 96.

Atkins, Robert. "The Art World & I Go On Line," *Art In America,* December 1995, pp. 58–65, 109.

Braham, Robert. "The Digital Blackout," *IEEE Spectrum,* July 1995, pp. 51–63.

Brand, S. *The Media Lab: Inventing the Future at MIT.* (New York: Viking Penguin, 1987).

Foust, John. "3-D Steps Forward," *Byte,* July 1995, pp. 123–124, 126, 128, 130.

Hapgood, Fred. "The Media Lab at 10," *Wired,* November 1995, pp. 142–145, 196, 198.

Heim, Michael. *The Metaphysics of Virtual Reality.* (New York: Oxford University Press, 1993.)

Pickover, Clifford. *Computers and the Imagination: Visual Adventures Beyond the Edge.* (New York: St. Martin's Press, 1991).

Riding, Alan. "Video Artists Meet Today's Software," *The New York Times,* December 26, 1995, pp. B 1– B 2.

Schlender, Brent. "Steve Jobs' Amazing Movie Adventure," *Fortune,* September 18, 1995, pp. 154–156, 160, 164, 168, 172.

Taylor, Dave. "Creating Web Pages," *Computerworld,* October 16, 1995, pp. 104–105, 109, 112.

Vacca, John R. "The Outer Limits, Virtual Reality on the Internet," *Internet World,* March 1995, pp. 42–44, 46–47.

Wood, Chris. "Canadian Made," *Maclean's,* June 24, 1996, pp. 38–43.

Artificial Intelligence: A Brief Introduction

Dennett, Daniel C. *Consciousness Explained*. (Boston, MA: Little, Brown and Company, 1991).

Dreyfus, H. L. *What Computers Can't Do, Second Edition*. (New York: Harper & Row, 1979).

Feigenbaum, E. A. and McCorduck, P. *The Fifth Generation*. (Reading, MA: Addison-Wesley, 1983).

Goldsmith, Jeffrey. "The Last Human Chessmaster," *Wired,* February 1995, pp. 120–123, 167–170.

Graubard, S. T. (ed.). *The Artificial Debate: False Starts, Real Foundations*. (Cambridge, MA: MIT Press [Daedalus Special Issue], 1988.)

Hebb, D. *The Organization of Behavior*. (New York: Wiley, 1949).

Moody, Todd C. *Philosophy and Artificial Intelligence*. (Englewood Cliffs, NJ: Prentice-Hall, 1993).

Penrose, Roger. *Shadows of the Mind: A Search for the Missing Science of Consciousness*. (New York: Oxford University Press, 1995).

Rosenberg, Richard S. "Artificial Intelligence in the Real World: A Critical Perspective." *Proceedings of the Ninth Canadian Conference on Artificial Intelligence,* AI '92, May 11–15, University of British Columbia, Vancouver, BC, pp. 22–29.

Schank, R. *The Cognitive Computer*. (Reading, MA: Addison-Wesley, 1984).

Searle, J. *Minds, Brains and Science*. (Cambridge, MA: Harvard University Press, 1984).

Shrobe, H. and the American Association for Artificial Intelligence (eds.). *Exploring Artificial Intelligence: Survey Talks from the National Conferences on Artificial Intelligence*. (San Mateo, CA: Morgan Kaufmann, 1988).

Sterling, Leon and Shapiro, Ehud. *The Art of Prolog*. (Cambridge, MA: The MIT Press, 1986).

"The Grandmaster's Nemesis." *The Economist,* December 23, 1989, pp. 95–96.

von Neumann, J. *The Computer and the Brain*. (New Haven, CT: Yale University Press, 1958).

Weizenbaum, J. *Computer Power and Human Reason*. (San Francisco, CA: Freeman, 1976).

Winograd, T. and Flores, F. Understanding Computers and Cognition: A New Foundation for Design. (Norwood, NJ: Ablex, 1986).

CRITICISM AND HISTORY

The clock not the steam engine is the key-machine of the modern industrial age. For every phase of its development the clock is both the outstanding fact and the typical symbol of the machine: even today no other machine is so ubiquitous . . .

The clock, moreover, served as a model for many other kinds of mechanical works, and the analysis of motion that accompanied the perfection of the clock, with the various types of gearing and transmission that were elaborated, contributed to the success of quite different kinds of machines . . .

The clock, moreover, is a piece of power-machinery whose "product" is seconds and minutes: by its essential nature it dissociated time from human events and helped create the belief in an independent world of mathematically measurable sequences: the special world of sciences.

Excerpt from *Technics and Civilization* by Lewis Mumford, © 1934 by Harcourt Brace Jovanovich; renewed in 1961 by Lewis Mumford; reprinted by permission of Harcourt Brace & Company.

INTRODUCTION

Computers did not suddenly appear. Technological innovation does not arise from thin air. There are strata of previous technological achievements and economic and human resources. We frequently assume that our times are unique and that only our particular genius could have brought forth such wonders. Many craftsmen, inventors, and scientists laid the necessary groundwork for the modern computer. Its history extends from the invention of the abacus to the designing of the Jacquard loom and beyond.

> There is a time when the operation of the machine becomes so odious, makes you so sick at heart that you can't take part; you can't even passively take part, and you've got to put your bodies upon the gears and upon the wheels, upon the levers, upon all the apparatus and you've got to indicate to the people who run it, to the people who own it, that unless you're free, the machine will be prevented from working at all. (Mario Savio, Berkeley, December 2, 1964.)

For many, this quotation was the rallying cry of the protest movement of the 1960s and early 1970s in the United States. It seemed to express the feelings of many that the state was a powerful, oppressive machine grinding up its young to further its single-minded aims. The issue here is not politics, but this perception of technology in control. It is necessary and important to confront the criticisms raised, if not to answer them completely.

COMMENTS ON TECHNOLOGICAL CHANGE

Technological progress is like an axe in the hands of a pathological criminal. (Albert Einstein [1879–1955])[1]

The following two points of view—two caricatures, perhaps—define the conflicting poles of the debate.

Computers are just tools. We as their inventors and users decide what we shall do with them. They are more complex and have greater potential than other tools but you should never forget that ultimately that is what they are. All statements to the contrary are alarmist.

A computer is not just another tool. Computers can carry out activities that previously only people could do. Furthermore, by virtue of their enormous speed and capacity they can give unpredictable results when applied in new areas. They already endanger privacy, employment, even freedom. Although previous tools posed some of these difficulties, the computer represents not just more of the same but an obvious quantum jump.

You may not have yet formed an opinion on this issue. In fact it may be premature to expect it. Even if you agree with the first viewpoint, you might in daily life be expected to defend that view again and again as the computerization of society proceeds and new issues crop up. Computers are here and now. Can we still shape our own destiny?

Computers are in a real sense a natural continuation of technological development, and there exists a large body of commentary on the effects and dangers of technology itself. Important scholars have provided a number of incisive insights and warnings.

Machine analogies can be readily perceived in human situations. For Lewis Mumford, the slave population involved in building the pyramids can be seen as a mega-machine, the individual humans analogous to cogs and gears, each performing a limited repeatable task. Siegfried Giedion views the assembly line in a similar manner. In one of his most damning criticisms of modern technology he shows how bread has evolved from nourishing food to a convenient, well-packaged, food product. The claim that technology is neutral and merely a tool that can be used for good or ill is subjected to a major critique by Jacques Ellul. Norbert Wiener points out that just by virtue of its size and speed the computer can go beyond being a tool and in some sense create a new reality. These critics have been concerned with technology in general, with computers only the most recent development.

In an important article published in 1969, John McDermott describes technology as "the opiate of the educated public, or at least its favorite authors."[2] He gives a representative list of the fruits of the cornucopia as seen by a number of the so-called prophets of technology, as follows: [3]

> An end to poverty and the inauguration of permanent prosperity (Leon Keyserling), universal equality of opportunity (Zbigniew Brzezinski), a radical increase in individual freedom (Edward Shils), the replacement of work by leisure for most of mankind (Robert Theobald), fresh water for desert dwellers (Lyndon Johnson), permanent but harmless social revolution [and] the final come-uppance of Mao-Tse-tung and all his ilk (Walt Rostow), and, lest we forget, the end of ideology (Daniel Bell).

This brief characterization of points of view should be fleshed out. In all the uproar over the wonders of technology, there should be a place for a few wise voices with a message of caution and concern. This book explores the impact of recent computer developments. Beyond the initial, obvious benefits, future problems may indeed lurk. It is worth listening to the group of critics, historians, and commentators that includes Mumford, Giedion, Ellul, and Wiener, the old, but honorable guard, as well as Weizenbaum, Postman, and Birkerts, the newer critics.

Lewis Mumford

A major social critic and the grand old man of the environmental movement, Mumford is also a distinguished historian of technology. In a long series of books beginning in 1922, he was especially concerned to establish the continuity of craftsmanship and technology down through the ages. Furthermore, he attempted to catalog and analyze the variety of forces technology brings to bear against the maintenance of humanity in everyday life. Power, centralization, autocracy, mechanization, and control are a few of the key words that only begin to suggest the many issues that have exercised him for so many years. It is difficult to do justice to a lifetime of scholarship in so brief a space.

Here we are concerned with Mumford's analysis of the impact of computers and automation. He is disturbed not so much by the physical replacement of workers as by the elimination of the human mind and spirit from the process of production. The spirit suffers because of the elevation of computer decision making and the parallel subordination of individual initiative. The system or organization becomes all-knowing and all-powerful. The individual—as scientist, engineer, manager, or consumer—must abide by the established rules even if there is a loss of a human way of life.

For Mumford, the computer itself and its role in automation is just one more step along a road of constrained human choice. He has traced the enslavement of people from the building of the pyramids, under an organizational scheme that he likens to a machine, to the development and refinement of the modern assembly line. It is not inevitable that technology be used to enslave society (even assuming that we feel enslaved), because decisions as to its use must frequently be made consciously. If we have the knowledge and the will, we can structure society so that spontaneity and choice are encouraged and even rewarded. But if computers are left to make what are fundamentally human decisions, the consequences may be indeed serious, because computers may be programmed to return only those results desired by the leaders and managers.

In contrast to these perceived limitations in computers, strenuously challenged of course by most computer enthusiasts, Mumford offers a paean to the human brain:[4]

> Unfortunately, computer knowledge, because it must be processed and programmed, cannot remain constantly in touch, like the human brain, with the unceasing flow of reality; for only a small part of experience can be arrested for extraction and expression in abstract symbols. Changes that cannot be quantitatively measured or objectively observed, such changes as take place constantly all the way from the atom to the living organism, are outside the scope of the computer. For all its fantastic rapidity of operation, its components remain incapable of making qualitative responses to constant organic changes.

Siegfried Giedion

The major work of the architectural and social critic Siegfried Giedion, *Mechanization Takes Command*[5] appeared in 1948, before computers had achieved a significant presence. He is concerned with the process by which traditional human activities have gradually been assumed by machines to the obvious detriment of the final product. He is interested in "the elimination of the complicated handicraft."[6] An important example is the making of bread, long a central enterprise of human existence. From the beginnings of agriculture and the cultivation of wheat, the preparation of bread has been a necessary and honorable activity. The connection of humans with the organic is well exemplified through bread, its manufacturing (i.e., making by hand), distribution, and consumption. Riots have been provoked by scarcity of bread or slight increases in its price. The images conjured up by the simple phrase "the breaking of bread" are suggestive of basic human relations: sharing, participating, a sense of community, a willingness to understand, and a desire to reaffirm historical continuity.

The problem is, the quality of bread today is highly suspect. For the most part in North America, it looks and tastes like cardboard. Few remember, or even care, what a treat real bread can be. The story begins with the mechanization of kneading, clearly a strenuous activity requiring pulling and pushing and the use of feet as well as hands. In the late eighteenth century, the French pharmacologist Antoine Augustin Pametier described kneading as a process in which flour, yeast, water, and air are sufficiently well mixed to produce a new substance. It is clear that kneading is physically difficult and an obvious candidate for mechanization. Mechanical rotary kneaders were developed as far back as the Romans, and experiments continued through the Renaissance into the industrial era. Surprisingly, however, complete mechanization did not take place until after 1925, with the introduction of the high-speed mixer in the United States. Whereas early machines simulated the action of human hands, the high-speed mixer has an agitator that "usually consists of two arms attached to simple steel bars, which perform sixty to eighty revolutions a minute."[7] In explaining why they have not been widely adopted in Europe, Giedion notes that the more delicate European wheats cannot accommodate the tremendous speed and shocks produced by these mixers. Beyond the efficiency of using the mixers, there was a stronger motivation: "the main reason seems to have been that the energetic mixing made possible the manufacture of a bread even whiter than before."[8]

The final stage in the process is baking. Again, over time a satisfactory form of oven evolved. It resembled an egg, a shape that proved economical and advantageous for uniform heat distribution. However, there were limitations involved in the method of heating, the means for sweeping out embers, and the problems of dealing with large quantities of bread. And so the shape, size, and method of heating evolved: steel plates replaced brick and gas heaters replaced coal. Still, mechanization was not complete because what was needed was an assembly line process to measure and allocate the ingredients, to mix them into dough, and to cut, weigh, mold, and position the individual portions on a conveyor belt ready for the oven. As early as 1840, the French had achieved the mass production of bread.

Other aspects of the mechanization process should be mentioned. Two basic ferments were used to make the dough rise, yeast and leaven. These underwent a number of chemical transformations to speed up the fermentation process, increasing the weight of the bread. For example, carbonic acid increased the speed of fermentation and human labor was thereby reduced. Additional chemicals were added to make bread look whiter. These additives were used as long ago as the mid-eighteenth century. Even the milling process to produce the flour was altered to produce a whiter, cleaner product. At the beginning of the nineteenth century artificial bleaching was introduced to decrease the aging process and improve the whiteness. More recently, vitamins have been added to replace the nourishment lost through the actions of the previous processes.

As a result of all these innovations, in North America the bread factory has largely replaced the bakery. The small egg-shaped oven has become the 100-foot tunnel oven. The complete process has been mechanized, from the mixing, in several stages, to the dividing, the rounding into balls, the molding, the placing into pans, and the high-speed fermentation to, finally, the baking of the bread in the oven on an endless conveyor belt. The cooling process is accelerated by artificial means, and the bread is sliced, packaged, and distributed.[9] One question remains: What has happened to the quality of the bread?

The technological process has certainly produced a bread of uniform quality, which, it is argued, the public demands, as the following quotation shows.[10]

> The bread of full mechanization has the resiliency of rubber sponge. When squeezed it returns to its former shape. The loaf becomes constantly whiter, more elastic, and frothier. . . . Since mechanization, it has often been pointed out, white bread has become much richer in fats, milk, and sugar. But these are added largely to stimulate sales by heightening the loaf's eye-appeal. The shortenings used in bread, a leading authority states, are "primarily for the purpose of imparting desirable tender eating or chewing qualities to the finished product." They produce the "soft velvet crumb," a cakelike structure, so that the bread is half-masticated, as it were, before reaching the mouth.

The story of bread teaches that in the face of increased mechanization there is a strong tendency for the natural to suffer. But is it inevitable? Visitors to San Francisco rave about its sourdough bread, which is mass-produced. French bread is world famous for its taste, texture, and smell and is usually sold by small, family-owned bakeries. Thus, technology is inextricably woven into the social fabric of a culture. If it is important to maintain the quality of bread, independent of issues of mass production and distribution, it will be maintained. Therefore, to understand how technology affects the quality of life it is necessary, at the very least, to understand how public opinion is formed and shaped and how it manifests itself in the accommodation of the new. However, there is one critic of technology who argues that we don't have a real choice.

Jacques Ellul

A French sociologist, Jacques Ellul has become one of the world's foremost critics of technology. His major work, published in France in 1954, appeared in the United States in 1964 under the title *The Technological Society*.[11] He presents a very grim picture, indeed. He views technology as an irresistible, mysterious force, far more menacing than either Mumford or Giedion have supposed. It has an ability to change every aspect of life that it encounters. First, it is necessary to understand what Ellul means by *technique*. It is similar to Giedion's *mechanization* but much stronger:[12]

> The term *technique,* as I use it, does not mean machines, technology, or this or that procedure for attaining an end. In our technological society, *technique is* the *totality of methods rationally arrived at and having absolute efficiency* (for a given stage of development) in *every field of human activity*. Its characteristics are new; the technique of the present has no common measure with that of the past. (Emphasis added.)

The sense of the term will become clearer as we continue.

Ellul argues that although techniques derive from crafts and methods prior to the eighteenth century, there has been a quantitative change, and technique has taken on a life of its own with its own internal logic. Initiated by the labors of past generations, it has somehow become a separate force with potentially terrible consequences. He presents four explanations of why technique was under control until the eighteenth century.

1. Only certain constrained areas were amenable to technique.
2. Other areas of life such as leisure, social intercourse, sleep, prayer, and play were more predominant.
3. Technique was local and spread slowly.
4. The geographical and historical isolation of societies permitted, indeed required, the flourishing of many different types of techniques.

The situation is different now—we face the new and terrible power of technique and its unremitting campaign against human individuality. Progress still depends on the individual, but only within the terms defined by technique. Thus, efficiency is of prime concern, and aesthetics and ethics are sacrificed. Progress is a concept inherent in the system and is largely unrelated to the desires or wishes of the people.

It almost seems as if technique is some kind of living, breathing monster out of control, our control at least, with its own aims and its own means of achieving them. What are some of the features of this monster?[13]

> [Technique] has been extended to all spheres and encompasses every activity, including human activities. It has led to a multiplication of means without limit. It has perfected indefinitely the instruments available to man, and put at his disposal an almost limitless variety of intermediaries and auxiliaries. Technique has been extended geographically so that

it covers the whole earth. It is evolving with a rapidity disconcerting not only to the man in the street but to the technician himself. It poses problems which recur endlessly and ever more acutely in human social groups. Moreover, technique has become objective and is transmitted like a physical thing; it leads thereby to a certain unity of civilization, regardless of the environment or the country in which it operates.

Here, in brief, are some of the characteristics of technique as it operates currently.

Rationality. Aspects of management such as standardization, division of labor, and quality control.

Artificiality. Technique creates an artificial world, denying and eliminating the natural world.

Automatism of Technical Choice. The human has no role to play. Technique acts and people observe.

Self-augmentation. Technique changes and evolves with no help or direct intervention by people.

Monism. Technique forms a single whole and its various components are self reinforcing.

The Necessary Linking Together of Techniques. An historical necessity operating in which the technique at one stage must follow the one at a previous stage.

Technical Universalist. Geographic—technique has been spread by commerce, war, and the export of technicians. Qualitative—technique has taken over the whole of civilization.

The Autonomy of Technique. A good example is the functioning of an industrial plant as a closed system that is independent of the goals and needs of the society in which it exists.

Since it is not really made clear how technique has evolved, it is certainly not clear what, if anything, can be done. In contradistinction to Ellul's unrelieved pessimism, evidence can be offered of how much life has improved over the years. The obvious decreases in hunger and sickness, the lengthening of the life span, and the increase in literacy are proof of the fruits of technology. Ellul's critics would grant that all is not roses but on balance the good brought by technology far outweighs the ills.

Norbert Wiener

Called the father of cybernetics, Norbert Wiener was an important mathematician who had a deep concern about the possible social impact of his work. Cybernetics and automation are intimately related, as engineering is related to mathematics and physics. In fact, the subtitle of Wiener's very influential book, *Cybernetics, is Control and Communication in the Animal and Machine.*[14] The central notion in cybernetics is feedback. In this process, an action is maintained by continuously reducing the monitored difference between the current state and the desired state. This principle underlies much of industrial automation, hence Wiener's anguish over the fruits of his labor. He views automatic equipment as equivalent to slave labor, which means that humans in competition with the mechanical slaves must accept economic conditions equivalent to theirs. That is, employers will not pay their human workers more than the costs associated with robots performing equivalent work. He prophesied a period of serious unemployment when the new technology becomes pervasive.

Wiener was much less pessimistic about the future in the second edition of this book, which appeared some 13 years after the first. He felt that many of his concerns were starting to be accepted by the business world. The relation between technological change and unemployment is perhaps the central issue in assessing the impact of technology. There appears to be a general consensus that, initially, technological innovation may result in the loss of jobs but eventually more jobs are created than lost. (We return to this question in Chapter 10.) Wiener was troubled also by the ability of computers to produce unintended and unanticipated results. The problem results from a combination of factors, including the speed of the computer, the inadvisability of interfering with it during its computation, the narrowness of the program's scope, and the limitations of the data. Note that none of these elements has anything to do with whether a computer can exhibit intelligent behavior. The fundamental point is that computers operate so much faster than do humans that there is a basic mismatch in their interaction. We had better be very sure that the computer is doing what we have desired and intended.

Wiener offers a strategy much easier stated than carried out: [15]

> Render unto man the things which are man's and unto the computer the things which are the computer's This would seem the intelligent policy to adopt when we employ men and computers together in common undertakings. It is a policy as far removed from that of the gadget worshipper as it is from the man who sees only blasphemy and degradation of man in the use of any mechanical adjuvants whatever to thoughts.

Wiener feels that computers ultimately can be controlled for the benefit of society. But this sentiment seems to be expressed more as a caution—against the possibility of a terrible future if computers are not used wisely—than as a realistic expectation.

Joseph Weizenbaum

Twenty years ago, Professor Weizenbaum published a book, *Computer Power and Human Reason*,[16] that served as warning about the possible dangers of computers replacing humans in decision-making situations. He introduced the term, alien intelligence, to argue that no matter how intelligent computers may appear to be by virtue of advances in artificial intelligence, they should never be involved in human affairs:

> The concept of an intelligence alien to certain domains of thought and action is crucial for understanding what are perhaps the most important limits on artificial intelligence. But that concept applies to the way humans relate to one another as well as to machines and their relation to man. For human socialization, though it is grounded in the biological constitution common to all humans, is strongly determined by culture. All human cultures differ radically among themselves.[17] . . . Every human intelligence is thus alien to a great many

domains of thought and action. There are vast areas of authentically human concern in every culture in which no member of another culture can possibly make responsible decisions. It is not that the outsider is unable to decide at all—he can always flip coins, for example—it is rather that the basis on which he would have to decide must be appropriate to the context in which the decision is to be made. [18]

Although this argument has been viewed as an assault on the more arrogant segment of the AI community, the book itself presents an extended argument for the virtues of human reason and judgment over the power of computers and calculation. Weizenbaum heaps abuse upon computer hackers and the mentality that would view humans as replaceable by smart machines or perhaps as nothing more than smart machines. As such he continues in the tradition of those who value humans and human society above all, and who are alarmed by the degree to which society seems ready to accept technology and all its supposed benefits with little question.

Neil Postman

Mr. Postman has long been concerned with the relationship among culture, literacy, and technology with a general viewpoint that things are getting progressively worse. As he states in the Introduction to his book, *Technopoly:* [19]

> In fact, most people believe technology is a staunch friend. There are two reasons for this. First, technology is a friend. It makes life easier, cleaner, and longer. Can anyone ask more of a friend? Second, because of its lengthy, intimate, and inevitable relationship with culture, technology does not invite a close examination of its own consequences . . . Stated in the most dramatic terms, the accusation can be made that the uncontrolled growth of technology destroys the vital sources of our humanity. It creates a culture without moral foundation. It undermines certain mental processes and social relations that make human life worth living. Technology, in sum, is both friend and enemy.

Except for the last sentence quoted, Mr. Postman is in the tradition of Ellul in believing that technology at its worst is destructive of human values and in spite of its obvious benefits in many cases extracts an enormous price in return. Ellul has argued that there are no good and bad sides to technology, or rather *technique* in his terms, because technology does not really respond to human needs and desires, especially in its more advanced forms. However, Postman is willing to grant that there are benefits, but what exactly does his term Technopoly (the T is Postman's usage) encompass? He classifies cultures into three types, namely, tool-using, technocracies, and Technopolies, examples of which can be found in today's world. Technocracies are based on belief in modernity, the scientific method, rationalism, the power of knowledge, and secularism, in the sense that what people are able to accomplish and believe in is in no way limited by what God's design may be. Although his argument is lengthy, Postman claims that the US was certainly a technocracy by the end of the eighteenth century.

Currently, the US is the only country in the world to have become a Technopoly, albeit a young one. Postman suggests a couple of dates to mark this transformation: the rise of Henry Ford's empire being one and the Scopes "monkey trial" another. The first period is really the beginning of automation, the transformation of the workplace and the fundamental shift in the US economy. The second is more of a mind jump and a continuation of the process of science and technology triumphing over religion and mystical beliefs. As for a definition, Postman offers the following: "the submission of all forms of cultural life to the sovereignty of technique and technology."[20] At another point he writes, "Technopoly, in other words, is totalitarian technocracy . . . And it does so [eliminating alternatives to itself by making them invisible] by redefining what we mean by religion, by art, by family, by politics, by history, by truth, by privacy, by intelligence, so that our definitions fit its new requirements."[21] This a bleak picture, consistent with Ellul's worst case.

Sven Birkerts

One last critic will be presented, Sven Birkerts, a writer, a critic, and a teacher. Though his concerns do not appear to be of the same magnitude as the others, they are real and very worrisome, especially for literate people who worry about a generation or more that has been informed by electronic media and has little feeling for the printed word. Unfortunately, and with some irony, Birkerts' argument will be appreciated only by those who need no convincing, whereas those who might benefit from books seem lost to them and the cultural and historical matrix in which they are immersed. Thus, in the introduction to his book, *The Gutenberg Elegies,* he notes: "As the printed book, and the ways of the book—of writing and reading—are modified, as electronic communications assert dominance, the 'feel' of the literary engagement is altered. Reading and writing come to mean differently; they acquire new significations."[22] As noted, the argument as developed can make sense only to those already sharing many of Birkerts's very strong convictions. Here in a nutshell is his central concern:[23]

> For, in fact, our entire collective subjective history—the soul of our societal body—is encoded in print. Is encoded, and has for countless generations been passed along by way of the word, mainly through books. I'm not talking about facts and information here, but about the somewhat more elusive soft data, the expressions that tell us who we are and who we have been, that are the record of individuals living in different epochs—that are, in effect, the cumulative speculations of the species. If a person turns from print—finding it too slow, too hard, irrelevant to the excitements of the present—then what happens to that person's sense of culture and continuity?

It is curious that the Internet community defines itself by its impatience with traditional media, its conviction that the Internet represents a new frontier, a break with the past, a venture without traditional constraints. Books are the past, digital flows of information are the present, and as for the future, more and faster is all that matters. Subtleties, nuances, layers of meaning and inferences, the richness of language are casualties of the technological imperative for speed, efficiency, sensation, and endless gadgets and toys.

These views of the social critics range from apprehension to horror. The easy response to them is, yes there have always been problems, yes there will be more problems, but we are in control of our own destiny. The debate will continue and will probably increase in intensity as the presence of computers both singly and in networks is more strongly felt. In all likelihood, the discussion will turn on whether or not the computer in its most prevalent form—the microprocessor—represents a quantitative change in technology. The final word in this section, reminding us that concern about technology is not a recent phenomenon, goes to the nineteenth-century social philosopher John Stuart Mill, who suggests the following image:[24]

> Suppose that it were possible to get houses built, corn grown, battles fought, causes tried, and even churches erected and prayers said by machinery—by automatons in human form—it would be a considerable loss to exchange for these automatons even the men and women who at present inhabit the more civilized parts of the world, and who assuredly are but starved specimens of what nature can and will produce. Human nature is not a machine to be built after a model, and set to do exactly the work prescribed for it, but a tree, which requires to grow and develop itself on all sides, according to the tendency of the inward forces which make it a living thing.

The Ring of Optimism

> The fact is, that civilization requires slaves. The Greeks were quite right there. Unless there are slaves to do the ugly, horrible, uninteresting work, culture and contemplation become almost impossible. Human slavery is wrong, insecure, and demoralizing. On mechanical slavery, on the slavery of the machine, the future of the world depends.[25]

As most of this book is a study in success of the computer in its incredibly wide variety of forms and applications, we hardly need to pause to praise it. Nevertheless, these few words of cheer should be welcome as a clear statement of technology as the servant of the people who invent it, develop it, and employ it to serve the needs of everyone. About one hundred years later, this view was reinforced by Herbert Simon, winner of the Nobel prize in economics in 1978 and one of the fathers of artificial intelligence. Simon views technological change from the unique combined vantage point of economist, computer scientist, and cognitive psychologist. In a ringing challenge, Simon presents probably one of the most optimistic and encouraging statements of the technological vision:[26]

> It is to realize, perhaps for the first time in human history, that we are a part of the world; that we are a part of this vast machinery; that man is not outside nature, that man is not above nature, but that man is a part of nature.
>
> If we can make peace with ourselves on those terms, it will have at least one desirable byproduct: As we design new technology, as we make use of our knowledge about the world and the knowledge that we are gaining about ourselves, about our thinking processes, through research in AI and cognitive simulation, we will realize that we have to apply our technology in a way that keeps man's peace with the universe in which he lives, instead of conceiving our technology as a weapon with which man can wage war on the rest of nature.

One can almost hear the trumpets. But of course, Simon is not a solitary voice. George Gilder, Nicholas Negroponte, Alvin and Heidi Toffler, James Naisbitt, Kevin Kelly, John Perry Barlow, Andrew Grove, Howard Rheingold, and many others are projecting, to varying degrees, future visions of the technology harvest. Common to many is the centrality of networks, the economic power of information, and the new frontier of virtual communities with new political structures. Witness the following print media cover stories:

Newsweek
- February 27, 1995. Technomania: The Future Isn't What You Think: Cyberdemocracy, Intelligent Agents, Online Sex, Tracking a Hacker, Virtual Surgery, Interactive Movies and Music
- December 25, 1995/January 1, 1996. The Year of the Internet

Time
- Spring 1995. Special Issue: Welcome to Cyberspace: Strange Sounds and Sights, Intimate Strangers, Haves vs. Have-Nots, Confessions of a Cyberholic, Virtual Washington, It's a Wired, Wired World
- July 3, 1995. Cyberporn. Exclusive: A new study shows how pervasive and wild it really is. Can we protect our kids—and free speech?

Scientific American
- Special Issue 1995. The Computer in the 21st Century: Products and Services for Computer Networks, Networking, Government in Cyberspace, Computers, Networks, and the Corporation, Civil Liberties in Cyberspace

Business Week
- Special 1994 Bonus Issue. The Information Revolution: How Digital Technology is Changing the Way We Work and Live: The Information Economy, The Enabling Economy, The New Face of Business, The Information Society.

Maclean's (Canada)
- January 29, 1996. Plugging Into The Future: How the Internet of tomorrow will transform people's lives

Utne Reader
- March–April 1996. Cyberhood vs. Neighborhood: Are computer networks *real* communities? (Are Neighborhoods?)

A common theme runs through all these stories: big changes are on the way and while there may be some minor problems, the future is unbounded, replete with an ever-increasing stream of technological goodies. One final and important version of this vision has been articulated by the Progress and Freedom (PF) Foundation, which suddenly became known in 1995 because of its connection to Speaker of the House of Representatives, Newt Gingrich. Its mission statement includes the following:

> Progress is the belief that Mankind has advanced in the past, is presently advancing, and will continue to advance through the foreseeable future.
>   No idea is more American, no idea has played a more central role in the development of Western, and more recently, American Civilization. No idea is more important to our collective future, and no idea has suffered more from the cultural nihilism of the past 30 years than the idea of progress. . . .

That explains the mission of The Progress & Freedom Foundation: To restore, to renew and to recreate America's sense of its future, a future woven inextricably with the ideas of progress and freedom. It has been said that "The best way to predict the future is to create it." Creating ideas that will define America's future is what the Foundation has set about to do since its inception in April 1993. [27]

The PF Foundation is probably best known for a document it released in 1994, titled, "A Magna Carta for the Knowledge Age."[28] Its four coauthors—Ms. Esther Dyson, Mr. George Gilder, Dr. George Keyworth, and Dr. Alvin Toffler are widely known. Dr. Keyworth, a former Science Advisor to President Ronald Reagan, is chairman of the PF Foundation; Ms. Dyson is a prominent computer consultant and president of the Electronic Frontier Foundation, and Mr. Gilder and Dr. Toffler are very well-known writers, lecturers, and futurologists. The term Magna Carta was very cleverly chosen to indicate that the document contains a list of new rights appropriate for our new and exciting time. One thing to keep in mind, however, is that the original Magna Carta was an agreement, in 1215, between the barons and the King John of England over respective rights and powers and indeed only by default was relevant to the lives of most of the common people. This is not to deny the obvious importance of the Magna Carta in the history of achieving civil liberties. This modern Magna Carta envisions a revolutionary change as the Knowledge Age arrives, as the following excerpt from the Preamble demonstrates:

> But the Third Wave, and the *Knowledge Age* it has opened, will not deliver on its potential unless it adds social and political dominance to its accelerating technological and economic strength. This means repealing Second Wave [based on oil, steel, and auto-production] laws and retiring Second Wave attitudes. It also gives to leaders of the advanced democracies a special responsibility—to facilitate, hasten, and explain the transition.
>
> As humankind explores this new "electronic frontier" of knowledge, it must confront again the most profound questions of how to organize itself for the common good. The meaning of freedom, structures of self-government, definition of property, nature of competition, conditions for cooperation, sense of community and nature of progress will each be redefined for the Knowledge Age—just as they were redefined for a new age of industry some 250 years ago.

Of concern to the authors are such issues as the ownership of property (different), the marketplace (even more open), freedom (more and different), community (different and more diverse), and the role of government (much less regulation and more competition, increasingly distributed and decentralized). Such sentiments are emphasized in the final words of the authors:

> Yet there are key themes on which this constituency-to-come can agree. To start with, liberation—from Second Wave rules, regulations, taxes and laws laid in place to serve the smokestack barons and bureaucrats of the past. Next, of course, must come the creation—creation of a new civilization, founded in the eternal truths of the American Idea.

More trumpets.

A BRIEF HISTORY OF COMPUTERS

Computers in the future may weigh no more than 1.5 tons. (*Popular Mechanics,* 1949)

The next few pages will sparkle with such catchy names as ENIAC, EDVAC, UNIVAC, EDSAC, MARK 1, and others. They are the names of the earliest real computers, developed about 40 years ago. How they came to be is a fascinating, long, and involved story. There is a problem inherent in an abbreviated history—it may appear to be a series of inventions that were historically inevitable. The social forces, the burgeoning requirements of applied mathematics, and the demands made during times of war and peace—including the computation of ballistic tables, navigational aids, and census statistics—are discussed in the Additional Readings.

Before the Twentieth Century

Computing probably began with counting, and counting began with fingers and sticks and stones. The abacus, one of the oldest calculating devices, was known to the Egyptians as early as 460 B.C. and is still used today in many parts of the world. There are two classes of computing machines—*analog* and *digital*. An abacus is a digital device in which the positions of individual beads on wires represent numbers. In analog machines, the instantaneous value of a continuously varying physical quantity such as a length, voltage, or angular position represents a number. Before it was rendered obsolete by the pocket calculator, the slide rule was probably the most commonly used analog computing device. Its operation makes use of the fact that the product of two numbers is equivalent to the sum of their logarithms. By using a length on a stick to represent the logarithm of a number, multiplication is carried out by positioning two sticks appropriately. A traditional watch with face and hands is analog (no matter what process is used for positioning the hands), whereas one with only numbers that change in discrete jumps is digital. In this history the analog computer is a minor player.

Brian Randell, editor of *The Origins of Digital Computers,* divides their history into two streams: mechanical digital calculation and sequence control mechanisms.[29] These are the two major concerns of computation—how to actually perform a calculation and how to control sequences of calculations. Counting, the former, was of primary concern historically.

For centuries wheels with teeth or cogs in a linked train have been used to deal with addition that involves carries. The complete story includes the development of number systems, leading to the use of the decimal system in Europe. John Napier (1550–1617), best known as the inventor of logarithms, probably was the first person to use the decimal point in arithmetic operations. Until quite recently the credit for inventing the first calculator was given to the famous French philosopher Blaise Pascal (1623–1662). It is supposed that his impetus was to aid his father in performing calculations. In any case, at age nineteen he designed his first machine and by 1645 he had achieved a patent on it. The currently recognized first inventor, however, is Wilhelm Schickard of Tubingen (1592–1635), who apparently sent a set of drawings of a calculating machine to Kepler, the famous astronomer, in

1623. Who was first is not particularly important, since the idea and the necessary technology were in the air. The historical record is probably incomplete. The real importance of a new invention is heavily dependent on the social environment in which it occurs.

Some thirty years after Pascal's invention Gottfried Leibniz (1646–1716), a great mathematician and universal thinker, designed the Leibniz wheel, a crucial component of mechanical calculators. His machine, which was not constructed until 1694, permitted multiplication and division as well as addition and subtraction and was much more efficient than previous devices. As useful calculating devices were developed, the impetus grew to refine and improve them in order to carry out even more complicated computations. Leibniz himself raised the banner for the relief of drudgery through technology.

Also the astronomers surely will not have to continue to exercise the patience which is required for computation. It is this that deters them from computing or correcting tables, from the construction of Ephemerides, from working on hypotheses, and from discussions of observations with each other. *For it is unworthy of excellent men to lose hours like slaves in the labor or calculation which could safely be relegated to anyone else if machines were used.* (Emphasis added.)[30]

Charles Babbage: The Difference Engine and the Analytical Engine

Over the next century a number of refinements took place in the basic calculator, but it was not until the mid-nineteenth century that a generally successful calculator became available. Charles Babbage (1792–1871), a most remarkable man—mathematician, inventor, and initiator of scientific management—flourished in this period. He clearly deserves the title "father of the computer," although his story is one of generally unfulfilled ambition. In 1821, he became interested in building a "Difference Engine" to automate the calculation of algebraic functions by using successive differences. A story describes the moment of its inception. Apparently Babbage was checking some calculations with John Herschel (the son of Sir William Herschel, the discoverer of Uranus) when Babbage remarked, "I wish to God these calculations had been executed by steam." Herschel simply replied, "It is quite possible." (Steam was the major power source of Babbage's time.)

In 1835, before his Difference Engine was completed, Babbage conceived of a much more powerful, general purpose computer that he called the Analytical Engine.[31] In the end, neither machine was completed, for a variety of reasons—lack of sufficient financial resources, technical requirements beyond the skill available, and a design that underwent too-frequent change. There is little doubt, however, that Babbage at this early date envisioned a machine of such scope that its power would not be realized for more than a hundred years. His design included a memory store, an arithmetic unit, punched card input and output, and a mechanism that provided enough power of control to do iteration and branching. Following his death, others tried to build similar machines with little success. When successful machines were finally built, some of their designers were aware of his work; others were not. In the final analysis, Babbage appears to have been a cranky genius with ideas impossible to realize—for both economical and technical reasons—in his time.

No history of this period would be complete without mention of Augusta Ada, Countess of Lovelace (1816–1852), the only child of the poet Lord Byron, and a person of some mathematical ability. In 1840, when Babbage presented a series of lectures in Italy on his machine, they were attended by a young engineer, L. F. Menabrea. Ada translated his notes on the lectures and added comments of her own. Her work is the major account of the Analytic Engine. She may also have been the first programmer—she included a program to compute Bernoulli numbers, an important task for many physical problems. Her description of the engine is quite lyrical, not surprising for the daughter of a poet.

> We may say most aptly that the Analytical Engine weaves *algebraic patterns* just as the Jacquard loom weaves flowers and leaves. Here, it seems to us, resides more originality than the Difference Engine can be fairly entitled to claim.[32]

It appears that even the idea of a computer provoked in her mind the possibility that people might readily believe in the creative powers of such machines. She was at pains to disabuse the public of such a thought.

> It is desirable to guard against the possibility of exaggerated ideas that might arise as to the powers of the Analytical Engine. In considering any new subject, there is frequently a tendency, first, to *overrate* what we find to be already interesting or remarkable; and, secondly, by a sort of natural reaction, to *undervalue* the state of the case, when we do discover that our notions have surpassed those that were really tenable.
> The Analytical Engine has no pretensions whatever to *originate* anything. It can do whatever we *know how to order it* to perform. It can *follow* analysis; but it has no power of *anticipating* any analytical relations or truths. Its province is to assist us in making available what we are already acquainted with.[33]

What did Babbage achieve in the end? He did not build his Analytical Engine, but he did anticipate much of what would follow. He failed to realize his vision, probably because of his restless mind, the limitations of contemporary technology, and the lack of an obvious need for the projected computing power. He continually designed more advanced machines while the struggle was still on to realize his earlier designs. Still, his intellectual achievement was monumental.

Control of Computation

Ada's reference to the Jacquard loom relates to the second theme in our history of computers—sequence control mechanisms. The problem is twofold: (a) how to represent numbers and develop a mechanism for performing arithmetical operations on them, and (b) how to carry out sequences of calculations without human intervention, which could only restrict operational speeds. The automata discussed in Chapter 2 were generally controlled by a rotating pegged cylinder or a disc with holes, much as contemporary music boxes are. The problem of how to actually control a process by a mechanism essentially external to that process first arose in the weaving industry.

It was probably a man called Basile Bouchon who in 1725 used a perforated tape to control the weaving of ornamental patterns in silk. This idea was refined over the years by a number of inventors, including Jacques Vaucanson, the creator of the remarkable mechanical duck. The most important contribution was made by Joseph Marie Jacquard

(1752–1834). Building on the work of Vaucanson, Bouchon, and others, he designed a system of control that used a connected sequence of punched cards. The holes in the card determined whether or not vertical hooks controlling the warp threads were used in the pattern being woven. By the end of the nineteenth century looms with 400 or 600 hooks were quite common. As early as 1812, there were approximately 11,000 Jacquard looms in France.

In 1836, Babbage adopted the Jacquard card mechanism not only for entering numbers into the machine but most importantly for controlling the sequence of operations necessary to carry out the calculations. It was easier to punch up a set of cards, he reasoned, than to make changes directly within the central core of the computer. Once the cards were made they could be used again whenever the particular computation was desired. Clearly this is much easier than physically altering the computer itself. Babbage anticipated the notion of a fixed machine performing computations under the direction of a program. It is interesting that a technological advance in one area turned out to be influential in quite another one. The story resumes in the United States, where for the most part the electronic computer was first invented and subsequently refined.

Near the end of the nineteenth century in the United States, the demands made on the Census Office became quite burdensome. The 1870 census was the first to make use of mechanical equipment of a rather simple kind. The key figures were John Shaw Billings, who was in charge of the 1880 census, and Herman Hollerith (1860–1929), who worked for the Census Office from 1879 to 1883 and later supplied the tabulating equipment for the 1890 census. There is some controversy over who should be given credit for the tabulating machine concept. It seems that Billings suggested the idea of using punched cards to represent information but Hollerith actually built the machine. Billings apparently mentioned that he was inspired by the Jacquard loom principle. In any case the machines, patented by Hollerith in 1889, won a competition and were used in the 1890 census to punch and process approximately 56 million cards. Hollerith's machines, in an improved version, also were used in the 1900 census. However, relations between his company and the Census Bureau (the name was changed in 1903) deteriorated so much that for the 1910 census the Bureau used its own machines, which were developed by James Powers.

After Hollerith left the Census Office, he formed a company in 1896 called the Tabulating Machine Company. In 1911 it merged with two other companies to form the Computer–Tabulating–Recording Company. Thomas J. Watson, Sr., formerly with National Cash Register, became president in 1914. Ten years later he changed the company's name to International Business Machines (IBM). In the same year in which Hollerith's company merged, James Powers formed his own company, Powers Tabulating Machine Company, on the basis of patents received while he was employed by the Census Bureau. This company eventually merged with Remington Rand in 1927. Thus, the rivalry of Powers and Hollerith at the turn of the century gave rise to two companies that were rivals in the development of the electronic computer.

Birth of the Modern Computer

Babbage's machine did not die with him—his son attempted to raise money to complete it. (All that remains is a number of incomplete sections.) Others were influenced. Percy

Ludgate, an Irish accountant, attempted to build his own Analytical Engine in 1903. He died in 1922 leaving only a 1909 sketch describing his design. The Spaniard Leonardo Tores Y Quevedo (1852–1936) wrote an interesting paper in 1914 outlining a program-controlled device in the spirit of Babbage's Analytical Engine. He was also well known for his endgame chess-playing automata. As we move into the 1930s, the story starts to become rather complicated. Historians are still uncovering and evaluating claims for machines and devices. Furthermore, secret work done during World War II, especially work on the Colossus project undertaken in England, is gradually being declassified only now. It was a very exciting and interesting time—social and political conditions were ripe for the building of the first computer.

Before the first digital computer was developed there were a variety of analog computers in operation designed to solve specific problems. The most important of these, called the differential analyzer, was built at the Massachusetts Institute of Technology (MIT) by Vannevar Bush in 1931. Its purpose was to solve differential equations arising from several areas of mathematics. More important, perhaps, was its influence on computational endeavors elsewhere. For example, a version of the differential analyzer was built at the Moore School of Electrical Engineering at the University of Pennsylvania between 1933 and 1935. This effort provided the crucial experience from which the first electronic computer emerged some ten years later. As a side effect, MIT's commitment to analog computers, at the expense of digital ones, probably began at that time.

Electromechanical Computers

It is generally agreed that the first electronic computer was built at the Moore School under the direction of John Mauchly (1907–1980) and John Presper Eckert, Jr. (1919–1995). Called ENIAC (Electronic Numerical Integrator and Computer), it was built between 1943 and 1946. There were others, however, who claimed to be the first. The common factor of such claims was that the device was not electronic but electromechanical; that is, it relied on a mixture of electrical and mechanical components. Unfortunately, the first of those had very little impact on the development of computers in general. In fact, it was not until after World War II that the important work of Konrad Zuse (1910–1995) became known. He began in Germany to design electromechanical calculating aids in 1934; by 1938 he had produced the Z1, a somewhat unreliable mechanical computer. With the help of Helmut Schreyer he succeeded in building the Z3, "a floating point binary machine with a 64 word store. This computer, since it was operational in 1941, is believed to have been the world's first general purpose program-controlled computer."[34] Zuse continued his work during the war, but resources were not made available to extend his design. He made another important contribution with the design (in 1945) of a programming language called Plankalkul. This work also was not as influential as it should have been because it was unknown at the time. In the United States, important work on digital computers was initiated at the Bell Telephone Laboratories in New Jersey under the direction of George Stibitz. It is not surprising that Bell would be interested in computers, nor that they would be based on the relay circuit technology already in place in the telephone system. Stibitz and his associates began their research in 1937 and produced the first model, called the Complex Number Computer, in 1940. This so-called Model I was followed by a number of computers over the years: Model II, the Relay Interpolator, Model III, a relay calculator, the Ballistic Computer, and finally Model V in 1946. This last model was a general purpose computer under program control. Even though it was slow, it did permit programs to be changed easily and was quite reliable as well.

Another important early development in computer technology was the work of Howard Aiken (1900–1973). In 1937, while an instructor at Harvard, he convinced IBM to begin the design of a computer. Together with three IBM employees—C. D. Lake, F. E. Hamilton, and B. M. Durfee—Aiken built the Harvard Mark 1, or Automatic Sequence-Controlled Calculator, in 1944. Basically a mechanical computer, it was more than 50 feet long, perhaps the largest ever built. More important than the machine itself, probably, was the fact that it was an entry point for IBM into the world of computers. After this machine, Aiken went on to build a series of machines at Harvard based on mechanical components. When questioned many years later about his reluctance to use electronic components, he replied that he knew that electronics were the way to go but that they were unreliable at first and he preferred the dependability of mechanical systems. At IBM the development of machines continued with the Pluggable Sequence Relay Calculator, installed in 1949, and the SSEC (Selective Sequence Electronic Calculator), completed in 1948 under the direction of Wallace Eckert. The series of computers that followed launched IBM into world leadership.

ENIAC: The First Electronic Computer

The work of Aiken and Stibitz was well known to the designers of the ENIAC, as was that of John V. Atanasoff, who had built a special-purpose computer to solve systems of simultaneous linear equations. In fact, Mauchly visited Atanasoff at Iowa State University in 1941 to see his computer and invited him to come to the Moore School. There has been much controversy about how much ENIAC owed to Atanasoff. Mauchly in later years called Atanasoff's computer a "little gizmo." A court ruling in 1973, resulting from litigation between Honeywell and Sperry Rand over the ENIAC patent, was not clear-cut. The ruling, issued in October of 1973, stated, "Eckert and Mauchly did not themselves first invent the automatic electronic digital computer but instead derived the subject matter from one Dr. John Vincent Atanasoff."[35] Nevertheless, the judge acknowledged Eckert and Mauchly as the inventors of ENIAC, and Atanasoff's work did not change the ENIAC patent claims.

Two of the participants have written books about the development of this first electronic computer.[36] Herman Lukoff, an engineer, and Herman Goldstine, a mathematician, together with Arthur Burks and John von Neumann, were involved in the development of the ENIAC and successor machines. The Moore School had gotten involved with computers—albeit analog ones—in 1933, with the construction of a differential analyzer. John Mauchly, a physicist interested in the possibilities of electronic means of computation, joined the Moore School in the fall of 1941. Eckert, an electrical engineer employed as an instructor at the Moore School, was supportive of Mauchly's interests. In August 1942 Mauchly wrote a memo, "The Use of High Speed Vacuum Tube Devices for Calculating," which has been called by Randell, "surely one of the most important documents in the history of computers."[37] The Moore School had by this time become involved with the Ballistics Research Laboratory of the US Army Ordnance Department. Captain Herman

Goldstine, acting as liaison officer, helped convince the US government to sign a contract with the Moore School in 1943 to develop an electronic calculating machine for computing ballistic tables. The machine was completed in the fall of 1945 and dedicated on February 14, 1946.[38] It was a monster. Incorporating over 18,000 vacuum tubes, 70,000 resistors, and 10,000 capacitors, 100 feet long, 10 feet high, and 3 feet deep, it consumed 140 kilowatts in operation.

Thus, 1996 was the fiftieth anniversary of the public unveiling of ENIAC. This event has been celebrated in a number of ways and certainly is an appropriate time to consider the impact of this remarkable machine. On a very sad note, the last three major computer pioneers, whose work began in the 1930s, namely John Atanasoff, John Presper Eckert, and Konrad Zuse all died in 1995.

The Stored Program Concept

The next major step was to control the computer's actions by means of a program stored in its memory. If this could be done, programs could be manipulated just like data. Even more important, the computer could become involved in the preparation of programs themselves through the development of assemblers, compilers, and operating systems. (The latter are themselves programs that reside in the computer and permit the running of user-written programs.) As in many other areas of computer invention, the question of who was responsible for the stored program concept is somewhat unclear. Currently, there is general agreement that John von Neumann is the person to whom most of the credit belongs. Some facts are clear: The idea did emerge in the ENIAC group and it was expressed in print in a draft report dated June 30, 1945, written by von Neumann on the proposed EDVAC. Von Neumann (1903–1957) was one of the supreme geniuses of the twentieth century. He made major contributions to such diverse areas as the foundations of mathematics, quantum mechanics, game theory, hydrodynamics, and the foundations of computer organization and software. Contemporary computers have been described as von Neumann machines. However, there is some question about the origin of the ideas in the 1945 report.

Apparently, the stored program concept emerged in group discussions during the ENIAC project. Von Neumann first became involved with work at the Moore School when taken there by Goldstine in August of 1944. It is his opinion that von Neumann did make the major contribution, but it is unfortunate that the draft report did not acknowledge the work of others, and thus became known as the von Neumann report. Goldstine claims that von Neumann did not expect it to be widely circulated before he produced a revised version. Others have not been so agreeable.

Mauchly himself tried to set the history straight. In late 1979 he stated that as early as April of 1944 he and Eckert had planned to include both programs and data in the same memory. Furthermore, they discussed these plans with von Neumann in September of that year when he first came to the Moore School.

> We started with our basic ideas: there would be only *one* storage device (with addressable locations) for the *entire* EDVAC, and this would hold both data and instructions. All necessary arithmetic operations would be performed in just one arithmetic unit. All control functions would be centralized.[39]

Von Neumann quickly understood the nature of these ideas and reformulated them in his own terms, using such biological references as organs and neurons. Mauchly insists that von Neumann was merely rephrasing ideas developed by himself and Eckert. In any case, the von Neumann report does contain the first known program for a stored program digital computer; it happens to be a sorting program.

The Moore School went on to complete the EDVAC and delivered it to the Ballistics Research Laboratory near the end of 1951. Mauchly and Eckert left to form their own company, the Electronic Control Company, in late 1946. (The name was changed to Eckert-Mauchly Computer Corporation in 1947.) Problems with patent disputes and the constraints of the university environment had led to this separation. They conceived UNIVAC (a Universal Automatic Computer) but its development required continued research supported by contracts. In 1949, they completed a computer called BINAC—the first operational stored-program electronic computer that used magnetic tapes rather than punch cards—for the Northrup Aircraft Company. In 1950 Eckert and Mauchly sold their company to Remington Rand because of financial problems. The following year the UNIVAC I was completed and used for the computation of the 1950 US census. In 1955 Remington Rand merged with the Sperry Corporation and continued to manufacture the UNIVAC series. (The UNIVAC name was discontinued in 1983.)

Developments in England

In 1946, von Neumann and Goldstine went to the Institute of Advanced Studies at Princeton University and began to work on a new computer, the IAS. The early 1950s saw the beginnings of the computer explosion, as computers were developed at a number of research institutions in the United States and elsewhere.

The MARK 1, developed at Manchester under F. C. Williams and T. Kilburn, was probably the first stored program computer to be operational. It was a rather primitive machine and is important mainly for the concept it embodied and for the fact that its development was fairly independent of the Moore School effort.

Another significant project in England was the computer built at Cambridge University under the direction of Maurice Wilkes, called EDSAC (Electronic Delay Storage Automatic Calculator). This machine was based on the EDVAC principles—Wilkes had attended an important series of lectures at the Moore School in 1946. The EDSAC has been called the first practical stored program computer to be completed. It executed its first program in May 1949.[40] Finally, the classified work done at Bletchley Park during World War II has recently been disclosed. A computer called COLOSSUS was developed there under the leadership of Professor Newman and Mr. Flowers, with a major contribution by Alan Turing (1912–1954).[41] Turing was later involved with the ACE computers built at the National Physical Laboratories at Teddington.

No history of computing would be complete without mention of Alan Turing. His name has been associated primarily with a theoretical construct called the Turing machine, which he created to explore general issues of computation. More recently his contributions to the design of actual computers, especially his work on a highly secret coding machine called Enigma, have been made public. From a theoretical and a practical perspective, Turing is certainly one of the fathers of the modern computer.

The Rise of IBM

The age of the computer had arrived and growth was explosive. IBM quickly established its dominance and its name became synonymous with the computer. How this happened has been debated, but no one disputes the fact that IBM is the major company in the field and has been so for many years, both in the United States and worldwide. More recently, IBM has been less dominant in the wider information processing industry because of the importance of software and the phenomenal growth of the Internet. Of all the factors contributing to its success, the most important was probably its organizational structure, which was highlighted by a large, well-motivated, and dedicated sales staff. The company stressed a well-trained and responsive sales and service division. Its availability and concern did much to carry its customers through the early uncertainties of the commercial computer age. In the 1960s the industry was described as IBM and the Seven Dwarfs. The dwarfs in 1967 were Sperry Rand (later Sperry Corporation), Control Data Corporation, Honeywell, RCA (Radio Corporation of America), NCR (National Cash Register), General Electric, and Burroughs. In 1971, General Electric sold its computer hardware operation to Honeywell but maintained its computer services division and has recently shown strength in specialized computer equipment. RCA sold its computer operations to Sperry in 1971. Consolidation continued into the 1980s and 1990s; in 1986 Sperry merged its computer operations with Burroughs to form UNISYS, Honeywell sold its computer business to Groupe Bull (France), with a share to Japan's NEC, and on May 6, 1991, AT&T acquired NCR for $7.4 billion.

In the mid-1990s, the number two company in the world was Fujitsu, far behind IBM in data processing revenues, as can be seen in Figure 3.1, which shows the growth curves of some of the leading computer companies over the past few years. It should be noted that among the ten leading companies in data processing revenue in 1995, six were American—IBM (1), Hewlett-Packard (3), Digital (6), AT&T (7), Compaq (8), and EDS (9); and four were Japanese—Fujitsu (2), NEC (4), Hitachi (5), and Toshiba (10). Just four years previously, Groupe-Bull (France), Siemens (Germany), and Olivetti (Italy) were in the top ten, while Compaq, EDS, and Toshiba were not. A number of US companies, among the most prominent names in the computer industry, seem to be in serious decline. For example Control Data, once second only to IBM, has now dropped to number 92 worldwide with revenues of $524 million. Other companies that have lost significant market share are Wang, Data General, Unisys, and Texas Instruments (all United States), Siemens (Germany), Olivetti (Italy), and Groupe-Bull (France). Among companies whose revenues in data processing have grown substantially during the 1990s are EDS, Compaq, AT&T, Microsoft, and Sun Microsystems (United States), and Toshiba (Japan).

Computers are usually categorized by size and power. Supercomputers are at the top, then mainframes, followed by minicomputers, workstations, and personal computers at the bottom. There are no precise dividing lines, and as the power of workstations continues to increase they exert an upward pressure on the minicomputer market, as minicomputers once did to mainframes. Sun, the leading company in the workstation market, has challenged both Digital and IBM by producing computers that are smaller, faster, and cheaper. Indeed in the fourth quarter of its fiscal year ending in June 1990, Digital an-

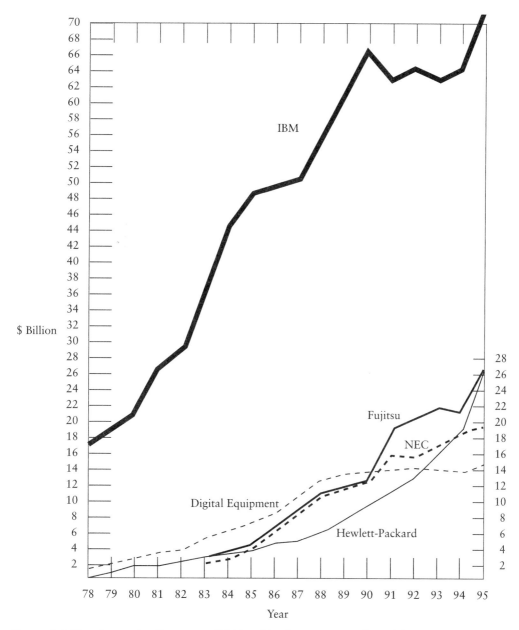

FIGURE 3.1 Data Processing Revenues of IBM and its Competitors. Adapted from *Datamation*, June issues, 1979–1996. © Datamation, reprinted with permission of Reed Elsevier Inc.

nounced its first loss in 33 years; 1994 was even worse with a loss of over $2 billion. As previously mentioned, IBM remains the dominating force in the computer industry and, in spite of various setbacks, is likely to hold its position into the foreseeable future. For example, it was number one in 1995 in most of the submarkets of the computer industry. Table 3.1 illustrates IBM's domination over its leading challengers. In the workstation market, IBM is currently in second place closely behind the leader Sun. Just five years earlier, IBM was in fifth place. Although, it has lost its leading position in the PC market to Compaq, it is close behind. Notwithstanding Microsoft's well-advertised leadership in operating system and applications software, its revenue is 60% of IBM's in that category.

One important measure of IBM's ability to recreate itself, in spite of possibly crippling setbacks is its shift from primarily a mainframe company (so-called "Big Iron"), to a much more diversified one. For example between 1993 and 1995, its overall revenue rose from $62.7 billion to $71.9 billion, while its revenue mix changed as follows:[42]

SOURCE OF REVENUE	1993	1995
Mainframes, Mainframe Software, Maintenance	54%	43%
Services, PCs, PC Software, Workstations	46%	57%

After years of major losses in net income in the early 1990s, profits rose from a staggering loss of over $8 billion in 1993 (including massive write-offs for early retirements) to $2.8 billion in 1994, to almost $4.2 billion in 1995, an extraordinary turn around.

Questions have been raised about the effect of such a powerful force on other companies in the industry and, more importantly, on the development of the field itself. Indeed, many of IBM's practices have become *de facto* standards.

TABLE 3.1

IBM AND ITS LEADING COMPETITORS IN SELECTED MARKETS IN 1995.
DATA TAKEN FROM *DATAMATION* (CAHNERS PUBLISHING CO.)
JUNE 15, 1996[43]

Markets (1995)	IBM's Revenues ($billions)	Leading Competitors' Revenues ($billions)	
Services and Support	20.1	EDS	12.4
Software	13.0	Microsoft	7.4
Desktops*	12.9	Compaq	9.2
Peripherals	10.1	Hewlett-Packard	8.6
Large-Systems: Mainframes	6.5	Fujitsu	5.1
Servers	6.5	Hewlett-Packard	3.7
Datacom	2.9	AT&T	3.3

*The Desktops category includes PCs, workstations, and laptops.

THE EMERGENCE OF THE CHIP

If the aircraft industry had evolved as spectacularly as the computer industry over the past 25 years, a Boeing 767 would cost $500 today, and it would circle the globe in 20 minutes on five gallons of fuel. [44]

If the automobile business had developed like the computer business, a Rolls Royce would now cost $2.75 and run 3 million miles on a gallon of gas. [45]

The History

The modern computer developed from a mechanical calculator into an immense electronic machine with thousands of vacuum tubes that occupied a large room. The power requirements were enormous and the issue of reliability was of paramount concern. When ENIAC was completed in 1946, it was generally believed that only a very few computers would be necessary to serve the computational needs of the nation. Developments were already underway, however, to change the basic structure of computers. As early as 1945, Bell Laboratories began research to develop electronic devices useful for telecommunications. Leading this research team were William Shockley, John Bardeen, and Walter H. Brattain. They were awarded the Nobel prize for physics for their invention, in 1947, of the point contact transistor. This device was not an instant success, because it operated over a limited range of frequencies, could amplify only to a limited degree, had limited stability, and was expensive to manufacture. It would have been difficult to predict at this point the shape of things to come.

As an electronic component, the vacuum tube generates a great deal of heat in operation, requires considerable power, and occupies a relatively large space. The advantages of the semiconductor are striking: low power requirements, minimal heat generation, and above all microscopic size. The semiconductor, as its name suggests, has conductive properties between those of a conductive material such as copper and an insulating material such as plastic or rubber. The first transistor was made of germanium, as was the second, called the junction transistor. Both were developed by Bell in 1951. Eventually silicon came into wide use, first for transistors and later for integrated circuits, or chips.

Over the next few years developments were rapid, and prices fell correspondingly. The basic motivation for miniaturization, however, did not derive from the requirements of computer engineers. It was the basic need of the US space and missile programs for compact, durable, and light components that motivated the drive for miniaturization. Developments were further accelerated by a combination of advances in scientific knowledge and the growth of scientific entrepreneurship.

Transistors were first used in hearing aids in the early 1950s. It was not until 1955 that the first all-transistor radios appeared. Much more importantly, in that same year IBM introduced a computer in which over 1000 tubes had been replaced by more than 2000 transistors. In addition to the virtues of the transistor already noted, there is one additional important point that had great implications for the future.

The great advantage of the transistor, an advantage scarcely appreciated at the time, was that it enabled one to do away with the separate materials—carbon, ceramics, tungsten and so on—traditionally used in fabricating components. At the same time the transistor raised the ceiling that sheer complexity of interconnections was beginning to place on system design. . . . The transistor was the first electronic component in which materials with different electrical characteristics were not interconnected but were physically joined in one structure.[46]

The next natural step was to include more than one transistor in the same physical structure. Once this idea was articulated, developments took place very rapidly. The integrated circuit includes—on a single chip of silicon—transistors, diodes, resistors, and capacitors, all connected in a functional circuit.

Once it was introduced, the integrated circuit business grew rapidly worldwide, with nearly $1 billion in sales in 1970 and $3.6 billion in 1976. These figures are dramatic in more ways than one since there has been a corresponding reduction in prices over these years and an increased number of active elements per circuit. For example, the cost per bit (binary digit) of random-access memory has declined an average of 35% per year since 1970.[47] Furthermore, from a single bit per circuit in 1959, the growth curve has been from 1K (1024) in 1970, to 4K in the mid-1970s, to 16K in the late 1970s, to 32K shortly after, followed by 64K in the early 1980s to the 256K bit memory in 1983, to the 1 megabit DRAM in the late 1980s, the 4 megabit DRAM in the early 1990s (selling for about $12),[48] and the 16 megabit DRAM in the mid-1990s. (The letter K is an abbreviation for 1024 but is typically used as 1000; a megabit is one million bits; DRAM means Dynamic Random Access Memory.) The 64M DRAM is expected by 1998.[49] The benefits of integrated circuits are as follows:

- They are cheaper
- Labor and materials are saved by not having to make large numbers of connections
- The integrated connections are more secure; hence, less maintenance is required
- Power and space requirements are drastically reduced, resulting also in savings on cooling fans and transformers
- Quality control is improved

In 1964 Gordon Moore, one of Robert Noyce's colleagues at Fairchild, suggested that the complexity of integrated circuits would continue to double every year. Moore's law is apparently still in effect and augurs well for improvements into the late 1990s.

The Microprocessor

So far we have discussed the development of circuits that have either been preprogrammed to carry out well-defined functions or are available for memory purposes. One of the most significant technological innovations of our time took place in 1971 at Intel, a semiconductor company founded two years earlier by Robert Noyce and others in Santa Clara, California. M. E. Hoff, Jr., a young engineer, invented an integrated circuit that is essentially equivalent to the central processing unit of a computer. Consider the following description:

Hoff's CPU [Central Processing Unit] on a chip became known as a microprocessor. To the microprocessor, he attached two memory chips, one to move data in and out of the

CPU and one to provide the program to drive the CPU. Hoff now had in hand a rudimentary general-purpose computer that not only could run a complex calculator but could also control an elevator or a set of traffic lights, and perform any other tasks, depending on its program.[50]

Intel brought out its first microprocessor chip, the 4004, in 1971. A larger model, the 8008, followed in 1972. Near the end of 1973 came the second generation 8080 chip, more than twenty times faster than the 4004. This last chip formed the basis for the personal computer bonanza that followed. Other companies—such as Rockwell International, National Semiconductor, Texas Instruments, and Motorola—soon entered the microprocessor derby.

In early 1989, Intel introduced its new microprocessor, the i486, successor to the 386 (technically the 80386) and two to four times faster. At that time, Intel sold a less advanced version of the 386, the 386SX, to computer manufacturers for $89 while the new i486 sold for $950. 386SX-based computers could be bought for $1500, a remarkable price given their power, and yet another indication of the rapid pace of development. One more startling indication is that although the 386 contained 375,000 transistors, the i486 had over one million. Less than one year later, TRW and Motorola (which makes the 6800 series of chips for the Apple Macintosh and Sun computers, among others) announced a "superchip" with about four million transistors:

> Two hundred million operations per second mean the (chip) is the computational equivalent of some supercomputers that fill an entire room, require elaborate refrigeration systems and weigh several tons. . . . Commercial successors of the superchip could find use in a wide variety of applications where high speed, small size and great computing power and reliability are needed. Among these are computer-aided design, medical diagnosis, plant process control and complex imaging.[51]

New chips continue to appear at a regular rate including Intel's Pentium chip, the microprocessor of choice for most of the world's personal computers and the Power PC chip developed by Motorola for Apple's Power Macintoshes. Motorola's Power PC 620, available in 1996, has nearly seven million transistors and is about the size of a fingertip.[52] Powerful computers are required to help design, build, and verify the increasingly complex chips under development. Such incredible increases in power and decreases in size seem to occur with such regularity in the computer industry that we tend to forget how remarkable these achievements are and how great an impact they continue to have on our lives.

The Semiconductor Business

The semiconductor business is perhaps the crowning jewel of the American industrial system. Its important early growth period was fostered by the US Department of Defense, which subsidized developmental costs. As it coincided with the emergence of scientific entrepreneurship, the US lead was ensured. The semiconductor industry has an economic impact far beyond its own domain, because of the multiplier effect. That is, a piece of equipment depending on semiconductors is likely to cost many times more than the integrated circuit itself.

That almost mythical community, Silicon Valley (named for the basic material of semiconductors) is a region running from Palo Alto south to San Jose along San Francisco Bay. Home of a number of chip manufacturers, personal computer companies, and peripheral-device companies, it has achieved worldwide fame as a source of innovation and expertise in the incredible explosion of microelectronics technology. Its achievements have been so overwhelming that other regions of the United States and the world have sought to plant seeds for their own Silicon Valleys.

The tradition of scientific entrepreneurship in the Valley is not new. As far back as 1939, David Packard and William Hewlett formed an electronics company, Hewlett-Packard, which in 1995 had total revenues of over $31.5 billion. The initial impetus of the phenomenal postwar growth of Silicon Valley came from William Shockley, one of the inventors of the transistor. He left Bell Laboratories and moved to Mountain View, California to set up Shockley Semiconductor Laboratory in 1955, which attracted a number of young, ambitious engineers and physicists. One of these was Robert Noyce, who (with seven others) left Shockley two years later to form Fairchild Camera and Instrument. The Silicon Valley syndrome of old companies spawning new ones was well under way.

After a few years, the next generation of offspring was born: National Semiconductor in 1967, Intel (founded by Noyce) in 1968, and Advanced Micro Devices in 1969. These are among the "Fairchildren" of Fairchild alumni. Not only has the semiconductor flourished in Silicon Valley; a whole range of computer-related companies have found the atmosphere congenial. Large mainframe corporations such as Tandem Computers and Amdahl were founded there.

Even on its own terms, the semiconductor market, including memory chips and microprocessors, has grown enormously; for example, worldwide sales in 1995 increased about 40% over 1994 to $155 billion.[53] Market share is almost equally divided between North America (39.8%) and Japan (39.5%) with the rest of Asia (mainly Taiwan and South Korea) at 12.1% and Europe at 8.6%. Both Taiwan and South Korea have plans to expand their productive capacity substantially to meet the processing demands of the next generation of multimedia computers. This growth will certainly pose a challenge to North America and Europe in the highly competitive and highly volatile semiconductor market.

In the personal computer market, Apple had been an outstanding success story, with sales increasing from $165 million in 1980 to over $11.3 billion in 1995. Other computer manufacturers have their home in Silicon Valley, including the leader in workstations, Sun Microsystems, whose sales increased from $115 million in 1985 to over $6.5 billion in 1995. Many disk drive manufacturers such as Seagate, Conner, Quantum, and Tandon are also neighbors. Although Silicon Valley has become a metaphor for "high tech" success, there are other important areas in the United States with similar achievements. On the east coast, Route 128 near Boston is the home of Digital Equipment, Wang, Prime, and Data General, all computer companies, as well as Lotus, a leading software house. The St. Paul-Minneapolis area is the home of Control Data and 3M. In Texas, Compaq is another success story in the personal computer market and the world leader in personal computer sales. Compaq's revenues have increased from $111 million in 1983 to almost $15 billion in 1995. In the Dallas-Fort Worth area are EDS, a major force in computer services, and Texas Instruments.

The success of all these regions depends on a number of factors, including a critical mass of nearby scientific expertise: Stanford University and the University of California at Berkeley for Silicon Valley, Harvard and MIT for Route 128, and the University of Minnesota for the St. Paul-Minneapolis area. In addition, other important factors are an existing base of technological skills, managerial skills, and venture capital resources, all of which have made Silicon Valley, especially, a much envied world center of microelectronics. There is, however, the downside to paradise, such as pollution, job alienation, a roller-coaster economy, unaffordable housing, and minimal job security and job loyalty.

The Personal Computer

Almost exactly 30 years after the first electronic computer made its appearance, the first personal computer (PC) was marketed. Since then, sales have been phenomenal. In the United States, sales for 1981 (excluding software and peripherals) reached $1.4 billion; they were up to $2.6 billion in 1983, and approximately $6 billion in 1985. Worldwide sales were $6.1 billion in 1982 and soared to $37.4 billion in 1989. By 1994, the top ten PC manufacturers in the US had combined sales of almost $40 billion. All this has been made possible by the microprocessor, but the idea of making a computer at a price low enough to sell to an individual, coupled with the belief that the computer would have sufficient appeal for that individual, is a product of American scientific and business genius.

As mentioned previously the major success story of the personal computer, discounting IBM's achievements and Compaq's success in riding on IBM's coattails, is Apple, founded in Silicon Valley by Steven Wosniak and Steven Jobs, then in their early twenties. In the by-now familiar Valley legend, Wosniak built the first machine in his parents' garage. (Interestingly, Jobs left Apple (or was pushed) in 1985 and in 1987 announced a new computer from his company, NeXT, Inc.) The first Apple machine was marketed in 1976 and by 1983 its sales had exceeded $1 billion, climbing above $11 billion by 1995 and propelling it to eleventh place in the worldwide computer market. (Compaq, growing faster had climbed to number 6.) Recently, however, Apple has experienced financial problems. Other players in the personal computer game are Acer, Dell, Gateway, Packard Bell, AST Research, AT&T, Digital, and Hewlett-Packard. As previously noted, IBM waited until 1981 to enter the market but did so with a splash.

We are living in a time when computers are numbered in the millions. They are no longer the private preserve of the government, large businesses, and research institutions. Extraordinary power is becoming available to a wide segment of society. How that power will be distributed and used, and to what ends, is a question yet to be answered. One application of that distributed power that is rapidly achieving the status of the familiar and the commonplace is the Internet.

THE INTERNET

Is it a fact, or have I dreamt it—that, by means of electricity, the world of matter has become a great nerve, vibrating thousands of miles in a breathless point of time? (Nathaniel Hawthorne, *The House of the Seven Gables*)

The Internet is a vast computer network, linking computer networks around the world, so therefore a network of networks. As described in Chapter 1, it originated from ARPANET, an experimental network financed by ARPA (Advanced Research Products Agency of the Department of Defense) in the late 1960s. Its purpose was to link geographically distributed researchers with shared interests via a relatively high-speed network to facilitate collaborative efforts. Its design was motivated by the necessity to function even during wartime conditions and it is therefore very resistant to interruptions, however serious. Its growth over the first few years was slow as more and more researchers came online. In fact by 1977 there were about 100 hosts on ARPANET. Although ARPANET itself was discontinued in 1990, other networks such as CSNET, founded by the National Science Foundation in 1980, and BITNET started a year later, took up the burden for a much wider audience than Defense Department researchers. Notable events include the introduction of the UNIX operating system in 1969 (Ken Thompson and Dennis Ritchie at AT&T Bell Labs), the first e-mail program that same year (Larry Roberts), and the beginning of work on the TCP/IP (Transmission Control Protocol/Internet Protocol) protocols (Vinton Cerf and Robert Kahn) in 1974. Another definition of the Internet, therefore, is the network of all networks that communicate by means of TCP/IP.[54]

The growth of the Internet began to take off in the late 1980s as the number of hosts seemed to increase exponentially. The Internet Society[55] estimated that there were over 16.1 million hosts worldwide on the Internet as of January 1997. Compare this number to the figure for July 1989, namely 130,000. What is far more difficult to determine is the number of people who have access to the Internet and its multitude of offerings. A number as high as over 40 million has appeared but there exists considerable doubt as to its accuracy. Whatever the number, it is large and growing. In addition, commercial networks such as CompuServe, America Online, and Prodigy have millions of customers and can also access the Internet. It is the apparent success of the Internet that gave rise to a vision, the Information Highway, of a broad-band network linking homes, schools, government, and business with a two-way communication system, able to download even movies in real time. Earliest mention of this vision occurred in 1991, with a fuller picture emerging in 1993, but at this time, it remains just a vision.

SUMMARY

There is a rather simple dichotomy between the view that technology is neutral, just a tool, and the view that it can create serious problems independent of the intentions of the developers. Critics of the unrestricted use of technology include Lewis Mumford, who is very concerned about the dehumanizing aspects of automation; Siegfried Giedion, who argues that technology in the pursuit of efficiency may be achieved at the loss of quality and traditional human skills; and Jacques Ellul, who presents an enormously pessimistic view of technology (or *technique*) as an all-powerful force independent of human control. More recently, Joseph Weizenbaum, Neil Postman, and Sven Birkerts, among others, have focused on computers and related technologies and expressed their concerns about negative impacts.

Charles Babbage, an irascible genius of nineteenth-century England, essentially invented the modern computer. He was unable to build it because of limitations in the technology of the time and his continual changes of the conception.

The modern electronic computer generally is acknowledged to have been invented at the Moore School of Electrical Engineering, at the University of Pennsylvania, by John Mauchly and John Presper Eckert in 1945. Called ENIAC, it was funded by the Department of Defense and motivated by the computational needs of wartime research and development. Other contributions were made in the United States, England, and Germany, and their history is only now becoming clear. IBM (a name synonymous with the computer) has had phenomenal growth and impact on the industry and despite its ups and downs still leads in sales in most categories.

The major triumph of technology in the third quarter of the twentieth century may well be the integrated circuit, usually called the chip. Another phenomenon of our times is the personal computer, which provides enormous computing power at relatively low cost and small size. But the 1990s have also been witness to the growth and incredible popularity of the Internet, as it has moved out of the research environment into mainstream consciousness. The impact of these technological innovations is impossible to predict, but the opportunities they present will have a significant impact on society, for both good and ill.

NOTES

1. Collected in online quotation list. Copyright: Kevin Harris 1995.
2. John McDermott. "Technology: The Opiate of the Intellectuals," *New York Review of Books,* July 31, 1969, p. 25.
3. *Ibid.*
4. Lewis Mumford. *The Myth of the Machine: The Pentagon of Power.* (New York: Harcourt Brace Jovanovich, Inc., 1970), p. 273.
5. Siegfried Giedion. *Mechanization Takes Command.* (New York: Oxford University Press, 1948).
6. *Ibid.*, p. 5.
7. *Ibid.*, p. 172.
8. *Ibid.*
9. For a detailed description, see Samuel A. Matz, "Modern Baking Technology," *Scientific American*, November 1984, pp. 122–126, 131–134.
10. *Op. cit.,* Giedion. *Mechanization Takes Command*, p. 198.
11. Jacques Ellul. *The Technological Society*, 1964; reprint ed. (New York: Vintage, a division of Random House, 1967).
12. *Ibid.*, p. xxv.
13. *Ibid.*, p. 78.
14. Norbert Wiener. *Cybernetics: Control and Communications in the Animal and Machine, Second Edition.* (New York: MIT Press and Wiley, 1961).
15. Norbert Wiener. *God and Golem.* (Cambridge, MA: MIT Press, 1966), p. 73.
16. Joseph Weizenbaum. *Computer Power and Human Reason.* (San Francisco, CA: W. H. Freeman and Company, 1976).
17. *Ibid.*, p. 224.
18. *Ibid.*, p. 226.

19. Neil Postman. *Technopoly: The Surrender of Culture to Technology.* (New York: Vintage Books, A Division of Random House, 1993), p. xii.
20. *Ibid.,* p. 52.
21. *Ibid.,* p. 48.
22. Sven Birkerts. *The Gutenberg Elegies: The Fate of Reading in an Electronic Age.* (Boston, MA: Faber and Faber, Inc., 1994), p. 6.
23. *Ibid.,* p. 20.
24. John Stuart Mill. *On Liberty.* (Boston, MA: Ticknor and Fields, 1863), p. 114.
25. Oscar Wilde. *The Soul of Man under Socialism and Other Essays.* (New York: HarperCollins, 1970), p. 245.
26. Herbert A. Simon, "Prometheus or Pandora: The Influence of Automation on Society," *Computer,* November 1981, p. 91.
27. The Progress and Freedom Foundation, "Mission Statement." Accessed from the Web page with URL: <http://www.pff.org/pff/miss.html> on February 20, 1996.
28. The Progress and Freedom Foundation, "Cyberspace and the American Dream: A Magna Carta for the Knowledge Age." Release 1.2, August 22, 1994. Accessed from the Web page with URL: <http://www.pff.org/pff/position.html> on February 21, 1996.
29. Brian Randell, ed., *The Origins of Digital Computers, Selected Papers.* (New York: Springer-Verlag, 3rd edition, 1982), pp. 1–7.
30. Gottfried Liebniz, as quoted in Herman H. Goldstine, *The Computer from Pascal to von Neumann.* (Princeton, NJ: Princeton University Press, 1972), p. 8.
31. A letter from Babbage to Adolphe Quetelet, dated April 27, 1835, is apparently the earliest known reference to the Analytical Engine. For a fascinating study of the torturous process of historical attribution as well as the pitfalls of publication, see J. A. N. Lee, "On "Babbage and Kings" and "How Sausage Was Made:" And Now for the Rest of the Story," *IEEE Annals of the History of Computing,* **17** (4), Winter 1995, pp. 7–23.
32. Countess Lovelace's translation of "Sketch of the Analytical Engine invented by Charles Babbage, Esq. By L. F. Menabrea, of Turin [1842], appeared in *Taylor's Scientific Memoirs,* Vol. III, together with her editorial notes. It is reprinted in B. V. Bowden (ed.), *Faster Than Thought: A Symposium on Digital Computing Machines.* (England: The Pittman Press, 1971) (original edition 1953), p. 368.
33. *Ibid.,* p. 398.
34. Randell, *Ibid.,* p. 160.
35. As quoted in Nancy Stern, *From Eniac to Univac.* (Bedford, MA: Digital, 1981), p. 4. The original source is E. R. Larson, Findings of Fact, Conclusions of Law and Order for Judgment (sic), File No. 4-67 Civ. 138, Honeywell Inc. vs. Sperry-Rand Corp. and Illinois Scientific Developments Inc., US District Court, District of Minnesota, Fourth Division, Oct. 19, 1973.
36. Herman Lukoff, *From Dits to Bits: A Personal History of the Electronic Computer.* (Portland, OR: Robotics, 1979). Herman Goldstine, *The Computer from Pascal to von Neumann.* (Princeton, NJ: Princeton University Press, 1972).
37. Randell, *Ibid.,* p. 297.
38. See the Spring 1996 issue of *IEEE Annals of the History of Computing,* **18** (1) for several papers "Documenting ENIAC's 50th Anniversary."
39. John Mauchly, contribution to "Readers' Forum," *Datamation,* October 1979, p. 217.
40. Randell, *Ibid.,* pp. 379–380.
41. John A. N. Lee and Golde Holtzman. "50 Years After Breaking the Codes: Interviews with Two of the Bletchley Park Scientists," *IEEE Annals of the History of Computers,* **17** (1), 1995, pp. 32–43.
42. Ira Sager. "It's Hot! It's Sexy! It's . . . Big Blue?" *Business Week,* March 4, 1996, p. 39.

43. "The Datamation World 100, Section Breakout." June 15, 1996. As accessed from the Web page with URL: <http://www.datamation.com/PlugIn/issues/1996/june15/06blist.html> on July 13, 1996. The data shown in Table 3.1 was extracted from the data provided for each of the top 100 companies. © Datamation, reprinted with permission of Reed Elsevier Inc.

44. Hoo-min D. Toong and Amar Gupta. "Personal Computers," *Scientific American,* December 1982, p. 87.

45. "The Computer Moves In," *Time,* January 3, 1983, p. 10. Copyright 1983 Time Warner Inc. Reprinted by permission.

46. F. G. Heath. "Large Scale Integration in Electronics," *Scientific American,* February 1970, p. 22.

47. Robert N. Noyce. "Microelectronics," *Scientific American,* September 1977, p. 67. This influential paper presents important reasons for the success of the integrated circuit.

48. Jaikumar Vijayan and Stewart Deck. "Glut of Memory Chips Pushes Prices Down," *Computerworld,* February 19, 1996, p. 32.

49. C. Dan Hutcheson and Jerry D. Hutcheson. "Technology and Economics in the Semiconductor Industry," *Scientific American,* January 1996, p. 61.

50. Gene Bylinsky. "Here Comes the Second Computer Revolution," *Fortune,* November 1975. Reprinted in Tom Forester (ed.), *The Microelectronics Revolution.* (Cambridge, MA: The MIT Press, 1981), p. 6.

51. "Computer Superchip 'Impressive'," *The Vancouver Sun,* January 4, 1990, p. B 4.

52. Hutcheson and Hutcheson, p. 62.

53. "Saving Chips from Market Dips," *The Economist,* January 20, 1996, pp. 63–64.

54. Stan Kulikowski. "Timeline for a Network History." As posted on comp.society.cu-digest, June 10, 1993. Message-ID: <1993June24.233217.3449@chinacat.unicom.com>.

55. The Internet Society is a nongovernmental international organization for global cooperation and coordination for the Internet and its internetworking technologies and applications. The Society's individual and organizational members are bound by a common stake in maintaining the viability and global scaling of the Internet. They comprise the companies, government agencies, and foundations that have created the Internet and its technologies as well as innovative new entrepreneurial organizations contributing to maintain that dynamic. Visit their home pages to see how Internet innovators are creatively using the network. The Society is governed by its Board of Trustees elected by its membership around the world. The Internet Society is accessible at the Web site with URL: <http://www.isoc.org>.

ADDITIONAL READINGS

Comments on Technological Change

Bell, Daniel. *The Coming of the Post-Industrial Society.* (New York: Basic Books, 1983).

Benedikt, Michael. *Cyberspace: First Steps.* (Cambridge, MA: The MIT Press, 1991).

Frankel Boris. *The Postindustrial Utopians.* (Cambridge, United Kingdom: Polity Press, 1987).

Kelly, Kevin. *Out of Control: The Rise of Neo-biological Civilization.* (Reading, MA: Addison-Wesley, 1995).

Kuhns, William. *The Post-Industrial Prophets.* (New York: Harper & Row, 1971).

Masuda, Yoneii. *The Information Society as Post Industrial Society.* (Bethesda, MD: World Future Society, 1981).

Mander, Jerry. *In the Absence of the Sacred: The Failure of Technology & the Survival of the Indian Nations.* (San Francisco, CA: Sierra Club Books paperback edition, 1992).

Negroponte, Nicholas. *Being Digital.* (New York: Alfred A. Knopf, 1995).

Nora, Simon and Minc, Alain. *The Computerization of Society.* (Cambridge, MA: The MIT Press, 1981).

Reinecke, Ian. *Electronic Illusions: A Skeptic's View of Our High-Tech Future.* (New York: Penguin, 1984).

Shallis, Michael. *The Silicon Idol: The Micro Revolution and Its Social Implications.* (New York: Oxford University Press, 1984).

Stoll, Clifford. *Silicon Snake Oil.* (New York: Doubleday, 1995).

Winner, Langdon. *Autonomous Technology: Technics-out-of-Control as a Theme in Political Thought.* (Cambridge, MA: MIT Press, 1977).

Winner, Langdon. *The Whale and the Reactor: A Search for Limits in an Age of High Technology.* (Chicago, IL: University of Chicago Press, 1986).

A Brief History of Computers

Augarten, Stan. *Bit by Bit: An Illustrated History of Computers.* (New York: Ticknor & Fields, 1984).

Blohm, Hans, Beer, Stafford, and Suzuki, David. *Pebbles to Computers: The Thread.* (Toronto, Canada: Oxford University Press, 1986).

Burks, Alice R. and Burks, Arthur W. *The First Electronic Computer: The Atanasoff Story.* (Ann Arbor, MI: The University of Michigan Press, 1988).

Flamm, Kenneth. *Creating the Computer: Government, Industry, and High Technology.* (Washington, DC: The Brookings Institution, 1988).

Hinsley, F. H. and Stripp, Alan (eds.). *Codebreakers: The Inside Story of Bletchley Park.* (New York: Oxford University Press, 1993).

Lavington, Simon. *Early British Computers.* (Bedford, MA: Digital Press, 1980).

Lee, J. A. N. *Computer Pioneers.* (Los Alamitos, CA: IEEE CS Press, 1995).

Lundstrom, David. E. *A Few Good Men from Univac.* (Cambridge, MA: MIT Press, 1987).

Metropolis, N., Howlett, J., and Rota, Gian-Carlo. *The History of Computing in the Twentieth Century.* (New York: Academic Press, 1976).

Mollenhoff, Clark R. *Atanasoff: Forgotten Father of the Computer.* (Ames, IA: Iowa State University Press, 1988).

Polson, Ken. "Chronology of Events in the History of Microcomputers," 1996. Accessed from the Web page with URL: <http://www.islandnet.com/~kpolsson/comphist.htm> on September 26, 1996.

Williams, Michael R. *A History of Computing.* (Englewood Cliffs, NJ: Prentice-Hall, 1985).

The Emergence of the Chip

Braun, Ernest and MacDonald, Stuart. *Revolution in Miniature: The History and Impact of Semiconductor Electronics.* (Cambridge, United Kingdom: Cambridge University Press, 1978).

Hanson, Dirk. *The New Alchemists: Silicon Valley Fever and the Micro-Electronics Revolution.* (New York: Avon, 1983).

Hayes, Dennis. *Behind the Silicon Curtain: The Seductions of Work in a Lonely Era.* (Boston, MA: South End Press, 1989).

Rogers, Everett M. and Larsen, Judith K. *Silicon Valley Fever: Growth of High-Technology Culture.* (New York: Basic Books, 1984).

Siegel, Lenny and Markoff, John. *The High Cost of High Tech: The Dark Side of the Chip.* (New York: Harper & Row. 1985).

The Internet

Anthes, Gary H. "The History of the Future," *Computerworld,* October 3, 1994, pp. 101, 104–105.

"Internet & Beyond," Special Report, *Byte,* July 1995, pp. 69–92.

Kehoe, Brendan P. *Zen and the Art of the Internet: A Beginner's Guide.* (Englewood Cliffs, NJ: Prentice-Hall, 1991).

Kroll, Ed. *The Whole Internet: User's Guide and Catalog.* (Sebastopol, CA: O'Reilly & Assoc., 1992).

Mitchell, William J. *City of Bits: Space, Place and the Infobahn.* (New York: HarperCollins Publishers, Inc., 1995).

4

THE BUSINESS WORLD

American business has a voracious appetite for more and better information.

Mark Klein, "Information Politics," *Datamation* (Cahners Publishing Co.), August 1, 1985.

INTRODUCTION

A major part of the June 5, 1971 issue of *Business Week* was devoted to a serious overview of computers in business.[1] The underlying sentiment was that computers are wonderful tools but they must satisfy traditional business principles, they must be used wisely, and they tend to generate their own special problems. Technology is changing rapidly, prices are falling, machines are getting faster and smaller, and software to deal with many of the pressing problems of business will soon be available. Minicomputers (minis) were the big news, much cheaper than mainframes but with more computing power for the dollar. And computers were being used everywhere:

Process Control and Manufacturing. Steel plants, automobile factories, the aerospace industry

Education. Business schools, high schools, and elementary schools

Financial Institutions. Banks, credit card systems, the stock market

Government. Social security administration, research, defense department (3,200 computers, and the electronic battle field), economic modeling

A list for today would be similar but much longer, as would be the list of concerns and aims. Our purpose in this chapter is to trace the evolution of data processing systems—their problems, their uses, and their future. The term data processing has evolved into the more ambitious concept, information processing or information technology, and industry managers need management information systems. These systems will provide instant information, decision-making advice, forecasts, statistics, graphs, and tables. With a terminal on the desk, the manager can access all these forms of business information directly, or so the story goes. Computers and associated technologies have thus changed the way companies are managed, with such descriptions as the virtual corporation and the re-engineering of the company receiving considerable attention.

Among the potential future benefits of computers, none has been as acclaimed as the automated office. There has been a call for the office to be transformed by computers and communication networks to decrease paperwork and increase productivity. The personal computer, which has slipped into every nook and cranny of the company, will continue to play an important role. Networking, both within companies and globally, is becoming a major factor in the business world. Also of increasing importance is the Internet and especially the World Wide Web, as a necessary advertising and sales tool, offering many potential benefits. Such networks are expected to play a crucial role in future business applications, as envisioned by many promoters of the Information Highway. The impact of computerization on the organizational structure of companies is an issue, as are the fears of some office workers about the potential industrialization of the office and the accompanying loss of jobs.

The Year 2000

But all is not efficiency, productivity, and organization: What about the coming chaos associated with the year 2000? Because computers began to be used heavily in the 1960s, a shortcut was introduced with respect to the computation of ages, years, and dates in innumerable databases. Simply put, if Mary was born in 1953 and it is currently 1997, her age can be computed by subtracting 1953 from 1997 (within one year). It requires less computer memory, a vital concern in the 1960s, 1970s, and 1980s, and less computation to carry out the subtraction as 53 from 97, if only two digits are stored for the year of birth and the current year. In many thousands of databases, both public and private, this latter strategy has been followed for forty years with the result that a simple and effective process, if not amended, will result in chaos in the year 2000, and subsequently. The age in the previous example will not be 47. It could be −53, it could be zero if negative results have been excluded, or it could cause a system crash if negative results permeate the database. To deal with this apparently simple problem will require a very expensive fix. The Gartner Group, Inc. makes the following points:[2]

- Worldwide costs to address the Year 2000 change: $300 billion to $600 billion. This cost includes inventory and finding and fixing date fields as well as testing. It does not include changing forms to accommodate the extra date field.
- Fix-it costs per line of code: $1. This cost does not include documentation, training and final implementation testing.

The Gartner forecast has been disputed of course, especially the prediction that correcting the problem will provide an enormous boost for mainframe sales, but there does exist a general agreement that it is a problem that must be addressed and one whose solution will not be cheap.[3] Just to reinforce the concern, here are some reasons that investors could suffer from year 2000 problems because all transactions are heavily dependent on the accurate recording and use of dates:[4]

- Clearing and settlement of transactions could break down.
- Stocks held electronically and checking accounts could be wiped out.
- Customers might be denied access to their accounts.
- Deposits or trades might not be credited to an account, and customers' funds would not be available.
- Interest might not be properly credited to accounts.

THE EARLY YEARS: DATA PROCESSING SYSTEMS

It is a capital mistake to theorize before one has data. (Arthur Conan Doyle)

The computer is almost synonymous with business. After use in military applications, the first computer sales were to business. Since then (more than forty years ago) business, in all its multifarious interests, has become the major user of computers. Some of the uses are obvious: payroll, accounts receivable, sales records, inventory control—management of all the basic records and computations needed to operate a business. As computer technology evolved and was in fact actively spurred on by the rising expectations of the business community, the range of uses expanded rapidly to meet both perceived and anticipated needs.

The Evolution of Data Processing

Cyrus Gibson and Richard Nolan described the goals of managers in introducing computer facilities and the resulting organizational problems that have arisen.[5] They were interested in methods and techniques for improving these facilities in response to the changing requirements of a company. In 1974, they argued that there are four stages of electronic data processing (EDP) growth and that it follows the classic S-curve from an initial to a mature phase. The first stage, accounting applications, reflects the replacement of manual methods by the computer with the primary goal of cost savings. Succeeding stages are characterized by a flowering of new possibilities that exploit the power and speed of computers. Stage 2 shows a "proliferation of applications in all functional areas" such as cash flow, budgeting, inventory, and sales. Stage 3 is consolidation, as the applications of Stage 2 are accommodated and control is emphasized. In Stage 4 more sophisticated software appears, focused on the database with a variety of online activities, as well as financial and simulation models.

It is instructive to remember, again, that not too many years ago when the population was not much smaller than it is today, bills were received, payments were acknowledged, payrolls were computed and disbursed, and society functioned more or less as it does currently, without computers. The arrival of the computer, however, meant that management had the potential systems capacity to engage in an enormous variety of new activities. This power would translate into quicker, more, and possibly better service for the customer, more (not always better) controls, better forecasts, and new ways of evaluating information. A new version of Parkinson's Law, that work expands to fill the time available, has arisen: Applications expand to fill the computer power available. (A corollary might be that ambition expands even faster.) For example, simulation and financial models represent complex applications made possible only by computers.

Simulation models are used to study complex systems for which exact mathematical analysis is too difficult. Companies trying to gauge market trends or determine crucial factors in the production process may decide to develop computer programs that simulate the situation of interest. Such programs are designed to simulate relevant features of the real world and study their interaction, because the world is too complex and cannot usually be modified to serve desired purposes. Care must be taken that important and relevant variables are recognized and properly interrelated. The underlying model must be carefully constructed and subsequently evaluated to ensure that the results produced are meaningful and significant.

Simulation is a powerful tool for science, government, and industry, but it must be used carefully. In the early 1970s, a considerable controversy arose in the wake of the publication of *The Limits to Growth,* a report that warned of a coming breakdown of the industrial world due to shortages in fuels and raw materials.[6] The report, based on a simulation model, was criticized for ignoring certain information, badly estimating the importance of some of the parameters, and ignoring crucial relations among selected variables. Currently a similar debate rages over the greenhouse effect and the concern that unless we curtail the production of carbon dioxide, a byproduct of industry and automobiles, we will have to confront the effects of higher temperatures around the world. If company policy is to be based on the results of simulations, management must be convinced of their accuracy—a nontrivial requirement. Even so, the use of simulations has become another important weapon in management's operational and planning arsenal.

Financial planning models depend on sophisticated mathematical models that have been designed to predict medium- and long-term events. Such models have become quite useful and important and would not be possible without computers. Their construction requires mathematical, financial, and programming skills. As computer systems have become more powerful these models have taken on a new significance. They can be responsive to changing world conditions and permit managers to make quick decisions. It is interesting to consider the current situation in which the major financial institutions all depend on sophisticated financial models to carry out their activities. To the best programs go the spoils.

One of the major advances of the 1970s was the development of online systems. An online system permitted almost instantaneous access to, and response from, the computer in contrast to the previous batch systems that required overnight runs to process daily activities. For example, a banking system permits online access when the teller can update an account directly from a terminal or personal computer. With online systems, management can have rapid access to personnel information, customer information, and sales information. It should be noted that an online system typically permits access to several hundred, if not thousands of users. Such a facility requires a large mainframe computer, or more recently, a distributed system with many small and powerful computers linked in a client-server configuration.

Gibson and Nolan pointed out a number of the problems associated with the growth of EDP systems in general. One of the earliest was the location of the data processing division within company organization and the implications of this decision. A data processing center could be a branch of the financial division, a service center accommodating a number of departments, or an autonomous division with its own vice president. Each of these had its own advantages and disadvantages for the company, for middle management, and for the employees. Not uncommonly, the first computer appeared in the finance department, since there were immediate applications in accounting. Soon other departments such as sales, marketing, production, and research saw in the computer an important and necessary instrument. In some cases the large investment in computing resources was jealously guarded by the financial department, and part-time release to other departments may not have been sufficient. Pressure arose for either a central independent computer facility or center to which all divisions or departments would have equal access, or a computing facility directly responsible to other users. In the former case, the center would be just another company division responsible to the president and in competition for resources in its own right. In the latter, the center would be a service department expected to provide whatever might be required and dependent on its clients for its budget. Clearly, different organizational roles imply differing degrees of responsibility. Computer professionals may be either technicians or part of the executive hierarchy.

Five Generations of Computers

One of the best overviews of the early evolution of computer systems has been provided by Frederic G. Withington, a vice president at Arthur D. Little Incorporated, and a long-time student of data processing systems.[7] He outlines five generations of computers, the first being 1953–1958 and the last 1982–ongoing. (The first three generations run from 1953 to 1974, the year the article was written. The last two represent predictions whose accuracy can be better determined at present.) The names of Withington's generations are instructive.

The first three periods represent the initiation and consolidation phase—new hardware, new software, traditional applications, changing organizational structure, and consolidation of the new technology. Withington predicted that the fourth generation, information custodians, would be characterized by very large file stores (databases), general purpose data manipulators, and centralized control with logistic decisions moving to headquarters and tactical decisions moving out. The forecast was actually quite accurate, with a couple of exceptions. The software did not evolve as rapidly as expected, although time-sharing systems did predominate. In the area of hardware, Withington did not, and could not be expected to, anticipate the personal computer explosion.

The last generation, action aids (beginning about 1982), he supposed would make use of new hardware such as magnetic bubble, laser-holographic technology, and distributed systems. Laser-holographic technology has yet to make its presence felt in the computer industry. Most computer companies have given up on magnetic bubble memories, but distributed systems have become the predominant architecture, albeit several years after the predicted date. Less centralized computing was anticipated, but the overwhelming integration of computing and communications could hardly have been expected. Furthermore, developments in office automation promise to revolutionize the basic operation of business. Other important contributions will include management information and decision analysis systems, aids to managers and executives at every level of the company.

IT Industry Evolution

One last view of the evolution of IT (Information Technology) presents "four waves of change." These persist from their years of initiation into the indefinite future as new waves wash over them and add to their effects. This view is more complex than the previous one, which seems to suggest a more-or-less linear sequence of successively more advanced technologies, with their associated organizational impacts. Table 4.1 presents a summary of the discussion in IS Priorities: As the Information Highway Begins. [8]

We seem to be in the age of the Information Society; not the official one however, but the beginning of what many would characterize perhaps as the Internet Age, a definite precursor to the fully blown vision encompassed in the term Information Society.

Guidelines for Growth

The transition from computer management to data resource management is an important step. Clearly, the situation changes as the range of applications grows, access diversifies via remote terminals and independent workstations, and more and more activities depend on the ready availability of information. In a natural way, the computer is thus transformed into a multifunctional information resource that is no longer the preserve of a designated division but is far-reaching and integrated into all the operations of the organization. Information in a variety of forms is now accessible—on modern systems, by all levels of management, whether or not they are near the computer, technically sophisticated, or have financial, managerial, marketing, or sales expertise.

In 1979, Richard Nolan extended the stages of data processing growth from four to six. [9] He considered the growth in knowledge and technology, organizational control, and the shift from computer management to data resource management—a necessary broadening of computer applications. It is obvious that the growth of knowledge exerts an important

TABLE 4.1

EVOLUTION OF INDUSTRY INFORMATION TECHNOLOGY.

Technology	Focus	Years of Duration	Number of Users
Mainframes and minicomputers	Large institutions	From 1964–1981 (until about 2010)	10,000,000 worldwide
PCs, LANs, open systems	Individuals at Work, at School, at Home	From 1981–1993 (past 2030)	Over 80,000,000
Information highways	Pervasive IT connectivity	From 1993–2010 to ?	Over 100,000,000
Information society	Converged, all-digital, multi-media context	From 2010– ? to ?	Over 150,000,000

influence on the direction and nature of further developments. In terms of organizational control, management must determine a balance between tight and so-called slack control. In fact, this balance will vary depending on the stage of growth. For example, to facilitate growth the control should be low and the slack should be high, but as the system matures both should be high. Nolan bases his results on a study during the 1970s of many companies that passed through all the stages except the last one.

And what of the predictions for the 1990s and beyond? The previous decade witnessed enormous technological and organizational changes, as companies struggle to accommodate an endless flow of new hardware and software. Arguments have raged about centralization versus decentralization, fulfilling user needs or management's directives, control, massive investment in technology with little obvious payoff, aging and fragile software investment, and an unpredictable and rapidly changing world economy. Given the basic and continuing importance of information to management, it is worth paying attention to the words of Peter Drucker, one of the world's foremost experts on management theory and practice. In a 1988 paper,[10] Drucker notes that for the most part computers are still being used to facilitate traditional computational efforts; that is, to "crunch conventional numbers," but that as a company, especially a large one, moves from "data to information, its decision processes, management structure, and even the way its work gets done begin to be transformed." Consider Drucker's definitions:[11]

> Information is data endowed with relevance and purpose. Converting data into information thus requires knowledge. And knowledge, by definition, is specialized . . . The information-based organization requires far more specialists overall than the command-and-control companies we are accustomed to.

And Drucker argues that competition demands that companies "will have to convert themselves into organizations of knowledge specialists."

If it sounds a bit too theoretical so far, perhaps we should turn to an industry practitioner:[12]

> As the companies reorganize for the '90s they are also exploding some myths. Chief among these is the notion that decentralization, the theme of the 1980s, will be the favored organizational approach to the emerging global marketplace. The pundits couldn't be more wrong, the executives reveal. Centralized control will increase, new centralized functions and entrepreneurial teams will arise.

There seems to be a considerable difference of opinion about the directions that business organizational structures will move in response to developments in information systems. Interestingly enough, when 50 US information systems executives were asked to rate 18 issues in order of importance they chose the following (in descending order of importance):[13]

- rapport and credibility with senior management,
- knowledge of the business,
- strategic systems opportunities,
- long-range vision and plan, and
- skills mix and motivation of IS personnel.

In recognition of significant difficulties associated with the automation of the office, *Fortune* devoted the cover of its May 16, 1986 issue to the provocative claim, "The Puny Payoff from Office Computers."[14]

> Have the millions of computers purchased by U.S. businesses brought any overall improvement in productivity? Surprisingly, the best information available says no . . . [O]n a national scale, business's investment of hundreds of billions of dollars in computers has failed to bring about a discernible improvement in productivity.

A number of reasons have been proposed to support this claim. These include the argument that computerization involves a long learning curve, that it may require a reorganization of the work process to realize significant gain, and simply that computers have been oversold so that they are misapplied in many applications. From another point of view, only the massive adoption of computers has prevented businesses from hiring many more people to maintain the same productivity levels.

Almost five years later the problem had not gone away, as a survey by the consultants Index Group reports ". . . the problem looming largest in the minds of corporate computer jockeys is convincing their colleagues to change their business practices to take advantage of office automation."[15] The startling statistic is that between the years 1980 and 1989, while the share of office equipment as a percentage of capital equipment rose from 3% to 18%, the productivity of office workers remained essentially unchanged. Over the same period the productivity of blue collar workers has increased substantially. We will have more to say about the difficult subject of productivity measurement later, but one final observation from the Index Group is particularly relevant: ". . . only about one-third of projects alter business practices. Most of the rest merely turn paper shufflers into computer-printout shufflers."[16]

More recently, it has been claimed that productivity has actually increased but that adequate tools and measures have not been available so that the by now familiar misconception is unjustified. Thus Professor Bakos of the University of California at Irvine presents the following reasons for the unacknowledged productivity gains:[17]

- It is ludicrous to blame computers for inadequate productivity in that period. [the 1980s] Computer investments in the 1970s and 1980s pale in comparison to the trillions of dollars of machinery, buildings and other assets that had accumulated over several decades.
- Any earlier move [prior to the 1990s] between computers and productivity would have been dwarfed by the impact of movements in oil prices and interest rates, changes in the tax code or fluctuations in the economy.
- Much of the productivity shortfall of the 1980s was a mirage anyway. Our tools for measuring productivity—designed for counting bushels of wheat and Model Ts off Ford's assembly line—are blunt when called upon to measure the tremendous improvements in service, quality, convenience, variety and timeliness.
- [A] recent comprehensive study of productivity of 380 large firms that together generate yearly sales in excess of $1.8 billion . . . found that computers . . . were significantly *more* [original emphasis] productive than any other type of investment these companies made.

If we can agree that computers have boosted productivity, the question that must be asked is why. There are no definitive answers but there are some possible ones. The real payoffs come about because the effective use of computers requires a substantial reorganization of the work process. In another study that attempts to determine the reasons for the wide fluctuations in computer-buying behavior by large companies, the authors suggest the following:[18]

> . . . the biggest reason for business's computer-buying behavior was that companies had to reorganize their business practices to take advantage of the new technology and had to tailor new software for their workers. They faced significant adjustment costs, and the process was painfully slow.

Two interesting answers to the productivity question seem to follow from this conclusion:[19]

- . . . the road to technical progress will need to be cleared by managers solving the intractable problems of corporations just as they have since the age of the Medicis.
- Why [have] the so-called social returns from the spread of computer technology—increased wealth or leisure from greater productivity— . . . been so slow to materialize? At first companies simply applied computer speed to old-fashioned work designs—paving the cowpaths, as it were. Really turbocharging productivity required basic re-design of work. And that took time.

The final words in this section will go to Richard Walton, distinguished and informed scholar of information system design and implementation. In a book written about eight years ago but still relevant, Walton makes the claim, consistent with the previous comments, that the effective implementation of advanced information technology (IT) in organizations "is a function of integrating the technical aspects of IT systems *and* [emphasis added] the social aspects of the organization."[20] To elaborate, we include a few additional comments, recognizing that they barely do justice to this important book, which proposes a detailed framework for the implementation of advanced IT.[21]

He notes that certain principles have been recognized early on in the implementation of IT:

- project champions,
- top management support,
- good relationships between developers and user departments,
- user involvement,
- adequate organizational resources,
- communication, and
- supportive organizational climate.

But more recently, these principles have been extended in the following ways:

- Top management should do more than merely support projects it approves. IT should develop and promulgate a broad version of IT, a vision capable of inspiring and guiding specific IT projects.
- Users are increasingly viewed as legitimately influencing design as well as installation activities.

- Advanced IT has "dual potentialities." For example, IT "can either routinize work or it can widen the discretion of users; it can strengthen hierarchical control or facilitate self-management and learning by users."

RECENT YEARS: INFORMATION TECHNOLOGY

Knowledge is of two kinds. We know a subject ourselves, or we know where we can find information on it. (Samuel Johnson)

Knowledge itself is power. (Francis Bacon [1561–1626])

It is not my intention to provide a comprehensive overview of information technology (IT) or Information Systems (IS) in business, even if that were possible given space constraints. Rather it will be possible only to indicate the current state of certain aspects of IT, such as groupware, workflow, and knowledge management, and to highlight possible trends. My purpose therefore is to present a number of current issues and approaches to integrating IT in the workplace.

General Background

In mid-1994, the cover of *Fortune* magazine read, "Managing in a WIRED WORLD."[22] This announcement seemed to herald the arrival of computer networks as a major organizational theme in the management world. This special report, also subtitled as *Fortune's* guide to Information Technology, surveyed such issues as managing, dealing with information overload, a survey of stationary and portable PCs, the role of telecom, or the office communication network, an overview of new products, ideas and, of course, investments. Just to indicate how much more information is available and accessible to the point of overload in today's offices, a few numbers are provided:[23]

- Change, since 1983, in numbers of computers in U.S. offices: +25,000,000
- Change, since 1987, in number of U.S. E-mail addresses: +26,250,000
- Messages left on voice mailboxes last year: 11,900,000,000
- Change, since 1987, in number of fax machines in U.S. offices and homes: +10,000,000
- Change, since 1987, in number of secretaries in the U.S.: −521,000
- Change, since 1987, in annual sales of over-the-counter pain relievers: +$500,000,000

A sampler of opinions follows to capture the swirl of issues surrounding the contemporary management problem:[24]

- Bill Raduchel, chief information officer of Sun Microsystems: "E-mail is a major cultural event—it changes the way you run the organization."
- Susan Falzon, a principal at CSC Research & Advisory Services in Cambridge, Massachusetts: "When work is carried out through networks, an organization's structure changes whether you want it or not. I can't find a single case where it doesn't happen."

... "In a network, supervision changes. There's less supervision of the content of the work, more supervision of a person's overall performance and career."

- Robert Walker, chief information officer at Hewlett-Packard: "With the ability to share information broadly and fully without filtering it through a hierarchy, we can manage the way we always wanted to.". . . Every month H-P's 97,000 employees exchange 20 million e-mail messages.
- Warns Helene Runtagh, CEO of General Electric Information Services: "The worst of all worlds is clinging to hierarchical behavior while bringing in network-based communications. You're in for a decade of chaos, frustration and poor financial results."

You might think that by examining a company's expenditures in IT and its overall performance it would be possible to determine what the best strategy might be with respect to the optimal deployment of computing resources. This is just what Paul Strassmann, a chief information officer at several major corporations and a writer for *Computerworld,* did, using data derived from a study of *Computerworld's* Premier 100 companies over a period of two years. These companies are renowned for their effective use of IT. Some of Mr. Strassmann's conclusions are given here:[25]

- They don't show any trend towards massive outsourcing.
- Excellent corporations deploy information technology in several ways. Many rely on mainframe computing, using older machines. Some spend a great deal on server hardware and PCs. Some devote up to half their budgets to systems development and systems engineering, and others coast along on program maintenance.
- Excellence is gained through the accumulation of company-specific know-how, for which company-based information management is indispensable.

In a following report, Mr. Strassmann makes the claim that expenditures in IT are not the determining factor in a corporation's success: "After twenty years of research I have found that computers do indeed add a great deal of value to well managed companies. But, computers are not an unqualified blessing. Identical machines, with identical software will make things worse if the enterprise is mismanaged."[26] In support of this assertion, he states that,[27]

> The proof of these assertions is that computer expenditures and corporate profits show no correlation whatsoever. I can state also that it is unlikely that any such relationship can be ever demonstrated. Computers are only a catalyst. Business values are created by well organized, well motivated and knowledgeable people who understand what to do with all of the information that shows up on the computer screens. It would be too much to hope that such a phenomenon would be a universal characteristic of all businesses.

These last remarks were based on a 1994 study of five hundred corporations in the US, Canada, and Europe. A scatter plot of Return on Equity versus Information Technology spending per employee for a statistically unbiased sample shows no correlation, as mentioned.

In Chapter 2, Isaac Asimov's three rules for robotics were given as an example of how technology could be constrained to serve people but not harm them, by building into the 'positronic brains' of robots a fundamental limitation on their exercise of power. Well, a project manager at a large company proposed a similar set of laws to govern the relationship between users and their Information Systems (IS):[28]

- Law No. 1: IS can't harm the business, or through inaction let the business come to harm.
- Law No. 2: IS must obey the orders given it by a user, except where such orders conflict with the first law.
- Law No. 3: IS must always protect its own existence, except where this would conflict with the first and second laws.

The first law encourages a proactive stance for IS, the second a re-examination of underlying assumptions prior to the initiation of new applications, and the third among other things would discourage outsourcing (a position consistent with Strassmann's findings).

To continue with this emphasis on the value of promoting a human-centered approach to the management of IT, we turn to the important work of Thomas Davenport, a partner and director of research at Ernst & Young's Center for Information Technology and Strategy in Boston. Mr. Davenport has written at length about the importance of people in the managing of IT and the benefits to be gained when their abilities, skills, and concerns are effectively addressed and employed. With the focus on gathering, storing, manipulating, and disseminating information in computers and over computer networks, a simple idea is occasionally lost, namely that much of what is valuable and important does not reside in machines but rather is part of the working intellectual capital of organizations and resides in the people. In Davenport's own words, here are a few of the ten "Information Facts of Life:"[29]

1. Most of the information in organizations—and most of the information people really care about—isn't on computers.
2. Managers prefer to get information from people rather than computers; people add value to raw information by interpreting it and adding context.
4. All information doesn't have to be common; an element of flexibility and disorder is desirable.
6. If information is power and money, people won't share it easily.
8. To make the most of electronic communications, employees must first learn to communicate face-to-face.
10. There's no such thing as information overload; if information is really useful, our appetite for it is insatiable.

Knowledge Management

This section is the first in this chapter to discuss a number of labels that have been applied to the employment of IT in the corporation, in conjunction with a specific management strategy that is claimed to improve efficiency, productivity, competitiveness, and whatever else seems important at the time. Thus knowledge management, the virtual corporation, the reengineered corporation, and other similar terms have been fashionable, with more and varied approaches ready to make their appearance. They are based on a variety of beliefs in the importance of knowledge to the successful corporation, the need to access and employ that knowledge, and the role of IT in that undertaking.

From a regular column by Joseph Maglitta in *Computerworld,* we learn that knowledge management is "the emerging discipline of systematically and actively managing and leveraging the vast stores of knowledge and information that exist in a typical company. 'Knowledge' refers to systems, processes, and know-how."[30] The answer to the question, "How does it affect IS [Information Systems]?" provides a boost to the development of technology, namely, "Depending on the organization and culture, technology groups lead knowledge management efforts or play an integral role as enabler. Some backers say knowledge management offers a promising, natural next stage of evolution for many IS groups."[31] The recognition of the value of company information is not a new idea but its identification, extraction, and employment in a number of areas including sales and marketing by means of advanced IT is new.

More than six months later, Maglitta attempted to characterize the importance of knowledge management as follows:[32]

> Although approaches vary, knowledge management in general tries to organize and make available important know-how, wherever it's needed. This includes processes, procedures, patents, reference works, formulas, "best practices," forecasts and fixes. Technologically, intranets, groupware, data warehouses, networks, bulletin boards and videoconferencing are key tools for storing and distributing this intelligence.

These technologies will be discussed later in this chapter but given the importance of Japan in modern management techniques, it is worthwhile to review briefly a recent book in this area.[33] Based on studies of a number of companies including Nissan Motor Co., the authors echo Strassmann's comments, reported previously, that there are definite limits to the value of information systems. We should emphasize that technology in and of itself cannot do the job; only people can and they can do it better by employing technology in appropriate ways. Thus the goal for modern management is to discover the best way to organize good people to use advanced technology effectively. In summarizing the approach advocated by the Japanese authors, including a cautionary view towards IT, correspondent Rob Guth notes that part of the reason that IT is not emphasized is that many Japanese corporations trail their US counterparts in its adoption. Consider the following remarks:[34]

> Knowledge management in the West has risen hand-in-hand with technologies such as groupware, whiteboarding and videoconferencing, but tacit knowledge is difficult to verbalize, represent digitally or store in a database. It is the stuff of metaphors and analogies and is better communicated face to face, the authors say ... Knowledge-creating companies rely on redundancy (of information and responsibilities, for instance) as a means of "encouraging frequent dialogue and communication" from which tacit knowledge can be converted to usable, explicit knowledge ... Middle managers are the heroes of a company's knowledge creation, according to Nonaka and Takeuchi. Yes, the same stratum held as the source of corporate inefficiency sits between front-line workers—those with useful reserves of tacit knowledge—and upper management. This is the layer in a company where knowledge creation occurs, the authors argue ... Middle managers mediate between the "what should be" of upper management and the "what is" of the real world.

Organizational Issues

The focus here is on the debate between two organization structures—centralization versus decentralization. More questions will be raised than answered but that is to be expected given the rapid changes in technology and the curious mirroring of technological architectures by organizational structures. The simple, perhaps simplistic, version of this relationship is that when mainframes personified computing, the organizational structure almost by necessity was strongly centralized. As time-sharing systems replaced batch processing, the rigid central control began to weaken and appeared to have ended as the age of personal computing dawned in the early 1980s. Then distributed computing arrived and decentralization seemed to be in full swing aided and abetted by the growing importance of the client-server strategy. This technology is obviously dependent on the enormous hardware advances resulting from the power of microprocessors as implemented in the by-now ubiquitous workstation. The trend seemed inevitable: more personal computers, both desktop and portable, more remote computing, and where necessary mainframes for large databases, resulting in less centralized control. Or so it seemed.

However, two long-time observers of the computing scene have some interesting views to offer about the inevitability of this trend. In this regard, the following views of John Rockart, director of the Center for Information Systems Research at MIT, are particularly relevant:[35]

> Global companies must compete and manage supplies and personnel worldwide, yet their local offices need enough decision-making autonomy to respond to local customers and market conditions. That means that IS must develop worldwide standards and centralize information technology purchasing, while making sure that locals have the authority to meet local business and technology needs. This is the force driving the move to "federal" IS organizations, which explicitly divide authority for information technology between central IS and local users . . .
>
> We will go to major centralized network and systems management and to centralized help desks. but it will take a while . . .
>
> Rockart believes the old trend toward dispersing spending and standards-setting authority is ending, as companies seek to contain costs and gain economies of scale . . .
>
> Corporations are standardizing on software packages and centralizing support functions such as finance and purchasing . . .
>
> Centrally managing servers is the sensible thing to do, Rockart says. It's cheaper than having local server gurus handling each server. "We are clearly seeing a larger number of 'server farms' in what used to be the glass houses."

Mike Braude is senior vice president and chief research officer, Gartner Group, a major IS consultant. Although he agrees with Rockart about many issues, he does have his own perspective and concerns:[36]

> From 1985 to 1995, PCs and client server moved too far away from centralized computing. Companies were rebounding from their past dependence on the IS priesthood. Today, companies are turning away from totally decentralized client/server or network computing,

Braude says. The expense and difficulty of managing decentralized computing is one factor. The immobility of mainframe applications and their data is another. However, the pendulum will never swing all the way back. For the next five years and beyond, enterprises will struggle to find the appropriate balance . . .

Traditional data centers are now being asked to manage departmental/distributed systems in a centralized manner. In part, that's because companies have yet to find systems and network software that do an adequate job of managing decentralized systems in a decentralized manner.

Obviously the presentation is partial and incomplete but nevertheless, it is highly suggestive that change is in the offing and that the coupling of computer architecture and organizational structure is by no means predetermined.

Workflow

Two benefits of recent developments in IT facilitate the tracking and monitoring of work, Workflow, and the efforts of individuals to cooperate on projects, Groupware. Both of these seem to have unlimited potential for enhancing the work process in an important way, albeit if employed in a spirit of commitment to basic human values. But first we examine the current state and promise of these technologies.[37]

WORKFLOW software automates and tracks the flow of documents and work processes through a company. The focus is on how work normally moves through an organization— the process—instead of on the specific information. There is a consensus today that you can break workflow products down into four groupings:

- *Production workflow:* deals with transaction-oriented, high-value, repetitive processes such as insurance claims or accounts receivable . . .
- *Collaborative workflow:* deals with high-value, non-repetitive, generally nontransactional-oriented processes such as new product development, sales-force automation or technical document assembly . . .
- *Administrative workflow:* deals with low-value processes generally connected to routine office work such as travel expense reporting, budgeting and purchase approvals . . .
- *Ad hoc workflows:* deals with low-value processes, generally connected to routine office work such as FYI routing, review and approval. Lots of ad hoc products are e-mail-based . . .

The trend is to include, or rather embed, workflow software in a broad range of applications programs so that it can be used directly in the programming environment. As more software is implemented in an object-oriented framework, workflow components will be integrated as a system of rules. Another perspective on workflow is based on the following definition by Thomas Koulopoulos, author of *The Workplace Imperative:*[38]

. . . as a toolset for the proactive analysis, compression, and automation of information-based tasks and activities. Think of the office environment as an information factory, or more specifically, a process factory . . . The connection of . . . office tasks creates a value chain that spans internal and external task boundaries. In this architecture, workflow attempts to streamline the component of the factory by eliminating unnecessary tasks, saving time, effort, and costs associated with the performance of those tasks and automating the remaining tasks that are necessary to the process.

So far the emphasis has been on the technological aspects of workflow but as previously mentioned, nothing will work unless "Human Factors" are taken into account. Thus the following considerations are crucial to the success of the workflow process:[39]

- *Involving the Users.* [You] mustn't underestimate the importance of soliciting input from the actual users of the system . . . An added benefit of involving users while designing the workflow is that you build in user support and ownership of the application from the start.
- *Setting Expectations.* It is important that you set realistic expectations for your users . . . If expectations have been set acknowledging that there will be problems initially but that over the course of a few weeks it will get easier, and if the potential benefits are clearly explained, people are more likely to get over the hurdles quickly.
- *Training.* . . . these are group solutions which rely heavily on everyone knowing exactly how the application works and what is expected of them.
- *Importance of Piloting.* Try to select a representative group as your pilot so that you can determine the issues most likely to affect the organization at large.
- *Building Buy-in at All Levels.* In order for strategic workflow applications to succeed, you need buy-in at the top . . . buy-in at the executive level . . . [b]uy-in at the management level is equally important . . . you absolutely must have buy-in at the user-level.
- *Rewarding Usage.* Users must perceive an added value to using the new application.

Groupware

Say the word groupware to information systems professionals and the response is likely to be Lotus Notes, software that permits individuals at different locations to share online ideas and writing projects. So for some, groupware is related to collaborative computing, or "information technology used to help people work together more efficiently," or "computer-based systems that support groups of people engaged in a common task and that provides an interface to a shared environment."[40] There appear to be two major current approaches that depend on such existing and independently effective technologies as e-mail, bulletin boards, discussion forums, electronic meeting and scheduling programs, shared databases, and multiauthoring document tools. The two approaches are characterized as follows:[41]

- *GroupSuite Model.* [It] parallels the desktop suite model in which several products are tightly integrated and provide a [somewhat] common user interface into a suite of applications. These products typically provide the basic functionality most companies are looking for today in Groupware including group calendar and scheduling, electronic forms, information sharing, email and workflow automation . . . GroupSuites strive to provide group productivity by providing ubiquitous access to information, tools for document sharing and tools that organize information in a meaningful way. [Best example is Novell's GroupWise]

- *Information/Communication (InfoComm) Model.* In this new model the user is presented with relevant information regardless of its origin, where it is located, or the application. Users are capable of storing, accessing, managing, and analyzing information from a wide variety of sources without having to think about where it is physically stored and what applications are needed to manipulate it . . . It may be stored on a server in another department or even on a worldwide web server at some other company. In this new environment the user is only concerned with the information. The best example of this model today is Lotus Notes.

The potential power of such collaborations is enormous and the growth in popularity of the Web provides an additional possibility for organizations that wish to foster distributed collaborative computing, although for the next while, Lotus Notes probably provides the best environment. Committed managers, who wish to encourage cooperative computing efforts, should also explore the impact on the altered workplace.

Virtual Corporation

As this discussion proceeds, keep in mind that our aim here is not an in-depth exploration of modern business organization, but rather an introduction to the role of computer and telecommunications technology in that organization. As such, the emphasis is on identifying the uses to which computers have been put, how successful these have been, their impact on the social environment, and reasonable projections of future developments. The tools, applications, and approaches discussed so far provide ways to perform work better, to improve the monitoring process, and to take advantage of valuable company knowledge, presumably with the goal to transform the corporation in some fundamental manner. The corporate transformational models that have been proposed over the past few years rely heavily on these tools. The so-called virtual corporation, the result of a strategy for converting an inertia-bound company into a flexible, adaptive, efficient, and productive one, adopts the word "virtual" in part from its use in computer technology as a software-implemented real-world phenomenon. *The Virtual Corporation* is the title of a book by William Davidow and Michael Malone [42] that both introduced the term and defined its potential. As we might expect, it is not particularly easy to define this rather abstract and elusive concept. First, however, it is necessary to define the simpler notion of a virtual product, namely, "The ideal virtual product or service is one that is produced instantaneously and customized in response to customer demand." [43] In somewhat more detail, the following is offered: [44]

A virtual product (the term will be use to mean both physical products and services) mostly exists even before it is produced. Its concepts, design, and manufacture are stored in the minds of cooperating teams, in computers, and in flexible production lines. While the *perfect* virtual product can never exist, there is little doubt that many will come close . . . formerly well-defined structures [are] beginning to lose their edges, seemingly permanent things starting to continuously change, and products and services adapting to match our desires . . . the ability to make them will determine the successful corporations of the next century.

Based on this idea of a virtual product, the virtual corporation can be thought of as a highly adaptive, highly flexible organization, which can respond rapidly to changing market conditions, changing technology, changing demand, and changing regulations in order to design, develop, test, and market the perceived right product or service at the right time. It is as if in the context of automobile production, new designs would result in the instantaneous creation of appropriate assembly lines with the simultaneous disappearance of no longer needed ones. Design, development, and production teams would appear as needed and diffuse into the corporation at large when their mission has been accomplished. Davidow and Malone offer the following formulation:[45]

> . . . it will appear almost edgeless, with permeable and continuously changing interfaces between company, supplier, and customers. From inside the firm the view will be no less amorphous, with traditional offices, departments, and operating divisions constantly re-forming according to need. Job responsibilities will regularly shift as will lines of authority—even the very definition of employee will change, as some customers and suppliers begin to spend more time in the company than will some of the firm's own workers . . . will require taking a sophisticated information network that gathers data on markets and customer needs, combining it with the newest design methods and computer-integrated production processes, and then operating this system with an integrated network that includes not only highly skilled employees of the company but also suppliers, distributors, retailers, and even consumers.

Business Week recognized the arrival of the "Virtual Corporation" as a "new model that uses technology to link people, assets, and ideas in a temporary organization. After the business is done, it disbands."[46] In this overview, the virtual corporation is characterized as "a temporary network of companies that come together quickly to exploit fast-changing opportunities." In more detail, five important features are highlighted:

- *Technology.* Informational structures will help far-flung companies and entrepreneurs link up and work together from start to finish. The partnership will be based on electronic contracts to keep the lawyers away and speed the linkups.
- *Excellence.* Because each partner brings its "core competence" to the effort, it may be possible to create a "best-of-everything" organization. Every function and process could be world-class—something no single company could achieve.
- *Opportunism.* Partnerships will be less permanent, less formal, and more opportunistic. Companies will band together to meet a specific market opportunity and, more often than not, fall apart once the need evaporates.
- *Trust.* These relationships make companies far more reliant on each other and require far more trust than ever before. They'll share a sense of "co-destiny," meaning that the fate of each partner is dependent on the other.
- *No Borders.* This new corporate model redefines the traditional boundaries of the company. More cooperation among competitors, suppliers, and customers makes it harder to determine where one company ends and another begins.

In 1996, the book *Going Virtual*[47] touted the virtues of the virtual organization, providing a detailed how-to manual for executives who still want to achieve a lean, flexible organization. The possibly enduring mantra to be derived from this guide to the eager-to-change is "Transitioning to a virtual organization is like redesigning an airplane while it's flying. Don't become so focused on your destination that you fail to keep the airplane up in the air." [48]

Reengineering

Almost in tandem with the advice to produce the "Virtual Corporation," was the more popular challenge to "Reengineer the Corporation," by using a variety of methods to transform a moribund organization to a dynamic, responsive one. Again, technology—computers and telecommunications systems—will play a necessary and vital role. The gurus of this call-to-arms are Michael Hammer and James Champy,[49] chairmen of influential management consulting firms, whose book *Reengineering the Corporation* appeared in 1993 as a manifesto for change; indeed the word manifesto appeared in the subtitle of their book. They leave no doubt with respect to the kind or magnitude of the change they say is absolutely required:

> Business reengineering means putting aside much of the received wisdom of two hundred years of industrial management. It means forgetting how work was done in the age of mass market and deciding how it can best be done now. In business reengineering, old job titles and old organizational arrangements—departments, divisions, groups, and so on—cease to matter. They are artifacts of another age. What matters in reengineering is how we want to organize work today, given the demands of today's markets and the power of today's technologies.[50] . . .

> Reengineering, we are convinced, can't be carried out in small and cautious steps. It is an all-or-nothing proposition that produces dramatically impressive results. Most companies have no choice but to muster the courage to do it. For many, reengineering is the only hope for breaking away from the ineffective, antiquated ways of conducting business that will otherwise inevitably destroy them.[51]

The idea caught on. *Fortune's* cover story on August 23, 1993 trumpeted: "Reengineering the Company: It's Hot, It's Happening, It's Now, How it Works—and Doesn't." Some four months later, *Business Week's* cover announced "The Horizontal Corporation: Hierarchy Is Dying. In the new corporate model, you manage across—not up and down. Here's how."[52] Inside the magazine, a plethora of organizational models were described, with such entertaining names as Starburst, a graph with multicolored nodes; Shamrock, a three-leafed shamrock; Pizza, a graph in a pizza shape with a center and radial arcs connecting subcenters; and Inverted Pyramid, labelled from top to bottom with operate, enable, and create. Clearly, a major attempt was in progress to recreate organizational models for the Information Age. Hammer and Champy describe how work will change in the reengineered company as follows:[53]

- Work units change—from functional departments to process teams.
- Jobs change—from simple tasks to multi-dimensional work.
- People's roles change—from controlled to empowered.
- Job preparation changes from training to education.
- Focus of performance measures and compensation shifts—from activity to results.

- Advancement criteria change—from performance to ability.
- Values change—from protective to productive.
- Managers change—from supervisors to coaches.
- Organizational structures change—from hierarchical to flat.
- Executives change—from scorekeepers to leaders.

And finally, a few remarks about the role of IT in reengineering from the perspective of the early 1990s (and these are not surprising):[54]

- A company that cannot change the way it thinks about information technology cannot reengineer. A company that equates technology without automation cannot reengineer. A company that looks for problems first and then seeks technology solutions for them cannot reengineer.
- Reengineering, unlike automation, is about innovation. It is about exploiting the latest capabilities of technology to achieve entirely new goals.
- . . . the real power of technology is not that it can make the old processes work better, but that it enables organization to break old rules and create new ways of working—that is, to reengineer.
- The sheer capacity of increasingly *affordable* computing power creates new application possibilities for companies. [original emphasis]

More recently, a new term has achieved currency, Business Process Reengineering or Innovation (BPR or BPI). Actually it "has been practiced as a formal discipline since the early 1920s. Then it was known as 'Methods and Procedures Analysis,' always searching for new ways of restructuring work flows or improving business organization."[55] This term seems to have superseded Hammer and Champy's original idea of reengineering and has been defined as follows:[56]

Business Process Innovation (BPI), also called Reengineering, is an approach to dramatically improve operating effectiveness through redesigning critical business processes and supporting business systems, as opposed to incremental improvement. It is a radical redesign of key business processes that involves examination of the fundamental process itself. It looks at the details of the process, such as why the work is done, who does it, where is it done and when. By focusing on examining the process of producing the output, it is an examination of the process's ability to add value.

Given the enormous amount of publicity associated with BPR, it is appropriate and even necessary to conclude this section with the cautionary voice of Paul Strassmann, who has been around long enough to be wary of the latest fad, no matter how enthusiastically it has been hailed as a cure for many illnesses, real and imagined:[57]

Reengineering is certainly not a breakthrough in management thinking, but a convenient bandwagon on which management and consultants could readily hop in search of a quick remedy to unfavorable financial health of U.S. industrial corporations that had been festering for a long time. A wholesome by-product of this rush is the long overdue reinstatement of the primacy of business process analysis that was neglected during three decades of over-emphasis on computer systems and prior to that two decades of socio-psychological experimentation. It has also freed funds for innovative computer-aided business analysis tools which make business process improvement and systems analysis much easier to do.

What's On the Horizon?

Maybe Strategic Planning is back, at least in the opinion of *Business Week*. Presumably after years of downsizing and reengineering, it is time to "wring more profits out of those streamlined operations. So what's making a comeback? You guessed it: strategic planning." [58] The article is rife with tales of missed opportunities, with pointed remarks directed at Apple and IBM. Key points in the new agenda for strategic planning are presented as follows: [59]

- *Value Migration.* The movement of growth and profit opportunities from one industry player to another.
- *Coevolution.* The notion that by working with direct competitors, customers, and suppliers, a company can create new businesses, markets, and industries.
- *White-Space Opportunities.* New areas of growth possibilities that fall between the cracks because they don't naturally match the skills of existing business units.
- *Strategic Intent.* A tangible corporate goal or destiny that represents a stretch for the organization. It also implies a point of view about the competitive position a company hopes to build over the coming decade.
- *Business Ecosystem.* System in which companies work cooperatively and competitively to support new products, satisfy customers, and create the next round of innovation in key market segments.

What happened to computers, Information Technology, and knowledge?

BUSINESS ISSUES AND MANAGEMENT INFORMATION SYSTEMS

In the ordinary business of life, industry can do anything which genius can do, and very many things which it cannot. (Henry Ward Beecher)

In the previous section, the topics addressed were somewhat abstract and the discussion turned on activities aimed at transforming the entire organization. Now we turn to more detail about some of the techniques actually employed by corporations to improve efficiency through technology. This survey is selective and is meant to highlight just a few of the many directions that modern business operations have explored in the process of attempting to reengineer themselves effectively. It is to be expected that computers and computer networks will play an important role.

Retail Operations

By its very nature, selling requires identifying those who will buy as well as those who might buy. Manufacturers make products but retailers must sell them, taking advantage of their closeness to the consumer and their knowledge of what sells. The largest retailers in the world have discovered that very large, carefully arranged stores can not only sell but earn enormous profits as well. Witness the enormous success of Wal-Mart, the world's largest retailer with sales of more than $93 billion in 1995. As noted in a "Survey of Retailing," [60] computers have finally begun to pay off after more than a decade and a half of capital investment. Some of the benefits are obvious, namely, inventory control, accurate sales statistics, general store management, and itemized profit margins. But there is much more as the growth of massive retail giants around the world has coincided with the growing importance of IT to this branch of the business world.

Some of the more sophisticated applications depend on the fact that with computers, "a well-managed retailer should no longer be lumbered with stock that may not sell, or run out of items customers want to buy," . . . "Computers have at last enabled clever retailers to exploit the closeness to the customer and control of the shelves that have always been their strongest points," and "Computers have allowed retail managers to exercise closer control over much more extended store chains." [61] The success of Wal-Mart, whose first store opened in 1962, is based to a great degree on the informed use of computers. From its inception in Arkansas, Wal-Mart used computers to construct a distribution system to gain the attention of major producers who had no reason to pay attention to a relatively small company. Computers played a major role in the following way: [62]

> By the early 1980s Wal-Mart had not only set up computer links between each store and the distribution warehouses; through a system called EDI (electronic data interchange), [more later] it also hooked up with the computer of the firm's main suppliers. The distribution centers themselves were equipped with miles of laser-guided conveyor belts that could read the bar codes on incoming cases and direct them to the right truck for their outward journey. The final step was to buy a satellite to transmit the firm's enormous data load . . .

> The first benefit was just-in-time replenishment across hundreds of stores. This has since been refined further, using computer modeling programmes to allow the firm to anticipate sales patterns. The second benefit was cost.

Many companies are modernizing their sales systems, after having addressed the automation of "manufacturing, inventory control, purchasing, and accounting." [63] Key issues in assembling a modern sales system are: [64]

- *Opportunity management systems* help sales reps manage sales opportunities, track those in the sales pipeline, and make forecasts.
- *Sales configuration systems* help companies put together accurate orders by configuring products, pricing, and financing in conjunction with each other.
- *Marketing encyclopedia systems* maintain repositories of all marketing information, including product literature and pricing. Sales reps can even call up videos of reference accounts to pitch products to potential customers.
- *Team sales solutions* require telemarketing and field sales integration tools, while low-end sales configuration software supports rapid order entry.
- *Sales management systems* provide traditional account management so companies can keep track of data in a variety of ways.

The consumer information accumulated by large companies in enormous databases has become an invaluable resource for targeting customers, predicting trends, setting trends, and tailoring buying and distribution in a more precise fashion. Later in this chapter, we examine the use of consumer data usually referred to as data mining. In addition, we discuss the role of such computer networks as the Internet in facilitating marketing.

Training

All the discussion presented up to this point rests on a major unspoken assumption: there exists a well-trained workforce able and ready to employ the new technology effectively. Furthermore, as the technology and management structure evolve, there must be a well-designed training program in place to ensure that employees are up-to-date. Training and a well-trained workforce are crucial in maintaining the well-being of the organization, in improving its flexibility, and in positioning it to take advantage of a rapidly changing marketplace. Of course, to maintain a lean and mean company, it will be necessary to dismiss redundant employees, that is, those whose presence is made expendable by the very efficiencies achieved through the ongoing training regimen.

Even though the benefits seem obvious, as with all other business costs, the expenditures must be justified. Costs for training include those for new employees as well as for maintaining current employees at state-of-the-art knowledge. Training methods employ conventional classroom environments supplemented with computer-based training delivered over local networks or over the Internet. Regardless of medium, the crucial concern is return on investment, which raises the question: How can management determine whether or not its investment in training its employees is worthwhile? Consider the following "commonly used training evaluation techniques:" [65]

> *Control Groups.* Job performance and business results for trained employees are measured against a group of nontrained workers in comparable jobs.
>
> *Management Objectives.* Managers identify and assign values to the new skills and capabilities they expect employees to get from training. These values are translated into dollars and compared with the cost of training.
>
> *Regression Analysis.* Nontraining factors that may affect job performance are identified, measured, and statistically exclude in order to isolate the effect of training on employee performance.
>
> *Case Analysis.* The job performance of one or more course graduates is tracked before and after training and compared with expected training-related improvements to draw conclusions about the effect of training on all employees.
>
> *Cost-Based Analysis.* Employee costs are used to calculate business benefit. Foe example, if the fully-loaded cost of one programmer is $80,000 per year and training increases programmer productivity by 20%, the company gains $16,000 per year for each programmer it trains.

Training managers and computer staff to use and even develop new software is only part of the picture. To complete it requires comprehensive end-user training so that the entire organization can benefit from new developments. The field of end-user training has been receiving considerable attention from researchers, training consultants, and companies because of the obvious payoffs. The basic goal is "to produce a motivated user who has the basic skills needed to apply what has been learned and then to continue to learn on the job."[66] Some of the issues involved in end-user training are "the determination of training needs," evaluation of "training materials and methods," "the method of training delivery—face-to-face, computer-based, or some combination," "evaluation of training and learning immediately after training [and] longer-term effects of training," "the effects of social influences . . . on the learning process," and "end-user learning (rather than training), transfer of learning to the workplace, and computer-based approaches to learning and training."[67]

Security

Computers and computer networks are obviously indispensable to the functioning of companies, but they are vulnerable in a number of ways to both external and internal threats and their very success requires companies to institute a variety of measures to improve security and limit unwanted access. A survey conducted by the American Society for Industrial Security[68] revealed some interesting results, such as that 77% of stolen proprietary information is done by "employees and other trusted parties," more than 85% of companies "do not monitor the use of e-mail or the Internet," and about 50% of companies "do not properly dispose of proprietary material, have no written policies/procedures, have no written policies for information systems security."

This same organization released a study in early 1996, "Trends in Intellectual Property Loss,"[69] in which they traced the loss of company information between 1993 and 1995, based on a survey of "700 incidents reported by 113 companies." The claim is that the value of "misappropriated information" over this period totaled about $5.2 billion, including "strategic plans ($1.4B), research and development information ($1.35B), manufacturing processes ($566M), marketing plans ($460M), intellectual property ($440M), financial data ($360M), [and] merger/acquisition data ($179M)." Given the finding that 77% of thefts are by trusted parties, only so much can be done to reduce the number of incidents perpetrated by outsiders. Within companies, secure audit trails, priority access levels, and other measures must be routine and any unexpected activities monitored and followed up. To deal with external access attempts, the following safeguards must be in place:[70] user ids (identification) and secure passwords, tokens and one-time passwords, dialback facility to ensure an approved client, firewalls to filter incoming traffic, and encrypted files, if all else fails.

Definitions and Characteristics of Management Information Systems

What is a management information system (MIS)? There are many conceptions and definitions depending on who is doing the defining and to what purpose. One of the foremost figures in the development of MIS, Gordon B. Davis, has supplied a definition of what MIS should be:[71]

> . . . an integrated man/machine system for providing information to support the operations, management and decision-making functions in an organization. The system utilizes com-

puter hardware and software, manual procedures, management and decision models, and a database.

In 1985, some eleven years after this definition, Davis and coauthor Margrethe Olson provided the following updated definition of MIS:[72]

> . . . an integrated, user-machine system for providing information to support operations, management, analysis and decision-making functions in an organization. The system utilizes computer hardware and software; manual procedures; models for analysis, planning, control and decision making; and a database.

It is fairly clear that, at least in the view of Davis and Olson, not much had changed in eleven years, a somewhat surprising situation given such enormous technological developments as PCs, networking, workstations, spreadsheets, word processing, laser printers, fiber optics, Fax, cellular phones, and more. In any case, MIS is not easily characterized. An MIS must incorporate expertise from a variety of areas such as organizational theory, economics, accounting, statistics, and mathematical modeling, to say nothing of computer hardware and software. It sounds incredibly ambitious and it is. In the view of many, the open-ended expectation engendered by such descriptions is one of the major reasons why any working system is felt somehow to be short of the mark, no matter what it actually accomplishes.

What are the components of such systems and what functions do they (or are they supposed to) perform? One way of viewing an MIS is as a pyramid structure. At the bottom is the routine transaction processing that occupies a good deal of the computer power of the system (recall that such activities as payroll and accounting were the first application of computers, beginning in the mid-1950s). The next level is concerned with supporting day-to-day activities at the operational level, whereas the third level represents a jump to tactical planning and decision-making. At the top level the MIS concept is fully expressed, with a wide array of resources for strategic planning and management decision-making.

The pyramid—transactions, inquiries, planning, and decision-making—sits on top of the data. Where do the data reside? The problems of representation, structure, organization, and integrity of data have occupied much attention in both the research and business communities. Gradually the notion of a database management system (DBMS) has evolved and this concept is fundamental to MIS. The DBMS must be responsible for manipulating data, on demand, by the variety of application subsystems supported by MIS. DBMS theory is currently a very active research and development area, with relational databases the most commonly used.

The decision-assisting models at the top level of the pyramid have evolved into a major component of MIS usually referred to as decision support systems (DSS). These are discussed in the next subsection. In general, models may be used to deal with such areas as inventory, personnel selection, new product pricing, and budgetary control. Four major areas have contributed heavily to the conception and evolution of MIS:[73]

Managerial Accounting. This area deals with such issues as cost analysis, assignment of responsibility, the provision of reports at a variety of levels, and budgetary information.

Operations Research. This discipline is concerned with determining optimal decisions by using mathematical models and procedures in a systematic and specific way. Some of these mathematical techniques are linear programming, queuing theory, game theory, decision theory, and statistics.

Management and Organization Theory. This research area is concerned with reaching satisfactory solutions, constrained by the human limitations on the search for solutions. The behavioral and motivational consequences of organizational structure and systems within organizations are also a concern.

Computer Science. Advances in hardware, software, algorithms, networks, and distributed processing have an impact on the realization and power of MIS.

As we might expect, a number of criticisms have also surfaced. Many of these revolve around the issue of centralization versus decentralization of the information resources, of the computer facilities, and of the analysis and modeling systems. In a sense, certain of these problems have become academic in the age of distributed computing that was brought in by advances in computer technology and communications. But the organizational issues remain—of access, and of smaller specialized databases versus larger uniform ones. In a paper examining the changes in MIS over the 15 year period from 1980 to 1995, the authors admit that[74]

> The areas of progress are significant and substantial. Yet the surprising lack of progress over the past 15 years is disturbing. MIS has an increasingly polyglot set of reference disciplines. The cumulative tradition in the field is still elusive, however, it is emerging in some research areas. More MIS research is carried out and published, but only read by MIS researchers themselves, bringing in to question relevance to practitioners. When added to the fact that important new issues have arisen, the future of the MIS research community appears to remain problematic.

One of the early criticisms of MIS was that it was not a true discipline but rather a collection of "reference disciplines." This criticism has persisted and means that success of the MIS enterprise is both difficult to achieve and evaluate since it depends on achievements in other areas. Furthermore, in 1980 the primary concern was with information itself; currently it is with both the flow of information through the organization as well as its uses. In addition, "the IS community, both practitioners and scholars have focused on two other highly visible types of dependent variables which have been tackled directly rather than through the use of surrogates: (1) The impact of MIS on corporate strategy and (2) The impact of MIS on "bottom-line" performance."[75]

Recent proposals have suggested that the time may be fast approaching when most executives sitting at their own desks will be able to call up any data they desire, in any form they wish, from personal computers that are part of a large, complex computer network. However, until that time arrives, a number of issues still need to be considered.

Decision Support Systems and Executive Support Systems

One direction that developments in MIS have taken is toward decision support systems (DSS). An early definition of DSS follows:

> Decision Support Systems . . . represent a point of view on the role of the computer in the management decision making process. Decision support implies the use of the computer to:
>
> 1. Assist managers in their decision processes in semistructured tasks.
> 2. Support rather than replace, managerial judgment.
> 3. Improve the effectiveness of decision making rather than its efficiency.[76]

Rockart and De Long wrote a book in 1989 titled *Executive Support Systems*,[77] and the designation ESS has become more commonly used. Whatever the name, the idea of executives having hands-on access to information via PCs or terminals is not yet generally acceptable, but gradually more and more upper management executives are demanding to see the data prior to massaging by their support staffs. There are good reasons for this growth, as Rockart and De Long note:[78]

1. Use of information technology to support executives makes good managerial sense. Despite the complex, unstructured, and unpredictable nature of their work, there are many logical applications of IT which can effectively support executive tasks.

2. The technology, both hardware and software, is rapidly improving. Applications for managers that were technically impractical and too costly only a few years ago have now become significantly easier to implement.

3. More and more top managers have become computer literate . . . many middle managers who have come to rely heavily on computers in their jobs are now being promoted to the executive ranks.

Of course there are a number of reasons against the adoption of ESS, including the following: as currently structured, ESS do not fit today's management styles or needs; further they cannot provide the type of information needed most by executives—verbal, anecdotal, nonformal and therefore difficult, if not impossible, to capture in a program; there are perhaps negative properties associated with the new technology—manipulating numbers via spreadsheets and simulations may mislead as to what is actually being accomplished, and communication facilities are useless unless a desire to communicate exists; more concretely, many attempts to implement working ESS have failed.[79]

Expert Systems

Probably the greatest commercial impact of artificial intelligence (AI) has been in the area of expert systems (ES). In the past few years, ES have become the most visible and highly publicized product of the entire AI enterprise. Indeed, they can be characterized as an almost independent discipline. They have been applied in a wide and growing number of domains including medicine, education, finance, industry, and the military. In their simplest form, they consist of a body of knowledge, typically quite narrow but necessarily deep, and a reasoning apparatus, or engine, that is able to use this knowledge to perform a range of activities including answering questions, predicting events, offering warnings, or identifying meaningful patterns.

Beyond this rather limited overview, work in ES can be divided into two broad categories: implementation of specific expert systems employing so-called shells, and research in diverse areas associated with basic problems in AI such as knowledge representation, reasoning in general and reasoning with respect to uncertainty, knowledge acquisition among domain-specific experts, programmers, and others operating within the constraints of a commercially available ES shell. The emphasis on knowledge acquisition dominates because of the need to translate informal expertise into the requirements of the shell's knowledge representation formalism. The inference strategy and problems of uncertain information are predetermined within a given shell and therefore must be accepted by the user.

The availability of shells of varying degrees of complexity has resulted in an explosion of ES. Many companies, from the very small to the very large, have built ES to capture some part of their corporate expertise. Systems abound, as described by Feigenbaum, McCorduck, and Nii,[80] in such major companies as IBM, Digital Equipment, Toyota, American Express, Sears, Frito-Lay, and Texas Instruments, and are increasing at a rapid rate. Probably the most well-known and the most successful are the systems XCON (eXpert CONfigurator) and XSEL (eXpert SELector), developed at Digital Equipment to configure computer systems automatically and to assist interactively in the selection of saleable parts, respectively. One testimonial comes from David Wise, a senior system analyst at Frito-Lay, Inc.: ". . . although expert systems software is not yet mature and can't do everything you want it to do, it does enough. We've been very satisfied; our payback has been millions of dollars and the ability to make better decisions."[81] The applications are seemingly endless but the following are representative: medical diagnosis, computer configuration, mineral prospecting, oil well analysis, stock market decision-making, financial analysis and planning, insurance analysis, electromechanical fault-finding and repair, and military analysis and decision-making.

Expert systems are also referred to as knowledge-based systems (KBS), with the subtle implication that other business software is somehow devoid of, or seriously impoverished with respect to, basic business knowledge. Of course, all software must incorporate "knowledge" in a variety of forms to perform adequately. The claim for ES must be regarded as a claim for an approach that explicitly separates knowledge from how it is used so that incremental growth can take place in a coherent fashion. In addition, the acquisition of knowledge as an ongoing joint enterprise of specialists and programmers is a unique contribution. Of particular significance to executives is the growth of sophisticated ES in financial planning. Such systems represent yet another important component in the gradually growing tool kit of computing resources for executives.

THE OFFICE OF THE FUTURE

A paperless office has about as much chance as a paperless bathroom. (Anonymous)

Office Automation

What is sometimes called the "electronic office" will be brought about by "office automation" or by the use of "office information systems." It will eliminate paper, promote electronic communication, isolate workers and break down social interaction, reproduce industrial automation in the office, decrease wasted time in preparing documents, and generally improve productivity. Such are the claims made by proponents and the critics.

What is included under the general term "office automation?" The definition we use, taken from Mowshowitz some years ago, is given here: [82]

> Office automation is the use of information technology in an office environment to create, process, store, retrieve, use, and communicate information in the performance of managerial, professional, technical, administrative, and clerical tasks.

Although not part of the definition, the usually understood reason for introducing office automation is to *improve* performance, but there are other reasons, such as to facilitate a new service that would be impossible without the technology, or to reinforce management's control. In any case, this definition does capture a general overview of office automation. More specifically, some of the office functions made possible by computers and associated technology follow, but first let's look at a spectrum of traditional office activities:

- Answering the telephone and handling messages
- Typing written and dictated material
- Filing and retrieving material
- Copying letters and reports
- Opening and handling mail
- Scheduling meetings and travel plans
- Billing and accounting
- Processing internal memoranda
- Miscellaneous—organizing parties, selecting gifts, buying take-out lunches

In addition, higher level functions include the following:

- Conducting research
- Monitoring market changes
- Drafting original documents
- Utilizing resource people
- Dealing with middle and upper management

What are the current and proposed functions of the electronic, or automated, office? They are many and diverse, but a number have been mentioned by most observers. Consider the following categories.

Word Processing. This application involves the use of computer-aided facilities to enter, manipulate, and edit text, typically via a personal computer, either standalone or in a network.

Electronic Mail. This is a system for transmitting messages in text, Fax, or voice. There are five different delivery systems:

1. Common carrier-based systems and public postal systems
2. Fax

3. Personalized computer-based message systems
4. Communicating word processing systems
5. Internet

Database Management Information Retrieval. The ability to store and retrieve large amounts of information under a variety of conditions has made computers irreplaceable in the office and has created a new industry—the marketing of information.

Spreadsheets. No single application, with the exception of word processing, has had as great an impact in companies. Employees from all levels of the organization are able to model cash flow, expenses, accounts receivable, and other economic factors in order to explore a variety of what-if scenarios. Thousands of variables can be included. The demands of spreadsheet users for ever more powerful personal computers became a driving force in the PC industry.

Desktop Publishing. The ability to produce sophisticated in-house brochures, newsletters, advertising material, and reports has saved businesses considerable amounts of money, driven the development of low-cost laser printers, challenged traditional composition and printing methods, and facilitated grassroots publishing.

Computer-Aided Design/Computer-Aided Manufacturing (CAD/CAM). Economical tools have been developed to permit engineers and draftsmen to design and manufacture new products using desktop computers. These are programs that facilitate the drawing and manipulation of precise and detailed diagrams in 3D and color on high-resolution monitors.

Experts Systems and Decision Support. As discussed previously, these systems are assuming increasing importance to management and the ability to run them on PCs and workstations will accelerate this process.

Graphics. The development of special programs, high-speed processors, and high-resolution color monitors and laser printers has resulted in the widespread use of graphics in design, documents, and video.

Teleconferencing. The use of telecommunication systems permits simultaneous communication over long distances via audio, computers, video, or combinations of these for distributed meetings.

Activity Management. This category includes systems such as electronic tickler (reminder) files and automated task-project management to track, screen, or expedite schedules, tasks, and information.

Other possibilities include the following:

- Electronic blackboards for broadcasting messages
- Electronic calendars for scheduling
- Computerized training to provide employees with up-to-date information and introduce new skills via CD-ROM, VCRs, and interactive systems

- The portable office, including communication links—modems, Fax, and cellular telephones—portable computers, computers with pen-based entry rather than keyboards, and paging devices
- The home office as a means for increasing the flexibility of work arrangements

and, of course

- The design, implementation, and use of Web pages on the Internet, a rapidly growing and potentially useful technology

If all this sounds rather overwhelming, it should, because one of the major components of the so-called information revolution is the electronic office. Much of the work force is currently engaged in white-collar jobs, and what happens in the office matters a great deal. Most white-collar workers use computers and the market for information technology is enormous and growing. Worldwide sales of information systems and services by the top 100 suppliers in 1995 totaled $439.1 billion, up 19% over 1994.[83] Although not all these sales are to businesses, a substantial number are.

The Personal Computer in the Office

Sometimes the pace of technological development confounds the best-laid plans of management for an orderly progression in the evolution of data processing facilities. Such is the case with the personal computer, which has become a basic fixture in the office. Originally designed for hobbyists, the market for the personal computer began to grow rapidly in the early 1980s and reached into schools, homes, small businesses, and executive offices. Early versions of microcomputers were quite limited and were used primarily to do simple accounting, maintain customer lists, and keep records of correspondence. But the machines and the associated software quickly became much more sophisticated and were soon performing such functions as budgeting, inventory management, word processing, and spread-sheet calculations. In small businesses, the role of the microcomputer was relatively straightforward, namely, to automate many of the functions previously executed by secretaries. In the medium-to-large company the issue was much more complicated.

As the number of PCs has grown rapidly, a variety of problems has emerged. The basic concerns are with who controls purchases and keeps track of them, and who decides when to lease instead of buy, when to sell, and what software to use. These decisions are especially important when PCs and PC software represent a substantial capital investment. With the arrival of laptop computers, additional problems have arisen, with respect to communications, maintenance, and security. Probably of most importance is availability—who gets them and for how long? These problems are significant given the growing popularity of laptops. One interesting aspect of laptop use is that although some companies have permitted access from the field to electronic mail and other nonsensitive services, they have restricted access to the mainframe for practical security reasons.

Probably of greater importance than laptops is the movement of workstations from the research environment into the commercial world. Although it is difficult to define the distinction between workstations and PCs, especially those at the top of the line, it can be said that they are faster, with high resolution monitors, and typically run under the UNIX operating system. The current leaders are Sun Microsystems, Hewlett-Packard, Digital Equipment, and looming as always, IBM. Workstations are important in distributed computing applications grounded in the client/server model as opposed to the more common host-based model used in mainframes or large minicomputers. They also play an important role as Internet hosts and Web servers.

On the Road to Better Communications

In the early days, computers were locked away in antiseptic rooms guarded by a cadre of initiates who were the sole custodians of programming, data preparation, and result reporting. As the number of people who had direct access to the computer increased, greater demands were made on the managers of computer facilities to provide easier access and better, more readable output. The development of time-sharing systems gave many people better access, but it has been certain improvements in hardware and especially in software that have, in fact, opened up access to computers.

Graphics and Imaging

Since the business of management is to make decisions based on all the available information, it is important to reduce the effort of gathering, processing, and displaying that information. Recently, technology and software developments have combined to make graphics facilities widely available to both information processing professionals and executives. For most managers, graphics presentation is a needed relief from pages of texts and tables. As someone remarked, a computer image is worth a thousand printouts. The benefits claimed for computer graphics are straightforward: saving of time in the production, interpretation, and communication of data, and assistance in management decision-making provided by visual information that is much easier to assimilate. Interactive graphics systems also encourage managers to explore the available information more extensively. Graphs, charts, and bar diagrams are readily available.

We should distinguish between graphics, the creation and manipulation of computer generated images, and imaging, the representation of paper documents as special computer files. An important early instance of imaging began in 1988 when American Express included with its billing statements "laser-printed, reduced facsimiles of the original receipts, including signatures. The reproduced forms were not photocopies, but rather digitized electronic images printed in the billing statements."[84] Scanners are used to convert documents directly into computer files that can then be manipulated—printed, included in other documents, retrieved, and mailed electronically. The uses of computer graphics are very widespread including CAD/CAM applications, architectural design, multimedia, desktop publishing, geographical maps, and scientific visualization.

Many of these applications serve the important purpose of condensing and distilling large amounts of data in order to improve the decision-making process. By employing a distributed system with either a large mainframe to store data and several linked graphics terminals to display it or a network of graphic workstations and servers, management can reduce costs and increase convenience. Therefore, graphics is rapidly becoming an important component of the automated office as well as an important management tool and thus a means to improve productivity. Decreasing costs and improved power are also significant factors in the widespread use of graphics equipment.

E-Mail

At its simplest, e-mail is the sending of a message from one computer to another, over a network, perhaps over a long distance. But what makes e-mail so successful is its ease of use, its low cost, its asynchronous nature that permits delayed response, and its universal acceptance. There are problems in its use, however, and these will be described. The editor-in-chief of *Datamation*, Kevin Strehlo, hails e-mail as a transforming technology. He also hails it as "the glue that binds most virtual organizations," claims "that having had an unchanging e-mail shingle for quite some time has kept me from losing touch with key professional acquaintances," and admits that "even my personal life is being dominated by e-mail today."[85] The lives of many people are seriously affected by e-mail; for example, the Electronic Messaging Association estimated that "Some 776 billion e-mail messages criss-crossed the globe last year [1994] and that number is expected to hit 1 trillion this year [1995]."[86]

In some cases, e-mail may be too successful, to the degree that measures must be taken for self-preservation. It is not too difficult to be overwhelmed by a large stream of e-mail. For example, "Jack Suess, associate director of computing at the University of Maryland in Baltimore County . . . gets an average of 1,200 electronic-mail messages a week—and spends four hours a day just responding."[87] The term information overload seems appropriate. How can anyone deal with such a volume of messages on a regular basis without detracting from other aspects of work and play? As we might expect, there are technological solutions, namely filtering and sorting, but these are not very sophisticated. Some systems will place messages in predefined folders organized by subject matter and source. What is lacking so far is the ability to sort on the basis of importance to the recipient, where the notion of importance is both context-sensitive and time-sensitive, but work is in progress.

In a final note from Paul Strassmann and a cautionary one, he states that "I have found no correlation whatsoever between the extent of e-mail availability and the information productivity of firms, as measured by the ratio of economic value-added/estimated total cost of information," and further cautions firms to "view e-mail as part of a much larger package of how people share information, rather than as an isolated application."[88]

PDAs (Personal Digital Assistants)

The evolution of computers from mainframes to minicomputers to workstations to personal computers to laptops seems to have culminated in a class of very small, palm-sized computers called personal digital assistants (PDAs), or pen-based devices. In 1993, Apple introduced its first version in this class, called the Newton, with a well-advertised handwriting recognition program. There were some problems with the technology, most significantly that it did not work very well or, in fact, so badly that it was near useless, but Apple and other companies such as AT&T, Hewlett-Packard, Fujitsu, Motorola, Casio, and Sony have persisted. One surprising success story is Palm Computing's Pilot. Apple introduced its MessagePad 120 in 1995 with improvements in handwriting ability, much more computing power, better desktop synchronization, and more application software. They have found favor in applications requiring mobility, appointment scheduling, note-taking, and where portability is a premium. Although there continues to be resistance because of unfulfilled promises and limited performance, PDAs are clearly a part of the computing picture and their use will increase as technology improves, especially in the area of wireless connectivity.

Wireless Communication

A report produced by the Yankee Group, a Boston consultant, predicts steady progress in the growth of wireless technology. More specifically, ". . . by the end of this decade, wireless communications, particularly the cellular and personal communications services (PCS) voice and data networks, will be well on the way to wide-scale market acceptance . . ." [89] Consider the following details of this forecast as shown in Table 4.2. [90]

The report also notes that although PCs are relatively easy to use, portable or mobile computing is still somewhat forbidding and costs for both are still high. Clearly, the future holds an increasing role for wireless communication, especially with a growing proliferation of satellites that will provide improved global access. The office of the future may not be paperless but it will almost certainly be without walls.

Videoconferencing and Teleconferencing

Traditional videoconferencing involved rented or leased television studios and closed circuit television to link geographically distributed individuals. It was a very expensive way to exchange information and not a very productive one either. The current technology of choice is called desktop videoconferencing, a technology that currently depends heavily on LANs (Local Area Networks). As Peter Cassidy notes, "Given the complexity of the application, which carries voice, video, and a mix of data, there is no single solution for rolling out desktop videoconferencing. In fact, moving too quickly now could preempt the benefits that will accrue once standards for LAN-mediated videoconferencing technologies are finally in place." [91] The technical quality is not equivalent to broadcast television, because desktop systems operate at 15 frames per second not 30 per second, but the convenience of being able to interact with colleagues from the comfort of your own workstation overweighs the somewhat jerky images on the screen. Also bandwidth requirements may

TABLE 4.2

WIRELESS COMMUNICATION FORECASTS.

Wireless Technologies	1997	2000
Cellular/PCs	39 million	62 million
Paging	34 million	55 million
Enhanced specialized mobile radio (ESMR)	3 million	6 million
Mobile data	5.9 million	9.9 million
Portable computers	20 million	38 million

severely compromise the other functions delivered by the LAN. Many developments are underway to address some of the current problems including the use of ISDN lines, international standards to improve interoperability, and reduced hardware and software costs.

EDI (Electronic Data Interchange)

As more companies have computerized their internal operations, it has become inevitable that intercompany communications would move from paper (mail) and telephone to the computer. This process is encouraged by the globalization of industry and the growth of worldwide communications networks. It seems to make good business sense that companies that depend upon one another should be able to facilitate this interaction by computer networks, that is, electronic data interchange (EDI). As in many other areas, EDI growth is fueled by the need to obtain a competitive advantage and to respond to customer needs. Many companies and government agencies require that all suppliers and customers use EDI. A formal definition of EDI is provided by Phyllis Sokol, a pioneer in EDI standards:[92]

> Electronic data interchange (EDI) is the INTER-COMPANY COMPUTER-TO-COMPUTER communication of STANDARD BUSINESS TRANSACTIONS in a STANDARD FORMAT that permits the receiver to perform the intended transaction.

Instead of generating a transaction on paper and then mailing it to a receiver, who then enters the data into a computer and runs an application program, the sender generates the transaction by computer, transmits it via a computer network, and the receiver simply has to run the application program on this transmitted data. By the previous definition, the data must be transmitted both in a standard form and for standard business transactions. Thus electronic mail would not be considered as part of EDI because it is unstructured.

A more recent definition, albeit from the European community, is given as follows:[93]

> EDI is a new technology linking information technology across organizational boundaries. However there has been no single technical breakthrough which has suddenly made electronic trading possible. Rather, EDI implementation flows from the marshaling of diverse resources—teleco standardisation of business data—to form communities trading electronically . . . Electronic trading requires organizations to cooperate, agreeing the form of electronic messages and collectively committing themselves to invest in the technical and organizational adjustments necessary. EDI thus differs from many other information technologies in that organizations cannot implement it in isolation. In practice this requires negotiation among enterprises which may have little history of cooperation.

For larger companies, EDI has become a way of doing business because of the requirements established among large and medium-sized corporations. To be responsive to market demands, to control inventory, and to mesh supplier production with the more precise needs of clients ensures that the growth of EDI will penetrate to even smaller companies.

Data Mining and Knowledge Discovery

Imagine a chain of supermarkets that builds up a database of purchases with complete details about date, time of day, store address, geographic location, items purchased, associated prices, coupons used, sales items, cashier identification, payment method, if credit card then kind, and if point-of-sale card then issuer. In very little time, an enormous database, sometimes called a data warehouse emerges. Of course, no imagining is necessary as almost every major retailer has such a warehouse. It is an article of faith that such massive collections of data must be useful beyond such obvious purposes as keeping track of the relative popularity of house brands versus national brands or the frequency of use of different credit or debit cards. The process of extracting useful information out of this mass of data "ore" is called data mining, an obvious analogy. A more precise definition is: [94]

> Data mining, *the extraction of hidden predictive information from large databases,* is a powerful new technology with great potential to help companies focus on the most important information in their data warehouses. Data mining tools predict future trends and behaviors, allowing businesses to make proactive, knowledge-driven decisions. The automated, *prospective analyses* offered by data mining move beyond the analyses of past events provided by retrospective tools typical of decision support systems. Datamining tools can answer business questions that traditionally were too time consuming to resolve. They scour databases for hidden patterns, finding predictive information that experts may miss because it lies outside their expectations.

Many companies are involved in providing products to perform data mining. Given the data warehouse, data mining requires large computer systems, typically with multiprocessor or parallel hardware, and appropriate algorithms, derived from research efforts in Artificial Intelligence, related to learning, and from ongoing work on large databases. For example, IBM has developed a data mining product called Intelligent Miner, "a toolkit that developers and data analysts can use to discover trends within data." [95] A version of this system, Advanced Scout, was used by the New York Knicks to improve their scoring against the Charlotte Hornets in an NBA game. The program used data made available on an "NBA electronic bulletin board."

In the context of retail marketing just mentioned, data mining could reveal hidden patterns that would not otherwise be apparent and this possibility is what drives research and investment. The rewards may be great. Consider the following: [96]

> *Automated prediction of trends and behaviors.* Data mining automates the process of finding predictive information in large databases. Questions that traditionally required extensive hands-on analysis can now be answered directly from the data—quickly. A typical example of a predictive problem is targeted marketing. Data mining uses data on past promotional mailings to identify the targets most likely to maximize return on investment in future mailings. Other predictive problems include forecasting bankruptcy and other forms of default, and identifying segments of a population likely to respond similarly to given events.

THE INTERNET AND THE WORLD WIDE WEB

The Internet is so big, so powerful and pointless that for some people it is a complete substitute for life. (Andrew Brown)

Introduction

The Internet is either the best thing to happen to retail marketers since television or it is a money sink with no major return on investment in the foreseeable future. Without doubt, providers of various services such as Netscape, the Web browser, and Yahoo, the search engine, made enormous amounts of money for their founders when they went public. But for the companies that have established a presence on the Internet, usually by means of Web sites, the results are quite mixed. Keep in mind that the pace of technological innovation over the past three or four years, especially with respect to the Internet, has been quite amazing. Thus, it is not surprising that there is considerable debate about future directions, both within the software community and the vast and growing user community. In a cover story on technological trends, *Fortune* writer David Kirkpatrick argues that the influence of the Internet will be pervasive in all aspects of computer technology; as such he predicts the following "opportunities:"[97]

- A shakeup in the PC market
- A computer in every room
- The growth of intranets (Internet-like networks within corporations)
- Increased competition among Internet-based companies
- Survival of commercial online companies such as America Online
- Continued success of Microsoft and Intel in spite of predictions that the Internet has made them vulnerable
- The growth of wireless computing
- Chipmakers will continue to flourish, except perhaps for plain memory manufacturers

Everything is available for purchase on the Internet, although the growth of an Internet economy is slower than anticipated. The Software Publishers Association released its Fifth Annual Consumer Study on April 22, 1996 and one of the key findings is relevant for the issue at hand. For example, the following reveals current activity habits on the World Wide Web:[98]

> Online and Internet use increased. Seventy percent of PC households reported owning a modem. Of modem owners, 46 percent subscribe to an online service, and an additional 26 percent use the Internet through another type of gateway, such as an office, educational institution or gateway provider. Seventy-seven percent of Internet users report accessing the Web. Once there, research/reference [39%], entertainment [35%] and education sites [26%] are visited by the greatest number of respondents. [Other uses are travel (18%), computers/software (15%), financial (12%), and sports (12%)]

Further note that "Survey results show the use of home personal computers increased slightly in 1995, with penetration of PCs reaching 34 percent by January 1996, representing 33.9 million households, up from 32.6 million the same period a year ago."[99] Simple arithmetic shows that 23.7 million households own modems and of these about 11 million subscribe to an online service and 6.2 million use the Internet, with 4.75 million of the latter having accessed the Web. Thus, the target market for retailers is actually quite small, independent of other factors that might currently limit the use of the Web as a marketplace, such as transactional security and ease of use. Keep these issues in mind as the discussion proceeds.

World Wide Web

The WWW, or simply the Web, has been described earlier and there are many books and Web pages[100] that provide an excellent overview. The present purpose is to describe the current and potential business uses of the Web within and without the organization. First a few examples of some Web uses may be suggestive of future directions. When two-way computer systems were envisioned, one of the first few applications anticipated was the selling of entertainment tickets online. By June 1996, Ticketmaster offered nationwide ticket-selling over the Internet. By accessing its Web pages, viewers can learn about events and then purchase tickets for any show, anywhere in the US.[101]

When the automobile appeared, the buggy whip industry soon disappeared. The rise of the Internet as a retail marketplace may hasten the reduction in the number of car dealers. Between 1970 and 1996, the number of car dealers fell from about 31, 000 to fewer than 23,000[102] and it is now possible to purchase a car over the Internet. It is much easier to compare prices, models, and features by performing a Web search than by driving around and talking to dealers. From the dealers' and manufacturers' point of view, selling over the Net can cut marketing costs substantially. Given the significance of the automobile industry to the economy as a whole, a substantial change in the way cars are marketed and sold will have a strong ripple effect in the marketplace.

In a sampling of opinions of five experts, *Wired* magazine asked about the likelihood of electronic shopping becoming an important economic factor. When asked "Will a Sears-caliber mass retailer dominate online shopping?" the response was "unlikely" by two experts and "1998, 2007, and 2010" by the three others.[103] One other question asks when 20 percent of groceries will be bought electronically, that number being the necessary level to ensure that online shopping is a real alternative. The answers varied between 2000 and 2015, with "Several experts not[ing] that the Peapod grocery shopping and delivery service—an online shopping system in use by Safeway in San Francisco and Jewel in Chicago—is already up and running."[104]

Business Opportunities

There seems to be a general consensus that the Web is good for business, but what is much less clear are the working details. The technology is largely in place; the user base, however, is still relatively small, and cautious. In an interview with *Fortune* magazine, author Mary Cronin was asked, "The Internet is such a visible, flashy phenomenon. But it often seems to have more style than substance. Has corporate America figured out how to use the Internet?"[105] Her answer is given as follows:

> Companies are hitting the wall in terms of what they're getting from the Internet. Managers I talk to say, "Okay, we're seeing a large number of hits on our Web site—but what is that doing for our business? Is that making any kind of significance difference for us?" Most

likely, if the only thing the company is doing is putting product info and advertising on the Web, the answer is no.

This is a good time to step back and ask, "How is the Internet going to change my industry? How are other people using it successfully? What are some of the models that are out there that can really help not just one specific application or another, but the entire organization?"

So far a very general description of the Web has been presented in terms of commercial applications. However, we can take advantage of existing scholarship to better characterize the real possibilities that the Web offers to a variety of business interests. Hoffman, et al. have proposed the classification of commercialization opportunities into the following six types:[106]

Integrated Destination Site

1) *Online Storefront:* direct sales through an electronic channel via an electronic catalog or other, more innovative format.
2) *Internet Presence Sites:* Flat Ads, Image, and Information: provide a virtual "presence" for a firm and its offerings. They may also serve to signal to current and prospective customers and competitors that the firm is on the cutting edge.
3) *Content:* Fee-based, Sponsored, and Searchable Database: In Fee-based content sites, the provider supplies and/or pays for content which the consumer pays to access. Sponsored content sites sell advertising space to reduce or eliminate the necessity of charging fees to visitors. Merchants or advertisers pay a provider for information placement in an organized listing in a Searchable Database. The unit of analysis is a person, service, or information source, all of the same type.

Web Traffic Control

4) *Mall:* The Mall site typically constitutes a collection of online storefronts, each of which may contain many different categories of goods for sale. The provider charges rent in exchange for the virtual real-estate and may offer a variety of services to the storefront.
5) *Incentive Site:* The Incentive Site represents a unique form of advertising that attracts a potential customer to a site. The objective is to pull the user to the commercial site behind it, thus helping marketers generate traffic to their Web sites.
6) *Search Agent:* The purpose of Search Agent sites is to identify other Web sites through keyword search of a database that extends throughout the Web. Software agents are used to generate and/or assist the search through the database.

Note that none of this existed before 1993 and that with such a rapidly evolving technology, classifications, predictions, and scholarly analyses are to be treated with considerable care. Since the original technology was developed with no concern for commercial applications, it is not surprising that there is some resentment in the old Net community about the current obsession with money-making enterprises. With a long tradition of getting information, software, games, images, and music for free, it will require something of a major shift in mind-set to convince users that they should begin to pay. The ubiquitous presence of large corporations on the Web accentuates a feeling of being overwhelmed even in this self-created environment by rapacious, profit-seeking conglomerates.

The availability of color images, still and motion, sound, hypermedia links, and near instantaneous response, certainly presents a medium that offers much to both consumers and retailers, but some barriers will have to be overcome. Among these are the following:[107] "ease of access" problems such as limitations of "bandwidth," "finding a [satisfactory] service provider," and the slow "diffusion of the computer hardware/software/modem bundle into the home." "Secondary barriers [include] ease of use, price [of access], and risk [in transactional communications with respect to] privacy and security." Some "barriers to firm adoption arise from the Web measurement problem [numbers and demographics], no established criteria for judging the success of Web sites, [and the need for] critical mass."

Services and the Internet

Identifying services as a special class of retail activities is important because advocates of a wired world claim that making services available online will be a major feature of the future Internet and certainly one of the driving forces behind the development of the National Information Infrastructure (NII), otherwise known as the Information Highway. One important service area is real estate and indeed there has been a growth in the number of Web sites offering properties around the country. The Web is ideal in providing information about house features, maps indicating distances from neighborhood services such as schools, hospitals, police, and firefighters, and neighborhood income distributions.

An interesting report was issued in late 1994 by the US government's Information Infrastructure Task Force on the role of services on the NII. Very briefly, "NII services provide capabilities for electronic creation and diffusion of information needed to satisfy a diverse set of applications."[108] NII services include the following provisions for the user and for the supplier of services:[109]

> *User*
> • Searching, discovering, updating, transforming, and retrieving useful information
> • Building and maintaining electronic repositories of information
> • Creating and distributing information electronically
> • Executing and recording commercial, legal, financial, and other business transactions; and
> • Supporting collaborative work efforts among collocated or remote individuals
>
> *Supplier*
> • Enable new application product offerings without requiring the creation of all of the supporting software
> • Facilitate the encoding and transport of data between locations and between networks
> • Translate data from one language representation to another; and
> • Support the migration of existing data files, data bases and programs from older legacy systems to more modern systems

The report includes three recommendations encouraging government support for research and development in facilitating the use of the NII for services. Indeed, in Recommendation 3, it is urged that, "Government, industry, and academia should work closely together in pursuit of an advanced architectural framework for the NII services layer that supports interoperability while enabling individual, commercially competitive solutions." [110]

The Intranet

The cover of *Business Week,* February 26, 1996, advertised a special report on "The Intranet" (not another feature piece on the Internet). Also on the cover: "The Internet revolution has come home—to internal corporate networks. Cheap flexible "intranets" are spreading everywhere—and becoming a new management tool." [111] If 1995 has been hailed as the year of the Internet, then for many companies, 1996 could be considered the year of the intranet, an Internet-like structure or better perhaps an internal Web, providing all the features of the World Wide Web but accessible only within the company. Claims are rampant that intranets are a much more efficient means to distribute company information of all kinds than traditional systems. Consider the following features available on intranets and the benefits of these features: [112]

Application Feature Set
- rapid prototyping (can be measured in hours or days)
- scalable (start small, build as needs, requirements allow)
- easy navigation (internal home page provides links to information)
- accessible via most computing platforms
- can integrate distributed computing strategy (localized web servers residing closer to the content author)
- can be tied in to "legacy" information sources (databases, existing word processing documents, groupware databases)
- extensible to a variety of media types (audio, video, interactive applications)

Benefits to These Features
- inexpensive to start, requires little investment either in dollars or infrastructure
- significantly more timely and less expensive than traditional information (paper) delivery
- distributed computing strategy uses computing resources more effectively
- users familiar with link metaphor from surfing experiences
- open platform architecture means large (and increasing) number of add-on applications available

These benefits have not been lost on Information Technology managers. One prediction is that while expenditures for Internet Web server software will increase to about $2 billion dollars in 1998 (from about $500 million in 1995) intranet server software will rise to $8 billion (from the same 1995 base). [113] Although the benefits are obvious, there are, as in most things, some drawbacks. For example, "multiple browser support" will be a fact of life, "hardware upgrades" will still be required, "application development" is still necessary, "reengineering" to take advantage of the intranet is mandatory, "management" will still have to be concerned with new security problems, the new technology will demand "integration with legacy systems," and there will be no way to avoid the usual "screwups and restarts." [114]

SOCIAL ISSUES

Significant changes are occurring in the organizational structure of companies as a result of information technology. It is also affecting the nature of office work. The actual role of the technology is not always easy to identify, however. The crucial factor in evaluating the office environment is the attitude of management, its goals, its methods, and its expectations for the new equipment. Ostensibly, the primary reason for introducing, and continuing the introduction of, computers and communications systems is to increase productivity. More machines should mean fewer people doing the same work and therefore an increase in individual productivity. As sales expand, additional people or even more equipment may be necessary. The very presence of the computer creates the real possibility of providing a wide range of new services to the public and new tools to management. Thus productivity may not increase as rapidly as expected and staff reductions may not take place. Nevertheless, management may succeed in implementing, by means of the technology, a number of its tactical as well as strategic goals.

From one point of view, management's long term goal is to control every aspect of the production process, whether in the factory or the office. Of course, this position derives from an analysis of factory work, in which things are the end result of the process. In the office, it is not so easy to measure either productivity or control but several issues have arisen that indicate to some that control is the foremost concern. Among these are electronic monitoring, health, and deskilling. These issues will be extensively discussed in the section *The Changing Nature of Work* in Chapter 10, but an introduction will be made next with respect to the previously discussed reengineering process. The Internet offers access to information directly related to work objectives but it also permits access to social, political, and entertainment material that management may feel is not an appropriate activity from 9 to 5.

Reengineering and People

One of the original founders of the reengineering movement was Thomas Davenport, now a distinguished professor at the University of Texas. In a remarkable article published in late 1995, he offers his unique insight on the incredible success of reengineering from the late 1980s to the mid 1990s, when its popularity substantially decreased. Admitting that it was clearly oversold as a basic answer to all the ills of US corporations, he claims that one of the major problems was that it was frequently implemented in complete disregard for its impact on employees, their feelings, and even their very jobs. "Reengineering didn't start out as a code word for mindless bloodshed. It wasn't supposed to be the last gasp of Industrial Age management."[115] Professor Davenport's most relevant and provocative remarks follow:[116]

> When I wrote about "business process redesign" in 1990, I explicitly said that using it for cost reduction alone was not a sensible goal. And consultants Michael Hammer and James Champy, the two names most closely associated with reengineering, have insisted all along that layoffs shouldn't be the point. But the fact is, once out of the bottle, the reengineering genie quickly turned ugly.

So ugly that today, to most business people in the United States, reengineering has become a word that stands for restructuring, layoffs, and too-often failed change programs. . . .

Reengineering treated the people inside companies as if they were just so many bits and bytes, interchangeable parts to be reengineered. But no one wants to "be reengineered." No one wants to hear dictums like, "Carry the wounded but shoot the stragglers"—language that makes workers feel like prisoners of war, not their company's most important assets. . . .

The 1994 CSC Index "State of Reengineering Report" had the answer: 50% of the companies that participated in the study reported that the most difficult part of reengineering is dealing with fear and anxiety in their organizations; 73% of the companies said that they were using reengineering to eliminate, on average, 21% of the jobs; and, of 99 completed reengineering initiatives, 67% were judged as producing mediocre, marginal, or failed results.

In 1996, the term downsizing gained common currency, as several large, very profitable, high-technology companies announced sizable workforce reductions.

Appropriate Use of the Internet

Should there be guidelines within corporations as to who should have access to the Internet and what if any restrictions should be imposed on what employees can access during working hours? Given that the workplace, the computers, and the communication costs are borne by management, it seems on the surface that management should and indeed has the responsibility to set guidelines, but what is not so clear is how management should determine if the guidelines are being followed. In an informal poll, on *Computerworld's* Web site during February 1996, of 153 visitors who responded 25% agreed that "it should be the IS department's responsibility to monitor online use" while 75% disagreed. And whereas 53% acknowledged that their "company [had] a policy for end users who go on the Internet," only 23% enforced it.[117] The following is a checklist of concerns that should be taken into account by management before it implements a monitoring strategy:[118]

- *Create a policy that's in line with your corporate culture.* Employees who are used to autonomy will resent restrictions and monitoring more than those who are accustomed to stringent control of corporate resources.
- *Remember that full benefits of the Internet have yet to be realized.* A staffer who appears to be wasting time surfing Web sites could be looking for innovative ways to improve job performance, serve customers more effectively, or generate new revenue.
- *If you intend to monitor employee usage of the 'net, the Electronic Communications Privacy Act requires that you publicize that policy.* It's possible that simply notifying your employees of your policy may be sufficient to protect you legally, but it's always better to get consent, says Barry Weiss, a partner at Gordon & Glickson, a law firm in Chicago.
- *Beware of being too dictatorial.* IS erred in that direction during the PC revolution; the result was virtual anarchy among users. An attempt to rein in users too tightly could instigate a similar revolt.

Software exists to determine the Web sites visited by employees as well as what is downloaded from those sites. Presumably, employees that use company time to download pornography will be discouraged if informed that management has installed such monitoring software and is prepared to use it. There are of course other activities that might not please management such as exploring entertainment sites or participating in nontechnical newsgroups or listservs. However, a flexible and nonpunitive management policy may encourage a culture in which playtime does not detract from work and may even result in quality work, because of improved employee morale.

SUMMARY

The history of computers is very much intertwined with their role in business. From their earliest use in payroll and accounting to more recent applications in knowledge-based decision making, computers have become an integral component of the business community. Some of the business applications are in financial planning, processing orders, billing, simulations, and real-time computing.

Information processing has taken several organizational forms, both in response to technological developments and management structures. There have been many attempts to provide models to characterize the growth of data processing, with varying degrees of success. With the arrival of PCs and workstations, a certain measure of chaos has occasionally entered the picture.

Management information systems (MIS) have been advertised and anticipated for several years. They are supposed to support a variety of management and decision-making functions and they have succeeded in part, although not perhaps as the integrated systems envisioned by the data processing pioneers. More recently, MIS has evolved into decision support systems, executive information or support systems, and expert systems, the last being an application of work in artificial intelligence.

Opening up more ways of serving computing needs is the growth in distributed computing. From large mainframes to networks of minicomputers linked to mainframes, to PCs linked to minis linked to mainframes, to PCs linked to workstations in host-server systems, the opportunities are open-ended, but with many associated difficulties. Of paramount consideration is the communications hardware and software necessary to make such systems work.

As noted, PCs and workstations have appeared on the scene in large numbers, bringing computing power to everyone's desk (and home), but usually with little planning and overall control, at least until recently.

The so-called office of the future features electronic mail, word processing, database management, spreadsheets, desktop publishing, CAD/CAM, scheduling, and occasionally teleconferencing. The impact on employment and work structure has yet to be understood. A number of other technological advances are entering the world of business. Among these are graphics (for generating images and presenting data in novel and informative ways) and electronic data interchange to facilitate communication among companies. Progress has also been made in natural language interfaces to databases as well as voice communication and speech synthesis.

More recently, the Internet and the World Wide Web have begun to demonstrate their commercial possibilities. The Internet itself has served as a model for the distribution of computer resources within companies, the intranet. In a surprisingly short time, the Web has assumed increasing importance as a new medium for commercial enterprises.

NOTES

1. "Business Takes a Second Look at Computers," *Business Week,* June 5, 1971, p. 59.
2. Peter de Jager. "If You Start Now . . . You Just Might Make It," *Computerworld,* November 20, 1995, p. 97.
3. Craig Stedman. "Controversy Roils Over Year 2000 Conversion Toll," *Computerworld,* December 18, 1995, pp. 1, 111.
4. Leah Nathans Spiro. "Panic in the Year Zero Zero," *Business Week,* August 12, 1996, pp. 72–73.
5. Cyrus F. Gibson and Richard L. Nolan. "Managing the Four Stages of EDP Growth," *Harvard Business Review,* January-February 1974, pp. 76–88.
6. D. H. Meadows, D. L. Meadows, J. Randers, and W. W. Behrens III. *The Limits to Growth.* (New York: Universe, 1972).
7. Frederic G. Withington. "Five Generations of Computers," *Harvard Business Review,* July-August 1974, pp. 99–102.
8. IS Priorities As the Information Highway Begins, A Special Advertising Supplement in *Computerworld,* May 22, 1995. Table 4.1 is based on Figure 1 and the associated discussion.
9. Richard L. Nolan. "Managing the Crisis in Data Processing," *Harvard Business Review,* March-April 1979, pp. 115–126.
10. Peter F. Drucker. "The Coming of the New Organization," *Harvard Business Review,* January-February 1988, p. 46.
11. *Ibid.,* pp. 46–47.
12. Ralph Carlyle. "The Tomorrow Organization," *Datamation* (Cahners Publishing Co.), February 1, 1990, pp. 22, 23.
13. Clinton Wilder. "Foreign and U.S. Execs See Eye-To-Eye on Top IS Issues," *Computerworld,* May 22, 1989, p. 63.
14. William Bowen. "The Puny Payoff from Office Computers," *Fortune,* May 26, 1986, pp. 20–24.
15. "Managing Computers, A Lot to Learn," *The Economist,* March 3, 1990, pp. 64–65.
16. *Ibid.,* p. 65.
17. J. Yannis Bakos. "Are Computers Boosting Productivity? Yes!" *Computerworld,* March 27, 1995, pp. 128, 130.
18. Timothy F. Bresnahan and Shane Greenstein. "The Competitive Crash in Large-Scale Commercial Computing," National Bureau of Economic Research Working Paper No. 4901 as reported in Rob Norton, "What Slowed the PC Revolution," *Fortune,* March 6, 1995, p. 38.
19. Rob Norton. *Ibid.*
20. Richard E. Walton. *Up and Running: Integrating Information Technology and the Organization.* (Boston, MA: Harvard Business School Press, 1989).
21. *Ibid.,* pp. 1–2.
22. "Managing a WIRED WORLD," Cover Story, *Fortune,* July 11, 1994.

23. *Ibid.,* p. 62.

24. As quoted in Thomas A. Stewart, "Managing in a Wired Company," *Fortune,* July 11, 1994, pp. 44, 46, 47, 48.

25. Paul Strassmann. "The Myth of Best Practices," *Computerworld,* December 18, 1995, p. 88.

26. Paul Strassmann. "Computers Don't Make Money, People Do," *Computerworld,* February 19, 1996. Accessed at the Web page with URL: <http://www.strassmann.com/pubs/people-do.html> on March 31, 1996.

27. *Ibid.*

28. Michael Gentle. "Sci-Fi Lessons for IS and Users," *Computerworld,* December 11, 1995, p. 37.

29. Thomas H. Davenport. "Saving IT's Soul: Human-Centered Information Management," *Harvard Business Review,* (72:2), March–April 1994, p. 123.

30. Joseph Maglitta. "Smarten Up," *Computerworld,* June 5, 1995, p. 85.

31. *Ibid.*

32. Joseph Maglitta. "Know-How, Inc.," *Computerworld,* January 15, 1996, p. 73.

33. Ikujiro Nonaka and Hirotaka Takeuchi. *The Knowledge-Creating Company: How Japanese Companies Create the Dynamics of Innovation.* (New York: Oxford University Press, 1995).

34. Rob Guth. "Where IS Cannot Tread," *Computerworld,* January 22, 1996, p. 72.

35. Allan E. Alter. "Change in the Weather," *Computerworld,* February 26, 1996, pp. 78–79. This article has a leading question: "The wind is shifting again. Centralize or decentralize?"

36. *Ibid.*

37. Amy Malloy, Laura Hunt, and Lory Dix."So What's All This About Workflow?" *Computerworld,* October 30, 1995, pp. 93, 97.

38. Theodore M. Koulopoulis. *The Workplace Imperative.* (New York: Van Nostrand Reinhold, 1995). As quoted in Ronni T. Marshak, "The Business Imperative for Workflow & Business Process Reengineering," an advertising supplement in *Fortune,* February 19, 1996.

39. *Ibid.,* Marshak.

40. Nina Burns. "Groupware: A CNI Overview, " Creative Networks, Inc., 1995. Accessed from the Web page with URL: <http://www.cnilive.com/cni008.htm> on September 28, 1996.

41. *Ibid.*

42. William H. Davidow and Michael S. Malone. *The Virtual Corporation: Structuring and Revitalizing the Corporation for the 21st Century.* (New York: HarperCollinsPublishers, 1992).

43. *Ibid.,* p. 4.

44. *Ibid.*

45. *Ibid.,* pp. 5, 6.

46. "The Virtual Corporation," cover story, *Business Week,* February 8, 1993, pp. 98–103.

47. Ray Grenier and George Metes. *Going Virtual: Moving Your Organization into the 21st Century.* (Upper Saddle River, NJ: Prentice-Hall Professional Technical Reference, 1996).

48. William E. Eager. "Virtual Realities," *Computerworld,* April 1, 1996, p. 90.

49. Michael Hammer and James Champy. *Reengineering the Corporation: A Manifesto for Business Revolution.* (New York: HarperBusiness, A Division of HarperCollinsPublishers, 1993).

50. *Ibid.,* p. 2.

51. *Ibid.,* p. 5.

52. "The Horizontal Corporation," *Business Week,* December 20, 1993, pp. 76–81.

53. *Ibid.,* Hammer and Champy, pp. 65 ff.

54. *Ibid.,* pp. 83 ff.

55. Paul A. Strassmann. "The Roots of Business Reengineering," *American Programmer,* June 1995. Accessed at the Web page with URL: <http://www.strassmann.com/pubs/reeng/roots.html> on May 8, 1996.

56. "Business Process Innovation: What Is It? Accessed at the Web page with URL: <http://www.abs.uci.edu/depts/facil/renovate/bpi_what.html> on May 8, 1996.

57. *Ibid.*, Strassmann, June 1995.

58. John A. Byrne. "Strategic Planning," cover story, *Business Week*, August 26, 1996, pp. 46–52.

59. *Ibid.*

60. "A Survey of Retailing: Change at the Check-Out," *The Economist*, March 4, 1995, p. 5.

61. *Ibid.*, p. 4.

62. *Ibid.*, p. 6.

63. Emily Kay. "Selling Enters the Information Age," *Datamation*, May 1, 1995, p. 38.

64. *Ibid.*, p. 40.

65. Jeff Moad. "Calculating the Real Benefit of Training," *Datamation*, April 15, 1995, p. 45.

66. Deborah Compeau, Lorne Olfman, Maung Sei, and Jane Webster. "End-User Training and Learning: Introduction," *Communications of the ACM*, 38 (7), July 1995, p. 25.

67. *Ibid.*, pp. 25–26.

68. "Weaknesses in Corporate Information Security Policies," *Computerworld*, April 8, 1996, p. 64.

69. Discussed in Gary H. Anthes, "Hack Attack," *Computerworld*, April 15, 1996, p. 81.

70. Joe Devlin and Emily Berk. "Cracking the Remote Access Security Bonanza," *Reseller Management*, August 1995, pp. 63–66.

71. Gordon B. Davis. *Management Information Systems: Conceptual Foundations, Structure, and Development.* (New York: McGraw-Hill, 1974), p. 5.

72. Gordon B. Davis and Margrethe H. Olson. *Management Information Systems: Conceptual Foundations, Structure, and Development, Second Edition.* (New York: McGraw-Hill, 1985).

73. *Ibid.*, pp. 13–14.

74. Paul E. Cule and James A. Senn. "The Evolution from ICIS 1980 to AIS 1995: Have the Issues Been Addressed," Proceedings of 1995 Americas Conference on Information Systems, August 25–27, 1995, Pittsburgh. Available at the Web site with URL: <http://hsb.baylor.edu/ramsower/acis/papers/cule.htm>.

75. *Ibid.*

76. P. G. Keen and M. S. Scott Morton. *Decision Support Systems: An Organizational Perspective.* (Reading, MA: Addison-Wesley, 1978), p. 13.

77. John F. Rockart and David W. De Long. *Executive Support Systems: The Emergence of Top Management.* (Homewood, IL: Dow Jones-Irwin, 1989).

78. *Ibid.*, pp. 6–7.

79. *Ibid.*, pp. 7–9.

80. Edward Feigenbaum, Pamela McCorduck, and H. Penny Nii. *The Rise of the Expert Company.* (New York: Times Books, 1988).

81. Johanna Ambrosio. "Expert Systems Make Their Mark in Corporations," *Computerworld*, August 6, 1990, p. 10.

82. Abbe Mowshowitz. "Social Dimensions of Office Automation," in Marshall C. Yovits (ed.), *Advances in Computers, Vol. 25.* (New York: Academic Press, 1986), p. 336.

83. Susan Mael. "Datamation 100: 20th Anniversary Edition," *Datamation*, June 15, 1996. Accessed from the Web page with URL: <http://www.datamation.com/PlugIn/issues/1996/june15/06bdtm10frame.htm> on July 13, 1996.

84. "Imaging: Changing the Way the World Works," special advertising section, *Business Week*, April 2, 1990, p. 105.

85. Kevin Strehlo. "E-Mail Can Change Your Life," *Datamation*, April 15, 1995, p. 9.

86. As reported in Mitch Betts and Tim Ouellette, "Taming the E-mail Shrew," *Computerworld*, November 6, 1995, p. 1.

87. *Ibid.*

88. Paul A. Strassmann. "E-mail is Only One Path to Success," *Computerworld,* January 9, 1995, p. 35.

89. Mindy Blodgett. "Wireless Wins Market Share Slowly But Surely," *Computerworld,* January 15, 1996, p. 60.

90. *Ibid.* Table 4.1 is based on material in this source. Copyright 1996 by Computerworld, Inc. Framingham, MA 01701—Reprinted from Computerworld.

91. Peter Cassidy." Special Report: Videoconferencing, The Next Best Thing to Being There," *LAN Times,* December 1995. Accessed on the Web page with URL: <http://www.wcmh.com/lantimes/95dec/512a079a.html> on May 23, 1996.

92. Phyllis K. Sokol. *EDI: The Competitive Edge.* (New York: Intertext Publications/Multiscience Press, McGraw-Hill, 1989).

93. Ian Graham, Claire Lobet-Marais, David Charles. "Social & Economic Impact of Electronic Data Interchange (EDI)," Date unknown. Accessed from the Web site with URL: <http://www.ed.ac.uk/~ehja36/tedis_c9.html> on May 14, 1996.

94. Kurt Thearling. "An Introduction to Data Mining: Discovering Hidden Value in Your Data Warehouse," Pilot Software (Dun & Bradstreet). Accessed from the Web site with URL: <http://santafe.edu/~kurt/dmwhite.pdf> on May 22, 1996.

95. Dan Richman and Thomas Hoffman. "Digging for Data," *Computerworld,* April 18, 1996, p. 16.

96. *Op cit.,* Thearling, p. 2.

97. Based on David Kirkpatrick, "Riding the Real Trends in Technology," *Fortune,* February 19, 1996, pp. 54, 56–58, 60, 62.

98. "Fifth Annual Study of Computers in the Home," Software Publishers Association, April 22, 1996. Accessed from the Web page with URL: <http://www.spa.org/research/releases/press1.htm> on May 27, 1996.

99. *Ibid.*

100. "World Wide Web Frequently Asked Questions (FAQ)?" Accessed from the Web page with URL: <http://www.boutell.com/faq/>. Updated on a regular basis.

101. Mitch Wagner. "That's the Ticket," *Computerworld,* May 6, 1996, pp. 77, 81.

102. Alex Taylor III. "How to Buy a Car on the Internet . . . ," *Fortune,* March 4, 1996, pp. 164–168.

103. "The Future of Electronic Shopping," *Wired,* January 1966, p. 64.

104. *Ibid.*

105. "Getting Your Company's Internet Strategy Right," *Fortune,* March 18, 1996, pp. 72–74, 78.

106. This material is taken from Donna L. Hoffman, Thomas P. Novak, and Patrali Chatterjee, "Commercial Scenarios for the Web: Opportunities and Challenges," *Journal of Computer-Mediated Communication,* Vol. 1, No. 3, 1995. Accessed from the Web site with URL: <http://shum.cc.huji.ac.il/jcmc/vol1/issue3/hoffman.html> on May 12, 1996.

107. The material in the remainder of this paragraph is taken from the above paper.

108. "Services and the National Information Infrastructure," Technology Policy Working Group, Committee on Applications and Technology, Information Infrastructure Task Force, Washington, DC, December 2, 1994. Accessed from the Web page with URL: <http://nii.nist.gov/nii.html> on May 29, 1996.

109. *Ibid.*

110. *Ibid.*

111. Amy Cortese. "Here Comes the Intranet," *Business Week,* February 26, 1996, cover, pp. 76–79, 82–84.

112. Lee Levitt. "Intranets: Internet Technologies Deployed Behind the Firewall for Corporate Productivity," Intranet Society, INET'96 Annual Meeting. Accessed from the Web page with URL: <http://www.process.com/intranets/wp2.htp on May 17, 1996.

113. Zona Research as reported in Cortese, p. 84. Note that Forrester Research predicts that sales of Intranet software will reach only $1 billion by the year 2000. See Cyberatlas, The Internet Research Guide, "Intranet," April 8, 1996. Accessed from the Web page with URL: <http://www.cyberatlas.com/intranet.html> on May 16, 1996.
114. John Gantz. "Intranets: A Thicket of Hidden Costs," *Computerworld,* May 6, 1996, p. 37.
115. Thomas H. Davenport. "The Fad That Forgot People," *Fast Company,* Number 1, November 1995. Accessed from the Web page with URL: <http://www.fastcompany.com/fastco/Issues/first/Reengin.htm> on May 25, 1996.
116. *Ibid.*
117. Alice LaPlante. "'Net Cops," *Computerworld,* March 11, 1996, pp. 81–83.
118. *Ibid.,* p. 83.

ADDITIONAL READINGS

Introduction

Nocera, Joseph. "The Story of '00," *Fortune,* August 19, 1996, pp. 50–52, 54, 58, 60, 62.

The Early Years: Data Processing Systems

Allen, Brandt. "Make Information Services Pay Its Way," *Harvard Business Review,* January–February 1987, pp. 57–63.
Drucker, Peter. *The New Realities.* (New York: Harper & Row, 1989).
Vincent, David R. *The Information-Based Corporation.* (Homewood, IL: Dow Jones-Irwin, 1990).
Verity, John W. "Rethinking the Computer," *Business Week,* November 26, 1990, pp. 116–119, 122, 124.

Recent Years: Information Technology

"A Business Researcher's Interests: Business Process Reengineering/Innovation," a Web site maintained by Yogesh Malhotra, sponsored by the Association for Information Systems, with URL: <http://www.pitt.edu/~malhotra/interest.html>.
Champy, James. *Reengineering Management: The Mandate for New Leadership.* (New York: HarperCollins, 1995).
Hammer, Michael with Steven A. Stanton. *The Reengineering Revolution: A Handbook.* (New York: HarperCollins, 1995).
Hoffman, Thomas and Mitch Wagner. "Visions of Holiday $ugarplums," *Computerworld,* December 4, 1995, pp. 1, 147.
Strassmann, Paul. "Spending Without Results," *Computerworld,* April 15, 1996, p. 88.

Business Issues and Management Information Systems

Alexander, Michael. "The Real Security Threat: The Enemy Within," *Datamation,* July 15, 1995, pp. 30–31, 33.

"An Overview of Data Mining at Dunn & Bradstreet," DIG White Paper 95/01, Data Intelligence Group, Pilot Software, Cambridge, MA, September 1995. Accessed from the Web site with URL: <http://santafe.edu/~kurt/wp9501.pdf> on May 23, 1996.

Brandel, Mary. "Videoconferencing Slowly Goes Desktop," *Computerworld*, February 20, 1995, p. 81.

"End-User Training and Learning," several papers in *Communications of the ACM*, 38 (7), July 1995, pp. 24–79.

Port, Otis. "Computers that Think Are Almost Here," *Business Week*, July 17, 1995, pp. 68–71, 73.

Radding, Alan. "Getting a Grip on Handhelds," *Computerworld*, July 3, 1995, pp. 72–76.

Sproull, Lee and Kiesler, Sara. *Connections: New Ways of Working in the Networked Organization.* (Cambridge, MA: The MIT Press, 1991).

Thearling, Kurt. "From Data Mining to Database Marketing," DIG White Paper 95/02, Data Intelligence Group, Pilot Software, Cambridge, MA, October 1995. Accessed from the Web site with URL: <http://santafe.edu/~kurt/wp9502.pdf> on May 23, 1996.

The Internet and the World Wide Web

"The Accidental Superhighway: A Survey of the Internet," *The Economist*, July 1, 1995. Accessed from the Web page with URL: <http://www.economist.com/surveys/internet/index.html> on May 27, 1996.

"Electronic Commerce and the Internet," special section. *Communications of the ACM*, 39 (6), June 1996, pp. 22–58.

Hoffman, Donna L., and Novak, Thomas P. "A New Marketing Paradigm for Electronic Commerce," paper submitted for the Special Issue on Electronic Commerce for *The Information Society*, February 19, 1996. Accessed from the Web page with URL: <http://www2000.ogsm.vanderbilt.edu/novak/new.marketing.paradigm.html> on May 28, 1996.

Hoffman, Donna L., Kalsbeek, William D., and Novak, Thomas P. "Internet Use in the United States: 1995 Baseline Estimates and Preliminary Market Segments," Project 2000 Working Paper, April 12, 1996, Vanderbilt University. Accessed from the Web page with URL: <http://www2000.ogsm.vanderbilt.edu/baseline/1995.Internet.estimates.html> on May 28, 1996.

Leonard, Andrew. "Smart Money?" *Cyberspace Today*, Issue #3, June 22, 1995. Accessed from the Web page with URL: <http://www.cybertoday.com/ct/v1n4/feature.html> on May 7, 1996.

Rebello, Kathy, Armstrong, Larry, Cortese, Amy. "Making Money on the Net," Special Report, *Business Week*, September 23, 104–107, 110, 114, 118.

"A Survey of the Software Industry," *The Economist*, May 25, 1996. Accessed from the Web page with URL: <http://www.economist.com/surveys/software/index.html> on July 25, 1996.

U.S. Congress, Office of Technology Assesment, *Electronic Enterprises: Looking to the Future*, OTA-TCT-600 (Washington, DC: US Government Printing Office, May 1994). Available at the Web site with URL: <http://www.ota.nap.edu/>.

Social Issues

"Corporate Information Technology Policies and Procedures Survey," Gordon & Glickson PC, Chicago, IL, May 1996. Accessed from the Web page with URL: <http://www.ggtech.com/pdf/96041.pdf> on May 30, 1996.

Dern, Daniel P. "Just One More Click..." *Computerworld*, July 8, 1996, pp. 93, 96.

Scheier, Robert L. "Let Go!" *Computerworld*, June 3, 1996, p. 82.

— 5 —

MEDICINE AND COMPUTERS

The potential for new computing and telecommunications technologies to reduce the cost of delivering health care, while facilitating broad structural changes in the health care industry, may presage a rapid expansion in the application of information technologies to the health care system.[1]

INTRODUCTION

Medicine is, at its root, people helping people. Doctors skilled at diagnosis and treatment are expected, in our society, to recognize the health problems of their patients, recommend the best ways to treat them, monitor this treatment, and adjust it if necessary until full health returns or a stable condition is achieved. In the course of this process it may be necessary to prescribe changes in diet, administer drugs, use equipment to monitor various body functions, or perform surgery—in short, to apply any necessary technology to meet the perceived needs of the patient. This model for health care in the United States stresses treatment rather than preventive methods and is eager to employ expensive and sophisticated technology. Examples of the latter are open-heart surgery, dialysis machines, reproductive technologies, and computer-aided tomography (CAT) scanners.

The computer has been used in this system in a variety of ways. It has found a natural home in the health delivery system and has supported a kind of medical practice that emphasizes and depends upon high technology. These computers and computer networks have responded to the deeply felt concerns of hundreds of thousands of health care professionals working within the current system. On the other hand, some are concerned that loss of humanity and increase in alienation might result from the growing dependence on machines and the occasional replacement of human contact with computer interfaces.

The most natural and earliest use of computers in medicine was in record-keeping, billing, and payroll, as in other areas of society. In medicine, however, record-keeping serves a function beyond its immediate mundane use. The ability to access medical records in an information system can serve a research as well as a required therapeutic function. And with the growth of the Internet it is possible to access records from anywhere in the world. Beyond this very important function, the Internet also permits, indeed encourages, the establishment of kindred groups of patients and health professionals, to exchange in-

formation, offer advice, and support those in need. Medicine itself can be practiced remotely and over the past few years, considerable attention has been paid to the emerging
discipline called telemedicine.

Other important application areas for computers are cross-sectional image analysis
systems, medical education, and library access and research. Visually impaired, hearing
impaired, and physically disabled people have been important beneficiaries of technological developments. The computer and (even better) the microprocessor have opened up
a number of possibilities otherwise beyond their reach. There are now automatic devices
for communication and for answering the telephone or the door. Other devices can monitor the ill and alert doctors or nurses if help is needed. Besides these uses, computer programming itself is an occupation that can be practiced in the home. Video games are
being used in therapy for patients suffering from brain disorders as a result of strokes, tumors, and degenerative diseases. The games help improve hand-eye coordination, patient
alertness, attention, concentration, memory and perceptual motor skills. Patients seem to
be much more amenable to and even enthusiastic about a session with a video game than
with a traditional therapist. There are plans to tailor software more specifically for rehabilitation purposes in the video game context. All in all it sounds like a marriage made in
heaven.

MEDICAL INFORMATION SYSTEMS

> However, there is still no system that comprehensively facilitates the flow of all types of
> health information and symmetrically addresses the needs of clinicians, administrators, pol-
> icy makers, patients, and consumers. [2]

On the surface information systems appear to include just computer databases that store
information, programs to process user queries, and more programs to present the results
in a variety of forms. However, special demands on medicine have resulted in the development of information systems with appropriate properties. It may literally be a matter of
life and death that medical records be accurate, complete, and current. This requirement
is the most basic, but there are a number of subsidiary ones beyond patient care, namely
administration, accounting, monitoring and evaluation of service, research, and resource
allocation. Figure 5.1 is a recently implemented information system developed by the US
Department of Defense (DOD) for its worldwide medical service. DOD had announced the
Composite Health Care System (CHCS) in 1988, to be installed at 754 locations worldwide, ranging from large military hospitals to small clinics. [3] The system was intended to
automate patient administration, patient scheduling, nursing, order entry, clinical dietet-
ics, laboratory, radiology, and pharmacy. Each facility would have communications, maintenance, and operations support. Furthermore, it would be able to interact with other
DOD systems, such as the National Disaster Medical System and VA System, food service,
medical logistics, and tactical automation system.

The US General Accounting Office (GAO) has reviewed CHCS for several years in terms
of cost-benefit analysis, success in reaching stated goals, and recent technological developments in medical care systems. It described CHCS briefly in the following manner: [4]

CHCS is a comprehensive medical information system that Defense has developed to provide automated support to its military medical treatment facilities. As shown in Figure 5.1, the system is multi-faceted and complex, composed of nine integrated modules and shared capabilities, such as order-entry, results retrieval, and electronic mail. The modules are used to create and update the integrated patient database, which can be accessed by all authorized users.

This system actually has been implemented in "526 medical treatment facilities worldwide" and represents a considerable investment of about $2 billion. It is probably one of the most advanced medical information systems in existence and while GAO is concerned with its costs and certain of its functions, it is its description of the capabilities of CHCS that is of most interest. A very brief overview of the various modules follows:[5]

Capabilities shared by most CHCS modules include *order-entry,* which allows the entry of patient orders by health-care providers and ancillary support personnel; *results retrieval,* which allows direct access to test results performed under any module; and *electronic mail,* which allows users to communicate with each other.

The **Diatetics** module manages the order and delivery of patient dietary instructions.

FIGURE 5.1 Shared Capabilities and Modules of the Composite Health Care System.

(From "Medical ADP Systems: Defense Achieves Worldwide Deployment of Composite Health Care System," United States General Accounting Office, GAO/AIMD-96-39, April 1996. Accessed from the Web page with URL: <http://www.gao.gov/monthly.list/ai96039.pdf> on May 21, 1996.)

The **Clinical** module manages orders for patient care and the retrieval of test results. It contains checks against the patient's medical record for risks and contraindications, and issues a warning if necessary.

The **Laboratory** module manages data associated with clinical and anatomical pathology, and blood/chemical tests. This includes ordering tests, processing specimens, documenting test results, and supporting quality controls.

The **Patient Administration** module manages the registration of patients and their medical records.

The **Patient Appointment and Scheduling** module manages appointment schedules for clinics and health care providers. Its Managed Care Program submodule supports enrollment, provider network management, and health care finder activities.

The **Pharmacy** module manages the ordering and filling of prescriptions. It checks for drug interactions and allergies, and provides an automated inventory control capability.

The **Radiology** module manages the ordering and scheduling of diagnostic, radiologic, nuclear medicine, and radiation therapy testing, as well as the reporting of test results.

The **Medical Records and Image Files Tracking** module manages and tracks patient medical records and images.

The **Quality Assurance** module supports the identification and documentation of recurring problems related to patient care, and tracks their solutions and resolutions. It also provides management of provider case lists and training to support the credentialing process.

Thus, the modern medical information system serves many functions, from day-to-day operations to long-term record-keeping to a valuable research database for spotting unforeseen health trends. For example, Kaiser Permanente, "the nation's largest and oldest HMO," serves 2.4 million people in Northern California. After scanning information from diverse databases for its members, it created a single database for the 84,000 identified diabetics among its membership. Searching this diabetics database, an interesting discovery was made—"15 to 20% of Kaiser's diabetic patients aren't getting their eyes checked routinely"—even though "diabetes is the leading cause of blindness."[6] This simple example suggests that a much more effective use may be made of apparently routine data. One of the main payoffs for large comprehensive databases is to determine whether or not particular medical procedures are effective. This applies of course to the increasing use of expensive medical technologies. The research arm of the US Congress, the Office of Technology Assessment (OTA) produced a study to explore this issue.[7]

With health care costs exerting a growing pressure on government expenditures, one direction to reduce costs is to determine the effectiveness of accepted medical technologies. The OTA report provides a number of options including the following: [8]

1. Improving the efficient production of meta-analyses and other systematic reviews of existing studies, to make the best use of past efforts at clinical evaluation.

Encourage the National Library of Medicine to maintain a commitment to establishing comprehensive databases of published controlled clinical trials.

2. Conducting more, and more efficient, clinical trials that yield valid comparative information on health technologies already in use, to produce results directly useful to patient and clinician decisionmaking; and making valid, well-designed comparative studies an intrinsic part of ordinary practice in every setting.

Establish and maintain a comprehensive database of ongoing clinical trials sponsored by the federal government (and, where possible, private industry).

3. Encouraging greater comparative evaluations of newly introduced technologies.

There is more from the OTA in a particularly relevant report issued in 1995 with the title, *Bringing Health Care Online.*[9] A list of a diverse number of technologies that are quite relevant for health care are provided. Consider Table 5.1. These technologies are divided into groups starting with the collection of data by a number of new techniques involving different modalities and onsite data entry. Once collected, issues of storage medium, data compression (for medical images), and structured archiving arise. The stored data is useful in so far as it can be readily accessed independent of distance and size; thus, issues of telecommunication networks and protocols are of prime importance. Finally, use must be made of the data, and in this regard programs to synthesize, analyze, and infer relevant information are necessary. Such disciplines as artificial intelligence, data mining, database theory, and decision support systems are involved.

The obvious advantages of computer-based patient records as compared with paper records is pointed out and include such improvements that "the health care delivery process could be fully documented, health information could be unfettered," and "caregiving, research, and data administration could be knit together."[10] These observations are well known but it is clear that they represent some of the major benefits of Information Technology in the medical system and need to be emphasized. Once stored digitally, information is accessible from many points and available for many purposes.

As we have seen, many reasons have been given for the importance and usefulness of medical information systems, but perhaps one additional reason might be offered: Medicare. In 1968, Medicare was introduced to help the elderly pay their medical bills. Medicare payments have become a crucial factor in hospital finances and the entire health care system, accounting for about 40% of hospital billings in 1987. Tight restrictions on Medicare payments, however, because of the federal government's decision to limit hospital payments to a fixed amount to treat each illness, as well as pressure by major corporations to limit the costs of large insurance carriers, have forced the health care system to tighten its operations. Thus, hospitals are encouraged to treat illnesses as quickly and cheaply as possible to recover a greater proportion of their costs. This situation has motivated the development and implementation of medical information systems to help reduce costs and at the same time improve the quality of care.

Medical Databases

The National Library of Medicine (NLM) is the "principal resource for the collection, organization, and retrieval of scientific literature in the health and biomedical fields."[11] The

TABLE 5.1

KEY INFORMATION TECHNOLOGIES FOR HEALTH CARE.

Human-computer interaction	handheld computers
	handwriting recognition
	personal digital assistants
	speech recognition
	automated data collection
	structured data entry
Storage, processing, and compression	computer-based patient records
	magnetic stripe cards
	smart cards
	picture archiving and communications systems
	medical imaging
	optical storage
	image compression
	digital signal processors
	object-oriented software design
Connectivity	clinical information systems
	cabled, optical, and wireless networks
	Internet and electronic mail
	World Wide Web
	Integrated Services Digital Network (ISDN)
	frame relay
	Asynchronous Transfer Mode (ATM)
	client-server computing
	messaging and coding standards
	proprietary and consensus standards
	Medical Information Bus
Security	passwords
	fault tolerant computers
	redundant disk (RAID) systems
	authenticators
	encryption
	firewalls
Data distillation	decision support systems
	pattern recognition
	artificial neural networks
	knowledge-based systems
	relational databases
	knowledge discovery
	natural language processing
	encoders and groupers

Source: US Congress, Office of Technology Assessment, *Bringing Health Care Online: The Role of Information Technologies*, OTA-ITC-624 (Washington, DC: US Government Printing Office, September 1995), Table 2-1, p. 44. Also available at the Web site with URL: <http://www.ota.nap.edu/>.

library has long been concerned with the application of computers to information retrieval and in 1964 introduced MEDLARS (Medical Literature Analysis and Retrieval System), its computerized retrieval and technical processing system. This system maintains data files, provides online retrieval services, and produces computer-photocomposed publications. It includes "over 40 online databases containing about 18 million records." One of these databases, MEDLINE (MEDLARS online), first came into service in 1971 to provide online capability. The MEDLINE database is actually Index Medicus® online, "the monthly subject/author guide to articles in 3,000 journals." [12] Currently, the term MEDLINE is used to describe the database, not the online service, and in fact is the largest and most extensively used of all the Library's databases. Other databases contain information on ethical topics, cancer, chemical substances, epilepsy, health planning and administration, history of medicine, and toxicology. As of 1988, MEDLARS databases contained over 10 million journal article references and abstracts. The online network consists of over 14,000 institutions and individuals in the United States. The NLM is clearly an invaluable resource and conducted "some 7.3 million searches in 1995" in both the United States and around the world.

In the mid-1980s, the NLM introduced PC-based software, Grateful Med, that permits the search of almost the entire MEDLARS database via a user-friendly interface. On April 16, 1996 a new version, Internet Grateful Med, was introduced, which will permit health professionals around the world to access MEDLINE via the Internet and the World Wide Web.[13] As the rate of growth in medical knowledge continues to increase at a rapid rate, access to a comprehensive database such as MEDLINE becomes an indispensable aid to providing medical care. As the National Library of Medicine Director Donald A. B. Lindberg, M.D. noted, "Even a disciplined physician who reads two medical journals a night for an entire year before going to bed would find that he had fallen behind on his reading by over 550 years. Internet Grateful Med will be an indispensable tool for medical professionals to stay current with the latest in medical information." [14]

MEDICAL APPLICATIONS

> Improving the health care of Americans through the discovery and implementation of new medical technologies has been an explicit goal of the federal government for over a century. Since the 1970s, however, the government has also underwritten a less visible effort—the attempt to identify which health care interventions, among those in current use, work best.[15]

The computer has found a welcome home in medical diagnosis, treatment, and as an aid to the disabled or physically disadvantaged. Powerful tools have become available for exploring parts of the body previously accessible only through surgery. For patients in intensive care or on life-support systems, the availability of microprocessors has relieved nurses of the responsibility of constant surveillance. In such applications, the computer is indispensable because of both its computational power and its decision-making ability.

Body Imaging

Until fairly recently there were two basic methods for identifying and investigating problems within the human body: X-rays—with or without the use of ingested or inserted dyes or radioactive tracers—and surgery. Both methods have obvious drawbacks. Surgery is a traumatic invasion of the body and should be reserved for situations that demand the actual removal of diseased or damaged organs or tissues or the correction of problems. Its use as an exploratory tool should be minimized. Over the past twenty years a number of methods for producing images of various parts of the body have been developed, employing both invasive and noninvasive means. Probably the best-known is the computerized axial tomography or computer-assisted tomography (CAT) scanner.

CAT Scanners

The term *tomography* refers to "any of several techniques for making X-ray pictures of a predetermined plane section of a solid object, by blurring out the images of other planes."[16] In an ordinary X-ray picture, the X-ray source produces a diverging beam that passes through the body and falls on a photographic plate. Although it has proven to be an invaluable tool, conventional X-ray does have limitations in that there is little sense of depth, and soft tissues show up somewhat blurred. The CAT scanner uses X-rays to produce sharp, cross-sectional images of the human body. The patient lies horizontally on a table and is placed in the center of the apparatus, which consists of an X-ray source and collimator (a device to focus the beam) on one side, a detector and data acquisition system on the other. The body is kept stationary in the scanner while the apparatus rotates around a given section, generating X-rays that are registered by the detectors as they pass through the body. There is attenuation of the beams as they pass through body structures of varying densities. The actual cross-sectional image is produced by using a computer to carry out a complex summation of the various measurements made. Although various algorithms for producing cross-sectional images have been known for years, it is only when using a computer that the computation becomes feasible.

The CAT scanner has been hailed as a major, almost revolutionary advance in medical diagnosis. It is important that the X-ray exposure necessary to produce a cross sectional image is no greater than that for a conventional X-ray. Most major hospitals have acquired CAT scanners even though the price is of the order of $1 million. In fact it has become something of a controversial item, as there has been criticism of the unseemly haste with which hospitals have competed to purchase the latest and most expensive equipment. However, there is no denying that it has proven to be an important diagnostic tool.

Nuclear Magnetic Resonance (NMR) or Magnetic Resonance Imaging (MRI)

NMR (also known as Magnetic Resonance Imaging, MRI) produces images similar to those obtained by CAT scanners but also permits the actual observation of certain internal processes such as the movement of blood, the reaction of cancerous tumors to a particular therapy, multiple sclerosis, the action of heart and blood vessels, and various problems in tendons, ligaments, and cartilage.[17] All these observations can be accomplished without X-rays, the injection of hazardous dyes, or the use of radioactive isotopes. Nuclear magnetic resonance has been used for many years by chemists to analyze uniform solids and liquids. In its medical application, the patient is placed inside a large cylindrical magnet. In the plane of radiation, the magnetic field can vary between 1500 and 15,000 gauss (more than 15,000 times the magnetic field of the earth). Under the influence of the large magnetic field, the atomic nuclei of hydrogen, phosphorous, and other elements act as tiny bar magnets and align themselves in the direction of the field. When the radio frequency (RF) is removed, the tiny magnets return to their original positions and in the process emit characteristic RF signals. An antenna in the cylinder detects the radio waves and transmits them to a computer to be analyzed and presented as an image. Further information is available, because the computer can also determine the rate at which the nuclei return to their original positions. It is possible to obtain a sequence of images of the human heart with the valves opening and closing.

There are some disadvantages. Among these are cost—an NMR system sells for about $1.5 million, about 50% more than a CAT scanner. The system must be isolated from extraneous electromagnetic signals and magnetic substances. There may be a hazard to people with artificial joints and pacemakers. The long-term effect of high magnetic fields on the body is unknown. Pregnant women are currently being excluded from examination by NMR. It is being introduced more slowly than the CAT scanner, but the future holds much promise for its use.

Positron-Emission Tomography (PET) Scanners

As is often the case, new technology follows rapidly on the heels of the old. The use of a PET scanner requires the subject to ingest, or be injected with, a radioactive isotope, typically of oxygen, carbon, and nitrogen. The system detects the radioactive decay by means of special scintillation counters. These isotopes are called positron emitters, because as they decay they release positively charged particles that are annihilated after collision with electrons. Gamma rays result whose direction of travel can be detected very precisely, thereby revealing a great deal about the relevant body tissue. The patient is placed inside a ring structure containing an array of gamma ray detectors. The directions are identified and the computer comes into play to construct a cross-sectional image of the distribution of the positron emitter. The PET scanner has an advantage over the CAT scanner in that it is able to reveal the functioning of organs and tissues, not just their outline.

The PET scanner can be used to (a) monitor blood flow in certain areas of the heart (cardiology), (b) assess the intake of sugar in cancer tumors or the brain (neurology), the size and growth of cancerous tumors (oncology), and (c) study chemical reactions that may suggest schizophrenia or Alzheimer's disease. There are many fewer PET scanners than CAT scanners in use, and many of the results obtained so far are still experimental.

There are some problems associated with the widespread use of PET scanners. Short-lived isotopes are necessary to prevent the patient from receiving too large a dose of radiation while the scan is in progress. Isotopes with such short half-lives (between 2 and 110 minutes) must be produced on-site by a cyclotron. The need to have a cyclotron on hand increases the costs enormously, on the order of $2 million for a PET installation. Furthermore, at the present stage of development the interpretation of the data is a very complex process. It still requires the efforts of specially trained chemists, mathematicians, physicists, computer scientists, and doctors. Both PET and CAT scanners are subject to the criticism that they expose the body to excessive radiation from either gamma rays or X-rays.

A recent report, albeit by the industry group the Institute for Clinical PET, claims that a more frequent use of PET would result in major savings in Medicare and non-Medicare

health costs. Savings would arise because as a superior diagnostic tool, PET use would eliminate a significant number of invasive procedures as well as other diagnostic procedures.[18]

Medical Laser Spectroscopy

A new class of techniques to avoid invasive surgery is based on the use of specially designed medical lasers. "Current technology cannot detect flat sections of precancerous
colon tissue—a serious concern, since colon cancer kills more people in the United States
than any other form of the disease save that of the lungs."[19] In current practice, a device
known as an endoscope is inserted into the colon and a white light is shone through the
optic fibers in the device. The difficulty is that the examination of the surface of the colon
does not reveal the flat precancerous lesions rather than the raised ones. Researchers have
discovered that by shining a laser beam "of weak ultraviolet light on body tissue, [s]ome
of the light's photons cause molecules in the tissue to become momentarily excited, after
which they produce lower-energy photons with fluorescent wavelengths that return to the
light source." The distribution of wavelengths in the emitted light is dependent on the state
of the tissue's structure, an indication of the health or possibly cancerous state of the tissue. Experiments are also underway to direct short pulses of light into specific parts of the
body to determine the existence of tumors that would otherwise require surgery.

Storage of Images

As a variety of techniques have emerged for producing images of the body, an interesting
problem has arisen. Large numbers of images must be stored, cataloged, and made readily available for future reference. For example, "A 300-bed hospital generates about 1 gigabyte (8×10^9 bits) of picture information every day and is legally bound to hold it for
three to seven years—30 years in the case of silicosis or black lung disease, illnesses that
may have relevance to future lawsuits."[20] Diagnostic imagers could have been designed to
produce digital output, which would have facilitated the storage of the images and their
transmission over networks, but for commercial reasons this was not done; in addition,
when scanners were first introduced, high resolution monitors were not generally available
and film processing techniques and handling were. More recently a number of hospital and
medical research centers in the US, Japan, and Europe have begun to implement and routinely use picture-archiving and communication systems (PACS). In more detail, a definition follows:[21]

> PACS accepts pictures or images, with associated text, in digital form and then distributes
> them over a network. The components of a PACS include control computers and a commu-
> nication network, interfaces to imaging devices, storage media, display stations, and printers.

Some of the problems impeding the rapid growth of PACS are the quality of the resolution of digital images compared to film, the ability to view multiple films rapidly, and the
low cost of film equipment compared to display stations of requisite quality. To deal with
these issues, radiologists will have to accept digital images even though they are concerned
about the possibility of extraneous details being introduced during computation. Another
looming problem is the vast number of images that must be stored.

The real payoff for PACS is the ability to transmit quality images over varying distances: local-area networks (LANS) linking scanners, data storage devices, and display stations in one department; wide-area networks for linking LANs within hospitals and medical centers; and teleradiology networks for national and worldwide distribution. PACS had their heyday in the 1980s and as with many other computer technologies, the Internet has had a major impact. The idea is that the scanners themselves produce their images in a form compatible with Internet transmission.[22]

Electronic Monitoring

For the patient in the intensive care unit of a hospital, the immediate world is full of electronic hums and beeps, flashing lights, and video monitors. Many activities performed by nurses in the past are now being carried out by a combination of sophisticated electronics, microprocessors, and software. Many body functions can be monitored automatically and compared to desired (or dangerous) levels by specialized equipment that emits signals to warn the nurse if an emergency arises. This system relieves nurses of the stressful and tedious work of sitting at the bedside of critically ill patients. The patient can be assured of constant monitoring and the nurse can apply himself or herself to patients who are conscious of nursing efforts.

Is the practice of medicine becoming increasingly dehumanized? How far have we moved away from the image of the doctor or nurse hovering near the patient, deep in thought, full of compassion? Perhaps this image is overly romantic and has little to do with the actual quality of care. It is difficult to assume a critical stance when sophisticated monitoring systems that are responsive to the slightest changes in the well-being of patients are in use and there is less dependence on overworked and tired medical staffs.

Computers in Medical Education

Aside from the use of computer-aided instruction in medical schools (the importance of which should not be overlooked), a significant and interesting application has been medical robots. These devices are shaped like humans, covered with synthetic skin, and are chock full of electronics that simulate a variety of human functions. Controlled by computers, they are used to provide students with an opportunity to perform diagnostic tests before they are experienced enough to interact usefully with human subjects. As advances are made in robotics, these robots will become more sophisticated and more challenging for students. Improved computer graphics and multimedia have resulted in medical simulations that also provide excellent teaching aids.

Medical Expert Systems

At the heart of medical practice is the diagnosis, that somewhat mysterious process by which a doctor assimilates medical evidence—in the form of family history, symptoms, the results of tests, and direct verbal reports—and determines a course of treatment along with further tests to ascertain whether the patient is in fact suffering from a particular ailment. Although there have been significant advances in medicine, the determination of the nature, cause, and treatment of disease and disability is still often more art than science. The process depends heavily on the experience, knowledge, and skill of the attending physicians and sometimes on just plain luck. The educational process depends on teaching diagnostic skills by example, occasionally in stressful situations, with the hope that the novice will learn from the experienced.

In the past few years there has been a considerable effort to apply artificial intelligence techniques to the area of medical decision-making. There are several components to this research program: the acquisition of medical knowledge, the problem-solving system or inference engine that captures the decision-making strategy of the best doctors, a means of adding new knowledge and modifying old, and finally, a facility for natural communication. The earliest medical expert system, MYCIN, was designed at Stanford University in the early 1970s to recommend the appropriate antibiotics to treat bacterial infections. (MYCIN is a typical suffix for the names of antibiotics; for example, streptomycin and aureomycin).[23] More recently experts systems have been developed for more general-purpose use such as in the offices of general practitioners. Such a system is the "Explain software package developed by G. Octo Barnett of Harvard Medical School's Laboratory for Computer Science; it includes 2200 diseases and 5000 symptoms in its knowledge base."[24]

COMPUTERS AND THE DISABLED

3) For some individuals with disabilities, assistive technology devices and assistive technology services are necessary to enable the individuals
   (A) to have greater control over their lives;
   (B) to participate in, and contribute more fully to, activities in their home, school, and work environments, and in their communities;
   (C) to interact to a greater extent with individuals who do not have disabilities; and
   (D) to otherwise benefit from opportunities that are taken for granted by individuals who do not have disabilities. [25]

The processing power of computers and indeed of microprocessors has found a ready application in devices and systems to aid the paralyzed, the sensory impaired, and the severly disabled. And not a moment too soon given the surprisingly large number of disabled people in the US and elsewhere. The "first comprehensive disability survey ever undertaken by the [Commerce Department's Census] bureau" was done during 1991/1992 and reported in January 1994. Some interesting and challenging results of this survey, which excluded people in institutions, are:[26]

- 49 million Americans had a disability* in 1991–92, 24 million classified as severely disabled.
- More women (14.2 million) than men (9.9 million) had severe disabilities.
- Among the 27.3 million persons aged 15 and over with a limitation in a physical or daily living activity, the conditions most frequently mentioned as a cause of disability were

arthritis or rheumatism (7.2 million), back or spinal problems (5.7 million), heart trouble (4.6 million), lung or respiratory trouble (2.8 million), high blood pressure (2.2 million), stiffness or deformity of the foot, leg, arm or hand (2 million), and diabetes (1.6 million).

- Of the 48.9 million persons with a disability, 6 percent were less than 15 years old, 60 percent were 15 to 64 years old, and 34 percent were 65 years and older.
- The number of persons aged 15 and older who used a wheelchair was 1.5 million (919,000 women and 575,000 men). Another 4 million persons did not use a wheelchair but used a cane, crutches, or a walker and had used such an aid for six months or longer.
- Among persons aged 15 and older, 9.7 million had difficulty seeing the words and letters in ordinary newsprint even when wearing corrective lenses. Of this total, 1.6 million could not see the words and letters at all.
- The number of persons aged 15 and older who had difficulty hearing what was said in a normal conversation with another person was 10.9 million, and 924,000 or 8 percent of these persons were completely unable to hear what was said in such a conversation.

*A disability is defined by the Census Bureau as difficulty in performing one or more functional or daily living activities, or one or more socially defined roles or tasks. Persons who are completely unable to perform an activity or task, or who must have personal assistance were considered to have a severe disability.

The impact of computer technology is likely to be so significant that the visually impaired will be helped to see (albeit dimly), the hearing impaired to communicate, the physically disabled to move (albeit slowly and with difficulty), and the paralyzed to interact with the world, for both work and play. Technologies that can be used "to increase or improve functional capabilities of individuals with disabilities"[27] are called assistive technologies. Some obvious examples are motor-driven wheelchairs, hearing aids, computer keyboards with oversized keys, voice-activated electro-mechanical systems, and remote-controlled devices. More detail is provided next.

The Visually Impaired

Most advances in the treatment of blindness are still experimental. For the blind, help comes in two forms: technology to improve access to information, and a means for providing a crude form of vision. In the former case, an important development was the Kurzweil Reading Machine and other reading machines for that matter. A person places a book or printed page on its glass top. A scanning mechanism converts the print images to electrical signals that are processed by a computer program whose output device is a voice synthesizer. Such programs incorporate a large number of English phonological rules (how text might directly be converted to appropriate sound) and exceptions (under what conditions the general rules fail). The voice or voices are sometimes difficult to understand, but users report that in a very short time they become quite comfortable with one or more variations. In addition, controls allow the user to vary the pitch, spell out the letters in words that have not been understood, repeat previous words, and increase the number of words scanned per minute.

For years, vision researchers have been experimenting with artificial eyes, retinal implants, and even cortical implants. In somewhat more detail, work is proceeding along the following three fronts:[28]

- Enhanced vision, which refers to aids that process the image for maximum visibility and then present the information to still viable parts of an individual's seeing retina.
- Prosthetic vision, which presents processed visual information to the inner retina or visual pathways through electrical stimulation of the surviving neurons.
- Artificial vision, which processes and interprets visual information and presents the result to the individual through another sensory modality.

Work in the mid-1980s on virtual reality cameras suggested to researchers in the field of electronic vision enhancement that such cameras might serve as a platform for providing improved vision to the large numbers of visually impaired people for whom neither corrective lenses nor surgery are effective alternatives. The first state-of-the-art production model was produced by Visionics Corp. in 1994. It has "two components: the headset and a control unit which doubles as a battery pack and is worn around the waist. On the headset are three cameras based on charge-coupled devices (CCDs): two for orientation and a third for refined viewing."[29]

Digital Hearing Aids

Apparently, about 1.5 million hearing aids are sold annually in the US, but many are unused because of their general ineffectiveness in many situations. Recently, digital hearing aids have been introduced with the expectation that they will provide improved performance. Digital circuitry will be able to vary the amplification profile of the hearing aid to take into account more precise information about the range of individual hearing loss and the sound characteristics of typically encountered environments. One device, Oticon's 4-gram, DigiFocus, "Uses a microprocessor that operates at 14 million instructions per second. A miniature battery is expected to last 200 hours . . . [it] will have up to 100 software-controlled parameters," compared to "perhaps 10 adjustable parameters" for current hearing aids.[30]

Dyslexics

Those individuals who have trouble reading and writing but not speaking and listening are known as dyslexic. In an ideal technological world, their needs would be met by computer systems that could translate spoken words to text and then output those words, actually continuous text, as spoken language. Thus dyslexics could have the computer act as a transducer, bypassing the difficult task, for them, of comprehending printed text. The technical problems arising in this task are being pursued in Artificial Intelligence and more specifically in the subarea of speech understanding. The second part of the operation, text to speech, is being handled fairly well, as discussed previously, although continued work is necessary to improve the quality of the speech. The general speech to text problem is still an open one in spite of existing systems that permit suitably programmed computers to respond to spoken commands. Many functions performed by telephone operators have also been assumed by speech recognition systems. However, the success of such systems is based on a very restricted domain of discourse and an associated limited vocabulary. Under these conditions, speech recognition, not understanding, is not only possible but effective.

To increase their effectiveness a learning component can be included so that individuals can improve performance by training the system to respond to their particular speech patterns. Of course, when a dyslexic is in the process of training a system, he or she must correct the system when it outputs an incorrect word or phrase, a daunting task for a dyslexic. A number of commercial programs, such as DragonDictate and Kurzweil, now exist with the capacity to recognize up to 30,000 individual words. Furthermore, they permit direct input to such popular word processing programs as Word and WordPerfect. [31]

The Severly Disabled

Microprocessors are being used to control various parts of the environment of severely disabled people by translating spoken or other commands into actions. It is possible to place a disabled person at the center of a wondrous communication network. Through voice control such a person can summon television programs from around the world by requesting the satellite dish in the yard to be pointed in any given direction. With a minimal active vocabulary of about 300 words, it is possible to play video games, participate in a conference-type telephone system, use a video recorder, dictate letters, dim the lights, and even program a computer. A robotic arm can be hooked up to the system to provide a crude manipulative capacity. Additional capabilities are answering and dialing a telephone, opening and closing drapes, controlling an entertainment console and other appliances, and using a video camera to screen visitors and open the front door. The cost of such systems is not exorbitant, given the continually decreasing costs of microprocessors, memory chips, software, transducers, and effectors.

The computer itself has enabled a number of physically disabled people to express themselves in ways not previously possible. Cerebral palsy has prevented many people from speaking understandably or from controlling their arms and hands to write. Typing requires less motor coordination, particularly on specially designed oversize keyboards connected to personal computers. With special programming languages and software, such people can communicate more readily, and minds locked in uncooperative bodies can emerge. A number of children with disabilities have found the computer to be a liberating force that returns much for the little effort required to press a few buttons. For those unable to speak clearly, a computer can display their words as they are keyed in and make them heard through a speech synthesizer. The applications are growing daily as the physically disadvantaged become aware of the potentialities of the computer.

The Disabled at Work

In 1990 a comprehensive law was passed in the United States, The Americans with Disabilities Act (ADA), requiring employers, public institutions, and private companies to provide facilities sufficient to enable people with disabilities to enjoy all the benefits that the rest of society currently enjoys and usually takes for granted. Although the ramifications of this law are likely to be far-reaching and surely unpredictable, it is clear that the computer, or at least the microprocessor and associated input/output devices, will play an important role. What will also be important is that equipment, produced for the general public, be well-designed so that the physically disabled will also benefit from their use. This requirement receives added urgency given that almost 40 million Americans have disabilities. Specially designed computers with oversized keyboards and large monitors, and communication networks will permit the severely disabled to work and be educated at home. Speech synthesizers have been improved and their price lowered so that screen displays can be spoken for the benefit of people with visual impairments, software is available to translate from English to Braille for printing, light pens and joy sticks can replace or augment keyboards although adequate software is still in short supply, and speech recognition is an active research area for people with and without disabilities.

Other applications of microprocessors to aid the disabled include their use in wheelchairs to improve control, and electronic mail or specialized telephone equipment to permit the deaf to communicate. Part of the motivation for a revitalized concern for the disabled was the reauthorization by Congress in 1986 of the 1973 Rehabilitation Act, with the addition of section 508, "to insure that handicapped individuals may use electronic office equipment with or without special peripherals." The implication is that disabled government employees, including federal, state, and local, should have "access to the same databases, operating systems, and applications programs as anyone else in his or her department." [32]

In the several years since the passage of the ADA, expected resistance from employers has not materialized, even though the Act was necessarily accompanied with bureaucratic apparatus to ensure compliance. For example, within the federal government itself, the General Services Administration has prepared a detailed document to help managers, especially those involved in information processing, to fulfill their responsibilities under the Act: [33]

> People with limitations of vision, hearing, or mobility are ensured full access and integration to information resources at a level equivalent to people without disabilities when automated information environments offer the flexibility they need. This flexibility can be achieved in most information environments through off the shelf "drop in" or "add on" hardware and software enhancements that modify the common keyboard input and monitor output interactions familiar to most computer users. When a common keyboard requires too much dexterity, coordination or effort from an individual, it can be replaced or enhanced so that less effort is required. In addition to being more user responsive, this input capability may also offer portability, speech input, or a wireless connection to the computer. If a person can not use a monitor without undue effort and visual strain, the display contents are magnified or replaced with synthesized speech.

This document provides detailed requirements for accommodating users with visual, hearing, and mobility impairments. As for the private sector, a report studying the efforts of that retail giant Sears Roebuck and Co. is quite revealing. [34] This report involved an examination of employment practices at Sears prior to the ADA and after, as well as employee interviews. The following are the key findings of this study that probably go beyond the experiences discovered at Sears and that offer considerable hope for the disabled of the United States and elsewhere as well: [35]

(1) The impact of the ADA on American business is evolutionary, not revolutionary.

(2) Universal design and access, not retrofitted technology, fulfill the objective of including people with and without disabilities into productive work force participation.

(3) Efforts to educate management and the work force about the ADA and the capabilities of people with disabilities must be based on facts, not paternalism and myths.

(4) Starting from a base of ADA compliance, companies can look beyond compliance to transcendence by fostering independence, not handouts and dependence, and by providing meaningful career opportunities for people with disabilities.

(5) Far from creating onerous legal burdens, the ADA can provide employers and employees with a framework for dispute avoidance and resolution, not the explosion of litigation that some observers predicted.

One very significant example of the power of the computer to increase independence, and even productivity, is Stephen W. Hawking, the world famous Cambridge physicist, who suffers from amyotropic lateral sclerosis. Also known as Lou Gehrig's disease, it is a progressive motor neuron disorder that profoundly affects the muscular system and has forced Hawking into a wheelchair at an early age as well as reduced his speech to unintelligibility and finally silence because of an emergency tracheotomy. By using a computerized speech synthesizer that he controls with a hand switch, he is able to produce speech, albeit with an American accent.[36]

Access to Libraries

Libraries have long taken a leading rule in providing access to a wide range of information resources for the disabled. Access to the Internet has become yet one more service that libraries are expected to provide and this responsibility translates into appropriate computers and interfaces. As mentioned, it is now quite common to encounter magnified letters on computer screens, oversized keyboards, and raised platforms to accommodate wheelchairs. Other technological aids, or assistive technologies, are voice interfaces and Braille displays. Also of concern is the form of the user interface because depending on the nature of the disability, users may or may not be comfortable with graphics or text or sound. Courtney Deines-Jones recommends a few general guidelines to help library patrons with various disabilities to effectively employ the available technology:[37] "whenever possible" use "both textual and graphical interfaces," "usually, accommodations for people with cognitive disabilities parallel those for patrons with visual impairments," and provide "clear models of [Internet] search strategies, printed in large type and kept near the work stations."

A Very Personal Computer

The first cardiac pacemaker was implanted in a human in 1958, in Sweden, and the second a year later in the United States. These early devices emitted pulses in a fixed, regular pattern to overcome the condition known as heart block, in which the body's method for stimulating the heart operates intermittently. Unfortunately, this fixed-rate system of stimulation could occasionally cause the heart to beat too rapidly (tachycardia), resulting in death. Advances in design resulted in pacemakers that operated only on demand, when the body's natural stimulation failed. Eventually, pacemaker technology benefited from developments in microelectronics, and programmable microprocessors are currently being implanted. Physicians can vary such features as sensor-amplifier sensitivity, energy output per pulse, pulse width, pulse frequency, and delay between chamber pulses. In addition, system diagnostics are available over telephone lines to permit doctors to check the behavior of the pacemaker. Another innovation is a pacemaker that adjusts its rate in response to the patient's physical activity. One model determines this activity by measuring body motion and another is triggered by changes in blood temperature.[38]

There is a heart disorder called fibrillation, in which the heart suddenly goes into a chaotic state that restricts or stops circulation and can lead to death within a few minutes. Since action must be taken quickly, implantable defibrillators could save many lives by automatically detecting the onset of an attack. One current drawback is that they must be implanted during open-chest surgery, a traumatic and expensive operation. Under test is a procedure for implanting the electrodes into the heart transvenously, similarly to the way pacemaker leads are implanted.[39] In July 1995, an atrial defibrillator was tested for the first time, as part of a national clinical trial. The device was being tested for "functionality, programmability, and data collection."[40] The next important step under investigation would be a single device to combine a pacemaker, a device to control arrhythmia, or irregular beat, and a defibrillator. A recent survey of pacemaker developments predicts improvement in the analysis of arrhythmia, "based on greater circuit sophistication and the ability to link information from the atrial and ventricular leads into an independent determination of rate from an artificial sensor."[41]

The next decade holds much promise as the computational power of microprocessors increases. For example it is expected that soon five channels of information will be available to pacemakers, or to use a more general term, implantable cardiac devices; these sources of information are "atrium, ventricle, two artificial sensors and an antitachycardia sensing channel specifically for the detection of tachycardia." By the end of this century, pacemakers will have five channels to deliver shocks to stimulate the heart in various regions and for various purposes.

MEDICINE AND THE INTERNET

> The use of telecommunications to deliver health services has the potential to reduce costs, improve quality, and improve access to care in rural and other underserved areas of the country.[42]

The Internet has begun to have an impact on the practice of medicine and more is promised as one of the major payoffs of the Information Highway. The transmission of records, including medical images is a fact of life and has permitted doctors to share knowledge and experiences over long distances. The term telemedicine has come into use to describe the host of medical services remotely available. Not surprisingly, the growth of telemedicine has been accompanied by a number of problems, both social and legal, including privacy and accuracy of medical records, the licensing of physicians, the efficacy of long-distance treatment, and the allocation of costs. The Internet has also fostered the creation of self-help and advice groups to facilitate the sharing of medical information among patients and relatives of patients. Of course doctors and other health practitioners have found the Internet to be an invaluable resource as well.

Telemedicine

From a report by the now-defunct Office of Technology Assessment, "Telemedicine can be broadly defined as the use of information technology to deliver medical services and information from one location to another." [43] It is clear that the quality of medical care is not uniformly distributed across most countries or even within countries because of lack of expertise, lack of economic resources, and lack of political will. There is now a general belief that the use of information technology, especially communications technology as manifested in the Internet, provides the means to deliver high quality medical care to those regions previously ill-served. Thus telemedicine has the promise to reduce costs of medical delivery, to increase general access, and to improve the quality of care. But some issues must be resolved if the benefits of the widespread diffusion of telemedicine are to be realized. Therefore, consider the following issues:[44]

Reimbursement for Services
A critical issue for telemedicine is whether and how it will be reimbursed by Medicare/Medicaid and other third-party payers. In rural areas, up to 40 percent of physicians' patient base consists of Medicare/Medicaid patients. As one congressman testified at a 1994 hearing on rural health care:

Telemedicine is particularly important to rural health delivery systems . . . However, without the assurance of payment for telemedicine services, the full potential of telemedical technology will never be realized . . . This administrative roadblock prevents the development and expansion of these systems in rural America.

Lack of Research/Experience
Another barrier to telemedicine is the lack of research demonstrating its safety and efficacy, clinical utility, and cost-effectiveness. This is a problem for potential users, payers, and policy-makers. No one knows for certain which medical conditions are best suited to the use of telemedicine . . . Early experiments in telemedicine were terminated before they produced answers concerning its cost, impact on access, and effects on quality of care. Those projects did not end because they failed to achieve their objectives. Instead, the reasons included:
   1) lack of familiarity and limited experience with the systems,
   2) lack of institutional commitments to sustain them when outside funding ran out,
   3) lack of incentives for physicians to use the systems,
   4) limitations of the technology, and
   5) poor system planning and design.

Telecommunications Infrastructure

The technology exists to provide a wide variety of telemedicine services over regular telephone lines. In many rural areas, however, the telecommunications infrastructure does not provide a medical facility with sufficient bandwidth to carry the necessary signals for interactive video teleconsultations . . . Delivering health care to the home is increasingly important for people who need convalescent or chronic care. A public network that can provide two-way video, high speed data transfer, and graphics is required before a wide range of health services can be delivered directly to the home.

Legal/Regulatory

Remote diagnosis and treatment across state lines could bring differing laws and regulations into conflict. Telemedicine raises a number of legal issues related to privacy/confidentiality, licensing and credentialing, and liability that could represent significant barriers to its broader diffusion.

- *Privacy and Confidentiality*
  — Privacy in health care information has been protected in two ways: 1) in the historical ethical obligations of the health care provider to maintain the confidentiality of medical information, and 2) in a legal right to privacy, both generally and specifically, in health information.
  — Confidentiality involves control over who has access to information.

- *Physician Licensing*
  Physicians must be licensed by the states in which they practice. Telecommunication facilitates consultations without respect to state borders and could conceivably require consultants to be licensed in a number of states. This would be impractical and is likely to constrain the broader diffusion of telemedicine programs. In July 1994, the State of Kansas passed legislation requiring that out-of-state physicians who provide consultations using telemedicine be licensed in Kansas. The licensing problem for telemedicine could be addressed by the implementation of national licensing standards or the classification of physicians practicing telemedicine as consulting physicians, thereby circumventing state rules. For a start, such a national license could be provided to physicians who provide consultations to *underserved* populations.

- *Liability*
  The liability implications of telemedicine are unclear. At least two aspects of telemedicine could pose liability problems. One is the fact that, in a remote consultation, the specialist does not perform a hands-on examination, which could be regarded as delivering less than adequate care. The second aspect is that the use of compressed video, in which repetitious information is eliminated as the data are converted from analog to digital and back, may raise the issue of diagnosing with less than complete information. On the other hand, telemedicine may, in fact, decrease the threat of malpractice suits by providing better record keeping and databases, and the fact that taping the consultations will automatically provide proof of the encounter. Tapes could also help to prove the innocence of providers who are falsely accused.

This degree of detail is necessary to illustrate that what appears to be an obviously worthwhile and effective technological solution to a pressing need may be accompanied by a host of problems, some relatively easy to solve and some very difficult. Interestingly, most of the problems are not technical in nature. Most studies of telemedicine have recognized these problems and have called for cooperation among state and federal agencies, and professional organizations. Thus a report issued by the Western Governors' Association recognized six barriers to the successful implementation of telemedicine:[45] Infrastructure Planning and Development, Telecommunications Regulation, Reimbursement for Telemedicine Services, Licensure and Credentialing, Medical Malpractice Liability, and Confidentiality. To provide a flavor of the kind of steps necessary to make telemedicine a commonly available medium for health care delivery, consider the recommended actions to deal with the licensure barrier.

It is recommended that a broadly-based task force be established to draw up a "Uniform State Code for Telemedicine Licensure and Credentialing (similar in principle to the Uniform Commercial Code)."[46] This task force would have to be concerned with a variety of licensing issues such as licensing of doctors to practice telemedicine, the licensing of the networks themselves with respect to their adequacy, and reciprocity issues for interstate licensing. Those advocating a more rapid adoption of telemedicine argue that these barriers must be overcome so that people living in rural areas, especially, will be able to benefit from improved medical care. Furthermore, health care professionals will be in much closer and effective contact with their colleagues, thus alleviating concern with isolation and lack of familiarity with current medical theory and practice.

Other Internet Issues

Virtual Environments

One area of online medical technology not usually included under the term telemedicine involves the use of virtual environments in health care applications. Virtual reality was discussed earlier but for the present purposes, the following definition of virtual environments is necessary:[47] "interactive, virtual image displays enhanced by special processing and by nonvisual display modalities, such as auditory and haptic, to convince users that they are immersed in a synthetic space." More simply put, computer hardware and software are used to simulate a 3D world that can be effectively navigated and manipulated employing vision and touch-sensitive feedback. Some examples of the applications of virtual environments are given as follows:[48]

- Remote surgery. A surgeon, operating in a virtual environment, will cause a robot arm located elsewhere to operate on a patient. This technology does not yet exist.
- Surgeons can manipulate instruments inserted through a tube into a patient while viewing a television monitor showing a picture produced by a miniature television camera at the internal site.
- For educational purposes, a virtual environment can be created that permits students to simulate medical procedures such as inserting a balloon catheter into the heart.
- "Virtual environments are also used to reduce phobias, to develop skills, and to train those with disabilities. One example of the use of virtual environments for training is a program that substitutes virtual bus rides for the real thing so that disabled individuals can learn to use a public transportation system."

Family Medicine Online

This example is just one of many online discussion groups in the area of medicine ranging from self-help groups to professional societies. This group, Fam-Med, is concerned with "the use of computer and telecommunication technology in the teaching and practice of Family Medicine."[49] Family physicians who practice in all regions of the world are very much in need of contact with their counterparts to share ideas, receive technical and moral support, and remain as close to the current state of knowledge as possible. Information is shared not just among family physicians but among physicians and other primary care providers. In addition to electronic discussion groups, there are file archives, a gopher server, and a structured collection of useful Web links. Discussion groups are moderated and unmoderated, with the virtues and drawbacks of both forms of communication. Family physicians require large amounts of diverse information, given that their practice covers many medical subdisciplines. Thus the Internet serves a very important function both in connecting physicians over long distances and in providing them with quick access to relevant information.

SOCIAL ISSUES

> In the evolving information infrastructure, there may be a unique role for the federal government to play to assure that CHI [Consumer Health Information] "systems" are not used as tools to breach issues of patient confidentiality and privacy. The public should be able to access CHI in completely anonymous (e.g., at home or privately in libraries) or confidential (clinical practice settings) ways.[50]

Perhaps the most serious charge against the use of computers in medical care, or in the health delivery system, is that they tend to dehumanize the patient-physician relationship. This argument suggests that doctors will shunt patients towards computers to increase their income by treating more patients. For the foreseeable future, computers will not be treating people directly; they will be an adjunct to doctors, complementing their knowledge. But what about large information systems, in which the patient is just a record to be scanned, modified and, of course, billed. It is certainly possible for patients to be treated in a dehumanizing way in a large medical center. The question is whether or not the use of computers aggravates this situation. Critics of computers in medical care argue that by their very nature the machines, and the organizational structure in which they are embedded, tend to centralize control, diminish individual responsibility, and inevitably will decrease the human quality in the relationship. On the other hand, information systems that assume much of the routine clerical work in hospitals and offices should free conscientious physicians to spend more time with their patients.

Hardly anyone could disagree with the important applications made feasible by computers in body imagery, education, and devices for the disabled. Surely the ability to diagnose internal problems by relatively noninvasive means is an incalculable benefit. But even here, the haste with which hospitals rushed to acquire million-dollar machines made many uncomfortable. The motivation seemed to be a concern with status and prestige rather than the therapeutic benefits. CAT scanners seemed to typify a large-machine mentality at the heart of the US medical system. It was easier to purchase a large machine than to provide preventive medical care for the less fortunate members of the community. In the case of microprocessor-based equipment for the disabled, there should be no argument against the significant and beneficial changes made in the lives of such people. However, there seems to be an imbalance in that relatively large amounts of money have been made available for treatment and equipment for a relatively few individuals. On the other side it is argued that costs are high in the initial experimental phases, but in the long run many will benefit.

Let us explore these issues a bit further, given their importance and impact on the health care of the American public. Two obvious questions are how much technology has improved the overall level of health care and how much does medical technology contribute to the rising costs of health care? These are both very complex questions and no ready answers are available, but a study in 1994 sponsored by the Health Care Technology Institute (HCTI), financed by the Health Industry Manufacturers, reports the following:[51] "medical technologies—medical devices, pharmaceuticals, and medical procedures—contribute between 11 percent and 15 percent of the annual increase in US health care costs. General inflation, which has afflicted health care like a plague, accounts for half of the annual increase; 20 percent is due to health services price increases that exceed general inflation; and 10 percent is due to population growth." Although, the HCTI is obviously interested in promoting the increased use of medical technology, the study has not received critical comment.

Genetic Testing

One area of medical technology that has not been mentioned yet is genetic testing. The information derived from performing a wide range of genetic tests has considerable impact that affects individuals and society in many ways. For example consider the following issues associated with genetic testing reported in a recent study:[52]

- They have the ability to predict risks of future disease. Seldom however, does the predictability approach certainty.
- Often no independent test is available to confirm the prediction of a genetic test; only the appearance of the disease itself confirms the prediction.
- The results may confront prospective parents with options regarding reproduction, including, artificial insemination, prenatal diagnosis, termination of pregnancy, in utero treatment, or cesarean section instead of vaginal delivery.
- The results provide genetic information relevant to the future health of relatives.
- For many genetic disorders, no interventions are yet available to cure, prevent or ameliorate future disease. For some others, the interventions that are being tried have not yet been demonstrated to be safe and effective.
- People identified as at risk of disease may experience psychological distress, discrimination and stigmatization.
- Because the frequencies of disease related alleles differ between ethnic groups, the appropriateness of many tests, and the interpretation of the results, is influenced by the ethnicity of the person being tested.
- Most health care providers have received little training in genetics.

- The number of medical geneticists and genetic counselors to whom patients can be referred is likely to remain too small to cope with the potential volume of testing.

As more and more genetic information is accumulated, the potential for beneficial uses as well as misuses mounts. This rather simplistic observation has not been lost on the scientific community. Indeed, about 3% to 5% of the funding for the Human Genome Project is directed towards "identifying and addressing ethical issues arising from genetic research."[53] Three important concerns are privacy, autonomy, and the welfare of both the individuals and families involved.

Privacy of Medical Records

Particularly crucial is the question of privacy and confidentiality—how to guarantee the protection of medical records while permitting necessary access, especially when records are accessible over communication networks. The issue of privacy will be discussed at greater length in Chapter 9, but for the present it is important, at the very least, to recognize that care must be paid to medical records because of the very special kind of information they contain and because so many health care professionals and others have arguably well-identified needs. But there are many others who have apparent needs to access medical records as part of a process to construct a detailed profile of targeted individuals:[54]

> An unregulated market currently exists for the sale of personal information from public and private sources. Companies that sell personal data need not ask the permission from individuals in advance. This can create financial incentives for both members of a medical organization and outsiders to increase their income by disclosing personal information. In addition to the unregulated computerization and potential brokering of health care information, demands for such information stem from a variety of sources, such as peer-review committees, third-party payers, employers, insurers and others who use the information for non-health purposes. Through unauthorized interception, fundamentally private information may be disseminated into the public arena with devastating consequences. Health care information can influence decisions about an individual's access to credit, admission to academic institutions, and his or her ability to secure employment and insurance.

The fundamental question to be addressed is whether or not computers will improve the health delivery system both in terms of the quality of the care itself and the numbers of people involved: "The reliance on technology to solve what is essentially a complex social issue is not peculiar to medicine. Failure to recognize the interplay of social forces underlying a problem makes for inappropriate and wasteful uses of scarce resources."[55] Surely, many people have been helped and will be helped by medical technology, but will society as a whole be improved? Another way to focus on the use of computers in medical care is to ask if money spent on computers might better be spent on nurses. Are large amounts of money being used to help a relatively small number of people with expensive technology, to the detriment of the health care services available to many others? Given the rising costs of health care, computers are seen by many administrators as a way to control expenditures while maintaining a high level of service. These decisions about the welfare of citizens must be made by society at large. To enable that process, the role and impact of computers in medicine must be regularly monitored and assessed.

A recent study on health care, conducted by the US Council on Competitiveness, surely a hard-nosed, pragmatic organization, is revealing. The final comment of this chapter is taken from the last of a set of eight findings, reported in the Executive Summary of this document: [56]

> There is no "silver bullet" policy or technology that will address or accelerate the changes under way in the health care market. The persistent push of market forces and the increasing availability of new technology are fundamentally reshaping the US health care delivery system. The changes that are occurring and the concerns they are raising are complex and intertwined. While some technologies may hasten certain changes and some policies may provide incentives to adopt them, no single policy or technology can, by itself, successfully address each of them. Cultural adjustments take time to permeate, new technologies take time to penetrate, and proposed policy and regulatory changes must be carefully thought through and reviewed with affected stakeholders before they can be implemented. The transformation under way requires that many steps be taken on many fronts to ensure access to high-quality, cost-effective, patient-centered care.

SUMMARY

The practice of medicine is slowly being affected by the use of computers in record-keeping, diagnosis, treatment, the Internet, and research.

Beyond the direct application of storing patient records, medical information can serve a variety of needs, including medical research. Computer databases, which can be searched more easily than manual ones, can uncover trends and access individual records at a distance. Systems vary in range of functions, ease of use, and ability to accommodate new data processing responsibilities. In medical diagnosis, computers play a vital role in the new area of body imaging, which includes such systems as CAT scanners, PET scanners, and NMR systems. Other important computer applications are the automated electronic monitoring of patients and the use of medical robots for teaching purposes.

The linking of computers to communication systems and to physical manipulators has provided new opportunities for disabled people to escape the boundaries of their beds and homes. The Kurzweil Reading Machine helps visually impaired people to access material not available in Braille automatically and quickly. Other aids for people with disabilities are still in the experimental stage. New microprocessor-driven pacemakers are being used to deal with various cardiac problems. In addition, they facilitate long-distance patient monitoring and treatment.

The Internet has begun to be used for experiments in telemedicine—the delivery of health care over long distances. A variety of issues must be dealt with, however, before telemedicine can become more commonplace, such as legal responsibility and cost-sharing.

Some commentators have expressed concern that an increasing use of technology in the medical delivery system will lead to dehumanization of the doctor-patient relationship.

Large expenditures for medical technology have also been criticized as an allocation of resources away from the important needs of preventive care.

NOTES

1. U.S. Congress, Office of Technology Assessment. *Bringing Health Care Online: The Role of Information Technologies,* OTA-ITC-624. (Washington, DC: U.S. Government Printing Office, September 1995), p. 14 Also available at the Web site with URL: <http://www.ota.nap.edu/>.
2. *Ibid.,* p. 30.
3. "DOD's New Health Care System," *SIGBIO Newsletter,* 10 (3) September 1988, p. 81.
4. From "Medical ADP Systems: Defense Achieves Worldwide Deployment of Composite Health Care System," United States General Accounting Office, GAO/AIMD-96-39, April 1996, p. 2. Accessed from the Web page with URL: <http://www.gao.gov/monthly.list/ai96039.pdf> on May 21, 1996.
5. *Ibid.,* pp. 18–19.
6. Joan O' C. Hamilton. "Medicine's New Weapon: Data," *Business Week,* March 27, 1995, pp. 184, 186, 188.
7. U.S. Congress, Office of Technology Assessment. *Identifying Health Technologies That Work: Searching for Evidence,* OTA-H-608 (Washington, DC: U.S. Government Printing Office, September 1994). Available at the Web page with URL: <www.ota.nap.edu/pdf/data/1994/9414.pdf>. Note that the Office of Technology Assessment was terminated in 1995 by Congress. Its archive of reports are now available at this Web site.
8. *Ibid.* See Chapter 1, Summary.
9. *Op cit., Bringing Health Care Online: The Role of Information Technologies.*
10. *Ibid.,* p. 41.
11. U.S. Congress, Office of Technology Assessment. *MEDLARS and Health Information Policy,* OTA-TM-H-11 (Washington, DC: U.S. Government Printing Office, September 1982).
12. The National Public Library. Available at the Web page with URL: <http://www.nlm.nih.gov/publications/factsheets/nlm.html>.
13. " 'Internet Grateful Med' Goes on the World Wide Web," accessed from the Web page with URL: <http://www.nlm.nih.gov/new_noteworthy/press_releases/igmpr.html> on April 8, 1996.
14. *Ibid.*
15. *Op cit., Identifying Health Technologies That Work, Chapter 1.*
16. Richard Gordon, Gabor T. Herman, and Steven A. Johnson. "Image Reconstruction from Projections," *Scientific American,* October 1975, pp. 56–61, 64–68.
17. "What You Should Know About Magnetic Resonance Imaging," The Magnetic Resonance Imaging Center, The University of Iowa Hospitals and Clinics. August 28, 1995. Accessed at the Web page with URL: <http://vh.radiology.uiowa.edu/Patients/PatientDept/RadiologyBrochures/MR/MRI.WhatYouShouldKnow.html> on June 10, 1996.
18. "PET Impact on Medicare Costs and PET Impact on Non-Medicare Costs," Institute for Clinical PET, 1996. Available at the Web page with URL: <http://www.icppet.org/ImpactStudies.html>.
19. Laura van Dam. "New Medical Images," *Technology Review,* July 1996. Accessed from the Web page with URL: <http://web.mit.edu/afs/athena/org/t/techreview/www/articles/july96/reporter.html> on August 25, 1996.

20. William J. Dallas. "A Digital Prescription for X-Ray Overload," *IEEE Spectrum*, April 1990, pp. 33–36.

21. *Ibid.*, p. 33.

22. Robert B. Lufkin and Anne Scheck. "Fasten Your Seatbelt: MRI in For A Wild Ride, *Diagnostic Imaging*, 1996. Accessed from the Web page with URL: <http://www.dimag.com/feature.htm> on June 5, 1996.

23. Bruce G. Buchanan and Edward H. Shortliffe (eds.). *Rule-Based Expert Systems: The MYCIN Experiments of the Stanford Heuristic Programming Project.* (Reading, MA: AddisonWesley, 1984).

24. John A. Adam. "Medical Electronics," *IEEE Spectrum*, January 1996, pp. 92–95.

25. "Technology-Related Assistance for Individuals with Disabilities Act of 1988 as Amended in 1994," Public Laws 110–407 and 103–218, Section 2. Findings and Purposes. Available at the Web page with URL: <http://www.gsa.gov/coca/tech_act.htm>.

26. "Only Half of Persons with a Severe Disability Have Private Health Insurance, . . ." press release, Census Bureau, January 28, 1994. Accessed from the Web page with URL: <http://gopher.census.gov:70/0/Bureau/Pr/Date/cb94-13.txt> on June 10, 1996.

27. Albert M. Cook and Susan M. Hussey. *Assistive Technologies: Principles and Practice.* (St. Louis, MO: Mosby-Year Book, Inc., Date Unknown). Available at the Web page with URL: <http://www.asel.udel.edu/at-online/publications/chapter.html>.

28. Gislin Dagnelie and Robert W. Massof. "Toward an Artificial Eye," *IEEE Spectrum*, May 1996, pp. 20–29.

29. *Ibid.*, p. 28.

30. John A. Adam. "Medical Electronics," *IEEE Spectrum*, May 1996, p. 93.

31. Ian Litterick. "Computers and Speech," to appear as a chapter in *Computer Support for Adult Dyslexics* to be published by Dyslexia Computer Resource Centre in 1996. Accessed from the Web page with URL: <http://www.dyslexic.com/overview.html> on June 10, 1996.

32. Susan Kerr. "For People with Handicaps, Computers = Independence," *Datamation*, May 1, 1988, pp. 39–40, 42, 44.

33. "Managing Information Resources for Accessibility," Center for Information Technology Accommodation (CITA) of the Information Technology Service, General Services Administration (GSA). December 1995. Available at the Web site with URL: <http://www.gsa.gov/coca/front.htm>.

34. Peter David Blanck. "Communicating the Americans with Disabilities Act, Transcending Compliance: A Case Report on Sears, Roebuck, and Co." (Washington, DC: The Annenberg Washington Program in Communications Policy Studies of Northwestern University, 1994). Available at the Web site with URL: <http://www.annenberg.nwu.edu/pubs/sears/sears1.htm>.

35. *Ibid.*

36. Peter H. Lewis. "A Great Equalizer for the Disabled," *The New York Times, Education Life*, November 6, 1988, pp. EDUC 61, 63.

37. Courtney Deines-Jones. "Access to Library Internet Services for Patrons with Disabilities: Pragmatic Considerations for Developers," *Information Technologies and Disabilities*, Vol. 2, Num. 4, 1995. Also available at the Web site with URL: <http://www.rit.edu/~easi/itd/itdv02n4/article5.html>.

38. Elizabeth Corcoran. "Medical Electronics," *IEEE Spectrum*, January 1987, pp. 66–68.

39. Karen Fitzgerald. "Medical Electronics," *IEEE Spectrum*, January 1989, pp. 67–69.

40. "Atrial Defibrillator Tested for the First Time in Milwaukee," Doctor's Guide to the Internet, July 28, 1995. Accessed from the Web page with URL: <http://www.pslgroup.com/dg950731.htm> on June 6, 1996.

41. Seymour Furman. "A Brief History of Cardiac Stimulation and Electrophysiology—The Past Fifty Years and the Next Century," from Keynote Address at NASPE (the North American Society of Pacing and Electrophysiology) 1995. Available at the Web site with URL: <http://webaxis.com/heartweb/history3.htm>.

42. *Op cit., Bringing Health Care Online,* p. 161.

43. *Ibid., Bringing Health Care Online,* p. 159.

44. *Ibid.,* pp. 177–184.

45. "The Western Governors' Association Telemedicine Action Report," 1995. Accessed from the Web page with URL: <http://www.arentfox.com/telemed.western.html> on May 30, 1996.

46. *Ibid.*

47. Judi Moline. "Virtual Environments in Health Care, a White Paper for the Advanced Technology Program of the National Institute of Standards and Technology," October 1995. Also available at the Web page with URL: <http://nii.nist.gov/virt_env_doc/>.

48. *Ibid.*

49. "Fam-Med, An Internet Resource and Discussion Group on Infrmation Technology in Family Medicine," June 27, 1995. Accessed from the Web page with URL: <http://apollo.gac.edu/> on June 5, 1996.

50. Kevin Patrick and Shannah Koss. "Consumer Health Information White Paper," Health Information and Application Working Group, Committee on Applications and Technology, Information Infrastructure Task Force, May 15, 1995. Accessed from the Web page with URL: <http://nii.nist.gov/chi.html> on June 4, 1996.

51. William Hoffman."Taking the Pulse of Medical Technology," *Minnesota Medicine,* November 1994. Accessed from the Web page with URL: <http://pro.med.umn.edu/bme/bme_article1.html> on June 10, 1996.

52. "Interim Principles Task Force on Genetic Testing," NIH-DOE Working Group on Ethical, Legal, and Social Implications of Human Genome Research, March 1996. Available on the Web site with URL: <http://infonet.welch.jhu.edu/policy/genetics/>.

53. "Five Years of Progress in the Human Genome Project," *Human Genome News,* 7 (3–4), September-December, 1995. Available at the Web page with URL: <http://www.ornl.gov/TechResources/Human_Genome/publicat/hgn/v7n3/04progre.html#els>.

54. Sonya Savkar and Robert J. Waters. "Telemedicine—Implications for Patient Confidentiality and Privacy," *Health Information Systems and Telemedicine,* 1995. Accessed from the Web page with URL: <http://www.arentfox.com/telemed.5.html#article.2> on June 1, 1996.

55. Abbe A. Mowshowitz. *The Conquest of Will: Information Processing in Human Affairs.* (Reading, MA: Addison-Wesley, 1976), p. 140.

56. "Highway to Health: Transforming U.S. Health care in the Information Age." (Washington, DC: Council on Competiveness, March 1996). Also available at the Web site with URL: <http://nii.nist.gov/coc_hghwy_to_hlth/title_page.html>.

ADDITIONAL READINGS

Medical Information Systems

Bennahum, David. "Docs for Docs," *Wired,* March 1995, pp. 100, 102, 104.

Garner, Rochelle. "A Medical Moon Shot?" *Computerworld,* April 10, 1995, pp. 78–79, 80.

Grossman, Jerome H. "Plugged-In Medicine." *Technology Review,* January 1994, pp. 22–29.

Kennedy, Maggie. "Integration Fever." *Computerworld,* April 3, 1995, pp. 81, 84–85.

Kolata, Gina. "New Frontier in Research: Mining Patient Record," *The New York Times,* August 9, 1994, p. A 10.

Wallace, Scott. "The Computerized Patient Record," *Byte,* May 1994, pp. 67–68, 70, 72, 74, 76.

Medical Applications

Blanck, Peter David. "Celebrating Communications Technology for Everyone," *Federal Communications Law Journal,* Vol. 47, Num. 2, December 1994. Also available on the Web page with URL: <http://www.law.indiana.edu/fclj/v47/no2/blanck.html>.

"Magnetic Resonance Imaging FAQs," FONAR, Melville, NY, March 5, 1996. Accessed from the Web page with URL: < http://www.fonar.com/faq.html> on June 10, 1996.

Computers and the Disabled

Adam, John A. "Technology Combats Disabilities," *IEEE Spectrum,* October 1994, pp. 24–26.

Kobetic, Rudi. "Advancing Step by Step," *IEEE Spectrum,* October 1994, pp. 27–31.

Norman, Richard A., Maynard, Edwin M., Guillory, K. Shane, Warren, David J. "Cortical Implants for the Blind," *IEEE Spectrum,* May 1996, pp. 54–59.

Stipp, David. "New Hope for the Heart," *Fortune,* June 24, 1996, pp. 108–112.

Wyatt, John and Rizzo, Joseph. "Ocular Implants for the Blind," *IEEE Spectrum,* May 1996, pp. 47–53.

Medicine and the Internet

Assi, Mona and Kim, Rebecca. "Oklahoma Telemedicine Network: A Case Study of Telemedicine," 1995. Available at the Web Site with URL: <nii.nist.gov/pubs_list_and_abstract.html>.

Fisher, Lawrence M. "Health on Line: Doctor Is In, and His Disk Is Full," *The New York Times,* June 24, 1996, pp. C 1, C 8.

Gross, Neil. "Seasick in Cyberspace," *Business Week,* July 10, 1995, pp. 110–111.

Patrick, Kevin and Koss, Shannah. "Consumer Health Information 'White Paper'," Information Infrastructure Task Force, Working Draft, May 1995. Available at the Web site with URL: <http://nii.nist.gov/chi.html>.

Social Issues

"A Survey of the Future of Medicine," *The Economist,* March 19, 1994, pp. 1–18.

"Avoiding the Crisis: Protecting the Confidentiality of Patient Data in a Healthcare Information Network Environment," Gordon & Glickson P.C., 1995. Accessed from the Web page with URL: <http://www.ggtech.com/pdf/96032.pdf> on May 25, 1996.

Magnusson, Paul. "Give Medicare a Shot of Managed Care," *Business Week,* June 24, 1996, p. 122.

Symonds, William C. "Whither a Health-Care Solution? Oh, Canada," *Business Week,* March 21, 1994, pp. 82–83, 85.

— 6 —

COMPUTERS AND EDUCATION

. . . [A]lthough new interactive technologies cannot alone solve the problems of American education, they have already contributed to important improvements in learning. These tools can play an even greater role in advancing the substance and process of education, both by helping children acquire basic skills and by endowing them with more sophisticated skills so that they can acquire and apply knowledge over their lifetimes.

US Congress Office of Technology Assessment, *Power On! New Tools for Teaching and Learning,* 1988.

INTRODUCTION

In 1866, the blackboard was hailed as a revolutionary device certain to have a significant impact on the educational process. Since then, "revolutionary" changes have appeared more frequently: radio in the 1920s, film in the 1930s and 1940s, language laboratories and television in the 1950s, the computer beginning in the 1960s, and in the mid-1990s, the Internet and the World Wide Web. Claims for the last two have been mounting ever since. Computers and the Internet will allow students to learn at their own pace. They will not be judgmental, impatient, or unsympathetic. Appearance, social class, and race are irrelevant.[1] The teacher will be free to devote quality time to those with real need while others acquire information, review material, take tests, or even play games. The computer will keep track of the student's progress, produce grades and averages, suggest additional material, and alert the teacher to any potential or actual problem. More and more material will be made available on an ever-increasing number of subjects on the Web. The computer itself and the Web will excite students, igniting their native curiosity and natural desire to learn. New programming languages and systems will appear, opening up innovative and challenging environments. In short, it is claimed, teaching and learning will never be the same.

The growth in the number of computers in use in the schools during the 1980s has been significant. From 1981 to 1987, the percentage of schools with at least one computer grew as follows: elementary schools, from 10% to 95%, junior high schools, from 25% to 97%, senior high schools, from 43% to 98%.[2] The total number of computers in public schools rose from 250,000 in 1983, to 2.4 million in 1989, to 3.5 million in 1992.[3] There is, however, considerable variance in these figures, ranging from wealthy private schools to poor inner city ones and from old technology to more recent models. Thus as of 1992, almost

50% of all computers in schools were (really) old (8-bit) machines—mainly Apple II+, IIc, and IIe's—and only 22% were relatively up-to-date—such as Macintoshes and IBM ATs 80286, 386, and 486—although none of these computers are in wide use today.[4]

The most recent surveys about student computer use in school and at home are from the Bureau of the Census, reporting 1993 data in early 1995. For purposes of comparison, data from 1984 and 1989 are also included. Among the highlights are the following:[5]

- In 1993, more than two-thirds of all students in grades 1–12 used a computer either at home or at school, with a majority, 66 percent, using a computer at school.
- The percentage of students in grades 1–12 using a computer at school more than doubled between 1984 and 1993, increasing from 31 to 66 percent. Twenty-seven percent of students used a computer at home in 1993, up from 13 percent in 1984.
- Whites were more likely than blacks or Hispanics to use a computer either at home or at school, both in grades 1–6 and in grades 7–12. In 1993, approximately 40 percent of blacks and Hispanics in grades 1–6 did not use computers at all compared to 20 percent of their white counterparts.
- Between 1984 and 1993, the proportions of students in grades 7–12 who used a computer either at home or at school increased at similar levels across family income. On one hand, the gain for low income students can be explained primarily by their increased use of computers at school, which rose 32 percentage points; on the other, the gain for high income students can be explained by their increased use of computers at school, which rose 30 percentage points, and at home, which rose 29 percentage points.

Clearly, the number of computers has been increasing over the years and more and more students have been using them both at school and at home. It remains to explore how much time students spend at the computer; that is, how integrated computer use is into the curriculum at large, how effective computers are in the education process (a very difficult question to answer), and how newer technologies, such as connection to the Internet are being used.

There are probably more than four million computers in use in schools today, a mixture of dated and newer technologies, but based on 1992 data, average weekly use in elementary schools is about one and three quarter hours, increasing to about two hours in middle schools, and reaching about three hours in high schools.[6] What are they doing? It depends when the question is asked because teachers have been given mixed advice about how best to use computers. What still seems to be the case is that time spent learning how to use computers considerably exceeds time spent using computers in traditional academic subjects. More on this later. Consider Table 6.1, produced by Joseph Becker for the Office of Technology Assessment.

As companies rapidly introduce and expand their computer systems, it becomes a matter of survival for employees, including management, to acquire computer skills. In response to such needs a number of institutes and schools, known as "virtual business schools" have appeared to serve this market. Much of the instruction, assignments, and consultation is carried out over a computer network. The result is a flexible, asynchronous system of instruction and communication, an important consideration for busy executives. They can pursue their education at their desks, at home, and in their free time. Though currently expensive, home education over computer networks may be a significant part of future education systems.

TABLE 6.1

Timeline of Changes in the Prevailing Wisdom of "Experts" about How Teachers Should Use Computers in Schools.

	1982
Teachers are told to:	*Teach students to program in BASIC.*
Rationale:	"It's the language that comes with your computer."
	1984
Teachers are told to:	*Teach students to program in LOGO.*
Rationale:	"Teach students to think, not just program."
	1986
Teachers are told to:	*Teach with integrated drill and practice systems.*
Rationale:	"Individualize instruction and increase test scores."
	1988
Teachers are told to:	*Teach word processing.*
Rationale:	"Use computers as tools, like adults do."
	1990
Teachers are told to:	*Teach with curriculum-specific tools (e.g., history databases, science simulators, data probes).*
Rationale:	"Integrate the computers with the existing curriculum."
	1992
Teachers are told to:	*Teach multimedia hypertext programming.*
Rationale:	"Change the curriculum—students learn best by creating products for an audience."
	1994
Teachers are told to:	*Teach with Internet telecommunications.*
Rationale:	"Let students be part of the real world."

Source: From H. J. Becker, "Analysis and Trends of School Use of New Information Technologies," Office of Technology Assessment contractor report, March 1994.[7]

Before engaging in an exploration of the influence of the Internet and the World Wide Web on education, it is worth reviewing past and present attempts to use computers in significant ways as part of the education process. Computer-assisted instruction is a well-known term, but what does it include and how well has it worked? A well-publicized, much acclaimed computer learning environment is provided by the language LOGO. It arose out of research carried out by artificial intelligence researchers. The LOGO environment is supposed to liberate the young from the constraints of traditional educational methods. Although less popular currently, lessons of cooperation and the development of problem solving skills are a LOGO legacy worth considering.

From the elementary school to the university, computers are playing an ever-increasing role both as part of traditional education and as a new focus for investigation. The popularity of the Internet has seemed to present unlimited possibilities for extending and improving education, if only schools can connect, a nontrivial problem given the costs of more sophisticated equipment and more sophisticated expertise. Nevertheless, yet another technology is being hailed as the solution to what ails education and indeed as a necessary next step to prepare students for the information-rich society that awaits them in the twenty-first century.

COMPUTER-ASSISTED INSTRUCTION (CAI)

> Available data suggest that in secondary schools, computers are used relatively infrequently for teaching and learning in traditional academic subjects, far less than in classes focused on teaching students *about* computers.[8]

Any discussion of computers in education in the 1980s is inevitably sprinkled with an alphabet soup of names: CBE, CAI, CAL, and CML. CBE is a very general term standing for computer-based education and includes all the others as subcategories. The basic division is along instructional and noninstructional lines. The major component of noninstructional uses is data processing, including record keeping, inventory control, and attendance and employment records. Some of the noninstructional applications are described as follows:

Computer-Assisted Testing (CAT). The computer is used solely as a testing medium. It is possible to take advantage of the computer's abilities to provide imaginative tests or merely to use it as a substitute for manual testing.

Computer-Assisted Guidance (CAG). The computer is used as an information retrieval system to provide career guidance for graduating students. It does not add to students' skills or knowledge but may encourage them to take certain courses to help with their future career plans.

Computer-Managed Instruction (CMI). The teacher uses the computer to plan a course of study, tailored for the student, that consists of computer sessions, readings, and testings. The computer keeps track of the student's performance and provides regular reports, highlighting problems and accomplishments. (In Great Britain, this application is called computer-managed learning, CML.) In somewhat more detail, CMI is based upon a set of well-defined learning objectives, often tied in with a particular set of textbooks. The computer is used to test mastery of these objectives and provide learning prescriptions for each child based upon individual placement within the objectives. After each prescription is followed, the child is retested and a new set of learning prescriptions is generated based upon the test results.

These applications are useful and important, but the most interesting and potentially far-reaching work is being done in the areas of CAI and CAL (computer-assisted learning). Before launching into a detailed examination of some of the important work in this area, it may be helpful to first present a brief overview. In a historical survey of computer applications in education, Kurland and Kurland define the following phases in the development of educational computing:[9]

CAI Delivery Systems. As computers moved from the office to the classroom, the earliest of the major CAI systems began in 1959. The underlying intellectual foundation was behavioral learning theory, and these systems had the flavor of programmed learning; that is, a bit of new material, a few questions, a review, and then more of the same. The technology was based on large time-sharing systems with centralized software development.

The Micro Invasion and the Decentralization of Computers. The major systems such as PLATO had little market penetration when microcomputers made their appearance in the early 1980s. At first the style of software followed the previous systems but then diversification rapidly took place and new styles emerged.

LOGO and the Emergence of the Computer as a Tool to Think With. The computer and appropriate software to facilitate new ways of thinking was the next development, led by Seymour Papert of the Massachusetts Institute of Technology (MIT). LOGO was first implemented on mainframes and later, in the early 1980s, on microcomputers.

The Computer Literacy Movement—Schools Attempt to Regain Control. The movement was towards awareness of computers (history, components, applications, and some social issues) and computer programming (LOGO, Basic, and Pascal). There was a growing concern, however, with the superficiality of the approach.

The Computer as Tool—Word Processing and Personal Productivity. The emphasis on programming was decreasing and more attention was directed, in the mid-1980s, toward application programs to assist productivity in writing, business, and general education through word processing, databases, and spreadsheets.

Incorporation of Computers into the Mainstream Curriculum. Microcomputer software was being introduced at an enormous rate and two conflicting views were in competition: to strengthen the existing curriculum or to change it in response to the new technology, including video and CD-ROMs, as well as very powerful microcomputers and networks.

Now we can return to a somewhat more leisurely examination of the dimensions and scope of CAI, still a component of computer applications in education.

Varieties of CAI

Simply put, CAI is the use of the computer directly in the instructional process as either a replacement for or complement to books and teachers. CAI has been a factor in education for a long time—since the 1960s at least—as a much-heralded but never quite perfected educational system. Because of the premature introduction of CAI software, many educators have become quite cautious about the claims for such systems. However, with the pervasiveness of microcomputers, the demand to install CAI systems in schools has become overwhelming.

There are several varieties of CAI. In the basic mode of drill and practice, the computer asks a question, receives the answer, and provides an appropriate response. If the student's answer is correct, positive feedback is provided, usually in the form of an affirming comment to the student. If the answer is incorrect but belongs in a class of expected answers, a variety of responses may be selected. Finally, if the answer is incorrect and the system cannot deal with it, it must repeat the original question and supply the answer, or go on to a new but similar question. In the second case, the question may be repeated with an encouraging remark, or a new question is posed based on the student's perceived difficulty. Because the computer can be programmed to keep track of each student's individual performance over a long period of time, at any given session it can work on those areas that need special attention and also boost the student's ego by reinforcing performance in areas of past success. Clearly, drill and practice are helpful when simple facts are to be learned in a structured context. Most available CAI software is of the drill and practice mode, but with considerable variation and ingenuity.

Tutorial systems for CAI are much more complex, since in this context new information is being delivered. At each stage the program can supply some general piece of information, a fact, an example, or a question to test the student's comprehension. As the major purpose of tutorial programs is to teach, they must have some way of determining what the student probably knows, what his or her difficulties are, and how the material can best be presented. In such programs, the knowledge typically is represented in a tree structure, and the presentation involves following the branches exhaustively. By precisely defining a local context, this tree organization helps identify the problems that the student may be having.

There are other aspects of this approach to CAI. For instance, more than one answer to a question may be acceptable, and the program must be prepared to deal appropriately with different responses. Furthermore, it must be able to produce sequences of questions that explore some area in detail, and such sequences may depend on the nature of the intervening questions. Clearly, the preparation, design, and realization of tutorial programs is a complex task, and it is not surprising that the overall quality of such programs could be better. As the material to be presented becomes more difficult, the problem of presenting it also becomes more of a challenge. Tutorial programs are increasingly useful as they allow more flexible input by the student. This input may include the ability to ask limited questions. Once again the influence of artificial intelligence will become increasingly important, as programs become able to communicate more readily with users. In addition to facility in natural language, the more advanced programs will need abilities in problem solving, knowledge representation, and inferencing.

Simulations are useful for studying processes so complex that it is difficult to determine the specific impact of individual variables. For example, suppose we are interested in studying traffic flow at a busy intersection. A computer program can be written to capture the important features of the intersection—the traffic light sequence, and estimates of traffic density in each direction—defined by the average expected occurrence of a vehicle in a given small time interval. How is the backup of traffic related to the arrival rates and the traffic light patterns? To facilitate this investigation, a simulation program will accept values for the input numbers and then display the resulting behavior as it unfolds over time, preferably using graphics. In more advanced applications, students will be able to construct the simulation domain themselves out of a building block set of components, to study not only the system behavior but how well it has been modeled. As the simulation unfolds, the system may ask the student about decisions involved in selecting values and about expectations that the student has about its behavior. Simulations are designed for more than the acquisition of factual knowledge. They encourage students to discover for themselves how something works. They have been used extensively in the physical and biological sciences as a substitute for and supplement to actual laboratory experiments, as well as in the social sciences to model such processes as presidential elections.

As video games established an incredible appeal and excitement outside the educational establishment, it was inevitable that the schools would begin using them to teach children. Games minimize any fears children may have about sitting in front of a terminal. They can be tailored to young children and to teenagers, who are enormously fascinated with them. They are challenging, almost hypnotic, and—if properly handled—can be an open door to most other forms of CAI. Some games can be combined with a question-and-answer feature to reinforce certain concepts. Others can be presented as a kind of puzzle for which the student must figure out the rules. How significant an impact games will have on education is still an open question.

A 1987 survey of the distribution of educational software by type, with 7,325 programs included out of more than 10,000 available, showed that 51% were skills practice, 33% tutorial, 19% educational games, 15% rote skill, and 11% tool programs (for example, word processors and databases).[10] The sum is greater than 100% because some programs have been assigned to more than one category. The more advanced and potentially important applications, such as conceptual demonstration and development, hypothesis testing, and simulation totaled only 17%, with simulation itself at 9%. Thus, it might appear that the major contribution of the computer to education is to facilitate traditional skills practice and rote drill in a flashier style than that provided by traditional textbooks. The software market is quite lucrative and will continue to grow whether effective or not. A survey reported in August 1996, noted that "American schools will spend $738 million on educational software in calendar year 1996, representing a 17.5% increase from 1995, . . . By the year 1999, sales of instructional software to K–12 customers will total $1.14 billion, SIMBA projects."[11]

COMPUTER-ASSISTED LEARNING (CAL)

> . . . some teachers use technology to support more student-centered approaches to instruction, so that students can conduct their own scientific inquiries and engage in collaborative activities while the teacher assumes the role of facilitator or coach. Teachers who fall into the latter group are among the most enthusiastic technology users, because technology is particularly suited to support this kind of instruction.[12]

CAL promotes a vision of the computer as a learning resource and as a stimulus for the imagination of the child, a powerful friend able to follow commands and respond to requests. The major figure in CAL is Seymour Papert, Leg Professor of mathematics and of education at the Massachusetts Institute of Technology. He has made major contributions in cognitive psychology and artificial intelligence. Earlier in his career, he worked with Jean Piaget, the eminent child psychologist. From these experiences have emerged some important ideas on how children might learn by using a computer—an ideal instrument, given its power to stimulate and to be whatever the child desires. The programming language Papert designed permits even young children to do very inventive things.

LOGO: A New Way of Learning?

The development of LOGO (or Logo) emerged from research in three areas: AI, psychology (based on the important work of Jean Piaget), and computer science in general. Seymour Papert and his colleagues at MIT began to put their ideas about education into effect. They are concerned with such issues as helping people (a) to build various computational models as a method of learning, (b) to interact with these models as a means to improve performance, and (c) to develop a sense of wanting to learn how instead of bemoaning one's deficiencies. We can learn in several ways: by being told directly, by reading, by being helped, and by discovering things ourselves. Traditional teaching methods are based on the first two; the LOGO approach is based on the last two, together with the notion of the model, which is derived from research in AI.

It is important in the design of intelligent systems to develop appropriate models of both the problem and the solver. The model of the solver must include a representation of the problem-solving strategy, a representation of the problem domain, a means of evaluating the performance of the solver, and finally a strategy for improving (or in computer talk, debugging) the solver. As systems have been developed within this framework, a new appreciation has been gained—about learning, about the importance of adequate models, and about what a computer language must be able to do to represent problems and provide procedures for solving them.

In the area of education, especially that of children, the principles embodied in the LOGO concept include such important features as ease and simplicity of expression, explicit representation of fundamental programming ideas, and immediate feedback. Programs can be written very simply by children, but this in no way limits the power of these programs. As children grow in sophistication and become more experienced, the language permits them to extend and build on their previous work in a natural way.

Perhaps the most important aspect of LOGO's usefulness has been the immediate response it provides to the student. The most popular LOGO environment is turtle graphics. (LOGO programs can be written to drive music synthesizers and physical mechanical devices also called turtles, but graphics is the most common output form.) The screen may be visualized as a field on which a small, triangular object, a turtle, can move under program control. The turtle can be given a heading, a number of unit steps to take, and directed whether or not to leave a track. (LOGOs designed for different computers may have additional different properties.) By suitably directing the turtle—and this is, of course, what a program does—it can be made to produce a pattern on the screen.

One very important aspect of the use of LOGO in schools is its impact on the social environment. The traditional classroom has one teacher and many learners, and the flow of knowledge is directed from the teacher to the students. In an environment rich in self-discovery, new and interesting possibilities arise. For example, students can help one another learn by sharing individual knowledge, asking interesting questions, and working together in common pursuits. Papert speaks to this issue in *Mindstorms*.[13]

By building LOGO in such a way that structured thinking becomes powerful thinking, we convey a cognitive style one aspect of which is to facilitate talking about the process of thinking. LOGO's emphasis on debugging goes in the same direction. Students' bugs become topics of conversation; as a result they develop an articulate and focused language to use in asking for help when it is needed. And when the need for help can be articulated clearly, the helper does not necessarily have to be a specially trained professional in order to give it. in this way the LOGO culture enriches and facilitates the interaction between all participants and offers opportunities for more articulate, effective, and honest teaching relationships.

The notion of a "LOGO culture" is quite interesting, for it suggests a shared language, common interests, and common goals. This LOGO culture may more properly be spoken of as a subculture of the rapidly growing computer culture, in which children can share ideas and enthusiasms. In the last section, we will look more critically at claims and counterclaims for the supposed virtues of LOGO.

Evaluation of Current Technologies

In late 1995, the RAND Corporation's Critical Technologies Institute (CTI) completed a study of educational technology for the US Department of Education. A report was presented by James Kulik of the University of Michigan, which attempted to evaluate the current state of computer-based instruction by a careful survey of a number of independent studies. Although the studies surveyed employ differing definitions of computer-based instruction and evaluate the success of programs in differing ways, it still seems possible to draw some conclusions about the effectiveness of educational technology. As Professor Kulik states, "At least a dozen meta-analyses have been carried out to answer questions about the effectiveness of computer-based instruction . . . each of the analyses yielded the conclusion that programs of computer-based instruction have a positive record in the evaluation literature."[14] In somewhat more detail, he states:[15]

- Students usually learn more in classes in which they receive computer-based instruction. The analyses produce slightly different estimates of the magnitude of the computer effect, but all the estimates were positive.
- Students learn their lessons in less time with computer-based instruction. The average reduction in instructional time was 34% in 17 studies of college instruction, and 24% in 15 studies of adult education.
- Students also like their classes more when they receive computer help in them.
- Breaking studies of computer-based instruction into conventional categories clarifies the evaluation results. One kind of computer application that usually produces positive results in elementary and high school classes is computer tutoring. Students usually learn more in classes that include computer tutoring. On the other hand, precollege results are unimpressive for several other computer applications: managing, simulations, enrichment, and programming.

Another RAND study suggested more reasons why it is difficult to make definitive statements about the contributions that educational technology can make to the overall learning process. Thus the following comment is quite revealing:[16]

The review that we made of evidence of the effectiveness of educational technology reaffirmed our initial impressions. By traditional evaluation standards, the most satisfying evaluation data are those generated in laboratory or controlled clinical settings using well-specified and implemented treatments and readily measured outcomes. When technology is removed from such settings and becomes more nearly a tool to be used by students and teachers than a treatment in itself, or when the outcomes sought become richer and less precisely measurable, assessment becomes much more difficult and the results less satisfying from a technical point of view.

This study provides evidence that schools with sufficient technological resources can create interesting, challenging, and effective environments. Exactly how effective is difficult to determine as is the cost-effectiveness of the technology. Thus, it is not surprising that definitive statements about educational technology are scarce and detailed recommendations for action are limited in number and scope. Nevertheless, a few of the findings of this study are interesting, seemingly obvious, trivial, and provocative, even suggesting directions for future research:[17]

1. Educational technology has significant potential for improving students' learning.
2. Extensive use of technology in schools has the potential to promote significant school restructuring and expand the time and motivation for student learning.
4. Data from a study by the IEA [International Education Association] in 1992 suggested the availability of technology in schools serving poor, minority, and special needs populations did not appear to lag substantially behind the averages of schools taken as a whole. However, to the extent that technology enables learning outside the school, large disparities in the access of students of different class and ethnicity to technology is a matter of concern.
6. The costs of ubiquitous use of technology are modest in the context of overall budgets for public elementary education but moving to such use requires significant and potentially painful restructuring of budgets.
7. When technology is deeply infused in a school's operations, teachers tend to assume new roles and require new skills. There is a strong consensus among the experts we consulted that neither the initial preparation of teachers nor the current strategies for continued professional development have been effective in developing these skills.

COMPUTER LITERACY AND THE INTERNET

I find television very educational. The minute somebody turns it on, I go to the library and read a good book. (Groucho Marx [1890–1977])

Computer Literacy

The idea that people should be knowledgeable about computers in today's society hardly seems controversial. However, the details of various proposals to implement this idea have aroused some disagreement. The term commonly used to characterize a heightened awareness about computers and their role in society is computer literacy. Comparisons with the notion of general language literacy are unavoidable and frequently misleading.

Various definitions of the term have been proposed, some of which draw parallels to literacy as it refers to language skills and a minimal level of competence in some domain. Ronald Anderson and Daniel Klasson of the Minnesota Education Computing Consortium (MECC) define computer literacy as "whatever understanding, skills, and attributes one needs to function effectively within a given social role that directly or indirectly involves computers."[18] The given social role is meant to encompass general well-being as well as specific achievements.

In the schools, at all levels, the debate continues over the definition, importance, and relevance of computer literacy. Critics are wary of pandering to the newest, flashiest technology. In a delightful parody several years ago, Bill Lacy, the president of Cooper Union, described the repercussions of the introduction of the pencil (later in colors and with eraser) into medieval Europe. Its introduction in schools met with the following responses: "Just because they have a pencil doesn't mean they have a lot of education going on," and "I don't know why my kid needs a pencil to learn French. We *are* French." Evaluating the claims made for computer literacy in the midst of the widespread publicity surrounding computers is not an easy task. Schools are under pressure by parents to provide their children with the best chance for a prosperous life, and that certainly includes computers.

Many universities and colleges are requiring as a condition of graduation that students take at least one course in what is sometimes called computer appreciation. Typically, this course includes an introduction to computer programming; a survey of computer applications, such as a word processor, a spreadsheet, and a database program; a familiarization with a few associated social issues; and more recently, an introduction to the Internet and the World Wide Web. It is felt that every person, to be a functioning and responsible citizen, must be aware of the role of computers in contemporary society. The debate about the usefulness of computers in the curriculum turns on such issues as the intellectual content of computer literacy courses, the benefits of computer programming for the average student, the supposed transferability of computer skills, improved job prospects, and the usefulness of the Internet in schools and later in work. Definitive answers are not yet available, but a number of voices have been raised against the uncritical acceptance of the concept of computer literacy for everyone. Other issues arise at the primary and secondary school level, in relation to computer programming, computer-assisted instruction, and computer games.

Many commentators have argued that for most people, learning to program is neither necessary nor beneficial. The long-term trend is toward sophisticated, user-friendly software such as word-processing and financial planning programs. Programming is not a skill easy to acquire or practice. It is unlikely that very many people, besides professionals and eager hobbyists, will program on their own. Thus, the major aim of the computer literacy movement should not be for every student to learn how to program skillfully.

The primary emphasis in computer literacy should be in the historical, economic, legal, and philosophical areas. Computers must be seen in their historical context—as part of an ongoing technological process. The economic and legal implications of their use are a rich source of material for exploring many important social issues. It would be a mistake to focus on the computer itself, because treating even such a marvelous machine in isolation can result in only superficial understanding. This is a real danger, if computer literacy courses are taught by programmers with little experience in other areas. The pressure to offer such courses may result in ill-conceived projects. Public pressure is a reality, however, and many schools have responded with such courses, and even programs, in computer literacy. The popularity of the Internet has added further fuel to the debate. It is seen by some as a wonderful educational and research tool that increases student access to information beyond that provided by teachers and local libraries. Others see it as a colossal waste of time, a vast melange of flash and glitter, requiring considerable experience and sophistication to be useful. Its potential is unlimited, however, and with careful instruction and discipline it is an invaluable resource and a major addition to the intellectual climate both within and without educational institutions.

Connecting to the Internet

In the fall of 1995, the US Department of Education commissioned a survey to determine "the types of advanced telecommunications equipment and services that are currently available in public schools and the specific locations of the equipment; current computer networking capabilities in public schools; the number of schools that have plans to connect to wide area networks; the formal role groups have in developing telecommunications plans; and the various barriers that limit schools' acquisition or use of advanced telecommunications."[19] This survey included 917 nationally representative schools. Among the findings are the following:[20]

- Fifty percent of US public schools now have access to the Internet . . . This percentage is up from 35 percent just 1 year ago.
- Access to the Internet varies by school characteristics . . . Only 31 percent of schools with large proportions of students from poor families (71 percent or higher eligibility for free or reduced-price lunches) have access to the Internet, compared to 62 percent of schools with relatively few students from poor families (less than 11 percent eligibility). Access is also related to school enrollment size—from 39 percent for schools with fewer than 300 students to 69 percent for schools with 1,000 or more students. Secondary schools (65 percent) are more likely than elementary schools (46 percent) to be linked to the Internet.
- Although half of the nation's public schools already have access to the Internet somewhere in the building and three-fourths of those without access have plans to connect, only 9 percent of all instructional rooms (classrooms, labs, and library media centers) are currently on the Internet . . . This is a three-fold increase compared with fall 1994, when only 3 percent of all instructional rooms had access to the Internet.
- Schools indicate that the school district (63 percent) and teachers and other staff (38 percent) are the two groups most likely to play a large formal role in developing the school's telecommunications program . . . While only 7 percent indicate that parents play a large role, 31 percent cite parents as playing a moderately active role. This is up from 1994, when only 4 percent of public schools indicated that parents played a large role, with 17 percent reporting they played a moderate role . . .
- Of the schools with Internet access [50%], 93 percent have e-mail, 83 percent can access resource location services, 80 percent have World Wide Web access, and 73 percent can

access news groups . . . While e-mail is the most widely available Internet service in schools, a higher proportion of schools with other Internet services make these other services available to students. Seventy percent of schools with World Wide Web access make it available to students, 62 percent of schools with resource location services make it available to students, and students can avail themselves of news group services in 51 percent of the schools with news group access. Only 41 percent of schools with e-mail provide access for students.

This study and others are part of a major campaign to wire America's schools, one of the widely hailed benefits of the Information Highway. In fact, President Clinton has made it a public priority to connect schools, to realize the expected significant improvement in the educational system for all American children, rich and poor, urban and rural, black and white. In June 1995, the National Telecommunications and Information Administration, the White House's chief agency for promoting the National Information Infrastructure (NII), released a report that advocated not just connecting schools but libraries and hospitals as well and has made its presence felt with "Congress, the States, local governments, private industry, public interest groups, and the public institutions themselves."[21] Since January 1994, when Vice President Gore announced the "Administration's commitment to connect every classroom, library, hospital, and clinic in the United States to the NII by the year 2000," the White House has taken every opportunity to argue for its vision. Thus it is no surprise to read the following passages from this report:

> As the transition to a knowledge-based economy accelerates, America's children must have access to communications and information technologies in the classroom. Without these tools, American children will lack the necessary computer skills to compete in the 21st Century. Deploying computers in classrooms and connecting them to the NII will enhance the learning process by providing students and teachers with access to information and teaching materials from around the world. In addition, as a result of the fiscal constraints and rising costs facing public schools, information technologies that offer new opportunities, efficiencies, and improvements in the education process are highly desirable.[22]

> By connecting public institutions to the NII, traditionally unserved and underserved groups, including the poor, ethnic and racial minorities, rural Americans, and disabled individuals, will have greater opportunities to access and benefit from the NII. To accelerate strategic development of the NII and to ensure widespread civic participation, the Administration has created shared-funding programs and has encouraged public-private partnerships.[23]

The commitment to connection will not be cheap however, even if some cable and telephone companies follow through on their promises to install telecommunication services at low or even no cost. One estimate provides a one-time capital connect cost of "$9.4B–$22.05B . . . with annual maintenance costs of $1.8B–$4.6B. At the per pupil level, this is equivalent to $212–$501 in one time installation costs and an ongoing annual cost of $40–$105."[24] There could be significant cost savings if schools coordinate their expenditures on a statewide basis or if the federal government plays a major role, but even with these, overall costs, especially network support and maintenance will remain high.

On February 1, 1996 Congress passed the Telecommunications Act of 1996 (signed into law by President Clinton one week later) that promised sweeping changes to the broadcast, cable, and telephone industries. This legislation will be discussed in more detail in Chapters 8 and 11, but for now its implications with respect to education will be briefly reviewed. Secretary of Education Robert W. Riley testified before the Federal Communications Commission on April 12, 1996 about the impact of the Telecommunications Act on education. He made the following blunt statement:[25] ". . . every effort should be made to give our nation's schools and libraries free access to the new telecommunications world that is now emerging or at least access at substantially discounted or affordable rates." He argued that such a step was necessary because of the obvious economic payoffs resulting from providing students with such important skills. Low cost or free access would hasten the implementation of necessary, basic changes in the education system, and an obvious argument for self interest would be that schools would create a vast reservoir of potential consumers receptive to the offerings of the Internet marketplace.

Some Examples of the Use of the Internet

The current discussion has been largely theoretical with respect to the advantages and costs of connecting to the Internet. A few examples of actual use and benefits may be helpful. Consider the following examples from various schools across the United States:[26]

- *E-mail Literature Project, Pennsylvania State University.* In 1994, a group of graduate education students from Pennsylvania State University (PSU) designed an e-mail literature project to link their seven classrooms spanning elementary, middle, high school, and university education. For this project, each class read a children's book with a similar theme (prejudice and conflict), and in small groups, corresponded with another class by e-mail "in character."
- *Long Beach Elementary School, Michigan City Indiana, "MayaQuest."* Dan Buettner, an adventure journalist who holds three cycling world records, toured the [Mayan] ruins with his brother, an archaeologist, a photographer, and a satellite dish that was strapped to his bike. Teachers and students around the world tapped into MayaQuest (through the Internet) to read weekly postings from the expedition team as well as their interviews with archaeologists and other local scientists.
- *Atchison Middle School, Atchison Kansas.* Students have keypals in Salinas, California, and Buffalo, New York . . . Atchison's students are also participating in . . . [an] AOL [America OnLine] project, "Seasoned Stories." Students correspond with other students across the country and then interview a senior citizen about a memory related to a particular season of the year. Students' stories are then published online and later in hardbound form.
- *Distance Learning, Baltimore City School District.* [M]oveable, solid satellite dishes are being installed at seven Title I schools in the district in order to provide new foreign language and math courses. Distance Learning Associates, a private company which is bringing together eight satellite providers for the project, will provide 6,000 hours of programming and training for the entire staff of each school.

There are many more examples but these should indicate the possibilities. It should also be noted that in the student-oriented examples, technology is not replacing teachers but rather is extending the power of imaginative teachers and curious students to explore the world in ways not previously possible. Well-trained teachers, assisted by technical staff, operating with adequate equipment, connected to the Internet, and financed with adequate operating funds are the basic necessities for success in the wired world.

Lifelong Learning on the Internet

Education is usually considered in the context of educational institutions—elementary schools, high schools, vocational schools, colleges, and universities—but considerable learning goes on in the workplace as well as in company-sponsored classrooms. Many people have a vision of lifelong learning as a combination of institutionalized instruction and the individual pursuit of knowledge. Traditionally, libraries have played a very important role in enabling motivated individuals to pursue their interests in a self-directed manner. Now with the emergence of the Internet, and the explosive growth of information, it is not unrealistic to consider that self-education is accessible beyond the confines of formal institutions. One early proposal is called TeleRead, "a nonpartisan plan to get electronic books into American homes—through a national digital library and small, sharp-screened computers—in an era of declining literacy."[27] It is writer David Rothman's vision to have an online library of books, not just public domain ones currently available on a number of Web sites, but newly published ones for which copyright still applies and that would be readily accessible for a small fee. Such a scheme could provide supplementary resources for schools as well and would operate in parallel with the school system.

COMPUTERS IN HIGHER EDUCATION

A teacher affects eternity; he can never tell where his influence stops. (Henry Adams [1838–1918])

Teachers open the door, but you must enter by yourself. (Chinese Proverb)

Computers first made their presence in education felt at universities, both as research tools and as objects of study. Not long after the first electronic computer, ENIAC, was built at the Moore School of the University of Pennsylvania, students were being instructed in the intricacies of computer design and programming. Electrical engineering departments turned their attention to transistors, semiconductors, integrated circuits, and communications. New departments of computer science were founded, to instruct students in the care and feeding of computers—that is, programming—and to carry out research in such areas as operating systems, the theory of computation, numerical analysis, and artificial intelligence. Many important innovations have come from the universities—time-sharing systems, programming languages (such as LISP, Pascal, and Basic), graphics devices (SKETCHPAD), numerical packages, and a variety of intelligent systems. The universities have filled an important function in training large numbers of computer professionals and in introducing several generations of other students to computers long before computer use became fashionable in the wider society. This role was recognized quite early by computer companies. Among these, IBM was the most prominent in recognizing the fact that early exposure to a given computer system would be a major influence in subsequent choices made by the students when they established themselves in the outside world. This realization produced a strategy that worked exceedingly well and contributed to IBM's dominance in the computer industry.

More recently, computer companies including IBM, Apple, Digital Equipment Corp. (DEC), Hewlett-Packard (H-P), Silicon Graphics, and Sun have again begun to respond to opportunities at the universities. These range from special purchase plans for students and faculty, and outright gifts of hardware, software, and maintenance to joint development projects including software and operating systems for existing machines, and the design and development of new machines and networks. A number of universities require their students, upon beginning their studies, to purchase computers under very favorable financial arrangements. These include Carnegie-Mellon University (which for years has had very close relations with DEC), MIT, Dartmouth, Drexel University in Philadelphia, Clarkson College in Potsdam, New York, and Rensselaer Polytechnic Institute in Troy, New York. In addition, the number of students entering university with their own computers is increasing. For example, among incoming freshmen at the University of Michigan, 50% own computers, at Pennsylvania it is 60%, and at Stanford and U.C.L.A. it is 65%.[28]

The intention is clearly that every student be able to use a computer in a variety of interesting ways beyond straight programming: to check for assignments in a course, to prepare and submit assignments (via a file accessible only to the instructor), to browse the catalog file of the library and even reserve books, to take tests and exams, and to exchange messages, via electronic mail, with fellow students and professors. All this can be done from a computer, or terminal, in the student's own room or from one of the many workstations distributed around campus. Hard copies are available from fast printers near the work stations. Such systems require extensive and sophisticated computer networks permitting thousands of users to simultaneously access computers ranging from workstations to mainframes.

Universities that have forged research and development contracts with computer vendors often argue that the relationship is beneficial for both parties, because it keeps universities at the cutting edge of technologies, to say nothing of acquiring computers at bargain prices, and permits computer and software companies to experiment with new ideas in a relatively sophisticated market. However, the growing relationship between universities and big business raises serious questions about autonomy, ethics, and responsibility. Can a university researcher simultaneously be responsible to his or her university, discipline, students, and corporate sponsor? What about the free and open circulation of research results when industry has proprietary interests? Going one step further, a number of university researchers have themselves formed companies, to develop commercial applications of their own research efforts and to consult with industry in their areas of expertise. This development is not new and there are arguments in favor of cooperation between academia and business, but there are potential dangers. Researchers must be careful not to exploit their students' work for financial gain or use results achieved with the help of government funds for private profit. Computer science is quite a lucrative field and there is considerable temptation for university researchers with these backgrounds to jump into the marketplace.

Another important player in the university computing research environment is the US government, in two major forms, the National Science Foundation (NSF) and the Department of Defense's (DOD) Defense Advanced Research Projects Agency (DARPA). NSF funds basic research in the sciences but its level of funding is considerably below that provided by DOD. For example, most of the federal funding for computer science at the prestigious universities, the University of California at Berkeley, Carnegie-Mellon, MIT, and Stanford comes from DOD. Furthermore, the military tends to support applied research related to various mission-oriented projects. Thus, to a significant degree the goals of the defense establishment shape the nature of research undertaken at the major universities of the country and hence the academic curriculum. Some researchers bemoan this state of affairs, but most recognize the political realities to the degree that there is considerable concern about the impact of cutbacks in military research budgets as a result of the easing of international tensions. Of course, given the unpredictability of world politics and the internal imperative for growth and innovation, the possibility of a peace dividend may not be realized and research funds may not be threatened.

The Virtual University

Given that universities are at the forefront of technological innovations, it is to be expected that new forms of delivering instruction at the post-secondary level are emerging. More and more universities are turning to the World Wide Web (WWW or the Web) as a way to provide instruction to supplement the typical lecture system. In fact, entire courses have been placed on the Web, permitting students access to lecture material at any time and from any place. Students have been encouraged to treat the course Web site as a living document by adding their own links to material discovered in the process of answering assignments or carrying out research projects. Thus, every student can potentially benefit from every other student's efforts. In such a situation, education can become a genuinely cooperative enterprise involving teachers and students alike. There is more: Courses mounted on the Web are also available around the world so that we might expect to see international competition among universities. In fact many universities now accept admission applications over the Web. There is a danger of uniformity as the globally renowned universities make their presence felt everywhere. How will local colleges and universities compete? They will have to provide a variety of services—hands-on experiences, local special conditions, direct personal attention—not available to distant institutions. It does seem to be the case that educational institutions will have to be flexible, imaginative, and perhaps lucky, to survive in a networked world.

One government sanctioned effort is taking place in the western United States as a consortium is developing plans for a Western Virtual University to be operating by June 1997. Such a university is expected to respond to a number of goals, including the following:[29]

> . . . expanding access to a broader range of postsecondary education opportunities for citizens of the West; reducing the costs of providing these opportunities and providing a vehicle for cost sharing; providing a means for learners to obtain formal recognition of the skills and knowledge they acquire through advanced technology-based learning—at home, on the job, or through other means outside the formal educational system; shifting the focus of education to the actual competence of students and away from "seat time" or other measures of instructional activity; creating high performance standards that are

widely-accepted and serve to improve the quality of postsecondary education; and demonstrating new approaches to teaching and assessment that can be adopted by more traditional colleges and universities.

Electronic Publishing

It is the job of professors not only to transmit knowledge by teaching but to add to knowledge by publishing their research findings in journals and monographs. Traditionally, these hard copy media have been a relatively slow way to disseminate knowledge and they have become increasingly expensive (especially journals), as rising subscription costs have been countered with falling numbers of subscribers, thereby establishing a deadly spiral. For many scholars, the Internet offers a way out of this dilemma by providing rapid turnaround in the refereeing process, reduced printing and mailing costs because paper has been removed from the process. In fact it is possible to only download or print individual articles of interest rather than entire journals, also a cost-saving measure. It may be possible for universities to become publishers of scholarly information as well as course material. These activities are happening now and will only increase as the advantages of electronic publishing become more obvious and a variety of technical and legal problems are resolved.

ISSUES AND PROBLEMS

I know of no safe depository of the ultimate powers of society but the people themselves; and if we think them not enlightened enough to exercise their control with wholesome discretion, the remedy is not to take it from them, but to inform their discretion by education. (Thomas Jefferson, letter to William Charles Jarvis, 1820)

One of the fundamental criticisms leveled against computer-assisted instruction is that an infatuation with hardware has minimized the concern about the educational merits of the courses. Critic after critic has bemoaned the poor quality of the material. As the market has grown, the rush to produce software has resulted in a lowering of quality. Perhaps some serious problems with educational theory itself also exist, and it is unreasonable to expect CAI to produce wondrous results. Another problem frequently ignored is the difficulty of obtaining qualified teachers who know how to use available hardware and software to their best advantage.

Other important issues include the impact of computers and computer use on the social organization of the classroom, as a byproduct of such aids to computer learning as LOGO, the tendency of the new technology to exclude girls and women or to minimize their contributions, and the role of technology in aiding the disabled.

Impact of CAI

Because of the many dimensions of the instructional process, it is difficult to determine the effectiveness as well as the drawbacks of educational technology. This observation was made earlier but it is useful to be reminded that powerful technologies do not operate independently of the environment in which they are immersed. In analyzing data obtained from a "study of social and organizational factors affecting technology and school reform," Barbara Means reports that two of the nine schools reviewed, with seemingly similar motivations, resources, and skills, diverged strikingly in the results achieved. She was thus led to make the following recommendations for the successful implementation of educational technology: [30]

- jointly developed school goals and technology's place in fulfilling them;
- adequate technology access provided in regular classes;
- technical support readily available and non-judgmental;
- professional growth opportunities, recognition, and rewards provided for exemplary technology use by regular teachers;
- technology use as a choice, not by fiat;
- mechanisms for teacher choice in what technology to use and how to use it;
- opportunities provided for teachers to work together; and,
- supported time for teachers to learn to use technology and to design technology-supported learning activities.

Technology will not be effective unless the people issues are taken into account in a meaningful way.

LOGO and the Classroom

The claims for the virtues of LOGO have been loud, insistent, and consistent since the late 1970s when it was first introduced. For example, two strong supporters, Maddux and Johnson, make the following claims for teaching children to program in LOGO: [31]

- Logo can provide a success [sic] experience for children who are accustomed to failure.
- Interesting things can be done with Logo by children who have received only a brief orientation to the language.
- The self-correcting nature of programming eliminates the need for adult correction for students who are sensitive to such correction.
- Logo may help promote social interaction and peer acceptance among children who are deficient in these important characteristics.

But perhaps the most controversial claim is that LOGO will improve general problem solving abilities, that there will be a transference from programming skills to conceptual skills in other disciplines, and that LOGO will unlock the natural curiosity and desire to learn inherent in all children, independent of their social and economic backgrounds—a sweeping claim, to say the least. Is there any evidence in support of all these claims?

An important early study of LOGO was carried out in two classrooms in an independent school in Manhattan by researchers from Bank Street College's Center for Children and Technology, between September 1981 and February 1984. One classroom included eight and nine year olds, and the other, eleven and twelve year olds, all of mixed socioeconomic backgrounds and achievement levels. Space does not permit a discussion of the experiments and methodology of this lengthy and careful study, so we will limit our presentation to a report of the most salient results. [32]

1. Teachers had a great deal of difficulty deciding on their approach to the use of LOGO in the classroom, between a structured environment and an environment to promote self-discovery.
2. Over the course of two years, students varied greatly in their interests and accomplishments. Teachers had difficulty in reaching those students who did not naturally take to the language.
3. Many students found the underlying logical structure of LOGO formidable and were unable to overcome their difficulties to the point that they could write even simple programs.
4. Teachers had difficulty rationalizing the role of LOGO into the ongoing classroom work. "Is Logo a legitimate part of the curriculum? And, if so, does it fit in as programming or math, or does it belong elsewhere? What can students be expected to learn from their efforts involving Logo: specific programming or math concepts, general problem-solving skills, or both?"

In the Introduction to the second edition of *Mindstorms,* Seymour Papert briefly and unapologetically responds to his critics, first by claiming that problems that may have arisen in applying ideas discussed in the 1980 edition are probably related to the mode of presentation rather than to the ideas themselves. Furthermore, to those academic critics whose response to Papert's apparent claims that " 'working with computers' would *cause* change in how children think," was to engage in experiments to prove him wrong, he responds with the following:[33]

I make no such claim anywhere in the book, but I may have made a mistake in waiting until chapter 8 before saying emphatically that I was not making it. What I was saying, and still say, is something slightly more subtle: I see Logo as a *means* that *can, in principle,* be used by educators to *support the development* of new ways of thinking and learning. However, Logo does not in itself produce good learning any more than paint produces good art.

Gender Issues

Prior to the arrival of the computer, girls were not expected to do well in science and mathematics, and these expectations were often self-fulfilling, as the educational system did not encourage their participation in these areas. Some of the computer concerns related to gender are equal access, gender-bias in expectations, and stereotypical computer programs and games. In terms of computer use in the schools, statistics show that males and females had roughly equal access in 1993 from kindergarten to the end of college an improvement from 1989 figures. The percentage of participation by both males and females across their entire educational history increased from 27% in 1988 to 42.7% to 59% in 1993.[34] In spite of these results, there are the concerns listed previously. Experiments conducted at the University of British Columbia in 1993 attempted to explore the following widely held views about differences between boys and girls with respect to computer games:[35]

COMMONLY HELD VIEWS ABOUT BOYS	RESEARCH RESULTS
(a) electronic games and boys' behavior while playing them contain elements of aggression, violence, competition, fast-action, and speed;	(a) while violent games are popular, many boys prefer games that challenge them mentally;
(b) electronic games encourage anti-social, "loner" behavior; and	(b) there appears to be little connection between anti-social behavior and electronic game playing; and
(c) boys who play electronic games are susceptible to becoming so devoted to playing games that they neglect other areas of their lives, such as school, physical activity, and family.	(c) many boys who play electronic games have interests also in music, programming, reading, and school.

So boys are actually more open and have a wider range of interests than is usually recognized. One can only hope that the game-playing software companies would recognize this observation and act accordingly.

The National Center for Educational Statistics produced a report in 1995 surveying the educational progress of women over the past twenty years. Although the word computer appears only twice in the context of physical sciences, mathematics, and engineering as areas in which women were much less likely than men to have taken bachelor's degrees, the general findings are that "women have made substantial educational progress. The large gaps between the education levels of women and men that were evident in the early 1970s have essentially disappeared for the younger generation."[36] But it should be noted that women are under-represented in the hard sciences. However, gains in education have not translated into gains in the marketplace, yet. As of 1993, "the average earnings of female high school graduates aged 25–34 were more than one-third lower than those of male graduates of the same age. Similarly, female college graduates earn, on average, salaries that are 80 percent of what their male counterparts receive."[37]

The Technological Fix

Computers are a valuable and undoubtedly useful tool. They have an important role to play in the educational system, as they do in the rest of society. But they are only one part of the educational process. As Joseph Weizenbaum has said, "Children may not be motivated in school because they're hungry or they've been abused at home or for any number of reasons. Simply introducing computers avoids the question of why children may not be motivated in school. It converts a social problem into a technological problem and then tries to solve it by technical means."[38]

In a study on the future impact of technology on education, the question is asked: "Is there a 'down side' to technology?" The following responses are provided as possible areas of concern:[39]

- Downsizing of the teaching force as staffing patterns are altered. (Many workshop participants felt that major changes in staffing, . . . would be challenged by teachers and administrators who faced possible job loss.)

- Greater inequalities in knowledge and skills among different groups of students due to differential access to technological resources. Will adding more technology to the most technologically advanced schools exacerbate discrepancies between the technology "haves" and "have nots," creating inequalities in access to information between students who attend the "have not" schools and students who attend the "have" schools?
- Concerns about whether learning through technology is always the best way for students to learn. Will an over-emphasis on technology mean that students who would benefit from direct, traditional instruction get lost in the shuffle of changing approaches to teaching and learning?
- Potential harmful influences from opening the sheltered class to the outside world. Telecommunications networks could give students easier access to questionable or dangerous elements, such as pornography on the Internet.

The limitations of technology in providing the answer to educational problems are revealed in a simple insight underlying what has come to be called the Comer process, after Dr. James Comer, a Yale University psychiatrist: "... a child's home life affects his performance in school, and ... if schools pay attention to all the influences on a child, most problems can be solved before they get out of control. The Comer process ... encourages a flexible, almost custom-tailored approach to each child."[40] These observations seem so obvious and so unglamorous compared to high technology that it is not surprising that it has taken so long for adequate attention to be paid to them. One interesting point with respect to the arguments made for technological solutions is that there are other claims to massive expenditures to maintain the educational infrastructure. For example, "Based on estimates by school officials in a national sample of schools, we project that the nation's schools need about $112 billion to repair or upgrade America's multibillion dollar investment in facilities to good overall condition."[41] Will there be enough money to satisfy all the basic needs of the educational system?

Hopefully, the computer, when properly used, can be a liberating force, fostering what Ivan Illich, a well-known critic of technological fixes, calls conviviality.[42] Illich does not mention computers explicitly, but they have the potential to be tools for conviviality par excellence through the growing use of electronic mail, multimedia, teleconferencing, and other information and communication resources, such as the Internet and the World Wide Web.

SUMMARY

Computers are rapidly becoming a pervasive feature of the educational scene. Will they transform education or are they just one more educational novelty, as were radio, film, and television?

Almost all the schools in America have computers. They are used to teach programming and such subjects as arithmetic, geography, history, and so forth. They are also used to play games. The market for hardware and software is large and growing. Apple is currently leading, followed by a variety of PCs. Television and magazine advertisements by these manufacturers and others suggest to parents that their children will suffer if computers are not made available to them at school and at home.

Computer-based education can be divided into a number of categories. The major areas are computer-assisted instruction (CAI) and computer-aided learning (CAL).

CAI includes such activities as drill and practice, tutorial (in which new material is presented), simulation (a means to explore the behavior of complex systems), and games. CAL puts the computer itself at the center of the learning experience, not as a tool to acquire knowledge in other areas. It is argued by CAL's foremost proponent Seymour Papert, one of the creators of the programming language LOGO, that an understanding of some of the important principles associated with programming can improve a child's performance in other areas of the curriculum. Some reported experiments have not supported this claim.

At universities, computers are being used in almost every area of instruction. Some universities are requiring that incoming students purchase or lease their own microcomputers. They will be used for word processing, assignments, library searches, and communicating with fellow students and professors. Comprehensive communication systems to support the growing number of computers have been initiated at most universities. The growing relation between universities and the Department of Defense is of some concern given the amount of military funding received by computer science researchers. Also of concern is the degree to which industry is cooperating in joint research efforts with faculty members and the impact of such efforts, as well as the military influence, on the academic program.

Computer literacy is a controversial area with many opinions about whether or not it constitutes a legitimate discipline. Other areas of computer applications in education have not yet proven their value. They seem to improve the rate of acquisition of knowledge in certain fact-driven areas, but even here they seem to be no more cost effective than other methods of instruction or remediation. The Internet, as in many other areas is becoming an increasingly important factor in education. Access to a vast extended library is just one of the many ways that students and their teachers can participate in a shared learning experience.

There is a basic concern that computers will be viewed as a technological fix to educational problems that are rooted in socioeconomic difficulties.

NOTES

1. Recall the famous *New Yorker* cartoon of a few years ago, with a dog at a terminal speaking to another dog: "On the Internet, nobody knows I'm a dog."
2. *Power On! New Tools for Teaching and Learning.* OTA-SET-380. US Congress, Office of Technology Assessment. (Washington, DC: US Government Printing Office, September 1988), p. 36.
3. *Teachers and Technology: Making the Connection.* OTA-EHR-616. US Congress, Office of Technology Assessment. (Washington, DC: US Government Printing Office, April 1995), p. 92. (Also available at the National Academy Press OTA Archives Web page with URL: <http://www.ota,nap.edu/pdf/data/1995/9541.PDF>.)
4. *Ibid.*, Figure 3–3, p. 95.
5. "The Condition of Education, 1995," US Department of Commerce, Bureau of the Census, October Current Population Surveys, January 30, 1995. Accessed from the Web page with URL: <http://www.ed.gov/NCES/pubs/CoE95/05txt.html> on June 20, 1996.

6. *Op cit., Teachers and Technology,* pp. 101–102. Note that the students themselves actually reported much less time spent using computers; 24 minutes per week in grade 5, 38 minutes in grade 8, and 61 minutes in grade 11.

7. *Ibid.,* p. 104.

8. *Ibid.,* p. 103.

9. D. Midian Kurland and Laura C. Kurland. "Computer Applications in Education: A Historical Overview," in Joseph F. Traub, Barbara J. Grosz, Butler W. Lampson, and Nils J. Nilsson, *Annual Review of Computer Science, Vol. 2.* (Palo Alto, CA: Annual Reviews Inc., 1987), pp. 317–358.

10. *Ibid., Power On!,* p. 20.

11. "Schools Will Spend $738 Million on Educational Software in 1996," news release, August 1996. Accessed from the Web page with URL: <http://www2.simbanet.com/simba/whatnew/whats1.html#EMSM9> on September 10, 1996.

12. *Op cit., Teachers and Technology,* pp. 1–2.

13. Seymour Papert. *Mindstorms: Children, Computers, and Powerful Ideas,* Second Edition. (New York: BasicBooks, A Division of HarperCollins Publishers, 1993), p. 180. (First Edition, 1980).

14. Arthur Melmed (ed.), "The Costs and Effectiveness of Educational Technology: Proceedings of a Workshop," Critical Technologies Institute, RAND Corporation, DRU-1205-CTI, November 1995. Also available at the Web page with URL: <http://www.ed.gov/Technology/Plan/RAND/Costs/cover.html>.

15. *Ibid.,* Section: Effectiveness.

16. Thomas K. Glennan and Arthur Melmed. "Fostering the Use of Educational Technology: Elements of a National Strategy," RAND Corporation, MR-682-OSTP, 1996. Available at the Web site with URL: <http://www.rand.org/publications/MR/MR682/contents.html>.

17. *Ibid.,* Chapter 5, Summary and Conclusions.

18. Ronald E. Anderson and Daniel L. Klasson. "A Conceptual Framework for Developing Computer Literacy Instruction." (St. Paul, MN: Minnesota Educational Computing Consortium, November 5, 1980), p. 7.

19. "Advanced Telecommunications in US Public Elementary and Secondary Schools, 1995," National Center for Education Statistics, US Department of Education, NCES 96–854, February 1996. Also available at the Web site with URL: <http://www.ed.gov/Technology/starrpt.html>.

20. *Ibid.*

21. "Connecting the Nation: Classrooms, Libraries, and Health Care Organizations in the Information Age," National Telecommunications and Information Administration, US Department of Commerce, June 1995. Available at the Web site with URL: <http://www.ntia.doc.gov/connect.html>.

22. *Ibid.,* Executive Summary.

23. *Ibid.,* Introduction.

24. Russell I. Rothstein and Lee McKnight. "Technology and Cost Models of Connecting K–12 Schools to the National Information Infrastructure," MIT Research Program on Communications Policy, Massachusetts Institute of Technology, 1995. *Technical Horizons in Education Journal,* October 1995. Also available at the Web site with URL: <http://far.mit.edu/Pubs/k12costs/CSTB.pdf>.

25. "Oral Statement of Richard W. Riley, US Secretary of Education before the Federal Communications Commission," April 12, 1996. Accessed from the Web page with URL: <http://www.ed.gov/Technology/fcc12.html> on June 1, 1996.

26. "Expanding the Classroom Through E-mail & the Net," *FOCUS on Education,* First Quarter 1995–1996. Accessed from the Web page with URL: <http://www.ed.gov/Technology/Focus/edfocus2.html#Telecommunications> on June 20, 1996.

27. "TeleRead Home Page." Available from the Web page with URL: <http://www.clark.net/pub/rothman/telhome.html>.

28. Katie Hafner. "Wiring the Ivory Tower," *Business Week*, January 30, 1995, p. 63.

29. "Goals and Visions for a Virtual University," May 1996. Accessed from the Web page with URL: <http://wga-internet.westgov.org/smart/vu/vu.html> on June 21, 1996.

30. *Ibid.*, "The Costs and Effectiveness of Educational Technology: Proceedings of a Workshop," November 1995, Implementation Issues and Strategies Section.

31. Cleborne D. Maddux and D. LaMont Johnson. *Logo: Methods and Curriculum for Teachers.* (Binghamton, NY: The Haworth Press, 1988), p. 13.

32. Jan Hawkins. "The Interpretation of Logo in Practice," in Roy D. Pea and Karen Sheingold (eds.), *Mirrors of Kinds: Patterns of Experience in Educational Computing.* (Norwood, NJ: Ablex Publishing Corp., 1987), pp. 3–34.

33. *Ibid., Mindstorms,* p. xiv.

34. Taken from Table 415—Student use of computers, by level of instruction and selected characteristics: October 1984, 1989, and 1993, Digest of Education Statistics, US Department of Commerce, Bureau of the Census, Current Population Survey, October 1984, 1989, and 1993, unpublished data. (This table was prepared April 1994.) Accessed from the Web page with URL: <http://www.ed.gov/NCES/pubs/D95/dtab415.htm> in June 1996.

35. Joan Lawry, Rena Upitis, Maria Klawe, Ann Anderson, Kori Inkpen, Mutindi Ndunda, David Hsu, Steve Leroux, and Kamran Sedighian. "Exploring Common Conceptions About Boys and Electronic Games," Technical Report 94–1, March 1994, Department of Computer Science, University of British Columbia, Vancouver, B.C., Canada, V6T 1Z4.

36. "The Educational Progress of Women, " Findings from The Condition of Education 1995, National Center for Education Statistics, US Department of Education, NCES 95-768, November 1995. Accessed at the Web page with URL: <http://www.ed.gov/NCES/pubs/finding5.pdf> in June 1996.

37. *Ibid.,* p. 1.

38. Joseph Weizenbaum as quoted in Alison B. Bass. "Computers in the Classroom," *Technology Review,* April 1987, p. 61.

39. *Education and Technology: Future Visions.* US Congress, Office of Technology Assessment, OTA-BP-EHR-169. (Washington, DC: US Government Printing Office, September 1995). Also available at the Web page with URL: <http://www.ota.nap.edu/pdf/data/1995/9522.PDF>.

40. Michel Marriott. "A New Road to Learning: Teaching the Whole Child," *The New York Times,* June 13, 1990, pp. A1, B8.

41. "School Facilities: Condition of America's Schools," United States General Accounting Office, GAO/HEHS-95–61, February 1995, Washington, DC. Available at the Web page with URL: <http://www.access.gpo.gov/cgi-bin/waisgate.cgi?WAISdocID=8204831730+1+1+0&WAIS-action=retrieve>.

42. Ivan Illich. *Tools for Conviviality.* (New York: Harper & Row/Perennial Library, 1973).

ADDITIONAL READINGS

Introduction

"Reinventing Schools: The Technology is Now," Washington, DC: National Academy of Sciences, 1995. Also available at the Web site with URL: <http://www.nap.edu/nap/online/techgap/welcome.html>.

Computers in Education

"21st Century Teachers," President Clinton's Educational Technology Initiative, May 1996. Available at the Web site with URL: <http://www.ustc.org/21stcentury/index.html>.

Losee, Stephanie. "How to Make Your Child PC Literate," *Fortune,* November 24, 1994, pp. 161–162, 164, 168, 172.

Nash, Kim. "Whiz Kids," *Computerworld,* May 8, 1995, pp. 1, 97–99.

Computer Literacy and the Internet

Blumberg, Roger. "Ex Libris," *The Sciences,* September/October 1995, pp. 16–19.

Bruning, David. "Students in Cyberspace," *Astronomy,* October 1995, pp. 48–53.

"The Future of Networking Technologies for Learning," Office of Educational Technology, US Department of Education, May 24, 1995. Available at the Web site with URL: <http://www.ed.gov/Technology/Futures/>.

Learning to Work: Making the Transition from School to Work. US Congress, Office of Technological Assessment, OTA-EHR-637. (Washington, DC: US Government Printing Office, September 1995). Available at the Web site with URL: <http://www.ota.nap.edu/pdf/data/1995/9548.PDF>.

"The Learning Connection," Benton Foundation, Winter 1995. Available at the Web site with URL: <http://cdinet.com/cgi-bin/lite/Benton/Goingon/learning.html>.

"NLII—National Learning Infrastructure Initiative," EDUCOM, January 1996. Available at the Web site with URL: <http://www.educom.edu/index.html>.

Reinhardt, Andy. "New Ways to Learn," *Byte,* March 1995, pp. 50–52, 54–56.

David Rothman. "TeleRead: A Virtual Central Database without Big Brother," in Robin P. Peek and Gregory B. Newby (eds.), *The Electronic Frontier.* (Cambridge, MA: The MIT Press, 1996). Also available at the Web page with URL: <http://www.clark.net/pub/rothman/teleread.html>.

Computers in Higher Education

Byrne, John A. "Virtual B-Schools," *Business Week,* October 23, 1995, pp. 64–65, 68.

"The Internet: Re-engineering Peer Review," Science and Technology Section, *The Economist,* June 22, 1996. Accessed from the Web page with URL: <http://www.economist.com/issue/22-06-96/st1.html> on June 27, 1996.

Issues and Problems

Miller, Leslie, Chaika, Melissa, and Groppe, Laura. "Girls' Preferences in Software Design: Insights from a Focus Group." *Interpersonal Computing and Technology: An Electronic Journal for the 21st Century,* 1996. Accessed from the Web page with URL: <http://www.helsinki.fi/science/optek/1966/n2/miller.txt> in June 1996.

Gokhale, Anuradha A. "Collaborative Learning Enhances Critical Thinking," *Journal of Technology Education,* (7:1), Fall 1995. Available at the Web site with URL: <http://scholar.lib.vt.edu/ejournals/JTE/jte-v7n1/gokhale.jte-v7n1.html>.

— 7 —

GOVERNMENT AND COMPUTERS

All government, indeed every human benefit and enjoyment, every virtue, and every prudent act, is founded on compromise and barter. We balance inconveniences; we give and take—we remit some rights that we may enjoy others. . . . Man acts from motives relative to his interests; and not on metaphysical speculations.

Edmund Burke, Speech on Conciliation with America, March 22, 1775

INTRODUCTION

Governments exist to serve their citizens, and presumably computers are playing a role in this endeavor. How, and for what purposes, do governments use computers? Their primary activity is record-keeping—the gathering, entering, maintenance, processing, and updating of files on individuals, families, organizations, and companies. The government actually might be thought of as *the* great record-keeper, whose insatiable appetite for information arises from the belief that the continual accumulation of information inevitably leads to the provision of better services. The US government is the single largest user of computers. Many of the applications are well known—taxation, social security, census, law enforcement, national security and defense, energy, health, education and welfare, agriculture, and so forth.

Clearly, the government is more than simply a user of computers. By virtue of being such a major purchaser of computer technology, the government tends to set standards and shape the form of future developments. The needs of the Census Bureau played an important role in the early development of the computer. In carrying out its responsibility for the nation's security, the Department of Defense (DOD) has spurred research and development in integrated circuits, programming languages, operating systems, security methods, and fault-tolerant designs. The National Aeronautics and Space Administration (NASA) is concerned with such issues as miniaturization, low power consumption, high reliability, and resistance to the effects of vibration and weightlessness.

These technical innovations are important and have done much to make the United States the leading technological country in the world. But more recently, there has been an attempt to paint the federal government as too big, too intrusive, too remote and unresponsive, and a danger to individual rights. In this context, technological sophistication may be seen as a threat, as an all-powerful government bent on discovering more about its citizens by means of modern technology and thereby controlling their behavior. This extreme viewpoint usually is seen as characterizing a far-right segment of the US political spectrum, but it also is consistent with views expressed by many long-time Internet users who are very concerned about government attempts to prevent nonregulated encryption schemes to be publicly used. In addition, the government has attempted to regulate content over the Internet as prescribed in the Telecommunications Act of 1996. (See Chapters 11 and 12 for a more detailed discussion.) Curiously, this area of government intervention is supported by many religious fundamentalist and right-wing organizations.

The election of a Republican majority in both houses of Congress in 1994 seemed to signal a general public consensus to downsize government. Of particular interest, the Speaker of the House, Newt Gingrich, believed that the new interactive technologies would permit a smaller government to determine more directly the wishes of the electorate and to perform its information processing more efficiently and effectively. The term cyberdemocracy has been proposed as a way of characterizing a new form of democracy facilitated by national information networks such as the proposed National Information Infrastructure, or Information Highway. *Time* magazine was not overly taken with this vision of the future noting that,[1]

> One problem with all this enthusiasm about electronically wiring the citizenry to the Washington policymaking machine is that in a sense it's already happened. Politicians are quite in touch with opinion polls and have learned not to ignore all the radio talk-show hosts, with their ability to marshal rage over topics from Hilary to the House post office . . . "Electronic Town Halls" have always faced one major rhetorical handicap: the long shadow of America's Founding Fathers. The Fathers explicitly took lawmaking powers out of the people's hands, opting for a representative democracy and not a direct democracy.

It has yet to be determined whether or not real economies of scale can be achieved by advanced technologies, but even earlier, the Clinton administration had launched its National Performance Review with the goal being to control the growth of government. Technology, primarily information processing systems, the Internet, and the World Wide Web, is expected to play the major role. It is too early to tell whether or not these efforts are more than window dressing but an interim report will be made later in this chapter.

Another area of growing importance is the increasing involvement of computers in the political process. This new development in the use of computer technology makes it possible to produce detailed mailing lists of voters who will respond as desired to specific issues. The use of computer models to predict voter behavior is also increasing in popularity, and of course every candidate of substance has a Web site, replete with speeches, position papers, voting profile, and endorsements. Opinions are solicited from interested browsers, thereby providing issues of most concern to a certain group of potential supporters.

Computer applications related to the nation's defense include the computerized battlefield, the use of computers in war games, security needs, and cryptographic development.

Many other areas of activity that involve computer applications and the role of government will be dealt with in further chapters. Because government is intricately involved in so many phases of society, it is inevitable that government-related issues turn up in many areas. In relation to computers and the law, such issues as the legal protection of software, the use of computers by law enforcement agencies, and computer crime, are paramount. The federal government is being called upon to take an active role in promoting and aiding the development of manufacturing strategies for American industry. In the communications industry, the Telecommunications Act of 1996 will have significant repercussions with respect to the computer networks spanning the country. Finally, one of the public's major concerns is the question of privacy of computer records. This extremely important issue (discussed in Chapter 9) includes problems of government legislation and related issues such as freedom of information. Consider the following role envisioned for government in a recent book published by the National Research Council:[2]

> Regardless of political sentiments about its role in general, government at all levels will inevitably be a major player. Government agencies at state and federal levels participate in almost every information-related role pursued by the private sector publisher, user, network manager, innovator. Governments have additional responsibilities by virtue of their constitutional obligations as arbiter, regulator, convener, and even leader in the interest of equity and an efficient, productive society. The federal government has unique responsibilities with respect to the transnational issues arising in the global information infrastructure (GII) and advancing the national technology base through support for research and development.

INFORMATION PROCESSING: COMPLEXITY AND BUREAUCRACIES

The Paperwork Reduction Act of 1995 requires the Office of Management and Budget's Office of Information and Regulatory Affairs (OIRA) to set a goal of at least a 10-percent reduction in government wide paperwork burden for fiscal year 1996 and goals for each agency that reduce burden to the "maximum practicable" extent. It also requires agencies to follow certain procedures in developing information collections, including a 60-day notice and comment period.[3]

Information Technology in the Federal Government

The General Accounting Office (GAO), Congress's watchdog over government expenditures, issues a variety of reports on a regular basis in response to requests for information about practices of government departments and agencies, as well as to determine compliance with applicable legislation. In mid-1995 in response to a request from Congress, GAO issued a report on government spending for information technology with emphasis on information technology related problems. Table 7.1 is a summary of GAO findings for the fiscal years 1994, 1995, and 1996.

In a preface to the report, the GAO offers a number of explanations, limitations, and warnings. Consider the following:[4]

(1) the total amount of federal IT spending is unknown, since the Office of Management and Budget (OMB) does not collect comprehensive IT budget data on a government wide basis;
(2) federal agencies do not generally break out IT obligations as separate line items in their budget documents, but they include this information within program or administrative costs;
(3) OMB reported that executive branch agencies plan to obligate about $26.5 billion in IT-related funds in fiscal year (FY) 1996;
(4) OMB does not require the reporting of some potentially significant types of IT spending, resulting in billions of dollars in unreported spending;
(5) IT-related obligations have increased by about $4 billion since FY 1991, despite the decline in defense obligations;
(6) 11 federal agencies have IT-related problems serious enough to be categorized as high-risk; and

TABLE 7.1

CATEGORIES OF IT-RELATED OBLIGATIONS.[5]
(DOLLARS IN THOUSANDS)

Category	Fiscal year 1994 (actual)	Fiscal year 1995 (estimated)	Fiscal year 1996 (planned)
Equipment:			
Capital purchases	$3,774,079	$3,788,099	$4,765,481
Other equipment	1,082,442	899,530	836,632
Software:			
Capital purchases	879,413	810,650	968,194
Other software	260,284	242,582	260,652
Services	3,555,609	3,609,024	3,590,876
Support Services	7,766,616	8,545,627	8,761,938
Supplies	599,802	592,116	621,105
Personnel	5,360,095	5,828,311	5,902,884
Other (Defense only)	217,114	180,931	189,595
Intra-government payments	4,845,980	5,200,719	5,295,272
Intra-government collections	(4,884,703)	(4,870,382)	(4,703,030)
Total	$23,456,731	$24,827,207	$26,489,599

Source: Office of Management and Budget.
– Personnel includes compensation and benefits for both civilian and military government personnel who perform IT functions 51% or more of their time.
– Intra-governmental payments for all IT services within agencies and between agencies and state and local governments.
– Intra-governmental collections for all IT services within agencies and between agencies and state and local governments.

(7) these IT-related problems warrant increased congressional oversight to ensure that top agency management takes corrective action.

The interpretation of these comments is both revealing and disturbing in a number of ways, given the very large amounts of money spent on IT. The GAO based its report on data collected by the Office of the Management of the Budget (OMB) but unfortunately OMB's data is not comprehensive. Within agencies, it may be difficult to identify all the IT-related expenditures.

Thus, the actual amount spent by the federal government on IT is unknown and probably unknowable. For example, in its accounting process OMB does not include "IT embedded in weapons systems." The Department of Defense has independently offered an estimate that the associated costs may vary between $24 billion to $32 billion annually, numbers greater than the totals shown in Table 7.1. Point (6) is particularly disturbing because the identified agencies perform such critical functions as air traffic control, income tax processing, modernization of the weather service, Department of State security, and claims modernization for veterans benefits. For several years, new systems, under development, have been rife with problems including major cost overruns, lengthening implementation periods, and failure to meet specifications. These problems have prompted Congress to declare IT programs in the 11 federal agencies as high risk.

Automated Bureaucracy

Even before computer systems became prevalent, governments regularly were subject to the criticism that they were too bureaucratic. The most straightforward interpretation of this charge is that bureaucracies frequently are so concerned with rules and procedures that they forget that their purpose is to deal with people and their problems. Thus, it is feared that computer systems will serve bureaucratic interests, not the public's, by further shielding government workers from direct responsibility. Furthermore, how do such systems affect the quality of decisions? Are citizens still assured of due process when computers are part of the decision-making process? Can the high-level policy makers in Congress and the executive branch be sure that the bureaucracy is accountable?

It may be useful to provide more detail on the activities of the Office of Management of the Budget (OMB), given authority over federal information functions under the Paperwork Reduction Act of 1980. Within OMB, the Office of Information and Regulatory Affairs (OIRA) was established with specific authority over "general information policy, reduction of paperwork burden, federal statistical activity, records management activities, the privacy and security of records, agency sharing and dissemination of records, and the acquisition and use of automatic data processing and telecommunications and other information technology for managing information resources."[6] With respect to information policies for the federal government, the 1980 Act specified the following:[7]

1. The development, implementation, and oversight of uniform information resources management policies and guidelines.
2. The initiation and review of proposals for legislation, regulations, and agency procedures to improve information management.

3. The coordination, through budget review and other means, of agency information practices.
4. The promotion of greater information sharing among agencies through the federal information locator system (FILS), the review of budget proposals, and other means.
5. The evaluation of agency information practices.
6. The oversight of planning and research regarding the federal collection, processing, storage, transmission, and use of information.

These information policies are meant to accomplish the main purpose of the Paperwork Reduction Act—to reduce the amount of paper the government handles. Just transforming paper into computer memory is not the answer. More computers do not necessarily mean less information is handled; in fact, quite the opposite may be the case. Thus, OMB is obliged by the Act to determine "whether the collection of information by an agency is necessary for the proper performance of the functions of the agency, including whether the information will have practical utility for the agency." Beyond its responsibility for paperwork clearance, OMB must

- prepare an inventory of all information collection activities,
- assign agencies as the primary collectors for other agencies,
- determine the goals for the reduction of information collection,
- monitor compliance with the recommendations of the Commission on Federal Paperwork,
- design and operate FILS, and
- report to Congress on an annual basis.

A major thrust of the Act is to reduce the paperwork burden on the general public by minimizing the government's requirements for information. In 1986, the Act was amended by the Paperwork Reduction Reauthorization Act, which called for additional reductions in the collection burden:[8]

1. [OMB was] directed to establish goals for agencies to reduce Federal paperwork burdens by five percent for each of the next four consecutive years beginning with FY 1987,
2. [the Act] clarified the treatment of paperwork requirements contained in regulations as being similar to other information collections, and
3. expanded the opportunities for meaningful public comments on agency information collection.

Continuing in this vein and not deterred by the lack of success, Congress passed the Paperwork Reduction Act of 1995 that[9]

... establishes a broad mandate for agencies to perform their information resources management activities in an efficient, effective, and economical manner. To assist agencies in an integrated approach to information resources management, the Act requires that the Director of OMB develop and implement uniform and consistent information resources management policies; oversee the development and promote the use of information management principles, standards, and guidelines; evaluate agency information resources management practices in order to determine their adequacy and efficiency; and determine compliance of such practices with the policies, principles, standards, and guidelines promulgated by the Director.

In mid-1996, the GAO released a report, casting serious doubts on the paper reduction enterprise; in fact, it was noted that the burden placed on the general public had "increased significantly since 1980, both government wide and in particular agencies."[10] One agency alone, the Internal Revenue Service "accounted for about 80% of the total paperwork burden of nearly 7 billion hours."

In parallel with these efforts, in 1993 the Clinton Administration launched an initiative to reform government, called the National Performance Review (NPR), sometimes referred to as reinventing government. It has been claimed that two years later much has been accomplished: considerable savings have been locked in, government is less intrusive, and Congress has passed a number of NPR-related laws.[11] In a review of past accomplishments and a look to the future, the NPR offered the following next steps for reinventing government while "Governing in a Balanced Budget World:"[12]

1. Convert to Performance-Based Organizations. Give agencies that deliver measurable services a greater degree of autonomy from governmentwide rules in exchange for greater accountability for achieving results.
2. Improve Customer Service Dramatically. Challenge all agencies to set service goals so everyone in America will see that government service is better. The heads of the 11 agencies with the greatest customer contact are making public commitments to improve selected services; they have created World Wide Web home pages as a means for receiving direct input.
3. Increase the Use of Regulatory Partnerships. EPA and other agencies have successfully piloted a noncoercive partnership approach that focuses on meeting environmental goals rather than on complying with regulatory red tape. Expand existing pilots in EPA, OSHA, and other regulatory agencies so this partnership approach becomes the mainstream strategy for federal regulatory agencies.
4. Create Performance-Based Partnership Grants. Develop federal-state-local partnerships that are based on results rather than process.
5. Establish Single Points of Contact for Communities. Establish a single point of contact for the nation's larger communities.
6. Transform the Federal Workforce. Reform the civil service system, increase investment in the workforce to create "learning organizations," and give senior executives more tools and make them accountable for achieving results.

Although part of the improvements will be derived by cutting red tape more extensively, others will take advantage of new and forthcoming technologies to facilitate communication between the public and the government. Note, however that point 3 may result in less effective enforcement if regulatory agencies become too close to the companies that they are expected to regulate.

Problems at the Internal Revenue Service (IRS)

The activities of the IRS affect every taxpayer in the country, a rather large number given that some 120 million individual returns were filed annually in the 1990s. Reports of problems at the IRS appear with some regularity—witness 1985 when problems with the computer system threatened to bring operations to a halt. As discussed previously, the IRS was identified by the GAO as having a high-risk IT problem and the press has not overlooked such major difficulties. Thus, *Business Week* warned, "Perhaps most troubling, the agency's vaunted Tax Systems Modernization (TSM) program—designed to replace its outdated system with a state-of-the-art network employing digital imaging—is in disarray."[13] Here are more details about the TSM problem from the GAO:[14]

> How can IRS design, acquire, and maintain computerized systems that streamline operations and are secure?
> By the end of fiscal year 1995, IRS will have spent over $2.5 billion on its $8 billion TSM initiative to streamline selected tax processing functions. Yet, the overall design of TSM remains incomplete, and IRS is continuing to automate existing functions with limited demonstration of how or if the pieces of the system will fit together to improve tax processing. Given such concerns and budget constraints, the Congress reduced IRS' fiscal year 1995 budget request by $339 million. In making decisions on IRS' fiscal year 1996 budget, the Congress will need to know whether the management of TSM has improved.

In fact, Congress cut the IRS budget by an additional $160 million for 1996. It is somewhat ironic that the IRS, which should be a prime beneficiary of electronic networks as a means of automating its enormous workload as well as providing a convenient and efficient service to its captive clientele, should be having so much difficulty implementing an appropriate system to do just that. In July, 1996, the IRS informed "1.2 million companies that they must begin paying business taxes electronically by year's end."[15] Many of these companies do not know about these electronic filing requirements nor do they have proper software. The IRS continues its unfortunate record of alienating the public into the network age.

Trouble with Air Traffic Control Systems

As another example of the problems involved in implementing sophisticated information systems, especially those operating in safety-critical environments in real-time, no better example could be chosen than air traffic control systems, previously identified as high-risk by the GAO. In 1988, the cost of the Federal Aviation Administration's (FAA) Advanced Automation System (AAS) was estimated at $2.6 billion, an estimate that more than doubled to $5.9 billion by 1993, reaching $6.9 billion the following year.[16] By mid-1995, no new systems had yet been installed, with 1998 given as a target for the delivery of the first system: ". . . the aviation agency is under renewed pressure to update its creaky 30-year-old backup systems. This is because the FAA has been going through a formal air traffic control system modernization effort since 1981 but still doesn't expect final delivery of the first of 20 systems until 1998."[17] The FAA, recognizing the serious problems it faced because of increasing failures in old mainframes, announced in late July 1995 that it would "begin installing new mainframes at air route traffic control centers in October 1997 more than a year earlier than it planned."[18] These systems, however, would still be running old software because "[t]he FCC said it could no longer wait until new software is written as part of its planned $4.8 billion overhaul of the nation's air traffic control system."[19]

Thus, the hardware part of the IT equation is being addressed but the state of software remains a serious problem.

Just to gain an appreciation of the size of the task that the FAA confronts, consider that its air traffic control system handles 220 million flights annually. Of these, "246,000 are delayed because of weather, 4,000 are delayed because of equipment failures," and [the FAA claims that] "Air traffic control systems are 99.43% reliable."[20]

Applications in Congress

Up to this point, our discussion has been focused on information technology in the federal government, meaning the executive branch and departments, but for years Congress and other legislative bodies have been developing information systems to aid in their work. Robert Lee Chartrand of the Congressional Research Office, in reviewing the progress made over the past several years, has noted that most of the recommendations made in 1966 for improved applications have indeed been implemented. Among these are the following: status of pending legislation, direct access to legislative research, current information on issues up for vote, current schedule of committee meetings and hearings, histories of committee action, selected readings of interest to each congressman, and constituent information.[21] More recently and not surprisingly, Congress has witnessed the appearance of microcomputers, electronic mail, Fax, telecommunication facilities, graphics equipment, and of course, the Internet as a means of presenting information to, and hearing directly from, constituents.

It is expected that both houses of Congress would gradually acquire all the technology necessary to keep up with the growth in activities and the demands on available time. Of particular interest is how the technology has permitted, and indeed encouraged, aggressive moves into new practices that were not previously possible. Consider the following applications and the impact that they have both on the operation of Congress, as a whole, and the performance of individual Representatives and Senators:[22]

Legislative Analysis Applications. These include straightforward information retrieval—bibliographic citations as well as full text—and the use of advanced models to delineate consequences of proposed legislation. Note that such systems tend to move Congress towards more equity with the executive branch, especially with respect to information matters.

Record-Keeping Applications. Among these are electronic voting in the House of Representatives, which by facilitating the voting process has resulted in an increased number of votes and has enabled the closer monitoring of voting behavior, permitting the exercise of party discipline.

Congressional Communication. Members of Congress receive vast numbers of letters, telephone calls, Faxes, telegrams, and e-mail messages from their constituents and other interest groups, from their colleagues, and from their staffs. One aim of the communication application is to serve Congressional members' self-interest by promoting their images to maintain or to further their political ambitions. One example is the use of computers and laser printers to produce typewriter-quality letters in vast numbers, individually targeted to voters, in response to the rapidly increasing volume of congressional mail.

What does seem obvious is that the advantage of incumbents in the electoral process has been increased by the use of information technology. Those attempting to unseat current officeholders also face a publicly supported technological network at the service of the current Representative or Senator. The next section contains more on this topic.

Databases for Delinquents and Offenders

Government databases, both state and federal, increasingly are being used to monitor or track individuals who may be dangerous to society or who may be delinquent with respect to financial obligations and whose location may not easily be ascertained. Thus, the US Department of Justice plans to implement "a computerized national registry of sex offenders by 1999."[23] This is one more example of what is called a "bad guy" database; existing examples include doctors who have been convicted of malpractice and parents who do not pay child support. The basic idea is to provide a central repository that can be accessed anywhere in the country to ensure that such individuals do not find a new place to practice or a new place to hide.

THE POLITICAL PROCESS

> As the happiness of the people is the sole end of government, so the consent of the people is the only foundation of it. (John Adams)

> Politics is the art of looking for trouble, finding it, misdiagnosing it and then misapplying the wrong remedies. (Groucho Marx)

In their simplest applications, computers are used to register voters prior to elections and to tabulate the results on election night. As a consequence of the nationwide census held every ten years, election boundaries must be redrawn to reflect the new population distribution. Computers play an important role in this process of reapportionment and have aroused considerable controversy for their alleged technological contribution to gerrymandering. They are also employed to sample public opinion, predict the outcome of elections, and maintain detailed lists of supporters. More recently, candidates and political parties have placed their opinions and positions on the Web to make them readily available to current supporters and to attract new ones. Fears have been voiced that the political party with sufficient money to afford the best computer and telecommunication resources and designers will have a major advantage in the electoral process. But then again, what has really changed? The skillful use of financial resources can be a major determining factor in the outcome of political contests.

Beyond the use of computers and the Internet for these purposes, possibilities that could radically transform the entire electoral process as well as the functioning of government itself are on the horizon. In a wired world, citizens could be regularly polled for their opinions, given adequate security procedures. They could, in fact, cast votes on a number of issues, a generalization of the referendum process usually in place for congressional elections in some states or for call-back votes in others. This form of instantaneous democracy is a powerful tool, whose operation must be carefully studied before it is implemented. That is, great care must be taken not to have technology drive potentially radical changes in both the electoral process as well as the governing process, without considerable study and discussion.

Getting Elected

It requires a great deal of money to get elected to political office, and indeed the role of fund-raiser has achieved a high profile in election campaigns. Traditionally, supporters have been identified and then canvassed for contributions before and during the campaign. But increasingly sophisticated fundraising methods have been developed that take advantage of the computer's power. Mailing lists of supporters are carefully organized in terms of ethnic background, income, education, age, sex, and opinion on a number of issues. Also stored in the computer are texts of fundraising letters, each focusing on a particular issue. Such systems are maintained by the political parties and by corporate political-action committees (PACs), legislated by Congress to collect money for political candidates. Whenever a political issue surfaces, the appropriate letter form is selected, and "personally" addressed by the computer to those supporters with an appropriate profile.

These techniques have also been used to mobilize support for political causes, in which case letters and telegrams are solicited rather than money. A system for this purpose requires a moderately sized computer, considerable storage, a high-speed printer, folding-sealing-stamping equipment, and people to do data entry. The ability to target voters along ethnic, regional, religious, or any other lines results in more efficient fundraising and more effective pressure tactics. But the public should be aware of what lies behind current solicitation practices.

The low price of personal computers means that they are now readily available for almost every political campaign in the land, even though computer expertise may be expensive. Something like 50,000 individuals are elected in each election cycle. Besides the important fundraising activities, computers are also used to plan the candidate's schedule, organize press releases, plan questionnaires, and schedule volunteer workers. Basic financial programs can be used to monitor donations and expenditures to ensure that sufficient funds are available for the entire duration of the campaign. A number of software packages have been developed exclusively for use in election campaigns to analyze previous election results, keep track of supporters, and perform financial analysis.

What Does the Voter Want?

Nowadays, people are asked their opinion about everything: their favorite soap operas, television show, and politician. There are public polls such as Gallup, Harris, and Roper, and many private ones are done for elected officials as well as candidates. The computer now is used to store survey results and to perform sophisticated statistical analyses and projections. Over the years, models have been constructed that can predict with reasonable accuracy, on the basis of a careful sampling of voter preferences, the outcome of elections on the local, state, or federal level. A danger of such models is that both elected officials and candidates for political office will begin to tailor their opinions in the directions determined by the models. A basic problem for elected officials will be heightened—to vote their conscience or to represent the political views of their constituency, when these are in conflict.

There were not many experiments in electronic polling of people at their homes prior to the widespread popularity of the Internet. In Columbus Ohio, in the early 1980s, about 30,000 homes, under an experimental system called QUBE (now terminated), were wired to a central computer by a two-way communication system. QUBE was used to sample public opinion in a quick and painless fashion. A question put to the subscribers appeared on their television set. Viewers would press either the yes or no button on their handsets as the vote was being taken. Each home on the network was briefly scanned, the votes accumulated, and the results would appear on the screen in a few seconds. Could (or should) such a polling method be used within the current political system? Consider the comments of political scientist, Jean Bethke Elshtain, at the time, criticizing this voting model as an:[24]

> interactive shell game [that] cons us into believing that we are participating when we are really simply performing as the responding "end" of a prefabricated system of external stimuli . . . In a plebiscitary system, the views of the majority . . . swamp minority or unpopular views. Plebiscitism is compatible with authoritarian policies carried out under the guise of, or with the connivance of, majority views. The opinion can be registered by easily manipulated, ritualistic plebiscites, so there is no need for debate on substantive issues.

Another experiment begun in the pre-Internet age is the Public Electronic Network (PEN) in Santa Monica, California. It was hailed as the "first free, government-sponsored public electronic network in the nation," with the following goals: "to deliver an alternative method of communication between residents and city government; to enhance and provide equal access to civic services; to develop an electronic forum for issues and concerns of residents; and to extend to the community the opportunity to use computer communications tools."[25] It went into operation early in 1989 and attracted over 1,200 citizens in the first seven months, well above expectations. What is most attractive about PEN is that it permits people to carry out typical government functions, such as purchasing licenses, without standing in line. It also permits a ready expression of community views, but it has failed in providing an online discussion forum, mainly because of a phenomenon that is quite rampant on Internet newsgroups, namely, flaming. A few participants tend to dominate the discussion and to discourage others by a steady stream of lengthy and abusive messages.

In the last few years with the public's discovery of the Internet and the startling growth in use, electronic polling has become much more of a real possibility. Polls are a regular feature on the Internet, whether voting for Web page layouts, songs, pinups-of-the-week, or presidential candidates. Of course, these polls are highly unscientific as there are no demographic controls and they have little effect other than to provide marketing information, but a sufficient level of security could be in place to limit voting to registered voters. In this case, would it be used by governments, and if so how and to what end?

Many questions must be answered before so-called instantaneous or electronic polling can become part of the democratic process. The fundamental issue turns on whether or not democracy can function as an extended Athenian marketplace. Supposedly, democracy began in Athens, where the citizens of that city state (not the women nor the slaves) decided issues of concern in open debate and public vote. Perhaps modern communication networks and computers can recreate the best features of that noble experiment. As we might expect, there would be a number of problems. How is a question to be formulated? How is the voting process itself to be monitored to ensure that only legitimate voters actually vote? How is the security of the central computers to be guaranteed? All these questions may be beside the main point—what benefits actually will accrue by integrating electronic polling into the current system?

One person in the forefront of the debate about electronic voting is Lorrie Cranor. One of her arguments in favor of electronic voting is that traditional voting methods, at least in North America, do not offer enough alternatives. Because one can vote only for one candidate, a concern exists about "wasting the vote" in a race involving more than two candidates. So in the 1992 election, it is claimed that "there were a lot of people who said that they were Perot supporters, but they felt that Perot didn't have a very good chance of winning. So as not to waste their vote, they voted for their second-choice candidate. And so at some point either the day before the election or the week before or even the day of the election, they evaluated Perot's likelihood of being able to win and decided that they weren't going to vote for him."[26] Cranor has proposed an electronic system, Sensus, that guarantees privacy and security and permits the voter to express a "declared voting strategy:"[27]

> you express a statement of strategy which explains how you want to vote. So, for example, this statement of strategy would indicate whether you would prefer to vote for, say, your second choice candidate instead of your first choice candidate, if your first choice candidate didn't have very much chance of winning. And you wouldn't have to decide before the election whether or not your first choice candidate had enough chance of winning. This would be decided for you by the computer, basically optimizing your strategy so that you would cast the best vote to get the most possible value for your vote when the votes were actually counted.

The role of the computer is to take into account each voter's strategy combined with the current vote tally and cycle through this process until everyone is as close to being satisfied as possible. Clearly, this approach encourages more candidates to run for office and is possible only with electronic voting. The extension of electronic voting to the legislative process seems to have very little support, certainly not from politicians, even if the many associated problems could be solved.

How Are the Votes Counted?

On the face of it, computerized voting and counting would seem to promise efficient, quick, and error-free reporting of election results, and for the most part it does, as it has become the dominant method of running elections:[28]

> During the past quarter of a century, with hardly anyone noticing, the inner workings of democracy have been computerized. All our elections, from mayor to President, are counted locally, in about ten thousand five hundred political jurisdictions, and gradually, since 1964, different kinds of computer-based voting systems have been installed in town after town, city after city, county after county.

But a number of worrisome cases suggest that program errors and manipulation may be more endemic than previously realized. In an ongoing study since 1984, the State of Illinois has reported finding errors in the counting instructions of one fifth of all computer programs examined. Apparently the local testing programs, which use only about fifty votes, had not uncovered these errors. Thus, a piece of program code that *kicks in* after a few hundred votes could be inserted into a counting program to produce whatever results are desired. Instead of paying people to vote a certain way, as has been done, programs could be altered to steal elections, unless adequate safeguards are in place.

In the summary to his study of computer voting, Roy Saltman offered the following cautionary remarks:[29]

> While vote-tallying using telephones or stations similar to automatic teller machines is technologically feasible, the decision to implement such a system must be based on more fundamental factors. Any installed system must meet political and economic requirements as well as technical requirements of accuracy and reliability. Political needs include equal access by individuals, the ability to verify registration, and the ability of the voters to vote in secret without intimidation. Internal controls must be implementable to demonstrate the correctness of the reported results.

Some five years later, Saltman pointed out that although the "US Congress is ultimately responsible for setting the rules governing the conduct of Federal elections i.e., for President and Vice-President, and its own membership," it has done almost nothing to institute procedures to deal with irregularities, the effects of new technologies, and other problems. As he notes, "this deficiency seriously inhibits the conduct of necessary scientific and engineering research, prevents the orderly development of alternatives for policy selection, and provides no center of expertise for dissemination of computer security and other important techniques to local administrators charged with the actual conduct of registration and voting."[30]

Who Won?

For many people, the most exciting and interesting part of the election process is election night, as the returns are presented to the nation over the television networks. In reporting the 1984 election, for the first time the networks used real-time computer graphics to display the results. Certain graphic information such as the candidates' pictures, maps of the states, and the forms of charts and graphs were prepared in advance. As the returns flooded in, the existing graphic information was combined with the new information and presented in a variety of colors and forms. A spokesman for CBS news noted, "In 1984, for the first time, we will be able to do true real-time, data-dependent images and animation."[31]

Computer models for predicting election outcomes on the basis of interviews with selected early voters have come under some criticism. In 1984 the landslide for President Reagan was anticipated quite early, but there was little surprise as most polls had predicted such a result. In the 1980 presidential election, however, many voters in the western part of the country apparently did not bother voting because the television networks declared President Reagan an early winner. Although these lost votes probably did not affect the presidential election, they did have an effect on local and state elections. It has been suggested that early computer predictions should not be announced until the polls have closed everywhere. In Canada, voting results are not announced until the polls have closed, so that on the West Coast late voters will not be influenced by reports in the East. Staggered hours might be a solution. In any event, the power of computer models, as well as the early report of results, to affect the electoral process must be recognized and steps must be taken to minimize the impact.

THE NATION'S DEFENSE

> Digitization of the battlefield is part of a major effort to reshape the Army and, thus, it is one of the Army's highest priorities. The Army hopes to identify how digitization will improve combat power and how to change its organizational structure, doctrine, and tactics to take advantage of digitization.[32]

A major responsibility of the federal government is to defend the nation from both internal and external enemies. This is certainly reflected in the fact that the defense budget is the major component of the total budget. The Department of Defense (DOD), with its vast resources, has taken a lead in the development of both computer hardware and software. Much of the early research in integrated circuits was funded by DOD for military purposes. Given the sheer size of the military establishment, problems of organization are serious. There is enormous difficulty in coordinating a worldwide enterprise consisting of millions of soldiers and civilian personnel and billions of dollars of equipment, while maintaining a high degree of military preparedness.

To maintain its large investment in advanced systems and to support new and risky projects, the Pentagon, in 1958, established an agency, DARPA (Defense Advanced Research Projects Agency), originally called ARPA, to fund research and development. This agency has had a major impact on semiconductors, computers, communication systems, applications, and artificial intelligence developments over the past 30 years. It has also exerted an enormous influence over the kind of research funded at US universities and has thereby shaped the growth of computer science departments from their very inception.

The Computerized Battlefield

In the 1982 conflict between Britain and Argentina over the Faulkland Islands, a single $200,000 computer-guided missile, the French Exocet, demolished the British destroyer Sheffield, a $50 million warship. The power of computer-age weapons was frighteningly revealed. The general class of weapons with microprocessors are called precision-guided munitions (PGMs). Probably the most publicized and sophisticated of the PGMs is the cruise missile. It is programmed to fly a ground-hugging route to its target to avoid most radar, and has a microcomputer aboard with detailed topographic information about its route. During flight this computer can compare information received from its sensors with its programmed knowledge to keep the missile on course. Future versions are expected to be able to recognize their designated targets when they arrive, to reduce the possibility of being deceived by camouflage. After a 1,500-mile trip the cruise missile can hit a ten-foot-square target.

With weapons this smart, how necessary are people? Perhaps the goal of the next stage of warfare planning will be to remove people from the battlefield. Wars of the future might be fought with computer-controlled aircraft in the sky and robots on the land. Robots with radio receivers and transmitters could lead troops into battle or into dangerous forays where the risk of death is high. Visions of the future battlefield go beyond even these possibilities to what *Time* has called "Cyberwar," waging "war by mouse, keyboard and computer virus."[33] It is only natural that the Information Age should spawn Information Warfare by means of "Info Attacks" plotted by "Cyberstrategists" with critical Information Technology, both private and public as the targets. Instead of waging traditional warfare against an enemy, the following components of an Info Attack may be used by the US:[34]

- *Electromagnetic pulse.* Delta Force Commandos infiltrate the enemy's capital and detonate a non-nuclear electromagnetic-pulse (EMP) device the size of a suitcase. The EMP bomb, placed next to the central bank, fries the electronics of the bank's computer and communications systems, bringing most financial operations to a halt.
- *Microbes.* The CIA inserts computer viruses into the switching networks for the country's phone system, causing massive failure. To perpetuate the degradation over a longer period, specially bred electronics-eating microbes are fed into the system.
- *Jamming.* Air Force electronic jamming planes break into the communications equipment of the enemy army and begin to overwhelm its generals with incorrect information, rendering the system almost useless.
- *Psychological warfare.* The Air Force's Commando Solo psy-ops plane jams signals for the government television station and inserts in its place a "morphed" TV program, in which the enemy leader appears on the screen and makes unpopular announcements, alienating him from his people.
- *Logic bombs.* Logic bombs shut down the computers that run the country's air-traffic control system and route its railroads. Planes end up at the wrong airports. Rail cars carrying military supplies are misdirected.

But if warfare does break out, the foot soldier will be outfitted with a bewildering array of electronic aids, including helmets with night-vision sensors, voice activation for a computer built into the body armor, a transmitter/receiver to send information back to headquarters and to receive new intelligence; body armor to protect against chemical or biological hazards; and, a weapon that can transmit still-frames to the high command and is connected to the helmet to aid in locating the enemy.

The Army's plans to develop the "Digital Battlefield" have been reviewed by the General Accounting Office, which notes that this will be carried out "by creating a vast network of computers, sensors, and communications systems that would provide a common picture of the battlefield from soldier to commander simultaneously . . . and [at an] estimated $4 billion cost."[35] The GAO is concerned about the following issues:[36]

> The Army's plan to digitize the battlefield is expensive, contains many risks, and lacks specific, measurable goals for the series of large-scale experiments that are to be conducted. The Army is planning to conduct a series of experiments from 1995 to 1997, including a brigade-level experiment in 1997 at a cost of $258 million, without having had a success-

ful battalion-level experiment . . . The Army faces numerous technical, program, cost, and schedule risks in implementing its master plan for battlefield digitization. These risks are integration, software development, hardware costs, unknown quantity requirements, communications, and interoperability with other command and control systems.

In other words, the Digital Battlefield may not just be around the corner; it is more theory than practice, and it will be very expensive.

The Strategic Defense Initiative

The possibility of nuclear war has been a fact of existence for most of us. It represents the terrifying vision of a technology that, once created and implemented, inevitably is loosed upon the world.

On March 23, 1983, President Reagan delivered his now famous "Star Wars" speech, launching the Strategic Defense Initiative. Its goal was the development of a comprehensive defense system to identify, intercept, and destroy all or most of an enemy's ballistic missiles. The debate over the feasibility of such a system and its impact on the current strategy of mutual deterrence has been raging ever since. Of course since the break-up of the Soviet Union, the threat to world peace has decreased substantially and some have argued that SDI, or the threat of a functioning SDI was a contributing factor to this momentous event. The financial costs of competing with the US may have created such a strain within the economy of the Soviet Union that its political and military will may have faltered and finally crumbled. Nevertheless, the effort to achieve a working SDI has had an impact in a number of areas and is therefore worth recounting.

It was clear at the outset that enormous computational resources would necessarily be involved in the Star Wars project. Thus, it is not surprising that the computer science community was split by a debate over the practicality of such a project and the morality of participation in its development. The decision whether or not to work on defense-related activities is of course not unique to computer scientists. The most obvious example is that of the many physicists who, after the dropping of nuclear bombs over Japan at the end of World War II, were reluctant to contribute to the development of hydrogen weapons. The role of scientists in service to the military is an old story rife with tales of ambition and regret.

In discussing the various issues associated with the Strategic Defense Initiative (SDI), the emphasis will be mainly on computer software; the very real and difficult physics problems will not be mentioned. Many critics of SDI have recognized that the most serious area of concern is software—the programs that are intended to direct the many computers in the wide variety of tasks necessary to make the system work. SDI will place unprecedented demands on software, to such a degree that many computer scientists publicly have expressed serious doubts about it ever working. And it must operate correctly the very first time it is used. Anyone familiar with writing even short programs knows that such an event is almost nonexistent: "Because of the extreme demands on the system and our inability to test it, we will never be able to believe, with confidence, that we have succeeded. Most of the money spent will be wasted." [37]

In 1988, the Office of Technology Assessment (OTA) of the US Congress issued a comprehensive classified study together with an unclassified version "to determine the technological feasibility and implications, and the ability to survive and function despite a preemptive attack by an aggressor possessing comparable technology, of the Strategic Defense Initiative Program . . . This study shall include an analysis of the feasibility of meeting SDI software requirements."[38] Consider the following items from the principal findings of this important study:

Finding 1. After 30 years of BMD (Ballistic Missile Defense) research, including the first few years of the Strategic Defense Initiative (SDI), defense scientists and engineers have produced impressive technical achievements, but questions remain about the feasibility of meeting the goals of the SDI.

Finding 2. Given optimistic assumptions (e.g., extraordinarily fast rates of research, development, and production), the kind of first-phase system that SDIO [*Strategic Defense Initiative Organization*] is considering might be technically deployable in the 1995–2000 period . . . such a system might destroy anywhere from a few up to a modest fraction of attacking Soviet intercontinental ballistic missile (ICBM) warheads.

Finding 4. The precise degree of BMD system survivability is hard to anticipate.

Finding 7. The nature of software and experience with large, complex software systems indicate that there may always be irresolvable questions about how dependable BMD software would be and about the confidence the United States could place in dependability estimates. Existing large software systems, such as the long-distance telephone system, have become highly dependable only after extensive operational use and modification. In OTA's judgment, there would be a significant probability (i.e., one large enough to take seriously) that the first (and presumably only) time the BMD system were used in a real war, it would suffer a catastrophic failure. . . . The relatively slow rate of improvement in software engineering techniques makes it appear unlikely to OTA that the situation will be substantially alleviated in the foreseeable future.

Finding 8. No adequate models for the development, production, test, and maintenance of software for full-scale BMD systems exist . . . Experts agree that new methods for producing and safely testing the system would be needed. Evolution would be the key to system development, requiring new methods of controlling and disseminating software changes and assuring that each change would not increase the potential for catastrophic failure. OTA has found little evidence of significant progress in these areas.

The inclusion of these extensive quotations is necessary and important in order to indicate the scope of the software engineering task facing the designers of SDI. SDIO seems to have recognized the enormous difficulty of its task: "If deployed, SDS (Strategic Defense System) will be more complex than any other system the world has seen."[39] The software manager, Colonel Charles W. Lillie agreed that "the software development and testing practice lags up to 10 years behind the state of the art. But he asserted that the SDI office has recently taken several steps to shorten the lag."[40] In addition, SDI officials have argued that previous military systems have been used without compete testing, and they point to the Aegis ship defense system. OTA has also noted that computer simulations will be difficult to mount because of the lack of real-world data on nuclear explosions in outer space, multiple enemy missile launches, and unpredictable countermeasures by the enemy as well. In a bizarre example of military strategic thinking, indulged in by OTA, the following backhanded support of SDI is proposed: "But unless the Soviets had secretly deployed coun-termeasures, such as a software virus planted by a saboteur programmer, the Soviets could not be certain that a SDI software would *not* work, and therefore *might* be deterred from attack,"[41] (emphasis added). Thus, expenditures of billions of dollars have already been made, and more will follow under a continuing renamed program, to produce a system whose reliability is highly suspect, which cannot be adequately tested, and whose major impact has probably already been felt in the collapse of the Soviet Union.

On May 13, 1993, the Department of Defense declared that funding for SDI had ended and that the "Star Wars" program was dead, but one month later, having undergone a name change to "Ballistic Missile Defense Organization," it was alive and apparently well "and may cost taxpayers another $30 billion by the end of the century. The program has already cost $33 billion. . . . Clinton-Aspin request[s] for SDI-related programs is $3.8 bil-lion."[42] In the 1996 Presidential campaign, Star Wars seems to have become a political issue. Congressional Republicans have been trying to pass the Defend America Act, which is seen as the old missile defense system of the Strategic Defense Initiative, under a new name. Robert Dole has argued: "If I ask most people what would you have the President do if there was an incoming missile, ballistic missile, you would say shoot it down. We can't because President Clinton opposes it. And we support it."[43] President Clinton is sup-porting a less costly version of this proposal.

Security from Information Attack

As previously mentioned, part of the repertoire of resources of the "Computerized Battle-field" involves attacks on information systems, including the destruction or alteration of important data. Such attacks against the US Department of Defense (DOD) have already occurred:[44]

> Attacks on Defense computer systems are a serious and growing threat. The exact number cannot be readily determined because only a small portion are actually detected and re-ported. However, Defense Information Systems Agency (DISA) data implies that Defense may have experienced as many as 250,000 attacks last year. DISA information also shows that attacks are successful 65 percent of the time, and that the number of attacks is dou-bling each year, as Internet use increases along with the sophistication of "hackers" and their tools.

Many of these attacks are harmless, but some may be extremely dangerous and efforts must be taken by DOD to increase security, a difficulty given that "Defense has to protect a vast and complex information infrastructure: currently, it has over 2.1 million comput-ers, 10,000 local networks, and 100 long-distance networks."[45]

ISSUES AND PROBLEMS

The investments reported here have the potential to revolutionize the way the public inter-acts with government. This revolution can be achieved through the development and deployment of interactive, multimedia applications that are accessible through kiosks as well as other available delivery mechanisms, such as personal computers.[46]

Many issues could be discussed but the emphasis will be on the following: fallible military technologies, the responsibility of the federal government for the electronic dissemination of public information and services, and an example of a serious Internet side effect for state and local governments. Other issues such as the growing number of government databases and their impact on privacy is examined in Chapter 9. Also discussed later in this book (Chapter 13) are the very difficult questions associated with ethical and professional conduct. As noted previously, many scientists have long struggled with whether or not to engage in research that directly or indirectly has military applications. Computer scientists have had to face similar questions in recent years.

A Terrible Accident

One important example that high technology is not infallible and that the consequences can be dreadful is the incident that occurred in July of 1988 in the Persian Gulf. At that time, the prime enemy was Iran, and the cruiser USS Vincennes, in the mistaken belief that it was under attack, shot down an Iranian airliner, killing 290 civilians. The Vincennes was equipped with the most advanced technology available, the $1 billion Aegis system, under which the captain issues commands from the Combat Information Center (CIS), a windowless room deep within the ship, connected to the outside world by radar and communications systems and relying on computers to process and display information rapidly. The information available to the captain was instantaneous and accurate and yet 290 people died. Why? The simple lesson is that too much data may overwhelm sound judgment, especially under battle conditions, exactly when such an advanced system is designed to make its major contribution.

After studying the computer tapes, Navy investigators judged the data to be accurate but found that two "key misperceptions led to the skipper's decision to shoot."[47] A radar operator reported that an F-14 fighter was headed directly towards the Vincennes, even though radar showed it climbing on a typical flight path. This report must be understood in the context of well-known previous events in the Gulf, specifically the attack on the frigate Stark by the Iraqis in 1987, which resulted in the loss of 37 sailors. The Stark captain's hesitant response in the face of a possible attack created a subsequent urgency not to let it happen again. Thus, a preconceived scenario was in place, and even when someone in the CIS announced that the radar blip might be a commercial airliner, it was noted but not really factored into the decision process. One recommendation was to improve computer displays to show an aircraft's altitude beside its radar track. The larger lesson is that human memories and emotions, heightened by stressful battle conditions, may compromise even the most sophisticated information technology system with dire consequences for all.

Many of these concerns were forgotten in the aftermath of the Gulf War, fought during January and February of 1991. Considerable publicity was directed towards "smart weapons," such as the Tomahawk cruise missile and the Patriot antiballistic missile. In fact, computers were seen as a major factor in the surprisingly quick and overwhelmingly massive victory over Iraq. High technology received an enormous boost, and increased funding for a new generation of weapons was assured. At the same time, we should note two points: the actual technology was developed in the 1970s and early 1980s, and a postwar analysis raised serious doubts about the actual effectiveness of computer-based weapons.

The Dissemination of Federal Information

The Federal government collects, processes, and distributes vast amounts of information used by all segments of the public. Until fairly recently, most of this material was hard copy, or ink on paper, frequently published by the General Printing Office or the National Technical Information Service. Many types of information, however, such as technical, statistical, scientific, and reference may best be stored and disseminated by electronic means. For example, reference information such as Bureau of the Census statistics reports could be made available on optical disks. The crucial issues under discussion are how to maintain ready access to electronic media and how to define the respective roles of the government and private information handlers in the electronic dissemination of information. Many of these questions were defined and discussed in a comprehensive report issued by the Office of Technology Assessment in 1988; some of the problems and challenges are given as follows:[48]

- At a fundamental level, electronic technology is changing or even eliminating many distinctions between reports, publications, databases, records, and the like, in ways not anticipated by existing statutes and policies.
- Electronic technology permits information dissemination on a decentralized basis that is cost-effective at low levels of demand.
- Technology has outpaced the major government-wide statutes that apply to Federal information dissemination.
- The advent of electronic dissemination raises new equity concerns since, to the extent that electronic formats have distinct advantages (e.g., in terms of timeliness, searchability), those without electronic access are disadvantaged.
- *Technological advances complicate the Federal Government's relationships with the commercial information industry . . . the privatization of major Federal information dissemination activities has not yet been demonstrated to be either cost-effective or beneficial for important government functions.* [Emphasis added.]

There was disagreement within the government over how much and how fast information dissemination should be privatized, not whether or not it should be. Within the Office of Management of the Budget (OMB), officials argue that government agencies should release information only in bulk form, similar to the activity of wholesalers in consumer goods, whereas the private sector should act as retailers, packaging the information to meet market demands, the argument being that information companies are much more flexible and responsive than government bureaucracies. In opposition to this view, such groups as the American Civil Liberties Union and Computer Professionals for Social Responsibility claim "that information technology could greatly improve the public's ability to draw on government data. They call for new policies that would encourage the fed-eral government to provide user-friendly access to its statistics and public records."[49] The battle is joined, largely on ideological and profit-motivated grounds. It appears that no comprehensive solution is in the offing, but rather a case-by-case approach in which the government is expected to provide services in those areas that are not economically viable for the private sector.

In the past few years, governments have taken advantage of the Internet as an efficient and relatively economic way to circulate information. Reports, studies, speeches, minutes of meetings, online conferences, and other types of information are made available shortly after they appear or even while they are taking place. The public, or at least that growing part of it with access to the Internet, now expects to find needed government information on demand. In a report to Congress, the Government Printing Office has made proposals about how to continue the process of making more information electronically available via the Federal Deposit Library Program (FDLP). The mission for the FDLP is "to provide eq-uitable, efficient, timely and dependable no-fee public access to Federal Government in-formation within the scope of the program."[50] Currently, a number of libraries across the country have been chosen to act as repositories for Federal information, providing ready access to all Americans. The report identifies four ways in which the GPO can bring elec-tronic information into the FDLP:[51]

- GPO can identify, describe and link the public to the wealth of distributed Government information products maintained at Government electronic information services for free public use.
- GPO can establish reimbursable agreements with agencies that provide fee-based Gov-ernment electronic information services in order to provide free public access to their in-formation through the FDLP.
- GPO can "ride" agency requisitions and pay for depository copies of tangible electronic information products, such as CD-ROM discs, even if they are not produced or procured through GPO.
- GPO can obtain from agencies electronic source files for information the agencies do not wish to disseminate through their own Government electronic information services. These files can be made available through the *GPO Access* services or disseminated to depository libraries in CD-ROM or other tangible format.

There appears to be some intention to continue the tradition of making as much govern-ment information as possible available to online users, but those interested in limiting the role of government in this area will continue to urge for more private sector involvement.

Delivering Services to Americans

Clearly not only information but government services as well can be delivered over elec-tronic networks. The Clinton-Gore initiative, the National Information Infrastructure (NII), is intended to dramatically change the way society operates, including the way gov-ernment agencies perform their functions. Thus, a series of reports and studies have been carried out outlining possible government policies in a wide variety of areas. Among these are the impact of telecommunications policies on rural areas and on Native Americans as well as how metropolitan America will be affected by the new technologies. References to these reports are given at the end of this chapter, but one example of a new way by which government can respond to requests and provide information in an efficient and timely fashion has been referred to as the interactive kiosk solution:[52]

- One-stop shopping-meeting customer needs by resolving all issues in one visit; no "arcade" of kiosks.
- 24-hour/7-day access-available at the customer's convenience.
- Universal reach and coverage-ready access for all people, using whatever technology is at their disposal. Kiosks will be located in areas designed to best meet the public's needs.
- On-line information and transactions-"real time" networked access to the most current and correct government information and the ability to complete product orders and personalized queries.

The Interagency Kiosk Committee, a coalition among federal agencies, has made several recommendations including pilot studies of easy-to-use, conveniently located kiosks to gather valuable public feedback, joint federal, state, and local participation, close coordination among federal agencies, and a commitment to carry through. In addition, it notes that, "Kiosks are one of a number of delivery channels for government services. The Committee recommends proceeding with the development of an electronic government services delivery system using kiosks as the initial interface to begin implementing the technical and support infrastructures that will maximize service delivery through many technologies."

A Negative Situation for State and Local Governments

For the most part, the Information Highway will be beneficial for both government and citizens and should provide better and more efficient services and access to information of all types. At least, this appears to be the accepted wisdom, although many technological spin-offs are impossible to predict and almost impossible to undo. For example, consider the following: "According to the US Advisory Commission on Intergovernmental Relations, an estimated $3.3 billion in state and local sales taxes are now lost due to untaxed mail order sales from out-of-state firms."[53] With the expected growth of commercial activities on the Internet and its successor, this amount will increase substantially. In addition, the Supreme Court has ruled that "interstate mail-order firms [are] exempt from state sales taxes." Furthermore, in California, because of Proposition 13, state and local governments "are extremely dependent on sales taxes to fund their budgets." What all this means is that as Internet commerce increases, and it will, many states and local governments will find their sales tax revenue declining. If in-state and local business suffer because of reduced sales, they may lay off employees or even shut down, further exacerbating the problem. Possible solutions are the following:[54]

- Centralize revenue collection to state and national levels.
- Scale back and even eliminate sales taxes as a revenue source.

- Legally prohibit "subsidy abuse" by local governments in competition for business location.

SUMMARY

Government is probably the largest single user of computers. These uses are incredibly varied and their impact is felt throughout society. The Federal Government has purchased and continues to purchase an enormous number of computers. It exerts considerable pressure on the market to conform to its requirements. Governments gather, store, and process vast amounts of information. The public may be concerned about how this information is safeguarded and how it is used. As the bureaucracy depends more heavily on computer systems, it may become less responsive to the needs of the public it is supposed to serve. It may hide behind the computer instead of providing human answers. Congress also has benefited from the use of computers and communication networks in a variety of ways.

More recently, the electoral process has witnessed the introduction of computers for purposes of identifying targeted special-interest groups and funding. The television networks use computers to monitor the voting process and, more controversially, to predict the outcomes as early as possible. Voting and counting by computer is becoming more common with all the attendant risks of program error and even fraud. The Internet has begun to play a role in this area as candidates set up Web sites to disseminate their views, post press releases, and receive comments from their supporters and opponents.

The Department of Defense (DOD) is the largest user of computers within the Federal Government. The DOD has launched major programs to modernize its control and command structure and its weaponry, including advanced programs in artificial intelligence to equip airplanes and tanks with sophisticated computer systems. Major funding for AI has come from DOD, in pursuit of improvements in battlefield capabilities. Important and expensive research and development efforts such as the Strategic Defense Initiative and the Strategic Computer Initiative have been launched, with a significant impact on computer science research and education. Given the important role of computers in the detection and recognition of large-scale military threats, some people have expressed a deep concern that accidental war may occur because computer systems will respond before humans can intervene. In spite of assurances by the government that humans will always retain ultimate responsibility, the ability to respond quickly is a high priority for military decision makers.

Finally, there is a considerable controversy over the role of the Federal government in disseminating electronically stored information. The debate turns on the balance between the respective responsibilities of the private and public sectors in providing information, gathered by the government, to the public. The past few years have witnessed the sudden appearance of numerous Web sites to provide the public with up-to-date government reports, news releases, as well as the status of legislation, and the complete text of bills. The influence of DOD in the growth of computer science has been well documented. What is of concern is whether or not this influence has been, and will continue to be, of benefit to the field, its practitioners, and the country.

NOTES

1. Robert Wright. "Hyperdemocracy," *Time*, January 23, 1995, pp. 41–46.

2. *The Unpredictable Certainty: Information Infrastructure Through 2000,* NII Steering Committee, National Research Council. (Washington, DC: National Academy Press, 1996). Available at the Web site with URL: <http://www.nap.edu/nap/online/unpredictable/>.

3. "Paperwork Reduction: Burden Unlikely to be Met," US General Accounting Office, GAO/T-GGD/RCED-96-186, July 5, 1996. (Gaithersburg, MD: GAO Document Distribution Facility), p. 3. Available at the Web page with URL: <http://www.access.gpo.gov/cgi-bin/waisgate.cgi?WAISdocID=6796319722+4+1+0&WAISaction=retrieve>.

4. "Information Technology Investment: A Governmentwide Overview," US General Accounting Office, GAO/AIMD-95-208, July 7, 1995. (Gaithersburg, MD: GAO Document Distribution Facility). Available at the Web page with URL: <http://www.access.gpo.gov/cgi-bin/waisgate.cgi?WAISdocID=2459617961+16+0+0&WAISaction=retrieve>.

5. *Ibid.*

6. "Paperwork Reduction: Mixed Efforts on Agency Decision Processes and Data Availability," US General Accounting Office, GAO/PEMD-89-20, September 1989, p. 11.

7. *Ibid.*

8. "Managing Federal Information Resources, Seventh Annual Report Under the Paperwork Act of 1980." (Washington, DC: Office of Management of the Budget, December 1989).

9. "Management of Federal Information Resources," Circular No. A-130 (Revised), February 8, 1996, Office of Management of the Budget. Available at the Web site with URL: <http://www1.whitehouse.gov/WH/EOP/OMB/html/circulars/a130/a130.html>.

10. "Paperwork Reduction: Burden Reduction Goal Unlikely to Be Met," testimony before the Committee on Small Business, US Senate, US General Accounting Office, GAO/T-GGD/RCED-96-186, July 5, 1996. Available at the Web page with URL: <http://www.access.gpo.gov/cgi-bin/waisgate.cgi?WAISdocID=6796319722+4+1+0&WAISaction=retrieve>.

11. "Introduction," National Performance Review, September 7, 1995. Accessed at the Web page with URL: <http://www.npr.gov/homepage/228e.html> on June 29, 1996.

12. "Reinvention's Next Steps: Governing in a Balanced Budget World," National Performance Review, March 4, 1996. Accessed at the Web page with URL: <http://www.npr.gov/homepage/272a.html> on June 29, 1996.

13. Dean Foust. "The IRS Is Badly Overtaxed," *Business Week,* April 15, 1996, p. 46.

14. "IRM/General Government Division Issue Area Plan, Fiscal Years 1994–1996," Accounting and Information Management Division, US General Accounting Office, GAO/IAP-95-8, March 1995. (Washington, DC: US General Accounting Office). Available at the Web page with URL: <http://www.access.gpo.gov/cgi-bin/waisgate.cgi?WAISdocID=696729821+38+1+0&WAISaction=retrieve>.

15. Gary H. Anthes. "IRS to Require Electronic Filing," *Computerworld,* July 15, 1996, p. 28.

16. Gary H. Anthes. "Air Traffic Takes Another Turn," *Computerworld,* April 25, 1994, p. 79.

17. Tim Ouellette and Steve Moore. "FAA's Reliance on Ancient Backup Systems Raises Concern," *Computerworld,* July 31, 1995, p. 14.

18. Gary H. Anthes. "FAA Speeds Plan to Replace Traffic Control Systems," *Computerworld,* August 7, 1995, p. 16.

19. *Ibid.*

20. Gary H. Anthes. "Revamp Flies Off Course," *Computerworld,* August 5, 1996, p. 28.

21. Robert Lee Chartrand. "Information Technology in the Legislative Process: 1976–1985," in Martha E. Williams (ed.), *Annual Review of Information Science and Technology (ARIST),*

Volume 21. (White Plains, New York: Knowledge Industry Publications, Inc. for the American Society for Information Science, 1986), pp. 203–239.

22. Stephen E. Frantzich. "The Use and Implications of Information Technology in Congress," in Karen B. Levitan (ed.), *Government Infostructures.* (Westport, CT: Greenwood Press, 1987), pp. 27–48.

23. Craig Stedman. "Feds Track Sex Offenders with Database," *Computerworld,* September 2, 1996, p. 24.

24. Jean Bethke Elshtain. "Interactive TV—Democracy and the Qube Tube," *The Nation,* August 7–14, 1982, p. 108.

25. "Providing Community Service via Civic Computer Network: A Case Study of Public Electronic Network, Santa Monica, CA," Center for Strategic Communications, Benton Foundation, Document #259, February 1995. Accessed from the Web page with URL: <http://www.cdinet.com/cgi-bin/bold?/Benton/Goingon/Csc/civic.html+politics> on July 1, 1996.

26. "Virtual Democracy: Is the Internet the Ultimate Voting Booth," an interview with Lorrie Cranor, *Off the Record,* February 6, 1996. Accessed from the Web page with URL: <http://www.mediapool.com/offtherecord/vot_tran.html> on July 1, 1996.

27. *Ibid.*

28. Ronnie Dugger. "Annals of Democracy: Counting Votes," *The New Yorker,* November 7, 1988, p. 40.

29. Roy G. Saltman. "Accuracy, Integrity and Security in Computerized Vote-Tallying," *Communications of the ACM,* **31** (10), October 1988, pp. 1191, 1218.

30. Roy G. Altman. "Assuring Accuracy, Integrity and Security in National Elections: The Role of the US Congress," Conference on Freedom and Privacy, February 12, 1993. Accessed from the Web page with URL: <http://www.cpsr.org/dox/conferences/cfp93/saltman.html> on July 1, 1996.

31. Tekla S. Perry. "TV Networks Vie for Viewer's Votes," *IEEE Spectrum,* October 1984, p. 68.

32. "Battlefield Automation: Army's Digital Battlefield Plan Lacks Specific Measurable Goals," Report to Congressional Committees, US General Accounting Office, GAO/NSIAD-96-25. (Gaithersburg, MD: US General Accounting Office, November 1995), p. 4. Available at the Web page with URL: <http://www.access.gpo.gov/cgi-bin/useftp.cgi?IPaddress=wais.access.gpo.gov&filename=ns96025.pdf&directory=/diskb/wais/data/gao>.

33. Douglas Waller. "Onward Cyber Soldiers," *Time,* August 21, 1995, pp. 30–36.

34. *Ibid.,* pp. 32–33.

35. *Op cit.,* Battlefield Automation.

36. *Ibid.,* pp. 1, 3.

37. Professor David Parnas, a distinguished software engineer, in his statement of resignation from a nine member Star Wars advisory panel on computing, as quoted in Philip Elmer-Dewitt, "Star Wars and Software," *Time,* July 22, 1985, p. 39. See Chapter 13 for more of Professor Parnas's views, especially with respect to professional responsibility.

38. *SDI: Technology Survivability and Software. Summary,* US Congress, Office of Technology Assessment, OTA-ISC-354. (Washington, DC, May 1988).

39. From a SDI report on the National Test Facility as quoted in John A. Adam, "Star Wars in Transition," *IEEE Spectrum,* March 1989, p. 37.

40. *Ibid.*

41. *Ibid.,* p. 38.

42. "Star Wars Still Alive," *Boston Globe,* June 21, 1993. Accessed from the Web page with URL: <http://www.cpsr.org/cpsr/cpsr_21st_century_project/star_wars_alive> on July 6, 1996.

43. "Star Wars—The Sequel," transcript of a PBS Newshour debate, June 4, 1996. Accessed from the Web page with URL: <http://web-cr01.pbs.org/newshour/bb/military/star_wars_6-4.html> on July 6, 1996.

44. "Information Security: Computer Attacks at Department of Defense Pose Increasing Risks," Report to Congressional Requesters, US General Accounting Office, GAO/AIMD-96-84. (Gaithersburg, MD: US General Accounting Office, May 1996).

45. *Ibid.*

46. "The Kiosk Network Solution: An Electronic Gateway to Government," Interagency Kiosk Committee, Date Unknown. Accessed from the Web site with URL: <http://www.wings.usps. gov/kioskweb.html> on May 29, 1996.

47. David Griffiths. "When Man Can't Keep Up with the Machines of War," *Business Week,* September 12, 1988, p. 36. Russell Watson, John Barry, and Richard Sandza, "A Case of Human Error," *Newsweek,* August 15, 1988, pp. 18–20.

48. *Informing the Nation: Federal Information Dissemination in an Electronic Age,* US Congress, Office of Technology Assessment, OTA-CIT-396. (Washington, DC: US Government Printing Office, October 1988), pp. 8–9.

49. Henry H. Perritt, Jr. "Government Information Goes On-Line," *Technology Review,* November–December 1989, pp. 60–67.

50. *Study to Identify Measures Necessary for a Successful Transition to a More Electronic Federal Depository Library Program,* GPO Publication 500.11. (Washington, DC: US Government Printing Office, June 1996). Available at the Web page with URL: <http://www.access.gpo.gov/ su_docs/dpos/rep_cong/images/report.pdf>.

51. *Ibid.,* p. 26.

52. *Op cit.,* The Kiosk Network Solution.

53. Nathan Newman. "Prop 13 Meets the Internet: How State and Local Governments Are Becoming Road Kill on the Information Superhighway," Center for Community Economic Research, University of California, Berkeley, August 1995. Accessed from the Web page with URL: <http://garnet.berkeley.edu:3333/budget/tax-internet/taxart3b.html>. on May 7, 1996.

54. *Ibid.*

ADDITIONAL READINGS

Introduction

Making Government Work: Electronic Delivery of Federal Services. US Congress, Office of Technology Assessment, OTA-TCT-578. (Gaithersburg, MD: US Government Printing Office, November 1993). Available from the Web page with URL: <http://www.ota.nap.edu/pdf/data/1993/ 9333.PDF>.

"The Nation-State is Dead. Long Live the Nation-State," *The Economist,* December 23, 1995–January 5, 1996, pp. 15–18.

Information Processing: Issues and Problems

Blodgett, Mindy and Sharon Gaudin. "Chasing Deadbeats Online," *Computerworld,* July 29, 1996, p. 29.

"Government Information Technology Services (GITS), Working Group Accomplishments Report," The Department of the Treasury, US, June 1996. Accessed from the Web page with URL: <http://www.ustreas.gov/treasury/initiatives/work/final.html> on August 25, 1996.

"Improving the Flow of Information to Congress," Report to the Ranking Member, Committee on Labor and Human Resources, US Senate, US General Accounting Office, GAO/PEMD-95-1, January 1995. (Gaithersburg, MD: US General Accounting Office). Available at the Web page with URL: <http://www.access.gpo.gov/cgi-bin/waisgate.cgi?WAISdocID=729222313+1+0+0&WAISaction=retrieve>.

"Information Technology: Best Practices Can Improve Performance and Produce Results," Testimony before the Subcommittee on Government Management, Information Technology and Technology Committee on Government Reform and Oversight, US House of Representatives, US General Accounting Office, GAO/T-AIMD-96-46, February 26, 1996. (Gaithersburg, MD: US General Accounting Office). Available at the Web page with URL: <http://www.access.gpo.gov/cgi-bin/waisgate.cgi?WAISdocID=696729821+35+1+0&WAISaction=retrieve>.

"Management Reform: Implementation of the National Performance Review's Recommendations," US General Accounting Office, GAO/OCG-95-1, December 1994. (Gaithersburg, MD: US General Accounting Office). Available at the Web page with URL: <http://www.access.gpo.gov/cgi-bin/waisgate.cgi?WAISdocID=725591777+1+0+0&WAISaction=retrieve>.

The Political Process

Cranor, Lorrie Faith. "Electronic Voting: Computerized Polls May Save Money, Protect Privacy." *Crossroads: The ACM Student Magazine,* 2 (4), April 1996. Accessed at the Web page with URL: <http://www.acm.org/crossroads/xrds2-4/voting.html> on July 1, 1996.

Goff, Leslie. "The Webbing of the President," *Computerworld,* September 2, 1996, pp. 79–80.

Schwartz, Evan L. "Direct Democracy: Are You Ready for the Democracy Channel?" *Wired,* 2.01, January 1994, pp. 74–75. Accessed from the Web page with URL: <http://www.eff.org/pub/Activism/E-voting/democracy_online.article> on July 1, 1996.

"Telecommunications and Democracy," Communications Policy Briefing #4, The Benton Foundation, 1994. Accessed at the Web page with URL: <http://cdinet.com/Benton/Catalog/Brief4/brief4.html> on July 1, 1996.

The Nation's Defense

Anthes, Gary H. "Info Warfare Risk Growing," *Computerworld,* May 22, 1995, pp. 1, 16.

Bellin, David and Chapman, Gary (eds.), *Computers in Battle—Will They Work?* (New York: Harcourt Brace Jovanovich, 1987).

Broad, William J. "From Fantasy to Fact: Space-Based Laser Nearly Ready to Fly," *The New York Times,* December 6, 1994, pp. B 5–B 6.

Broad, William J. *Teller's War: The Top-Secret Story Behind the Star Wars Deception.* (New York: Simon & Schuster, 1992).

Commercial Multimedia Technologies for the Twenty-First Century Army Battlefields: A Technology Management Strategy. National Research Council, 1995. (Washington, DC: National Academy Press). Some of the material was accessed from the Web site with URL: <http://www.nas.edu> on June 10, 1996.

Crock, Stan. "Star Wars Junior: Will It Fly?" *Business Week,* July 15, 1996, pp. 88–89.

Distributed Interactive Simulation of Combat. US Congress, Office of Technology Assessment, OTA-BP-ISS-151. (Washington, DC: US Government Printing Office, September 1995). Available at the Web page with URL: <http://www.ota.nap.edu/pdf/data/1995/9512.PDF>.

Molander, Roger C., Riddile, Andrew S., and Wilson, Peter A. *Strategic Information Warfare: A New Face of War*. National Defense Research Institute. (Santa Monica, CA: RAND, 1996). Available at the Web site with URL: <http://www.rand.org/publications/MR/MR661/MR661.pdf>.

Patton, Phil. "Robots with the Right Stuff." *Wired,* 4.03, March 1996, pp. 148–151, 210, 212, 214.

Port, Otis, Magnusson, P., Payne, S., Smart, T., Levine, J. B., Schine, E., and Oster, P. "The High-Tech War Machine," *Business Week,* February 4, 1991, pp. 38–41.

Virtual Reality and Technologies for Combat Simulation—Background Paper. US Congress, Office of Technology Assessment, OTA-BP-ISS-136. (Washington, DC: Government Printing Office, September 1994). Available at the Web page with URL: <http://www.ota.nap.edu/pdf/data/1994/9444.PDF>.

Issues and Problems

"Information Superhighway: An Overview of Technology Challenges." Report to Congress, US General Accounting Office, GAO/AIMD-95-23. (Gaithersburg, MD: US General Accounting Office, January 1995). Available at the Web page with URL: <http://www.access.gpo.gov/cgi-bin/waisgate.cgi?WAISdocID=696729821+22+1+0&WAISaction=retrieve>.

Katz, Randy. "Professor Katz Goes to Washington." *Communications of the ACM,* 39 (5), May 1996, pp. 13–17.

"Survey of Rural Information Infrastructure Technologies." National Telecommunications and Information Administration, US Department of Commerce, NTIA Special Publication 95–3, September 1995. Accessed through the Institute for Telecommunications (ITS) Home Web page with URL: <http://www.its.bldrdoc.gov> on May 25, 1996.

The Technological Reshaping of America. US Congress, Office of Technology Assessment, OTA-ETI-643. (Washington, DC: US Government Printing Office, August 1995). Available at the Web page with URL: <http://www.ota.nap.edu/pdf/data/1995/9541.PDF>.

Telecommunications Technology and Native Americans: Opportunities and Challenges. US Congress, Office of Technology Assessment, OTA-ITC-621. (Washington, DC: US Government Printing Office, August 1995). Available at the Web page with URL: <http://www.ota.nap.edu/pdf/data/1995/9542.PDF>.

Thomborson, Clark. "Role of Military Funding in Academic Computer Science," in Bellin and Chapman (eds.), *Computers in Battle—Will They Work?,* pp. 283–296.

— 8 —

COMPUTERS AND THE LAW

Bad laws are the worst sort of tyranny.
Edmund Burke (1729–1797)

The first thing we do, let's kill all the lawyers.
William Shakespeare, *King Henry VI Part II*

INTRODUCTION

A given technological innovation will inevitably secure its place in society as the existing system of laws is expanded to accommodate it. What is remarkable about computer technology is how fast this process has occurred and how many interesting and important legal issues have arisen. As we have noted, computer professionals and legal professionals share at least one thing: they both have an extensive and impenetrable jargon. In a very short time a new subdiscipline has come into being, usually called computer law. One lawyer (Thomas Christo) has argued that it is wrong to speak of computer law when in fact there is just the *Law*.[1] Nevertheless, a number of universities do offer courses in computer law and there are several journals in this area. What, then, are some of the issues that currently fall within the purview of computer law?

There are several major areas of concern. Computer crime involves the use of the computer, with or without computer networks, to steal or embezzle money in a manner that could not easily have been done otherwise. There are also such crimes as stealing computer time, unlawful access to files, the acquisition of privileged information, and the corruption or actual destruction of computer files. This last activity has probably become the most highly publicized, as terms such as "virus," "worm," and "hacker" have penetrated the public consciousness. Although much computer crime has traditionally been perpetrated in banks, small and large companies, and government bureaucracies, viruses have had a direct impact on the ordinary citizen at home. Computer viruses seem to arrive as regularly as biological ones and occasionally with devastating effect.

The second major area concerns the relation between copyright and patent law and the legal protection of software. Much has been written about whether or not current law can be used in this area. There is the problem of distinguishing between the central idea captured in a program and the program itself. Other problems are occurring as the distinction between hardware and software becomes increasingly blurred. How do we protect programs implemented in ROM (read only memory)? There are questions about the copying of the masks used to manufacture microprocessor chips or, what is more subtle, the determination of the underlying logic by reverse engineering. Considerable legal wrangling has taken place over the "look-and-feel" of application and system interfaces, although the courts finally seem to have made a definitive decision.

It would indeed be surprising if the coming of the Internet had not generated a number of legal issues or at least cast well-known ones in a new light. Probably the issue that has generated the most publicity is the question of free speech and the concern with the unfettered flow of pornographic material over the Internet. The passage of the Telecommunication Act of 1996 was directed mainly at permitting technologies such as telephone, cable, and the broadcast media to compete under a weakened regulatory structure. (More details are provided in Chapter 11.) But also included in the legislation was the Communications Decency Act, an attempt to prevent "indecent" material on the Internet and local bulletin boards from finding its way into the hands (eyes?) of children. The attempt to regulate content over the Internet has aroused vigorous opposition and once again, the sanctity of the First Amendment has become the major rallying cry.

Private networks such as CompuServe and America Online have dealt with court challenges to their status, either as broadcasters such as the television stations or networks, or as common carriers such as telephone companies, either local or long distance. This distinction is crucial with respect to the responsibility, if any, that they have for the content of the material they carry. Around the world some countries have also been concerned about the content of material carried on the Internet, and there have been attempts at interceding and controlling unwanted information. Defenders of an unregulated world have argued that it is impossible to control the Internet, which itself was designed to operate under extreme physical disruptions and indeed to route transmissions around such impediments. Furthermore, it is argued that this unique means of global communication should not and cannot be subject to the laws of another era.

Other legal issues have arisen on the Internet and more particularly on the World Wide Web. The highly linked world of the Web has given urgency to the task of determining a new structure for intellectual property rights in a digital and widely distributed format. Many countries are in the process of revising their copyright and patent acts to deal with these challenging and novel conditions. And there is more. What about online harassment and libel, and the spread of ethnic, racial, gender, and religious hate material? What about the availability of information on how to make simple bombs?

Developments in information processing have also affected the way law is practiced. Legal information retrieval systems help the lawyer in case preparation. Research is in progress to model legal reasoning in computer programs and to develop expert systems (ES) in various branches of case law, both examples of applied artificial intelligence. Courtrooms have taken advantage of IT to facilitate access to information, as viewers of the O. J. Simpson trial might recall; up-to-the-minute-information was also available over the Internet. Even legal counsel was remotely available: "Each day, [defense attorney Alan] Dershowitz participates electronically in the O. J. Simpson double-murder trial in Los Angeles from his office or home in Massachusetts."[2]

The computer has, of course, created new business for lawyers, such as liability litigation resulting from software errors in both application programs and ES. Evidence derived from computer printouts or long discarded hard drives can and has been used in litigation. Even supposedly erased information can be recovered by computer specialists. "One man has been sentenced to death in a kidnapping and murder case following the electronic recovery by police of ransom notes which had been previously deleted from computer disks."[3] The computer itself, in a desk publishing environment with a scanner and a high quality color laser printer, has become an important tool for counterfeiting checks, certificates of all kinds, and even currency.

Other legal issues arrive in different contexts. The privacy issue with relation to computers has resulted in several pieces of legislation in the US and in the context of the Internet created a number of serious concerns (see Chapter 9). Important legal problems arise around electronic funds transfer systems, transborder data flows, government regulation of the computer and telecommunication industries, the control of technology transfer as well as the ongoing controversy over the US government's attempts to control the standard for encryption strategies necessary to secure online transactions (see Chapter 11).

COMPUTER CRIME

The "1996 CSI/FBI Computer Crime and Security Survey" offers some evidence [of the seriousness of the problem]. For example, 42% of respondents acknowledged that they had experienced unauthorized use of computer systems within the last 12 months. And we're not talking about users playing solitaire on company time—respondents reported a diverse array of attacks from brute force password guessing (13.9% of attacks) and scanning (15% of attacks) to denial of service (16.2% of attacks) and data diddling (15.5% attacks). (Richard S. Power in testimony before US Senate Committee on Government Affairs, June 5, 1996.)[4]

One of the more glamorous products of the new technology is the crime story. Hardly a day passes without a report that yet another computer system has been broken into and money has been taken, or that a new virus from the East will begin destroying files in PCs in two weeks; discussions of computer security and new antiviral programs abound. The glamour factor used to arise because computers seemed to be so formidable that any breakdown in their security was clearly noteworthy. Now, with so many computers in homes and small businesses, a new virus has enormous economic and social impact. For stories dealing with violations of large computer networks, a "David and Goliath" image emerges of the lonely, clever computer programmer or hacker, cracking the all-powerful system, thought to be invincible up to now. Many people are quite sympathetic to the human-versus-machine success story even if a crime has been committed. Given that crimes are indeed being perpetrated, however, measures must be taken to prevent them; security must be improved; and both professionals and the public at large must be educated about the dangers of such crimes.

Using computers to commit crimes is not the only way they are associated with unlawful activities. Sabotage can be directed towards the computer installation itself to uncover information useful to crack various security codes. The computer can be the target of people who object—for political, social, and economic reasons—to the growing influence of computers in everyday life. The attack might be directed towards the communication network in which the computer is embedded—for example, phone lines might be tapped and Internet communications monitored. These possibilities have stimulated an ongoing concern with computer security. Besides safeguarding the physical system, the data itself may need to be protected.

A Few Definitions

It is helpful to clarify a number of terms used in the discussion of computer crime. The following definitions represent a compromise between technical details and general understandability. One cautionary note: be careful about definitions that push biological analogies too far.

Virus. Simply put, a virus is a program that can insert executable copies of itself into other programs. In more detail, a computer virus must satisfy the following properties:

1. It must be capable of modifying software not belonging to the virus by attaching its program structure to the other program.
2. It must be capable of executing this modification on a number of programs.
3. It must have the capability of recognizing this modification in other programs.
4. It must have the ability to prevent further modification of the same program upon recognition of previous modification.
5. Modified software produced by the virus must have attributes 1–4.[5]

Bacterium. This is a program designed to cause a system to crash; that is, to cease operation without warning, thereby causing the loss of data. A bacterium does not attach itself to other programs but replicates itself to the limit of system capacity, preventing other legitimate programs from running.

Worm. A worm searches a computer system for idle resources and then disables them, not by replication of its own code, as do viruses and bacteria, but by systematically erasing various locations in memory. Thus the system is unable to function as designed.

Trojan Horse. This appears to be a useful program but it contains within it hidden code that may have a destructive function. Viruses are typically spread by Trojan Horses. On the other hand, a programmer may include a "trap door" in the Trojan Horse to permit subsequent tampering; for example, a way to get into the system around the security envelope. (More detail is given later in this section.)

Time Bomb. Also called a logic bomb, this is one of the preceding infections modified to become operative on a given date or after its host program has run a certain number of times. Note the Burleson program described in the next section is a time bomb.

Hacker. This is a term with multiple meanings that have changed over time. Consider the following descriptions of a hacker:

1. A programmer who works long hours and seems to be strongly motivated by, and infatuated with programming
2. A compulsive programmer who is driven to find solutions to problems, claimed to be extremely difficult or even impossible
3. A programmer who produces programs that are not particularly elegant and represent a collection of patches, or hacks, rather than a coherent whole; such programs are difficult to maintain, modify, or verify
4. A programmer who breaks into systems to prove that it is possible, and that no system can resist his or her efforts; such a hacker is sometimes called a cracker
5. A programmer who is a variant of 4 but in addition feels that society benefits by his or her actions in that hidden information is brought to light or proprietary software is made available to the entire community of programmers

Perhaps it is more instructive to let this particular Internet subcommunity define itself:[6]

- Hackers are the "wizards" of the computer community; people with a deep understanding of how their computers work, and can do things with them that seem "magical".
- Crackers are the real-world analogs of the "console cowboys" of cyberpunk fiction; they break in to other people's computer systems, without their permission, for illicit gain or simply for the pleasure of exercising their skill.
- Phreaks are those who do a similar thing with the telephone system, coming up with ways to circumvent phone companies' calling charges and doing clever things with the phone network. All three groups are using emerging computer and telecommunications technology to satisfy their individualist goals.
- Cypherpunks: . . . think a good way to bollix "The System" is through cryptography and cryptosystems. They believe widespread use of extremely hard-to-break coding schemes will create "regions of privacy" that "The System" cannot invade.

One attorney, who specializes in computer and communications law, prefers to use the term "rogue programs" to cover all these types of deviant programs and the term "computer rogues" to describe all individuals who devise, implement, and implant such programs as well as those who commit other crimes by using computers.[7] Donn Parker, an expert on computer crime, prefers to use the term computer abuse. He defines it as follows: ". . . any incident involving an intentional act where a victim suffered or could have suffered a loss, and a perpetrator made or could have made gain . . . associated with computers."[8]

Some Examples

As of early 1995, some 3,000 computer viruses, or perhaps 6,000, have been documented.[9] Attacks by hackers, or crackers, or inside assaults by employees are difficult to document because companies find it distasteful and embarrassing to admit (publicly) that their security has been breached.[10] Nevertheless, there are some indications, mainly as a result of surveys in which individual information is not identifiable, of how serious a problem intrusions into computer systems may be. One 1992 study by USA Research Inc., a technology consulting firm reported the following:[11]

- [T]he number of unauthorized intrusions detected in US workplace computers grew from 339,000 in 1989 to 684,000 in 1991.
- Intruders altered or destroyed data or software in 42% of the cases . . . studied, at a cost of $82 million in 1989 and $164 million in 1991.

In 1996, the Computer Security Institute, based in San Francisco, produced a survey on computer crime in cooperation with the FBI, which is interested in investigating, "violations of Computer Fraud and Abuse Act of 1986, including intrusions to public switched networks, major computer network intrusions, privacy violations, industrial espionage, pirated computer software and other crimes where the computer is a major factor in committing the criminal offense."[12] This very large survey received responses from 428 organizations and included the following highlights:[13]

- 42% have experienced some form of intrusion or other unauthorized use of computer systems within the last 12 months. Over 50% of those who experienced intrusions, or attempted probes of their internal systems, traced those intrusions to on-board employees. Unauthorized probes were also prevalent from remote dial-in sources and Internet connections. In terms of frequency of intrusions, 22 of the respondents indicated that they had experienced 10 or more "attacks" on their system within the past year.
- Attacks from US-owned corporate competitors are of serious concern. Over 50% of respondents cited US corporate competitors as a likely source of attacks ranging from eavesdropping to system penetration and reported that information sought in recent attacks would be of use to US-owned corporate competitors.
- The most significant concern of respondents in regard to eavesdropping, system penetration and attacks in which intruders forge a return address to gain access (known as spoofing) centered on independent hackers and external "information brokers" as likely sources. Disgruntled employees and corporate competitors were the next most significant concern in these categories.

Here, then, are a few examples of some classic computer crimes presented for purely academic interest, of course.

The Burleson Revenge. In September 1985, Donald Gene Burleson, a programmer at a Fort Worth, Texas brokerage house inserted a special program into the company's computer that later caused 168,000 sales commission records to be suddenly deleted. Mr. Burleson had been dismissed three days before this event. He was charged and later "convicted of computer abuse under the Texas Penal Code which permits a felony charge to be filed if the damage exceeds $2,500 from altering, damaging, destroying data, causing a computer to malfunction or interrupting normal operations."[14] He was fined $11,800 and sentenced to seven years probation.

The Pakistani Brain. During the period early 1986 to late 1987, shoppers (mostly American) purchased such brand-name software as Lotus 1-2-3 and Word Star at prices as low as $1.50 per disk at Brain Computer Services in Lahore, Pakistan. The brothers Alvi, owners of the store, also included, for free and of course unknown to the purchasers, a piece of hidden software, a virus, on each disk, which destroyed data and left behind the message, "WELCOME TO THE DUNGEON—Amjad and Basit Alvi." The copying of Pakistani disks was so extensive that before long, about 100,000 disks were so infected. Only disks bought by Americans were infected and Basit offered the reason, "Because you are pirating, you must be punished."[15] On a purely technical level, the virus designer, Amjad, is recognized widely as highly skilled and the virus as very elegant.

Breach of a Classified System. San Francisco, January 17, 1990—"Federal authorities today charged three men in California with engaging in a widespread pattern of breaking into Government and telephone company computers and obtaining classified information from a military computer. The prosecutor said the case might represent the first intrusion into a classified military computer by trespassers."[16]

Global Threat. "Three Australians have been arrested on charges of tampering with computers in the United States and Australia in a case that computer specialists say raises troubling questions about the vulnerability of technology to intruders operating beyond American borders and laws."[17]

Computergate. On September 7, 1990, John Kohler, executive director of the New Jersey Republican General Assembly staff resigned, admitting, contrary to previous denials, that he knew about "improper access to Democrat staff computer records."[18] Apparently the actual culprit was fired earlier in the year.

In testimony before a Senate Subcommittee, Richard G. Power, editor, Computer Security Institute, reported the following incidents:[19]

- In 1994, IBM, General Electric and NBC were hacked over Thanksgiving Day weekend. The alleged perpetrators, a mysterious group dubbing itself "The Internet Liberation Front" caused major disruptions.
- In 1995, Citibank was hit by Russian hackers who illegally transferred over $10 million to separate accounts around the world, using a laptop PC.
- Recently, a former software engineer for Intel Corporation pled guilty to charges that he stole Pentium chip production secrets, worth millions of dollars, and gave them to a rival computer company.
- Also, in recent weeks, it was revealed that several employees of the Social Security Administration allegedly passed information on 11,000 people (including their Social Security numbers and mothers' maiden names) to a credit card fraud ring.
- In another widely reported incident, FBI investigators armed with a court-ordered wiretap and a sophisticated program called Intruder Watch (I-Watch), tracked down an alleged hacker who had compromised computer networks at many sensitive sites including Harvard University, NASA, and the Los Alamos Naval Laboratory.

Two Important Cases

We will discuss two cases that have generated considerable publicity in more detail than the previous group, because of their importance and significance for security purposes.

The INTERNET Worm

The most publicized and most discussed case of computer crime in recent years is known as the INTERNET worm, although all the early reports referred to it as a virus. Its importance goes beyond the event itself in November, 1988, to include possible legal repercussions, as lawmakers strive to formulate comprehensive legislation to deal with present and future threats to computers and networks. On September 26, 1988, *Time's* cover story was on computer viruses, and on August 1, 1988, *Business Week's* cover asked the question, "Is Your Computer Secure?" and mentioned hackers, viruses, and other threats. [20]

Curiously enough, within a rather short period, on November 4, 1988, a front page story in *The New York Times* announced " 'Virus' in Military Computers Disrupts Systems Nationwide." [21] Over the next few weeks, stories appeared on a regular basis in many newspapers and magazines, and on television. Consider the following headlines on front-page pieces by John Markoff of *The New York Times*:

- November 5: Author of Computer 'Virus' is Son of US Electronic Security Expert: Cornell Graduate Student Described as 'Brilliant'
- November 6: How a Need for a Challenge Seduced Computer Expert
- November 8: Loving Those Whiz Kids: Mischief Like the Computer 'Virus' Release Comes from Group That Is Indispensable
- November 9: The Computer Jam: How It Came About (p. 38)

The initiator of the INTERNET worm was Robert T. Morris, a graduate student in computer science at Cornell University in Ithaca, New York. On the evening of November 2, 1988, the first of about 6,200 computers allegedly affected, on a network of about 60,000, gradually slowed down or ground to a halt, as an unknown program began seizing computer resources. The activity began initially on ARPANET, a computer network created for academic users by the Defense Advanced Research Projects Agency (DARPA). It then spread to the MILNET, an unclassified network of the Department of Defense, and finally to the global Internet. All of these networks and others are connected by gateways across North America and indeed the world. Some local systems broke connections with the network as word of the unprecedented disaster spread and thereby avoided being infected. Within about 48 hours, life was back to normal everywhere.

The impact was so wide-ranging—NASA Ames Laboratory, Lawrence Livermore National Laboratory, The Massachusetts Institute of Technology, Stanford University, the Rand Corporation, among others, were affected—that the uproar in the research communities was deafening. The costs of containing the damage, clearing out the memories, and checking all programs for signs of the rogue program were estimated at $96 million, then $186 million, up to $1 billion. Final estimates were considerably more sober, closer to $1 million and 2000 computers affected. [22]

In John Markoff's first report on November 4, he described a telephone call to *The New York Times* in which the unidentified caller, claiming to be an associate of the culprit, a university student, said that the program was an experiment that went awry. According to the caller, the worm, cleverly written except for the error that caused the explosion, exploited three flaws in the common operating system of computers on the networks. The next day the culprit was identified as Robert T. Morris, the son of one of the government's leading experts on computer security, chief scientist at the National Computer Center in Bethesda, Maryland, a branch of the National Security Agency. One of the flaws was in the basic electronic mail handling program, *sendmail,* which permits computers on the networks to communicate with one another. Another was a utility program, *fingerd,* which is called to identify users at a given location; this was its most successful means of migration. The last method was to guess passwords in order to gain access to trusted hosts where it might be able to migrate. What was disturbing to many of the users is that these flaws were generally known but were not exploited because that would have been a violation of collegiality, a breakdown in a system of trust shared by a large community.

Mr. Morris was indicted on July 26, 1989 by a federal grand jury in Syracuse, New York and accused under the Computer Fraud and Abuse Act of 1986 (see discussion later in this chapter) of gaining access to federal interest computers, preventing authorized access by others, and causing damage in excess of $1,000. The fact that there was a delay of more than six months between the date of the incident and the indictment suggests that government lawyers were in some disagreement over how to frame the charges. This uncertainty is probably the major legal legacy of the INTERNET worm, as the government has considered amending current legislation to be more comprehensive and relevant. The trial began on January 16, 1990, and on January 23, a federal jury found Mr. Morris guilty of intentionally disrupting a nationwide computer network, the first jury conviction under the 1986 act.[23] On May 5, 1990 a federal judge fined Mr. Morris $10,000, placed him on three years' probation, and ordered him to perform 400 hours of community service. The judge stated that prison punishment did not fit the crime, although the act provided for up to five years in prison. An appeal was heard on December 4, l990.[24] "On March 7, 1991, the US Court of Appeals for the second circuit court upheld Robert's conviction. In the autumn of 1991, the Supreme Court refused to hear the case."[25]

Kevin Mitnick: A True Compulsive or a Gifted Hacker

In early January 1989, Kevin Mitnick was arraigned in Los Angeles, held without bail, and charged with such crimes as illegally accessing computers at Digital Equipment Corp. and at the University of Leeds, in England, and stealing computer programs and long-distance telephone services. His trouble with computers and the law actually began in 1981 when he and friends physically had broken into a pacific Bell phone center. He was even able to change the credit rating of the judge in the 1989 case, which explains, in part, why he was denied bail and prohibited from making telephone calls. He was charged and convicted under the Federal Computer Fraud and Abuse Act of 1986, one of the first so treated, and sentenced to 12 months in jail, six months in a residential treatment program and three years of probation.[26] Given that he did not even own a computer, he was not fined. As you might have guessed, his career was not over.

In September 1992, Mitnick was being investigated by the FBI for possible illegal access to a commercial database and two month later a warrant was issued for "his arrest for having violated the terms of his 1989 probation. There were two charges: illegally accessing a phone company computer, and associating with one of the people with whom he'd originally been arrested in 1981."[27] Mitnick eluded arrest and while on the run managed, among other actions, "to wiretap the telephones of the FBI agents who were searching for him."[28] On Christmas Day in 1994, a computer at the home of security expert Tsutomu Shimomura in San Diego was broken into and files removed. Mitnick left taunting messages on Shimomura's answering machine and used some of the files taken from his computer to break into other systems. Some of these files turned up about a month later in the account of another well-known computer person, Bruce Koball, on the WELL, a Sausolito, California network. Koball got in touch with John Markoff of *The New York Times* and Shimomura, who within about two weeks was able to trace Mitnick to a Raleigh, North Carolina location where he was arrested by the FBI. He is awaiting trial in Los Angeles charged with numerous counts of computer and telecommunications fraud.

One serious concern arising out of Mitnick's adventures was the ease with which he was able to penetrate a variety of Web sites and accounts on supposedly secure systems. Certainly, efforts to increase the volume of commercial traffic over the Internet must take into account the security problems that have once again come to the fore.

The Computer Fraud and Abuse Act of 1986

The original act, the Counterfeit Access Device and Computer Fraud and Abuse Act of 1984 was signed into law by President Reagan in October 1984 as part of the Comprehensive Crime Control Act of 1984. In 1986, it was amended with the Computer Fraud and Abuse Act. The 1986 Act prohibits six types of computer abuse and provides for three types of felonies. The following computer abuses are defined as criminal conduct {§1030(a)(1)-(6)}:

(1) Knowingly accessing a computer without authorization and obtaining restricted information with the intent to use that information to the detriment of the United States.

(2) Intentionally accessing a computer without authorization and obtaining information in the financial record of a financial institution.

(3) Intentionally, without authorization to access any computer of a department or agency of the United States, access[ing] such a computer of that department or agency that is exclusively for the use of the Government of the United States or, in the case of a computer not exclusively for such use, is used by or for the Government of the United States and such conduct affects the use of the Government's operation of such computer.

(4) Knowingly, and with intent to defraud, accessing a Federal interest computer and obtaining something of value, unless the value so obtained is limited to the use of computer time.

(5) Intentionally accessing a Federal interest computer without authorization, and by means of one or more instances of such conduct altering, damaging, or destroying information in any such Federal interest computer, or preventing authorized use of any such computer or information and thereby causing damage in excess of $1,000 or damaging records.

(6) Knowingly, and with intent to defraud, trafficking in computer passwords.

Number (5) is the section under which Morris was charged and convicted. Although the number of computer-related crimes seems to have increased significantly, only a few convictions have taken place under this Act. There seems to be a number of limitations, both in the language of the Act and in the very nature of computer crime, that make such crimes difficult to prosecute. In the first instance, the Act focuses on computers used and owned by government departments without acknowledging the vast number of corporate computers equally likely to be abused. Access alone is not a crime, unless information is obtained, and neither is browsing, or the looking at files without causing damages.[29] Viruses or worms were not anticipated in the Act. Since many technical issues arise, prosecutors may have difficulty in dealing with such cases. Gathering evidence may also be difficult without violating the privacy of individuals whose files are on the system under investigation. One final point is that the Act does not require that intent to defraud or cause damage be proven; thus any unauthorized access to a government computer system could leave the perpetrator subject to criminal charges.

Other Related Issues: Education, Hackers, and Civil Liberties

Actions independent of new special-purpose legislation may be helpful and indeed necessary. Many have called for an education program, especially among computer scientists, to point out the underlying impact of violations of computers and networks. Stressing privacy issues may convince some potential violators that their actions could undermine the civil liberties of their colleagues. Furthermore, reaction to unauthorized access of individuals and programs may result in the introduction of constraints that severely limit the free flow of information, to the detriment of the considerate and law-abiding majority of users.

It must be acknowledged, however, that a small community exists, simplistically described as hackers, who maintain their *right* to enter any system for any purpose they deem appropriate. In an electronic forum held over a nationwide bulletin board in early 1990, a number of hackers expressed a variety of opinions on breaking into systems, perusing files, and the "virtues" of privacy.[30] Among the opinions expressed is a version of the "means justify the end" for hackers; that is, breaking into a system is warranted if the purpose is useful, a position countered by the analogy of entering an unoccupied house if there is something inside it of use to the perpetrator. Many hackers argue that the very concept of secret information is offensive and that if it were not collected, there would be no need to protect it. Thus, they claim that their role must be to "liberate" the data, to defeat the notion of secure systems, and thereby to inhibit the open-ended collection of information.

Despite the hackers' seemingly democratic principle of information for the people, their self-indulgence emerges, loud and clear: we define the issues, we say what is right and wrong, and by virtue of our skills, we reserve the right to act in whatever way we wish. How representative are these opinions? It is impossible to know, but even if they come from a very small minority, it is a highly skilled and a highly motivated one.

As a final point in support of those concerned that law enforcement officials will overzealously pursue and persecute possible offenders in response to increased computer crime, or at least increased publicity, this case is offered. Early in 1990, the Justice Department indicted Craig Neidorf, 19, also known as "Knight Lightning," on charges of having downloaded the 911 emergency computer program from Bellsouth Telephone Company, obtained illegally, to his computer at the University of Missouri, and then editing it for inclusion in his bulletin-board newsletter for computer hackers, called Phrack.[31] The trial began in Chicago near the end of July. Sheldon Zenner, Neidorf's attorney argued that his client "was merely a journalist using an electronic bulletin board to disseminate a 'meaningless . . . bureaucratic' document. . . . Mr. Neidorf never broke into any computer system, never stole any file and never profited from this. . . . He is not a hacker—he's a journalist."[32] Four days into the trial, federal prosecutors dismissed charges against Mr. Neidorf because prosecution witnesses admitted that Mr. Neidorf had not been involved in the theft and further that the document itself was widely available; it could be purchased from Bellsouth for $13 although the indictment claimed that it was valued at $79,449.[33] The protection of free speech by the First Amendment must include electronic communication in its various forms, and reasonable approaches to dealing with computer crime must be employed.

The Morris case seems to have spurred only a few isolated efforts by industry and government to improve security, in spite of the enormous publicity the case received. As mentioned earlier, various initiatives were undertaken in the House and Senate to strengthen legislation related to computer viruses. In addition, in May 1990, law enforcement agencies attempted to confront suspected computer crime by a number of raids across the US, code-named Operation Sundevil. Only one indictment was delivered, and serious questions were raised about the rights of computer users and bulletin board operators, whose computers were seized.

Security Procedures

As in many other areas of life, prevention is far better than detection, indictment, and possible conviction. What steps can administrators of computing facilities take to ensure the physical security of the system itself, and the security of the communications network?

Physical security involves the computer itself, the peripheral equipment, and the rooms and buildings, including furniture, storage media, and terminals. Obvious care must be taken with respect to fire, water, earthquakes, explosions, and other natural causes. Special care must he taken to control access by people in order to safeguard the equipment and physical surroundings. It is necessary to require identification badges for those individuals who work in restricted areas. There must be alternative power supplies as well as back-up systems to be used in case of damage. An entire subindustry has grown up to advise companies in physical security and to supply security equipment. As the dependency of society on computers increases, it becomes a basic necessity to take steps to guarantee physical security.

System security involves the basic operation of the computer itself. The issue is access—to the computer, the associated files, sensitive production programs, and even the operating system. The basic controls used to restrict access are computer identification numbers (IDs) and passwords. Within this system there may be privileged function levels, including user and program access control. An ID is typically issued by the computing center; it is the user's responsibility to choose a password as a second level of security. The operating system of the computer will permit access only to identifiable IDs and passwords. Once on a system, the ordinary user is restricted to his or her own files and system programs, including programming languages and library functions. Individual users may provide other users with access to their files, where access may mean reading the file, writing into it, or both. The operating system must ensure individual user security as well as protect itself from unauthorized access. There are a number of by-now traditional means of cracking system security.

The Business Software Alliance suggests the following measures to protect against viruses in computer networks: [34]

- Only purchase and use original software.
- Develop guidelines—and monitor—the installation of new software.
- Educate users about the dangers of computer viruses.
- Make backups of all programs and information stored on servers.
- Control access to servers and networks.
- Control software rights granted to users.
- Scan servers regularly to look for possible viruses.
- Protect workstations from outside access.
- Offer additional MIS and systems administrator services.

Security, especially in computer networks, has become a dominant topic among computer professionals. As attacks increase, especially over the Internet, calls for increased security multiply as do companies selling such basic products as firewalls to isolate systems from unwanted and unauthorized access. One of the most important surveys on security is carried out by the consulting company, Ernst & Young and the industry magazine *Information Week*. The third annual survey conducted during August and September 1995 produced a number of interesting results, including the following: [35]

- Management attention to information security has improved. Compared to the prior year:—more respondents noted that security is "extremely important,"—reporting relationships of security professionals to senior management have strengthened, and—management awareness was noted less frequently as an obstacle to information security.
- Organizations are increasingly embracing client/server technology and processing mission critical systems on LANs and UNIX-based systems. And these systems are most often connected to central computing resources. But a growing number of organizations are not satisfied with the overall security of these client/server environments.
- Business use of the Internet is increasing as is concern over Internet security. One in five Internet-connected organizations reported an attempted or successful break-in to their organization via the Internet in the past year.
- Over two-thirds of the respondents encountered a virus over the past year. Fortunately only a small portion of the viruses caused financial loss.
- Over the last two years, nearly half of the organizations suffered an information security-related financial loss, with inadvertent errors the most frequently noted source of loss. But over 80% were unable (or unwilling) to estimate the dollar value of the loss.
- Three-quarters of respondents have formal information security policies, but less than half have on-going security awareness or education programs for employees.

Money Laundering

At the beginning of its report on technologies to control money laundering, the Office of Technology Assessment notes, [36]

Crime can be highly profitable. Money generated in large volume by illegal activities must be "laundered," or made to look legitimate, before it can be freely spent or invested; otherwise, it may be seized by law enforcement and forfeited to the government. Transferring funds by electronic messages between banks—"wire transfer"—is one way to swiftly move illegal profits beyond the easy reach of law enforcement agents and at the same time begin to launder the funds by confusing the audit trail.

One of the major problems facing law enforcement officials is tracking down money acquired in illegal activities. To avoid drawing attention to themselves, criminals must make it appear that the money in their possession has been obtained in traditional legal ways; that is, the money must be laundered to remove any trace of its criminal origins. As defined in an Office of Technology Assessment Report, "To launder money is to disguise the origin or ownership of illegally gained funds to make them appear legitimate. Hiding legitimately acquired money to avoid taxation also qualifies as money laundering. Federal agencies estimate that as much as $300 billion is laundered annually, worldwide. From $40 billion to $80 billion of this may be drug profits made in the United States."[37] There appear to be three basic steps in money laundering:[38]

- placement—introducing cash into the banking system, or into legitimate commerce;
- layering—separating the money from its criminal origins by passing it through several financial transactions, for example, transferring it into and then out of several bank accounts, or exchanging it for travelers' checks or a cashier's check;
- integration—aggregating the funds with legitimately obtained money or providing a plausible explanation for its ownership.

With the vast amounts of money flowing over computer networks, considerable pressure has been placed on law enforcement officials to detect the transmission of laundered money. It is also expected that the Internet will be used for money laundering, a situation that creates a problem for users wishing to preserve their privacy in financial transactions. This conflict lies in part at the heart of the debate over the government's plans to have access to much encrypted communication. As for current proposals to determine whether or not wire transfers involve laundering, the following are four categories of analysis technologies:[39]

- *knowledge sharing* to disseminate profiles of money laundering activities quickly, reliably, and
- *wire transfer screening* to determine where to target further investigations,
- *knowledge acquisition* to construct new profiles for use during screening,
- *data transformation* to produce data that can be easily screened and analyzed.

Part of the mandate under which this investigation was carried out was to determine if current artificial intelligence techniques were sufficiently well advanced to detect money laundering over wire transfer systems. Unfortunately, no such techniques were found to be adequate in terms of accuracy, efficiency, minimizing the burden placed on the transfer system, minimizing the threat to law-abiding citizens, and cost of development. Other proposals that are perhaps less glamorous are computer-assisted examination of wire transfer records by bank regulators and targeted access to wire transfers for FinCEN (Financial Crimes Enforcement Network), a financial crime data analysis and intelligence agency that is also responsible for administering the Bank Secrecy Act. In the first case, the bank examiners would use AI-based programs to examine all wire transfers at all banks and in the second, "banks and wire transfer systems would be required to provide wire transfer records electronically to FinCEN in response to its specific requests, provided the data requested are from a limited period (e.g., not over two years old)."[40] The OTA report takes great pain to present approaches that do not compromise the legitimate interests and rights of companies and individuals, or foreign countries.

THE LEGAL PROTECTION OF SOFTWARE

> Congress shall have Power . . . To promote the Progress of Science and useful Arts, by securing for limited Times to Authors and Inventors the exclusive Right to their respective Writings and Discoveries. (The Constitution of the United States, Article 1, Section 8, 1788)

The framers of the Constitution would have been surprised by the development of computers. The attempt to characterize software in order to design appropriate legal protection has been a long and torturous process that is by no means complete. Computers themselves are readily protected under patent law, as they are certainly inventions. But problems have arisen even here because of the difficulty in determining how to safeguard the masks used to produce integrated circuits. The major concern, however, lies with computer software, more specifically with applications programs. Congress has passed legislation that provides penalties for those who infringe upon the safeguards granted by patents or copyrights. There is the protection afforded by case law to protect trade secrets, and there is the law of contracts. Each has different background, advantages, and disadvantages.

One of the problems in protecting programs is a basic question of definition. As Gemignani has pointed out a program may be viewed as

> a particular form of expression of a flowchart or algorithm, a process for controlling or bringing about a desired result inside a computer, a machine part or completion of an incomplete machine, a circuit diagram of an incomplete machine, a circuit diagram or blueprint for a circuit board, a data compilation, a code writing. . . .[41]

The list does not end there. All the key terms in the constitutional mandate—limited time, author, inventor, and discovery—must be interpreted in the present context.

The growing debate over software protection is a part of the larger issue of protecting intellectual property rights. The big stakes in this area are of course related to technology, a clear indication of its importance. For example, some important cases of the 1980s are given here:[42]

- 1985: The Polaroid challenge against Kodak over violations of the patent for instant cameras is successful, and damages of $909.5 million were awarded on October 12, 1990, considerably less than the anticipated award of $10 billion.
- 1987: Corning Glass Works wins a patent suit against Sumitomo over the design of optical fibers.

- 1988: Fujitsu agrees to pay IBM over $1 billion over copyrights for mainframe operating systems but gains access to newer versions of this software.
- 1989: A five year suit between NEC and Intel ends when a judge rules that microprocessors can be copyrighted (and Intel lost its claim because it neglected to print the copyright symbol), but that the functions of a chip can be duplicated without a violation.

The 1990s have witnessed similar suits, and within the computer industry, the area of "look and feel" of computer interfaces in general and application program interfaces in particular dominated the first half of the 1990s. Actions were taken by Apple against Hewlett-Packard and Microsoft, by Xerox against Apple, by Lotus Development Corp. against Paperware Software International and Mosaic Software (Lotus won this case in June 1990), and by Lotus against Borland International. These cases will be discussed in a following section. It is clear that the once relatively dormant area of patent and copyright law has become energized as developments in the computer industry continue to accelerate. However, the new arena for litigation is obviously the Internet and World Wide Web as very complex issues of protection for digital forms of information are emerging.

The economic stakes are very high: The Business Software Alliance's (BSA) Annual Survey reported that estimated worldwide software piracy in 1994 totaled $15.2 billion, up from $12.8 billion in 1993. Part of the increase was due to an additional $335 million from 23 countries not included in the 1993 survey.[43] The BSA uses the term piracy rate to mean the percentage of total sales represented by the piracy number. Thus, for example, Europe's piracy losses were about $6 billion with an average piracy rate of 58 percent; Asia's numbers were $4.3 billion and 68 percent. The three countries with the largest losses were the US with $2.8 billion and 35%, Japan with $2 billion and 67%, and Germany with $1.8 billion and 50%. These losses are very high, but keep in mind that BSA represents the software industry and for purposes of influencing public opinion and public policy, it is to its advantage to report high numbers.

Patents

Obtaining a patent is a long and involved process, but it does confer considerable advantages—a monopoly on use, as well as considerable tax benefits. Are computer programs patentable? The relevant portion of the US Code, section 101, states: "Whoever invents or discovers any new and useful process, machine, manufacture, or composition of matter, or any new and useful improvement thereof, may obtain a patent therefore, subject to the conditions and requirements of this title."[44] Thus, a program would have to be considered a programmable process or a programmed machine. The statute further confers, "the right to exclude others from making, using, or selling" the invention. As the US Patent and Trademark Office comments, "What is granted is not the right to make, use, or sell, but the right to exclude others from making, using, or selling the invention."[45] The history of attempts to patent programs is rife with controversy, confusion, and a basic inability to define the nature of a relatively new technology.

Companies and individuals wishing to patent their software are confronted by a tangled situation. The Patent Office has consistently rejected most patent applications. The Court of Customs and Patent Appeals generally has supported attempts to patent software. The Supreme Court has usually overturned decisions by the Court of Customs and Patent Appeals and has not clarified the question of the patentability of software. And, finally, Congress has so far not passed necessary and appropriate legislation. In 1968, the Patent Office made an official statement: "Computer programs per se . . . shall not be patentable."[46] In the following year, the Court of Customs and Patent Appeals, in hearing a patent appeal, set aside this opinion.[47] Since then a series of cases have proceeded to the Supreme Court, which consistently rejected patent claims until the case of Diamond v. Diehr in 1981. In this case, Diehr applied for a patent for a process for molding raw uncured synthetic rubber into cured products. This process involved measuring temperatures, using a computer to determine cure times, and opening a press accordingly. The Patent Office rejected the claim, and the Court of Customs and Patent Appeals reversed the rejection, arguing that the mathematical formula was embodied in a useful process. The Supreme Court upheld this opinion in a five-to-four decision. Three basic points of law emerged from the Court's opinion.[48] First, the mere inclusion of a mathematical formula, or programmed computer does not invalidate a claim. Second, in this claim, it was stated, "the respondents [did] not seek to patent a mathematical formula." Third, the claims sought "only to foreclose from others, the use of that equation in conjunction with the other steps in their claimed process." Before the Diehr decision, out of about 100,000 patent applications filed each year only about 450 were for program patents. However, patent applications for software increased considerably in the 1980s.[49]

The battle to obtain software patents continued, with many applications first rejected, then appealed, then accepted, then rejected yet again. Given that the basic objection to software patents is that because programs are very close to mathematical formulae and these are not patentable, neither are programs; creative applications have argued for software embedded in a machine, device, or process. This strategy has worked in that 4,569 software-related patents were granted in 1994 in such areas as networking (623), operating systems (558), graphical user interfaces (223), and databases (173).[50] However, many complaints about the process, heightened by the events associated with the 1994 case *In re Alappat,* involving a series of disallowals, approvals, and appeals,[51] resulted in the US Patent and Trademark Office (PTO) issuing new "Examination Guidelines for Computer-Related Inventions."[52] The crucial issues resulting in a change of approach by the PTO are given as follows:[53]

> . . . a patent may be granted for a claim directed to software technology if the claim, as a whole, is directed to a machine that carries out a function that the patent laws were designed to protect. Decisions issued after Alappat suggest that patent protection of software technology may be extended to "electronic structures" and to machines having a memory device containing a specified data type. Consistent with these recent cases, Patent Examination Guidelines proposed by the Patent Office appear to permit the issuance of patents claiming a computer program stored in a storage medium, such as a floppy disk. An "electronic structure" represents patentable subject matter.

There are a number of advantages and disadvantages to the patent process with respect to software protection. Patent protection is broad and long-term (17 years). Independent development is no defense against an infringement charge. However, there are some serious disadvantages. Obtaining a patent is a long and costly process. Protecting a patent may also be quite costly. One important concern about patent applications is whether or not the entire program must be included to meet disclosure requirements. The simple answer is that flow charts or block diagrams, sufficiently detailed and complete, will suffice, but in the new guidelines mentioned previously, the emphasis on utility requires that examiners must

- Determine what the applicant has invented by reviewing the written description and the claims. Identify any specific embodiments of the invention that have been disclosed, review the detailed description of the invention and note the specific utility that has been asserted for the invention.
- Pay particular attention to the specific utility contemplated for the invention—features or elements of the invention that are necessary to provide the specific utility contemplated for that invention must be reflected in the claims.
- A failure to limit the claim to reflect features of the invention that are necessary to impart the specific utility contemplated may also create a deficiency under Section 112, first paragraph.

Copyright

A new Copyright act was enacted in 1976 and became effective in 1978. The new law was not meant to apply to computer software issues until a report was issued by the National Commission on New Technological Uses of Copyrighted Works (CONTU). On the basis of CONTU's recommendations, the Computer Software Copyright Act of 1980 was enacted. It contained the following definition:[54]

> A "computer program" is a set of statements or instructions to be used directly or indirectly in order to bring about a certain result.

(The noted author John Hersey, a member of CONTU, objected strenuously to the recommendation to provide copyright protection to programs. He argued that a program is not a "writing" in the Constitutional sense.) Permission was granted to an individual user to make copies or changes in a copyrighted program, for back-up purposes. In Section 102(a) of the Copyright Act the definition of what can be copyrighted is as follows:

> Copyright protection subsists . . . in original works of authorship fixed in any tangible medium of expression, now known or later developed, from which they can be perceived, reproduced, or otherwise communicated, either directly or with the aid of a machine or device.

A number of cases since 1978 have clarified some of the issues of copyright protection. Its advantages are (a) it is easy to obtain—inexpensive and quick; (b) it is appropriate for works that have wide circulation; (c) it endures during the author's lifetime plus 50 years; and (d) preliminary injunctions may possibly be much more easily obtainable than for possible patent violations. Nevertheless, there are some serious drawbacks. There are still some open questions about what is actually covered. For example, are object programs embodied in ROMs? What about the source program on tape? The scope of protection may be uncertain. For example, can you reproduce copyrighted subject matter in order to develop an object that cannot be copyrighted? Since software is widely proliferated, it will be difficult to enforce copyrights. Can the masks used to produce integrated circuits be copyrighted?

This last question can be answered: yes. In 1984, Congress passed the Semiconductor Chip Protection Act to protect the technology embodied in chips and the associated masks. Congress was concerned that chips and masks, representing one of the major achievements of American ingenuity, were vulnerable to copying and decided to create explicitly a new form of intellectual property protection to help stimulate continued investment in new chip design. The copying of chips is prohibited; however, the reverse engineering of masks is permitted. Both chips and mask works are defined and the requirements for protection of masks delineated.[55]

Proving that infringement has occurred, under the Computer Software Copyright Act, may be extremely difficult. It is necessary to demonstrate that copying has taken place and that this constitutes an improper appropriation. The Act does permit a user to copy a program for private use. Improper use must be adjudged by a lay person, not a technical expert. The most critical issue arises from a statement issued by the Supreme Court in 1954: "Protection is given only to the expression of an idea—not the idea itself." Several important cases will be considered to illustrate the nature of the issues associated with software copyright cases.

Important Copyright Cases

Whelan Associates, Inc. v. Jaslow Dental Laboratories

This is the first of two cases relevant to the current impassioned debate on the "look and feel of computer user interfaces." Although not really a user interface case at all, Whelan is important because of the scope of its judicial decision. Jaslow hired Whelan to write a program to computerize Jaslow's office procedures, with a view to marketing it to other labs. Jaslow would pay development costs, Whelan would own the rights, and Jaslow would get a royalty on sales. Jaslow aided in the design, even tailoring the interface to his own methods. The program, Dentalab, written in an obsolete language to run on an IBM mainframe, was delivered in 1979. A few years later Jaslow wrote his own version of the program called Dentacom, in BASIC, to run on PCs, without studying Whelan's code. When he began marketing his PC program, Whelan sued for copyright infringement.[56]

Although Whelan seemed to be concerned only that Jaslow had copied the underlying structure of her program, the similarity in interfaces became an important issue. In 1985, the court found for Whelan on all issues. With respect to copyright infringement, the court found "that the Dentacom system [Jaslow's program], although written in another computer language from the Dentalab, and although not a direct transliteration of Dentalab, was substantially similar to Dentalab because its structure and overall organization were substantially similar."[57] The decision was appealed and Whelan's victory upheld but the appellate court decision introduced a measure of confusion in that it ruled that screen displays that were similar were indications that the programs were also similar. The results of this case were evaluated by Pamela Samuelson, a professor of law, as follows:[58]

The structure of the program was expression [of the idea] because it wasn't part of the general purpose or function of the program and because there were other ways for Jaslow [the defendant] to have structured such a program besides the way that Whelan had structured hers, so it was an infringement for Jaslow to have used a similar structure to Whelan's.

Broderbund Software v. Unison World

In another important case settled just a few months after Whelan, in 1986, Broderbund Software prevailed over Unison World in a decision that established that " 'the overall structure, sequencing and arrangement of screens' in the user interface of a program are protected by copyright, or—broader yet—that a test of the 'look and feel' to an ordinary observer is applicable to software cases generally . . ."[59] This raises the question, however, of what is required of a user interface so that it can exist independently of the working parts of a program. Answers are slowly being proposed in current cases, of which the most stunning decision is that in Lotus Development Corp. v. Paperback Software International and Mosaic Software.

Lotus Development Corp. v. Paperback Software International and Mosaic Software

This case was brought in February 1987 by Lotus, the very successful developer of Lotus 1-2-3, the leading spreadsheet for IBM PCs and compatibles. Paperback and Mosaic also produce spreadsheets, but their software sells for $99 each compared to Lotus at $495. Lotus charged that the two companies had copied its screen format, a grid-like image, as well as its keystroke sequences, or macros. In his ruling in favor of Lotus, on June 28, 1990, federal judge Keeton stated, "I conclude that a menu command structure is capable of being expressed in many if not an unlimited number of ways, and that the command structure of 1-2-3 is an original and non-obvious way of expressing a command structure."[60] The immediate implication of this verdict is that once a program becomes a *de facto* industry standard, it will be extremely difficult for new products to challenge its dominance, if they are unable to employ a compatible interface. In the middle of October, Paperback Software announced that it would "stop marketing its VP Planner product line by December 1 and pay Lotus Development Corp. $500,000 for violating its 1-2-3 spreadsheet copyrights . . . [Paperback] also agreed not to appeal a June federal court ruling. . . ."[61] Following up on its courtroom success, Lotus launched a suit against Borland International, the maker of the spreadsheet Quattro Pro, also selling for $99; however, the issue was that Quattro had as an option the 1-2-3 menus and commands as an alternative to its own interface. The eventual result of this case would be to end the "look-and-feel" debate, but not in the way that Lotus had anticipated. Before describing the outcome of this case, it may be helpful to explore the implications of the debate itself.

The Interface Debate

Considerable debate had erupted within the industry and elsewhere about the merits of copyright protection of interfaces, as once guaranteed by the courts. Simply put, those supporting copyright protection argue that the original designers must have their work protected in order to earn a reasonable return on their investment, to encourage the design of new and innovative systems, and to attract and keep bright designers. Those in opposition might argue that copyright protection impedes innovation by freezing designs that may not be optimal, unfairly rewards those who happen to be first but not best, and discourages the free exchange of ideas for the benefit of all. Pamela Samuelson's response to the Lotus decision was expressed in a characteristically blunt fashion:[62]

> I am a lawyer. I interpret cases for a living. I have read Judge Keeton's opinion carefully and I have worked very hard to figure out what it means. I would tell you what it means if I could understand it, but I cannot. And neither can anyone else. So anyone who says he or she is sure the Lotus decision is a very narrow one and only makes copying the whole of someone else's interface illegal is giving his opinion and making a prediction . . .

A considerably more radical position was taken by a founder of The League for Programming Freedom, Richard Stallman, a renowned MIT programmer and recipient of a MacArthur Foundation fellowship.[63] Stallman argued that software should not be copyrighted but should be freely available to everyone. This is based on the notion of a community of programmers, all of whose tools and products are shared resources. One fear of copyright can be seen by drawing an analogy with typewriters. If the typewriter interface (i.e., the specific keyboard layout) could be copyrighted, each manufacturer would be required to produce a different layout. For computers, interface copyright inevitably will lead to greater incompatibility. "Anything which impedes standardization impedes the social penetration of technology."

Apple Computer, Inc. v. Microsoft Corp. and Hewlett-Packard Co.

A preliminary decision in Apple Computer's suit against Microsoft and Hewlett-Packard for copyright infringement of its interface was won by Apple in March, 1991, much to the displeasure of Stallman. However, Apple ultimately lost its suit in 1994 and ironically the seeds of this loss were sown in 1985, when an agreement between Apple and Microsoft ended an earlier Apple suit over Windows 1.0. Apple "granted Microsoft a license to use the visual displays in Windows 1.0 in future programs. Microsoft, in turn, granted Apple a license to use any new visual displays created by Microsoft. The programs in suit are based on a desktop metaphor with windows, icons, and pull-down menus that can be manipulated on the screen with a device called a mouse."[64] Thus Judge Rymer, of the Court of Appeals for the Ninth Circuit, ruling against Apple, said, "to the extent that later versions of Windows and HP's NewWave programs use the visual displays in Windows 1.0, such use is authorized and cannot infringe."[65] Despite strenuous objections, Apple's arguments were dismissed. Indeed, Judge Rymer claimed that Apple's basic ideas, "the graphical user interface in a desktop metaphor, use of windows to display multiple images and facilitate user interaction, iconic representation of familiar objects from an office environment, manipulation of icons to convey instructions and control operations, use of menus to store information or computer functions, and opening and closing of objects to retrieve or transfer data," are not protectable. Of course, Apple appealed to the Supreme Court and in February 1995, the Court refused to overturn the Court of Appeals decision, thus dealing a serious blow to protection in the "look-and-feel" debate.

Lotus Development Corp. v. Borland International, Inc.

Lotus first filed suit in 1990 against Borland, charging that Quattro Pro infringed on its copyright and won in a federal court some three years later. Borland appealed and the case was heard in the US Court of Appeals for the First Circuit in October 1994; the ruling came down on March 9, 1995, overturning the lower court decision. The Appeals Court's decision reversed the district court,[66]

> holding that the menu command hierarchy was a "method of operation" that is excluded from copyright protection under 17 U.S.C. § 102(b), because "[t]he Lotus holding that the menu command hierarchy was a "method of operation" that is menu command hierarchy provides the means by which users control and operate Lotus 1-2-3." Slip op. at 20. The court defined " `method of operation,' as that term is used in § 102(b) [as] the means by which a person operates something, whether it be a car, a food processor, or a computer." Id. Even to the extent that the menu command hierarchy included expression, the court denied that expression any copyright protection: "Accepting the district court's finding that the Lotus developers made some expressive choices in choosing and arranging the Lotus command terms, we nonetheless hold that expression is not copyrightable because it is part of Lotus 1-2-3's `method of operation.' " Id. at 23.

The court used an analogy based on VCRs (video cassette recorders) to explain its reasoning "in finding that the Lotus 1-2-3 command menu hierarchy was a 'method of operation' " by likening "it to the buttons on a VCR." The buttons on the VCR are themselves the "method of operation" of the VCR—their arrangement and labeling does not make them a "literary work" "nor does it make them an 'expression' of the abstract 'method of operating' a VCR . . . Lotus 1-2-3 depends for its operation on use of precise command terms that make up the Lotus menu command hierarchy . . . the arrangement of buttons on a VCR would not be copyrightable because the buttons are an uncopyrightable 'method of operation.' Similarly, the 'buttons' of a computer program are also an uncopyrightable method of operation.' "[67]

Lotus appealed to the Supreme Court which heard the case on January 8, 1996 and issued the following opinion on January 16:

> Per Curiam.
>
> The judgment of the United States Court of Appeals for the First Circuit is affirmed by an equally divided Court.

In other words, Lotus lost because in a tie 4-4 vote (Justice Stevens took no part in the decision) the Supreme Court let the decision of the First Circuit stand. Lotus petitioned for a rehearing and was denied on March 4, 1996. The lack of an opinion by the Supreme Court leaves many issues undecided, but for the present there is no look-and-feel basis for attempting to copyright user interfaces.

Trade Secrets

The most favored method of protection, at least up to fairly recently before the surge in copyright cases, has been under trade secret laws. As there is no federal trade secrecy legislation, the relevant laws have been established, not in a uniform manner, in the individual states. One definition of a trade secret is "any formula, pattern, device or compilation of information which is used in one's business and which gives him an opportunity to obtain an advantage over competitors who do not know how to use it."[68] Three conditions are necessary to legally protect a trade secret: novelty, secrecy, and value in business. Trade secret law appears to cover programs as "processes comprising inventions, with documentation protectable as ancillary 'know-how'."[69] Databases and documentation could also receive protection as information of value. An attempt has been made to establish uniform laws on trade secrecy—the "Uniform Trade Secrets Acts" were drawn up in 1979, approved by the American Bar Association in 1980, and adopted by Minnesota and Arkansas in 1981.

The main advantages of trade secrecy laws are that preliminary injunctions are obtained readily, the applicability over a wide range of subjects is relatively clear, protection applies to both ideas and expressions, the waiting period is brief, and the application remains in force for a long period. Among the disadvantages are the lack of uniformity across the United States, the stress on secrecy as a bar to progress, the lack of protection against independent development, the difficulty in maintaining long-term secrecy—especially for widely proliferated software, and possible preemption by the Copyright Act.

Other Methods

To protect software, an employer may make a contract with the relevant employees as part of the terms of employment, which may include such stipulations as no unauthorized copies and no public discussion of programs under development. Whatever the specific terms of a contract, an employee is expected to respect confidentiality. Associated with the sales or licensing of software, there may also be contractual arrangements controlling disclosure. In such a rapidly evolving industry, employees tend to move readily among companies. Contractual arrangements are a reasonable way to maintain software protection, but the restrictions must not be too severe or they will not be upheld by the courts.

Finally, to protect secrecy it is certainly advisable to improve the effectiveness of security procedures. Also technology may be employed to increase the difficulty of making unauthorized use of programs. The copying of disks may be made quite difficult by special built-in protection. For example, the software may be restricted to run only on certain machines. Additional methods of foiling would-be violators have been and could be devised.

LEGAL ISSUES ON THE INTERNET

'(a) Whoever—
'(1) in interstate or foreign communications—

'(A) by means of a telecommunications device knowingly—
'(i) makes, creates, or solicits, and
'(ii) initiates the transmission of, any comment, request, suggestion, proposal, image, or other communication which is obscene, lewd, lascivious, filthy, or indecent, with intent to annoy, abuse, threaten, or harass another person;

'(B) by means of a telecommunications device knowingly—

'(i) makes, creates, or solicits, and

'(ii) initiates the transmission of, any comment, request, suggestion, proposal, image, or other communication which is obscene or indecent, knowing that the recipient of the communication is under 18 years of age, regardless of whether the maker of such communication placed the call or initiated the communication;

'(C) makes a telephone call or utilizes a telecommunications device, whether or not conversation or communication ensues, without disclosing his identity and with intent to annoy, abuse, threaten, or harass any person at the called number or who receives the communications;

'(D) makes or causes the telephone of another repeatedly or continuously to ring, with intent to harass any person at the called number; or

'(E) makes repeated telephone calls or repeatedly initiates communication with a telecommunications device, during which conversation or communication ensues, solely to harass any person at the called number or who receives the communication; or

'(2) knowingly permits any telecommunications facility under his control to be used for any activity prohibited by paragraph (1) with the intent that it be used for such activity,

shall be fined under title 18, United States Code, or imprisoned not more than two years, or both.';

> TITLE V—Communications Decency Act of 1996, Section 502, Obscene or Harassing Use of Telecommunications Facilities.

If the area of computer law is relatively new and growing, and it is, then a major impetus to that growth is the host of issues that have arisen on the Internet and that continue to challenge society. Among these are such issues as intellectual property rights for digital media, free speech, harassment, libel, and telecommunications law with respect to responsibilities for carriers and broadcasters. There are too many issues to explore in depth at this point but it is necessary to describe these in order to understand how the publicity associated with the Internet and the Web either exaggerates certain problems or ignores others, thereby creating a distorted image of this complex and global phenomenon. It must be recognized that these issues are far more than legal ones and that they involve social, political, gender, religious, and other important concerns. In later chapters, we revisit some of these and explore them from other than a legal perspective.

Intellectual Property Rights Protection

Given that the preceding section has dealt with copyright and patent issues in considerable detail, it should be interesting to continue the discussion in the context of the Internet. In

September 1995, the US federal government's Information Infrastructure Task Force released a lengthy report, a White paper (incorporating detailed government proposals); the following selection is taken from the introduction:[70]

> This Report represents the Working Group's examination and analysis of each of the major areas of intellectual property law, focusing primarily on copyright law and its application and effectiveness in the context of the NII. The approach of this Report is to discuss the application of the existing copyright law and to recommend only those changes that are essential to adapt the law to the needs of the global information society. By providing a generalized legal framework, based on the extensive analysis and discussion of the way in which the law has been and should be interpreted, we can lay the groundwork for the rapid and efficient development of the NII.

The report states that only a few minor changes in current copyright legislation will be necessary to provide for the new medium of the Internet, but these "minor changes" have aroused considerable criticism. We should note that the report contained a legislative proposal, the "NII Copyright Protection Act of 1996," "to amend Title 17 to adapt the copyright law," that in fact was introduced into both the House and Senate. To its defenders, including film studios, and book and magazine publishers, the proposals are indeed minor and just clean up a few loose ends to ensure that copyright holders receive full value over the new media where it is so easy to download, store, and retransmit information. Perhaps the most vocal critic, first of the White paper and then of the legislation, is Pamela Samuelson, a professor at the University of California at Berkeley, with a joint appointment in Law and the School of Information Management and Systems. She wrote a highly critical article in *Wired* that attacked the proposed legislation in a vigorous and impassioned manner. For example, here is her interpretation of what she labels as the White paper's "maximalist agenda," namely, the attempt to control all aspects of a copyrighted work's transmission and use to obtain as much financial return as possible:[71]

- Give copyright owners control over every use of copyrighted works in digital form by interpreting existing law as being violated whenever users make even temporary reproductions of works in the random access memory of their computers;
- Give copyright owners control over every transmission of works in digital form by amending the copyright statute so that digital transmissions will be regarded as distributions of copies to the public;
- Eliminate "fair use" rights whenever a use might be licensed (The copyright maximalists assert that there is no piece of a copyrighted work small enough that they are uninterested in charging for its use, and no use private enough that they aren't willing to track it down and charge for it. In this vision of the future, a user who has copied even a paragraph from an electronic journal to share with a friend will be as much a criminal as the person who tampers with an electrical meter at a friend's house in order to siphon off free electricity. If a few users have to go to jail for copyright offenses, well, that's a small price to pay to ensure that the population learns new patterns of behavior in the digital age);
- Deprive the public of the "first sale" rights it has long enjoyed in the print world (the rights that permit you to redistribute your own copy of a work after the publisher's first sale of it to you), because the white paper treats electronic forwarding as a violation of both the reproduction and distribution rights of copyright law;

- Attach copyright management information to digital copies of a work, ensuring that publishers can track every use made of digital copies and trace where each copy resides on the network and what is being done with it at any time;
- Protect every digital copy of every work technologically (by encryption, for example) and make illegal any attempt to circumvent that protection;
- Force online service providers to become copyright police, will be responsible not only for cutting off service to scofflaws but also for reporting copyright crime to the criminal justice authorities);
- Teach the new copyright rules of the road to children throughout their years at school.

Of course, defenders, especially publishers, formed the Creative Incentive Coalition (CIC) to promote acceptance of the new copyright legislation. Among the members of CIC are publishers, television stations, motion picture producers, software producers, and computer companies, including McGraw-Hill, Time Warner, Turner Broadcasting, Microsoft, and IBM.[72] Their claim is that minor changes in existing copyright law are necessary to protect creators, but since CIC's members are corporations, it is clear who they are concerned about. Of course, Internet service providers and commercial networks have their own concerns. Consider the following three issues that William W. Burrington, director of public policy at America Online, Inc., would like addressed in the copyright bill being considered by the Senate:[73]

- Service providers and systems operators won't be liable for any copyright infringements when, like a telephone company, they provide only conduit services.
- Service providers must not be required to police file or message contents.
- It is the responsibility of copyright owners to notify service providers of copyright infringements and the responsibility of service providers to remove the infringing material.

The issue of who is responsible for content and over what, is a recurring theme for many Internet legal issues. For the typical online user, the potential threat that every byte viewed or downloaded will have to be paid for is a vision of the future definitely not worth the wait.

Free Speech

If anything has brought the Internet to the attention of the general public it is the flood of newspaper, magazine, and television stories on Internet pornography, on threats to children by sexual predators, on parents discovering that their children have been downloading images of group sex, and more. Perhaps nothing so typified this relentless attack on the Internet as a cesspool of depravity than the infamous cover story of the July 3, 1995 issue of *Time*:

CYBERPORN

EXCLUSIVE: A new study shows how pervasive and wild it really is.

Can we protect our kids—and free speech?

For the purposes of this discussion, we must begin with that most fundamental of statements regarding limitations on government interference in human affairs, the First Amendment to the US Constitution:

Congress shall make no law respecting an establishment of religion, or prohibiting the free exercise thereof; or abridging the freedom of speech, or of the press, or the right of the people peaceably to assemble, and to petition the government for a redress of grievances.

It should be obvious that freedoms guaranteed prior to the emergence of electronic means for distributing information should continue to receive the same protection and be subject to the same limitations. It also seems to be a truism that one of the earliest uses of any new communication technology is to portray pornographic images. The early movie industry was heavily censored, as was television. Now movies are classified and censored, broadcast television is censored and cable pay television is classified. Local online bulletin boards, depending on location, may contain hardcore pornography. The Internet makes a considerable amount of pornography available, for free in newsgroups, and for a price on the sex Web sites. Accessibility to these Web sites requires proof of age and a credit card. It should also be pointed out that a number of steps must be taken to view potentially offensive images. Appropriate sites or newsgroups must be selected and since images are stored in a binary coded form, appropriate decoders must be available. Thus, the Internet user may never encounter pornography just as the average shopper may never encounter pornographic videos or magazines, unless he or she seeks them out.

Obscenity laws exist and material that a court of law finds obscene can result in penalties for those who sell or transmit such material. The current Supreme Court definition of obscenity, the *Miller* test[74] requires that all of the following three conditions be met:

(1) The average person, applying contemporary community standards, would find that the work, taken as a whole, appeals to the prurient interest (in sex); and

(2) the work depicts or describes, in a patently offensive way, sexual conduct specifically defined by the applicable state (or federal) law; and

(3) the work, taken as a whole, lacks serious literary, artistic, political, or scientific value.

In the case of child pornography, purchasing or possessing is sufficient to incur criminal charges. Thus certain forms of information have been found by the courts to be indefensible by appeal to the First Amendment and although expressed in unequivocal terms— Congress shall pass *no* laws—the Courts have approved some laws, believing that under rare circumstances, compromises were necessary to achieve another social good. So the debate inevitably turns upon determining whether or not a given situation requires yet another special case exception to a general principle. To help sharpen the discussion, we will present a few examples that have aroused considerable publicity and that have contributed to a sense that perhaps the Internet should be regulated by content. Also keep in mind that by its very nature, regulating a worldwide system such as the Internet is a nontrivial task, actually an impossible one in the belligerent opinion of many long time Net aficionados.

The Jake Baker Case

Jake Baker was an undergraduate student at the University of Michigan when in October of 1994, he began posting stories on a Usenet newsgroup, alt.sex.stories, of a particularly violent and pornographic nature. One story apparently referred to a women that Baker knew from one of his classes. These stories were brought to the attention of university administrators, who had Public Safety officers search his room and computer account with his permission. It was discovered that Baker had been communicating by e-mail with an Arthur Gonda in Canada and that they were discussing the possibility of kidnapping someone, presumably to torture in a fashion described in the stories. Baker was suspended by University President Duderstadt and subsequently arrested by the FBI on February 9, 1995 and charged with violating 18 U.S.C. s 875(c): "Transmission in interstate or foreign commerce of a communication containing a threat to kidnap any person or any threat to injure the person of another."

This case has raised a host of issues, including the following:[75]

- *Privacy of victim.* Was Baker within his free speech/free press rights to use her name without her knowledge or permission?
- *Threats.* Does the story constitute a threat to Jane Doe? It is legally unclear whether a conversation regarding fiction between two other parties without her knowledge constitutes a threat.
- *Therapy.* Are Baker's stories a kind of psychological therapy? Baker claims that the stories help him to vent anger.
- *Role Playing in Creative Writing.* Was Baker role playing when he corresponded with Arthur Gonda? Was Baker writing about himself in his stories?
- *Obscenity.* Do Baker's stories have constitutional free speech/free press protection? Should they?
- *Due Process.* Did Baker receive due process from the University? Does Baker merit handling as a violent felon on the basis of his writing alone?
- *The Internet.* The Baker case would not merit much attention if it did not involve the Internet.
- *Internet as a publishing medium.* Did Baker abuse his posting privileges?
- *Internet crossing jurisdictional boundaries.* Was a crime committed by use of Internet media? How will this affect the future of the Internet?
- *Obscenity standards on the Internet.* Were Baker's stories inappropriate for the Internet?

This list covers just about all the issues that have arisen on the Internet over the past few years. Cases such as Baker's influenced the momentum being developed towards regulating legislation and the outcome of his case had an impact as well. On June 22, 1995, US District Judge Avern Cohen "dismissed the charges, citing the government's lack of evidence that Baker planned to act on his writings." In somewhat more detail, Judge Cohen noted that what the government failed to establish was the requirement stated in Kelner, 534 F.2d at 1027 of a "threat which on its face and in the circumstances in which it is made is so unequivocal, unconditional, immediate and specific as to the person threatened, as to convey a gravity of purpose and imminent prospect of execution."[76] This decision was widely hailed as a significant victory for the First Amendment on the Internet. On November 21, 1995, the Government filed an appeal of dismissal.

Time's Cover Story: The Marty Rimm Study

This *Time* cover story promised a great deal: "A research team at Carnegie Mellon University in Pittsburgh, Pennsylvania, has conducted an exhaustive study of online porn—

what's available, who is downloading it, what turns them on—and the findings (to be published in the Georgetown Law Journal) are sure to pour fuel on an already explosive debate."[77] The editors were well aware that their story would be influential: "If you think things are crazy now, though, wait until the politicians get hold of a report coming out this week." Up to the appearance of the *Time* cover story, it might have been claimed that most Internet pornography pieces were not only sensational but anecdotal with no real evidence of how pervasive or how hardcore the images carried on the Internet are. With the appearance of an academic study, it would now be possible to formulate regulatory policy based on hard evidence and its high profile in a major magazine would reinforce that process. Clearly, a lot was riding on the Carnegie-Mellon report, more commonly known as the Rimm study. The major findings as reported by *Time* are given as follows:[78]

- *There's an awful lot of porn online.* In an 18-month study, the team surveyed 917,410 sexually explicit pictures, descriptions, short stories and film clips. On those Usenet newsgroups where digitized images are stored, 83.5 percent of the pictures were pornographic.
- *It is immensely popular.* Trading in sexually explicit imagery, according to the report, is now "one of the largest (if not the largest) recreational applications of users of computer networks." . . .
- *It is a big moneymaker.* The great majority (71 percent) of the sexual images on the newsgroups surveyed originate from adult-oriented computer bulletin-board systems (BBS) whose operators are trying to lure customers to their private collections of X-rated material. There are thousands of these BBS services, which charge fees (typically $10 to $30 a month) and take credit cards; the five largest have annual revenues in excess of $1 million.
- *It is ubiquitous.* Using data obtained with permission from BBS operators, the Carnegie Mellon team identified (but did not publish the names of) individual consumers in more than 2,000 cities in all 50 states and 40 countries, territories and provinces around the world.
- *It is a guy thing.* According to the BBS operators, 98.9 percent of the consumers of online porn are men . . .
- *It is not just naked women.* Perhaps because hard-core sex pictures are so widely available elsewhere, the adult BBS market seems to be driven largely by a demand for images that can't be found in the average magazine rack: pedophilia (nude photos of children), hebephilia (youths) and what the researchers call paraphilia—a grab bag of "deviant" material that includes images of bondage, sadomasochism, urination, defecation, and sex acts with a barnyard full of animals.

No sooner had the story appeared than controversy erupted. Attacks both against *Time's* rush to publish an article based on a paper that had yet to appear in an academic journal[79] (although it was to be printed shortly) and against the paper itself were quickly mounted. The most important critique was authored by two professors at Vanderbilt University, Donna L. Hoffman and Thomas P. Novak. They produced criticisms of both the magazine article and the journal paper.[80] When considering the *Time* story, they are concerned that although the impression is made that lots of pornography is online (i.e., on the Internet), the data is derived primarily from adult Bulletin Board Systems (BBSs).[81] These are commercial enterprises that provide online access to explicit images, and subsequently the Internet comes into play as individuals post these images on newsgroups. The statement that there is "an awful lot of pornography online," is thus misleading. In fact, the *Time* article presents a much more accurate view but doesn't highlight it sufficiently, possibly because it would weaken the flood-of-pornography theme. Thus, the article notes, "the Carnegie Mellon study is careful to point out, pornographic image files, despite their evident popularity, represent only about 3 percent of all the messages on the Usenet newsgroups, while the Usenet itself represents only 11.5 percent of the traffic on the Internet."[82] The failure to make the arithmetic explicit is somewhat irresponsible, namely, that pornography therefore represents only about one third of 1% of all Internet traffic. And within this very small percentage, the amount of actual hardcore stuff is even smaller because the study's methodology included in the count, material such as text files, with comments by readers. Much more could be said, but the point is clear—for the public at large and some of their government representatives, the Internet must be cleaned up, even if government involvement is required.

Whose Community Standards? Amateur Action Bulletin Board

We review one last case that in and of itself is not significant, but could set a legal precedent that could reduce the content of the Internet to a level acceptable by only the most restrictive community in the US. Amateur Action BBS (AABBS) had been operated by Robert and Carleen Thomas from their home in Milpitas, California since February 1991. It provided typical services, including, e-mail, chat lines, public messages, and a large database of explicit images that patrons could download. Most of the images were scanned from sexually explicit adult magazines purchased in public adult book stores. In July 1993, a complaint was received about AABBS by the United States Postal Office from a person living in western Tennessee. A US Postal Inspector paid for a membership, accessed the BBS from Memphis after his account had been authorized by a phone call from Robert Thomas, and downloaded a number of GIF (Graphic Interchange Format) files that form the basis for six of the twelve charges subsequently laid against the Thomases. They were tried in federal court in Memphis under a 12-count indictment that included conspiracy to violate federal obscenity laws and "six counts under 18 U.S.C. § 1465 for knowingly using and causing to be used a facility and means of interstate commerce—a combined computer/telephone system—for the purpose of transporting obscene, computer-generated materials (the GIF files) in interstate commerce."[83]

The decision was appealed and heard in the US Court of Appeals for the Sixth Circuit, where the lower court decision was upheld. This case has serious repercussions for the Internet with respect to content and accessibility. The defendants claimed that they should not have been tried in Tennessee because they did not cause the GIFs to be transmitted there. This claim was rejected because of a precedent that the court recognized as applying in this case, namely, " 'Venue lies in any district in which the offense was committed,' and the Government is required to establish venue by a preponderance of the evidence."[84] The defendants further claimed that the community standards of their home location, namely northern California, should apply in the determination of whether or not the GIFs in question were legally obscene. Recall that the first part of the Miller test contained the requirement that "The average person, applying contemporary *community* standards . . ." must agree that the material under question is obscene. The Appeals Court found ample precedents that the relevant community could be " 'in any district from, through, or into which' the allegedly obscene material moves," that "[p]rosecutions may be brought either in the district of dispatch or the district of receipt," and that "it is not unconstitutional to subject interstate distributors of obscenity to varying community standards."[85] Thus the notion of community standards seems to have been extended in a devastating manner. Purveyors of pornography could be held, and probably will be held, to the most restrictive standards anywhere in the US and must be aware of those standards.

The defendants also claimed that the existence of computer networks required a correspondingly new definition of community standards, "one that is based on the broad-ranging connections among people in cyberspace rather than the geographic locale of the federal judicial district of the criminal trial. Without a more flexible definition, they argue, there will be an impermissible chill on protected speech because BBS operators cannot select who gets the materials they make available on their bulletin boards." This argument was also rejected. This case was appealed to the Supreme Court where the Circuit Court's decision was upheld. In the interim attention has shifted to the federal government's attempt to implement control over content on the Internet by legislation.

The Communications Decency Act of 1996

On February 1, Congress passed the Telecommunications Act of 1996 and it was signed into law one week later by President Clinton. It was a far-reaching attempt to deal with the new technologies that have dramatically altered the telecommunications industry in the past few years. (More will be said about the Act in Chapter 11.) The issue of interest, however, is Title V—Obscenity and Violence, Subtitle A—Obscene, Harassing, and Wrongful Utilization of Telecommunications Facilities; with the short title, the Communications Decency Act of 1996. The quotation at the beginning of this section provides the crucial words of the Act that have aroused so much controversy.

Although the passage of the Act was expected, as it had been debated for many months, many hoped that these provisions would be weakened or even deleted, but such was not the case as it passed both houses of Congress with overwhelming majorities. Within minutes of the enactment a suit was filed in federal court by the American Civil Liberties Union and 19 other organizations to enjoin several sections of the Act. Others in this group included the National Writers Union, Electronic Frontier Foundation, and the Electronic Privacy Information Center. A temporary restraining order was narrowly granted on the indecency provisions. On February 26, another suit was launched by a group, the Citizens Internet Empowerment Coalition (CIEC), led by the American Library Association and including Apple, CompuServe, America OnLine, Microsoft, the Association of American Publishers, and the Newspaper Association of America. The suits were joined the following day and the hearing began on March 21. In the interim, many sexually-oriented Web sites began displaying elaborate messages to forestall any legal responsibility.[86]

If February 8 was a black day for free speech on the Internet for many, then June 12 witnessed the sun breaking through. In a unanimous decision, the three-judge panel in Philadelphia found for the plaintiffs and declared the indecency provisions unconstitutional. As expected the government appealed and the case was argued before the Supreme Court on March 19, 1997. What was encouraging to the strong supporters of the First Amendment were the quality of the statements made by the judges in support of their decision. Thus the following examples are indicative of the unanimous sentiments of the judges:[87]

- The Internet may fairly be regarded as a never-ending worldwide conversation. The government may not, through the CDA, interrupt that conversation. As the most participatory form of mass speech yet developed, the Internet deserves the highest protection from government intrusion . . .
- Any content-based regulation of the Internet, no matter how benign the purpose, could burn the global village to roast the pig.
- Internet communication, while unique, is more akin to telephone communication than to broadcasting because as with the telephone an Internet user must act affirmatively and deliberately to retrieve specific information online.
- Just as the strength of the Internet is chaos, so the strength of our liberty depends upon the chaos and cacophony of the unfettered speech the First Amendment protects.
- The CDA will, without doubt, undermine the substantive, speech-enhancing benefits that have flowed from the Internet. The diversity of the content will necessarily diminish as a result. The economic costs associated with compliance with the Act will drive from the Internet speakers whose content falls within the zone of possible prosecution.

One final point is that all the judges were impressed by the development of programs such as CyberSitter, SurfWatch, and NetNanny, which give parents the ability to prevent their children from accessing selected Web sites. Although government lawyers admitted that such programs could help and were being improved, they were not prepared to admit that parents acting responsibly meant that direct intervention by government was unnecessary.

Content Responsibility: CompuServe and Prodigy

What responsibility do private networks such as CompuServe and Prodigy have over content? The previous section dealt with free speech issues but there are many things to be concerned about other than pornography. On October 31, 1991, US District Judge Peter Leisure held that CompuServe was not liable for information carried on an online forum it had created, that is, statements that might be defamatory could not be blamed on the service provider: and in the trial CompuServe did not dispute this point. Thus, this important ruling equated CompuServe and other similar networks to bookstores and newsstands, whose owners are not responsible for content unless they actually have specific knowledge beforehand.[88] In commenting on the importance of this decision, Caden and Lucas note that, "By labeling CompuServe as a distributor rather than a publisher, the court issued the first prominent legal decision concerning the culpability of on-line access providers. The decision encouraged growth within the Internet community by reducing the threat of liability to on-line access providers."[89]

In the case Stratton Oakmont v. Prodigy Services, Stratton sued Prodigy for libel because of statements posted about its president on a Prodigy bulletin board. In its ruling against Prodigy on May 24, 1995, the court found that Prodigy was acting as a publisher and was therefore responsible for content. It distinguished this case from the CompuServe one on the grounds that Prodigy advertised itself as responsible for content: "Prodigy promulgated content guidelines, used a software screening program, utilized Board Leaders [with the ability to monitor and censor incoming messages], and had an emergency delete function."[90] Prodigy could not have it both ways: it could not monitor content and claim its commitment to family values and then attempt to absolve itself of responsibility when information on its system was found to be libelous. Later in October, Stratton decided not to challenge new evidence that Prodigy planned to bring forward, leaving it to the judge to decide. Prodigy apologized for the offensive statements but continued to insist that it was not a publisher. In any case, the passage of the Communications Decency Act changed Prodigy's position, as the commentary taken from Blumenfeld & Cohen makes clear, " 'Good Samaritan' blocking of information that content providers or users find objectionable (on a purely subjective basis) is legalized, thus overturning a well-known case finding Prodigy liable for civil damages on account of a forum posting that defamed a company on the ground that Prodigy engaged in selective blocking of postings."[91]

OTHER DEVELOPMENTS

Liability and Malpractice

Suppose a navigator aboard an aircraft uses a computer, with appropriate application software, to plan a route that results in the aircraft's crashing into an unexpected mountain. Who is responsible? Among the candidates are the navigator, the pilot, the aircraft company, the computer manufacturer, and the software developer. The grounds for suit may include breach of warranty, breach of third-party beneficiary contract, negligence, and strict liability. In the last instance the programmer might be found liable, even though he or she was very careful in both the writing and debugging of the program. Under strict liability, a seller is liable for damages even if there is no contract between the seller and the person suffering the damages. As the dependence of society on computers grows, there will be a corresponding growth in litigation associated with computer malfunction, and it will be particularly interesting when the judgments of expert systems are challenged.

In a very important case, Diversified Graphics v. Groves, Diversified hired the consulting firm of Ernst & Whinney (now Ernst & Young) to recommend a turnkey computer system that could be operated without specially trained staff. It claimed that the system did not work as expected and many thousands of dollars were wasted in trying to make it satisfactory. Ernst & Whinney argued that in recommending a system it should be held only to an ordinary standard of care, not to a professional one. The jury, in finding for the plaintiff, Diversified Graphics, "held consultants from Ernst & Whinney liable for shirking the Management Advisory Services Practice Standards of the American Institute of Certified Public Accountants in their procurement of a turnkey system for Diversified Graphics."[92] In February 1989, the appeals court upheld the verdict. The strong message from this case is that even system programmers or application programmers as well as consultants will be held to professional standards.

Beyond programs or systems that fail to perform as advertised, there may be programs that actually cause physical harm. Computers in medical care can offer valuable services but there may be risks. For example, a heart monitor may produce an incorrect reading that results in a doctor prescribing incorrect treatment, or incorrect software may cause an X-ray overdose, as has actually happened. The case of Therac-25, a computerized radiation therapy machine, has become an important landmark in the development of risk management strategies and ethical responsibility. Therac-25 was developed by Atomic Energy of Canada Limited (AECL) as one of a series of radiation therapy machines and came into use in the mid-1980s. Between 1985 and 1987, six incidents occurred in which patients were given massive overdoses, resulting in death or injury.[93]

Determining liability in computer-related cases is still a developing area of law. One possibility is the application of "strict liability to health care providers as a *seller* of computer products." Another is that the program may be viewed as incidental to the services provided and perhaps negligence, under the principle of torts, may apply. Or new legal principles may be required when computers or computer networks are involved.

Sexual Harassment and Electronic Networks

A defense of free speech on electronic networks, the Internet to be more precise, has been made previously in this chapter but there are certain consequences that must be addressed. What if anything should be done about people who download sexually explicit images on workstations in public areas at work, in libraries, and in universities and colleges? The concern arises because others in the area at nearby computers may find these images offensive and disturbing, resulting in an interference with normal work. Beginning in the early 1990s, many educational institutions concerned with this problem took steps to restrict student access to suspect newsgroups as a way of dealing with the problem. Thus all newsgroups in the alt.sex hierarchy were cut off, including the so-called binaries, where most of the suspect coded images resided. However, this hierarchy contains many newsgroups that deal with sexual issues that in no way could be characterized as pornographic, even if a satisfactory definition of that term were possible. However, administrators at many institutions decided that censorship, although that term was rarely used in public, was the most effective way to deal with a burgeoning problem.

A detailed exploration of this situation was carried out by Rosenberg in 1993,[94] to argue that it should not be necessary to censor or suppress in order to achieve equitable environments. Having watchdog groups, regularly monitoring Usenet to determine if any non–alt.sex newsgroups were problematic, or if any new newsgroups might be offensive with respect to racial, ethnic, or gender concerns, is not appropriate for educational institutions. Thus, Rosenberg proposed, "six basic principles . . . that adhere strongly to the principle of free speech, as a hallmark of an open and democratic society . . . the first four principles are stated in the form of injunctions intended to serve administrative, pragmatic requirements while simultaneously serving free speech. The last two principles are an attempt to capture the benefits of electronic networks in a concise fashion, juxtaposed with the difficulties that organizations may have in enforcing the unenforceable."[95]

Administrative Principles

(1) Do not treat electronic media differently from print media, or traditional bulletin boards merely because they can be more easily controlled
(2) Do not censor potentially offensive material on networks; encourage the use of sexual harassment procedures, if appropriate
(3) Be aware of your responsibility with respect to the uses and misuses of your facilities. However, do not use cost of services as an excuse to censor and limit access
(4) Trust and educate people to be responsible

Social Principles

(1) Issues will proliferate beyond the ability of organizations to control them by rigid policies
(2) Occasional offensive postings do not detract from the benefits of electronic networks

It is recognized that "Placing the burden on women to invoke sexual harassment procedures may compound an already difficult situation. Fellow students or workers may attempt to trivialize the events and criticize the complainant's lack of camaraderie and unwillingness to be one of the gang. The increasing number of women who participate in network communication and computing in general may change the culture sufficiently so that offensive displays will no longer be accepted or tolerated."[96]

More Free Speech Issues

Two more issues will be introduced briefly. Although concern with free speech is a hotly debated topic in the US and several other countries, for the majority of the world's countries, many other matters take precedence. In the US, whatever assaults exist against a full exercise of free speech, there are constitutional guarantees and a strong commitment to them; unfortunately, such is not the case in most of the world. The international organization Human Rights Watch has issued a report that focuses on the global attack on free speech on the Internet. In the Summary to this report, the threat is clearly stated: "Governments around the world, claiming they want to protect children, thwart terrorists and silence racists and hate mongers, are rushing to eradicate freedom of expression on the Internet, the international "network of networks," touted as the Information Superhighway."[97] A few examples of these events are as follows:[98]

- China, which requires users and Internet Service Providers (ISPs) to register with authorities;
- Vietnam and Saudi Arabia, which permit only a single, government-controlled gateway for Internet service;
- United States, which has enacted new Internet-specific legislation that imposes more restrictive regulations on electronic expression than those currently applied to printed expression;
- India, which charges exorbitant rates for international access through the state-owned phone company;
- Germany, which has cut off access to particular host computers or Internet sites;
- Singapore, which has chosen to regulate the Internet as if it were a broadcast medium, and requires political and religious content providers to register with the state; and
- New Zealand, which classifies computer disks as publications and has seized and restricted them accordingly.

Human Rights Watch recommends that international agreements enshrine freedom of expression as a basic principle for a Global Information Infrastructure. This would include "prohibiting prior censorship of on-line communication, . . . [p]romoting the wide dissemination of diverse ideas and viewpoints from a wide variety of information sources on the GII. Ensuring that the GII enable individuals to organize and form on-line associations freely and without interference."

One category of pornography against which specific and severe legislation exists is child pornography, and the laws apply to the manufacture, sale, distribution, and possession. Accusations have been made that the Internet has become another distribution channel for this most despised material. Certainly BBSs exist that carry child pornography and some of the images have made their way to the Internet. There have been highly publicized police raids and a number of people have been arrested. In 1995, the US Congress passed the Sex Crimes Against Children Prevention Act of 1995 (SCACPA), and required that the United States Sentencing Commission report on the adequacy of federal penalties. In its report, the Commission noted that penalties had been increased over the previous two years and were quite severe, but the report also examined the role of the Internet. In surveying computer use among defendants in pornography cases with respect to trafficking and receipt, computers were involved in 22 out of 66 cases. In nine of these, "defendants posted notices of interest in receiving child pornography, and in four cases defendants posted notices regarding the availability of child pornography."[99]

Although the numbers are small, Congress viewed computer and computer networks as a growth area and in fact, the legislative history of the SCACPA indicated that Congress had the following concerns:[100]

(1) the wide dissemination and instantaneous transmission in computer-assisted trafficking of child pornography,
(2) the increased difficulty of investigation and prosecution by law enforcement officials,
(3) the increased likelihood that child pornography will be viewed by and harm children, and
(4) the potential for pedophiles to lure children into sexual relationships through the computer.

A Final Comment

Arguments about copyright and patent occur in the context of sophisticated technologies developed in advanced countries. However, in one context, the worldwide search for useful flora, fauna, and human genetic material, the arena is remote from the laboratory, the research institute, or the university. Claims of biological imperialism have arisen as researchers from the US have patented "a cell line found in the blood of the Hagahai [from Papua New Guinea] that acts as a vehicle for a type of human T-cell leukemia virus. The virus normally causes a severe form of leukemia. But the strain found in the Hagahai strain is benign . . ."[101] One of the researchers had arranged for the tribe to receive one-half of any royalties earned. So a naturally occurring blood strain of a primitive people has been patented, a concept presumably quite remote from their experience, for the benefit of a people with whom they are quite unfamiliar.

SUMMARY

The introduction of computers in significant numbers into society has brought the legal system problems of new crimes and new ways to commit old ones. Computer crime has become one of the most publicized aspects of computer use. The various crimes associated with computers are difficult to evaluate in terms of either magnitude or frequency, but it seems safe to say that the number and variety are increasing and the stakes are growing. Victimized companies, including banks, have been reluctant to publicize such crimes for fear of endangering their reputations for security. Nevertheless, enough cases have been documented to indicate that computer crimes can be quite subtle and difficult to detect.

More recently, computer viruses and worms have taken the center stage, causing severe disruptions of systems and networks and loss of files for individual computer users. The most publicized case was the INTERNET worm initiated by Robert Morris, a Cornell graduate student, late in 1988. Although found guilty, Morris's actions prompted a flurry of congressional activity towards new legislation to deal with viruses and worms. The range of crimes made possible by computers is so wide that precise definition has proven elusive.

Legislation has been passed in various states to deal with computer crimes, but it was only in late 1986 that Congress passed the Computer Fraud and Abuse Act to provide penalties for illicit access to computers. The current generation of computer crimes seems to be less concerned with property-based activities and more focused on reckless behavior, which puts other users at risk. To deal with unauthorized entry, a variety of security methods have been proposed to protect against both physical and electronic trespassing. Only authorized staff should be able to gain direct entry to the computer. A system of passwords and priority levels should be used to restrict unauthorized sign-ons via remote terminals.

The development of software and computers must be protected against illegal copying to ensure that developers are properly rewarded for their work and to encourage others to enter the marketplace. Traditional means of protecting intellectual property are copyrights and patents. Patent protection for programs was first recognized in a 1981 Supreme Court decision but it has taken several years for the Patent Office to be receptive to software applications. First in 1980 and then in 1984, the Software Copyright Act extended copyright protection to computer programs. Also in 1984, Congress passed the Semiconductor Chip Protection Act to protect chips and the masks used to produce them. Of recent concern has been the attempt by some software and hardware companies to protect the "look and-feel" of their user interfaces. In 1990, Lotus Development, the developer of the 1-2-3 spreadsheet program won an important suit to copyright its interface and command structure but subsequently, this decision was overturned.

The Internet has become the target of a number of attacks that threaten its openness and traditional frontier mentality. At the top of the list is the concern in the press, certain religious groups, law enforcement officials, and politicians that the Internet is rife with obscene material that must be controlled. The passage of the Communications Decency Act in 1996 was a clear demonstration by elected officials in an election year that they were serious about outlawing questionable material. Other important legal issues relate to the protection of digital material by the extension of copyright law to this domain, the liability of Internet Service Providers, and harassment of Internet users.

NOTES

1. Thomas K. Christo. "The Law and DP: A Clash of Egos," *Datamation,* September 1982, pp. 264–265, 267–268.
2. Joseph Maglitta. "IS at O. J. City," *Computerworld,* May 15, 1995, pp. 90–91, 94.
3. Raphael Winick. "Searches and Seizures of Computers and Computer Data," *Harvard Journal of Law and Technology,* 8 (1), Fall 1994, pp. 75–128. The reference for this case is Commonwealth v. Copenhefer, 587 A.2d 1353 (Pa. 1991).
4. "Testimony of Richard G. Powers, editor, Computer Security Institute, before the Permanent Subcommittee on Investigations, US Senate Committee on Governmental Affairs, June 5, 1996. Accessed from the Web page with URL: <http://www.gocsi.com/csi/testify.htm> on July 10, 1996.
5. R. Burger. "Computer Viruses: A High-Tech Disease, Second Edition." (Grand Rapids, MI: Abacus, 1988), p. 15. As referenced in James Tramontana, "Computer Viruses: Is There a Legal 'Antibiotic'?" *Rutgers Computer & Technology Journal,* 16 (1), 1990, note 26, p. 255.
6. "alt.cyberpunk Faq list." Accessed from the Web page with URL: <http://bush.cs.tamu.edu/~erich/alt.cp.faq.html > on July 13, 1996.
7. Anne W. Branscomb. "Rogue Computer Programs and Computer Rogues: Tailoring the Punishment to Fit the Crime," *Rutgers Computer & Technology Law Journal,* 16 (1), 1990, p. 4.
8. Donn Parker. *Crime by Computer.* (New York: Scribner's, 1976), p. 169.
9. Gary H. Anthes. "InVircible: Invincible or Irresponsible?" *Computerworld,* June 5, 1995, p. 41. Laurent Belsie, "Computer Virus Update: Newer Strains Defy Experts," *The Christian Science Monitor,* March 3, 1995, pp. 3–4.
10. An interesting bit of historical trivia is associated with computer crime statistics. In 1973, in a speech to the American Society for Industrial Security, Robert V. Jacobson, president of International Security Technology, Inc. reported that, "According to an unpublished study of white-collar crime in the United States, 86.2% of computer crime in 1972 was never detected!" This figure gained great currency in the computer crime lecture and publication circuit. However, as Mr. Jacobson admits, "At the time it never occurred to me that people would miss the irony. After all how could one generate an estimate with three figure accuracy about undiscovered events?" Special Interest Group on Security Audit & Control Review, Association for Computing Machinery, Spring 1987, pp. iii–v.
11. Wade Roush. "Hackers: Taking a Byte Out of Computer Crime," *Technology Review,* April 1995. Accessed from the Web site with URL: <http://www.mit.edu/techreview/www/> on June 15, 1995.
12. "1996 Computer Crime and Security Survey," Computer Security Institute, May 1996. Accessed from the Web page with URL: <http://www.gocsi.com/csi/iss_t.htm#Computer Crime> on July 10, 1996.
13. *Ibid.*
14. *Op. cit.,* Branscomb, p. 18.
15. Philip Elmer-DeWitt. "You Must Be Punished," *Time,* September 26, 1988, p. 54.
16. Andrew Pollock. "3 Men Accused of Violating Computer and Phone Systems," *The New York Times,* January 18, 1990, pp. A1, A17.
17. John Markoff. "3 Arrests Show Global Threats to Computers," *The New York Times,* April 4, 1990, pp. A1, A16.
18. "Computergate Hits New Jersey," *Computerworld,* September 17, 1990, p. 147.
19. *Op. cit.,* "Testimony of Richard G. Powers."
20. Katherine M. Hafner, et al. "Is Your Computer Secure?" *Business Week,* August 1, 1988, pp.

64–67, 70–72, and Philip Elmer-DeWitt, "Invasion of the Data Snatchers," *Time,* September 26, 1988, pp. 50–55.

21. John Markoff. "'Virus' in Military Systems," *The New York Times,* November 4, 1988, pp. 1, 13.

22. *Op. cit.,* Branscomb, p. 7.

23. John Markoff. "Jury Convicts Student Whose Program Jammed Computers," *The New York Times,* January 23, 1990, p. A13.

24. John Markoff. "Computer Intruder Gets Probation and Fine But Avoids Prison Term," *The New York Times,* May 5, 1990, pp. 1, 8. "Morris Appeal Due," *Computerworld,* November 12, 1990, p. 8.

25. Katie Hafner and John Markoff. *Cyberpunk: Outlaws and Hackers on the Computer Frontier.* (New York: Simon & Schuster, A Touchstone Book, 1992), p. 346. This book contains considerable detail about the INTERNET worm case as well as the activities of Kevin Mitnick in the 1980s.

26. *Op. cit.,* Branscomb, pp. 18–21 and "Drop the Phone," *Time,* January 9, 1989, p. 15.

27. Taken from an excerpt from Tsutomo Shimomura with John Markoff, *Takedown: The Pursuit and Capture of Kevin Mitnick, America's Most Wanted Computer Outlaw by the Man Who Did It.* (New York: Hyperion, 1996). The excerpt was accessed at the Web page with URL: <http://www.takedown.com/bio/mitnick.html> on July 11, 1996.

28. John Markoff. "Cyberspace's Most Wanted: Hacker Eludes F.B.I. Pursuit," *The New York Times,* July 4, 1994. Accessed from the Web page with URL: <http://www.takedown.com/coverage/most-wanted.html> on July 11, 1996.

29. Christopher D. Chen. "Computer Crime and the Computer Fraud and Abuse Act of 1986," *Computer/Law Journal* X (1) Winter 1990, pp. 71–86.

30. "Is Computer Hacking a Crime?" *Harper's Magazine,* March 1990, pp. 45–57. A transcript of selections of a nationwide forum held on a computer bulletin-board over an 11-day period, including a variety of perspectives.

31. Michael Alexander. "Babes in High-Tech Toyland Nabbed," *Computerworld,* February 12, 1990, p. 8.

32. Michael Alexander. "Hacker Trial Begins in Chicago," *Computerworld,* July 30, 1990, p. 8.

33. Peter H. Lewis. "Can Invaders Be Stopped But Civil Liberties Upheld?" *The New York Times,* September 9, 1990, p. 12 F, and Michael Alexander. "Dial 1-800 . . . for Bellsouth 'Secrets'," *Computerworld,* August 6, 1990, p. 8. The three individuals who actually broke into the Bellsouth Corp.'s computers to obtain the proprietary information were not so fortunate. They were sentenced, on November 16, 1990, to terms varying from 14 months to 21 months in prison plus fines of $233,000 each. Reported in Michael Alexander. "Hackers Draw Stiff Sentences," *Computerworld,* November 26, 1990, pp. 1, 99.

34. "The VIRUS: A Computer Toxin," Washington, DC: Business Software Alliance, October, 1995. Accessed from the Web page with URL: <http://smash.paxnet.com.au/~dippy/9510/art4.htm> on July 10, 1996.

35. The 3rd Annual Ernst & Young/Information Week Information Security Survey, 1995. Accessed from the Web page with URL: <http://www.ey.com/us/isas/infosec.pdf> on July 10, 1996. The 3rd Annual Ernst & Young/Information Week Information Security Survey was conducted during August and September, 1995. The survey questionnaire was sent to over 13,000 Information Week subscribers in North America, representing mostly larger organizations in a cross section of industries. Over 1,300 responses were tabulated. 59% of respondents were from organizations with more than 2,500 employees. 85% of respondents were either IS Heads or CIOs (42%), direct reports of CIO (31%), or heads of information security (12%).

36. *Information Technologies for Control of Money Laundering,* US Congress, Office of Technol-

ogy Assessment, OTA-ITC-630. (Washington, DC: US Government Printing Office, September 1995). Available at the Web site with URL: <http://www.ota.nap.edu/>.

37. *Ibid.*, pp. 2–3.

38. *Ibid.*, pp. 3–4.

39. *Ibid.*, pp. 51–52.

40. *Ibid.*, p. 139.

41. Michael C. Gemignani, *Law and the Computer.* (Boston: CBI, 1981), p. 84.

42. Paula Dwyer, et al. "The Battle Raging Over 'Intellectual Property'," *Business Week*, May 22, 1989, p. 89. Keith H. Hammond. "What Will Polaroid Do with All That Moola?" *Business Week*, October 29, 1990, p. 38.

43. "Piracy and the Software Market," Annual Survey [1994 Results], Business Software Alliance, April 1995. Accessed from the Web page with URL: <http://198.236.7.124/Piracy/1994ww.htm> on July 12, 1996.

44. David Bender, *Computer Law: Evidence and Procedure.* (New York: M. Bender, 1982), p. 4A–2.

45. "What is a Patent?" US Patent and Trademark Office. Accessed from the Web page with URL: <http://www.uspto.gov/web/patinfo/what_is_a_patent.html on July 12, 1996.

46. As quoted in Gemignani, *Law and the Computer,* p. 102.

47. *Ibid.*

48. As quoted in Bender, *Computer Law,* pp. 4A-7–4A-8.

49. J. Michael Jukes and E. Robert Yoches. "Basic Principles of Patent Protection for Computer Software," *Communications of the ACM,* **32** (8), August 1989, pp. 922–924.

50. Mitch Betts. "Feds to Ease Software Patent Guidelines," *Computerworld,* April 17, 1995, p. 20.

51. Curtis L. Harrington. "Computer Program Patentability Update," no date. Accessed from the Web page with URL: <http://www.wweb.net/comart/curt/update.html> on July 12, 1996.

52. "Examination Guidelines for Computer-Related Inventions," Patent and Trademark Office, 1995. Accessed from the Web page with URL: <http://www.uspto.gov/web/software/files/guides.doc> on July 12, 1996.

53. W. Scott Petty. "Yes Virginia, the US Patent Office Grants Software Patents!" *Georgia Computer Law Section Newsletter,* Winter 1996. Accessed from the Web page with URL: <http://www.kuesterlaw.com/comp4g.htm> on July 12, 1996.

54. *Op. cit.,* Bender, p. 4A–31.

55. Frederick L. Cooper III. *Law and the Software Marketer.* (Englewood Cliffs, NJ: Prentice-Hall, 1988), pp. 91–96.

56. Pamela Samuelson. "Why the Look and Feel of Software Interfaces Should Not Be Protected by Copyright Law," *Communications of the ACM,* **32** (5), May 1989, pp. 563–572.

57. Paul R. Lamoree. "Expanding Copyright in Software: The Struggle to Define 'Expression' Begins," *Computer & High Technology Law Journal,* **4** (1), January 1988, p. 62.

58. *Op. cit.,* Samuelson, p. 567.

59. *Op. cit.,* Lamoree, p. 78.

60. As quoted in John Markoff. "Lotus Wins Copyright Decision," *The New York Times,* June 29, 1990, p. C 3.

61. Patricia Keefe. "Paperback Pulls Spreadsheet, Won't Appeal Lotus Victory," *Computerworld,* October 22, 1990, p. 7.

62. Pamela Samuelson. "How to Interpret the Lotus Decision (And How Not to)," *Communications of the ACM,* **33** (11), November 1990, p. 32.

63. Prepared by Richard Stallman and Simson Garfinkel for the League for Programming Freedom. "Against User Interface Copyright," *Communications of the ACM,* **33** (11), November 1990, pp. 15–18.

64. Neil Boorstyn. "An Analysis of Apple Computer, Inc. v. Microsoft Corp. and Hewlett-Packard Co., 35 F3d 1435 (1994, CA 9)," reprint of article contained in *The Copyright Law Journal*, no date. Accessed from the McCutchen On-Line Web site with URL: <http://www.mc-cutchen.com/IP/IP_2105.HTM> on July 13, 1996.

65. *Ibid.*

66. Jesse M. Feder. "Lotus v. Borlund 3/9/95 1st Cir. Decision," accessed from the Web page with URL: <http://www.panix.com/~jesse/lotus.html> on July 14, 1996.

67. *Ibid.*, Id. at 26–27.

68. Bender. *Computer Law*, p. 4A–78.

69. *Ibid.*, p. 4A–79.

70. *Intellectual Property and the National Information Infrastructure.* The Report of the Working Group on Intellectual Property Rights, Information Infrastructure Task Force. (Washington, DC: US Patent and Trademark Office, September 1995). Available at the Web site with URL: <www.uspto.gov>.

71. Pamela Samuelson. "The Copyright Grab," *Wired*, **4.01**, January 1996, p. 136. Accessed from the Web page with URL: <http://www.hotwired.com/wired/whitepaper.html> on February 26, 1996.

72. "Coalition Supports Digital Update of Copyright Laws," Creative Incentive Coalition, 1996. Accessed from the Web page with URL: <http://www.cic.org/hears.html> on February 7, 1996.

73. Gary H. Anthes. "Cyber Copyright Issue Sparks Fierce Debate," *Computerworld*, May 20, 1996, p. 28.

74. Enunciated in *Miller v. California* (413 U.S. 15 [1973]).

75. "What's the Big Deal over Jake Baker?" The Jake Baker Information Page. Accessed from the Web page with URL: <http://krusty.eecs.umich.edu/people/pjswan/Baker/big.deal.html> on July 17, 1996. Note that the Jake Baker Information Page will be moved to the MIT SAFE Archive with URL: <http://www.MIT.edu:8001/activities/safe/home.html>.

76. "United States v. Jake Baker and Arthur Gonda," United States District Court, Eastern District of Michigan, Southern Division. Accessed from the Web page with URL: <http://ic.net/~sber-aha/baker.html> on July 17, 1996.

77. Philip Elmer-DeWitt. "On a Screen Near You: Cyberporn," *Time*, July 3, 1995, p. 32.

78. *Ibid.*, p. 34.

79. Marty Rimm. "Marketing Pornography on the Information Superhighway: A Survey of 917,410 Images, Descriptions, Short Stories, and Animations Downloaded 8.5 Million Times by Consumers in Over 2000 Cities in Forty Countries, Provinces, and Territories," *Georgetown Law Journal*, 83, June 1995, pp. 1849–1934. Accessed from the Web page with URL: <http://trfn.pgh.pa.us/guest/mrtext.html> on July 11, 1995.

80. Donna L. Hoffman and Thomas P. Novak. "A Detailed Analysis of the Conceptual, Logical, and Methodological Flaws in the Article: 'Marketing Pornography on the Information Super-highway,'" July 2, 1995. Accessed from the Web page with URL: <http://www2000.ogsm.vanderbilt.edu/rimm.cgi> on July 17, 1996.

81. Donna L. Hoffman and Thomas P. Novak. "A Detailed Critique of the TIME Article: 'On a Screen Near You: Cyberporn' (DeWitt, 7/3/95)," July 1, 1995 (version 1.01). Accessed from the Web page with URL: <http://www2000.ogsm.vanderbilt.edu/dewitt.cgi> on July 17, 1996.

82. *Op. cit.*, Elmer-DeWitt.

83. "United States v. Thomas," 1996 FED App. 0032P (6th Cir.). Accessed from the Web page with URL: <http://www.law.emory.edu/6circuit/jan96/96a0032p.06.html> on July 17, 1996.

84. *Ibid.*

85. *Ibid.*

86. "Bodacious Babes in Lingerie." Accessed from the Web page with URL: <http://www.shout.net/~odin/tamali/> on April 28, 1996. Here is the warning:

FIRST AMENDMENT PRIVACY CURTAIN. PLEASE READ THIS!

To protect the world from viewing adult-oriented material without their consent, and to protect the viewing of adult-oriented material by minors, we require all viewers to read and certify to the following:

By entering this site you are certifying that you are of legal adult age and are entering this website with full knowledge that it contains adult oriented material.

Furthermore you are certifying that the viewing, reading, and downloading of the images in this website do not violate the community standards or the laws governing your street, village, city, town, county, state, province or country.

By continuing, you certify that you know your local laws and furthermore know that they do not prohibit the viewing of sexually explicit materials. Ignorance is not a valid defense.

You also certify that you are wholly liable for any false disclosures and responsible for any legal ramifications that may arise from viewing, reading, or downloading of images or material contained within this website and that the web site creator and their affiliates can not be held responsible for any legal ramifications that may arise as a result of fraudulent entry into or use of this website and/or material contain herein.

These pages are provided for adult entertainment and educational purposes, and are not designed to promote prurient interests. The web site creator does not censor, or warrant the information presented here. Furthermore, a listing is not to be construed as any type of implied endorsement for the authors or services of the listed pages or the information contained thereon.

In addition to the above statements, you must also certify the following:

* I am at least 21 years of age;

* The sexually explicit material I'm viewing is for my own personal use and isn't to be viewed by minors or anyone else but myself;

* I am not a US POSTAL OFFICIAL or LAW ENFORCEMENT AGENT or acting as an agent thereof, attempting to obtain any evidence for the prosecution of any individual or CORPORATION or for the purpose of entrapment;

* I desire to receive and haven't notified the POSTAL SERVICE or any OTHER, GOVERNMENTAL AGENCY to intercept sexually explicit material;

* I recognize I can stop receiving such material at any time by logging off and not returning;

* I believe, that as an adult, I have the unalienable right to read and/or view any type of material that I choose;

* The web site creator has no editorial power over the pages contained herein and therefore cannot be held responsible for their contents;

* That at no time, will minors be subjected to said material of any kind;

* By going to our home page and/or by looking at any of the pictures on this site you are agreeing that the pictures contained herein are not obscene or offensive in any way nor could ever be construed to be so, nor could any sexually explicit material of any kind ever be considered obscene or offensive. You also certifying that the material presented here is not illegal or considered obscene in your street, village, community, city, state, province or country. If you are unsure, do not continue.

* All of the above is understood and the following is true.

DISCLAIMER OF LIABILITY: The web site creator, is not liable to the users of this service or to its listed participants for the content, quality, performance or any other aspect of any information provided by the listed participants and transmitted by this service or for any errors in the transmission of said information. Nor is the web site creator, responsible to any person for any damages arising in any manner out of the use of this service.

INDEMNIFICATION: The user and/or the listed participants shall indemnify and hold harmless the web site creator, and their officers and employees, from and against any claims, liabilities, losses, costs, damages or expenses (including attorney's fees) arising from the user's use of or participation in this service or the information contained thereon.

I am at least 21 years of age. I consent to viewing any adult-oriented material that I may be exposed to as a result of following this link, and it is legal to view such material in my jurisdiction.

I certify that all statements on this page are true!

I can not, or do not agree with one or more of the above statements!

All models are at least 18 years old or older, depicting sexually attractive women. If you are not interested in such material please forget this address and remove it from your bookmark file.

87. "ACLU v. Reno," Full Text of Opinion, June 12, 1996. Accessed from the Web site with URL: <http://www.epic.org> on June 13, 1996.

88. "Cubby v. CompuServe." October 31, 1991. Accessed from the Web page with URL: <http://www.eff.org/pub/CAF/law/cubby-v-compuserve.summary> on July 8, 1996.

89. Marc L. Caden and Stephanie E. Lucas, "Accidents on the Information Superhighway: On-Line Liability and Regulation," *University of Richmond Journal of Law & Technology*, 2 (1), 1996. Accessed from the Web page with URL: <http://www.urich.edu/~jolt/v2i1/caden_lucas.html> on June 15, 1996.

90. *Ibid.*

91. "Overview of the Telecommunications Act of 1996," Blumenfeld & Cohen—Technology Law Group, February 1996. Accessed from the Web page with URL: <http://www.technology-law.com/techlaw/act_summary.html> on February 25, 1996.

92. J. J. Bloombecker. "Malpractice in IS?" *Datamation*, October 15, 1989, p. 85.

93. Nancy G. Leveson and Clark S. Turner. "An Investigation of the Therac-25 Accidents," *IEEE Computer*, 26 (7), July 1993, pp. 18–41. Reprinted in Deborah J. Johnson and Helen Nissenbaum (eds.). *Computers, Ethics & Social Values*. (Englewood Cliffs, NJ: Prentice Hall, 1995), pp. 474–514.

94. Richard S. Rosenberg. "Free Speech, Pornography, Sexual Harassment, and Electronic Networks," *The Information Society*, 9 (4), October–December 1993, pp. 285–331.

95. *Ibid.*, p. 287.

96. *Ibid.*

97. "Silencing the Net: The Threat to Freedom of Expression On-line," Human Rights Watch, 8 (2), May 1966. Accessed from the Web page with URL: <gopher://gopher.igc.apc.org:5000/00/int/hrw/general/27> on May 11, 1996. Human Rights Watch is a nongovernmental organization established in 1978 to monitor and promote the observance of internationally recognized human rights in Africa, the Americas, Asia, the Middle East, and among the signatories of the Helsinki accords.

98. *Ibid.*

99. "Sex Offenses Against Children: Findings and Recommendations Regarding Federal Penalties,"
     United States Sentencing Commission, June 1996, p. 29. Accessed from the Web page with
     URL: <http://www.ussc.gov/main/scac.pdf> on June 24, 1996.
100. *Ibid.,* p. 27.
101. Theresa Riordan, "Patents: A Recent Patent on a Papua New Guinea Tribe's Cell Line Prompts
     Outrage and Charges of 'Biopiracy'," *The New York Times,* November 27, 1995, p. C 2.

ADDITIONAL READINGS

Introduction

Himelstein, Linda. "The Snitch in the System," *Business Week,* April 17, 1995, pp. 104–105.
Maher, Stephen T. "Lawfutures, or, Will You Still Need Me, Will You Still Feed Me, When I'm Sixty
     Four?" *Richmond Journal of Law & Technology,* VI (April 10, 1995). [http://www.urich.edu/~
     jolt/v1i1/maher.html].

Computer Crime

Alexander, Steve. "The Long Arm of the Law, *Computerworld,* May 6, 1996, pp. 99–100.
Cavazos, Edward A. and Morin, Gavino. *Cyberspace and the Law: Your Rights and Duties in the
     On-Line World.* (Cambridge, MA: The MIT Press, 1994).
Denning, Peter J. *Computers Under Attack: Intruders, Worms, and Viruses.* (Reading, MA: Addi-
     son-Wesley, ACM Press, 1991).
"Information Security: Computer Hacker Information Available on the Internet." US General Ac-
     counting Office, GAO/T-AIMD-96-108. (Gaithersburg, MD: US General Accounting Office, June
     5, 1996). Available from the Web page with URL: <http://www.access.gpo.gov/cgi-bin/useftp.cgi?
     IPaddress=wais.access.gpo.gov&filename=ai96108t.pdf&directory=/diskb/wais/data/gao> on July
     20, 1996.
International Review of Criminal Policy. United Nations Manual on the Prevention and Control of
     Computer-Related Crime, no date. Accessed from the Web page with URL: <http://www.ifs.uni-
     vie.ac.at/~pr2gq1/rev4344.html> on July 10, 1996.
Littman, Jonathan. *The Fugitive Game: Online with Kevin Mitnick.* (Boston: Little, Brown and Com-
     pany, 1996).
Lohr, Steve. "A Virus Got You Down? Who You Gonna Call?" *The New York Times,* August 12,
     1996, pp. C 1, C 4.
Quittner, Joshua. "Cracks in the Net." *Time,* February 27, 1995, pp. 32–33.

The Legal Protection of Software

Brandel, William. " 'Look and Feel' Reversal Reignites Copyright Fight," *Computerworld,* March
     13, 1995, pp. 1, 15.
Cole, Rodger R. "Substantial Similarity in the Ninth Circuit: A 'Virtually Identical' Look and
     Feel'?", Apple Computer, Inc. v. Microsoft Corp., 35 F.3d 1435 (9th Cir. 1994)." *Santa Clara
     Computer and High Technology Law Journal,* 11 (2), July 1995, pp. 417–428.
Ferranti, Marc. "Vhat a Deal!" First in a Two-Part Series on Software Piracy Overseas. *Computer-
     world,* July 24, 1995, pp. 1, 77–79.

Guth, Rob and Uimonen, Terho. "S.O.S. (Save Our Software)." Last in a Two-Part Series on Software Piracy Overseas. *Computerworld,* July 31, 1995, pp. 87–89.

"Lotus Development Corporation v. Borland Int'l, Inc." *Berkeley Technology Law Journal,* February 9, 1996. Accessed from the Web page with URL: <http://server.Berkeley.EDU/lvb/lvbindex.html> on May 15, 1996.

Myers, Joseph. "Apple v. Microsoft: Virtual Identity in the GUI Wars. *University of Richmond Journal of Law & Technology,* V, April 10, 1995. Available at the Web page with URL: <http://www.urich.edu/~jolt/vlil/myers.html>.

Legal Issues on the Internet

Baker, Jonathan D. and Oblon, Michael A. "Intellectual Property and the National Information Infrastructure (The White Paper)." 1996. Accessed from the Web page with URL: <http://roscoe.law.harvard.edu/courses/techseminar96/course/sessions/whitepaper/whitepaper.html> on July 15, 1996.

de Grazia, Edward. *Girls Lean Back Everywhere: The Law of Obscenity and the Assault on Genius.* (New York: Vintage Books, A Division of Random House, 1993).

"Eight Myths About the NII Copyright Protection Act." Creative Incentive Coalition, 1996. Accessed from the Web page with URL: <http://www.cic.org/myths.html> on February 26, 1996.

Festinger, Jonathan B. "Mapping the Electronic Highway: A Survey of Domestic and International Law Issues," *University of British Columbia Law Review,* 29 (2), 1995, pp. 199–250.

Godwin, Mike. "LaMacchia Case Reveals a Federal Attitude Problem," *Internet World,* March 1995. Accessed from the Web page with URL: <http://www-swiss.ai.mit.edu/6805/articles/dml/godwin-internet-world-march95.html> on July 8, 1996.

Gordon, Mark L. and McKenzie, Diana J. P. "A Lawyer's Roadmap of the Information Superhighway," *John Marshall Journal of Computer & Information Law,* XII (2), Winter 1995, pp. 177–230.

Hawkins, Gordon and Zimring, Franklin E. *Pornography in a Free Society.* (New York: Cambridge University Press, 1988).

Lewis, Peter. "Company Says Electronic Mail Was Opened to Find Pornography," *The New York Times,* September 15, 1995, p. A 16. Accessed from the Web page with URL: <http://www-swiss.ai.mit.edu/6805/articles/computer-crime/FBI-AOL-NYT-9-15-95.txt> on July 8, 1996.

Lewis, Peter. "Judges Turn Back Law to Regulate Internet Decency," *The New York Times,* June 13, 1996, pp. A 1–A 16.

Litman, Jessica. "Revising Copyright Law for the Information Age." *Twenty-Third Annual Telecommunications Policy Research Conference,* October 2, 1995. Accessed from the Web page with URL: <http://swissnet.ai.mit.edu/6805/articles/int-prop/litman-revising/revising.html> on July 15, 1996.

Loundy, David J. "Revising the Copyright Law for Electronic Publishing," *Journal of Computers & Information Law,* XIV (1), Fall 1995, pp. 1–46.

Okerson, Ann. "Who Owns Digital Works? Computer Networks Challenge Copyright Law, But Some Proposed Cures May Be as Bad as the Disease," *Scientific American,* July 1996. Accessed from the Web page with URL: <http://www.sciam.com/0796issue/0796okerson.html> on July 26, 1996.

"The Property of the Mind," *The Economist,* July 27, 1996. Accessed from the Web page with URL: <http://www.economist.com/issue/27-07-96/wbsf1.html> on July 30, 1996.

Quittner, Joshua. "Free Speech for the Net," *Time,* June 24, 1996, pp. 46–47.

Samuelson, Pamela. "The NII Intellectual Property Report." *Communications of the ACM,* 37 (12), December 1994, pp. 21–27. Accessed from the Web page with URL: <http://alberti.mit.edu/arch/4.207/texts/samuelson.html> on July 15, 1996.

Samuelson, Pamela. "Regulation of Technologies to Protect Copyrighted Works," *Communications of the ACM,* **39** (7), July 1996, pp. 17–22.

Sansom, Gareth. "Illegal and Offensive Content on the Information Highway, A Background Paper, Industry Canada, June 19, 1995. Accessed from the Web site with URL: <http://info.ic.gc.ca/info-highway/ih.html> on July 11, 1995.

"The Wired Trilogy: The White Paper Ain't Perfect, But It's Not the Disaster Naysayers Make it Out to BE. *Information Law Alert: A Vorhees Report,* **3** (20), December 20, 1995. Accessed from the Web page with URL: <http://roscoe.law.harvard.edu/courses/techseminar96/course/sessions/whitepaper/voorhees.html> on July 15, 1996.

Yang, Catherine. "How Do You Police Cyberspace?" *Business Week,* February 5, 1996, pp. 97, 99.

Other Developments

Arnold-Moore, Timothy. "Legal Pitfalls in Cyberspace: Defamation on Computer Networks." *Journal of Law and Information Science,* 5 (2), 1994, pp. 165–209.

McGraw, David K. "Sexual Harassment in Cyberspace: The Problem of Unwelcome E-mail," *Rutgers Computer & Technology Law Journal,* **21** (2), 1995, pp. 491–518.

"Patent Blather." *The Economist,* November 25, 1995, p. 87.

─── 9 ───

PRIVACY AND FREEDOM
OF INFORMATION

The makers of our Constitution undertook to secure conditions favorable to the pursuit of happiness. . . . They sought to protect Americans in their beliefs, their thoughts, their emotions and their sensations. They conferred, as against the Government the right to be let alone—the most comprehensive of rights and the right most valued by civilized men. To protect that right every unjustifiable intrusion by the Government upon the privacy of the individual, whatever the means employed, must be deemed a violation of the Fourth Amendment.

Justice Louis D. Brandeis, Dissenting, Olmstead v. United States, 277 U.S. 438, 1928

INTRODUCTION

The following are excerpts from newspaper and magazine articles in the United States and Canada and from Web pages:

- Workplace privacy has always been a sensitive issue that weighs a boss's right to know what's going on in the office against an employee's right to be left alone. But in Illinois that delicate balance has been upset by a new state law that permits bosses to eavesdrop on employees' work phones. As originally conceived by telemarketers and retailers, the law was intended solely to enable supervisors to monitor service calls for courtesy and efficiency. But on its way to Republican Governor Jim Edgar for a Dec. 13 signing, the measure was reworked to embrace any listening in that serves "educational, training or research purposes" without defining inappropriate monitoring. [1]
- DocuSearch. "We find people and information about them." Now any Internet-savvy individual can locate lost friends, track down debtors and deadbeats, or discover the secrets of the people with whom you associate. It's all totally professional, completely legal, and entirely confidential. For the information-impaired the world can be a dangerous place. . . . [2]
- Privacy on data networks is a complex issue. It includes thorny questions about anonymity—who should be allowed to be anonymous in network interactions, under what circumstances. . . . It also includes consumer privacy where people who go online

are targets for a new breed of direct marketers eager to use technology to collect and sell every scrap of personal information they can.[3]

- Delta police launched an internal investigation Wednesday into allegations that someone on the force used the RCMP [Royal Canadian Mounted Police] computer system to obtain information about pro-choice activists. . . . The investigations were prompted by fears that the computer was being used to run checks on the ownership of cars parked regularly outside Vancouver abortion clinics.[4]

- Metromail Corporation is a large database marketing company with over $200 million in annual sales. It gathers and sells information about your family to marketers, the government, and individuals. It is a subsidiary of the printing giant, R. R. Donnelley and Sons Company, a $6.4 billion corporation. . . . Now Metromail is in trouble again. It has been exposed for selling information about children over a "900" number and online. The company has been providing access to the names, home addresses, and ages of millions of children to any stranger for $3 a minute. It also sells the information on children through mailing lists and its advertising boasts of "3,200 innovative sources" for information on babies.[5]

- Lexis-Nexis, one of the nation's leading private information brokers, has discontinued a new on-line offering that provided access to millions of individuals' Social Security numbers, after an onslaught of complaints from customers and the credit information bureau that originally supplied the data. . . . "We have very few legal rights regarding the collection and use of personal data when it's done by a private enterprise," Joel R. Reidenberg, [associate professor at Fordham University Law School and a specialist in information privacy] said.[6]

Probably the single most frequent charge leveled against computers is that they rob us of our privacy. Banks of computer disk drives and tapes are envisioned in some back room, on which the intimate details of the lives of many people are stored. Government agencies, law enforcement officials, insurance companies, banks, schools, credit agencies, and many others have access to private information about most people in society. This situation was true before the arrival of computers, but somehow the computer has added a significant new element—whether it is due to the computer's ability to store and search rapidly through vast amounts of data, the image of the computer as a malevolent force, the economic benefits available to companies that are able to target precisely large segments of the population, or the general trend in society towards the accumulation of information that computers make possible.

Privacy Surveys

The national research firm, Louis Harris & Associates, has been conducting surveys on American attitudes toward privacy since 1970, with assistance by Dr. Alan Westin of Columbia University. These surveys represent the most comprehensive attempt to gauge US public opinion on the issue of personal privacy and technological impact, over an extended period of time.[7] Figure 9.1 shows a rising concern by the public about threats to their personal privacy over the period 1977 to 1995. The rise between 1970 and 1978 probably reflects the post-Watergate and post-Vietnam disillusion with government. The rise to near 80% during the conservative Republican administrations of Presidents Reagan and Bush is somewhat more difficult to explain. The surveys from 1990 on suggest a continuing dis-

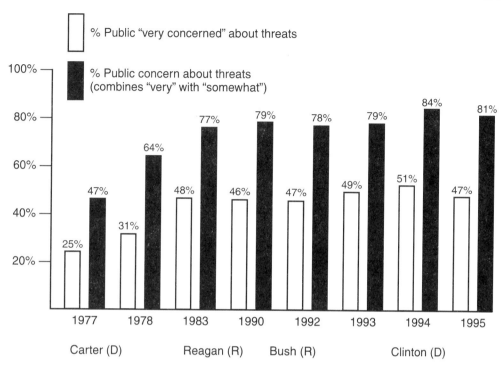

FIGURE 9.1 Concern by the US Public about Threats to Their Personal Privacy.

1. For 1977, the Harris question asked: "Now some people tell us they are concerned about what's happening to their personal privacy—the right to live their own life without others knowing more about it, or intruding into it, more than is absolutely necessary. I'd like to know if you've ever thought about that. Would you say you are very concerned about the loss of personal privacy, somewhat concerned, only a little concerned, or not concerned at all?"

2. For 1978, 1983, 1990, 1992, 1993, 1994, and 1995, the Harris question asked: "How concerned are you about threats to your personal privacy in America today?" (very concerned, somewhat concerned, not very concerned, not concerned at all).

Sources: A national opinion survey conducted for Equifax Inc. by Louis Harris & Associates and Dr. Alan F. Westin, Columbia University. Equifax Inc., 1600 Peachtree Street, Atlanta, Georgia 30302.

trust of institutions and a concern that control over personal information has been lost to credit bureaus, Web servers, and government. The distrust of large institutions of all kinds may be rooted in a realization that very little personal information remains private, that government seems to have an insatiable need to collect more and more information, that in the private sector, banks, credit bureaus, and direct marketing companies also seem driven to reap economic benefits from large, detailed databases on consumers, and that the technology permits, and indeed encourages the collection and rapid processing of vast amounts of data.

To explore some of these issues more carefully, it is helpful to look at a few of the results of five surveys, to monitor the changes in opinion between 1978 and 1995. One prob-

TABLE 9.1

RESPONSES FROM QUESTIONS ON COMPUTERS AND PRIVACY FROM THE YEARS
1978, 1983, 1990, 1993, 1995.

Questions	Responses	1978[a]	1983[b]	1990[c]	1992[d]	1995[e]
1. Do you feel that the present uses of computers are an actual threat to personal privacy in this country or not?	Yes No Not sure	54% 33% 12%	51% 42% 6%	—	68% 28% 3%	—
2. Consumers have lost all control over how personal information about them is circulated.	Agree Disagree Not Sure			71% 27% 3%	76% 20% 3%	80% 19% 2%
3. My rights to privacy are adequately protected today by law or business practice.	Agree Disagree Not Sure			46% 51% 3%		45% 54% 2%
4. In the year 2000— consumer privacy protection . . .	Will get better Will get worse Will remain same				12% 55% 32%	16% 41% 42%
5. Technology has almost gotten out of control	Agree Disagree Not sure	43% 41% 15%		45% 53% 2%		63% 36% 1%

Sources:
(a) Louis Harris and Associates and Dr. Alan F. Westin, *The Dimensions of Privacy: A National Opinion Research Survey of Attitudes Toward Privacy* (for Sentry Insurance, New York: Garland Publishing, 1981).
(b) Louis Harris and Associates, *The Road after 1984: The Impact of Technology on Society* (for Southern New England Telephone, December 1983).
(c) A national opinion survey conducted for Equifax Inc. by Louis Harris & Associates and Dr. Alan F. Westin, Columbia University. Equifax Inc., 1600 Peachtree Street, Atlanta, Georgia, 1990.
(d) Louis Harris & Associates and Dr. Alan F. Westin, *Harris-Equifax Consumer Privacy Survey 1992* (for Equifax Inc., 1992, 1991).
(e) Louis Harris & Associates and Dr. Alan F. Westin, *Equifax-Harris Mid-Decade Consumer Privacy Survey 1995* (for Equifax Inc., 1995).

lem is that the targeted groups varied somewhat over the years so that strict comparisons are not possible. Also as the general public has become more aware of computers, primarily through direct exposure to personal computers, the level of sophistication has increased, especially among professionals. With these caveats consider Table 9.1, which reveals some of the fears and concerns of the general public.

This table represents only a very small and carefully selected part of several quite extensive surveys. A few points are clear, however, as follows:

- The general public is clearly concerned about computers and their effect on privacy (see questions 1, 2, 3, and 4).
- It is surprising how many people accept the idea that technology has almost gotten out of control (see question 5).
- Note that in 1995, most people did not feel that their privacy rights were adequately protected (see question 3). Combined with the response to question 4, there is a clear perception that personal privacy is seriously threatened and no relief is in sight. One possibility is that government play a stronger role but in the atmosphere of general distrust of government, this direction taken by many European countries is unlikely. (Much more on this topic will be provided later in the chapter.)

In the 1993 Equifax survey, concerned with "Health Information Privacy," the following question was asked: "If national health care reform is enacted, which of these two approaches do you favor to safeguard the confidentiality of individual medical records? Some responses are shown in Table 9.2.

Thus, with respect to the privacy of medical information records, which arrived on the political agenda in 1996, there was public sentiment in 1993 for government intervention.

Earlier in the 1990 Equifax survey, when asked whether they believe that lists of consumer information should be sold, 69% of the public (out of a base of 2254) say that it is a bad thing and only 28% are favorable. More specifically, when asked if direct marketing companies should be permitted "to ask credit reporting bureaus to screen their computerized files for those who meet the requirements and then supply just the customer's name and address . . . [without obtaining] the customer's advance permission," 76% of

TABLE 9.2

RESPONSES TO A QUESTION ON THE ROLE OF GOVERNMENT IN PRIVACY PROTECTION.

	Total Public	Total Leaders	Hospital CEOs	Health Insurer CEOs	Congressional Aides
Base:	1000	651	101	45	70
	%	%	%	%	%
Enact comprehensive federal legislation that spells out rules for confidentiality of individual medical records in such a system or	56	58	65	45	66
Continue with existing state and federal laws and professional standards on confidentiality, disclosure and security	39	41	35	55	33

Source: A national opinion survey conducted for Equifax Inc. by Louis Harris and Dr. Alan F. Westin, Columbia University. Equifax, Inc., 1600 Peachtree Street, Atlanta Georgia.

the public find this an unacceptable practice, while 23% find it acceptable. Not surprisingly, among the direct marketing people sampled the reverse is found—it is acceptable to 75% and unacceptable to only 21%.[8]

Clearly, there is a deep concern among most segments of society about the growing number of records being held in both private and government databases. The US government maintains databases containing many billions of individual records, probably over 20 for each American. Credit bureaus, including TRW and Equifax, hold records on most Americans, and Canadians as well; they are used mainly to verify applications for credit, such as for life insurance, mortgages, and consumer loans. These records are now being used, as mentioned previously, for other purposes by direct marketing companies, whose very existence depends on treating information as a commodity, to be bought and sold, independent of the wishes of the people themselves. The government records are needed for the various agencies to carry out their responsibilities. In the not too distant past, however, various departments did establish databases to collect information on individuals who were perceived as a possible threat to the stability of government. Such activities could inhibit the free exercise of constitutional rights.

Privacy is a cultural, philosophical, and political concept. The formulation of legislation in this area clearly depends on how privacy is viewed and valued. Concern with privacy did not begin with computers. As Edward Coke (1552–1634), an English writer on the law, put it, "A man's house is his castle." The common person and the king should be equal with respect to the security of their home. The computer seems to have added several important new wrinkles to this principle. The collection, storage, and retrieval of large amounts of private information, by credit bureaus, for example, has become a major industry.

In response to a variety of problems associated with violations of privacy, legislation has been enacted in the United States to guarantee certain rights. Such piecemeal legislation addresses some issues, but leaves others open. Given that there is a deep cultural component to the question of privacy, it is not surprising that different types of legislation exist in other countries. There also seems to be less distrust of government in western Europe, Australia, New Zealand, and elsewhere which helps explain why countries have enacted comprehensive data protection laws administered by commissioners. As the Internet grows in importance and perhaps evolves into the Information Highway, enormous amounts of personal information will be gathered in commercial and other transactions. How will governments respond? This question has been extensively studied in North America and Europe and a variety of proposals and recommendations will be explored.

The term *freedom of information* is generally applied to the concept that governments must make the information they collect accessible to the public at large unless they can demonstrate a pressing need for secrecy. The explication of this idea requires a distinction between privacy and secrecy. In general, governments are reluctant to reveal their operations. Eventually legislation was passed in the United States to provide public access to government under a set of regulations, the Freedom of Information Act.

Finally, future privacy issues will arise in connection with new technological developments. Given varying national privacy laws, international agreements will have to be developed to deal with the flow of data across borders. It seems that everywhere we turn, someone or some group is asking questions and gathering information. How was it used, who has access and for what purposes, and what rights do the people, about whom the information was gathered, have?

THE NATURE OF PRIVACY

> A man has a right to pass through this world, if he wills, without having his picture published, his business enterprises discussed, his successful experiments written up for the benefit of others, or his eccentricities commented upon, whether in handbills, circulars, catalogues, newspapers or periodicals. (Jurist Alton B. Parker, Decision, Robertson v. Rochester Folding Box Company, 1901)

Privacy as a social issue has long been a concern of social scientists, philosophers, and lawyers. The arrival of the computer has sharpened this concern and made concrete a number of threats to personal privacy. But what does the word privacy mean? Is privacy a right?

> Privacy is the claim of individuals, groups or institutions to determine for themselves when, how, and to what extent information about them is communicated to others.[9]

Alan Westin, the author of this statement, has probably made the most important recent contributions to both the definition and scope of the meaning of privacy in the age of computers. In fact, this definition is arguably the most common one in current use. Westin's definition has been criticized because it formulates the definition in terms of a claim. The counter-argument is that privacy "is a situation or freedom about which claims may be made."[10] This dissension may appear to be the usual legal hairsplitting, but it seems to suggest that the Westin definition represents an activist view that privacy should be a right. Two other criticisms of the Westin definition are that it limits the concept of privacy to information control, and only information about the individual who makes the claim, at that.

It is not surprising that information and its control feature so prominently. After all, the forthcoming information age will certainly catapult individual privacy to the forefront of civil liberty issues (if it has not done so already). Information is not the only thing that comes to mind when we think of privacy, however. Also important are being alone or alone with our families, not being exposed to displays we consider offensive, and the right not to have our behavior regulated (for example, the right to use contraceptives, or to have an abortion). These issues arise in connection with such privacy problems as surveillance by the use of wiretapping, electronic bugs, long-range microphones, and television cameras; possible censorship of the public media; and the tension between individual behavior and the demands of society.

The concept of privacy can be given three aspects: territorial privacy, privacy of the person, and privacy in the information context.[11] Territorial privacy refers to the very basic notion that a physical area surrounds a person that may not be violated without the acquiescence of the person. Laws referring to Peeping Toms, trespassers, and search warrants have been enacted to safeguard territorial privacy. The second category, in some sense, is concerned with protecting a person against undue interferences such as physical searches and information that violates his or her moral sense. The third category is the one most relevant here, as it deals with the gathering, compilation, and selective dissemination of information.

Privacy and Information

To live in contemporary society is to leave, stored in records held by institutions, a trail of the following kinds of information:

- Vital statistics (birth, marriage, death)
- Educational (school records)
- Financial (bank records, stock portfolio, mortgages, loans, insurance)
- Medical (health records, AIDS status, psychiatric reports)
- Credit (credit cards, credit record, purchases)
- City government (house taxes, improvements)
- Employment (earnings, deductions, work record)
- Internal revenue (taxation, deductions, earnings)
- Customs and immigration (passports, visas, customs payments)
- Police (arrests, convictions, warrants, bail, paroles, sentences)
- Welfare (payments, history, dependents)
- Stores (credit record, purchases)
- Organizations (membership, activities)
- Military (service record, discharge status)
- Motor vehicles (ownership, registration, accident record)

This list represents only a sample of the kinds and sources of information being held about the average citizen. The computer has made it possible to store an enormous amount of information and to retrieve it in an efficient manner. Most of these listed records are held by government institutions at all levels. This fact is seen by some critics as evidence of the insatiable appetite of government to know more and more about its citizens. In the private domain there has been a corresponding increase in the amounts and uses of information, as anyone who has received unsolicited mail, samples, and charitable requests knows.

In recognition of this explosion in information, the concept of privacy has undergone some changes. Inevitably there will be disclosures of information—if not, why has it all been collected? How can the rights of the affected person be protected? Perhaps the prior question is what should these rights be? A basic statement appeared in 1973, in an important US government report, as follows:[12]

> An individual's personal privacy is directly affected by the kind of disclosure and use made of identifiable information about him in a record. A record containing information about an individual in identifiable form must, therefore, be governed by procedures that afford the individual a right to participate in deciding what the content of the record will be, and what disclosure and use will be made of the identifiable information in it. Any recording, disclosure, and use of identifiable personal information not governed by such procedures must be proscribed as an unfair information practice unless such recording, disclosure or use is specifically authorized by law.

This statement does not describe what information should be stored, or what the controls for its use should be, but it does argue for the legal establishment of privacy rights for the individual. Subsequent legislation did delineate and incorporate some of these rights by regulating the behavior of record-keepers.

The general public in the United States is concerned about threats to personal privacy, and this worry is growing, as Figure 9.1 illustrates. Many people would claim that there is a basic human need for privacy. Not all basic human needs are defended in law, however. It has been recognized that individual privacy, in its many manifestations, is a basic prerequisite for the functioning of a democratic society. In this light, the recommendations made in the 1973 government report have served as a basis for subsequent legislation. In fact, they have almost assumed the status of a "Bill of Rights" for privacy and are known as the "fundamental principles of fair information practice:"[13]

- There must be no personal-data record-keeping systems whose very existence is secret.
- There must be a way for an individual to find out what information about him is in a record and how it is used.
- There must be a way for an individual to prevent information about him that was obtained for one purpose from being used or made available for other purposes without his consent.
- There must be a way for an individual to correct or amend a record of identifiable information about him.
- Any organization creating, maintaining, using or disseminating records or identifiable personal data must assure the reliability of data for their intended use and must take precautions to prevent misuse of the data.

Records have been kept on individuals from time immemorial, but the use of computers has introduced a change in kind as well as in degree. Records can now be transmitted easily over long distances, searched efficiently, and merged if desired. Since the cost of storage is cheap, more data can be stored and so more is collected. As more information is collected, more uses are made of it, as if the availability drives the need. There seems to be an insatiable appetite for information in both the private and public domains. Since these trends are likely to accelerate in the future, we can gain much by trying to understand the various implications of contemporary threats to privacy.

Government Threats and Constitutional Protection

Individual privacy is threatened by the possible use of government databases for surveillance. Such use may inhibit the free exercise of constitutionally guaranteed rights, such as freedom of speech and petitioning the government for the redress of grievances. With private databases, such as those maintained by the large credit bureaus, the impact could also be quite serious. Without credit, a car, house and life insurance, and a mortgage are not available. A suspect credit rating may limit your type of employment, housing, and children's educational possibilities. Quite clearly, the misuse of information by others could have a devastating effect on your life. With the increasing use of information systems to store personal records, the imbalance between the individual and the "system" has grown. It is therefore incumbent upon the record-keeper to establish guidelines to insure the protection of individual privacy.

The Privacy Commission, set up after the passage of the Privacy Act of 1974, enunciated the three necessary objectives of a privacy protection policy as follows.[14]

Minimize Intrusiveness. This involves creating a balance between what is demanded of an individual and what is provided in return.

Maximize Fairness. This will make sure that information stored about an individual is not used unfairly.

Create Legitimate, Enforceable Expectations of Confidentiality. It is most important to guarantee that recorded information is subject to the most stringent security procedures.

Constitutional Guarantees

Some very complex privacy issues are highlighted by the First, Fourth, and Fifth Amendments to the Constitution. These amendments are concerned with the following rights and guarantees:

First Amendment. Freedom of religion, speech, the press, peaceable assembly, and the right to petition for redress of grievances.

Fourth Amendment. No unreasonable search and seizure by the federal government.

Fifth Amendment. A person may not be compelled to testify against himself or be deprived of life, liberty, or property without due process.

By the collection of large amounts of data and surveillance of individuals and groups (as discussed earlier), the government could inhibit the freedoms of speech and assembly guaranteed in the First Amendment. Threats to these rights have occurred in the past, against both active and passive participants in political meetings and demonstrations. A basic challenge arises whenever threats to First Amendment rights surface: "What have you got to worry about if you haven't done anything wrong?" Unfortunately, the collection of data by the government, as well as surveillance, can be repressive in itself, in that it creates the impression that an activity is not proper and that participants ought to reconsider their actions. In some cases, information has been used directly to affect the employment of individuals. First Amendment rights are crucial to maintaining a democratic society, and any attempts to limit them must be forestalled.

The interrelation between information systems and the Fourth Amendment turns on such issues as the use of personal or statistical data as a reason for search and seizure, the information itself as the object of the search, and the use of the system to facilitate the search and seizure. With the use of criminal record information systems, police may carry out searches on the basis of instantaneous access to the database. Courts may be concerned about whether such information provides reasonable cause. Computer systems could be employed to monitor the shopping activity of individuals by accessing appropriate financial transactions systems. This activity would be much more intrusive than personal observation could be.

Possible Fifth Amendment violations may arise when data collected for one purpose is used by the government as evidence in an unrelated case. Another problem may arise in the use of criminal records in computer models to predict criminal behavior. Individuals' rights could be denied on the basis of predictions, not actual unlawful actions. Since these records may include statements by the persons being modeled, self-incrimination is a definite possibility. More constitutional issues associated with databases and privacy will surface in the future.

Computer Matching

A final example of the possible misuse of the data that is collected and stored in government databases is particularly worrisome. It points out that the arrival of the computer literally has created new avenues for the exercise of bureaucratic power. The term *computer matching* probably reached public consciousness in late 1977, when Joseph A. Califano, Jr., the Secretary of Health, Education, and Welfare, announced a new program, "Project Match," to reduce welfare violations. The idea was to match computerized lists of federal employees against computerized lists of state welfare rolls. Any person whose name appeared on both lists, a so-called hit, would be a likely candidate for welfare fraud investigation.

The Privacy Act of 1974 (discussed later in this chapter) embodied the principle that information collected about individuals for certain purposes cannot be used without their consent for unrelated purposes. An individual's consent is not required if the information is to be used either in a manner consistent with the original purpose—the "routine use" provision—or for a criminal investigation. Computer matching has been justified by appeal to the routine use exception. In response to criticisms about the extensive use of computer matching, the Office of Management and Budget (OMB) drew up a set of guidelines in 1979. These have not satisfactorily addressed the critical issues, in the opinion of many critics.

In 1984, Richard P. Kusserow, Inspector General of the Department of Health and Human Services, argued that computer matching is just another necessary weapon in the government's arsenal against waste and fraud. Because the cost of such fraud is so enormous, the government is entitled to take whatever measures it deems necessary to protect the rights of innocent taxpayers. The Reagan Administration revised the OMB guidelines in 1982, they claimed, to "streamline paper-work requirements and reiterate requirements for privacy and security of records."[15] The government maintains that privacy safeguards are in place and that computer matching is not a threat to civil liberties. The critics argue that the safeguards are inadequate and that computer matching represents one more serious step in the erosion of personal privacy.

In 1986, the United States General Accounting Office (GAO) issued a report reviewing the activities of federal agencies in implementing the provisions of the Privacy Act of 1974. Although computer matching is not explicitly mentioned in the Act, the OMB revised guidelines were an attempt to address some of the concerns raised by increasing government use of this technique. In the conclusions to the report, GAO notes that[16]

> Although computer matching is one of the most controversial activities generating privacy concerns, agencies (1) did not have current, complete data on the extent of matching programs, (2) did not always follow OMB's matching guidelines, and (3) differed in interpretation of the matching guidelines as to whether programs needed to be reported to OMB.

In addition, two component agencies exempted their matching programs from OMB's guidelines. We found no evidence that OMB was previously aware of these discrepancies.

Without addressing the privacy concerns associated with computer matching, GAO makes the following bureaucratic recommendations to ensure that the OMB guidelines are effectively enforced:[17]

- Computer matching guidelines should specifically state that agencies are to annually report to OMB all participation in matching programs initiated in prior years but conducted on a recurring basis. This would contribute to more complete data in OMB's Annual Report to the Congress.
- Computer matching guidelines should provide for public notice of computer matching programs conducted by organizations not covered by the act when Privacy Act systems of records are disclosed by federal agencies.
- Computer matching guidelines should instruct agencies to notify OMB when like IRS [Internal Revenue Service] and OCSE [Office of Child Support Enforcement], they believe they are exempt from OMB guidelines. This would provide OMB with the opportunity to review and concur. [What about the possibility of refusal on occasion?]

Hearings were held on computer matching in the Senate in 1986 and in the House the following year. On October 18,1986 the Computer Matching and Privacy Protection Act was enacted (and took effect in 1988). It is discussed later in this chapter, in the section on Privacy Legislation.

OMB most recently revised its guidelines, OMB Circular No. A-130, in February 1996 in response to the passage of the Paper Reduction Act of 1995. The guidelines are quite detailed with respect to the requirements for computer matching activities. For example, two of the many requirements are:[18]

(3) For each matching program, an indication of whether the cost/benefit analysis performed resulted in a favorable ratio. The Data Integrity Board should explain why the agency proceeded with any matching program for which an unfavorable ratio was reached.

(4) For each program for which the Board waived a cost/benefit analysis, the reasons for the waiver and the results of the match, if tabulated.

One example of the kind of information that must be provided in advance of proceeding with a matching exercise is taken from a Department of Education proposal to "compare USPO (United States Postal Office) payroll and ED delinquent debtor files for the purposes of identifying postal employees who may owe delinquent debts to the federal government under programs administered by the Department of Education. The pay of an employee identified and verified as a delinquent debtor may be offset under the provisions of the Debt Collection Act of 1982 when voluntary payment is not made.[19] It is also noted that the matching program will last at most for 18 months and will not start until May 1996.

Private Databases

Let us not overlook a significant fact . . . people tend to state their case most favorably when they know that the information they supply will be the basis of their having their application granted. . . . It is essential that we be permitted to verify the information presented to us by the applicant through the credit bureaus and others. . . .[20]

A great deal of information is gathered by the private sector. Educational, employment, medical, financial, and insurance records all require protection to ensure privacy. Probably of greatest importance in the average citizen's life is the use of credit information. When an individual opens a charge account, applies for a credit card or life insurance, or takes out a loan, personal and financial records are created. Apparently, credit bureaus first opened their doors in the early 1890s to provide services for specific businesses. They produced reports in various forms on individuals applying for credit. As of the end of 1989, credit bureaus contained some 500 million consumer credit files, more than one, on the average, per adult, and in 1988, they issued about 450 million credit reports.[21] To appreciate the increase in information gathering and storing, consider that, "The typical consumer is on at least 25 marketing data bases. Some land on upwards of 100. There are more than 15,000 specialized lists containing 2 billion consumer names—each representing a potential sale."[22]

PRIVACY LEGISLATION

Section 602.
(b) It is the purpose of this title to require that consumer reporting agencies adopt reasonable procedures for meeting the needs of commerce for consumer credit, personnel, insurance and other information in a manner which is fair and equitable to the consumer, with regard to the confidentiality, accuracy, relevancy, and proper utilization of such information in accordance with the requirements of this title.[23]

Transactional Data Protection

Lawmakers frequently respond to public pressure by formulating legislation to deal with agreed-upon abuses. Since 1968, a series of laws have been passed that deal in the broad sense with credit protection where this includes a variety of financial matters. Coupled to these financial activities is a concern with the privacy of the associated information, or the transactional data, and laws have been passed to protect this data from improper use. Among these laws are the ones shown in Table 9.3.

Space precludes the discussion of all these laws, so we will focus on one of the earliest, the Fair Credit Reporting Act of 1970, and briefly describe the most recent ones, the Cable Communications Policy Act and the Video Protection Act.

Fair Credit Reporting Act

. . . to insure that consumer reporting agencies exercise their grave responsibilities with fairness, impartiality, and a respect for the consumer's right to privacy. (Fair Credit Reporting Act, 1970)

In 1967, the first Congressional hearings were held to address threats to personal privacy by some credit bureaus: false records, biased records, outdated material, and errors in data

TABLE 9.3

A SELECTION OF TRANSACTIONAL DATA PROTECTION LAWS.

Law (date enacted)	Purpose
1. *Consumer Credit Protection Act* (1968)	To state clearly the cost of borrowing.
2. *Fair Credit Reporting Act* (1970)	To permit the correction of mistakes on credit records.
3. *Currency and Foreign Transactions Reporting Act (Bank Secrecy Act)* (1970)	To keep certain records on individuals and to report certain types of financial transactions to the government.
4. *The Right to Financial Privacy Act* (1978)	To limit some of the broad interpretations of the Bank Secrecy Act.
5. *Tax Reform Act* (1976)	To restrict governmental use of tax information for other purposes.
6. *Debt Collection Act* (1982)	To regulate the federal government's release of personal information on bad debts to credit companies.
7. *Cable Communications Policy Act* (1984)	To protect the privacy of subscribers to cable television.
8. *Video Protection Privacy Act* (1988)	To protect records of individual borrowers held by video rental stores.
9. *Telemarketing Consumer Protection Act* (1994)	To prevent fraudulent or harassing telemarketing practices.

entry. The Fair Credit Reporting Act (FCRA) was passed in 1970 and came into law in April 1971. Below is a brief overview of the main points of the Act:[24]

Accuracy of Information. Credit agencies must take all reasonable steps to guarantee the accuracy of reports in collection, storing, and processing.

Obsolete Information. Certain information must not be included after a number of years have elapsed: bankruptcies, 14 years; suits and judgments, 7 years; criminal arrest, 7 years.

Limited Uses of Information. This point specifies the conditions under which an agency may supply a report. Examples are credit, employment, licensing, legitimate business needs, court order, and with written instructions from the concerned individual.

Notices to Individuals. If the results of the report adversely affect the individual, he or she must be notified and supplied with the name and address of the relevant agency. If an investigation is to be undertaken, the affected individual must be notified.

Individual's Right of Access to Information. The individual has a right to be fully informed about all information held about him or her (except for medical records), and the sources and recipients of the information—for the previous two years for reasons of employment, and six months for others.

Individual's Right to Contest Information. An individual can dispute the information held on him or her, which may require a reinvestigation. If the disagreement is not resolved, the agency must permit the individual to include a brief statement in the file.

In 1976, FCRA was criticized by the federal district court judge in Minnesota in the case Henry v. Forbes:[25]

> The Act does not provide a remedy for all illicit or abusive use of information about consumers . . . individuals are not protected against the abuse of the credit reporting apparatus unless their circumstances are within the narrow bounds of coverage under the Act . . . [The individual has] no remedy unless the information were used in violation of common law privacy rights (requiring highly public, outrageous conduct to make a cause of action).

Another set of criticisms can be summarized as follows: considerable vagueness exists with respect to who has access to the credit data. It permits disclosure to "anyone with a legitimate business need for the information in connection with a business transaction involving the consumer."[26] The FCRA requires the credit agency to provide an inquiring consumer only with "the nature and substance of all information," and does not permit him or her to inspect the file in person. The importance of the accuracy of the information collected, stored, and disseminated is not recognized in the Act. And finally, the Act is directed only at credit reporting agencies and not at other institutions that may request the information.

In September 1989, *Business Week's* cover story, "Is Nothing Private?" revealed what to many Americans was a confirmation of their worst fears that nothing is private. An editor signed up with two super credit bureaus, using the small lie that he needed to run credit checks on one or two prospective employees. For $20 apiece, one of the super bureaus produced credit reports based on just the names and addresses of two of his colleagues. It gets more interesting. For an initial fee of $500, the editor was able to access the super bureau's database from his home computer. He ran two names through the system—Representative Richard J. Durbin (D-Illinois) and Dan Quayle, the vice president of the United States. These requests did not set off alarms and reports were produced. Various innocuous tidbits about J. Danforth Quayle, with a Washington address, turned up including that he has a big mortgage and that he charges more at Sears, Roebuck & Co. than at Brooks Brothers, and what his credit card number is. A spokesman for the vice president said, "We find the invasion-of-privacy aspect of the credit situation disturbing. Further controls should be considered."[27]

In the early 1990s, unsuccessful attempts were made to update the Act but differences among credit bureaus, direct marketers, and consumer and privacy advocacy groups could not be resolved. Linda Himmelstein reported on one proposal: "The Consumer Reporting Reform Act addresses access to, as well as accuracy and privacy of, consumer credit information. Among other things, the bill provides consumers with a free credit report annually and allows them to opt out of having their personal data used for marketing purposes."[28] There is no new privacy protection for consumers even though they have made it clear that they require additional protection. Thus, in a survey of 4,000 Americans carried out by Yankelovich Partners, "45% of consumers strongly feel legislation is needed, compared with a 23% figure five years ago." [29] The study also found that, "66% feel it is a serious privacy violation for a firm to sell a mailing list without permission of the people listed. Moreover, 55% called unsolicited fundraising phone calls a privacy violation."

Finally, from a survey conducted in spring 1996, the following results are of interest: [30]

- Survey respondents were split fairly equally between being "greatly, somewhat, slightly or not at all" concerned about whether their name was on mailing lists.
- A whopping 83% of the survey participants said there should be a law requiring an opt-in procedure for names to be included on mailing lists.
- 50% of the general survey audience indicated that data on credit card ownership and credit limits should not be collected.
- 55% of the group's mail order buyers said they want their credit data to be off-limits.

Cable Communications Policy Act of 1984

This important Act extended privacy protection to subscribers of cable television and would apply as well to interactive systems carried over cable. Subscribers to cable television may create a record of programs paid for, purchases made for home shopping, and other services as well. The Internet, the Web, private systems such as America Online and CompuServe (see Chapter 12), permit subscribers to take advantage of a number of services, including banking, reservations to musical, theatrical, film, and sporting events, bulletin boards, electronic mail, and news and information sources. Every action by a subscriber leaves a trail, gradually accumulating a record of preferences and interests that direct-mailing companies, advertisers, and even criminal investigators may find useful. The consumer needs protection and hence the passage of this Act. Some of the provisions of the Act are given below: [31]

- Cable operators have to provide subscribers to cable television services with a separate annual written statement, which clearly and conspicuously states the nature, uses, disclosures, retention periods and rights of access concerning the identifiable personal information to be collected with respect to the subscriber.
- A subscriber has to furnish prior written or electronic consent before a cable operator can use the cable system for the collection and disclosure of identifiable personal information, except that the cable company may collect, use, and disclose personal information in order to provide legitimate business services to the subscriber or to respond to a court order, and may disclose names and addresses, if the subscriber has had an opportunity to prohibit or limit such disclosure.
- A "governmental entity" may obtain such access pursuant to a court order, only if in a court proceeding it has offered "clear and convincing evidence" that the subject of the information is reasonably suspected of engaging in criminal activity, that the information sought would be material evidence in the case, and that the subject of the information is afforded the opportunity to appear and contest such entity's claim.

Video Privacy Protection Act of 1988: The Bork Bill

In 1987, when Robert Bork had been nominated by President Reagan to the Supreme Court and was being considered by the US Senate, a reporter obtained unauthorized access to the video rental list of his family. Presumably, the purpose was to uncover evidence that Mr.

Bork, or his family, rented questionable (read pornographic) movies as a way of further discrediting his nomination. Congress acted quickly to protect the privacy of video renters. Individual laws of this kind, however well-motivated, are indications of the lack of a well-thought, comprehensive approach to consumer privacy protection in the United States.

Government Personal Privacy Protection

> . . . privacy is at the heart of liberty in a modern state and is essential for the well-being of the individual. For this reason alone, it is worthy of constitutional protection, but it also has profound significance for public order. The restraints imposed on government to pry into the lives of the citizen go to the essence of a democratic state. (R. v. Dyment [1988], 45 C.C.C. [3d] 245 at 254)

Privacy Act of 1974

The passage of the Privacy Act of 1974 was the culmination of many studies and hearings, but the Watergate scandal was probably the major factor in its approval. The crucial elements of this Act, which applies to the departments, agencies, offices, and administrations of the federal government are given below:[32]

> The purpose of this Act is to provide certain safeguards for an individual against an invasion of personal privacy by requiring federal agencies, except as otherwise provided by law, to . . .

(1) permit an individual to determine what records pertaining to him are collected, maintained, used or disseminated by such agencies;

(2) permit an individual to prevent records pertaining to him obtained by such agencies for a particular purpose from being used or made available for another purpose without his consent;

(3) permit an individual to gain access to information pertaining to him in federal agency records, to have a copy made of all or any portion thereof, and to correct or amend such records;

(4) collect, maintain, use, or disseminate any record of identifiable personal information in a manner that assures that such information is current and accurate for its intended use, and that adequate safeguards are provided to prevent misuse of such information;

(5) permit exemptions from the requirements with respect to records provided in this Act only in those cases where there is an important public policy need for such exemptions as has been determined by specific statutory authority; and

(6) be subject to civil suit for any damages which occur as a result of willful or intentional action which violates any individual's rights under this Act.

With respect to subsection (5), records maintained by the CIA, any law enforcement agencies, prosecutors, courts, correctional institutions, or probation or parole authorities are exemptions as defined in the act. Because police work depends so heavily on informers, these records must be excluded from general access. Also exempt are records involving national defense or foreign policy, specific statute exclusions, trade secrets, and the protection of the president. Many other categories are given in the act. It also required the establishment of the Privacy Protection Study Commission, to conduct a study of the data-banks, automated data processing programs, and information systems of governmental, regional, and private organizations to determine the standards and procedures in force for the protection of personal information.[33]

Implicit in all the legislation discussed so far is an after-the-fact philosophy. The assumption is that computerized personal record systems are here to stay, and it is only necessary to regulate their use to limit the worst abuses. The law is employed to establish procedures and provide recourse for injured parties. The prior question of whether there is justification and need for a particular database has not been legally addressed. Any government agency can decide to set up a record-keeping system whenever it wishes. Most of the critical energy in the privacy issue has been directed toward the adequacy of procedures rather than the prior question of need, and this attitude has persisted into the privacy discussion with respect to the Internet and the anticipated Information Highway.

Family Educational Rights and Privacy Act

In contrast to the omnibus approach of the Privacy Act, the Family Educational Rights and Privacy Act (FERPA), passed in 1974, was directed at educational records. This law gives the parents of minors and students over 18 the "right to inspect and review, and request correction or amendment of, an education record."[34] Educational institutions must inform parents and students of their rights and must draw up appropriate procedures to conform with the regulations of the Act. Since there are over 60 million students, this act covers a great number of people. A privacy law in this area was necessary, because in addition to grades, conduct, and attendance information, some schools keep track of the family life—its stability and economic and social level—and social life of the student, including relationships and membership in churches. The file may also contain psychological test data and teacher evaluations. The unauthorized use of this data could seriously affect the student's life both in and after school.

Schools tend to divulge personal information readily to other schools, law enforcement officials, and for research purposes to the government. Frequently, the interests of the student are secondary. The desire to collect more and more information seems to be increasing, because records are heavily used in decision making. This trend is especially strong in those institutions with large numbers of students. In many postsecondary institutions there is a history of cooperation with law enforcement officials, especially with respect to information about student radicals. It was this rather slipshod treatment of student records, with little access for students or their families, that motivated the passage of FERPA.

Privacy Protection Act of 1980

This Act defines regulations to be followed by law enforcement agencies in acquiring print media records, but it also provides "special protection against search and seizures of materials in the possession of the media and their representatives by federal, state, and local law enforcement agencies. Such materials are subject to seizure by law enforcement agencies *only* if the custodian of the materials is suspected of criminal activity or to prevent the death, serious bodily injury, or destruction of evidence."[35] Reporters may sue for damages if they feel that their right to privacy has been compromised.

Computer Security Act of 1987

This Act creates a means for establishing minimum acceptable security practices for federal computer systems. Responsibility was originally assigned to the National Bureau of Standards (now the National Institute of Standards and Technology, NIST) to develop standards and guidelines to guarantee the security and privacy of the federal computer system, with technical advice provided by the National Security Agency (NSA). The Office of Management of the Budget (OMB) has been working with NIST and NSA to assure the effective implementation of the Act. For example, in 1988, OMB issued guidance to agencies on computer security planning; it co-sponsored a workshop for federal employees on implementing the training and planning portions of the Act; in March of 1989, the inaugural meeting of the Computer System Security and Privacy Advisory Board established by the Act was held; and NIST and NSA reached an agreement that formalized their working relationship in computer security.[36]

Computer Matching and Privacy Protection Act of 1988

This Act amended the Privacy Act to require a biannual report by the president concerning the administration of the law. It was motivated by a concern with the increasing number of computer matches being carried out by various government agencies. In the opinion of Professor David Flaherty, a renowned privacy expert, the Act has a limited scope, "applying only to the 'computerized comparison of records for the purpose of (i) establishing or verifying eligibility for a Federal benefit program, or (ii) recouping payments or delinquent debts under such programs.' It does not apply to matches performed for statistical, research, law enforcement, foreign counterintelligence, security screening, and tax purposes."[37] The Act contains some measures to protect privacy, however: agencies wishing to carry out matching programs must design written agreements describing how the resulting records will be used; affected citizens must be given prior notice in the *Federal Register:* "agencies cannot take steps to deny or cut off a benefit to a person on the basis of adverse data uncovered, unless they have validated their accuracy and offered the individual an opportunity to contest the findings [; and] agencies that conduct or participate in matches are required to create Data Integrity Boards, made up of an agency's own senior officials, to oversee and approve matches."[38] (See the previous section on Computer Matching.)

Communication Privacy Protection

Electronic Communications Privacy Act of 1986

Title 111 of the Omnibus Crime Control and Safe Streets Act of 1968, usually called the Wiretap Act, amended the 1934 Communications Act so that government officials at all levels could legally use wiretaps and other forms of electronic surveillance. This was in the spirit of the times to provide law enforcement agents with wider powers to combat crime. Technological developments such as cellular telephones, citizen band radios, and electronically transmitted information in computer-readable form have created new forms of communication not anticipated in the 1968 Act. Thus, the 1986 Act was enacted to deal with these deficiencies and includes digital communications, data communications, video communications, and a separate chapter on e-mail (electronic mail). Of primary concern with respect to privacy is an amendment that permits the government to contract out the task of monitoring communications pursuant to a court order. The ramifications of this amendment are quite complicated and beyond the scope of the present discussion, but what is clear is that "the infringement of privacy rights will be multiplied by an incalculable factor because of the use of contracting parties. Rather than delegating the responsibility for conducting these privacy-sensitive interceptions, Congress should have added additional staff to the law enforcement agencies charged with conducting interceptions."[39]

Also of considerable interest, given its increasing use, are the provisions with respect to e-mail. It is a criminal offense, in the words of the legislation, to either "intentionally [access] without authorization a facility through which an electronic communication service is provided; or intentionally [exceed] an authorization to access that facility." A fine line must be drawn to permit bulletin boards to function while protecting e-mail. Thus, criminal liability applies only if the person who gains access to a system actually obtains, alters, or prevents another's access to electronic communication. One final provision is that the Act "prohibits an electronic communications service provider from knowingly divulging the contents of any stored electronic communication."[40]

Communications Assistance for Law Enforcement Act of 1994 ("FBI Digital Telephony Bill")

After much debate and considerable opposition from privacy advocate groups, this Act, also referred to as the "FBI Wiretap Bill" was signed into law by President Clinton on October 25, 1994. "This law requires telecommunications carriers, as defined in the Act, to ensure law enforcement's ability, pursuant to court order or other lawful authorization, to intercept communications notwithstanding advanced telecommunications technologies."[41] Original opposition to this bill focused on the apparently increased convenience and powers of the FBI to monitor conversations remotely on telephone systems, that will be required by the law, for the first time in history, to reserve part of the capacity for surveillance purposes. Beside the enormous costs of this requirement, the relatively easy availability of surveillance technology may prove attractive to overzealous or rogue investigators. Subsequent to the passage of the Act, "the FBI is claiming that compliance with CALEA requires that telephone companies and other service providers in some regions of the country build in enough surveillance capacity so that "one percent" of all phone lines could be "simultaneously" wiretapped, calls isolated, and forwarded to the FBI."[42] One additional, but important change, is that up to now, wiretap statistics have been based on the number authorized and intercepted, but the implementation of this Act will shift the discussion to "percentages of total communications activity." The apparent fear of illegal or subversive uses of telephone systems, over which much of the Internet operates, has resulted in this legislation as well as other attempts to control and limit potentially encrypted communications. (See Chapter 11 for a discussion of the infamous Clipper Chip.)

An Overseas Example

There seems to be a general consensus that privacy legislation should be concerned with three broad areas: (1) the setting up of databases and collection of data, (2) procedures for regulating the management of the information, that is, the right of access and data correction, and (3) monitoring and enforcement schemes. Different countries have chosen to emphasize these aspects to varying degrees. A major criticism of the US system of privacy protection is the lack of regulation of private databases. There is nothing comparable to the data protection boards that exist in most European countries.

One country that has launched an approach to record-keeping at odds with the privacy concerns of the Western countries is Thailand. The Thailand Ministry of the Interior has created the Central Population Database (CPD), which "closely *tracks* the 55 million Thais living in 10 million households nationwide. The database, which is the only fully integrated demographics database system in the world, *can* be used to improve the country's standard of living."[43] (Emphasis added.) This comprehensive national database contains extensive demographic information, presumably permitting improved public health planning, educational planning, benefits administration, tax collection, and law enforcement. Obviously necessary is a system of national identity cards with personal identification numbers (PIN), containing a thumbprint and photograph. Soon every Thai will have a card, which will also be used for passport, immigration, and refugee control. The director of the CPD center in Bangkok, sensitive to charges of a Big Brother society claims, "It's a system that people need. They accept it. CPD complies with government privacy laws." The Central Population Database was the recipient of a *Computerworld Smithsonian Award* in 1990.

PRIVACY ISSUES ON THE INTERNET AND THE INFORMATION HIGHWAY

The NII promises enormous benefits. To name just a few, the NII offers the possibilities of greater citizen participation in deliberative democracy, advances in medical treatment and research, and quick verification of critical information such as a gun purchaser's criminal record. These benefits, however, do not come without a cost: the loss of privacy. Privacy in this context means "information privacy," an individual's claim to control the terms under which personal information—information identifiable to an individual—is acquired, disclosed, and used.[44]

The National Information Infrastructure (NII) is a major initiative of the Clinton administration and especially Vice President Albert Gore. A number of government structures have been created to stimulate, and assist in, the development of the NII, including the Advisory Council on the NII, the Information Infrastructure Task Force (IITF), and the National Telecommunications and Information Administration (NTIA). Let me briefly describe these. NTIA is an agency of the US Department of Commerce and is headed by

Larry Irving, Assistant Secretary for Communications and Information. NTIA's mandate is broad with such concerns as encouraging private investment, promoting and protecting competition, providing open access to the network, developing an international telecommunications policy, and promoting a minority telecommunications program. Among the specific programs are the Office of Spectrum Management, the Institute for Telecommunication Sciences, the Office of Telecommunications and Information Applications, and the Office of Policy Analysis and Development (OPAD). OPAD is concerned with universal service and open access, content regulation and the First Amendment, Electronic Commerce, and of interest for the present purposes, privacy. Thus the NTIA White Paper issued in February 1994 (Inquiry on Private Sector Use of Telecommunications-Related Personal Information) was developed by this office.

Three committees of the IITF have been established, the Telecommunications Policy Committee, the Applications Committee, and the Information Policy Committee, which has created three Working Groups, the most relevant being the Working Group on Privacy. A year after the IITF began its work, it issued a progress report, with relevant sections related to privacy and security concerns.[45] A major thrust of the administration's plan for dealing with privacy is actually to deal with the security aspect by an increased dependency on encryption. It is for this reason that it has devoted so much attention to a particular encryption strategy in spite of vigorous and sustained opposition from many quarters. Recall that the administration's plan is to require the use of a given standard, known colloquially as the "Clipper Chip" that will enable government security agencies, under strict legal guidelines, to access all communication over computer networks, including the IH.

It is important to be clear about the distinction between privacy and security. Privacy is a right and security is a means to ensure that right. In addition, confidentiality is a judgment that certain information should be specially treated and not publicly available. Thus once determining that certain communications are to be private, encryption might be chosen as the appropriate technology. In storing information electronically, special passwords may be required to access it. These are important and necessary, but lacking the prior commitment to ensure privacy, they represent an orthogonal concern. They will come into play after it has been decided, hopefully, that all communications on the IH are to be treated as private communications, subject to appropriate comprehensive legislation. One final point is that the debate about encryption strategies and the US government's role is obviously related to the privacy issue. If the government can unilaterally decide that it needs to decrypt a selected communication then obviously privacy is compromised. So the fight against the government's intention to make the use of the Clipper Chip mandatory is simultaneously a fight for personal privacy; this is how the controversy has generally been reported.

US Government Privacy Recommendations

To determine possible directions for the US to take in responding to its citizens' privacy concerns about the Internet and the IH, we briefly consider three sources. The first is a pair of reports produced by the now terminated Congressional Office of Technology Assessment (OTA). These studies were commissioned by Congress to propose options for the legislative branch in dealing with privacy and security issues on "network environments."[46]

In June 1995, the Privacy Working Group of the Information Infrastructure Task Force, a creation of the Clinton administration, released its final recommendations for privacy protection.[47] Finally, the National Telecommunications and Information Administration issued a final White Paper on privacy issues in the private sector in October 1995, after a year and a half of consultations.[48]

OTA Reports: Information Society and Privacy in Network Environments and Update

The first OTA report recognizes that the privacy of networked information held by the government may not be covered adequately by the Privacy Act and further notes the lack of a tradition in the US of comprehensive privacy legislation compared with Europe: "Although the United States does not comprehensively regulate the creation and use of such data in the private sector, foreign governments (particularly the European Union) do impose controls." Thus, in approaching the issue of privacy protection in the private sector for network environments, the report suggests that Congress might consider legislating standards comparable to existing OECD (Organization of Economic Cooperation and Development) guidelines or permit the "business community to advise the international community on its own of its interests in data protection policy." Another possibility is the creation of a Federal Privacy Commission, similar to data protection boards in Europe, to deal with privacy issues, but unlike the European model such a board is not intended to have any regulatory powers.

This commission would not have the responsibility to approve the requests of public or private agencies to engage in the collection and storage of personal information. It would not be required to monitor the operating procedures of such agencies. What also seems to be intended is basically an advisory function and not a regulatory one in the European model. What seems to be intended is the development of privacy guidelines that will minimally satisfy the European Union's policy on data protection for the international flow of information. That is, the motivating force appears to be economic not social. The second OTA report noted that the urgency to deal with the privacy problem had intensified. One comment, from a workshop whose results formed a major part of the report, is quite interesting: "Consumers are increasingly concerned with control of personal and transactional data and are seeking some protection from potential abuse of this information. Those participants who had been less inclined than most to trust the market on security issues found more comfortable ground on privacy, because few participants seemed to feel that the market will prioritize personal privacy."[49]

IITF Draft Principles for Providing and Using Personal Information

The IITF Working Group on Privacy notes that the National Information Infrastructure (NII), the Clinton Administration's term for the Information Highway, will by its very nature raise the privacy stakes beyond anything that has so far existed and therefore require more comprehensive privacy principles. Consider the following comments:[50]

(a) No longer do governments alone obtain and use large amounts of personal information; the private sector now rivals the government in obtaining and using personal information. New principles would thus be incomplete unless they applied to both the governmental and private sectors.

(b) The NII promises true interactivity. Individuals will become active participants who, by using the NII, will create volumes of data containing the content of communications as well as transactional data.

(c) The transport vehicles for personal information—the networks—are vulnerable to abuse; thus, the security of the network itself is critical to the NII's future success.

Thus, although a set of updated privacy principles for the Information Highway are the goal of this report, the Working Group argues that they should not be implemented as legislation. In the report, it is stated that the purpose of these Principles is to provide a "guide" for any groups, institutions, or governments that need to design privacy regulations or laws but that these Principles do not have "the force of law." This position is certainly consistent with the long-standing attitude of the US in opposition to broad and comprehensive privacy legislation and in favor of a piecemeal or sectoral approach, often resulting in legislation enacted under crisis situations or in response to a wellspring of public indignation. Thus the federal Privacy Act of 1974 seems to have been enacted as a result of the Watergate events with the basic intent to reassure the public that government would respect personal privacy only if specific legislation were in place. The Fair Credit Reporting Act (1970) can be seen as a response to public opinion concerned with the accuracy and misuse of credit records by credit bureaus, banks, insurance companies, and other institutions that depend upon personal credit reports.

These two paragraphs are quite revealing:

9. Moreover, the Principles are intended to be in accord with current international guidelines regarding the use of personal information and thus should support the ongoing development of the Global Information Infrastructure.

10. Finally, adherence to the Principles will cultivate the trust between individuals and information users so crucial to the successful evolution of the NII.

Paragraph 9 states that the Principles are "intended to be in accord with current international guidelines . . ." but given that they do not have the force of law it is not clear that a mix of voluntary guidelines will satisfy the countries of Europe that have adequate legislation in place. Paragraph 10 offers the plaintive hope that "adherence to the Principles will cultivate the trust between individuals and information users . . ." What evidence is there that voluntary codes work? How will individuals know which voluntary code is in effect and how its provisions differ or are similar to other voluntary codes? What recourse will they have if they feel that their privacy has been compromised? The good will of the "information user?"

Privacy and the NII: Safeguarding Telecommunications-Related Personal Information

The White Paper extols the promise of the NII, especially the enormous quantity of commercial activity to be generated. All of this activity has as one of its side effects the creation of a "paper" trail of personal data and as we just discussed, this data constitutes a wealth of extremely valuable marketing information. Existing applicable federal legislation is briefly reviewed with respect to privacy coverage and comments are solicited as to the adequacy of coverage for multimedia information and to the unrestricted use of secondary data. This position paper also points out that telephone transactions have become a rich source of data and that perhaps new regulatory policy is warranted. It notes that the "United States currently has no omnibus privacy law that covers the private sector's acquisition, disclosure, and use of TRPI (telecommunications-related personal information)." But not surprisingly its bottom line is not to recommend such legislation, at least not yet. Instead, the White Paper hopes for the following:

> As stated above, NTIA's proposed framework draws upon the IITF's Principles and has two fundamental elements—provider notice and customer consent. Under NTIA's proposed framework, each provider of telecommunications and information services would inform its customers about what TRPI it intends to collect and how that data will be used. A service provider would be free to use the information collected for the stated purposes once it has obtained consent from the relevant customer. Affirmative consent would be required with respect to sensitive personal information. Tacit customer consent would be sufficient to authorize the use of all other information.

> This approach, if embraced by industry, would allow service providers and their customers to establish the specific level of privacy protection offered in a marketplace transaction, **free from excessive government regulation**, so long as the minimum requirements of notice and consent are satisfied . . . For these reasons, NTIA believes that it is in the private sector's interest to adopt the privacy framework outlined in this paper, **without waiting for formal government action**. [emphasis added]

Formal government involvement in the marketplace regulation of privacy via appropriate legislation is not in the cards, even though western Europe, Canada (not yet but promised), and other countries have chosen this approach. The paper recommends a modified contractual approach to dealing with privacy concerns. Under a contractual approach, "companies would inform their customers about what sorts of personal information the firms intend to collect and the uses to which that information would be put. Consumers could then either accept a company's 'offer,' or reject it and shop around for a better deal." The modified contractual approach, favored by NTIA, "allows businesses and consumers to reach agreements concerning the collection, use, and dissemination of TRPI, subject to two fundamental requirements, provider notice and customer consent. Our recommended approach should adequately protect individuals' legitimate privacy interests without excessive government intervention in the marketplace." Finally to reinforce its view, NTIA offers both the carrot and the stick. It recommends that the modified contractual framework be grounded in the "principles of fair information practices released by the IITF's Privacy Working Group in June 1995." NTIA expects the private sector to implement this framework voluntarily but "If such private sector action is not forthcoming, however, that framework can and should form the basis for government-mandated privacy regulations or standards."

Although the efficacy of self-regulation or volunteerism has been previously discussed, it is worth remarking that information handlers readily propose and implement privacy policies to forestall possible government legislation. As remarked previously, it has been impossible so far to update the Fair Credit Reporting Act of 1970, originally enacted because of the misuse of personal information, including inaccuracies in collection. The credit reporting agencies would certainly have preferred to operate within rules of their own making; for one thing it would have been cheaper. Because of the current political atmosphere of apparent government mistrust, it is likely that self-regulation will become the wave of the future and it is also likely that individual privacy will continue to be under attack. However, it is also possible that events in the European Community may force North American governments to intervene in the personal information industries.

The European Privacy Directive

In June 1995, The European Community adopted the Privacy Directive, first drafted in 1992, that governs the handling of personal information within and without the European Community (EC). The significant part of this Directive for the present purposes is Chapter IV, Transfer of Personal Data to Third Countries. Article 25, Principles, reads in part:[51]

1. Member States shall provide that the transfer to a third country of personal data which are undergoing processing or are intended for processing after transfer may take place only if, without prejudice to compliance with the national provisions adopted pursuant to the other provisions of this Directive, the third country in question ensures an adequate level of protection.
2. The adequacy of the level of protection afforded by a third country shall be assessed in the light of all the circumstances surrounding a data transfer operation or set of data transfer operations; particular consideration shall be given to the nature of the data, the purpose and duration of the proposed processing operation or operations, the country of origin and country of final destination, the rules of law, both general and sectoral, in force in the third country in question and the professional rules and security measures which are complied with in those countries.

The simple version of item 1 is that no personal data can be transferred, from any member state of the EC to a third country unless that country's level of protection is adequate, where adequate means equivalent to that offered in the EC. Since no national privacy laws for the private sector are in existence in North America, it would seem to be the case that a confrontation is looming, but the Directive allows the possibility that adequate "professional rules and security measures" may be sufficient, or that satisfactorily agreed upon procedures that could be generalized may do as well. Thus, it is possible that the Privacy Directive may serve to spur the development of federal privacy laws or, more likely, special arrangements will be made between US companies and the EC for the protection of personal information.

FREEDOM OF INFORMATION

I therefore call upon all Federal departments and agencies to renew their commitment to the Freedom of Information Act, to its underlying principles of government openness, and to its sound administration. This is an appropriate time for all agencies to take a fresh look at their administration of the Act, to reduce backlogs of Freedom of Information Act requests, and to conform agency practice to the new litigation guidance issued by the Attorney General, which is attached.

Further, I remind agencies that our commitment to openness requires more than merely responding to requests from the public. Each agency has a responsibility to distribute information on its own initiative, and to enhance public access through the use of electronic information systems. Taking these steps will ensure compliance with both the letter and spirit of the Act. (William J. Clinton)[52]

The freedom of information issue exists in uneasy tension with the question of personal privacy. The freedom of information concept is concerned with the rights of citizens to obtain access to information held by the government. The desire to obtain information from the government may endanger the privacy of individuals about whom records are kept. Thus, the situation is such that the individual demands the right to know but at the same time wishes to guard his or her privacy.

It is recognized that the vast amounts of information collected by the government are used to serve the public—for administrative purposes and for planning and research. Research uses—frequently by external agencies, research groups, and universities—involve statistical data in which information about individuals cannot be identified. Although there are some problems, it is generally agreed that information used for such statistical purposes usually protects privacy, and it is readily made available.

The following problem areas arise:

- There must be a reconciliation between the freedom to obtain information from the government when that information contains personal information about other people. Should there be absolute guarantees on the privacy of personal data or should the release of such information be discretionary?
- There are currently restrictions on individuals obtaining access to information about themselves. How does this relate to a freedom of information scheme?
- Various individual access procedures should be consistent with some overall freedom-of-information concept.

The Freedom of Information Act

The federal Freedom of Information Act (FOIA) was passed in 1966, went into effect on July 4, 1967, and was subsequently amended in 1974 and 1976. Its basic principle is that any person may request access to government records and may make copies of the same. Certain records are exempt from disclosure. "Record" is taken to mean all the documents either in the possession of an agency or subject to its control. Some of the features of the FOIA are as follows:

- Requests must be made to the agency that holds the record—that is, any "executive department, military department, Government corporation, Government-controlled corporation, or other establishments in the Executive Office of the President or any independent regulatory agency."[53]

- If an agency refuses to provide the records within a ten-day period, appeal is possible, first to a higher level and then to a district court.
- A fee may be charged for searching, reviewing, and copying.
- Each agency is required to publish, in the *Federal Register,* information about its organization, access methods, rules of procedure, and so forth.

Not all agencies are required to respond to requests; in fact, there are nine exemptions. The first refers to national defense and foreign policy, and includes executive privilege as it relates to state secrets. A 1974 amendment directed the heads of agencies claiming this exemption to turn documents over to the courts for a final decision. Other exemptions include trade secrets and commercial information, internal personnel rules and practice, information limited by appropriate statutes, inter- and intra-agency memoranda, reports prepared in the course of regulating or supervising financial institutions, and geological and geophysical information. Two exemptions are particularly significant. Exemption (6) excludes "personnel and medical files and similar files the disclosure of which would constitute a *clearly unwarranted invasion of personal privacy.*"[54]

> . . . under normal circumstances, intimate family relations, personal health, religious and philosophic beliefs and matters that would prove personally embarrassing to an individual of normal sensibilities should not be disclosed.

Exemption (7) deals with law enforcement records. The original wording in the act was criticized because it permitted the withholding of just about any file labelled "investigatory." Amendments introduced in 1974 defined this exemption more precisely. In part, they exclude access to investigatory files if such access "constitutes an unwarranted invasion of personal privacy." This differs from Exemption (6) only in that it omits the word "clearly." The courts have not held this difference to be significant. The FOIA does protect privacy, but the distinction must be made between an individual requesting information about a third party or about himself or herself. The latter case has been dealt with under the terms of the various privacy acts. With regard to the former, the absolutist position would be to restrict all access to personal information about another individual. However, there seems to be general agreement that on occasion the cause of open government must have higher claim than that of personal privacy. For example, it may be necessary to examine information about public officials to determine if they are exercising their responsibilities as required by law. There is a "balancing" test in Exemption (6): For each request for access, privacy and confidentiality must be balanced. Appeal to judicial review is possible, and case law will determine appropriate guidelines over time. Another approach might be to specify, in advance, records for which privacy must be maintained and to exempt them absolutely from disclosure. This approach may not be satisfactory in all cases, as it makes no provision for the public's right to know in special circumstances.

Technological innovations have also had an impact on the operation of the FOIA. With the increasing computerization of Federal record-keeping, the question arises as to what constitutes a record under the FOIA. Vast amounts of information can be assembled from various distributed databases, organized under a variety of categories, and selectively printed. As Alan Westin has said, "It's as if you've created a great no man's land of information. Traditionally, thinking has been in terms of paper environments and without any sophistication about electronic information."[55] John Markoff, a writer on technology issues for *The New York Times* notes, "There are no explicit legal guidelines that agencies must follow when programming their computers to extract information asked for under the act. Nor are there guidelines on the form in which agencies must release the data. Some experts argue that unless issues involving computerized records can be resolved by the courts or by new laws, the lack of guidelines will become a common way for agencies to deny requests."[56] The interesting question is how much computing, if any, the government is required to do in order to respond to a request for information. On the other hand, the government could release enormous quantities of paper instead of using computers to produce a succinct, directed response. Thus, there is considerable interest in amending the FOIA to accommodate electronic information.

ISSUES AND PROBLEMS: PRESENT AND FUTURE

> Unlike in traditional processing of personal data where there is usually a single authority or enterprise responsible for protecting the privacy of their customers, there is no such overall responsibility on the Internet assigned to a certain entity. Furthermore there is no international oversight mechanism to enforce legal obligations as far as they exist. Therefore the user is forced to put trust into the security of the entire network, that is every single component of the network, no matter where located or managed by whom. The trustworthiness of the Net will become even more crucial with the advent of new software which induces the user not only to download programs from the Net, but also weakens his control over his personal data.[57]

Privacy as an issue will not disappear. In fact, it is becoming more pronounced as the computer makes even greater inroads into the functioning of society. Future problems are inextricably linked to the ability of the computer to process large amounts of information efficiently and rapidly. Although the computer, and more recently computer networks, have brought certain problems to the fore, the importance of privacy as a societal issue and its protection depends on a host of legal, political, and economic concerns. We briefly review a few issues to indicate the breadth of the ongoing assault on personal privacy.

Caller ID

Telephone companies around the country have made available to consumers a service commonly called Caller ID. Simply put, when a call is made, the receiver will be able to see the telephone number of the caller on a small liquid crystal display. Thus, by having access to the telephone number in advance, the receiver can decide whether or not to answer and in the case of obscene, threatening, or unwanted calls, to gain knowledge of the incoming number. On the other side, callers will be forced to reveal unlisted numbers thereby losing a certain measure of privacy. More advanced systems can automatically match the incoming call against a stored list of numbers and then display the name of the caller permitting the receiver to prepare a ready response. Of course the caller could use a public telephone to conceal his or her identity or take advantage of a newly available third-party service for rerouting calls at a cost. Caller ID seems to have obvious value but many concerned about privacy have voiced objections. Consider the following arguments against Caller ID made by Joseph Rhodes, Jr., a commissioner on the Pennsylvania Public Utilities Commission:[58]

- Unblockable Caller ID clearly violates the 'trap and trace' provision of the state wiretap act.
- Bell's other new "IQ services," like Call Trace, Call Return, and Call Back, provide virtually all the opportunity for reducing harassing and obscene phone calls. . . .
- Caller ID will be used by commercial operations to compile phone lists for phone solicitation.
- I believe that unblockable Caller ID will sooner or later cause the death or injury of a police officer doing undercover work or a person hiding from an abusive partner. [A reverse directory will make this possible.]

One commentator in favor of Caller ID suggests remedies to allay the fears of those concerned about loss of privacy. He suggests that telephone companies offer blocking free to anyone who wants it, with the knowledge that some abusive callers will be the first to take advantage of this option. By using call tracing, the numbers of unwanted callers can be trapped at the phone company.[59]

It was only in 1996 that California introduced Caller ID after a major public education program mandated by the California Public Utilities Commission (CPUC). The Commission "has also required that the phone companies make both Complete and Selective Blocking available to consumers at no charge (called Per Line and Per Call Blocking in other states)."[60] In addition, CPUC's education program, that included radio and TV announcements, full-page newspaper advertisements, and bill inserts, resulted in substantial public involvement expressed in a flood of calls to Pacific Bell and GTE. Public awareness was also evident in the results of a spring survey: "74% of those polled knew about Caller ID and [that] 67% were aware there is a way to prevent the delivery of their phone number to the called party." This effort provides a model for the education of the public prior to the introduction of a new technology. Given the high level of concern about personal privacy, it is no surprise that public awareness reached such heights.

New Surveillance Technologies

Most of the discussion so far has been directed towards information stored in computer databases and gathered over computer networks but other computer-facilitated technologies, some derived from military applications, have been diffusing into general use at a surprisingly fast rate. Familiarity is growing with "smart cards" which are very popular in Europe and will be more widely used in North America in the near future. Such a card contains a microchip and newer ones employ optical technology that permit the storage of medical records including X-ray images. An introduction to recent surveillance technology has been provided by David Banisar of the Electronic Frontier Foundation:[61]

- *Advanced microphones.* The FBI has already developed a solid-state briefcase-size electronically steerable microphone array prototype, that can discreetly monitor conversations across open areas.
- *Closed Circuit Television Cameras (CCTC).* Technical developments have increased the capabilities and lowered the cost of video cameras, making them a regular feature in stores and public areas. In the UK, dozens of cities have centrally controlled, comprehensive citywide CCTC systems that can track individuals wherever they go, even if they enter buildings.
- *Forward Looking Infrared (FLIR).* Originally developed for use in fighter planes and helicopters to locate enemy aircraft, FLIR can detect a temperature differential as small as .18 degrees centigrade. Texas Instruments and others are marketing hand-held and automobile- and helicopter-mounted models that can essentially look through walls to determine activities inside buildings.
- *Massive Millimeter Wave Detectors.* Developed by Militech Corporation, these detectors use a form of radar to scan beneath clothing. By monitoring the millimeter wave portion of the electromagnetic spectrum emitted by the human body, the system can detect items such as guns and drugs from a range of 12 feet or more.
- *Van Eck Monitoring.* Every computer emits low levels of electromagnetic radiation from the monitor, processor, and attached devices. Although experts disagree whether the actual range is a only a few yards or up to a mile, these signals can be remotely recreated on another computer.
- *Intelligent Transportation Systems.* ITS refers to a number of traffic management technologies, including crash-avoidance systems, automated toll collection, satellite-based position location, and traffic-based toll pricing. To facilitate these services, the system tracks the movements of all people using public or private transportation. As currently proposed by TRW, a leading developer of the technologies involved, the data collected on travel will be available for both law enforcement and private uses such as direct marketing.
- *Digital Cash.* Potentially, digital cash will create one of the most comprehensive systems for the collection of information on individuals. Using computer software and smart cards to replace physical cash, consumers can spend virtual money for small transactions such as reading an electronic newspaper online, making phone calls from pay phones, paying electronic tolls, buying groceries, as well as for any transaction currently done through credit cards.

A few words about Closed Circuit Television Cameras (CCTC) may be helpful in appreciating the frequently conflicting aims of surveillance technology. Its use is more advanced in Britain where some 120 towns and cities use CCTV for monitoring public areas. The employment of CCTV was motivated by Britain's infamous "soccer hooligans" in the 1960s and later by various kinds of social disorder, including race riots in 1984, union strikes in 1984–1985, 1989 riots in opposition to the government's poll tax, and ongoing terrorism by the IRA. To preserve order and to identify perpetrators, a massive introduction of CCTV has taken place. The claim is that crime has diminished, public spaces are much safer, business has improved, and the quality of street life has improved. Crime has diminished in some cities but whether the use of CCTV is the crucial factor is not known. However, most people seem to be willing to trade a certain measure of privacy, or at least public anonymity, for security. North America has been much more cautious than Europe in adopting CCTC but there are plans for trials.

Unregulated Databases

Companies have fired workers from jobs without cause, doctors have refused to take new patients who are able to afford medical care, and apartment managers have refused to rent to prospective tenants with regular jobs and sufficient income. Many similar cases have been documented with the common denominator that the companies, doctors, and managers have all taken advantage of special-purpose commercial databases directed towards their concerns. Companies can turn to databases to determine if any of their workers have filed a worker compensation claim elsewhere, as well as the disposition of the case. Other blacklists will provide information to physicians if a prospective patient has ever sued a doctor for malpractice, or will provide information to an apartment manager if a prospective tenant has ever brought a claim for a violation of tenant's rights. The data for these lists is openly available in tenants' courts, small claims courts, worker compensation hearings, and civil court proceedings. All that is required is sufficient staff to extract relevant information from these records and then enter it into the database. By focusing on large population centers, companies with comprehensive databases find a ready market for their services. And it is all legal; the only possible danger may result from inaccurate data. Credit bureaus, banks, cable companies, and video rental stores are all subject to a certain degree of regulation with respect to the privacy of their clients but uniform laws do not exist to protect the privacy of citizens in all their commercial activities.

The National Practitioner Databank

For years it has been difficult, if not impossible, to monitor the movements of health care professionals who, having been disciplined by one board, move to a new jurisdiction, leaving behind their flawed record and presenting themselves as competent professionals. In 1986, Congress passed a law to set up a national database, the National Practitioner Databank, of disciplinary actions taken against physicians, dentists, nurses, therapists, and other licensed health professionals. The databank, accessible to hospitals, licensing agencies, and other medical groups, but not the general public, will supply such information as professional misconduct (including making sexual overtures to patients), misdiagnosis, and mistreatment, but not personal matters such as arrests, nonpayment of taxes, or drug or alcohol abuse (except when professional performance is affected), malpractice payments, restrictions of privileges in hospitals and clinics, disciplinary actions by medical and dental societies, and state actions against hospitals and other health care institutions.

The data bank, popularly known as "docs in a box" opened for business on September 1, 1990, as names of offending health care professionals were entered. Doctors are permitted to inspect their own files and to enter explanatory statements, if they wish. The American Medical Association, which initially opposed the databank, now supports it but would like "nuisance suits" to be left off. Hospitals will have to improve their verification of doctors' records and to rationalize their disciplinary procedures, because of the serious consequences of including such actions in the National Databank. Presumably the public will benefit in that incompetent health practitioners will no longer be able to find new places to work where their past record is unknown. Here is an important case in which the need of hospitals to know about their staff's background, in order to provide competent medical care and to reduce costly malpractice suits, outweighs any claim to privacy by members of that staff.

Electronic Mail

An important component of office automation, electronic mail, or e-mail, was discussed in Chapter 4. Although it has proven to be an extremely useful communication tool and facilitates cooperation throughout the company, an important privacy issue has emerged, one strongly related to the growing concern with workers' rights. (See Chapter 10.) The basic question is to what degree management can monitor its employees' e-mail, either on an occasional or regular basis. A class action suit launched in August 1990 against Epson America Inc. for "allegedly violating its employees' privacy by intercepting their E-mail," was dismissed in January 1991 in a Los Angeles County Superior Court because "the company did not violate a state penal code prohibiting electronic eavesdropping on private communications."[62] Another suit was filed against Nissan Motor Corp. in January 1991 by two employees, again in California, accusing the company of intercepting their electronic messages and violating their privacy. Some companies argue that they reserve the right to intercept messages, without prior warning, as a means of ensuring that employees do not abuse the system with personal communications. What does seem necessary is that companies issue clear guidelines, based on discussions with their employees about the use and misuse of e-mail, and that both employees and employers adhere to them.

However, even a clear statement of operating procedures may not help employees. In a case decided in Pennsylvania in early 1996, Michael A. Smyth sued The Pillsbury Company for being wrongfully discharged, based on information obtained from Mr. Smyth's supposedly protected e-mail in spite of the fact that the company "repeatedly assured its employees, including plaintiff, that all e-mail communications would remain confidential and privileged. . . . Defendant further assured its employees, including plaintiff, that e-mail communications could not be intercepted and used by defendant against its employees as grounds for termination or reprimand."[63] The judge found for the defendant and the final paragraph of his decision is quite revealing:[64]

> In the second instance, even if we found that an employee had a reasonable expectation of privacy in the contents of his e-mail communications over the company e-mail system, we do not find that a reasonable person would consider the defendant's interception of these communications to be a substantial and highly offensive invasion of his privacy. Again, we note that by intercepting such communications, the company is not, as in the case of urinalysis or personal property searches, requiring the employee to disclose any personal information about himself or invading the employee's person or personal effects. Moreover, the company's interest in preventing inappropriate and unprofessional comments or even illegal activity over its e-mail system outweighs any privacy interest the employee may have in those comments.

More on employee rights in the next chapter.

Netscape's "Cookies"

This example is a preview of what may become commonplace on the commercial Information Highway and is just another step on the way to more efficient gathering of consumer information. Netscape's Navigator is the most commonly used Web browser, that software tool for locating Web sites, reading news, listening to music, watching movies, downloading information, and buying products. Existing software is able to determine several pieces of information about anyone who visits a Web site. Here is some of the information that was obtained from a visit to a demonstration Web site hosted by the Center for Democracy and Technology:[65]

Your name is probably . . . , and you can be reached at . . .

Your computer is a PowerMac.

Your Internet browser is Netscape.

You are coming from . . .

I see you've recently been visiting this page at

www.cdt.org.

But more could be obtained such as "your e-mail address, the exact files you viewed, and other detailed information gathered without your knowledge. And you reveal information to web site operators both directly and indirectly." Indirect methods gather this kind of information as well as information gathered by means of Netscape's Cookies, an overly clever name for "client-side persistent information," itself a euphemism for the following process: we gather information about your shopping habits and make it available for subsequent perusal by us, by downloading it without your knowledge onto your hard drive. Of course the official Netscape line is that "cookies are beneficial to the Web . . . shopping done via the Web could be gradually gathered in the cookies file, and then paid for (as if at a supermarket checkout) when the user enters the appropriate page. The concept can also be used to create a permanently customized view of a site—if you regularly have specific needs from a search engine, for example."[66] Thus its major motivation is convenience—it saves the user from having to reenter information that may be required for successive visits to a Web site. But there are drawbacks:[67]

John Yang, a research assistant in the geology department at Florida International University in Miami, said a Cookie program can be built to track the user's every move while connected to a particular server. This information can then be fed into a database to keep statistics on site usage so Webmasters can tailor a site to a particular user's interests.

Combine Cookie with JavaScript and a site's administrator could launch a very effective direct mail campaign without ever having asked the user for permission, Yang observed.

In more malevolent hands, these new tools can do far worse. For example, a Webmaster could pretend to be a particular site in order to retrieve a user's Cookie data without authorization. "If you use a server that does not encrypt its information, there is a real problem," Yang said.

It should be noted that Cookies are a feature on other browsers, including Microsoft's Internet Explorer and Quarterdeck's Mosaic 2.0. Finally, in response to the concern's expressed about possible invasions of privacy, Frank Chen, security product manager of Netscape, responded that steps were being taken to deal with the situation by first fixing security bugs in JavaScript and then dealing with making Cookies more secure. "He added that Netscape is looking at adding a feature that will either disable Cookie and JavaScript support or alert the user to their presence. 'You've got to be able to store some information on the client side in order to build robust client-server applications, but we also have to inform users of the types of information they will receive,' " Chen said.[68] Note that the emphasis on security issues finesses the justified privacy concern about why so much information must be gathered in the first place, without most users being aware of this process.

Possible Forthcoming Privacy Legislation

Two issues were in the forefront in 1996—children's privacy and medical records privacy. Various bills were being debated in Congress, including S. 1360, the Medical Records Confidentiality Act of 1995 (introduced by Senator Bennett on October 24, 1995), and the Children's Privacy Protection and Parental Empowerment Act of 1996 (Senator Dianne Feinstein and Rep. Bob Franks). The need for the protection of medical records is motivated by the following concerns: administrative errors that "misclassify, release, or lose information . . . computerization [of medical records means remote access and rapid dissemination of information] . . . Access by unrelated parties [including] insurance companies, drug companies; [and often unknown to patients,] when her or his patients have been subpoenaed."[69] Typically, to receive medical treatment it is necessary to sign a waiver that allows "the health care provider to release your medical information to government agencies, insurance companies, employers and others."[70]

Various groups concerned about privacy have opposed the Bennett Bill for a number of reasons, including the following:[71] "the bill preempts state statutes that provide general medical confidentiality protection, and all common law that pertains to medical privacy," "legislation also provides a statutory framework for the creation of information megabusinesses called 'Health Information Services.' These services will be able to compile individual lifetime medical records. Information from these records will then be redisclosed in both identified and de-identified forms for a widevariety of purposes," and "bill permits most disclosures without obtaining patient consent."

In the discussion in Chapter 8 on free speech on the Internet, the primary motivation for the passage of the Communications Decency Act was the perceived availability of, and easy access to, images and other material not appropriate for children. But children are also the targets of other activities that concern parents but have not received the same kind of publicity. The Center for Media Education has produced a report on threats to children from "Online Marketing" and recommends that for future marketing directed towards children, the following principles be observed:[72]

1. Personal information (including click stream data) should not be collected from children, nor should personal profiles of children be sold to third parties.

   2. Advertising and promotions targeted at children should be clearly labeled and separated
      from content.
   3. Children's content areas should not be directly linked to advertising sites.
   4. There should be no direct interaction between children and product spokescharacters.
   5. There should be no online microtargeting of children, and no direct-response marketing.

The Children's Privacy Protection and Parental Empowerment Act would deal with threats
to children resulting from the collection and exchange of information gathered about
them. Thus, the Act would do the following:[73]

   1. Prohibit the sale or purchase of personal information about children without parental
      consent
   2. Require list brokers and solicitors to disclose to parents, upon request, the source and
      content of personal information on file about their children.
   3. Require list brokers to disclose to parents, upon request, the names of persons or enti-
      ties to whom they have distributed personal information on that parent's child.
   4. Prohibit prisoners and convicted sex criminals from processing the personal information
      of children.
   5. Prohibit any exchange of children's personal information that one has a reason to be-
      lieve will be used to harm or abuse a child.

Although the issues of medical records and children's privacy protection are obviously important and legislation is necessary, the question raised throughout this chapter comes to
the fore: Why not put in place comprehensive privacy legislation to deal with both the private and public sectors?

Concluding Remarks

The right to privacy is not viewed as an absolute right, especially with respect to information. In fact, the word "privacy" does not appear in the Bill of Rights. The major thrust of
legislation has been to control, not to forbid, the collection and use of private information.
Information about any individual is not always in that individual's control. Rather it can be
gathered, stored, and disseminated by both private and public agencies. The law has provided protection, and we must continue to turn to the law for future protection. The distinguished jurist, William O. Douglas, referred to the police in the following quotation, but
he might just as well have been concerned with other institutions and groups in society:[74]

> The free state offers what a police state denies—the privacy of the home, the dignity and
> peace of mind of the individual. That precious right to be let alone is violated once the po-
> lice enter our conversations.

We briefly describe two last issues. One bold attempt to regain control over personal information was launched by Ram Avrahami, a subscriber to *U.S. News and World Reports*,
against that magazine in June 1995. He claimed that his "name is his personal property.
Virginia law prohibits anyone else from using his name for advertising purposes or purposes of trade without Mr. Avrahami's written consent." Simply put, *U.S. News and*

World Report and the *Smithsonian Magazine* exchanged mailing lists so that each magazine could attempt to attract the other's subscribers. Mr. Avrahami's position is that he did not give his explicit permission for his personal property to be used by the magazine. On June 11, 1996, Virginia Circuit Court Judge William Newman ruled in favor of *U.S. News and World Report*. He stated that Avrahami "is precluded from recovering damages because he failed to use reasonable means to have his name removed from mailing lists and affirmatively created this litigation by using a false name."[75] Direct Marketers heaved a sigh of relief as it was business as usual. However, Mr. Avrahami appealed on June 13.

Finally, what about identity cards? Given the concern with illegal immigration in the US there has been a renewed interest in identity cards. Americans have traditionally been repelled by the image of European police requiring individuals to produce their papers, but the attractiveness of a single, multipurpose number is being advocated again. In Europe, there has also been a movement towards the introduction of smart identity cards, presumably to be used to identify illegal residents. This issue is likely to be debated for the foreseeable future.

SUMMARY

The impact of computers on privacy is one of the major concerns voiced by the public at large. Although most people agree that computers have improved the quality of life, there is a definite apprehension that some form of an Orwellian 1984 society is not far off. Privacy is an important but difficult right to maintain when so much information about individuals is gathered and stored by both public and private agencies. Personal data must be safeguarded and used only for the purpose for which it was originally collected.

One of the fears of legitimate groups is that databases built up by government surveillance will be used to harass lawful activities. The increasing use of computer matching is of concern to civil libertarians, because the searching of computer records in order to turn up possible violations seems to be an action contrary to the presumption of innocence. Credit bureaus play a major role in the marketing of information. Because credit ratings are so important in almost every aspect of life, it is necessary to guarantee that such data is as accurate as possible and that individuals be informed as to its use.

In response to public concern, a number of Acts have been passed by the federal government to deal with the most serious violations. The European approach in the private sector is to establish government agencies to license and regulate companies that operate databases. The Internet provides new challenges to personal privacy as increasing numbers of users carry out commercial transactions. The much-discussed Information Highway will also gather enormous quantities of information about individuals. In contrast with the European approach, there seems to little willingness in the US to have government pass legislation to protect personal privacy.

Freedom of information occasionally conflicts with privacy rights, but balances must be struck to ensure that the public is able to obtain information about the actions of government.

NOTES

1. Jill Smolowe. "My Boss, Big Brother," *Time,* January 22, 1996, p. 38.
2. Accessed from the Web site with URL: <http:www.doccusearch.com/index.html> on March 28, 1996.
3. Denise Caruso. "Digital Commerce: As Privacy Grows Scarcer on the Internet, People Finally Start to Take Notice," *The New York Times,* June 3, 1996, p. C 5.
4. Kim Bolan. "Police Computer Used to Track Pro-Choicers, Report Alleges," *The Vancouver Sun,* January 5, 1995, p. A 1.
5. "Metromail—The Selling of Information on Kids," Klasskids Home Page, February 24, 1996. Accessed from the Web page with URL: <http://www.klaaskids.inter.net/pg-back.htm> on June 17, 1996.
6. Laurie J. Flynn. "Information Company Discontinues On-Line Access to Social Security Numbers," *The New York Times,* June 14, 1996, p. A 16.
7. Louis Harris and Associates and Dr. Alan F. Westin. *The Dimensions of Privacy: A National Opinion Research Survey of Attitudes Toward Privacy.* (for Sentry Insurance, New York: Garland Publishing, 1981). The poll was conducted between November 30 and December 10, 1978 and between November 27, 1978 and January 4, 1979.
   Louis Harris and Associates. *The Road after 1984: The Impact of Technology on Society.* (for Southern New England Telephone, December 1983). The poll was conducted between September 1 and September 11 and between September 7 and September 23, 1983.
   Louis Harris & Associates and Dr. Alan F. Westin. *The Equifax Report on Consumers in the Information Age.* (for Equifax Inc., 1990). This poll was conducted between January 11 and February 11 and between April 20 and April 30, 1990.
   Louis Harris & Associates and Dr. Alan F. Westin. *Harris-Equifax Consumer Privacy Survey 1991.* (for Equifax Inc., 1991). This poll was conducted between January 1 and July 8, 1991.
   Louis Harris & Associates and Dr. Alan F. Westin. *Harris-Equifax Consumer Privacy Survey 1992.* (for Equifax Inc., 1992, 1991). This poll was conducted between June 9 and June 18, 1992.
   Louis Harris & Associates and Dr. Alan F. Westin. *Harris-Equifax Health Information Privacy Survey 1993.* (for Equifax Inc., 1993). This poll was conducted between July 26 and August 26, 1993.
   Louis Harris & Associates and Dr. Alan F. Westin. *Equifax-Harris Consumer Privacy Survey 1994.* (for Equifax Inc., 1994). This poll was conducted between August 17 and September 4, 1994.
   Louis Harris & Associates and Dr. Alan F. Westin. *Equifax-Harris Mid-Decade Consumer Privacy Survey 1995.* (for Equifax Inc., 1995). This poll was conducted between July 5 and July 17, 1995.
8. *Ibid.* (Equifax 1990), pp. 69–70.
9. Alan F. Westin. *Privacy and Freedom.* (New York: Atheneum Publishers, 1967), p. 7.
10. Kent Greenwalt. "Privacy and Its Legal Protections," *Hastings Center Studies,* September 1974, p. 45.
11. Privacy and Computers. Department of Communications/Department of Justice, Canada. (Ottawa: Information Canada, 1972), p. 13.
12. *Records, Computers, and the Rights of Citizens.* US Dept. of Health, Report to the Secretary's Advisory Committee on Automated Personal Data Systems. (Washington, DC, 1973), pp. 40–41.
13. *Ibid.,* p. 41.

14. *Personal Privacy in an Information Society*. Report of the Privacy Protection Study Commission. (Washington, DC, 1977), pp. 14–15.

15. Richard D. Kusserow. "The Government Needs Computer Matching to Root Out Waste and Fraud," *Communications of the ACM,* **27** (6), June 1984, p. 543.

16. *Privacy Act: Federal Agencies' Implementation Can Be Improved.* United States General Accounting Office, GAO/GGD-86-107. (Washington, DC, August 1986), p. 47.

17. *Ibid.,* p. 49.

18. "Management of Federal Information Resources," Circular No. A-130, revised. Office of the Management of the Budget, Whitehouse, February 8, 1996. Accessed from the Web page with URL: <http://www1.whitehouse.gov/WH/EOP/OMB/html/circulars/a130/a130.html> on June 25, 1996.

19. "Computer Matching Program; Notice." Department of Education, April 17, 1996. Accessed from the Web page with URL: <http://www.ici.coled.umn.edu/register/education/4-29-96ed/ed1.htm> on July 20, 1996.

20. Written statement of J. C. Penney Company, Inc. to the Privacy Protection Study Commission, February 12, 1976, as quoted in *Personal Privacy in an Information Society,* p. 43.

21. "Resolved: Credit/Privacy Laws Need to Be Revised," *At Home With Consumers,* **10** (3), December 1989, pp. 2, 4. Published by the Direct Selling Education Foundation.

22. Bruce Horovitz. "Marketers Tap Data We Once Called Our Own," *USA Today,* Dec. 19, 1995, pp. 1A–2A, 4B.

23. Fair Credit Reporting Act, 602. FINDINGS AND PURPOSE, Public Law 91-508, as amended, November 6, 1978. Available at the Web page with URL: <http://www.nvi.net/search/fcra.html>.

24. *Op. cit., Records, Computers, and the Rights of Citizens,* pp. 66–69.

25. As quoted in Warren Freedman. *The Right of Privacy in the Computer Age.* (New York: Quorum Books, 1987), p. 14.

26. Richard F. Hixson. *Privacy in a Public Society: Human Rights in Conflict.* (New York: Oxford University Press, 1987), p. 220.

27. Jeffrey Rothfeder, Stephen Philips, Dean Foust, Wanda Cantrell, Paula Dwyer, and Michael Galen. "Is Nothing Private?" *Business Week,* September 4, 1989, p. 74.

28. Linda Himmelstein. "Attack of the Cyber Snoopers," *Business Week,* June 1994, pp. 134, 136, 138.

29. "Survey Shows Growing Concern Over Privacy Issue." *Direct Marketing Technology,* October 20, 1995. Accessed from the Web page with URL: <http://www.mediacentral.com/Magazines/Direct/Archive/10209501.htm> on July 23, 1996.

30. "Consumers Nervous About Privacy: DIRECT poll," *Direct Newsline,* June 17, 1996. Accessed from the Web page with URL: <http://www.mediacentral.com/Magazines/Direct-Newsline/OldArchives/199606/1996061701.html> on July 23, 1996.

31. David H. Flaherty. Protecting Privacy in Two-Way Electronic Services. (White Plains, NY: Knowledge Industry Publications, Inc., 1985), p. 102.

32. Section s.2(b) of the Privacy Act of 1974, 5 U.S.C., s.552a, passed as part of Pub. L. 93-579.

33. *Op. cit., Personal Privacy in an Information Society,* p. xv.

34. *Ibid.,* p. 413.

35. *Op. cit.,* Freedman. *The Right of Privacy in the Computer Age* (1987), p. 15.

36. *Managing Federal Information Resources.* Seventh Annual Report Under the Paperwork Reduction Act of 1980, Office of the Management of the Budget. (Washington, DC, 1989), pp. 35–36.

37. David H. Flaherty. *Protecting Privacy in Surveillance Societies: The Federal Republic of Germany, Sweden, France, Canada, and the United States.* (Chapel Hill, NC: The University of North Carolina Press, 1989), pp. 357–358.

38. *Ibid.*

39. Russell S. Burnside. "The Electronic Communications Privacy Act of 1986: The Challenge of Applying Ambiguous Statutory Languages to Intricate Telecommunication Technologies," *Rutgers Computer & Technology Law Journal,* **13** (2), 1987, p. 508.

40. *Ibid.,* p. 512.

41. "Federal Bureau of Investigation (FBI) Implementation of the Communications Assistance for Law Enforcement Act," Federal Register, Vol. 60, No. 36, February 23, 1995. Accessed from the Web page with URL: <http://cpsr.org/cpsr/privacy/epic/wiretap/fed_reg_notice.txt> on July 24, 1996.

42. "Oppose the FBI National Wiretap Plan!" Electronic Privacy Information Center (EPIC), February 14, 1996. Accessed from the Web page with URL: <http://www.epic.org/privacy/wiretap/oppose_wiretap.html> on July 24, 1996.

43. Carol Hildebrand. "Thailand's Database Aimed at Social Needs," *Computerworld,* July 30, 1990, p.14.

44. *Privacy and the National Information Infrastructure: Principles for Providing and Using Personal Information, Final Version.* Privacy Working Group, Information Policy Committee, Information Infrastructure Task Force, June 6, 1995. Accessed from the Web page with URL: <http://ntiaunix1.ntia.doc.gov:70/0/papers/documents/niiprivprin_final.txt> on October 23, 1995.

45. *The National Information Infrastructure Progress Report, September 1993–1994.* Information Infrastructure task Force, September 1994. Available on NII Virtual Library WWW site with URL: <http://iitf/doc.gov>.

46. *Information Security and Privacy in Network Environments.* US Congress, Office of Technology Assessment. (Washington, DC: US Government Printing Office, September 1994). Available on the Web page with URL: <http://www.ota.nap.edu/pdf/data/1994/9416.PDF>. *Issue Update on Information Security and Privacy in Network Environments.* US Congress, Office of Technology Assessment. (Washington, DC: US Government Printing Office, June 1995). Available on the Web page with URL: <http://www.ota.nap.edu/pdf/data/1995/9528. PDF>.

47. *Privacy and the National Information Infrastructure: Principles for Providing and Using Personal Information.* Information Infrastructure Task Force Working Group on Privacy, January 19, 1995. Available on the IITF Web site with URL: <http://iitf.doc.gov>.

48. *Privacy and the NII: Safeguarding Telecommunications-Related Personal Information.* NTIA, Office of Policy Analysis and Development, Washington, DC, October 1995. Available at the Web page with URL: <gopher://www.ntia.doc.gov:70/HO/policy/privwhitepaper.html>.

49. *Op. cit., Issue Update on Information Security and Privacy in Networked Environments,* p. 71.

50. *Op. cit., Privacy and the National Information Infrastructure: Principles for Providing and Using Personal Information.*

51. "Directive 95 on the Protection of Individuals with Regard to the Processing of Personal Data and on the Free Movement of Such Data." The European Parliament and the Council of Europe, June 15, 1995. Accessed from the Web page with URL: <http://www2.echo.lu/legal/en/dataprot/directiv/directiv.html> on May 15, 1996. An addendum to the Directive, referred to as the Recitals is available at the same Web page, except for the last part, <. . ./recitals.html>.

52. "Memorandum for Heads of Departments and Agencies, Subject: The Freedom of Information Act." The White House, Office of the Press Secretary, October 4, 1993. Accessed from the Web page with URL: <http://cpsr.org/cpsr/foia/white_house_foia_policy.txt> on July 25, 1996.

53. *Public Government for Private People, Volume 2.* The Report of the Commission on Freedom and Individual Privacy, Province of Ontario, Canada (Toronto, 1980), pp. 455–457.

54. *Ibid.,* p. 114.

55. As quoted in John Markoff. "Freedom of Information Act Facing a Stiff Challenge in Computer Age," *The New York Times,* June 18, 1989, p. Y 13.

56. *Ibid.*

57. "Data Protection on the Internet: Report and Guidance, Budapest Draft." International Working Group on Data Protection in Telecommunications, May 21, 1996. Accessed from the Web page with URL: <http://www.datenschutz-berlin.de/diskus/budaen.htm> on June 26, 1996.

58. Joseph Rhodes, Jr., is a Commissioner on the Pennsylvania Public Utilities Commission. His arguments (reprinted from *Privacy Journal,* Providence, RI, March 1990, pp. 4–5) are taken from a dissenting statement to the Commission, which approved the proposal by Bell Telephone of Pennsylvania to offer Caller ID services. This approval was challenged in the courts and in May 1990, the courts rejected Caller ID as a form of illegal wiretapping.

59. Peter Coy. "Why All the Heavy Breathing Over Caller ID," *Business Week,* June 18, 1990, p. 34.

60. Beth Givens. "Caller ID: The Case for Consumer Education," Privacy Rights Clearinghouse, University of San Diego, Center for Public Interest Law, June 18, 1996. Accessed from the Web page with URL: <http://www.acusd.edu/~prc/ar/callerid.html> on June 29, 1996.

61. David Banisar. "Big Brother Goes High-Tech," *Covert Action Quarterly,* Spring 1996. Accessed from the Web page with URL: <http://www.worldmedia.com/caq/articles/brother.html> on June 19, 1996.

62. Jim Nash and Maureen J. Harrington. "Who Can Open E-mail?" *Computerworld,* January 14, 1991, pp. 1, 88.

63. "Michael A. Smyth v. The Pillsbury Company," C.A. No. 95-5712, United States District Court for the Eastern District of Pennsylvania, January 18, 1996. Accessed from the Web page with URL: <http://www.epic.org/privacy/internet/smyth_v_pillsbury.html> on March 14, 1996.

64. *Ibid.*

65. "Who's Watching You and What Are You Telling Them?" Center for Democracy and Technology. Accessed from the Web page with URL: <http://www.13x.com/cgi-bin/cdt/snoop.pl> on June 1, 1996.

66. "Netscape's Cookies Crumble," *Australian Personal Computer Online—News,* April 1996. Accessed from the Web page with URL: <http://www.com.au/apc/9604/thenet/onnews.html> on May 13, 1996.

67. James Staten, "Netscape Tricks Raise Security Concerns," *MacWeek,* March 13, 1996. Accessed from the Web page with URL: <http://www.zdnet.com/macweek/mw_1011/gw_net_tricks.html> on May 13, 1996.

68. *Ibid.*

69. Taken from "Threats to Medical Record Privacy." Electronic Privacy Information Center (EPIC), 1995. Accessed from the Web page with URL: <http://www.epic.org//privacy/medical/threats.html> on July 27, 1996.

70. "How Private Is My Medical Information," Privacy Rights Clearinghouse Fact Sheet #8, March 1993. Accessed from the Web page with URL: <http://www.vortex.com/privacy/prc.med-8.Z> on July 27, 1996.

71. "Statement of Opposition to S. 1360, the So-Called 'Medical Records Confidentiality Act of 1995,'" American Civil Liberties Union of Massachusetts, Boston, MA, November 4, 1995. Accessed from the Web page with URL: <http://www.epic.org/privacy/medical/aclum.txt> on July 27, 1996.

72. *Web of Deception: Threats to Children from Online Monitoring.* Center for Media Education, Washington, DC. No Date. Accessed from the Web page with URL: <http://www.igc.apc.org/cme/kidadsreport.html> on July 27, 1996.

73. "The Children's Privacy Protection And Parental Empowerment Act of 1996: Legislative Summary." Accessed from the Web page with URL: <http://www.epic.org/privacy/kids/CPP-PEA_summary.html> on July 27, 1996.

74. William O. Douglas. Address to the American Law Institute, 1953.

75. Kathleen Kiley. "U.S. News Wins Landmark Privacy Suit," *Catalog Age Weekly,* June 13, 1996. Accessed from the Web page with URL: <http://www.mediacentral.com/Magazines/CatalogAge/Weekly/1996061303.htm> on July 23, 1996.

ADDITIONAL READINGS

The Nature of Privacy

Berry, Jonathan. "Database Marketing," *Business Week,* cover story, September 5, 1994, pp. 56–62.

Besson, Jim. "Riding the Market Wave," *Harvard Business Review,* 71 (5), September–October, 1993, pp. 150–160.

Branscomb, Anne Wells. *Who Owns Information? From Privacy to Public Access.* (New York: Basic Books, 1993).

Burnham, David. *The Rise of the Computer State.* (New York: Random House, 1983).

Hays, Laurie. "Using Computers to Divine Who Might Buy a Gas Drill," *Wall Street Journal,* August 16, 1994, pp. B 1, B 4.

Sadofsky, David. *The Question of Privacy in Public Policy: An Analysis of the Reagan-Bush Era.* (Westport, CT: Praeger Publishers, 1993).

Privacy Legislation

Bennett, Colin. *Regulating Privacy: Data Protection and Public Policy in Europe and the United States.* (Ithaca, NY: Cornell University Press, 1992).

Electronic Surveillance in a Digital Age. US Congress, Office of Technology Assessment, OTA-BP-ITC-149. (Washington, DC: US Government Printing Office, July 1995). Available on the Web page with URL: <http://www.ota.nap.edu/pdf/data/1995/9513.PDF>.

Privacy: The Key Issues of the 90's. A Direct Marketer's Guide to Effective Self-Regulatory Action in the Use of Information. (Washington, DC: Direct Marketing Association, Inc., October 1993).

Rothfeder, Jeffrey. *Privacy for Sale: How Computerization Has Made Everyone's Private Life an Open Secret.* (New York: Simon & Schuster, 1992).

van Bakel, Rogier. "How Good People Helped Make a Bad Law," *Wired,* 4.02, February 1996, pp. 133–135, 181–186.

"Visions for Privacy in the 21st Century: A Search for Solutions." Conference organized by The Office of the Information and Privacy Commissioner of British Columbia and The University of Victoria, Victoria, BC, May 9–11, 1996.

Privacy Issues on the Internet and the IH

Baig, Edward. "How to Practice Safe Surfing," *Business Week,* September 9, 1996, pp. 120–121.

Blackman, Joshua D. "A Proposal for Federal Legislation Protecting Informational Privacy Across the Private Sector," *Santa Clara Computer and High Technology Law Journal,* 9 (2), November 1993, pp. 431–468.

Issues and Problems: Present and Future

"The Anonymizer FAQ." Accessed from the Web site with URL: <http://www.anonymizer.com/> on June 1, 1996.

Frook, John Evan. "IA Scoop: Netscape Embraces Cookie in Launch of Personal Workspace," *Interactive Age Daily Media and Marketing Report,* April 4, 1996. Accessed from the Web page with URL: <http://techweb.cmp.com/ia/marketapr96/2apr4.htm> on May 13, 1996.

"Letter to Representative Bob Franks regarding H.R. 3508." Center for Democracy and Technology, June 4, 1996. Accessed from the Web page with URL: <http://www.cdt.org/privacy/children/Franks_let.html> on July 27, 1996.

Markey (D-MA), Representative Edward J. "Electronic Privacy and Children's Privacy," statement before the Federal Trade Commission, June 5, 1996. Accessed from the Web page with URL: <http://www.cdt.org/privacy/children/960605_Markey_stmnt.html> on July 27, 1996.

"The Medical Records Privacy Protection Act: A Discussion Draft." Medical Privacy Coalition. March 11, 1996. Accessed from the Web page with URL: <http://www.epic.org/privacy/medical/mpc_bill.html> on May 15, 1996.

Privacy Protection Principles for Electronic Mail Systems. Toronto, Ontario: Information and Privacy Commissioner, February 1994.

Poole, Robert and Williams, Derek. "Success in the Surveillance Society," *Security Management,* May 1996. Accessed from the Web site with URL: <http://www.securitymanagement.com/library/000138.html> on May 18, 1996.

Smith, Robert Ellis. "The True Terror Is in the Card," *The New York Times Magazine,* September 8, 1996, pp. 58–59.

━━ 10 ━━

EMPLOYMENT AND UNEMPLOYMENT

Any kind of machinery used for shortening labour—except used in a cooperative society like ours—must tend to less wages, and to deprive working men of employment, and finally, either to starve them, force them into some other employment (and then reduce wages in that also), or compel them to emigrate. Now, if the working classes would socially and peacefully unite to adopt our system, no power or party could prevent their success.

Manifesto, Cooperative Community, Ralahine, County Clare, Ireland, 1883 (on the introduction of the reaping machine)

INTRODUCTION

The most serious and complex problem associated with the impact of computers on society has to do with work. The basic and almost simplistic expression of this concern is the question, does technological change, create, or destroy, jobs? In the present context, technological change refers to innovations in computer and communications technology. Definitive answers are scarce; by way of focusing the debate, the arguments may be stated briefly as follows. Yes, the introduction of new technology may reduce the number of jobs in the directly affected industry. On the other hand, it may actually increase the number, because increased productivity resulting from the new technology will increase demand, and more workers will be necessary to satisfy it. Even if there is a net loss of jobs in a specific industry, it is argued, new jobs will be created in support areas for the new technology, in whole new industries resulting from unpredictable technologies, and in the service and white collar areas. For example, the introduction of robots will create a robot support industry to install, service, and monitor performance, to say nothing of design and manufacture. Jobs are eliminated in those industries that benefit from robots, but are created in the robot support companies. The common term for this effect is *job displacement*. The question about technology and jobs can be restated in terms of the economy as a whole, to take job displacement into account.

Assuming that new jobs will be created, will there be a sufficient number to take up the slack? It is likely that in factories that manufacture robots, robots themselves will be a major factor in production. The technology associated with computers is qualitatively different from previous technologies. It brings not only ways to do things more efficiently, but also the possibility of doing many things with very few workers. The possibility that many of society's needs could be satisfied with a significantly reduced work force is of concern to many people.

What about the theory that an unending chain of inventions and discoveries will always be part of our future, creating new products and new jobs? In our time such inventions and processes as Xeroxing, Polaroid cameras, video cassette recorders, personal computers, and more recently Web pages have certainly created new industries and jobs in design, manufacturing, marketing, sales, and service. In the past 200 years, since the beginning of the Industrial Revolution in England, enough jobs have been created, it has been claimed, to accommodate growth in population, increased urbanization and reduction of farm labor, and a rapidly accelerating chain of inventions. These observations apply mainly to the industrialized countries, but increasingly to the rest of the world.

Prior to the Industrial Revolution, most of the population was engaged in agriculture. With advances in farming machinery, fertilizers, and disease-resistant and weather-conditioned crops, productivity on the farm has soared. Currently, in the United States about 3% of the work force produces enough food for the entire country, as well as enormous quantities for export. Where did all the farm workers go? Most of them became blue collar workers in the rapidly growing industrial plants. Recently, the percentage of the work force in blue collar jobs has been decreasing. Most American workers are now employed in service and white collar jobs—that is, they do not produce things but work with people, paper, and information.

The expectation now is that as society moves from an industrial to an information base, the major source of new jobs will be in the office; in service areas such as restaurants, hotels, and entertainment; in the financial domain; and in government. The model of the future has a much-reduced labor force in production and an expanded number of people in the service and information areas. A serious problem with this view is the increasing rate of automation in the office. The introduction of computers, office networks, telecommunication systems, and Fax machines has a major improvement in office productivity as a goal, but fewer jobs as a byproduct. Of these, fewer will be the kind of low-skill jobs that have traditionally served as an entry point for many hundreds of thousands of workers.

Another major concern is with the changing nature of work. The Industrial Revolution spawned a number of responses from workers whose livelihood was threatened by the use of machines. Probably the most well-known were the Luddites, who flourished in the beginning of the eighteenth century. They are best known for having smashed newly introduced machines—in supposed blind opposition to progress, according to the conventional view. However, the well-known British historian E. P. Thompson has argued that:[1]

> At issue was the "freedom" of the capitalist to destroy the customs of the trade, whether by new machinery, by the factory-system, or by unrestricted competition, beating down wages, undercutting his rivals, and undermining the standards of craftsmanship.

Since that time there has been an uneasy relationship between the worker and new technology. While welcoming the relief from drudgery and dangerous work that machines have provided, the worker has been concerned first with becoming merely an adjunct to the machine and then being replaced by it. In many cases the machines themselves were dangerous.

This fear has grown, especially in the factory, as work has become organized under such principles as scientific management (Frederick Taylor) and the assembly line (Henry Ford). The reduction of production to a series of small, repeatable actions encouraged a belief that workers were easily replaceable, that their skills could be extracted, and that they would perform boring, routine tasks efficiently for many years of working life. The computer can be seen merely as the most recent phase of technology or as a new force that gives management a powerful tool for extending its control, whether in factory or office. Computers and communications systems may reproduce the factory model in the office— at least this is the fear of many workers. The relatively open social system in the office may be replaced by a rigid, highly structured environment in which the performance of the worker at the terminal may be closely monitored.

Within a month of each other in 1994, two of the major US business magazines had very similar covers:

THE END OF THE JOB
No longer the best way to organize work, the traditional job is becoming a social artifact. Its decline creates unfamiliar risks—and opportunities.[2]

The Economy is Changing.
Jobs are Changing.
The Workforce is Changing. Is America Ready?
RETHINKING WORK[3]

As we approach the end of the twentieth century, there is a sense that work of the future will be organized quite differently than it is currently. "The job is a social artifact, though it is so deeply embedded in our consciousness that most of us have forgotten its artificiality or the fact that most societies since the beginning of time have done just fine without jobs."[4] Thus as they move towards the future, companies will put more emphasis on the work to be done and less on the individual job labels of the workers. Thus as jobs vanish, the role of managers will require redefinition or may even disappear. The idea is that workers will be very flexible, open to new experiences, eager to learn, and willing to take risks for themselves and the company and that the company will depend much less on individual workers and much more on constantly shifting contractual arrangements. The role of computer technology is crucial in this shift but how it is used is not predetermined; rather, it depends on a number of economic and social concerns of management.

EXPERIENCES OF WORKERS

What is good for General Motors is good for the country. (Charles Wilson, Secretary of Defense under President Eisenhower)

Computers will make their presence felt in several ways in both factory and office. Computers have been used to automate various decision-making processes so that workers who formerly monitored ongoing production now must watch video terminals to see what is happening. The most dramatic innovation in the factory is the introduction of robots into the assembly line. In both factory and office, there may be problems in integrating people and machines in an efficient, safe, and productive manner, especially if the goals of management do not include concern about anything but profits and immediate return on investment.

Workers Voice their Concerns

> The men and women who do the hard work of the world have learned from him [Ruskin] and Morris that they have a right to pleasure in their toil, and that when justice is done them they will have it. (William Dean Howells, *Criticism and Fiction,* 1891)

It is useful and important to characterize the nature of the workplace as seen through the eyes of the workers themselves. The opinions of satisfied or indifferent workers, probably a majority, are sometimes neglected in favor of the angry or frustrated ones. Our interest is in real and potential problems, difficulties, and alienation, but how representative these angry voices are is a real question. It is also true that in times when unemployment rates are high, workers are less likely to complain openly.

What aspects of work are likely to be most affected by computers? In the words of a spot welder, in the early 1970s, in an automobile assembly plant,[5]

> I don't understand how come more guys don't flip. Because you're nothing more than a machine when you hit this type of thing. They give better care to that machine than they will to you. They'll have more respect, give more attention to that machine. And you know this. Somehow you get the feeling that the machine is better than you are. (Laughs.)

The theme of the machine receiving preferred treatment is likely to become more common. The machine referred to is in fact part of traditional assembly line equipment, which differs significantly from a new generation of equipment. Robots are a form of flexible automation that can be programmed to perform a variety of tasks. The relationship of the worker to such new machines will be different. Will workers perceive themselves as mere caretakers, or as surviving only until the next generation of even more sophisticated machines? Their concern derives from a real awareness of their place in the production process.[6]

> You really begin to wonder. What price do they put on me? Look at the price they put on the machine. If that machine breaks down, there's somebody out there to fix it right away. If I break down, I'm just pushed over to the other side till another man takes my place. The only thing they have on their mind is to keep that line running.

There is nothing unique about the American experience in this regard, of course. Witness the following account describing work in a Japanese automobile factory:[7]

> I have really been fooled by the seeming slowness of the conveyor belt. No one can understand how it works without experiencing it. Almost as soon as I begin, I am dripping with

sweat. Somehow, I learn the order of the work motions, but I'm totally unable to keep up with the speed of the line. My work gloves make it difficult to grab as many tiny bolts as I need, and how many precious seconds do I waste doing just that? . . . If a different-model transmission comes along, it's simply beyond my capacity. Some skill is needed, and a new hand like me can't do it alone, I'm thirsty as hell, but workers can neither smoke nor drink water. Going to the toilet is out of the question. Who could have invented a system like this? It's designed to make workers do nothing but work and to prevent any kind of rest.

One of the issues that is of increasing concern to many workers is job security. There is an increasing trend towards what has come to be called downsizing, the reduction of the workforce to reduce labor costs by taking advantage of technological innovations. Part of the process may be different contractual arrangements with workers. For example, consider the following remarks of an employee "laid off from her job as a bankruptcy collection agent, then taken on again as a contractor":[8]

I'm grateful to have work, and I'm happy with what I'm doing. I do a good job for them because I feel an obligation as a contractor. But I don't feel loyalty, not the old fashioned sense of loyalty we used to have. It's the realization that it's just not going to be the same ever again.

Some Historical Issues

The history of technological innovation and its effect on the workplace is complex. To begin with, it is almost impossible to discuss the history of work without assuming a particular political viewpoint. In its starkest form, the capitalist or free enterprise position argues that the constant pressure to increase productivity to meet competition results in increased investment in capital equipment. The worker is gradually relieved of a dangerous environment, decision-making responsibility, and the power to disrupt the productive process. From a Marxist point of view, the basic goals of capitalist management are simply to extract skills from workers and to achieve sufficient return on investment by reducing the cost of labor. Management also wants complete control over its workers—to use them as it wishes, independently of their needs and desires as human beings. Free enterprise spokesmen point out that industrialization has permitted workers to improve substantially their standard of living. Marxists argue that the price has been high—loss of autonomy, loss of skills, and loss of respect. Technological optimists predict that the age of computers will accelerate benefits, with more and cheaper goods available, less work necessary to maintain income levels (not in the cards for the foreseeable future, however), and improved living conditions for the Third World. A closer examination of the industrialization process reveals a rather disturbing long-term trend: Workers have been losing control, initiative, and skills.

An important examination of this process was carried out by Harry Braverman. Written from a Marxist point of view, his book has been recognized even by non-Marxist economists and sociologists as a valuable contribution to the history of labor studies.[9] In his view, the most important implication of the Industrial Revolution for the worker was loss of control. In the evolution of the craftsman working on his or her own to the worker on the factory floor, the distinguishing feature is loss of control—over pace of work, the individual steps, and the quality of the product. From this loss—this sale of one's labor—many consequences follow. The worker and the work process have been endlessly studied to improve efficiency, reduce costs, and (in Marxist terms) squeeze out the last drop of surplus labor.

Scientific Management

As enterprises grew larger the problems of organization became paramount. Near the end of the nineteenth century serious attempts were made to apply new techniques to the management of large and varied companies. Initiated by Frederick Winslow Taylor, this principled effort was called scientific management.[10] He bluntly stated that it was management's sole responsibility and duty to control every facet of labor's activity. Although previous thought and practice had recognized this domination, Taylor set out to demonstrate in painstaking detail how management could translate its power into the closely controlled supervision of the labor process. He based all his subsequent research on the notion of "a fair day's work"—apparently, the maximum amount of work a worker could do on a regular basis throughout his lifetime without damaging his health. In the eyes of management, when workers slow their pace, loaf, or talk, they fail to fulfill their potential, and here scientific management comes into play. The worker attempts to conceal from management how fast the work can actually be done; so management is paying a salary that does not correlate with the realities of the situation. Supervision and discipline that are vague and general will not be adequate as long as the workers themselves control the labor process. From first-hand experience, and a series of experiments that took 26 years, Taylor derived a precise formulation by which workers could carefully be instructed in each movement of their prescribed tasks.

Taylor's contributions can be summed up in terms of three principles, as follows:[11]

1. Dissociation of the labor process from the skills of the workers. Management should organize the labor process independently of the workers' knowledge and craft.
2. Separation of conception from execution. Basically, the task of the worker is to perform a series of prescribed actions that do not involve planning or decision making. The worker must not introduce his or her ideas into the labor process because this compromises management's control.
3. The use of the monopoly over knowledge to control each step of the labor process and its mode of execution.

The implementation of these principles involves the systematic planning of each production step and the careful instruction of workers in its proper execution. Scientific management and its successor theories became a dominant force in the growth of large industrial enterprises.

The Modern Assembly Line

At the turn of the century, the production of automobiles was essentially a craft. Individual mechanics would move around a stationary work site until the assembly of the automobile was complete. After Henry Ford introduced the Model T in 1908, the demand was so enormous that new production techniques were needed. In 1914, the first continuous assembly line was introduced at his Highland Park plant near Detroit. The improvements in productivity were astounding. Within three months an automobile could be assembled in about one-tenth the time, and "by 1925 an organization had been created which produced almost as many cars in a single day as had been produced, early in the history of the Model T, in an entire year."[12] The pay structure was flattened, and bonuses and incentives were done away with. They were no longer necessary to stimulate productivity, because the combination of the division of labor and the moving assembly line meant that management could precisely control the rate of production. The assembly line principle quickly spread to other industries and served as a foundation for industrial growth.

Worker reaction was decisive and negative: they left in large numbers as other work was available. In 1913, the turnover rate was 380% and a major unionization drive began. In response Ford increased pay to $5.00 per day, considerably above the going rate. This measure stemmed the flow of workers and introduced another feature to the industrial scene—the use of higher wages to limit possible disruptions. This strategy has also been one of the responses appropriated by labor unions as they confront potential and actual loss of jobs resulting from the introduction of computers.

COMPUTERS AND EMPLOYMENT

> They talk of the dignity of work. Bosh. The dignity is in leisure. (Herman Melville, *Redburn*)

Before examining computers and employment, it is useful to consider the broader perspective of technology in general.

Technology and Employment

> When large numbers of men are unable to find work, unemployment results. (Calvin Coolidge)

In a study by the National Academies of Sciences and Engineering and the Institute of Medicine on technology and employment in the US, published in 1987 but still very timely, the following principal finding was given:[13]

> Technological change is an essential component of a dynamic, expanding economy. The modern US economic system, in which international trade plays an increasingly important role, must generate and adopt advanced technologies rapidly, in both the manufacturing and nonmanufacturing sectors, if growth in employment and wages is to be maintained. Recent and prospective levels of technological change will not produce significant increases in total unemployment, although individuals will face painful and costly adjustments. Rather than producing mass unemployment, technological change will make its maximum contribution to higher living standards, wages, and employment levels if appropriate public and private policies are adopted to support the adjustment to new technologies.

In this carefully worded statement, the obvious is juxtaposed with the speculative. Yes, technology is important, no significant levels of unemployment will result, but "individuals" beware, and all will be fine if government and business cooperate. In the mid-1990s, this endorsement would likely ring hollow in the ears of the many employees "dehired" by several very profitable, high-tech companies.

As part of a comprehensive analysis on the relationship between technology and structural unemployment, the Office of Technology Assessment (OTA) of the US Congress was concerned with the problems of reemploying workers displaced by technology.[14] Clearly, changes in technology can be disruptive, making some jobs obsolete and reducing opportunities for others. But perhaps a definition of technology itself would be helpful. It certainly includes tools, devices, machines, and all manner of equipment, but it also includes a body of knowledge incorporated in processes, skills, routines, and organization of work and social groupings. This latter component is frequently overlooked when the impact of new hardware is evaluated. It is also important to understand the dependent concept of productivity. There are several definitions but labor productivity is typically defined as the goods or services produced per employee-hour. This measure depends crucially on capital investment in technology to reduce the labor component and thereby to increase labor productivity. That is, with more equipment or improved processes, fewer people may be needed to produce the same or greater amounts of products or services. One striking example may suffice: in 1950, some 244,000 operators were required to handle over 175 million long-distance calls; in 1980, about 128,000 operators handled over 2.64 billion calls, an increase in productivity of almost 60-fold. Of course such a dramatic increase was possible only with improved switching equipment, which resulted in a steep increase in the number of direct long-distance dialings. So in fact operators are probably not handling many more calls themselves, an observation that points out the weakness of the definition of labor productivity.

In any case, as OTA points out, labor productivity is only one factor in overall productivity and efficiency. Others include "good labor management relations, well-trained employees, improved design so that products can be made more easily and perform better, and higher quality in the sense of meeting design specifications more closely."[15] If the relationship between technology and productivity is complicated then the relationship between productivity and employment is equally complicated. In addition to technology, employment depends on international trade, domestic competition, changes in consumer preference, international relations, inflation, fiscal policy, and a host of other factors. Nevertheless, technology is a major factor and a country cannot hope to be competitive without employing advanced technology in its manufacturing and service industries. It is possible to see the impact of technology on the long-term shifts in the distribution of jobs by major occupational groups. For example, farm labor, which constituted over 70% of the labor force in 1820, was reduced to less than 50% by 1880, less than 40% by 1900, and is currently running at less than 3%, because of mechanization, fertilizers, and new crop varieties. Table 10.1 shows these changes for the major occupational groups.

The number of production workers has also declined, though not as sharply since the Second World War. Operatives, most of whom are semiskilled manufacturing workers, reached a peak of 20.4% in 1950 and then decreased to 14.2 % in 1980. Furthermore the proportion of production workers within manufacturing has decreased substantially; in

TABLE 10.1

PERCENTAGES OF TOTAL US EMPLOYMENT ACCOUNTED FOR BY MAJOR OCCUPATIONAL GROUPS, FROM 1900 TO 1980.

Occupational Group	1900	1920	1940	1960	1980
Professional and technical services	4.3	5.4	7.5	10.8	16.1
Managers and administrators	5.8	6.6	7.3	8.1	11.2
Salesworkers	4.5	4.9	6.7	7.1	6.3
Clerical workers	3.0	8.0	9.6	14.1	18.6
Craft and kindred workers	10.5	13.0	12.0	13.6	12.9
Operatives	12.8	15.6	18.4	18.9	14.2
Nonfarm laborers	12.5	11.6	9.4	5.2	4.6
Service workers	9.0	7.8	11.7	11.2	13.3
Farmworkers	37.5	27.0	17.4	6.0	2.8

Source: Technology and Structural Unemployment: Reemploying Displaced Adults. US Congress, Office of Technology Assessment, OTA-ITE-250. (Washington, DC, 1986), p. 331.

absolute terms, between 1979 and 1985, 1.7 million manufacturing jobs were lost. This decline will continue as fewer and fewer workers together with increasingly sophisticated technology and organizational structures produce all the goods required. The increase in clerical workers and professional and technical workers should also be noted as this increase still continues.

Future Jobs

Given the previous discussion, can anything be said about what the jobs of the future will be? One important question is whether or not high technology will be a major contributing factor to job growth. The Bureau of Labor Statistics, of the Department of Labor, regularly issues job projections, based on a sophisticated model. Tables 10.2 and 10.3 show the fastest growing occupations, in terms of percentage growth, between 1988 and 2000 and between 1994 and 2005, respectively, based on the moderate alternative projection. Some observations from these projections follow; for fastest growing occupations:

- For the 1988–2000 projection more than one-half of the 17 fastest growing jobs are health service occupations, reflecting an aging population with in-home and technological needs.
- Notice that the 1994–2005 projection, not surprisingly, includes 15 out of the 20 categories in the health and human services occupations.
- There is a rapid growth for occupations related to computer technology for both projections. The 1994–2004 projection includes systems analysts, computer engineers, and electronic pagination systems workers in the top ten.
- Most of the growth areas in the 1988–2000 projections were in service jobs: paralegals, securities and financial services, travel agents, etc.

TABLE 10.2

FASTEST GROWING OCCUPATIONS, 1988–2000, MODERATE ALTERNATIVE PROJECTION.
(NUMBERS IN THOUSANDS)

Occupation	Employment 1988	Employment 2000	1988–2000 Numerical Change	1988–2000 Percent Change
Paralegals	83	145	62	75.3
Medical assistants	149	253	104	70.0
Home health aides	236	397	160	67.9
Radiologic technologists and technicians	132	218	87	66.0
Data processing equipment repairers	71	115	44	61.2
Medical records technicians	47	75	28	59.9
Medical secretaries	207	327	120	58.0
Physical therapists	68	107	39	57.0
Surgical technologists	35	55	20	56.4
Operations research analysts	55	85	30	55.4
Securities and financial services sales workers	200	309	109	54.8
Travel agents	142	219	77	54.1
Computer systems analysts	403	617	214	53.3
Physical and corrective therapy assistants	39	60	21	52.5
Social welfare service aides	91	138	47	51.5
Occupational therapists	33	48	16	48.8
Computer programmers	519	769	250	48.1

Source: Monthly Labor Review. US Department of Labor, Bureau of Labor Statistics, November 1989, p. 60.

Tables 10.4 and 10.5 show those occupations with the largest job growth in terms of absolute numbers, respectively. Both represent the moderate alternative projection. Some observations from these projections follow; for largest job growth:

1988–2000 projection (Table 10.4)

- Retail growth—salespersons, retail will have the largest growth.
- Food-related jobs are among the fastest growing—waiters and waitresses, food counter, fountain and related, and food preparation.
- Health services are also growing very fast—registered nurses, nursing aides, orderlies, and attendants.

1994–2005 projection (Table 10.5)

- Service areas—cashiers, waiters, nurses, guards, teachers, teacher aides, receptionists, child care, workers etc. will predominate in job growth.
- Health service areas will also contribute in a major way to job growth.
- Only systems analysts in the high-tech area is among the top twenty!

TABLE 10.3

THE 10 FASTEST GROWING OCCUPATIONS, 1994–2005, MODERATE ALTERNATIVE PROJECTION.
(NUMBERS IN THOUSANDS)

Occupation	Employment		1994–2005	
	1994	2005	Numerical Change	Percent Change
Personal and home care aides	179	391	212	119
Home health aides	420	848	428	102
Systems analysts	483	928	445	92
Computer engineers	195	372	177	90
Physical and corrective therapy assistants and aides	78	142	64	83
Electronic pagination systems workers	18	33	15	83
Occupational therapy assistants and aides	16	29	13	82
Physical therapists	102	183	81	80
Residential counselors	165	290	126	76
Human services workers	168	293	125	75
Occupational therapists	54	3	39	72
Manicurists	38	64	26	69
Medical assistants	206	327	121	59
Paralegals	110	175	64	58
Medical record technicians	81	126	45	56
Special education teachers	388	593	206	53
Amusement and recreation attendants	267	406	139	52
Correctional officers	310	468	158	51
Operations research analysts	44	67	22	50
Guards	867	1,282	415	48

Source: "BLS Releases New 1994–2005 Employment Projections," Bureau of Labor Statistics, November, 1995. Accessed from the Web page with URL: <http://stats.bls.gov/emptab01.htm> on August 12, 1996.

From the point of view of high technology's contribution to employment, Tables 10.4 and 10.5 show that most of the new jobs in the next 12 years will definitely be traditional, low-skilled, service jobs: salespersons, janitors and cleaners, waiters and waitresses, general office clerks, secretaries, nurses aides and orderlies, home health aides, truck drivers, receptionists, cashiers, guards, and food counter and food preparation. Computer programmers and computer systems analysts are also included, but both make rather small contributions compared to the other occupation groups. Among the fastest growing occupations are paralegals, medical assistants, home health aides, medical records technicians, medical secretaries, and travel agents, again not exactly technology-rich jobs. As part of these projections, the Bureau of Labor Statistics estimates that manufacturing is expected to continue decreasing in its percentage of the work force, from 26.4 in 1988 to 24 in 2000. Note these figures are somewhat inflated because they include laborers as well. The

TABLE 10.4

Occupations with the Largest Job Growth, 1988–2000, Moderate Alternative Projection.
(numbers in thousands)

| | Employment | | 1988–2000 | |
Occupation	1988	2000	Numerical Change	Percent Change
Salesperson, retail	3,834	4,564	730	19.0
Registered nurses	1,577	2,190	613	38.8
Janitors and cleaners, including maids and housekeeping cleaners	2,895	3,450	556	19.2
Waiters and waitresses	1,786	2,337	551	30.9
General managers and top executives	3,030	3,509	479	15.8
General office clerks	2,519	2,974	455	18.1
Secretaries, except legal and medical	2,903	3,288	385	13.2
Nursing aides, orderlies, and attendants	1,184	1,562	378	31.9
Truck drivers, light and heavy	2,399	2,768	369	15.4
Receptionists and information clerks	833	1,164	331	39.8
Cashiers	2,310	2,614	304	13.2
Guards	795	1,050	256	32.2
Computer programmers	519	769	250	48.1
Food counter, fountain, and related	1,626	1,866	240	14.7
Food preparation workers	1,027	1,260	234	22.8
Licensed practical nurses	626	855	229	36.6

Source: *Monthly Labor Review*. US Department of Labor, Bureau of Labor Statistics, November 1989, p. 60.

1994–2005 projection also includes a decreasing representation for manufacturing:[16] "Manufacturing's share of total jobs is expected to decline, as a decrease of 1.3 million manufacturing jobs is projected. Manufacturing is expected to maintain its share of total output, as productivity in this sector is projected to increase. Accounting for one of every seven jobs in 1994, manufacturing is expected to account for just less than one of every eight jobs in 2005."

Clearly, the manufacturing sector will not provide the majority of new jobs in the economy and has not done so for some time. As shown, although high technology industries are growing very fast, they will not provide many new jobs in comparison to the more mundane areas. Three reasons are: the high technology sector is relatively small, its productivity is growing faster than many other manufacturing sectors, and many jobs created by US companies are actually off-shore, in the Far East, typically. The products of high technology—computers, microprocessors, communication equipment, robots and advanced manufacturing equipment, software, and computer peripherals—will improve productivity in application areas and so will have a deleterious effect on other manufacturing employment. The recession of the early 1980s resulted in the loss of some three million manufacturing jobs. Most of these will never be replaced.

TABLE 10.5

THE 10 OCCUPATIONS WITH THE LARGEST JOB GROWTH, 1994–2005,
MODERATE ALTERNATIVE PROJECTION.
(NUMBERS IN THOUSANDS)

Occupation	Employment		1994–2005	
	1994	2005	Numerical Change	Percent Change
Cashiers	3,005	3,567	562	19
Janitors and cleaners, including maids and housekeeping cleaners	3,043	3,602	559	18
Salespersons, retail	3,842	4,374	532	14
Waiters and waitresses	1,847	2,326	479	26
Registered nurses	1,906	2,379	473	25
General managers and top executives	3,046	3,512	466	15
Systems analysts	483	928	445	92
Home health aides	420	848	428	102
Guards	867	1,282	415	48
Nursing aides, orderlies, and attendants	1,265	1,652	387	31
School teachers, secondary	1,340	1,726	386	29
Marketing and sales worker supervisors	2,293	2,673	380	17
Teacher aides and educational associates	932	1,296	364	39
Receptionists and information clerks	1,019	1,337	318	31
Truckdrivers, light and heavy	2,565	2,837	271	11
Secretaries, except legal and medical	2,842	3,109	267	9
Clerical supervisors and managers	1,340	1,600	261	19
Child care workers	757	1,005	248	33
Maintenance repairers, general utility	1,273	1,505	231	18
Teachers, elementary	1,419	1,639	220	16

Source: "BLS Releases New 1994–2005 Employment Projections," Bureau of Labor Statistics, November, 1995. Accessed from the Web page with URL: <http://stats.bls.gov/emptab02.htm> on August 12, 1996.

As mentioned in the previous paragraph, in the early 1980s, recessions led to large-scale job losses, especially in manufacturing. Displaced workers were defined as those, who through no fault of their own, lost their jobs as well as their investment in training. However, in the last few years the focus has shifted from manufacturing workers to "the firing of middle managers, financial industry employees, and, with increasing automation in office equipment, clerical workers."[17] A survey carried out in 1988 revealed that between 1983 and 1988, 4.6 million workers over age 20 were displaced. This is a considerable number given that during this period total employment rose substantially. The most significant fact about this recent group of displaced workers is that the jobs they lost were less likely to have been in manufacturing industries. Thus we may be witnessing the first indication that information processing technology is having an impact on office employment.

If this is indeed the case then it may be now be the turn of a segment of white-collar workers to enter a long period of decline.

A somewhat more restrictive definition of displaced workers was used in 1994:[18] "Displaced workers are persons 20 years and older who were released from jobs because their plant or company closed or moved, there was insufficient work for them to do, or their position or shift was abolished." The survey reported that 4.5 million workers were displaced from their jobs between January 1991 and December 1993. These workers had to be employed for at least three years but if this restriction is removed, 9 million workers were displaced. Some of the other findings of this survey are of particular interest:[19]

- The manufacturing industry had the greatest number of displaced workers in the February 1994 survey, as in the prior surveys. Between 1991 and 1993, 1.5 million factory workers were displaced . . . about 1 of every 3 displacements in the early 1990s.
- Even though most of the job growth in the United States continues to be in the service-producing sector, substantial displacement occurs in these industries as well . . . Reemployment rates among workers who lost jobs in service-producing industries were higher than for those who lost factory jobs.
- Among occupations, the largest number of job displacements occurred among managers and professionals (1.2 million) and technical, sales, and administrative support workers (1.3 million).
- Workers in "blue-collar" jobs had smaller job losses in number but were overrepresented among the displaced compared with their share of employment.
- Of the displaced workers who lost full-time wage and salary jobs between 1991 and 1993 and who were employed again at the time of the survey, nearly 8 in 10 had found new full-time wage and salary jobs.

In summary, part of the cause of the unemployment, or displacement, discussed is the increasing tendency towards industrial automation as a means to improve manufacturing productivity and towards office automation as a means to improve white-collar productivity. For example, Japan—the world's leading country in the introduction of robots—has presented a serious challenge to other industrialized nations. The message is quite clear: increase productivity or cease to compete on the world scene, with an accompanying loss of jobs and a lowering of the standard of living. In some sense, while Japan may be seen to be exporting unemployment as well as VCRs, cameras, and television sets, the dilemma of industrialized countries may be seen as follows:

- Automate rapidly (thereby increasing unemployment, hopefully only temporarily) to compete internationally and perhaps restore the immediate loss in jobs with an increase in total production or in a lowering of service costs.
- Don't automate aggressively, to save jobs in the short run. However, because cheaper goods may be produced elsewhere, or cheaper services may be available elsewhere, domestic jobs will eventually be in jeopardy.

Early in 1996, AT&T announced that it would eliminate 40,000 jobs from a 300,000 person workforce, over the next three years. This followed a cut of 19,500 through early

1994. In fact, *Business Week* reported that "some 100,000 readditional telecommunications jobs will be eliminated in the next five years, atop the 250,000 cut since the Bell system breakup in 1984."[20] Also note that there have been substantial layoffs in the computer industry as well in recent years, including IBM (63,000 announced in July 1993), Digital Equipment (20,000, May 1994; 3,200, April 1993), NCR (7,500, November 1993), and Apple (1,300, January 1996; 2,500, July 1993).[21] Although the cuts in the computer industry came on the heels of substantial losses, those announced at AT&T occurred in the context of a healthy company with competitive and profitable divisions.[22] It is disconcerting that such high technology industries are not the engines of job growth. However, the continuous growth in innovative, relatively small companies is what drives employment in the technology sector.

So clearly the bulk of future jobs will not be produced in manufacturing but in the service area, especially in the sector that includes relatively low-paying jobs. Are we heading towards a society in which a relatively small percentage of the labor force produces sufficient food and manufactured goods and performs professionally in such areas as education, medicine, engineering, science, finance, computers and government, while most workers are involved in health services, food preparation and serving, custodial work, salesclerking, leisure, clerical work, and other relatively low-skilled and low-paying jobs?

Part-Time, Contingent, and Contract Workers

Another indication of the major changes that the labor force has undergone in recent years, and a trend that is very likely to continue, is the decrease in the number of regular employees and the increase in the number of part-time, contract, or contingent employees. The Bureau of Labor Statistics has been interested in this trend as well and conducted a major survey in February 1995. A simple working definition for contingent jobs is given as "jobs which are structured to last only a limited period of time." Other alternative work arrangements were also considered, namely, "those working as independent contractors and on-call workers, as well as those working through temporary help agencies or contract companies."[23] Results show that "between 2.7 and 6.0 million workers—a range of 2.2 to 4.9 percent of total employment—were in contingent jobs." The last figure includes both wage and salary workers and those workers who had no expectation of long-term employment. There were many other findings, including the following: "8.3 million workers (6.7 percent of the total employed) said they were independent contractors, 2.0 million (1.7 percent) worked "on call," 1.2 million (1.0 percent) worked for temporary help agencies, and 652,000 (0.5 percent) worked for contract firms that provided the worker's services to one customer at that customer's worksite."[24]

Clearly, weakening the contractual relations between workers and their employers must weaken worker loyalty and commitment. The following two quotations are indicative of a growing dismissal by management of the importance of a well-motivated, committed, and loyal workforce:[25]

- Workers are expensive. They can justify their employment if they can truly contribute to the value-added flow of the enterprise.
- In places like the US, you hire people who have the knowledge to go with the new technology, and you fire those who don't.

Recognizing this trend, *Business Week* columnist Keith Hammond wrote that "Corporate America has abandoned too easily the idea that keeping people in decent jobs is both important and possible." [26]

Another point of view argues that current trends are not unique or indicative of a disturbing direction in employer-employee relations. Economist Steven J. Davis found "That over a typical 12-month period, one in ten US manufacturing jobs disappears—and does not open up again at the same location within the following two years. Other jobs, however, are being created at the same time. The phenomenon of large-scale job destruction and creation has been part and parcel of the US economy and other market economies for as long as we have data." [27] However the process works, most people (64%) believe "that Congress can do something about it," and the figure rises to 78% for those "already hard-hit by a layoff." [28]

The Computer and the Office

There are at least two possibilities for the office of the future. The promising model includes an increase in productivity, more jobs, improved skills for office workers, and increased opportunities for executives. The pessimistic version suggests that the industrial model will be reproduced in the office, with rows of women at desks and terminals, automatically monitored by the computer, with a major reduction of the traditional social intercourse of the office. The clerical work force is heavily dominated by women: 62% in 1970, but 80% in 1980. Although the office and the typewriter have been a major source of employment for women, the next stage of technological innovation may not be so kind. In 1978 Siemens, a West German company, estimated that office automation could result in a reduction of the labor force by 25 to 30%. Occupations such as file clerk, bookkeeper, typist, and bank teller, which are predominantly filled by women, are the leading candidates for automation.

Interestingly enough, the term *word processing* was first introduced by IBM in the early 1960s to sell dictation equipment. In 1967, IBM also used it as part of an advertising campaign for its magnetic tape Selective typewriters. The goal for the future office is clearly stated in an encyclopedia entry for word processing (WP): "WP represents a further stage in modern society's application of automation, reaching beyond manufacturing and production lines into the office." [29]

Those who look forward to increased office automation, especially (but not exclusively) equipment manufacturers and software developers, have an optimistic view. In the long run the routine and ordinary will be automated, and the number of employees with higher technical skills will increase. Office work will be more satisfying as the drudgery is relegated to machines. The level of human interaction will rise among those employees who need to communicate and who have sufficient time. Besides word processing, office automation includes communication networks, electronic mail, scheduling of meetings, information retrieval, and other applications. The complete package will arrive in stages because of high capital costs as well as associated technical problems. Productivity improvements will not be spectacular and in fact may not initially appear to justify the expense and effort. Over the next few years the office will undergo a transformation that will affect work in many ways. The shape of the future is difficult to predict. A concerned and informed public can help to humanize the new technology.

The Computer and the Factory

A brief overview of the application of robotics will be presented here and in a later section the more inclusive area of industrial automation will be surveyed. The context is of course the impact of such advanced technology on both employment and work itself in the manufacturing plant. The focus is on robots because of their growing importance, but of course computers and computer networks have also had an impact.

What Is a Robot?

The major application of robots in the foreseeable future will be in the industrial environment. However, a small but steadily growing number of application areas does exist, including service robots for cleaning and vacuuming, and retrieving and delivering parcels and mail; telerobotics for use in dangerous environments such as mines, radioactive and chemically toxic areas, and in space and undersea situations; and medical robots for precise work in operations. Industrial robots are used for materials handling, spot and arc welding, assembly (mounting, screwing, bonding, sealing, gluing, and soldering), painting, casting, plastic moulding, and numerical control. The industrial robots after being appropriately programmed operate in an autonomous fashion, whereas most of the other applications require a human operator in more or less continuous control. Based on the industrial model, the following "semi-official" definition was adopted by the Robot Institute of America in 1979 and the International Federation for Robots in 1981:[30]

> A Robot is a reprogrammable multi-functional manipulator designed to move materials, parts, tools, or other specialized devices, through variable programmed motions for the performance of a variety of tasks.

This doesn't sound very much like C3PO or R2D2, but remember that industrial robots are designed for specific tasks in the factory. Before science fact meets science fiction, considerable research and development will be required.

Worldwide Distribution

Although the first robot patent was granted in the US and the first robot was manufactured in the US in 1961 by a company called Unimation (that no longer exists), the world leader in the manufacture and use of industrial robots is Japan. The lead is substantial no matter how robots are counted, whether by the definition given previously or by a simpler notion of pick-and-place machines. For example, at the end of 1994, the US base of installed robots was about 53,000 compared with "more than seven times as many in use," in Japan.[31] In the US there has been a considerable fluctuation in predictions of new robots coming online and the actual numbers produced and sold. The early 1980s promised a period of sustained growth but 1987 witnessed such a fall off that only one US robot maker, Adept Technology, survived. But sales began to pick up again in the early 1990s so that by 1995, more than 10,000 robots were shipped at a value of nearly $900 million, "a jump of 34% in units and 30% in dollars over 1994's record-setting pace. Robot shipments are up more than 128% since 1991, when the robotics industry began surging forward."[32]

The major trade association, Robotic Industries Association (RIA), is obviously very excited by the dramatic surge in the sale of robots:

> "The robotics industry's comeback in the 1990s is extraordinary," said Donald A. Vincent, Executive Vice President of RIA. "Today's robots are powerful productivity-enhancing tools that offer tremendous benefits to companies in virtually every industry. End users now have a better understanding of how robotics fits into an overall automation strategy, which has led to the creation of many new robot applications.

> "While the automotive industry remains the leading user, as evidenced by the strong orders for spot welding robots, we're encouraged by the big jump in demand for material handling robots which perform tasks such as packaging and palletizing in industries such as food and beverages, pharmaceuticals, glass, plastic bottles and containers, and various other consumer products," Vincent explained.

Why Use Robots? Work and Productivity

Robots have not been introduced into the workplace as rapidly as proponents had hoped or expected. Factors were reliability deficiencies in the available technology, high costs, high interest rates, and perhaps that their flexibility and efficiency were oversold. However, in reaction to the massive onslaught of "Japan Inc.," North America and Europe had come to view the robot as the key to restoring their lost economic superiority, at least with respect to manufacturing. Especially in the industry that had suffered the most—the US automobile industry—hopes for increased productivity have focused more and more on a large investment in improved industrial automation, including robots. Robots can affect the industrial process in the following ways:

- *Improvement of Productivity.* Increased plant operating time because of fewer shutdowns, ease of retooling, automation of small batch production.
- *Stability and Improvement in Product Quality.* Reduced quality variation, 24-hour working days with elimination of changeover problems.
- *Improvement in Production Management.* Reduction of manpower allocation problems, benefits of durability and accuracy of robots, overcoming of skilled manpower shortages.
- *Humanization of Working Life.* Release of people from dangerous, unhealthy, and monotonous work.
- *Resource Conservation.* Saving of materials by efficient robots, saving of energy by robots working in environment with reduced lighting, air conditioning, and so forth.

The very large, sustained budget deficits and trade imbalances in the US, and the relatively low rates of increases in productivity over the past twenty years (better more recently however) have given rise to a serious concern about America's future, especially in manufacturing. Many studies and books have appeared debating the weaknesses and strengths of the US economy, challenging the very idea of a post-industrial society, and arguing that manufacturing is fundamental to threatened US world economic leadership. The argument frequently turns on the issue of productivity, that it must be increased, and how that goal is to be achieved. For many industries, a major infusion of capital investment is required and robots, computers, and factory automation have become the symbols of the new manufacturing. Not unexpectedly, considerable debate exists with respect to the definition of productivity itself, especially in the service sector and also about what it will take to improve it.

Two kinds of productivity are usually considered: labor productivity and multifactor productivity. Labor productivity is expressed in terms of dollars of output (necessarily adjusted for inflation) per hours worked. Thus we can compare productivity within different industries in one country, or the same industry across different countries, or even among countries by taking the total output of the economy, the gross national, or gross domestic, product and dividing it by the total number of hours worked by all contributing workers. However, even though the phrase labor productivity is used, it is actually productivity that is being measured. Thus the Bureau of Labor Statistics (BLS) in one of its regular reports on productivity notes that[33]

> These productivity measures describe the relationship between real output and the labor time involved in its production. They show the changes from period to period in the amount of goods and services produced per hour. Although these measures relate output to hours at work of all persons engaged in a sector, they do not measure the specific contribution of labor, capital, or any other factor of production. Rather, they reflect the joint effects of many influences, including changes in technology; capital investment; level of output; utilization of capacity, energy, and materials; the organization of production; managerial skill; and the characteristics and effort of the work force.

Thus the definition supplied by the BLS is really appropriate for multifactor productivity "a composite measure of how efficiently an economy makes use of both labor and capital inputs. Growth in multifactor productivity reflects such factors as the introduction of new technology, improvements in skill and motivation of the work force, and better techniques of management and organization."[34] Other factors may be interest rates, the quality of the educational system, and the financial support for research and development by both government and industry. There seems to be a payoff in the introduction of capital investment in the manufacturing plant as shown by the size of the increases in the recent rate of manufacturing productivity. The 1995 increase was 3.7%, a small decrease from 1994's 4.2% gain.

Industrial Automation

A number of key terms to describe the various important areas of computerized manufacturing technology.[35]

* *Computer-Aided Design* (CAD). CAD serves as an electronic drawing board for design engineers and draftsmen, with applications in aircraft design, automobiles, and integrated circuits. Included in this heading are *computer-aided drafting* and *computer-aided engineering* (CAE). CAE is concerned with interactive design and analysis.

- *Computer-Aided Manufacturing* (CAM). CAM includes those types of manufacturing automation used primarily on the factory floor to help produce products. Some of the important subfields are *robots, numerically controlled* (NC) machine tools, and (of increasing importance) *flexible manufacturing systems* (FMS). Two other areas included in CAM are *automated materials handling* (AMH) and *automated storage and retrieval systems* (AS/RS).

- *Management Tools and Strategies.* These include most importantly, *computer-integrated manufacturing* (CIM) and *management information systems* (MIS) (see Chapter 4). CIM involves the integration and coordination of design, manufacturing, and management using computer-based systems. It is currently an approach to factory organization and management.

Robots are only part of the manufacturing process. The factory of the future is expected to be organized around (a) computers and sophisticated graphics systems at the design stage (CAD), and (b) computers, numerically controlled machines, routing systems, and robots at the manufacturing stage (CAM). CAD/CAM is not a well-defined production strategy, but rather a developing set of systems and strategies that are being applied to various aspects of the design and manufacturing process. It has taken off in recent years as both substantial improvements in hardware technology and research developments in graphics, computational geometry, and AI have provided enormous power at reasonable costs.

An exact definition of CIM is not possible, as most commentators characterize it as a concept or approach rather than a well-established manufacturing systems. Still it can be characterized in a variety of ways, by referring to two orthogonal organizing schemes: vertical and horizontal. Vertical integrated manufacturing, the most commonly understood reference to CIM, involves the use of CAD to design a product and a CAM system to produce it directly from the CAD instructions. The entire process, including inventory, shipping strategies, and production schedules, and other procedures that depend on MIS and CAP (computer-aided planning) systems, is controlled and regulated by CIM. The Horizontal approach, on the other hand, is concerned only with systematizing the manufacturing process itself—the computer control and coordination of equipment on the factory floor. This latter approach is also subsumed under the term flexible manufacturing systems (FMS). And as with robotics, one major objective is minimizing direct labor costs.

More recently the term "Agility" has gained popularity but its meaning is somewhat vague, as the following definitions indicate:[36]

- The ability to profit from rapidly changing, continually fragmenting, global markets for individualizable, customer value-based products and services.
- Agility is a new system of commercial competition, a successor to the still dominant system that developed around mass production-based competition once it was coupled to the modern industrial corporation. Like the latter, agility was made possible by the synthesis of innovations in manufacturing, information, and communication technologies with radical organizational redesign and new marketing strategies.
- Agility is a comprehensive, strategic, response to fundamental and irreversible structural changes that are undermining the economic foundations of mass production-based competition.

Present day technology permits more rapid response to changing market conditions, the ability to exploit niche markets and produce made-to-measure goods efficiently, and to take advantage of global production and communication systems.

Labor and Technology

In the United States, the introduction of robots, up to very recently, has taken place much more slowly than in Japan. As the pace has quickened, concerns of labor and management about the introduction of new technology have come to the fore. The economic difficulties in the US that began in the mid-1970s, when the average increase in manufacturing productivity was 1.4%, have convinced many manufacturers that only by reducing the labor component of production could they compete internationally. This viewpoint has been especially well articulated by the automobile industry, the major user of robots. One instructive and important example of the attempt to humanize the industrial workplace was provided by General Motors when in 1983 it announced a new subsidiary, called Saturn, that would produce quality automobiles as efficiently and cheaply as possible in order to meet Japan's challenge to world leadership.

The Saturn concept was to integrate computers into the entire production process from the office to the factory floor. One of the goals was to reduce the labor component per car from the then current level of 55 hours to about 20 hours. Robots would play a major role. Saturn "is going to advance significantly the state of the art in automated assembly. It will be the most robotized of any GM plant—and probably any plant in the world."[37] The plans were impressive: robots would position sheet metal for other robots to weld as car roofs. They would install windshields and rear windows and doors, they would attach wheels and install seats. Such applications would require the development of robots with advanced vision systems.

The vision of 1983 was not translated into reality until late 1990, when the first Saturn rolled into dealer showrooms. It was already clear in 1988 that massive expenditures on advanced production technologies centered on robots were not going to work. Instead of trying to produce a workerless "lights out" factory, Saturn will be focusing on building a car that can compete with the best Japan can offer. "We're still exploring, but Saturn is no longer an experiment. We're not a laboratory. We're not a social program. We're a business."[38] The Saturn plant in Spring Hill, Tennessee, intended to be the most technologically advanced of all the GM plants, may now be known as the most advanced in terms of management-worker relations:[39]

> The ranks of robots and armies of car-carrying automatic guided vehicles that populate GM's newest plants will be thinned. Instead Saturn is pouring its money [some $3.5 billion] into people management. It plans to hire exceptionally motivated workers, put them through intensive training, give them more say in how their jobs get done, and pay them a salary plus a performance bonus—just like Saturn executives.

In late 1990 as Saturn made its appearance, a great deal was riding on its success. Lester Thurow, dean of the Massachusetts Institute of Technology's Sloan School of Management argued that the importance of Saturn could not be overestimated. Its success, if it came, would show that the large, old bureaucracy could be pushed aside and a giant company could still adapt and learn, that management and labor could forge a new relationship, and that market share could be recovered.[40] However, failure would be devastating. As noted the enormous changes that have accompanied the Saturn project are not just technological. Some crucial points in the new relationship between management and labor at GM that thoroughly involves the United Auto Workers in every aspect of plant management are given as follows, and it is not an exaggeration to state that they are indeed revolutionary, especially in the context of a history of lengthy and bitter confrontation.

The work will be organized around 165 semiindependent work teams that have a great deal of decision-making power such as stopping the assembly line when a problem arises or interviewing and approving new members, or agreeing to any decisions affecting them. They will be salaried rather than hourly employees with part of their salary dependent on a formula that includes productivity, automobile quality and, of course, profits. Workers will "ride along on a moving wooden conveyor belt as they do their jobs, which enables them to concentrate on their work,"[41] rather than struggling to keep up with a line moving past them.

The Saturn plant is a unique GM experiment and an interesting gamble for an American institution not particularly known for its spirit of adventure. Given that it will take several years for Saturn to make a profit, the question arises as to whether or not management and labor relations can last the course. In an attempt to establish its independence, Saturn's advertisements make no mention of GM. Furthermore, it will try to tap the large reservoir of American animosity towards Japan that many believe lies just below the surface. If Saturn proves to be a quality car with the right price and styling it could achieve enormous success; if not, Japan will inexorably continue its move towards domination of the world automobile market. Perhaps this last sentiment is a bit melodramatic, as other issues are involved in which company and which country will predominate. Also significant and particularly humbling for GM, is that after years of spending billions of dollars to become more competitive, the answer is not just better machines but better people, more knowledgeable, more committed, more involved, and more motivated people.

Has it worked? In early 1994, *Business Week* reported that sales were slowing and inventories rising. Apparently, General Motors, short of cash, forced Saturn to cut back on advertising, slow down the rate of growth in new dealerships, and delay new products. Longer term prospects are also troublesome because expansion in needed capacity did not appear to be forthcoming. In 1993, Saturn started making profits but given GM's $5 billion investment, there was still a long way to go. On the other hand, customer satisfaction is very high, placing Saturn just behind Lexus and Infiniti, and "Saturn cars have among the lowest defect rates of any US brand. Half of its customers say they would have bought a foreign nameplate if Saturn hadn't been on the market."[42] More recently, GM announced that Saturn would be building a midsize car to add to its three similar small models. A new plant to be located in Wilmington, Delaware, would be required and although Saturn has still not recovered the initial $5 billion investment, its sales are once again very strong. "The secret to Saturn's success has been innovative production and retail programs rather than the cars themselves, which are solid but unremarkable.[43]

Social Concerns

The work of Frederick Taylor has been introduced and discussed; its influence has persisted to the present day. Indeed, the terms Taylorism and Fordism have come to stand for a style of management, predominantly American, that seeks to reduce substantially the worker's role in manufacturing. More recently two new terms have come into use, mainly in Europe, which have been employed to differentiate two approaches to the application of automated systems in the factory, namely, human-centered and technocentric. Although these approaches rarely appear in a pure form, of all countries in the world, the US is the most technocentric, the Saturn example notwithstanding. In somewhat more detail, the following characterizes the technocentric style:[44]

> It denotes an attempt to gradually reduce human intervention in the production process to a minimum and to design systems flexible enough to react rapidly to changing market demand for high quality products. Workers and technicians on the shop-floor are sometimes seen as unpredictable, troublesome and unreliable elements capable of disturbing the production and information flow which is best controlled centrally through computers. The "unmanned factory" is the ultimate goal. It represents the division of labor carried to its extreme whereby subdivided and simplified tasks executed by a mass of low-skilled labour are progressively taken over by increasingly flexible intelligent and versatile industrial robots and machines communicating among each other via networks and computers.

There are some serious questions about whether this goal is at all viable. Experience seems to show that to make flexible manufacturing systems work, highly skilled and motivated workers must be involved, able to deal quickly and effectively with breakdowns and other problems. Advocates of the technocentric approach might argue that it is only a matter of time until the technology is sufficiently well-refined to achieve the goals set for it.

The human-centered approach depends on the purposeful integration of people into the entire manufacturing process, from planning and design to execution, problem-solving, and redesign. Machines are valued for their role in replacing workers in dangerous and uncomfortable situations and in those involving endless repetitive actions, as well as for enhancing human abilities. People are valued for their creativity, adaptability, and special abilities to respond quickly to unforeseen events as well as their motivation, pride, and intelligence. Given that humans do make mistakes, that they do forget aspects of their jobs, that they do become irritated, and that they do lose concentration, is the answer to replace them with machines when this becomes possible? The question is badly formed, not just because people are invaluable, but because even with advanced technology, a well-trained and well-motivated work force provides the essential ingredient to make technology work.

Finally, we turn briefly to explore the question: What is the impact of robots on the quality of work and on the work environment? The answers are neither new nor surprising, especially given the Japanese experience. Almost every commentator on these issues has stressed one point: advanced planning and consultation with labor is necessary. It has been maintained that success often depends on paying special attention to the problems of displaced workers, gaining line management support for the change, and educating employees in the use of the equipment before installation. Unions would like to be informed early in the planning process, to be able to help their displaced members to be assimilated into new jobs. It also seems to be ordinary common sense that the workers who are actually going to be involved with the new machines should be consulted about the selection of these machines. Many companies—including Ford, Westinghouse, IBM, and even GM—have taken pains to consult with those workers who will be most affected by robots. This responsibility should be extended, however, to include retraining and compensation.

The Organization of Work

The contributions of Frederick Taylor to the organization of the productive process concerned scientific management, time studies, and the assembly line. His goal was to separate the planning process from the execution process. Management's prerogative is to decide how a product is to be manufactured and then assign workers specific tasks to perform. Because of this division of labor and the separation of thought and action, work on assembly lines has been characterized as boring, mind numbing, and alienating. The trade-off of job security and good wages for mediocre working conditions has been justified by many commentators of the labor scene. However, with the rise of Japan as a major world competitor, it became clear to many observers that the traditional means of production still dominant in the United States could not compete successfully. Many reasons have been offered for the Japanese success story: American aid; a modern industrial plant; a special relationship among government, business, and labor; new management techniques; a premium on quality control; the use of advanced technology such as robots; and the encouragement of worker participation in industrial decision making. Much has been written about the involvement of Japanese workers in the decision-making process. Workers are organized into groups for specific tasks and are permitted to carry out these tasks as they wish as long as production goals are met. On a regular basis, workers meet with management to suggest improvements in production. This system reverses the Taylor maxim. It must be working, or management would not continue to operate under such a system. In addition, management makes a long-term commitment to its workers—to train them appropriately and find alternative work if market conditions change.

Many of these methods actually originated in the United States and were imported into Japan, where they were enthusiastically accepted and widely used. In an interesting turn of events, the same methods are being returned to the United States. Unfortunately, the economic recession of the early 1980s has limited to a considerable degree the willingness of many companies to experiment. In fact, certain industries took advantage of high unemployment rates to renegotiate major changes in work rules with their unions. For example, in the steel, automobile, and airline industries, crews have been reduced in size and jobs enlarged with new duties. Management has gained more power to schedule work and required workers to give up relief periods in some cases.

Finally, what direct impact will computers have on the organization of work? In direct contradistinction to the problems associated with computers and workers, current approaches to the enhancement of work, sometimes referred to as computer-facilitated cooperative work, especially in the Scandinavian countries and Germany, offer a work place in which the computer, with appropriate software, provides the necessary resources to encourage workers to realize their full potential. The goal is to provide computer and communication facilities to enable people to perform their jobs better by cooperating with their fellow workers wherever they may be located. Management must be prepared to surrender part of its autonomy in the belief that a well-trained, well-motivated work force, operating with work-enhancing tools will produce better products and provide better services. Thus computer technology, in the view of supporters of the cooperative approach, can indeed be a liberating force in the work place, freeing people from the drudgery of routine work, and permitting them to produce quality work.

Whether management will be sufficiently enlightened to recognize this potential is questionable, for it will require a break with long-held beliefs and the exercise of a measure of trust that computers, as a new technology, are indeed different and that their potential is unlimited. The major component of the trust is actually in the workers, in their desire to excel, in their interest to explore the possibilities of the new technology; in other words, a return to workers of some degree of control over the work process. Experiments are in progress in many countries of the world to develop both software and hardware to realize some of these aims. However, in the real world, computers for the most part are not at all liberating. They are management's current tools to reinforce control, to extract knowledge, and to ultimately reduce the labor component to increase profits and minimize potential work disruption.

The Service Sector

> . . .A McDonald's outlet is a machine that produces, with the help of unskilled machine attendants, a highly polished product.[45]

The impact of computer technology in manufacturing and in the office has received most of the attention when a concern with employment and the changing nature of the work place is discussed. However, the service sector can benefit greatly from technology and given its overwhelming importance in the economy, serious attention must be paid to understanding something about its operation. First, the definition of services is usually given as that sector of the economy "whose output is not a physical product or construction, is generally consumed at the time it is produced and provides added value in forms (such as convenience, amusement, timeliness, comfort or health) that are essentially intangible concerns of its purchaser."[46] Note that services go beyond fast food and football, and include finance, communications, education, health care, transportation, legal assistance, entertainment, and travel. Most employment growth over the next few years is expected to be in the "service-producing industries: Over the 1994–2005 period, total employment is projected to increase by 14 percent or by 17.7 million, from 127.0 million in 1994 to 144.7 million in 2005. Service-producing industries will account for virtually all of the job growth. Only construction will add jobs in the goods-producing sector."[47]

Although capital investment in services has been growing rapidly, one of the concerns about such investment is that the desired payoff in terms of increased productivity generally has not been achieved. It is difficult to define productivity for services in general; nevertheless, carefully constructed measures can be produced for individual segments. In some of these areas, productivity has clearly increased (recall long-distance calls as well as the caveat) and in others it has not—if complaints about the limited return of office automation are to be believed.

As we noted, the service sector has been, and is expected to be, the job engine of the economy. The real question however is not just job numbers but job quality. As the Bureau of Labor Statistics has noted in its employment projections, "Health services, business services, and social services are expected to account for almost one of every two jobs added to the economy during the 1994–2005 period. Of the 10 fastest growing industries, nine belong to one of these three industry groups."[48] Furthermore none of these areas is likely to benefit from computer technology in any way that will improve job availability, wages, or quality of work. In addition, these are areas with an increasing frequency of part-time or contingency workers, which means that the jobs lack many of the benefits that provide a safety net in difficult times. Those parts of the service sector in such areas as communications, finance, insurance, and transportation will obviously benefit from increased capitalization in technology. Salaries will be higher, work will probably be more interesting, advancement more possible but in terms of the service sector as a whole, these areas do not provide a large percentage of the jobs.

TELECOMMUTING AND REMOTE WORK

Telecommuting costs often absorbed by employees can include:

1. Buying a larger house to create office space.
2. Purchase of office furniture and supplies.
3. Installation of extra phone lines.
4. Photocopiers, fax machines, printers.
5. Heating and air conditioning caused by the home being occupied more hours per day.
6. Business phone charges not refunded (long distance, 3-way calling, voice mail, etc.).
7. Equipment repairs.
8. Insurance.
9. Interior decoration.
10. Extra phone handsets and answering machines.[49]

Telecommuting: Electronic Cottage Industry

The phrase "electronic cottage,"[50] apparently first used by Alvin Toffler, conjures up visions of people working at home by means of computers and communications networks. The cottage part is a preindustrial vision of workers at home, performing piece work that they return upon completion to central locations and then pick up new supplies. Remnants of this mode of labor exist in the Western world today. In northern Scotland tweed fabrics are woven on home looms. In late 1984, the US Labor Department permitted home knitters to sell their work for profit. (They are still required to observe minimum wage and child labor laws. Much of this work is done in New England and had been illegal since 1942.)[51] Two other terms are occasionally used:[52] *telework,* organizational work performed outside of the normal organizational confines of space and time, augmented by computer and communications technology; and *telecommuting,* the use of computer and communications technology to transport work to the worker as a substitute for physical transportation of the worker to the location of the work.

A number of companies have chosen to encourage part of their staff to remain at home while performing their information processing activities. Other companies, not particularly in favor, have nevertheless permitted telecommuting as a way of hiring information systems staff in a highly competitive market. Estimates of the number of teleworkers are not easy to determine because some are employed by companies that have implemented a telework program, others are contract or part-time workers who telecommute, and still others have their own businesses and work out of their homes using computers and networks. Link Resources surveys households with respect to telecommuting issues. It estimates that "7.6 million people are telecommuting this year [1995] in one form or another, and the number is growing at 15 percent per year, though telecommuters with formal arrangements amount to only 1.6 percent of US workers."[53] This number represents company employees but Link also provides these numbers: "Additionally, there are 24.3 million self-employed home-based workers and 9.2 million after-hours home office workers, bringing the total of work-at-home residents to 41.1 million."[54] To appreciate the magnitude of the change, consider the following projections: "15 million telecommuters in 2002—about 10.5 percent of the workforce or 17.5 percent of information workers. This is a gain of 650 percent over the next 10 years [1992 to 2002], with half of the growth occurring in the last 3 years."[55]

Advantages and Disadvantages

Proponents of remote office work, or telecommuting, claim that an increasing number of employees will be working at home because it makes economic sense. Commuting is eliminated, which means savings in fuel costs, automobile pollution, time, and a general reduction in the stress associated with driving. Employees have an increased flexibility for arranging their working hours around their family responsibilities. People will be able to choose where they live independently of the need to be close to a job. There must also be advantages for the employer, or new working arrangements will not be implemented. Productivity improvements are supposedly a major reason for physically decentralizing work. One difficulty in measuring productivity is that more work may be accomplished because more time is being spent rather than because the worker is more efficient.

From management's point of view, employees may be easier to attract if flexible work arrangements are possible. If the number of staff at a central location is reduced, the building rental costs can also be reduced—a saving somewhat offset by increased telephone charges. However, for many women who want a career, there are problems about staying at home. It may appear to be convenient to work at home, but women who work there may not be taken seriously, even if child care can be adequately arranged. The problem is a general one for remote workers—if they are out of sight, will they be out of mind at promotion time?

In summary, a list of advantages, including some of those mentioned, consists of the following:[56] conserves energy (vehicle, highway, and office-related), reduces pollution, reduces land requirements for roads and parking lots, promotes safety, improves health by reducing driving-related stress, increases time spent with family, and permits choice of desired home location. Clearly some of the benefits claimed for telecommuting disproportionally accrue to the employer. For example, see the quotation at the beginning of this section.

Telecommuting and the Internet

It seems obvious that the Internet should facilitate many kinds of telecommuting and provide open-ended opportunity for working at home whether for companies or independently. There is some expectation that "the following developments will help support telecommuting and distance work:"[57]

- Web-based conferencing (documents, video, audio) that allows dispersed teams to share information and work together. Most of the technical tools available today are still a bit rough around the edges, but they will improve.
- Sun Microsystems' Java language will make it possible for remote workers to access a variety of applications no matter what PC platform they're using. Java is catching on quickly, so watch for Web site and intranet applications.
- The telecommunications bottleneck is still the biggest problem that most remote workers experience. The more stuff there is on the Web, and the more people there are trying to access it, the slower the access time and the greater the frustration. The debate about the relative pros and cons of advanced telecommunications "pipelines" such as ISDN, ADSL, and cable modems (among others) continues and grows. Whichever one, or ones of these options or others becomes more popular, it's clear that something has to happen so most of us can get beyond the 14.4 or 28.8 kbps that we rely on.

The number of Web sites has grown explosively and associated with this growth has been job creation in areas impossible to have foreseen even a few years ago. In addition to the companies that have created Web browsers, plug-ins, and application software, there is suddenly a professional expertise in Web page design (Webmeisters), maintenance, usage measurement, security, and marketing strategies. Many of these jobs are carried out in a distributed fashion which furthers the general growth in remote and distributed computing.

Some Social Concerns

A few years ago, one informed critic of telecommuting, Tom Forester, the author and editor of several books on technology and society, proposed the following reasons that telecommuting, as discussed in the late 1980s, would not necessarily grow as fast as proponents suggested:[58]

1. Not many people are or will be in a position to work at home in future because of space constraints and the nature of their occupations.
2. Of those who could work at home, not many will choose to do so, because homeworking suits only some people and not others. Even fewer people can cope with the psychological problems on a long-term basis.

3. We are thus most unlikely to see a major increase in homeworking (or the 'mass return home after the industrial revolution' envisioned by the electronic cottage theorists).
4. We may, however, see a small but steady increase in the number of people doing some rather than all of their work at home, as flexible working patterns become more widespread and more people seek to 'get the best of both worlds.'

Even now, it is not clear whether or not these predictions have any substance. More people are working at home as employees of corporations but the patterns are so diverse that it is difficult to identify specific trends. A column by Mitch Betts, *Computerworld's* senior editor, social and legal issues, described a few of the negative sides of telecommuting:[59]

- . . . the virtual office may be virtual death for your career because telecommuters can't play the game of office politics (Neal Thornberry, professor of industrial psychology at Babson College)
- An article in *Futurist* magazine warns that telecommuting "portends an environmental disaster of the first magnitude." Why? Because modem-toting expatriates from the city will buy all the rural open space and turn it into Yuppie homesteads that destroy forests and streams.
- . . . outfitting the teleworker isn't cheap. The cost to equip telecommuters exceeds $4,000 for initial installation and $2,100 in annual expenses . . . most telework will be done by "White-collar workhorses" who squeeze in a few extra hours of work at night, on weekends and while traveling. (Forrester Research in Cambridge, Mass.)

As with any technological innovation, the impact on the social lives of affected individuals is not easy to discern and may require considerable time for trends to become apparent, at which point it may be impossible to ameliorate the situation, even if it is recognized as being unsatisfactory.

THE RESPONSE OF UNIONS

With all their faults, trade unions have done more for humanity than any other organization of men that ever existed. They have done more for decency, for honesty, for education, for the betterment of the race, for the developing of character in man, than any other association of men. (Clarence Darrow)[60]

Labor unions are the worst thing that ever struck the earth because they take away a man's independence. (Henry Ford)[61]

Unions have their supporters and their detractors, but they are concerned about the welfare of a large but diminishing segment of the workforce. Their activities represent an attempt to protect the workers they represent from threats to job security and loss of benefits. How they perceive the challenge of technology is indicative of the feelings of the workers themselves as opposed to the intentions of management.

The unions have been caught in a difficult position. Faced with the loss of jobs during the recession of the early 1980s, unions have negotiated contracts in which hard-won concessions gained over the years have been given up. They have tried to protect current jobs for a reduced work force. In this context, technological change has not been in the forefront of most unions' bargaining positions. For some unions, however, the handwriting has been on the wall for quite a while. After a series of bitter strikes, the printers' union in New York settled for a contract that essentially means the end of the industry and the union. Typographers and printers have fallen victim to computerized composition and typesetting. At most newspapers, reporters can enter their stories directly into a computer, where they can be edited and subsequently put together in the paper's layout. In a significant technological innovation, the computer-stored information can be sent across the country, and indeed such papers as *The New York Times* and *USA Today* can be printed simultaneously in many parts of the country. Equally, if not more significant is the electronic distribution of newspapers over the Internet, a process that is beginning to take place.

As an example of the ability of management to take advantage of computer networks and the internationalization of labor, consider the operation of one "global office."[62] New York Life Insurance, finding it difficult to hire workers skilled enough to process insurance claims, has turned to rural Ireland. Insurance claims are sent daily to Ireland by air leaving Kennedy International Airport in the evening and arriving at Shannon Airport early the next day. They are then driven to Castleisland, 60 miles away, processed within seven days, and sent to a service center in New Jersey via a trans-Atlantic communications network linking computers in Ireland and the US. An explanation and perhaps a check is printed overnight and then mailed to the beneficiary. The system works because wages in Ireland, for comparable work, are about half those in the US and the unemployment rate in Ireland is about three times the US rate. This is only one example of the export of jobs made possible by international computer networks and global salary inequities and unemployment. It is one reason, among many, that labor unions in the US are consistently losing relative membership, as the work force grows.

Bureau of Labor Statistics figures show that the percentage of union membership among nonagricultural workers grew from 11.6% in 1930 to a peak of 35.5 % in 1945. This growth was not continuous and there was a dip in 1933, a sudden jump in 1937, and dips in 1940 and 1942. The decline was continuous from 1945 to the present except for a slight rise in 1952 and 1954. In 1978, membership was 23.6% but the total number at about 20 million had remained relatively constant over the previous five years. After 1978, the statistics include employee association membership as well and indicate that by 1982, the percentage had declined to 20.6 with about 19.8 million members.[63] By 1989, the percentage excluding the government sector stood at about 12%, rising to only 16% if government employees are included. Thus out of a work force of over 100 million, union membership had declined to about 16 million. The decline continued into 1995, with "9.4 million union members in private nonagricultural industries, where they constituted 10.4 percent of wage and salary employment, and 6.9 million in government (federal, state, and local), where they accounted for 37.8 percent of wage and salary employment."[64] Thus, although the nonfarm labor force increased to over 110 million, total union membership increased slightly to about 16.4 million.

Not only have the numbers decreased substantially but the composition of the membership has also altered dramatically, in a not surprising way to mirror the new reality. Thus there has been a movement away from manufacturing towards services. Between 1965 and 1995, the percent of private-sector workers who belong to unions fell from about 31% to slightly over 10%, and the percent of government workers who belong to unions rose from about 27% to 38% over the same period. And not surprisingly, as union membership has declined among blue collar workers, it has increased among workers in the service sector as this sector has grown in its overall proportion of the workforce. Thus unions have had to move away from their industrial roots and attempt to organize the growing numbers of service and white collar workers. This effort has created tensions within the union movement between blue collar and white collar workers, between private and public sector workers, and between a traditionally white, male-dominated institution and the large numbers of women, blacks, and Hispanics in the new labor force.

Union membership in Europe and elsewhere is considerably higher than in the US: For example in Italy, Australia, and Britain it stood at about 40% in 1990, while in Sweden it was over 80%, in Canada 37%, in Germany 36%, and in Japan 25%.[65] Although these numbers are considerably larger than the US numbers, they represent a decline except for a few countries such as Sweden, Italy, and Canada. One interpretation of the decline in US union membership is that the unions have been too successful, that the gap between union pay and nonunion pay has become so large that unionized companies are no longer competitive and companies have substantially increased their efforts to combat unionism.[66] Thus the advice to unions is to forego wages as their main focus in negotiations and move to other areas such as job security and benefits. In addition unions must come to terms with the fact of the increased numbers of part-time workers and their different needs as well as new compensation programs such as profit-sharing, employee stock option plans, and even joint ownership and management. Other reasons for the loss of union membership may be a reduction in average plant size—it is easier to organize workers in one large plant rather than several smaller ones—and perhaps a general mistrust of all institutions.

Given that the major impact of technology is in the information-intensive industries, the question that emerges is when, or perhaps if, unions will succeed in representing professionals whose work has been affected by computers. Up to now no major professional organization has adopted collective bargaining, except for the American Nurses' Association. Engineering societies seem to be too diverse and fragmented to fall under a single umbrella organization and also a large percentage, about one-third, are management. Professionalism also remains an obstacle given the common perceptions that unions are suitable only for factory workers.[67] Thus unions may find much more fertile areas among the large numbers of low-paid, relatively low-skilled data-entry clerks, office workers, and others whose work place environment has deteriorated because of computers and insensitive management. Even more, concern about possible dangers of radiation from computer terminals, or muscular damage from keyboard use could be negotiation issues for unions.

Unions and Technological Change

Given the difficulties that unions are having in organizing workers other than traditional blue collar ones, it should not be surprising that their views on telecommuting are not exactly supportive. The following concerns are taken from a report by the US General Services Administration:[68]

1. The union's continued ability to effectively represent telecommuters.
2. Equity in the selection of telecommuters (e.g. rank, performance ratings, residence, etc.).
3. Level of support (e.g. sophistication of equipment, clerical assistance, etc.).
4. Return of micro-management procedures and piecework assignment techniques.
5. Adherence to labor standards laws (e.g. overtime, safety, etc.).
6. Home inspections, electronic monitoring, and other potential invasions of the worker's privacy.
7. Efforts to convert career employees to contract personnel.

These items are a mixture of self-interest and traditional union concerns, which also extend towards the extravagant promises made for the Information Superhighway (IH). In a general expression of concern, the AFL-CIO (American Federation of Labor—Council of Industrial Organizations) calls on the government to ensure that all Americans benefit by having affordable access to the IH from their homes, schools, libraries, and community centers and that governments provide access to all their reports and services. It also points out that the US has lost jobs in the high-tech areas because of the increasing power of global communications systems, and argues that "government policy for the information superhighway should be directed at assuring that the workers who produce, disseminate and deliver information do so under good wages, standards and working conditions. Federal law should guarantee that they have a genuine voice on the job through independent trade unions and adequate protection of their privacy rights."[69]

One final statement about work and life, from a union, is an appropriate way to end this section.[70]

> Work, and not just income, is an essential condition of well-being in society. Through the activity of human work in all its forms, people should be able to realize their human dignity and self-expression, participate in social and economic life, secure decent personal and familial incomes, and contribute to the building of a more just world.

WOMEN, COMPUTERS, AND WORK

> One area in need of greater focus is the responsiveness of workplace practices to the needs of working women. A large scale survey of working women published by the Women's Bureau of the Department of Labor in October 1994 reported that, while most women are breadwinners and many are the sole support of their households, they are not getting the pay and benefits commensurate with the work they do, the level of responsibility they hold, or the societal contribution they make.[71]

The widespread use of computers and computer networks have provided, and are expected to provide, many jobs for women. The impact of computers on employment is also expected to affect women significantly, given their high representation in office work. Do computers represent new opportunities for women or will they merely reinforce the old inequities? An increasing number of women have been choosing careers in computer science and engineering. Society has tended to discourage women in the sciences, and how the schools react to the challenge will be very important to girls and women. Equally if not more important is whether or not the workplace climate has improved and if women can achieve success based on their proven abilities.

Early indications of the situation in schools are not encouraging. Girls are being excluded, either overtly or subtly, from computer-related activities. Arguments are formulated that girls are just not suited for computers, that their minds are not logical, and that if computer time is in short supply, boys should be given priority. Whether girls think differently from boys—girls (supposedly) intuitively, boys (supposedly) logically—is neither proven nor relevant, but actions based on this assumption, whether acknowledged or not, must be regularly examined and challenged. In almost every area of computer use—video games, computer courses at school, computer games—boys are in the majority and in effect define the associated culture. One feature of this culture is the excitement of shared expertise. If the environment were made less competitive and less aggressive, girls could be encouraged to participate more fully.

Another discouraging observation is that "The percentage of women getting Ph.D.'s in computer science has remained essentially level at 12% to 13% since 1980, with occasional small dips and swings. This is in contrast to all other fields of science, math, and engineering, which have all experienced increasing percentages of women earning Ph.D.'s. For example, during the same period the percentage of women receiving doctorates increased from about 9% to 17% in the physical sciences and from 25% to 36% in the biological sciences."[72] Consistent with these statistics is the existing situation in terms of the representation of women in the faculty of university computer science departments: "One-third of the computer science and computer engineering departments in the 1990 Taulbee survey had no female faculty at all."[73] However, more recently, the representation of women at the assistant professor level has begun to approximate their percentage of Ph.D.'s achieved.

Encouragement of girls in their formative years may increase the proportion of women in information systems but the trends are not encouraging. Currently, men outnumber women by more than a two to one majority in computer science. Women earn considerably less than men for comparable work and have a minuscule representation at the higher levels of corporations. Thus, a recent survey, reported in *Computerworld,* shows that the average salary of women Information Systems (IS) professionals is between $10,000 to $20,000 less than their male counterparts. "[W]omen have fewer advancement opportunities and on average receive lower ratings on their job performance than men. Women tend to be employed at lower levels of the organization, make less money and have greater intentions to leave."[74] A recent article in the *San Jose Mercury News*, close to Silicon Valley, provided striking examples of the marginal position of women in high-tech industries:[75]

- Last year, a Mercury News survey of the highest-paid executives at Silicon Valley's 150 largest public companies included no women.
- Another listing last year by Vanity Fair of the top 50 leaders of the Information Age included only one woman—Esther Dyson, chairwoman of the board of the San Francisco-based Electronic Frontier Foundation.
- A Mercury News survey of the 1995 annual reports of Silicon Valley's 15 largest companies found only 5.4 percent of the people listed as its top officers—board members, vice presidents and division heads—are women.

If professionals are facing a slowly changing work environment, what about the other end of the job spectrum? "The total number of secretaries in the United States dropped from 4 million in 1988 to 3.4 million in 1994. And while their numbers are now projected to start increasing again, general secretary jobs are likely to rise less sharply than US employment as a whole."[76] But what forecasts show is that over the period 1994 to 2005, stenographers, data entry keyers, and especially typist/wordprocessors will decrease.[77] Since women represent the bulk of employment in these categories, women will have fewer traditional entry level jobs available. Since the impetus is to acquire marketable skills, the problems women face in the educational system will have to be overcome if they are to continue the slow movement towards equity in the workplace. There is also the fear that increasingly, low-level data entry work will be contracted out to "giant data processing outfits, or what critics sometimes call 'electronic sweatshops.' "[78]

Professional women continue to face an unfair struggle for career advancement and adequate recognition of advanced degrees. There seems to be an unstated reluctance to choose equally qualified women over men for management positions. The explanation frequently offered, that men simply feel more comfortable working with men, does not do justice to the depth of the problem. Men tend to patronize women at a professional level. Women have only recently increased their representation in professional ranks and lack the widespread "old-boys" network that has traditionally provided contacts, support, and information for successful men. This situation is changing, as several women's organizations are now in operation: the Association of Women in Computing, the Society of Women Engineers, and the Aerospace Women's Committee, among others. These societies work to keep women informed of educational and professional opportunities, provide support in stressful situations, and actively promote the visibility of their members.

One group of women connected to the computer industry has generally been overlooked in the discussions of success stories—Asian women who may work in sweatshop conditions to produce microprocessors and peripherals. For example, wafers containing chips manufactured in the US are sent to Third World countries such as Thailand and Malaysia, where they are separated, have their leads soldered, and are then returned for incorporation into products. The work pays little by Western standards and produces considerable eye strain. Another very interesting example is the assembly of compact disk drives. One of the most successful companies in this area is Seagate Technology, Inc., with 1990 sales estimated at about $2.5 billion. Of its 40,000 employees in 1990, 27,000 were in Southeast Asia, about half in Singapore, and most of these were women. As Seagate chairman Alan Shugart says "In Thailand, there is a lot of close work under microscopes. It is pretty tough to find people in the US to do that kind of work."[79] The pay in Singapore in the early 1990s was about $2 per hour while in Thailand it started at 50 cents. Here is the description of one of the factories: "At one location, the employees, nearly all women, piece together drives while facing each other across three-by-three-foot tables. They rarely speak, rarely look up. One American Seagate manager described them as 'mini-robots' and then was cautioned by an aide to display more sensitivity."[80] Advances in technology sometimes rest on a foundation of human blood, sweat, and tears.

Job Safety: VDTs and Other Problems

The video or visual display terminal (VDT), or unit (VDU), is the most common piece of evidence of the increasingly widespread distribution of computers in the workplace and at home. Estimates vary but there are probably more than 50 million VDTs in use in the workplace today and the number is growing. Large numbers of workers, mainly women, have been spending many hours in front of VDT screens. Over the years a number of fears have been expressed about possible threats to health from long-term interaction with VDTs and keyboards. These concerns can be grouped into four main categories: visual, physical, psychological, and most controversial, radiation-related. The greatest fears have been aroused because of potential genetic defects. A number of incidents have been reported of what appear to be unexpectedly high rates of miscarriages and birth defects among women working with VDTs. During a one-year period between 1979 and 1980, at a Sears Computer center in Dallas, there were seven miscarriages and one premature infant death, in twelve pregnancies in one year. In the same period, four of seven babies born to VDT operators at the Toronto Star had birth defects.

Subsequent investigations have revealed that screens do not emit sufficient ionizing radiation to cause any damage but questions are being asked about the effects of electromagnetic fields (EMFs). Similar radiation is produced by electric blankets, electric razors, hair dryers, and other electric appliances, power lines, and the human body itself. There is considerable debate in the scientific community about the dangers of low-level radiation and the experimental evidence is at present inconclusive. The current opinion about the impact of magnetic radiation emitted by VDTs on pregnancy is "that most of the epidemiological studies suggest that VDT work is not associated with an increased risk of adverse pregnancy outcome. A few studies showed an excess of some adverse outcomes, but the effects of recall bias could not be excluded in these studies."[81] But a problem still exists because even though modern VDTs generally emit low levels of radiation, older units do not, and the safe levels are not generally agreed upon.

The question of the effect of EMFs on a variety of illnesses is still being studied and many questions are still open. Consider the following recent findings:[82]

- In some experiments, human cancer cells exposed to EMF exhibit increased resistance to attack by the body's cancer fighting white blood cells and the body's immune system. Further, a drop in the levels of melatonin have been reported in people sleeping with electric blankets. Melatonin is a hormone which controls the monthly female cycle and inhibits the growth of certain cancers.
- A study released in February, 1991 by the University of Southern California (USC) Los Angeles unexpectedly found an increased rate of leukemia among children who watch black and white televisions.
- Loomis and Savitz of the University of North Carolina reported a doubling of the expected breast cancer rates for women in electrical trades aged 45–54. (Microwave News, Nov/Dec 1993).
- Results from two studies conducted in Finland and one in Los Angeles indicate that people with a high occupational exposure to EMFs are at least three times as likely to develop Alzheimer's disease as those without significant exposure. (Network News, Aug/Sep 1994).

- Yet the experts agree only on one thing: no one knows the extent, nature and cause of health hazards associated with electromagnetic fields. Should we take comfort in published reports that the evidence is "not conclusive," or should we take steps now to mitigate public exposure to EMF even if the scientific jury is still out?

In late 1989, IBM began shipping VDTs with reduced electromagnetic emissions, while strenuously maintaining that existing VDTs posed no safety hazards. Careful statistical analysis of the clusters of birth defects, mentioned previously, indicate that such clusters are bound to occur by chance alone and do not demonstrate that there is a connection between birth defects and VDT work. Just to be safe the following advice seems entirely prudent:[83]

- Don't sit too close to your computer display. Keep at least an arm's length away from the screen, but remember that at this distance you will still be within the magnetic field. Computer monitors vary greatly in the strength of the magnetic fields which they emit, so you should check yours with an ELF and VLF meter.
- Rearrange your office work area so that you and your co-workers are not exposed to EMF from the sides and backs of each other's VDTs.
- Turn off your VDT when you are not using it.
- Consider purchasing a low radiation VDT which contains an active compensating coil, or a zero radiation display based on shielded LCD technology.

Although reproductive issues have received considerable attention, there are many other important health-related issues. Other problems are eye strain (even the formation of cataracts has been claimed), back, neck, arm, hand, and finger trauma. In some cases a solution is achieved by better background lighting, reduction of glare, proper height of tables and chairs, regular breaks, and the elimination of stress attributable to excessive monitoring. The vision problems that arise from extended work with VDTs include eye strain, fatigue, blurring, and double vision similar to those associated with other visually demanding work. There are other problems related to screen flicker and cursor blinking, which can cause headaches. The term *ergonomics* is used to describe the field of study concerned with the design of working environments to facilitate ease and safety of use (ergos: work and nomos: study of). Most organizations have adopted a set of procedures to prevent or alleviate physical and psychological problems that may arise in the extended use of computers. For example, the following guidelines were prepared by the Health and Safety Branch of the National Institutes of Health:[84] select eyeglasses for correct focal length, use an antiglare screen, keep eye-to-screen distance between 16–27 inches, take periodic stretch breaks, adjust chair back height and tension for lumbar support, adjust chair height so that thighs rest horizontally, adjust VDT angle and/or lighting to reduce neck/eye strain, and adjust keyboard height to 28–30 inches above floor.

A group of physical problems are associated with long-term use of the keyboard that are known under a variety of terms, namely, repetitive strain injuries, cumulative trauma disorder, VDT disease, and upper-limb disorders (ULD). One specific nerve disorder resulting from thousands of repetitive movements is carpal tunnel syndrome, a painful condition that may debilitate the hands and arms. In 1989, out of 284,000 occupational illnesses, 147,000 were repetitive motion disorders, up 28% over the previous year, making it the fastest growing occupational complaint.[85] In general ULD may involve damage to muscles, nerves, and tendons, as well as swelling and inflammation. It is important to recognize the onset of these disorders as they may be difficult to alleviate. Much more research needs to be undertaken but for the present, careful attention to furniture design, keyboard height and location, arm and wrist angles, and frequent breaks must be observed.

THE CHANGING NATURE OF WORK

> The man whose whole life is spent performing a few simple operations, of which the effects are perhaps always the same, or very nearly the same, has no occasion to exert his under-standing or to exercise his invention in finding out expedients for removing difficulties which never occur. He naturally loses, therefore, the habit of such exertion, and generally becomes as stupid and ignorant as it is possible for a human creature to become.[86]

The importance of work in our lives can hardly be overestimated and therefore anything that affects the many hours we spend working has an impact well beyond the work place. The physical and psychological challenges to the well-being of workers both in the office and the factory raise many important social issues. For all the talk about the potential lib-erating power of the new technology, there may be a price to pay, especially for women and especially in the office. More specifically, there is a growing concern with threats to worker autonomy and self-respect posed by various kinds of technology including drug testing, television and telephone surveillance, and sophisticated body searches. Of course careful attention must be paid to computer-based technology such as computer monitor-ing, which is only the most recent version of the process of determining base-line work lev-els and adherence to preestablished work regimens. Such monitoring is physically unob-trusive although the employee, typically a woman, must be constantly aware that every few milliseconds her activities are being measured. The result is usually an increase in stress level with detrimental psychological side effects.

Somewhat more abstract but obviously of concern is the growing uncomfortable relation between people and machines, especially when these machines may pose a challenge to human dignity. Thus it is all the more important that the introduction of sophisticated computers into the work place be accompanied by proper training, which stresses the long term benefits of computer-aided work and assures employees of their ongoing value. Part of the fear is that ultimately they will be replaced by the computer. Even though there is little likelihood of this occurring in the short run, sufficient evidence exists to warrant some apprehension. A more realistic concern is that an increasing number and variety of jobs will be deskilled—they will consist of nothing more than "tending" machines.

Deskilling

Does the introduction of new technology—computer systems, to be specific—raise or lower the overall skills of employees? The pessimistic viewpoint is that the new technology, for example, office automation, will certainly raise the skills of some of the workers, but most of the office staff will have a reduced range of responsibilities. Their work will be narrowly constrained to data entry—that is, sitting at a terminal all day, rapidly typing rows and columns of numbers. Under this scenario, skills have been reduced for many of these employees, most of whom are likely to be women. As jobs are deskilled, they are also re-classified and downgraded in terms of wage scales. Thus, entry level jobs will pay less and be less secure, more routine and monotonous. Consistent with this view is the assumption that office managers are always interested in maximizing volume and speed in data pro-cessing. The only restraints are side effects such as absenteeism, high turnover, poor qual-ity, or even sabotage. This view justifies the fears of many critics that management wishes to reproduce the factory model in the office.

Many women are concerned that the new automation will reinforce sex segregation in the office. With more women employed in routine jobs, their path for advancement will be much longer and more difficult. In fact, most women will have no opportunity for ad-vancement because there will be no opportunity to improve their skills. On the factory floor, many workers see their future as adjuncts to powerful, computerized machines. Here also deskilling is an issue. Fewer workers will be able to exercise a broad range of skills, and most workers will be narrowly constrained. From a historical point of view, the process of separating the actions of the worker from their planning and organization will culminate in the computerized factory where very few workers are required. An alternate scheme is to incorporate workers in the planning process to make use of their skills at the manufacturing level.

A number of government reports have appeared in the last few years that attempt to di-rectly address this issue of the impact of technological change on the workplace and the worker. Consider the following presentation of the debate:[87]

> Two opposing points of view are prominent
>
> - technological change leads to upgrading of skills, making for better jobs but also requir-ing more training or education, so that less skilled people may have trouble finding jobs;
> - or, on the contrary, that advanced technology de-skills jobs, making them narrower, more repetitious and perfunctory, and leaving workers as nothing but machine tenders at relatively low pay.
>
> A third view has also emerged:
>
> [T]echnological changes are increasing the quality and number of some higher level jobs while eliminating or downgrading middle-level positions, thus creating a skills gap be-tween lower and higher level jobs.

It is also important and necessary to point out that it is not just technology that affects the nature of jobs. The technology is implemented in a matrix of economic, historic, and so-cial forces that present a variety of decisions for management and labor. To succumb to a belief in technological determinism is to abrogate responsibility; certainly the range of de-cisions may be constrained but there are decisions to be made and both management and workers must cooperate, if possible, to produce a humane work place. Just a few years ago, the following advice on how to use their equipment and deal with their workers was recommended to factory managers:[88]

> If skills can be progressively built into machines, then workers need not be especially skilled themselves . . . [G]ear up for long production runs, buffer yourself with enough inventory to keep the lines moving, inspect for defects—if at all—at the end of those lines, treat workers primarily as a reservoir of costs that can be bled out under pressure as the need arises, and you will boost your market share, your profits, your stockholder's good disposition, your bond ratings, your own compensation, and the Nation's industrial health.

In 1985, the Panel on Technology and Employment was created by the Committee on Science, Engineering, and Public Policy of the Council of the National Academy of Engineering to study the impact of technological change on employment opportunities, productivity, and the quality of work life. It published its findings in 1987,[89] which included a comprehensive review of existing literature. When discussing worker skills it is necessary to distinguish between basic skills, those which workers have typically acquired before entering the labor force, such as literacy, problem-solving, and written communication, and job-related skills, typically provided by employers and required by employees to perform the job. Although studies have been carried out for more than fifty years, the overall results are surprisingly inconclusive:[90]

1. Process innovations in skill-intensive manufacturing processes often eliminated high-skill jobs and generated low-skill jobs. The opposite was true, however, for the adoption of data-and word-processing-technologies in offices, which eliminated low-skill jobs and created high-skill jobs.
2. No evidence [has been found] to support claims of significant upgrading or downgrading in aggregate skill requirements as a result of technological change.
3. [Using] educational attainment as a proxy for skill requirements . . . the educational requirements of projected 1995 jobs were virtually identical to those needed for 1982 jobs.
4. [T]he automation of high-skill jobs shifted their content from the direct operation of a machine to monitoring the operations of a different machine that was more nearly self-controlling . . . the changes resulting from new technology reduced skill requirements.
5. . . . [T]he shift toward increased responsibility required higher-order mental skills to ensure quick and appropriate responses to mechanical breakdowns.
6. . . . [T]he introduction of automated manufacturing technologies reduced the number of job classifications while broadening the scope of activities within each classification.
7. . . . .[A]utomation fragmented and standardized clerical work, requiring lower-level and narrower skills.
8. . . . [T]he introduction of minicomputers, personal computers, and higher-level programming languages has restructured office work . . . this worker will be responsible for a wider range of tasks . . .

In a study commissioned by the Department of Labor's Office of the American Workplace (and carried out by researchers at Harvard and Wharton Business Schools together with Ernst & Young), it was reported that "Lifting workers' skills while simultaneously implementing innovative workplace management solutions pays off in profits and competitiveness, . . ."[91] Important findings from this report, with respect to upgrading worker skills are worth noting:[92]

- Integrating business process and technology improvements with high performance work practices are the key to maximizing their benefits. Process practices, such as Just-In-Time inventory management, are most effective when implemented in conjunction with employee training and empowerment programs.
- Companies investing in employee development enjoy significantly higher market values, on average, than their industry peers.
- Companies with "above average" and early implementation of TQM [Total Quality Management] programs that included an element of employee empowerment were rewarded with significant share price increases.
- Companies which have adopted aggressive employee development and involvement practices—such as skills training and team-based management—make significantly larger productivity gains than those which do not.

It is clearly worth the investment by management to upgrade the skills of its employees to remain competitive and profitable.

Surveillance and Monitoring

The rights of workers in the workplace are not clearly defined. By providing jobs, management would seem to have power over its workers that threaten their basic civil liberties. For example, drug tests, polygraph tests, and psychological evaluation may be required to qualify for a job and to keep one. On the job, employees may be subject to television surveillance, telephone and computer monitoring, and even regular body searches. Professed reasons are to deter and detect criminal activities, to measure performance in order to establish basic rates of work, and to maintain such rates. Management maintains its right to control the labor process by whatever means it deems necessary. Workers argue that monitoring creates an atmosphere of suspicion and recrimination resulting in decreased productivity and unacceptable levels of stress.

Table 10.6 shows the kinds of monitoring and testing that have increased concern about the challenges to privacy and civil liberties in the workplace. It is taken from an Office of Technology report called The Electronic Supervisor.[93] The first three categories seem to be directed towards measuring work performance and are sometimes called work monitoring or work measurement, and are of primary concern in the present context. Others investigate more personal issues both in and outside the workplace and are beyond the scope of this discussion. A review of some of the following findings in the report reveals the depth of concern that this issue has raised (the numbers are as given in the report):[94]

2. Computer-based systems offer opportunities for organizing work in new ways, as well as means of monitoring it more intensively. Electronic monitoring is most likely to raise opposition among workers when it is imposed without worker participation, when standards are perceived as unfair, or when performance records are used punitively. Worker involvement in design and implementation of monitoring programs can result in greater acceptance by workers, but despite activities of labor unions in some industries and recent progress in labor-management cooperation in others, most firms do not have mechanisms to do this.

3. There is reason to believe that electronically monitoring the quantity or speed of work contributes to stress and stress-related illness, although there is still little research sepa-

TABLE 10.6

Some Categories of Behavior Subject to Monitoring, Measurement, or Testing.

Monitoring, Measurement, Testing	Performance	Behaviors	Personal Characteristics
Output: keystrokes, etc.	x		
Use of Resources: computer time, phone	x	x	
Communications contents: "eavesdropping"	x	x	
Location: cards, beepers, TV cameras		x	x
Concentration, mental activity: brainwave		x	x
Predisposition to error: drug testing		x	x
Predisposition to health risk: genetic screening			x
Truthfulness: polygraph, brainwave			x

Source: The Electronic Supervisor: New Technology, New Tensions. (Washington, DC: US Congress, Office of Technology Assessment, OTA-CIT-333, September 1987), Figure 1, p. 13.

rating the effects of monitoring from job design, equipment design, lighting, machine pacing, and other potentially stressful aspects of computer-based office work.

4. Monitoring the content of messages raises a different set of issues. Some employers say that service observation (listening to or recording the content of employees' telephone conversations with customers) helps assure quality and correctness of information and the protection of all parties in case of dispute. However, service observation also impacts the privacy of the customer, and workers and labor organizations have argued that it contributes to stress of the employee, and creates an atmosphere of distrust. Monitoring the content of electronic mail messages or personal computer (PC) diskettes also raises privacy issues.

It is obviously very difficult to obtain accurate statistics about how much monitoring goes on and who gets monitored. Typically, routinized work, and low-level work such as simple data collection are likely candidates for monitoring. Thus word processors, data-entry clerks, telephone operators, customer service workers, telemarketing workers, and insurance claims clerks are subject to monitoring, but certainly not all. Alan Westin, who produced a report used in The Electronic Supervisor, estimated that the great majority of clerical workers are not monitored (65 to 80 percent) and that most professional, technical, and managerial workers are not (95 percent or more). But note that if 20 to 35 percent of clerical workers are monitored this amounts to four to six million workers.[95]

In a survey reported in April 1996, some 84 of 300 Fortune 500 corporations responded to a series of questions with respect to their workplace privacy policies. Among the highlights of the findings are the following:[96]

Disclosures of Personal Employment Data
Seventy percent of the corporations have a policy concerning which records are routinely disclosed to inquiries from government agencies. As a result, the employees of 3 out of 10 corporations are left without such guidance.

Also, 7 out of 10 (70%) disclose personal information to credit grantors; almost one-half (47%) disclose it to landlords; and one out of 5 (19%) give the data to charitable organizations.

Informing the Individual
Over half of the corporations inform personnel of the types of records maintained (62%), and how they are used (56). Nearly half (49%) of the corporations responding find it necessary to collect information without informing the individual.

Three out of four (75) organizations check, verify, or supplement background information collected directly from personnel.

Authorizing Personal Data Collection
Nine out of ten (93%) companies obtain written permission from the individual when seeking information about him/her from a third party.

When written permission is not obtained, only 3 out of 10 (32%) corporations have a policy of informing an individual of the types of information sought; one of 4 (25%) tell them the techniques used to collect it; and 3 of 10 (29%) disclose the sources.

Use of Investigative Firms
Two-thirds (67%) of the organizations responding retain the services of an investigative firm to collect information concerning personnel. A quarter (25%) of these corporations do not review the operating policies and practices of the investigative firm.

Given that an increasing amount of communication in offices is taking place via electronic mail (e-mail), it behooves organizations to have well-defined policies in place. (Recall the e-mail privacy cases discussed in the previous chapter.) The following set of e-mail principles has been proposed by the Information and Privacy Commissioner of Ontario, Tom Wright, who administers the *Freedom of Information and Protection of Privacy Act* and the *Municipal Freedom of Information and Protection of Privacy Act* of the province of Ontario:[97]

1. The privacy of e-mail users should be respected and protected.
2. Each organization should create an explicit policy on the use of e-mail which addresses the privacy of the users.
3. Each organization should make its e-mail policy known to users and inform users of their rights and obligations in regard to the confidentiality of messages on the system.
4. Users should receive proper training in regard to e-mail and the security/privacy issues surrounding its use.
5. E-mail systems should not be used for the purposes of collecting, using and disclosing personal information, without adequate safeguards to protect privacy.
6. Providers of e-mail systems should explore technical means to protect privacy.
7. Organizations should develop appropriate security procedures to protect e-mail messages.

These principles should form the basis of an e-mail privacy statement for most public and private organizations.

SUMMARY

Of all the issues associated with technology, especially computers, the most important is work—how much, and what kind. The subject of jobs and computers will be with us for a very long time, and everyone will be affected.

The relation between technology and work is a complex one. Historically, except for periods of worldwide economic dislocations, technological innovation has not decreased the number of jobs. The open question is whether or not computers are a fundamentally different kind of technology. The contributions of Frederick Taylor and Henry Ford were key to the development of the assembly line. The separation of actual work from its planning has serious consequences for workers. The process continues, with the introduction of robots into the factory and computer networks into the office. The voices of the workers themselves should be listened to . What workers really want, whether or not they are dissatisfied, and the role of computers in their lives are issues of concern to society at large.

Which jobs will be most affected by computers and how? Granted that many jobs will be lost, where will the new jobs come from? Will there be enough? The number of blue collar jobs is decreasing. The number of service and information jobs is increasing. Agricultural jobs are now only about 3% of the total. Fewer people are producing the products and food for the entire country. How does office automation affect the social organization of the office? Computer networks have opened up new possibilities for distributing work and reducing the size of central offices. There are advantages to employers to having some part of their staff working at home, but the advantages to employees are somewhat more debatable

Unions are dedicated to the welfare of their members. Unfortunately, in recent difficult, economic times, job security has overridden considerations of working conditions, wages, and other benefits. However, some unions have attempted to include technological issues as bargaining issues in their contracts.

Women are affected by computers in many important ways because of their large representation in the office. Problems of job advancement, equal pay for equal work, and discrimination in the workplace and in academia exist. Serious questions have been raised about the physical, psychological, and long-term genetic effects of video display terminals. Other ergonomic concerns, such as glare, background lighting, and seating are more amenable to correction.

Some of the changes in the lives of workers and in the nature of their jobs as a result of the introduction of computers into the workplace have not been for the better. Considerable debate exists over whether or not the skill level of both workers and jobs have increased or decreased, the so-called deskilling issue. Also very serious is the increasing use of computer systems to monitor performance and to threaten individual privacy.

NOTES

1. E. P. Thompson. *The Making of the English Working Class.* (Middlesex, England: Penguin, 1980), p. 600.

2. William Bridges. "The End of the Job," *Fortune,* September 19, 1994, pp. 62–64, 68, 72, 74.

3. Keith H. Hammonds, Kevin Kelly, and Karen Thurston. "Rethinking Work," Special Report, *Business Week,* October 7, 1994, pp. 74–77, 80–81, 84–87.

4. *Op. cit.,* Bridges, p. 64.

5. Phil Stallings, as quoted in Studs Terkel. *Working* (New York: Avon paperback 1975), p. 223.

6. *Ibid.*

7. Described in Satoshi Kamata. *Japan in the Passing Lane.* (New York: Pantheon Paperback, 1983), p. 22.

8. Joan Young, Cantonsville, MD, as quoted in Hammonds et al., p. 85.

9. Harry Braverman. *Labor and Monopoly Capital: The Degradation of Work in the Twentieth Century.* (New York: Monthly Review Press, 1974).

10. Frederick Winslow Taylor. *The Principles of Scientific Management.* (New York: Norton Library, 1967). Originally published in 1911.

11. *Op. cit.,* Braverman, p. 147.

12. *Ibid.,* p. 147.

13. Richard M. Cyert and David C. Mowery (eds.). *Technology and Employment: Innovation and Growth in the US Economy,* Panel on Technology and Employment; Committee on Science, Engineering, and Public Policy; National Academy of Sciences, National Academy of Engineering, and Institute of Medicine. (Washington, DC: National Academy Press, 1987), p. 168.

14. *Technology and Structural Unemployment: Reemploying Displaced Adults,* US Congress, Office of Technology Assessment, OTA-ITE-250. (Washington, DC, February 1986), pp. 321–367.

15. *Ibid.,* p. 321.

16. "BLS Releases New 1994–2005 Employment Projections," Bureau of Labor Statistics, December 1, 1995. Accessed from the Web page with URL: <ftp://stats.bls.gov/pub/news.release/ecopro.txt> on March 9, 1996.

17. Diane E. Herz. "Worker Displacement in a Period of Rapid Job Expansion: 1983–87," *Monthly Labor Review,* May 1990, p. 21.

18. "Worker Displacement During the Early 1990s," Bureau of Labor Statistics, September 14, 1994. Accessed from the Web page with URL: <ftp://stats.bls.gov/pub/news.release/disp.txt> on March 9, 1996.

19. *Ibid.*

20. Mark R. Bruneau, consultant, as quoted in Catherine Arnst. "The Bloodletting at AT&T Is Just the Beginning," *Business Week,* January 15, 1996, p. 30.

21. "Apple Cutting 1,300 Jobs; Focuses on 'Best-of-Class'," *The Vancouver Sun* (Associated Press), January 18, 1996, p. C 5.

22. Edmund L. Andrews. "Job Cuts at AT&T Will Total 40,000, 13% of its Staff," *The New York Times,* January 3, 1996, p. A 1.

23. "New Data on Contingent and Alternative Employment Examined by BLS," Bureau of Labor Statistics, USDL 95-318, August 17, 1995. Accessed from the Web page with URL: <ftp://stats.bls.gov/pub/news.release/conemp.txt> on March 9, 1996.

24. *Ibid.*

25. The first quotation is by Stephen Roach, chief economist, Morgan Stanley, and the second by Luc Soete, Maastricht Economic Research Institute on Innovation and Technology. Both are taken from Bill Barol. "Staying Afloat," *Time Digital, Time's Technology Supplement,* April 15, 1996, TD 24–TD 30, TD 32.

26. Keith H. Hammonds. "The Issue Is Employment, Not Employability," *Business Week,* June 10, 1996, p. 64.

27. As described and quoted in Rob Norton. "Job Destruction/Job Creation," *Fortune*, April 1, 1996, p. 55.

28. From a poll conducted in late 1995 and reported in Elizabeth Kolbert and Adam Clymer, "The Politics of Layoffs: In Search of a Message." Sixth of seven articles on The Downsizing of America, *The New York Times*, March 8, 1996, p. A 13.

29. Edward W. Gore, Jr. in *McGraw-Hill Encyclopedia of Science and Technology*, Volume 14, Fifth Edition. (New York: McGraw-Hill, 1982), p. 708.

30. "Robot Institute of America Worldwide Robotics Survey and Directory," Robot Institute of America. (Dearborn, MI, 1982), p. 1.

31. "Demand for US Industrial Robots Surging," *Industry Flash*, **1** (4), December 5, 1994. Accessed from the Robotics FAQ Web page with URL: <http://www.hitex.com/FAQ/robotics/7.html> on August 4, 1996.

32. "Robot Sales Soar to New Records in 1995," Robotic Industries Association, February 21, 1996. Accessed from the Web page with URL: <http://www.robotics.org/whatshot.html> on August 4, 1996.

33. "Productivity and Costs: Preliminary Fourth-Quarter Measures and Annual Averages, 1995," Bureau of Labor Statistics, USDL 96-76, March 6, 1996. Accessed from the Web page with URL: <ftp://stats.bls.gov/pub/news.release/prod2.txt> on March 9, 1996.

34. Michael L. Dertouzos, Richard K. Lester, Robert M. Solow, and the MIT Commission on Industrial Productivity. *Made in America: Regaining the Productive Edge*. (Cambridge, MA: MIT Press, 1989), pp. 26–27.

35. *Computerized Manufacturing Automation: Employment, Education, and the Workplace*. US Congress, Office of Technology Assessment, OTA-CIT-235. (Washington, DC, April 1984), pp. 32–98.

36. "Agility Overview," Agility Forum, Date unknown. Accessed from the Web page with URL: <http://absu.amef.lehigh.edu/agility.html> on August 5, 1996.

37. Jimmy L. Haugen, vice president for automotive assembly systems, GMF Robotics Corp., as quoted in David Whiteside, et al. "How GM's Saturn Could Run Rings Around Old-Style Carmakers," *Business Week*, January 28, 1985, p. 128.

38. Saturn President R. G. "Skip" LeFauve as quoted in Alex Taylor III. "Back to the Future at Saturn," *Fortune*, August 1, 1988, p. 64.

39. Alex Taylor III, *Ibid.*

40. S. C. Gwynne. "Does US Industry Have the Right Stuff? GM's Saturn Division Aims to Show that America Can Still Compete," *Time*, October 29, 1990, p. 42.

41. *Ibid.*, p. 48.

42. David Woodruff and Kathleen Kerwin. "Suddenly, Saturn's Orbit Is Getting Wobbly," *Business Week*, February 28, 1994, p. 34.

43. Gabriella Stern and Rebecca Blumenstein. "GM Expected to Approve Mid-Size Saturn Model," *Wall Street Journal*, as reprinted in the Globe and Mail (Toronto, Canada), August 6, 1996, p. B 6.

44. Karl-H. Abel. *Computer-Integrated Manufacturing: The Social Approach*. (Geneva: International Labour Office, 1990), p. 6.

45. George Cohon, CEO of McDonald's Restaurants of Canada Ltd. as quoted in Report on Business Magazine, *Globe and Mail*, Toronto, Canada, April 1988, p. 14.

46. James Brian Quinn, Jordan J. Baruch, and Penny Cushman Paquette. "Technology in Services," *Scientific American*, December 1987, p. 50.

47. *Op. cit.*, BLS Releases New 1994–2005 Employment Projections.

48. *Ibid.*

49. Source unknown, but taken from a collection at the Web page with URL: <http://www.tele-worker.com/quotes.html> on August 8, 1996.

50. Alvin Toffler. *The Third Wave.* (New York: Bantam, 1981).

51. "Home Work," *Fortune*, December 10, 1984, pp. 10–11.

52. Margrethe H. Olson. "Organizational Barriers to Professional Telework," in Eileen Boris and Cynthia R. Daniels (eds.) *Homework: Historical and Contemporary Perspectives on Paid Labor at Home.* (Urbana and Chicago: University of Illinois Press, 1989), pp. 215–216.

53. As quoted in "On Telecommuting: A PS Enterprises Research Paper, PS Enterprises, 1995. Accessed from the Web page with URL: <http://www.well.com/user/pse/telecom.htm> on August 7, 1996.

54. As quoted in the Home Office Facts and Figures Web Page, Home Office Association of America, 1995. Accessed from the Web page with URL: <http://www.hoaa.com/hostats.htm> on August 8, 1996.

55. A projection of the US Department of Transportation as quoted in *Saving Energy in US Transportation*, US Congress, Office of Technological Assessment. (Washington, DC: US Government Printing Office, July 15, 1994). Available at the Web site with URL: <http://www.ota.nap.edu/>.

56. Richard P. Johnson, "Ten Advantages to Telecommuting," September 1994. Accessed from the Web page with URL: <http://128.165.144.22/Group/tsa10/rick_johnson/telebenefits.html> on August 7, 1996.

57. "Frequently Asked Questions (FAQs) on Telecommuting/Telework and Alternative Officing," Gil Gordon Associates, date unknown. Accessed from the Web page with URL: <http://www.gilgordon.com/faqs.html> on August 7, 1996.

58. Tom Forester. "The Myth of the Electronic Cottage," *Futures*, 2 (3), June 1988, p. 232.

59. Mitch Betts. "Telecommuting: The Dark Side," *Computerworld*, August 7, 1995, p. 55.

60. Clarence Darrow, in *The Railroad Trainmen*, November 1909.

61. Henry Ford (booklet distributed to Ford employees during CIO drive), as quoted in *Time*, August 20, 1945.

62. Steve Lohr. "The Growth of the 'Global Office'," *The New York Times*, October 18, 1988, p. 29.

63. Michael Goldfield. *The Decline of Organized Labor in the United States.* (Chicago: The University of Chicago Press, 1987), pp. 3–25.

64. "Union Members in 1995," US Bureau of Labor Statistics, USDL 96-41, February 6, 1996. Accessed from the Web page with URL: <ftp://stats.bls.gov/pub/news.release/union2.txt> on March 13, 1996.

65. "Adapt or Die," *The Economist*, July 1, 1995, pp. 54, 56.

66. "Workers of the World Disunite," *The Economist*, August 18, 1990, p. 57.

67. Sar A. Levitan and Frank Gallo. "Collective Bargaining and Private Sector Professionals," *Monthly Labor Review*, September 1989, pp. 24–33.

68. Adapted from Federal Interagency Telecommuting Centers, an Interim Report by the GSA, March 1995 by Telework Analytics International, May 7, 1996. Accessed from the Web page with URL: <http://www.teleworker.com/quotes.html> on August 8, 1996.

69. "Statement by the AFL-CIO Executive Council on The Information Superhighway," May 10, 1995. Accessed on the Web page with URL: <http://www.aflcio.org/estatements/may95/infsuphwy.txt> on August 7, 1996.

70. From the Facts, published by the Canadian Union of Public Employees, and reprinted in *The Globe and Mail,* Toronto, Canada, March 2, 1988, p. B 10.

71. "Report of The Commission on the Future of Worker-Management Relations," The Dunlop

Commission, US Departments of Commerce and Labor, Section 3, 1995. Available at the Web page with URL: <http://www.ilr.cornell.edu/lib/e_archive/Dunlop/>.

72. Maria Klawe and Nancy Leveson. "Women in Computing: Where Are We Now? *Communications of the ACM*, **38** (1), January 1995, p. 32.

73. *Ibid.*

74. Magid Igbaria, professor of information science at Claremont Graduate School, from results originally reported in *MIS Quarterly*, as quoted in Laura DiDio. "Sexism in IS: Not Gone, Not Forgotten," *Computerworld*, June 24, 1996, p. 84.

75. Janet Rae-Dupree and Dean Takahashi. "High-Tech Women Still Struggle," *San Jose Mercury News*, June 2, 1996. Accessed from the Web page with URL: <http://www.sjmercury.com/business/wom601.htm> on August 11, 1996.

76. Ilana DeBare. "Secretaries Take a Memo: No Computer Skills, No Jobs," part 3 of a series on Women in Computing, *The Sacramento Bee*, 1996. Accessed from the Web site with URL: <http://www.sacbee.com/news/projects/women/index.html> on August 9, 1996.

77. Bureau of Labor Statistics, *Monthly Labor Review*, November 1995.

78. *Op. cit.*, DeBare.

79. As quoted in Evelyn Richards. "Asia's Taskmaster: How One US Company Drives Employees," *The Vancouver Sun* (Canada) June 30, 1990, p. D 10. Originally published in *The Washington Post*.

80. *Ibid.*

81. "General EMF Health Effects. Video Display Terminal Magnetic Fields and Pregnancy Outcomes." *BENER Digest Update*, June 17, 1996. Accessed from the Web page with URL: <http://infoventures.microserve.com/emf/currlit/bu12482.html> on August 11, 1996.

82. George S. Lechter. "A Survey of Present Knowledge Concerning Low-Frequency Electromagnetic Radiation from Power Lines, Home Wiring, Appliances, Televisions and Computer Displays," *Medical Electronics*, 1994. Accessed from the Web page with URL: <http://www.milligauss.com/info.html> on August 11, 1996.

83. *Ibid.*

84. "Safety and Health Program for Video Display Terminal (VDT) Operators," Health and Safety Branch, National Institutes of Health, Safety Notes, Number 11, July 25, 1996. Accessed from the Web page with URL: <http://www.niehs.nih.gov/odhsb/notes/note11.htm> on August 11, 1996.

85. Mitch Betts. "Repetitive Stress Claims Soar," *Computerworld*, November 19, 1990, p. 1.

86. Adam Smith. *The Wealth of Nations*. (London: Everyman's Library, J. M. Dent & Sons Ltd., 1947), vol. II, p. 278.

87. *Op. cit., Technology and Structural Unemployment*, p. 336.

88. W. Abernathy, K. Clark, and A. Kantrow. *Industrial Renaissance: Producing a Competitive Future for America*. (New York: Basic Books, 1983).

89. *Op. cit.*, Richard M. Cyert and David C. Mowery (eds.). *Technology and Employment*.

90. These studies are all referenced in Cyert and Mowery, *Technology and Employment*, as follows:

1. P. M. Flynn. "The Impact of Technological Change on Jobs and Workers." Paper prepared for the US Department of Labor, Employment Training Administration, 1985.

2. K. I. Spenner. "The Upgrading and Downgrading of Occupations: Issues, Evidence, and Implications for Evidence," *Review of Education Research*, 55, 1985, pp. 125–154.

3. H. Levin and R. Rumberger. "Educational Requirements for New Technologies: Visions, Possibilities, and Current Realities," working paper 86-SEPI-2, Stanford Education Policy Institute, 1986.

   4.   Flynn. "The Impact of Technological Change on Jobs and Workers."
   5.   Larry Hirschhorn. *Beyond Mechanization: Work and Technology in a Postindustrial Age.*
         (Cambridge, MA, 1984).
   6.   National Research Council, Committee on the Effective Implementation of Advanced Man-
         ufacturing Technology. *Human Resources Practices for Implementing Advanced Manufactur-*
         ing Technology. (Washington, DC: National Academy Press, 1986).
   7.   B. Baran. "The Technological Transformation of White-Collar Work: A Case Study of the
         Insurance Industry. In H. Hartmann (ed.). *Computer Chips and Paper Clips: Technology and*
         Women's Employment., Volume 2, Case Studies and Policy Perspectives. (Washington, DC:
         National Academy Press, 1987), pp. 25–62.
   8.   *Ibid.*
  91.   "Study Finds Competitive Gains from Innovative Workplace Practices," Ernst & Young, June
         5, 1995. Accessed from the Web page with URL: <http://www.ey.com/us/work.htm> on July
         10, 1996.
  92.   *Ibid.*
  93.   *The Electronic Supervisor: New Technology, New Tensions,* US Congress, Office of Technol-
         ogy Assessment, OTA-CIT-333. (Washington, DC, September, 1987).
  94.   *Ibid.*, pp. 9–12.
  95.   *Ibid.*, p. 32.
  96.   David F. Linowes. "A Research Survey of Privacy in the Workplace," Institute of Government
         and Public Affairs, University of Illinois at Urbana-Champaign, April 1996. Accessed from the
         Web page with URL: <http://www.securitymanagement.com/library/000149.html> on May
         22, 1996.
  97.   "Privacy Protection Principles for Electronic Mail Systems," Information and Privacy Com-
         missioner/Ontario, Toronto, Canada, February 1994.

ADDITIONAL READINGS

Introduction

"The Downsizing of America," a seven part series, *The New York Times,* March 3, 1996 to March
    9, 1996.
Lerner, Sally. "The Future of Work in North America: Good Jobs, Bad Jobs, Beyond Jobs," *Futures,*
    March 1994. Accessed from the Web page with URL: <http://cs-www.uchicago.edu/discus-
    sions/cpsr/jobtech/future-of-work.html> on August 11, 1996.
Thompson, Paul. *The Nature of Work, 2nd edition.* (London, England: Macmillan Education Ltd.,
    1989).
Zuboff, Shoshana. *In the Age of the Smart Machine: The Future of Work and Power.* (New York:
    Basic Books, 1988).

Experiences of Workers

Aronowitz, Stanley. *False Promises.* (New York: McGraw-Hill, 1974).
Doray, Bernard. *From Taylorism to Fordism: A Rational Madness.* (London, England: Free Associ-
    ation Books, 1988).
Garson, Barbara. *All the Livelong Day.* (Middlesex, England: Penguin, 1977).

Littler, Craig R. (ed.) *The Experience of Work*. (Aldershot, Hants, England: Gower, 1985).

O'Toole, James. *Work and the Quality of Life*. (Cambridge, MA: MIT Press, 1974).

Stewart, Thomas A. "The Invisible Key to Success," *Fortune*, August 5, 1996, pp. 173–174, 176.

Computers and Employment

Aley, James. "Where the Jobs Are," *Fortune*, September 18, 1995, pp. 53–54.

Bjerknes, Gro, Ehn, Pelle, and Kyng, Morten (eds.). *Computers and Democracy*. (Aldershot, Hants, England: Avebury [Gower], 1987).

"Computer Science in Manufacturing," Special Issue of *Communications of the ACM*, **39** (2), February 1996.

Greenbaum, Joan. *Windows on the Workplace*. (New York: Monthly Review Press, Cornerstone Books, 1995).

Human Resource Practices for Implementing Advanced Manufacturing Technology. Committee on the Effective Implementation of Advanced Manufacturing Technology, Manufacturing Studies Board, Commission on Engineering and Technical Systems. (Washington, DC: National Academic Press, 1986). Accessed from the Web page with URL: <http://www.ul.cs.cmu.edu/books/human_resource/hum001.htm> on August 1, 1996.

Leontief, Wassily and Duchin, Faye. *The Future Impact of Automation on Workers*. (New York: Oxford University Press, 1986).

Olson, Margrethe H. *Technological Support for Work Group Collaboration*. (Hillsdale, NJ: Lawrence Erlbaum Associates, 1989).

Quinn, James Brian and Paquette, Penny C. "Technology in Services: Creating Organizational Revolutions," *Sloan Management Review*, winter 1990, pp. 67–78.

"A World Without Jobs," *The Economist*, February 11, 1995, pp. 21–23.

Telecommuting and Remote Work

Babcock, Charles. "Telecommuting: The Future is Now," *Computerworld*, March 13, 1995, p. 8.

Betts, Mitch. "Workers Slow to Accept Telecommuting," *Computerworld,* February 20, 1995, p. 97.

"The Future of Telecommuting," *Wired*, 3.10, October 1995, p. 68. Accessed from the Web page with URL: <http://www.hotwired.com/wired/3.10/departments/reality.check.html> on August 7, 1996.

Maglitta, Joseph. "Think Simple," *Computerworld*, May 13, 1996, pp. 77, 80.

Kugelmass, Joel. *Telecommuting: A Manager's Guide to Flexible Work Arrangements*. (New York: Lexington Books, 1995).

Pacific Bell Telecommuting Guide, date unknown. Accessed from the Web page with URL: <http://www.pacbell.com/products/business/general/telecommuting/tcguide/tcguide.pdf> on August 7, 1996.

"Telecommuting: A Quick Call Beats a Long Commute." Nando.net, the Associated Press, January 9, 1996. Accessed from the Web page with URL: <http://www3.nando.net/newsroom/ntn/info/010996/info8_1897.html> on August 7, 1996.

The Response of Unions

Commission on the Future of Worker-Management Relations, final report, US Departments of Commerce and Labor, December 1994. Accessed from the Web page with URL: <http://www.ilr.cornell.edu/library/e_archive/Dunlop/dunlop.contents.htm> on August 7, 1996.

Fox, Justin. "Big Labor Flexes its Muscles," *Fortune,* June 10, 1996, pp. 24, 26.

Garland, Susan B. and Regan, Mary Beth. "Workers Unite . . . Against the GOP," *Business Week,* June 24, 1996, pp. 34–35.

Heckscher, Charles C. *The New Unionism: Employee Involvement in the Changing Corporation.* (New York: Basic Books, 1988).

Montgomery, David. *Workers' Control in America: Studies in the History of Work, Technology, and Labor Struggles.* (New York: Cambridge University Press, 1979).

Women, Computers, and Work

Brodeur, Paul. "The Magnetic-Field Menace," *MacWorld,* July 1990, pp. 136–144.

Fierman, Jaclyn. "Why Women Still Don't Hit the Top," *Fortune,* July 30, 1990, pp. 40–42, 46, 50, 54, 58, 62.

Hemenway, Kathleen. "Human Nature and the Glass Ceiling in Industry," *Communications of the ACM,* 38 (1), January 1995, pp. 55–62.

Himmelstein, Linda. "Repetitive Stress Injuries: The Asbestos Case of the 1990s?", *Business Week,* January 16, 1995, pp. 82–83.

Pearl, Amy et al. "Becoming a Computer Scientist," a report by the ACM Committee on the Status of Women in Computer Science, *Communications of the ACM,* 33 (11) November 1990, pp. 47–57.

"The Uphill Struggle: No Rose Garden for Women in Engineering," *IEEE Spectrum,* May 1995, pp. 40–50.

The Changing Nature of Work

Ehn, Pelle. "Scandinavian Design: On Participation and Skill," Chapter 4 in P. S. Adler and T. A. Winograd (eds.). *Usability: Turning Technologies into Tools.* (New York: Oxford University Press, 1992), pp. 96–132. Accessed from the Web page with URL: <http://www.ilt.columbia. edu/ilt/papers/Ehn.html> on August 11, 1996.

Garson, Barbara. *The Electronic Sweatshop: How Computers Are Transforming the Office of the Future Into the Factory of the Past.* (New York: Simon and Schuster, 1988).

Grudin, Jonathan. "Computer-Supported Cooperative Work: History and Focus," *IEEE Computer,* May 1994, pp. 19–26.

Piller, Charles. "Bosses with X-Ray Eyes," pp. 118–123 and "Privacy in Peril," pp. 124–130, *MacWorld,* July 1993.

"Representations of Work," Special Issue of *Communications of the ACM,* 38 (9), September 1995.

Research Recommendations to Facilitate Distributed Work. National Research Council. (Washington, DC: National Academy Press, 1994). Accessed from the Web site with URL: <http://www. nap.edu/nap/online/distr_work> on June 10, 1996.

—————————11—————————

BUSINESS AND GOVERNMENT

The business of America is business.

Calvin Coolidge, Address to the Society of American Newspaper Editors, January 17,1925.

INTRODUCTION

In Chapter 4, a variety of applications of computers in the business world were presented and discussed. In Chapter 7, a similar exercise was carried out for the role of computers in government. The primary purpose in each of these cases was to focus on specific innovative uses within a given domain. Of course, many information processing problems do not respect arbitrary boundaries. Several issues naturally reside in the sometimes murky area between government and business.

The relationship between business and government has been long and complex. Most companies wish to pursue their activities with minimal interference from government, except perhaps when guaranteed loans are required on occasion, or when foreign companies are felt to have an unfair advantage. Government has a variety of responsibilities, among them the creation of a climate in which companies may compete openly and the protection of its citizens' welfare. To these ends, governments have to pass antitrust and consumer protection legislation. In countries where the state owns and manages all the major companies, the goals of these companies and the people are taken to be indistinguishable. And even in a free enterprise system, government has found it necessary, over the years, to intervene in the marketplace to ensure that all companies have a fair chance to compete. The following list of relevant issues illustrates some of these interventions:

Antitrust Cases. The US government charged IBM with antitrust violations in a suit that lasted 13 years until it finally was dropped in January of 1982. Microsoft was charged with unfair practices to maintain a monopoly position since the mid-1980s. The case was settled in July 1995, with rather minor restrictions imposed on Microsoft.

Regulation of the Telephone Industry. Up to fairly recently, long distance telephone lines were a monopoly run by AT&T (American Telephone and Telegraph). In January of 1982,

AT&T agreed to separate itself from a number of local telephone companies under an agreement arranged by the Federal courts. The agreement took effect on January 1, 1984.

Industry Standards. The government plays an important role in helping to set standards in the computer and communication industries (and other areas as well).

Auctioning the Airwaves. The Federal Communications Commission auctions segments of the radio spectrum to provide a variety of services.

Legal Protection of Software and Hardware. The government protects programs by such means as copyright and patent laws (as discussed in Chapter 8).

Protection of Privacy. Issues arising from the growth in the use of computer-based information systems have led to problems and legislation.

Electronic Financial Transactions Systems. Future regulation of the banking and financial industries must take into account the increasing use of computer and communication systems for banking services.

International Trade Agreements. The US government has negotiated specific high technology trade agreements with Japan; for example, a 1996 agreement on computer semiconductors.

Transborder Data Flows. As information becomes a major resource, governments must develop policies to control the flow of information across national borders. This process is complicated by differing national policies on privacy and freedom of information.

Technology Transfer. Individual countries are concerned with protecting their technological developments. In the United States this concern covers both economic competitors such as Japan and political ones such as China. In the United States open discussion of technical issues is a way of life, and restrictions will be resisted. In fact, restrictions on the export of strong encryption programs are currently being debated.

Thus, the federal government must intrude into the marketplace from time to time. In general, its policy is to set rules for the players, monitor the resulting performance, and take specific actions only if violations occur. This is the usual procedure for competitive industries such as computers, automobiles, and household appliances. In regulated industries such as the telephone system and radio, television, and cable systems, the government has traditionally exerted control by the issuance of licenses, their renewals, and the setting of rates. There has been much debate about the proper role of government, which acts from a variety of motives, ranging from the accommodation of public opinion to the exercising of a particular political philosophy.

The computer industry has grown very rapidly since 1945 and no company has been more successful than International Business Machines, at least until fairly recently. In fact, as of 1995, IBM was the fifth leading US company in sales at almost $72 billion, and fifth in profits at $4.18 billion, up 38% over 1994 (but down from $6.02 billion in 1991). As a further indication of its dynamism and flexibility, IBM became the world leader in income from sales of personal computers in 1983, having just entered the market two years earlier, and in 1995, after many ups and severe downs, it was still the major world player, although with a considerably reduced market share.[1] In one of the final acts of the Johnson administration, in early 1969 IBM was charged with a variety of antitrust violations. After much expense on both sides, the charges were finally dropped thirteen years later. How IBM's domination of the computer market was achieved and maintained was an important issue in the government's suit.

The other major government suit of the late 1970s and early 1980s was directed against AT&T. "Ma Bell," as it was sometimes called, had been a gigantic company composed of a number of local telephone companies, a long-distance service, a manufacturing division, Western Electric, and a world-famous research facility, Bell Labs. During the 1970s, AT&T's monopoly over long-distance service was challenged, and the result was a consent agreement between the company and the federal courts that required AT&T to divest itself of its local telephone companies. The subsequent growth of these companies, continued challenges in the long-distance market, new challenges from cable companies, and the phenomenal growth of the Internet and the World Wide Web, finally prompted Congress to pass a new Telecommunications Act in 1996 to deal with the impact of the new telecommunications technologies.

Since money plays such an important role in our lives, the new developments in banking and bill paying will have a significant impact. Already, automatic teller machines (ATMs) are everywhere and are changing long-established banking habits. Additional changes taking place now include: point-of-sale terminals (POS terminals), debit cards, smart cards, home banking, and regional, national, and global banking networks. Several social issues naturally arise with the growth in electronic banking. Among these are privacy, new possibilities for large scale theft and sabotage, system reliability, reduced competition, and consumer protection.

The rise in popularity of the Internet and its promise for the future has opened up a host of legal, social, and regulatory issues. In previous chapters, we have examined such issues as privacy and free speech as they relate to the Internet and in this and the next chapter, additional and equally important concerns are addressed. One example discussed later in this chapter is the restriction on the export of encryption programs as well as the government's attempts to impose a standardized encryption scheme to be used for communication over the Internet.

Of major concern to governments is the competitiveness of their industries in response to worldwide challenges. The United States is currently locked in technological combat primarily with Japan but increasingly so with Europe. Japan has made enormous advances since World War II, in becoming a major economic force and technological leader. It has invested heavily in new technology and now challenges the United States across a broad range of products and services, especially computers and microelectronics. In response, the US government, in the process of meeting its defense requirements, has sponsored research and development in many areas of high technology. Many economists and politicians have urged the development of a national plan to maintain economic superiority. The centerpiece of most proposals is a national resolve to continue world leadership in computer hardware and software. Except in times of war, national mobilization has not been a hallmark of US society; nevertheless, concern with competitiveness and productivity has never been greater.

Another important area of the economy in which some degree of government involvement has taken place are the nation's stock exchanges. Computers have made possible the trading of enormous quantities of securities very rapidly and have contributed to a certain degree of instability. The flow of information around the world via communication networks has become an important factor in the conduct of international business. This development coincides with the growth in multinational corporations and their increasing dependence on the rapid and efficient transmission of information. Because it is vitally interested in maintaining technological as well as military superiority, the government has initiated attempts to control technology transfer. More recently, as the Cold War has diminished because of the far-reaching changes in Eastern Europe, the West has reduced, and even removed, many of the restrictions on the export of computers.

INDUSTRY REGULATION

What is good for the country is good for General Motors and what's good for General Motors is good for the country.[2]

The US government has recognized two major forms of environments in which businesses can operate. One is the typical free marketplace situation in which companies compete against one another. The other is a monopoly situation, in which the government permits a single company to operate without competition, under an agreement that its rates will be regulated. Until fairly recently the telephone industry was the prime example of a regulated monopoly. An intermediate form is represented by the radio, television, and cable industries. Individual stations must apply for licenses, which are renewed at regular intervals if no violations occur. Governments have seen fit to try to ensure that the competition in the open marketplace is as unrestricted as possible. For example, in 1890 Congress passed the Sherman Antitrust Act in reaction to the activities of large railway and industrial trusts. In later years various companies—such as Alcoa Aluminum, American Tobacco, and Hughes Tool—were charged with antitrust violations. The longest antitrust case to date involved IBM.

IBM and the Computer Industry

Our industry is healthy and competitive, and IBM has not violated the antitrust laws.[3]

On January 17, 1969, the last possible day it could take action, the Justice Department of the Johnson administration launched an antitrust suit against IBM. Almost 13 years later, on January 8, 1982, the Justice Department of the Reagan administration dropped the longest antitrust suit in history. In the interim, many millions of dollars were spent in legal fees, 66 million pages of documents were collected, and IBM was somewhat restrained in its activities. The government originally charged IBM with monopolizing the computer industry. In general, industries dominated by a few large companies are certainly more stable but perhaps less innovative, although in the personal computer market, including software, competition and innovation are the hallmark, so far. Those who favor minimal government involvement in business point to the computer industry as an example of a successful and innovative field, neglecting to consider the influential role of the Department of Defense, the National Aeronautics and Space Administration, and the National Science Foundation. Nevertheless, even with the IBM giant, there has been room for Silicon Valley and Route 128.

Since it was the undisputed leader in the industry from the 1960s to the late 1980s, IBM's every move, announced or predicted, was carefully watched and evaluated. This situation had given IBM extraordinary power in manipulating the market to suit its own needs. The government's antitrust case depended, in part, on proving that certain practices of IBM in controlling the computer industry were illegal. For example, when competitors began marketing new models that were faster and cheaper than the current IBM versions, IBM might announce a price cut or its own new models. Generally customers were forced to wait until the details of IBM's new machines were released. Making inroads into IBM's domination was not easy under the best of conditions. To convince an IBM customer to switch, a price reduction in equipment would not be sufficient. It was necessary to guarantee that existing programs would continue to run properly on the new computer. Nevertheless, IBM's share of the market did slowly diminish. In response to the government's charges, IBM argued that its practices were commonly accepted in other businesses, that it did not really control the market, and that in such a technically active field no single company could ever maintain control for very long. Little did IBM know how true its words would turn out to be.

It had been felt that IBM had assumed a much less competitive stance during the years of the trial, to avoid the possibility of further charges. While IBM appeared to be dormant, though, there was considerable ferment below the surface. The best example of the "new" IBM was its stunning achievement in the personal computer market. From its introduction of the PC (Personal Computer) in 1981, IBM took the lead in dollar value of personal computers sold in 1983. IBM's worldwide domination of the computer market was described in Chapter 3. The IBM name once again demonstrated its worth in the personal computer area. First-time buyers found comfort in dealing with a company that had a proven track record and was not likely to go out of business. Because of its belief in the primacy of hardware and the urgent need to develop an operating system for its PCs, IBM entered into negotiations with a small software company called Microsoft. The introduction of DOS was a major boost in persuading businesses that the PC was more than a toy. If Apple, with its Macintosh introduced in 1984, promoted the idea of fun and ease of use, IBM's PCs, and a host of clones, countered with arguments intended to appeal to the business community.

Although IBM legitimized the PC, it did not anticipate that competing in this market would be substantially different from its traditional "big iron" experience. Furthermore, the incredibly rapid and sustained growth in this market favored smaller, more agile companies to the detriment of the older giants of the industry. For example, Digital Equipment was unable to compete in the PC market and its leadership in minicomputers suffered as did the company itself as more powerful PCs put considerable pressure on this segment of the industry. IBM itself ran into serious difficulties in the early 1990s as profits evaporated and losses mounted. In 1990, IBM's profits were slightly over $6 billion and it seemed that a return to the very profitable years of the mid 1980s was in the offing. But the following year IBM reported a loss of over $2.8 billion; 1992 was worse with a loss of $6.87 billion and in 1993 losses reached an incredible $8.1 billion, to which massive layoffs (about one-fifth of all employees in 1993) were a major contributor.

IBM's stock market value fell substantially as well and terms such as dinosaur, out-of-touch, lost cause, and stumbling giant were applied with increasing frequency. IBM's problems reverberated throughout the computer industry because so many companies depended on filling software and hardware niches. In fact, a whole industry has come into being that produces equipment compatible with IBM's; companies in this market are referred to as PCMs, Plug Compatible Manufacturers. Only the existence of a relatively stable industry, guaranteed by such a major company as IBM, would encourage the growth of PCMs. IBM's considerable difficulties attracted attention and its imminent demise was predicted by many. One example is the book by Charles H. Ferguson and Charles R. Morris, *Computer Wars: The Fall of IBM and the Future of Global Technology*.[4] One view of the future, presented in this book, should suffice:[5]

> It is probably not too late for Gerstner [appointed CEO in 1993] to arrest the slide, but the shadows are growing long. Without some dramatic action, IBM will rapidly decline to only about two-thirds of its present size, losing money all the way down. At this point, it will just be a carcass of a company—and something like Groupe Bull in France—fit only for an unsightly public dismemberment.

This grim prognostication may yet come to pass, but refusing to leave quietly, IBM seems to have turned the situation around in an unbelievably short time. Losses in 1993 were $8.1 billion but in the following year profits were $2.88 billion, a change of almost $11 billion! Growth was sustained in 1995 as profits reached almost $4.2 billion, hardly a performance to be expected from a company sounding the death rattle. A few more statistics from 1995 will reveal that IBM is still the overall dominant player in the worldwide computer industry.

IBM was first in revenue, with Fujitsu second, at $26.8 billion, trailing IBM by some $45 billion. In its annual rankings, *Datamation* divides the computer industry into seven categories. These are large-scale systems ("big iron" or mainframes), servers (minicomputers and large, special-purpose workstations), desktops (PCs, workstations, and laptops), software (system and application software), datacom (bridges, routers, and terminal servers), services (outsourcing, facilities management, IT consulting, contract programming, etc.), and peripherals (data storage, monitors, disk drives, printers, and add-on boards). IBM led in six of these categories, trailing only AT&T and NTT Data (Japan) in datacom revenues. (See Table 3.1.) At the risk of overusing the term, IBM has reinvented itself in a fundamental way, decreasing its traditional reliance on mainframes and increasing its revenue from services to the point that in 1995, its revenues from services were over $20 billion while those from large-scale systems were about $6.5 billion. To further its ability to compete in new, profitable areas, IBM purchased Lotus Development for $3.5 billion in June 1995. Lotus Notes has turned out to be a viable competitor for simple intranets in the effective use of company networks.[6]

In the first half of 1996, IBM's revenues were up slightly over the comparable period in

1995, but profits were down almost 30% to $2.12 billion.[7] This decrease was attributed to sharp drops in memory prices and currency and not to internal structural problems. Its success has been reflected in substantial improvements in its stock market share price, from about $40 in 1993 to nearly $120 near the end of February 1996. All in all a remarkable turnaround. One other piece of judicial action removed a restriction from the early days of the computer industry. In January of 1996, a Federal judge freed IBM "from most 40-year old restrictions on its ability to compete for computer services and related businesses." One other major company that has been viewed with some concern by its competitors and the US Justice Department because of its aggressive marketing activities and its monopolization of the operating system market for PCs is, not surprisingly, Microsoft, the world's second largest software company.[8]

Microsoft and the Software Industry

Microsoft's phenomenal growth and dominance in the software industry could not but help attract the interest of the Federal Trade Commission (FTC) and the US Department of Justice (DOJ) spurred on by the vocal complaints of competitors and some consumer groups. In November 1989, the FTC launched an antitrust investigation of Microsoft that resulted in deadlock when votes were taken on February 5 and July 21, 1993 on whether to file a complaint. When the FTC ended its inquiry on August 20, 1993, DOJ began its own investigation.[9] As reported in 1994, the government's concerns were as follows:[10]

- Whether Microsoft favored its applications division by providing information on undocumented application programming interfaces (API) in Windows, thus putting rivals such as Lotus Development Corp., WordPerfect Corp. and Borland International, Inc. at a disadvantage.
- Whether Microsoft's policy of requiring PC vendors to pay for DOS and Windows licenses for every processor they ship has the practical effect of excluding operating system vendors such as Novell and IBM.
- Whether Microsoft used its dominance in operating systems to coerce PC vendors into bundling its own applications with machines, thereby freezing out competitors.

It is crucial to the government's case to show that users were harmed by Microsoft's business practices "because the US Supreme Court has ruled that antitrust laws were designed to protect competition and consumer interests not to settle feuds between competitors."[11]

On July 15, 1994, Microsoft and the government came to an agreement to end the investigation, thereby placing Microsoft in the company of IBM and AT&T as "having been officially declared a monopolist by the US government."[12] The official charges filed by the Justice Department's Antitrust Division are as follows:[13]

- Per-processor contracts with PC makers that forced them to pay royalties for MS-DOS and Windows on every processor they shipped, even if the machine did not ship with that software. This forced PC makers selling non-Microsoft operating systems to pay two royalties one to Microsoft and one to its competition potentially making a rival system more expensive.

- Unreasonably long contracts with PC makers typically three to five years that included minimum commitments that effectively excluded rival operating systems from the market.
- Overly restrictive nondisclosure agreements to prevent third parties that test beta products such as Chicago from working on rival system software.

In essence, the Justice Department alleged that Microsoft has used these unfair practices to maintain a monopoly power in the operating systems market since at least the mid-1980s, with market share consistently in excess of 70%.

The proposed settlement was to apply to all Microsoft products except Windows NT Workstation or Windows NT Advanced Server under the following terms:[14]

- The proposed settlement prohibits Microsoft from using per-processor licenses and minimum purchase terms. Licenses are limited to one or two years.
- Nondisclosure agreements are limited to one year and may not prevent programmers from working on rival operating systems as long as Microsoft's proprietary information is not disclosed.
- Furthermore, Microsoft cannot require PC makers to purchase another Microsoft product as a condition for licensing a Microsoft operating system.
- The settlement will last for six and a half years after it is signed by the presiding judge. Microsoft agreed to abide by the settlement terms immediately.

There was considerable disagreement among rival companies, informed commentators, and the general public about who had won and whether Microsoft would really change its practices. Many felt that given a generally weak case, the government had done as well as it could while others, mainly small competitors, were angered by their perception that nothing had changed. In an editorial, *Business Week* complimented the DOJ because it "was able to use antitrust policy as a scalpel rather than a bludgeon."[15] Furthermore, the Clinton Administration was lauded and encouraged "to aggressively investigate allegations of monopolies and other activities that squelch competition."[16] Surprisingly, the agreement was not to become effective for more than a year after it had been signed.

In January 1996, US District Court Judge Stanley Sporkin, a former enforcement director at the Securities and Exchange Commission, entered the proceedings, because he believed that the settlement was not justified and a month later he rejected the agreed-upon consent degree, resulting in the unlikely alliance of Microsoft and the DOJ expressing anger and disbelief at his actions. A number of Microsoft's rivals made presentations that were accepted by Judge Sporkin. Among these were that the settlement was too narrow, insufficiently documented, minimally enforceable, and that "the government and Microsoft 'have been unable and unwilling to adequately address certain anticompetitive practices' the company has vowed to keep using."[17]

While Judge Sporkin was continuing his investigation, Microsoft was attempting to purchase Intuit, Inc., the maker of Quicken financial software, for $2 billion, in a hostile takeover. This deal was opposed by the Justice Department, which launched an antitrust lawsuit. Major banks were also opposed to the acquisition, because of their concern with a company as aggressive and skilled as Microsoft using Quicken over its proposed network to dominate home banking.[18] On May 20, 1995, Microsoft called off the proposed Intuit takeover. So at this point, Judge Sporkin's rejection of the almost one-year old antitrust settlement agreement between the government and Microsoft was being reviewed by the US Court of Appeals in Washington, and the Justice Department was considering the possibility of further antitrust charges related to "The Microsoft Network and/or other Windows 95 bundling practices."[19] The first of these was settled on June 18 when the federal court allowed the 1994 settlement, and two months later the consent degree was finally official.

DOJ's interest in Microsoft continues, however, as the following illustrates:[20]

> In the latest round between the two sides, the Justice Department has focused on the Windows 95 upgrade's tendency to displace 16-bit Internet browsers from rival companies. Should that form the basis of the Justice Department's complaint, however, antitrust specialists say the department will have a hard time proving its case.
>
> Hackles were initially raised after it was found that, upon installation, Windows 95 dislodges existing Windows-based Internet access software. Microsoft's critics cite the fact that Windows 95 overwrites users' Winsock DLL (dynamic link library) software, saying this constitutes evidence of anticompetitive behavior. Winsock (Windows sockets) software provides a link between client software and the Internet protocol (TCP/IP).

As long as Microsoft continues its aggressive behavior, it will attract the attention of the Justice Department and the ire of its competitors. For example, early in August 1996, Netscape Communications asked the DOJ "to investigate Microsoft Corp.'s Web server sales practices. Netscape claims that licensing and technical restrictions in how users may run World Wide Web server software on Microsoft's Windows NT operating system violate antitrust laws and give Microsoft an unfair advantage over Netscape and other rivals."[21]

AT&T and the Telephone Industry

> Mr. Watson, come here; I want you.[22]

The American Telephone and Telegraph used to be referred to as the largest company on earth, and it was not an exaggeration. On January 1, 1984, AT&T underwent the first and most momentous of a series dramatic changes, which have had, and will continue to have, a significant impact on society. The role of telephone systems has become crucial in the growth of computer networks both national and global, especially the Internet. Given the size and importance of AT&T, it is useful to trace its history, albeit briefly, to better understand the way in which telephone systems have become so dominant.

Alexander Graham Bell invented the telephone in 1876.[23] Bell Telephone Company, the predecessor of AT&T, was founded on July 8, 1877. Under the leadership of Theodore Vail, a shrewd and visionary businessman, AT&T was formed in 1885, after an early battle with Western Union. AT&T had purchased Western Electric as its manufacturing division and forced Western Union to withdraw completely from the telephone business. It then underwent a period of rapid growth, stringing telephone lines across the country, fighting off competitors, and purchasing independent telephone companies. By 1910, it had even achieved control of Western Union. In 1913, under the threat of antitrust action, an understanding with the Justice Department was reached, the Kingsbury Commitment, by which AT&T promised to sell its Western Union stock, desist from purchasing any additional competitors, and permit interconnection with independent companies. It seems inevitable that companies that come to dominate their industries will probably have used methods that violate antitrust legislation, or are at least borderline.

After the passage in 1921 of the Willis-Graham Act, which excluded telephone mergers from antitrust charges (if they were approved by the regulatory agencies), AT&T launched a new wave of acquisitions until by 1932 its market share had reached 79%. To protect its position, AT&T strongly advocated regulation, arguing that where there was no serious competition, public control should be in force. It prospered under the regulatory system, which after the passage of the Communications Act of 1934 included the Federal Communications Commission (FCC). In practice, regulation precluded the entrance of competitors and protected AT&T's monopoly. In 1956, after several years of dealing with a new antitrust suit filed in 1949, AT&T and the Justice Department agreed to a Consent Decree that generally accepted AT&T's position that the basic issues of the suit should be resolved by Congress. Existing arrangements were to continue, except that AT&T was not permitted to engage in any business other than the furnishing of common carrier communications services. Thus, AT&T and its subsidiary, Western Electric, could be involved only in regulated services. This seemed to confirm AT&T's mandate, but the new age of computer communications was fast approaching and AT&T seemed to be excluded.

Challenges to AT&T began to appear. In addition to the telephone, there are other kinds of terminal equipment: modems for connecting computers to communication networks, key telephone sets for small businesses with several lines, and Private Branch Exchanges (PBXs) for large businesses with internal switching centers. Telephone companies permitted only their own equipment to be connected to telephone lines. In 1966, the FCC ruled that though the telephone companies could set standards, they could not prohibit devices manufactured by other companies from being attached to their networks. Both PBXs and key telephone sets entered the competitive market. This was an important development because PBXs soon became the basic infrastructure of the office and its interface to the existing telephone system.

Perhaps the most significant assault on the existing telephone system was initiated by Microwave Communications Incorporated (now officially MCI), which applied in 1963 for the right to build a microwave system between St. Louis and Chicago. MCI planned to offer such services as voice, data, and facsimile (Fax) transmissions, in direct competition with AT&T. After initial approval by the FCC in 1966 and final approval in 1969, a court challenge by AT&T was instituted and withdrawn in 1971, more than seven years after the date of the original application. The telephone companies correctly anticipated that the MCI application would have immense repercussions far beyond its modest beginnings. Other companies entered the field and MCI itself soon expanded to a nationwide network, primarily providing private-line service. A dial-up call would use a telephone company's local lines to reach the nearest MCI office, then go over the MCI network to the destination city's MCI office, and finally over local telephone lines to the destination telephone. AT&T appealed to the FCC and was upheld, but eventually the case went to the courts. In May 1978, the Supreme Court supported a lower court ruling that overturned the FCC decision. Thus, after almost 100 years of operating as a monopoly, AT&T faced serious competition in the long-distance market.

Another challenge to AT&T's monopoly was the development of satellite-based communications systems and the blurring of the boundary between computer and communications technologies. Computer manufacturers began to compete with communications companies in the production of a range of products. The FCC had permitted a policy of free market competition in the satellite communication industry in 1972. AT&T was permitted to use domestic satellites for its public long-distance monopoly service but was not allowed to compete for three years in the private satellite market. In November 1974, convinced that new technology had made the Consent Decree of 1956 outdated, the Justice Department initiated the largest antitrust suit ever against AT&T. The suit argued that AT&T should be broken up into separate companies: Western Electric for Telephone equipment, Long Line for long-distance service, and the Bell operating companies (BOCs) for local service. Finally, on January 8, 1982, an agreement was reached between AT&T and the Justice Department along the lines suggested in the original suit.

> An historic agreement has been reached: AT&T agreed to a consent order divesting the company of all facilities used to provide local telephone service, and the Department of Justice dropped its antitrust case against the company.[24]

After divesting itself of its local telephone companies, AT&T was organized in two main divisions, as follows:[25]

- AT&T Communications.
  Long-distance. 1984 sales: $35 billion.

- AT&T Technologies. 1984 sales: $17 billion.
  AT&T Bell Laboratories: Research and development.
  AT&T Network Systems: Telephone equipment, manufacturing and sales.
  AT&T Technology Systems: Manufacturing and sales of components; for example, chips.
  AT&T International: Overseas marketing of equipment and services; foreign partnerships.
  AT&T Information Systems: Computers and business systems.

On January 1, 1985, AT&T Information Systems—set up as an arms-length, deregulated subsidiary by the government—was reorganized along three lines of business: computers, large business systems, and small business systems. The remaining parts of the AT&T empire—the 22 local operating companies, about two-thirds of its assets—were reorganized into 7 independent regional Bell operating companies, the Baby Bells: Pacific Telesis, US West, Bellsouth, Nynex, Bell Atlantic, Southwestern Bell, and Ameritech, and the Central Services Organization, a research and development division jointly owned by these companies and now called Bell Communications Research (Bellcore). AT&T has begun to compete in the office automation market. Its Information Systems division is in direct competition with such companies as Wang, Xerox, and Digital Equipment. In the communication switching equipment area, it competes with such companies as Northern Telecom (Canada), Rolm (US), and L. M. Ericsson, Philips, and Plessey (Europe), and in the long-distance carrier market its major competitors are MCI, GTE-Sprint, and Allnet.

It was expected, however, that the major confrontation would be with IBM, "The stage is set for a bout of worldwide dimensions: never before have two private corporations brought such resources and so many years of preparation into a head-on competition."[26] However, in spite of all this anticipation, no major confrontation occurred, although each company unsuccessfully attempted to move into the other's domain; in the end, each company was left to deal with challenges within its own industry.

Telecommunications in an Era of Rapid Change

The idea of a natural monopoly was introduced earlier in this chapter, and much of the discussion of the history of telephone companies turned on regulatory issues but with the introduction of powerful new technologies at such an incredible pace, natural monopolies no longer exist in the telephone industry and challenges can arise suddenly and unexpectedly. The recent history of AT&T is witness to this observation.

Ups and Downs of AT&T

In 1984 at the time of the divestiture, AT&T's income from long distance calling was 96% of a $34 billion market ($32.64 billion). By 1994, its market share had dropped to 61% but the market had increased to $64 billion, netting AT&T $39 billion. During the latter half of the 1980s and the first half of the 1990s, AT&T took a number of steps to improve its competitive position. In 1991, it took over the computer company NCR, in yet another attempt to gain a foothold in the computer industry. Once again this attempt proved unsuccessful; in 1995, AT&T announced its intention to spin off NCR as well as Lucent Technologies, the telephone equipment manufacturer, as separate companies, leaving AT&T as basically a long-distance service provider. Its 1995 revenues were about $80 billion in total, of which $43 billion were derived from long distance. AT&T also made a significant move into the Internet by announcing on February 27, 1996, "an offer for its 80 million residential long-distance customers: Five hours a month on WorldNet, its Internet access service, free—for 12 months."[27] While AT&T was restructuring itself the BOCs were not standing still.

They all began as local telephone companies in 1984 with about the same revenues of about $8 billion plus or minus a few hundred million, but over the years some have been more successful than others and have moved in a variety of directions to increase growth. For example, US West (1995 revenues of $9.48 billion), with "Its $10.2 billion takeover of Continental Cablevision and its 25% stake in Time Warner Cable gives [it] access to 13 million cable subscribers." Bell Atlantic (revenues $13.43 billion) is "A leader in developing technology to send video over phone lines, was first to enter long distance outside its region, and its wireless partnership with Nynex [another BOC] could lead to the first Bell megamerger. SBC Communications (formerly Southwestern Bell, revenues $12.67 billion) is "one of the nation's largest cellular operators"[28] and is trying to purchase PacBell (formerly Pacific Telesis, revenues $9 billion) for $17 billion. On a regular basis, these companies complained about AT&T's activities and petitioned state and federal regulators for permission to pursue new ventures. AT&T also argued that it was artificially constrained and limited in its ability to compete nationally as well as globally. Finally, in February 1996, congress passed the first comprehensive telecommunication legislation in sixty years.

The Telecommunications Act of 1996

The Act was signed into law by President Clinton on February 8, 1996. We have already discussed the most publicized part of the Act, the Communications Decency Act, but although its attempt to regulate content on the Internet has been challenged and rightly so, it would be a terrible shame if the rest of the Act, which will launch major changes in the US telecommunications system were not closely examined. First a brief overview of the Act itself, taken from the analysis of the law firm, Blumenfeld & Cohen:[29]

- *Telephone Service.* The Act overrules all state restrictions on competition in local and long-distance telephone service. The Baby Bells are freed to provide long-distance service outside their regions immediately, and inside their regions once completing a series of steps to remove entry barriers for local telephone competition.
- *Telecommunications Equipment Manufacturing.* The Act allows the Baby Bells to manufacture telephone equipment once the FCC approves their application for out-of-region long-distance.
- *Cable Television.* Telephone companies are permitted to offer either cable television services or to carry video programming for other entities via "open video systems." The Act substantially relaxes the rules governing cable television systems under the 1992 Cable Act.
- *Radio and Television Broadcasting.* The Act relaxes the FCC's media concentration rules . . . Television equipment manufacturers are required to equip all new TVs with a so-called "V-chip" ("V" for violence) allowing parental blocking of violent, sexually explicit or indecent programming.

A complementary view was expressed in the popular media, as *Newsweek* described the impact on the general public as follows:[30]

- *Long-Distance Phone Service.* The Baby Bells can now battle AT&T, MCI and Sprint for customers. Calls to Aunt Molly may cost less.
- *Local Phone Service.* Cable and long-distance companies can compete in local markets. Business customers are likely to feel the effects first.
- *Television.* Television makers will be required to install chips in TV sets that will allow viewers to block out violent and sexual programs.
- *Cable.* Customers in big metro areas could see higher bills when rate regulations are lifted. Smaller-city subscribers might be affected sooner.
- *Internet.* People who make indecent material available to minors will now face criminal penalties.

The motivation for this legislation originated from several sources. The Republican-controlled Congress was interested in lessening government regulation of industries that were taking advantage of such advanced technologies that distinctions among telephone, broadcasting, and cable systems had nearly vanished. That is, voice, music, images, and movies are all transmitted by bits moving over copper wires, fiber optics, coaxial cable, or through the air as satellite signals. Thus, distinct regulatory strategies for telephone, broadcast, and cable do not seem viable or supportable. The telephone companies, both local and long-distance want to compete independently of the distance the call covers and they want to carry all sorts of information and not be restricted in any way. In fact, they are developing technical methods for expanding the usable bandwidth of copper wire in order to carry movies and other information-intensive communications. Cable companies are interested in carrying telephone communications, having regulations over their pricing formulae, reduced or eliminated, and providing Internet access over high speed cable modems, which will require the provision of two-way data flow. Broadcast media want to reduce regulations over ownership, both vertical and horizontal. All can find in the Act possibilities to further their interests. Some even want the FCC removed, or at least its powers diminished, to permit the unfettered marketplace to decide the winners and losers.

AT&T's plans to divest itself of its computing (NCR) and equipment manufacturing (Lucent) divisions to concentrate on the long-distance market depend on deregulation. By the year 2005, AT&T would like to achieve revenues of $54 billion in long-distance, $30 billion in the local telephone market, $20 billion from wireless services, $13 billion from on-line services, and $15 billion from other markets, including video and universal cards, for a total of $132 billion, compared with about $80 billion in 1995.[31] However, AT&T will face competition in the long-distance market from many quarters, including the following:[32]

- *Dial-Around Companies.* These resellers allow customers to dial into a discount service on a call-by-call basis, using an access code. AT&T can spend millions to retain customers and still lose their business.
- *Prepaid Calling Cards.* Like the dial-around companies, prepaid calling cards give their customers a way to circumvent their long-distance carrier of record, again without giving AT&T any notification.
- *Local Telephone Companies.* Within three years, local telephone companies will be allowed to offer long-distance calling within their regions for the first time; they can already do so outside their home markets.
- *Internet Calling.* Only about 500,000 people worldwide use the Internet for some voice communication today. If glitches can be worked out, the Internet will provide flat-rate long-distance and international calling.

More detail about the use of the Internet for telephone, video, and broadcasting will be provided in the last section in this chapter. During 1997, the Federal Communications Commission will articulate the steps in the deregulation process. It is required to deal with a host of issues, including for example, "how much local phone companies can charge other firms to use their networks."[33]

On August 1, 1996, the FCC issued its first rules on local competition in the telephone industry in the wake of the Telecommunications Act. This is only the first step in developing the ground rules for local competition. The next two parts will deal with access charge reform and universal service reform. There is some consensus that in this round the long distance carriers achieved an advantage. With respect to reseller discounts, for example, "local phone companies must offer long-distance companies a discount of 17 to 25 percent off the retail price of any network service, so that these rivals could resell the service under their own brand names."[34] Long-distance companies will be able to purchase individual services and equipment from local providers rather than complete packages that the locals would have preferred to provide. However, current access charges that the long-distance companies must be pay will be kept in place for the time being.

It will take many years until the winners and losers in the corporate world are determined, to say nothing of the population at large. There is some hope that telephone rates both local and long-distance will decrease after decade-long increases. Encouraging competition by removing restrictions against who can enter which market should result in lower rates for consumers. Combined with advances in telecommunications technologies, the average citizen should be able to take advantage of many of the new services. However, nothing is given and the stakes are very high, with an estimate of $235 billion for the entire US telecommunications market in 2005.[35] From the US telecommunications companies' point of view, competition at home is only one part of the story. Because of a tradition of government-owned postal, telephone, and telegraph companies around the world, so-called PTTs, many of these now private, are formidable competitors. Thus, based on 1994 revenues, AT&T ranked second with telecommunications revenues of $43 billion. It trailed NTT, Japan ($60.1 billion) and is followed by Deutsche Telekom (Germany, $37.7 billion), France Télécom ($23.3 billion), and BT (UK, $21.3). Number six is Telecom Italia, followed by four US companies, GTE, BellSouth, Bell Atlantic, and MCI.[36] So the next few years will witness global competition, global arrangements, and cooperation, taking place at an unprecedented pace. The Internet is only the first stage in the establishment and continuous growth in worldwide communications.

ELECTRONIC BANKING AND FINANCIAL TRANSACTIONS

Legitimate businesses use wire transfers when sending very large sums or when the timeliness and certainty (irrevocability) of payments are of paramount importance—especially in foreign exchange transactions and securities trading. For routine payment for goods and services, they are more likely to use checks or automated clearing house (ACH) payments.[37]

Financial transactions are such a common occurrence in everyday life, it is not surprising that computers have found eager acceptance in the banking community. The sheer mass of numerical computations required to record, update, and process banking records has made the industry a major purchaser of equipment and employer of information processing professionals. Early applications involved the use of keypunches to prepare financial information that was then read into the computer. Accounts were then updated and financial statements produced. As software and hardware became increasingly sophisticated, banks modernized their method of operation. Tellers could enter transaction information into a local computer via terminals at the counter. For independent banks, this information would be useful directly; for branch banks, the local computer would send the information over a communication system to the central computer. The merging of computers and communication systems is a marriage made in heaven for financial institutions. Up to fairly recently, the common term used to refer to a host of services facilitated by computers and electronic networks was EFTS (Electronic Funds Transfer Systems). It is less commonly used now. The next step has been to permit customers direct access to their accounts directly or via the Internet.

Banking in America

In 1983, Stephen T. McLin, strategic planning chief, Bank of America, in commenting on how banks could reduce costs, noted that "the central challenge in retail banking . . . is 'to migrate customers from the brick and mortar system to electronic delivery systems'."[38] This challenge is being met, as we shall see, but first let's briefly review the development of retail banking. Banks can be chartered by both the federal government and the states. The history of banking reflects the tension between the desire of rural, frontier America for local control over banks and the seeming expansionist tendencies of the international banks. This confrontation has turned on the issue of branch banking—which banks can set up branches and what constitutes a branch bank. "By 1988, 45 states had passed some type of legislation permitting regional or nationwide branching. Many states allowed for the formation of regional compacts designed to give regional banks enough time to prevent themselves from being absorbed by the money center banks."[39] The past 25 years have witnessed considerable consolidation of banks, as the number of truly independent banks has decreased from 13,400 in the mid-1960s to 9,800 by the end of 1988. This trend will continue as deregulation of interstate banking continues, as banks close because of depressed regional economies, and as hostile takeovers become more frequent.

The Dimensions of Electronic Banking

Included under this heading is a multitude of processes, services, and mechanisms that depend on computers and communication systems for their operation. Some components have been in existence for quite a while, others have been introduced recently, and still others are in the planning stage. The full array will certainly change the way we shop, bank, and generally carry out our financial transactions. The impact on society will be in such areas as employment, privacy, social relations and patterns of interaction, centralization of control, financial transactions, and possible major consolidations of financial institutions.

Preauthorizations and Automated Banking

The following were probably the first procedures that could legitimately be referred to as instances of electronic banking:

- Direct deposits of regular payments: paychecks, royalties
- Direct payments of recurrent expenses: mortgages, loans
- Direct regular contributions: charity
- Payment of bills by telephone

Once a person authorizes deposits or payments, these are made automatically without further interaction. Typically, large companies would deliver tapes of employees salaries to banks for disbursement into appropriate accounts. Such tapes are of course generated by the companies' computers. Since these procedures do not require sophisticated computer techniques, they were instituted quite early in the course of electronic banking. Now, such information is transmitted over secure electronic networks.

The use of Automated Teller Machines (ATMs) for depositing and withdrawing money, transfers between accounts, and other services—and the authorization of credit and checks—have become a way of life for many people. They have proven to be convenient, easy to use, and extremely popular because of their availability at all hours of the day and night. For their part, the banks find that ATMs, which can operate 24 hours a day, save them a considerable amount of money because employees are not needed. The banks are encouraging the use of ATMs during regular banking hours as well, by reducing their staff size and reserving the remaining staff for special problems. Although ATMs permit a variety of banking functions, most are cash withdrawals. The direct economic benefits of ATMs are obvious, a much lower cost per transaction compared with a teller transaction.

Another part of electronic banking is the use of terminals to perform credit checks. Before authorizing a purchase, a store is able to verify electronically that a customer has sufficient funds on hand or that the balance available on a credit card is sufficiently large. This kind of checking can also be carried out by telephone, with only slightly more difficulty, but the communications networks necessary for electronic banking discourage the use of the telephone in this context.

POS (Point-of-Sale) Operations

The common feature of POS operations is that the electronic financial transactions are made directly at the time of purchase. Thus, instead of using cash, a check, or a credit card, the customer will have a debit card that, when placed in a POS terminal, transfers money from the customer's bank account to the store's. The card used in ATMs is really a debit card, since its use may result in instantaneous transfers into and out of bank accounts. If the customer has insufficient funds or lacks a line of credit, the purchase will not be completed. The widespread use of the debit card may be a major step along the way to the cashless society. Another important implication is the loss of the "float period" between the time a purchase is made and the time it must be paid for. The float period is not desirable for the banks, because it gives the customer use of the bank's money interest-free. In periods of high interest rates, substantial amounts of money are involved. With the debit card, the float period is effectively eliminated and at the same time payment to the vendor is guaranteed.

What benefits do debit cards have for consumers? Consider the following list proposed by Jane Bryant Quinn:[40]

1. For the prudent, debit cards are pure discipline. You don't spend more money than you have in the bank.
2. The cards can be easier to use than personal checks, especially in places where you're not known.
3. For couples with joint checking, debit cards eliminate the need to juggle two checkbooks or carry loose checks.
4. If you use a debit card for small purchases, you run no risk of paying interest on them. With a credit card, by contrast, interest might be due even if you pay off the bill at the end of the month. (That usually happens when you roll over debt or when your card has no grace period.)
5. If you're short of cash, a debit card can see you through a supermarket, a gas station, a fast food restaurant—places that generally don't take credit cards.

Debit cards are much more common in Europe and Japan than in the United States, and there is a variation—the prepaid card used to pay for a wide range of goods and services. The initial value of the card is coded on a magnetic strip and subsequent payments result in a corresponding reduction in its value. This type of card is now being tested in North America.

Automated Clearinghouse

A major part of the cost of processing a check is the physical movement of the check itself from the merchant, to a local bank, to a central clearinghouse, to the customer's bank, and eventually back to the customer, with perhaps additional stages involved. The replacement of all this paper processing by an electronic system is well under way. Such networks have been in existence for some time to facilitate the movement of money among financial institutions. Large networks of ATMs and POS services are being built. Banks are getting larger through mergers, acquisitions, and the formation of networks to permit customers access to banking services on a regional basis. Such growth is necessary if the costs of constructing both regional and national systems are to be financed.

Current Banking Technologies

A recent report on technology in the banking industry in 1995 found that "with nearly half of all banking transactions no longer involving human interaction, traditional banks are teaming up with other financial service organizations to create 'value networks' that offer customers many more service options, . . ."[41] In more detail, 56% of transactions were ordinary branch banking, 28% used ATMs, 10% telephone, 1% home banking, and 6% other. The forecast for 1998 shows a drop in branch banking to 41%, and increases in ATM use to 31%, telephone to 15%, and home banking to 6%. Another indication of the changing face of banking is that although "all the banks surveyed plan on opening up new branches—53% plan full-service branches and 42% plan mini-branches—although they will decrease the total number of branches." It is predicted that the banking industry will spend more than $21 billion on technology in 1998, up from $18.7 billion in 1995. More services will be available at branches, including mutual funds and insurance; these will also be available over ATMs at many banks by 1998.

One bank that has made history is a rather small bank in Pineville, Kentucky, the Security First Network Bank, that on October 18, 1995 became the first Internet bank approved by the government. How does the bank try to sell itself?[42]

- You'll save money. Our regular Internet checking accounts have no monthly fees or minimum balance requirements. You get 20 free electronic payments each month, unlimited check-writing privileges, and a free ATM or Debit card.
- You'll make money. Our Money Market and CD rates are some of the highest in the country. Our costs are lower, so we pass the benefits on to you.
- You'll save time. Paying your bills will take minutes, not hours. Who else lets you open a bank account from the convenience of your home, in less than five minutes?
- Peace of mind. All your transactions are protected by military grade security in use by the US Department of Defense and top intelligence agencies.

- SFNB's wide range of services. Have your electronic payments sent to anyone.
- No software to buy . . . ever. You can use your SFNB account any time, from any computer with Internet access, worldwide.
- No manuals to sift through. SFNB is so easy to use that one "walk" through our demo and you are ready to go. And SFNB interfaces with popular personal finance software, so you don't have to change your habits.
- Forget banker's hours and holidays. Our customer service reps are here 24 hours a day, 365 days a year at no charge to you.

Other banks, such as Wells Fargo and Bank of America have set up Internet access for their customers. However, Wells Fargo has embraced the Internet much more thoroughly than has Bank of America. Wells Fargo customers "can access [its] home page and look at current balances on their checking, savings, money market and 23 other types of accounts."[43] Bank of America has been much more cautious about providing access for its customers because of concern about adequate security over the Internet. Indeed, Wells Fargo will not permit its customers to transfer funds over the Internet until better encryption is available. Encryption is only one part of the security challenge; others include the following:

- Authentication—Certifying individual or company identity.
- Authorization—Dictating access levels once identity is verified.
- Confidentiality—Maintaining the secrecy of the contents of a transmission.
- Integrity—Guaranteeing that a transmission arrives in exactly the same form in which it was sent.
- Non repudiation of origin—Ensuring that when an entity sends an authenticated electronic communication it cannot later deny the origin or contents of the communication, e.g. an electronic credit card receipt.

Problem Areas

One of the byproducts of electronic banking is an increase in financial information. For example, the use of a POS terminal results in a record indicating that an individual spent a particular amount of money at a particular time and place. Because these records are created electronically and stored in computer databases, they are relatively straightforward to retrieve. Since electronic banking operates online and in real time (i.e., transactions take effect instantaneously) such systems could be used to locate individuals whenever they initiate a transaction. Furthermore, more institutions will have access to an individual's financial records. In 1978, Congress passed the Right to Financial Privacy Act, limiting the government's access to financial records. The act outlines the procedures necessary to obtain financial records such as the following:

- Customer authorization
- Administrative subpoena or summons
- Search warrant
- Judicial subpoena
- Formal written request, a copy of which is filed in court

The government must notify individuals that their financial records are being requested and advise them that they may under law have the right to attempt to keep those records from the requesting agency. Records obtained by one agency cannot be provided to any other government department or agency. Such legislation represents legitimate concerns about the increasing availability of private information, in this case financial, even though the act is primarily concerned with specifying the conditions under which the government *can* have access.

Technologies on the Horizon

Smart Cards

The credit or bank card, with its magnetic stripe on the back, has taken its place among the indispensable objects of modern life. It is used to obtain credit from a merchant and the credit card company, and cash from an ATM. A further significant change has already begun—the development and distribution of the smart card, a credit card-sized device containing one or more integrated circuit chips that perform the functions of a microprocessor, memory, and input/output interface. Such a card can contain an enormous amount of information about an individual and his or her commercial transactions. For example, "Germany has issued over 80 million smart cards to its citizens in conjunction with their national health care program; 60% of French people currently use smart cards."[44] Smart cards are very popular in Europe and Asia, although relatively unknown in the US. One industry consulting firm, Frost & Sullivan, estimated that the worldwide smart card market grew to $2 billion from $450 million in 1992. One unsophisticated form of the smart card is the stored value card, distributed by Visa International. It is a simple money substitute, useful for purchases under $10, and requires no identification.

An interesting application of smart cards is as an electronic purse that can be used to pay for services on the Internet. First, the card must be filled up at a specially equipped ATM and then it can be used online in the following manner: "After having reached an on-line service or mall that accepts the card, the customer browses and selects the goods or services he/she is interested in. On completion of his/her selection and confirmation of this to the vendor, the customer will be asked to insert his/her card into a card reader that attaches to the serial port of the computer."[45] This use of smart cards has several advantages including security, guaranteed payment, portability, anonymity to protect privacy, independent of banking accounts or credit limits, and immediate receipt of funds by vendor. One disadvantage is the necessity of a special-purpose card reader and another, of course, is the requirement that this approach must become generally available. The whole issue of secure payment systems for the Internet is obviously an important obstacle in the way of growth for commercial transactions. Various forms of electronic payment have been proposed, and a brief review follows.

Digital Cash

Products and services are available in abundance over the Internet; many are free, but most require payment and ironically, payment is usually off-line by means of a credit card, when using the telephone. A number of systems are either being used or discussed that will permit online payment. Among these are Cybercash, Digicash, First Virtual, and Mondex. First Virtual, for example, was launched in October 1994 and as of early 1996, it had about 90,000 customers worldwide. A First Virtual document describes how its security operates:[46]

> The FV Internet Payment System goes far beyond issues of cryptography and software; it uses a Virtual PIN to provide the first safe link between the world of credit cards, banks, processing agents and the Internet. The system features a secure "line" that separates buy-sell transactions on the Internet from secure banking transactions and financial operations done off the net. Customers simply register with FV and make on-line purchases from participating merchants using their Virtual PIN "above the line." All transactions are confirmed with the buyers via e-mail before being posted "below the line" to the credit card networks over separate, secure, dedicated lines that are not accessible from the Internet.
>
> Using FV PINcryption, credit card numbers are never sent over the Internet, and never typed into a computer connected to the Internet, thereby eliminating the need for encryption and significantly reducing the potential for fraud.

Currently, electronic purchases are a small percentage of purchases at large: $245 billion versus $5,150 billion in 1994—about 4.5%; and of these, $45 billion are over TV and cable TV, $140 billion are business-to-business, other online commerce is $60 billion, and Internet commerce is almost negligible.[47] It is estimated, however, that in 2000, Internet commerce will reach $600 billion out of a total of $1,650 billion in electronic purchases. This latter number would represent 16.2% of $8,500 billion in total purchases. The stakes are obviously very high and much of the growth of the Internet and whatever follows it, such as the Information Highway, will depend on a trusted, easy-to-use, and secure payments system.

Implications of Electronic Banking

There is growing feeling that with the increasing use of electronic networks in the commercial payment system and the anticipated increasing use of electronic cash, it will become impossible for governments to estimate with any sense of confidence, how much money is in circulation at any time. Computing the money supply is important for a number of monetary policies that fall under the responsibilities of central banks and governments. The inability to compute reasonable estimates may play havoc with the development of coherent fiscal policies. Consider the title of a recent book on electronic funds systems: *The Death of Money: How the Electronic Economy Has Destabilized the World's Markets and Created Financial Chaos*.[48] Here is the author's view of the situation:[49]

> Money is now an image. Simultaneously, it can be displayed on millions of computer screens on millions of desks around the world. But in reality it is located nowhere and needs no vault for safekeeping. Yet while money has no real location, it has created an environment that is paradoxically everywhere while taking up no physical space. An environment peopled by millions of investors, traders, bankers, money managers, stockbrokers, arbitrageurs, analysts, policymakers, and government officials—all observing and manipulat-

ing money from different video terminals around the world. A community where neighbors, colleagues, and competitors are accessible only through electronics.

THE INTERNET AND THE INFORMATION HIGHWAY

> While the use of encryption technologies is not a panacea for all information security problems, we believe that adoption of our recommendations would lead to enhanced protection and privacy for individuals and businesses in many areas, ranging from cellular and other wireless phone conversations to electronic transmission of sensitive business or financial documents. It is true that the spread of encryption technologies will add to the burden of those in government who are charged with carrying out certain law enforcement and intelligence activities. But the many benefits to society of widespread commercial and private use of cryptography outweigh the disadvantages. (Kenneth W. Dam, Chair Committee to Study National Cryptography Policy, Computer Science and Telecommunications Board, National Research Council, National Academy of Sciences and National Academy of Engineering, May 30, 1996)[50]

The issues to be explored relate to a variety of attempts by governments to influence or control material carried on the Internet or the methods used or proposed to ensure the security of Internet transmissions, namely encryption. In Chapter 8, two major areas of concern were explored, namely free speech and copyright. Free speech as an issue usually relates to the rights of individuals to make their opinions known and to have access to the opinions of others. Copyright determines the limitations of use by individuals and others of works not created by themselves. As such, although the distinction is not particularly significant, these areas were deemed to be treated appropriately in the general context of computers and the law. The issues under discussion in this section are more diffuse and varied and relate to perceived government imposed restrictions on business and organizations. Thus, these topics include the so-called Clipper chip debate (a restriction on access to preferred encryption choices by business and individuals), restriction on the export of computer technologies (including encryption software), terrorism concerns (including bomb-making instructions), and gambling.

The Clipper Chip

> A state-of-the-art microcircuit called the "Clipper Chip" has been developed by government engineers. The chip represents a new approach to encryption technology. It can be used in new, relatively inexpensive encryption devices that can be attached to an ordinary telephone. It scrambles telephone communications using an encryption algorithm that is more powerful than many in commercial use today.[51]

The issue is encryption—the need to transform communications into a secure form so that sender and receiver are assured that no third party has access and can determine the content. It is important for commerce that payments are secure, that money transfers are guaranteed, and that confidentiality is respected at all costs. Individuals want the same assurance for their private communications.

An Introduction to Cryptography

There will be no mathematics in this discussion; many fine books exist. The point is to provide just enough background to make the presentation meaningful. First a few definitions are in order.[52]

> *Encryption* is the transformation of data into some unreadable form. Its purpose is to ensure privacy by keeping the information hidden from anyone for whom it is not intended, even those who can see the encrypted data.
>
> *Decryption* is the reverse of encryption; it is the transformation of encrypted data back into some intelligible form.
>
> Encryption and decryption require the use of some secret information, usually referred to as a *key*. Depending on the encryption mechanism used, the same key might be used for both encryption and decryption, while for other mechanisms, the keys used for encryption and decryption might be different

Most of the concern with cryptography, the process of creating and using cypher systems, has been to ensure secrecy and verification, or authentication, a necessity for government security in many of its operations, including military, criminal, and espionage. With the rise of telecommunication networks as the preferred means for exchanging information, commercial and otherwise, these concerns have assumed prime importance in the private sector as well. In the preceding quotation, the term key is used and an elaboration of this concept follows.

The basic process of traditional cryptography was to encrypt the original document (plaintext) by a well-defined method such as permutation by a fixed amount (the key) into the cyphertext, which was then sent or carried to the intended receiver who would have to know the key (how many characters to permute the cyphertext) to recover the plaintext. Obviously, this kind of encryption, sometimes called weak encryption, is too simple and too easy to decrypt to guarantee secure transmission. More recently, strong cryptographic systems have come into use. In such systems, the strength lies not in the algorithm, such as permutation, but in the secrecy of the key. Thus the algorithm can be made public without affecting the security of the system, but only if the computational effort to compute the key is extraordinarily great. Private key cryptography involves a unique key for each pair of users and the security of the system depends upon both parties protecting the key. In 1977, the then National Bureau of Standards issued the Data Encryption Standard (DES) as a Federal Information Processing Standard and it is still in use.[53] The other modern approach is public key cryptography:[54]

> Private key (sometimes called asymmetric key or two key) systems use two keys: a public key and a private key. Within a group of users who exchange—for example, within a computer network—each user has both a public key and a private key. A user must keep his private key a secret, but the public key is publicly known; public keys may even be listed in directories of electronic mail addresses. If you encrypt a message with your private key, the recipient of the message can decrypt it with your public key. When you receive an encrypted message, you, and only you, can decrypt it with your private key.

RSA is the best known public key encryption system. It was invented by Ron Rivest, Adi Shamir, and Leonard Adelman in 1977 and is probably the most widely used authentication scheme. One more definition is required, namely key escrow system. Under such a system, some or all of the keys are kept in escrow by third parties: "The keys are released only under proper authority to allow some person other than the original sender or receiver to read the message. The US government is strongly supporting key escrow as a way to balance the needs for secrecy between communicating persons against the needs of law enforcement and national security agencies to sometimes read these encrypted communications (with proper legal authority)."[55]

The US Government's Clipper Chip

Although the government's proposals in cryptography have been referred to as the Clipper chip, the actual situation is somewhat more complicated. Clipper is, strictly speaking, one component of the Capstone project, which consists of four components in total: "Clipper (for bulk data encryption), a digital signature algorithm, a key exchange algorithm, and a hash function." So Clipper, in intent, is comparable to DES and incorporates in hardware an algorithm named Skipjack for use in low speed data/voice transmission. Thus the intent of the government is that the Clipper chip be installed in telephones and would therefore meet the demands of business and consumers for secure communications. But the very controversial part of its program is that the government would manage the key escrow system and would be able to decrypt selected communications if it could convince the courts that its need was justified because of national security requirements or the necessity to combat crime. One model for this proposal is the wiretap laws governing the use of such devices by law enforcement officials.

It was not surprising that many individuals and companies were opposed to the Clipper chip or that many did not trust the government to manage a key escrow system, but the strength and breadth of the opposition and the duration of its existence has been surprising. Nothing has united Internet users across the country (except perhaps for opposition to the Communications Decency Act) as opposition to the Clipper Chip has. Opposition united "almost all communications and computer industries, many members of Congress and political columnists of all stripes. The anti-Clipper aggregation is an equal opportunity club, uniting the American Civil Liberties Union and Rush Limbaugh."[56] In writer Steven Levy's estimation,[57]

> By adding Clipper chips to telephones, we could have a system that assures communications will be private—from everybody but the Government. An that is what rankles Clipper's many critics. Why, they ask, should people accused of no crime have to give Government the keys to their private communications? Why shouldn't the market rather than Government determine what sort of cryptosystem wins favor.

On the other hand, Dr. Dorothy Denning of Georgetown University, a leading expert on cryptography and data security supports the government's initiatives. In a debate with John Perry Barlow, a founder of the Electronic Freedom Foundation, she made the following argument: "The government needs a new encryption standard to replace DES. They came up with a very strong algorithm called SKIPJACK. In making that available, they didn't want to do it in a way that could ultimately prove harmful to society. So they came up with the idea of key escrow so that if SKIPJACK were used to conceal criminal activity, they would be able to get access to the communications."[58] John Perry Barlow's argument against Clipper is different than the one stated by Steven Levy. Barlow believes that, independent of the access to content that the government's system makes possible, what is of equal concern "is in the functional nature of the chip as designed to greatly enhance the ability of government to observe who we are calling, when, and from where, all fairly automatically and centrally."[59]

The American Civil Liberties Union raised constitutional issues in a letter it sent to the Computer System Security and Privacy Advisory Board on May 13, 1993. One of its arguments was that by holding the keys in a public key escrow system, First Amendment issues on restriction of free speech are raised: "Such a prohibition on encrypted speech is a direct restriction on speech and we do not believe that the government may, in effect, ban all encrypted speech, because encrypted speech that is evidence of crime may be unobtainable."[60] There are also Fourth and Fifth Amendment issues with respect to "requiring disclosure of the key to the government in advance of there being probable cause sufficient to entitle the government to seize an encrypted communication and to search and seize the key to such communication."[61]

Since April 1993, the government has tried to modify its original proposal in ways that might mollify its critics and still meet its ultimate aims, but with little success. On May 30, 1996, the National Research Council (NRC) released a report, requested by Congress, on the government's cryptographic policies. After extolling the virtues of cryptography for business applications, the NRC committee made the following strong recommendations:[62]

> The committee said that the government should explore "escrowed" encryption for its own use, but should not continue to aggressively promote this unproven technology to the private sector. In escrowed encryption, the decoding key would be held by a trusted third-party organization or institution. This is attractive to law enforcement agencies because with a court order, they could obtain the key and unlock even the most unbreakable code. However, many companies don't like the idea of giving a third party the key to all their secrets, even if the third party is considered trustworthy.
>
> The US government's current support of escrowed encryption as a technical pillar of its cryptography policy is inappropriate now, the report says, because there are many unresolved questions about this approach, such as the liability of third-party encryption. Even when these problems are resolved, adoption of escrowed encryption or of any other specific technology or standard by the commercial sector should be voluntary and based on business needs, not government pressure.

The impact on US companies goes beyond the concern with government access to encrypted communication; it also involves business, the export of high technology products.

ITAR (International Traffic in Arms Regulations)

The US government regulates the export of arms that employ advanced technologies that could harm the country. Included in the list of restricted exports are advanced computers and strong cryptosystems, implemented in either software or hardware. Encryption materials are included in Category XIII and require a license for export that must be approved by the Departments of State and Commerce, with input from the National Security Agency. What makes the problem of such great concern to business is that, "Export restrictions also apply to all products that contain cryptography, such as electronic mail, databases and data-compression products."[63] There is also a general perception that if a cryptosystem does receive an export license, it probably can be decrypted easily and is therefore not of much interest. What underlies this government policy is that US military, police, and espionage officials want to be able to access communications around the world, as well as in the US.

The authors of the NRC report, referred to previously, also noted that "current federal restriction on the export of encryption technologies allow only the export of relatively weak cryptography. This is done to protect the nation's ability to gather foreign intelligence. However, these export laws not only inhibit US companies from selling their best cryptographic technology overseas, but they also limit what is available in this country. Even though there are no legal limits on the kinds of encryption that can be sold in the United States, many companies find it impractical to develop and market different products for both US and overseas markets."[64] A group of members of Congress wrote a letter to the President arguing against the export restrictions. They referred to the Computer Systems Policy Project that "unless the US relaxes out-of-date export controls, the US technology industry will lose $60 billion in revenues and 200,000 jobs by the year 2000."[65]

One curious byproduct of bureaucratic decisionmaking is the special dispensation allowed to individuals traveling overseas with their portables in hand when these portables have strong encryption software aboard. Under the condition that such software is for personal use only, no license requirement is necessary.[66] Finally, a White House Fact Sheet on Anti-Terrorism Proposals revealed that the government's commitment to control strong cryptographic systems has not wavered:[67]

> We will seek legislation to strengthen our ability to prevent terrorists from coming into possession of the technology to encrypt their communications and data so that they are beyond the reach of law enforcement. We oppose legislation that would eliminate current export barriers and encouraging the proliferation of encryption which blocks appropriate access to protect public safety and the national security.

Terrorism

Among the many charges directed at the Internet is that it could be used by terrorist groups to plan their activities. Of course, similar accusations could be laid against telephone companies that carry conversations among known or suspected terrorists. Police forces have cautioned that bomb-making instructions are available on the Internet and that (more) restrictions are required to remove these or to impose severe penalties on those who post them and those who access them. It is forgotten or conveniently ignored that libraries have such information as well and yet who (except for the FBI perhaps) would suggest that librarians monitor borrowers to determine who is interested in weapons manufacture. Nevertheless, at a July 1996 meeting, the G7 (Group of Seven leading industrialized nations) adopted a set of measures to combat international terrorism. Among these, one was directed at the Internet: "6. note the risk of terrorists using electronic or wire communications systems and networks to carry out criminal acts and the need to find means, consistent with national law, to prevent such criminality."[68] This rather cryptic pronouncement is devoid of any hint of practical measures that might be undertaken and therefore serves to inflame popular sentiment against the Internet as a home for terrorists, to say nothing of pornographers, and child molesters[69] as well.

Gambling

Everyone likes to place bets, informally or at race tracks, gambling casinos, bingo parlors, and state lotteries. Apparently more than $500 billion was wagered in the US last year with net earnings by gambling establishments of about $40 billion.[70] Legal bets can be placed only locally as the Federal Interstate Wire Act "prohibits anyone in the gambling business from taking bets over a network—including the Internet—that crosses state or international borders."[71] Enter the Internet. It operates worldwide, it transmits information instantaneously, and sites can be established in one country and accessed from another. Thus a gambling facility could be established in the Caribbean, in Southeast Asia, or elsewhere, and Americans could place bets after setting up an account. One operation has been set up in Belize and requires that $1,000 first be wired to a bank located there. "Then, for $100, you must purchase a start-up kit, including special software, a card reader that attaches to your PC, and a smart card that holds your security and account information."[72] Kerry Rogers, the chief technical director claims that 4,000 people have registered, half from the US. It is unlikely that state governments will sit back and do nothing; we should probably expect a licensing process whereby betting-on-demand on the Internet will be established, and considerable tax money will flow to governments.

COMPETITIVENESS

Is the United States still competitive? If we are to believe the many journalists, economists, and historians who have written over the past ten years, the answer is, perhaps yes, but the future holds a diminished economic role internationally for the United States. Large trade deficits have become endemic; whole segments of the consumer electronics industry, such as television receivers, video cassette recorders, television cameras, and still cameras have vanished; the automobile industry has suffered a continuing reduced market share; major segments of the computer industry, such as memory chips, printers, laptop and notebook computers, and even supercomputers are being dominated by Japan; in international banking, Japanese banks have taken nine of the top ten positions, in 1995, in terms of total assets, with one German bank making the top ten. In all these areas, the trends do not favor the United States and some have even argued that the United States should forego international industrial competition and become the world's provider of services and handler of information. Opposing voices have argued that it is impossible for the United States to maintain world leadership without a strong and thriving industrial base, especially in the computer, communications, and information technology sectors.

The three major challengers to US dominance are Japan, Southeast Asia countries (South Korea, Taiwan, Singapore, Malaysia, and China itself), and Western Europe. Although one important factor in the Japanese success story is the intimate cooperation among business, government, and labor to achieve advances in carefully chosen areas, the US government has officially resisted the design of a national industrial policy as a way of focusing energy on well-defined goals. Nevertheless, certain steps have been taken to mount challenges, including cooperative efforts among leading computer companies, the control of the export of designated technologies, and government support of certain advanced technologies, especially the Internet. In fact, the Clinton Administration has made the promotion of the National Information Infrastructure (NII), also referred to more popularly as the Information Superhighway, the centerpiece of its high technology concerns.

The Japanese and Korean Challenges

In recent years books, television shows, and special issues of magazines have appeared, with some regularity, that purport to explain Japan to Americans. The work ethic of the Japanese is continually extolled in comparison to the well-publicized but unverified negative attitudes of the American worker. Characterizations of Japan are varied and numerous, including the following:

- The Japanese are copiers not innovators.
- Their success is based on unfair cooperation among government, industry, and labor.
- IQ tests show the Japanese to be smarter than Americans.
- They prevent fair competition by restricting entry to their domestic marketplace.
- They compete unfairly abroad by taking initial losses in order to penetrate a new market.
- Although they lost World War II, the Japanese obtained an advantage in the complete rebuilding of their industrial plant.

In the consumer electronics market, Japan and Southeast Asia are the world leaders in video cassette recorders, citizen band radios, stereo systems, color television sets, and compact disk players. In the application of new digital electronics to consumer products, they have shown the way and lead in 35 mm cameras, with self-focusing and automatic film advance, calculators, and watches. The quality of these products has totally reversed an earlier reputation for shoddy workmanship.

Other factors contributing to the success of "Japan, Inc." are a stable and hard-working labor force; progressive management (although there is some debate about how progressive); effective cooperation among business, government, and labor; a serious concern with productivity and quality; aggressive worldwide marketing coupled with a protectionist home policy; and a focus on consumer production under the US military security umbrella. However, in the early 1990s, the Japanese economy seemed to slow down, in part a victim of its own success as the yen increased in value against major world currencies, thereby pushing up the costs of Japanese products. Japan is still a formidable competitor but a closer examination of the assets of its major companies, both home and abroad, reveals that they may be overvalued by a considerable amount, as much as $7.7 trillion, of which $6 trillion is in overpriced real estate.[73]

Japan is also turning to its natural markets in the far east with results that create a large, impenetrable market resistant to Western control. In addition to the long term economic influence and power of Japan, South Korea has been growing rapidly in many high-tech areas. Consider the following indicators:[74]

- *Autos* Korea is already the world's fifth-largest auto manufacturer.
- *Semiconductors* Already dominant in 4-megabit DRAM semiconductors, Samsung, LG and Hyundai are expected to stay ahead of Japan in 16-megabit and 64-megabit generations.
- *Information Processing* Korean makers are attacking Japanese dominance of liquid-crystal-display industry; also gearing up massive production of CD-ROM drives.
- *Telecommunications* Increasing use of satellites and fiber-optic networks.
- *Nuclear Energy* Already ranking with France and Japan as one of the world's top three developers of civilian nuclear energy.

Thus, the challenge to the US in many of the technological areas that it first developed is worldwide, and how to maintain its overall dominance when the economic attacks are relentlessly mounted is an open problem.

An Industrial Policy

Governments regulate, monitor, allocate, draw up guidelines, enforce statutes, and generally attempt to create a favorable climate for business. Periodically, the US government involves itself more directly in business activities. For example, it guaranteed massive loans to the Chrysler Corporation to enable it to survive. In the early 1980s a number of voices urged the government to become a partner in future industrial development. The following reasons were among those offered:

- Japan's stunning industrial success has been attributed to the long-range planning and adequate financing provided by industry and government in cooperation with labor.
- High technology is so volatile and important to the economic well-being and security of the nation that government involvement is mandatory.
- Other more traditional industries such as steel and automobiles—the so-called smoke-stack industries—are seen as supplying fewer jobs in the future, and so the government is urged to stimulate other areas of the economy.
- The serious recession of the early 1980s has convinced many economists that active government participation in a national plan for growth is necessary to stabilize the economy in the future.
- The government has already been so involved in piecemeal economic activities—through its funding of research, its investment credits, its antitrust prosecutions, and its import/export regulations—that a coherent, long-range strategy is quite appropriate.

Critics maintain that the United States has arrived at its current dominant position precisely because the government has not become involved in a serious way in major business activities. Many prefer the government to act as a referee, not a player. They suggest that the strength of the free enterprise system is that it is self-regulating and that any interference by the government will disturb this system. They ask what special skills the government has to enable it to predict winners independent of market forces. This confrontation is not new, but current economic, social, political, and military factors have given it a new urgency.

Given that our focus is not on a national industrial policy in general but rather on efforts to promote and stimulate computer technology, the present discussion will be concerned with steps taken in this direction. Two periods will be examined, first the 1980s and the early 1990s, and second the mid-1990s and further.

US Actions: Phase I

Although no national policy has ever been enunciated by the US government, steps have been taken in the 1980s and early 1990s, such as the following:

- The Department of Defense, through DARPA (Defense Advanced Research Projects Agency), has supported research and development in a variety of military-related, high technology areas including artificial intelligence (smart land rovers, battle management systems, pilot's assistant, expert systems), integrated circuits, supercomputers, parallel processing, and neurocomputing.
- The Microelectronics & Computer Technology Corporation (MCC) was formed in 1982 by ten US computer and semiconductor companies (but not IBM) to share costs to develop the next generation of computers to exceed Japan's efforts. It now includes such industrial shareholders as "3M, AMD, Andersen Consulting, AT&T, Cadence, Ceridian Corporation, Digital, Eastman Kodak Company, General Electric, Harris, Hewlett-Packard, Honeywell, Lockheed Martin, Motorola, National Semiconductor, Nortel, Rockwell, and Westinghouse Electric Company."[75] MCC's mandate has changed from its early ambitious goal "to focus primarily on two areas: a high-volume electronics division that develops packaging, interconnect and display technology, and an enterprise integration division dedicated to building a global data-highway and accompanying networking and database technologies."[76]
- Sematech is a consortium of chip producers, founded in 1988, with 14 members in 1989, funded by its members and the Federal and Texas governments to attempt to restore the lost US lead in DRAM (dynamic random access memory) chips. The board of the Semiconductor Industry Association, with 37 members, unanimously approved this effort in 1989. A major source of funding is $100 million from the Pentagon. Both IBM and AT&T donated chip technology to the fledgling consortium: IBM, the design and manufacturing specifications for its 4-megabit DRAM, and AT&T, the technology for a l-megabit static RAM. Sematech suffered a major blow in June 1990 when its first chief executive, the legendary Robert N. Noyce, died. Sematech is funded by its member companies with matching federal funds. It has been very successful in regaining US leadership in the $77 billion semiconductor industry.
- The Federal government itself has sponsored related projects through many of its agencies such as the National Institute of Standards and Technology, that has funded research on semiconductor measurement technology. Up to 1996, the government has spent about $650 million on Flat Panel Display research.

US Actions: Phase II

The most common rhetoric over the past few years has been with reference to the Information Highway, a term apparently introduced by Vice President Al Gore.[77] This rhetoric has been accompanied by new government agencies, research funds, committees, reports, corporate mergers, legislation, and even more rhetoric. From the outset, the government projected its role as a facilitator not as a source of funds and this theme, in keeping with the tenor of the times, namely less government, was echoed in the myriad of reports that followed. For example, consider the following policy issues expressed in a meeting held by the National Academy of Engineering:[78]

(1) The government should help provide the vision for the way the NII will evolve and operate. Private industry should build, own, and operate the NII under competitive conditions.

(2) The government should provide incentives and opportunities, such as tax credits for investment in equipment, R&D, or worker training, to encourage the private sector to invest in and deploy new information technology. The government should continue to focus its direct support on precompetitive projects or applications that demonstrate and test new NII technologies.

(3) In order to realize the broad benefits of the multimedia revolution and the NII, there must be full and fair competition in all sectors of our communications and information industry, both domestically and internationally.

(4) Private industry must continue to play the lead role in working to define the interoperability standards of the NII. The government must continue to work with and represent industry in some international treaty organizations that develop standards. Jointly, we need to speed up the standards-setting process.

(5) Perhaps the broadest policy challenge is that of facilitating public acceptance of and comfort with the benefits of multimedia communications and the NII. This will require setting ground rules to protect electronically available intellectual property, creating a framework to ensure privacy and security of information, and establishing mechanisms to make these benefits available to the largest number of users. This last point is vital if we are to avoid having a nation of information "haves" and "have nots." The challenge, simply put, is to develop a new definition of universal service.

These views are reinforced in almost every document and speech about the NII or the IH. The final report of the US Advisory Council on the National Information Infrastructure was delivered in February 1996. It reviews the progress in building the IH, states many principles that should govern the variety of services to be provided, and makes a number of recommendations to guide continued development. About half of the membership of the Advisory Council was selected from the business community, with the remainder from unions, local public officials, and consumer and lobbyist groups. Thus it is to be expected that the views emerging from the Council will reflect commonly held positions of the business sector, mainly telecommunications and entertainment. The report states quite clearly that, "The private sector must have primary responsibility for the continued design, deployment, and operation of the Information Superhighway."[79] The role of government, at all levels. is to be a catalyst, through the use of research and development funds. Thus, the Federal Government should have the responsibility to:[80]

- Provide visionary leadership (publish best practices, give awards to technically competent schools ["CyberSchools"]);
- Provide support and funds for appropriate projects, including retraining, enhancement, and enrichment;
- Provide funds for precompetitive research and development;
- Promote partnerships and dialogue with the private sector (joint setting of standards, precompetitive research, pilot projects, etc.);
- Protect rights by clarifying and enforcing laws on intellectual property, security, and privacy and providing dispute-resolution mechanisms for the protection of rights;
- Promote public understanding through copyright awareness and similar campaigns;
- Encourage the private sector to take the lead in providing value-added information and services over the Information Superhighway;
- Stimulate Superhighway activity in its role as purchaser and user;
- Provide services where the services are not available in the private sector (such as public safety); and
- Protect and promote the country's interests internationally.

The NII Testbed, a consortium of 48 companies, universities, and national laboratories, in its 1996 report, presented the responses of its members to the question, "What is the greatest potential benefit of the National Information Infrastructure?" 68% answered "Will boost competitiveness of US companies;" 19% answered "Will improve US work-force through access to training and education;" 9% answered "Will improve government and public services;" and only 4% offered that it "Will provide consumer services to the home."[81] There does appear to be a consensus that although the government should act as a cheerleader with research funds, it should not attempt in any way to direct the growth of the IH. Its funds should be used to stimulate areas that may be to too speculative for the private sector but that may prove to have significant payoff. In other words, it should continue its relatively long tradition of funding research and development that industry may be wary of but that is welcomed by them, universities, and research institutions, nevertheless.

Final Comments

The debate over a national industrial policy has gone through several stages, but as the economist Robert Kuttner points out, the United States has had an industrial policy since the end of World War II and it has been implemented by the Pentagon, which subsidizes technological development every time it buys a new weapons system, supports a research project in a national laboratory, or contracts with the private sector through projects supported by DARPA. The Pentagon even can claim considerable success in such major innovations as integrated circuits, advanced composite materials, supercomputers, optics, computerized machine tools, telecommunications, and AI.[82] Many of the Pentagon needs are also important to society in general and should properly be supported by agencies other than the Department of Defense. Among these technologies are integrated circuits, robotics, fiber optics, biotechnology, and superconductivity.

   With all the discussion about revitalizing "our" (US) competitiveness, the Harvard economist Robert Reich asked, "Who is us? Is it IBM, Motorola, and General Motors? Or is it Sony, Thomson, Philips, and Honda?"[83] He describes two corporations: corporation A with headquarters in New York, with American top managers and directors but with most of its employees non-American, and much of its research and most of its manufacturing plants located outside of the United States; and corporation B, which is headquartered abroad, with most of its management foreign but most of its employees American, and much of its research and most of its manufacturing carried out in the United States. In improving US competitiveness, which corporation is most crucial? As Reich notes, "... the competitiveness of American-owned corporations is no longer the same as American competitiveness. Indeed, American ownership of the corporation is profoundly less relevant to America's economic future than the skills, training, and knowledge commanded by American workers—workers who are increasingly employed within the United States by foreign-owned corporations."[84] Thus the answer to the question, "Who is us?" is the American work force, not necessarily the American corporation, and this answer of course changes the terms of reference of any discussion about what steps, if any, the government should take with respect to US competitiveness. For example, by the early 1990s, Honda was manufacturing more cars in the United States than in Japan and will even be exporting cars to Japan. In fact, 10% of the US manufacturing work force is currently employed by foreign employers.

Another important move by Japan, beyond buying American companies and setting up partnerships with US firms to gain access to emerging technology, and building manufacturing plants within the United States, is the opening of research laboratories to carry out basic research in the United States. The crucial aspect of this venture is that Japanese companies intend to hire top US computer scientists to work in them by offering salaries considerably higher than the going rate. Academics may find these offers hard to refuse given current cutbacks in research funds and the promise of state-of-the-art equipment. Following the American model, the Japanese companies intend to establish their facilities near leading universities to attract US scientists.[85] Japanese influence in the United States is already of some concern because of their supposed excessive lobbying efforts in Washington on behalf of their economic interests.

Japan will not go away; neither will Europe nor that fast rising group of Asian contenders including South Korea, Taiwan, Singapore, Hong Kong, and Malaysia. What is clear is that to a lesser or greater degree, the US government will play an important role in America's economic future especially in the high technology arena, whether through the fiction of noninterference in the marketplace or overtly through direct support for emerging technologies. The size of its role may be smaller in monetary terms, however, given the republican control of Congress. Thus projections to fiscal 2002, from fiscal 1995, show that nondefense research and development spending will be reduced substantially, by about 34%, down from $34.3 billion to $22.5 billion.[86]

OTHER ISSUES

The Internet is essentially a network of networks and computers which have agreed to use a common protocol with which to communicate. These protocols can operate over a number of media, including copper wire, fiber optic cable and electromagnetic spectrum. Furthermore, the Internet's protocols operate independently of whether ASCII text, voice, video, graphical or other data is being carried within its packet-based mode of transmission. Thus, the Internet is a multi-media, transmission-technology independent form of communication.

Regulation should not be used to inhibit the further development of technology. It is in the public interest to allow the integration of voice, video, graphics and text applications.[87]

Stock Market Regulation

Sometimes called Black Monday, this event set off a flurry of accusations and was seen as yet another crime committed by Wall Street insiders and traders against the small investor:[88]

> From the close of trading on Friday, October 16, to its lowest point on Tuesday, October 20, a period of just 10 trading hours, the S&P 500 Index fell 22%. During the same 10 hours, the S&P Futures Index fell 36%. This precipitous drop in prices on October 19 and 20,1987, and the events that surrounded it, are now known as the Crash of 1987. The 1987 stock market plunge was the worst ever.

In the wake of the crash, studies were initiated by several authorities, including the Presidential Task Force (the Brady Commission), the Commodity Futures Trading Commission (CFTC), the Securities Exchange Commission (SEC), the General Accounting Office (GAO), the New York Stock Exchange (NYSE), and the Chicago Mercantile Exchange (CME). All these reports addressed two major questions: What caused the crash? Are the financial institutions flawed? The answers are surprising, especially in the light of the instant analyses following the crash. The SEC report does not answer the "what" and indeed says that the precise combination of causes may never be known. It was indirectly critical of computerized strategies that involved the simultaneous buying and selling of stocks and stock index futures.[89] (This practice is discussed later in this section.) The Brady Commission report notes (p. x), "The precipitous market decline . . . was 'triggered' by specific events: an unexpectedly high merchandise trade deficit which pushed interest rates to new high levels, and proposed tax legislation which led to the collapse of the stocks of a number of takeover candidates."[90] Note that nothing is said about the internal workings of the stock exchanges themselves. After analyzing all of these reports, the author of the opening quotation, Franklin Edwards of Columbia University, attempts to capture the common opinion, perhaps a generalization: ". . . a combination of speculative euphoria in world stock markets and serious underlying macroeconomic disequilibria set the stage for a crisis of confidence that inevitably would have, and finally did, precipitate a market break."[91]

In the early reactions to the crash, a likely major candidate was the computer in two respects; first as initiating and responding to trades in a manner that produced a frenzied, uncontrollable cycle of selling, and second as an inadequate record keeper and monitor of the overheated market. These charges were not supported by the subsequent studies. Nevertheless, immediately following the crash, the New York Stock Exchange suspended program trading ("Program trading exacerbated the decline"[92]), an act that falsely suggested a major contributing role for computers. Perhaps three definitions would be helpful at this point.[93]

Program Trading. Prior to the entry of computers, program trading involved the purchase or sale of a portfolio, or "basket" of stocks, as if the portfolio were a single stock. With the advent of computers, the term *computerized trading* is frequently used and the image of huge blocks of stock bought or sold with a single keystroke is evoked.

Stock-Index Arbitrage. Arbitrage is the simultaneous purchase and sale of similar securities on different markets in the hope of achieving a gain based on small differences in prices on the two markets. In the most popular form of arbitrage, called stock-index arbitrage, a portfolio of stocks is traded instead of a single stock. Traders prepare a basket of stocks that mirrors the Standard & Poor (S&P) stock index, and monitor the value of that index on the Chicago Mercantile Exchange, which deals in futures (i.e., in contracts to deliver a fixed quantity of stocks at a fixed price and a fixed time). Simultaneously, the value of the basket is monitored on the New York Stock Exchange, where the sum of the momentary values of each stock determines the overall value. Because of discrepancies that arise between these two markets and last only a few minutes, it is possible for a trader, by instantaneously issuing buy or sell orders for large baskets at values (e.g., between $10 and $100 million) to profit by moves of the two markets in opposite directions. It has been possible for vast amounts of money to be made by this process.

Portfolio Insurance. One way for an investor to hedge against losses is to program his or her own computer to monitor the instantaneous behavior of the portfolio. If it falls below a certain value, a warning can be triggered and the investor can issue a sell with a few keystrokes, or if it rises, the investor can issue a buy order. The computer program can issue such orders automatically if the conditions are well-defined. Portfolio insurance commonly is used by corporations, pension funds, endowments, and mutual funds.

Index arbitrage and portfolio insurance played some role in the crash, although they probably did not initiate it. The question for regulatory authorities such as the internal ones run by the Exchanges and especially the SEC, the federal agency responsible for the operation of all the nation's exchanges, is to ensure that all investors, large and small, have equal opportunity. The destabilizing impact of computers, if any, must be eliminated or reduced. Among the recommendations in the SEC study that are relevant to the use of computers are the following:[94]

- Program trading information should be publicly disseminated, and the NYSE's DOT (designated order turnaround) system should be enhanced.
- Better market-surveillance systems are needed.
- Various improvements should be made to increase the efficiency of the automated settlement systems used by clearing associations.

The creative use of computers to manipulate stocks in ways not previously anticipated will require regulators to exercise constant vigilance. To this end, the New York Stock Exchange (NYSE), the National Association of Securities Dealers (NASD), and the American Stock Exchange (AMEX) have invested in sophisticated computer programs to identify suspicious abnormal trading. Given the enormous number of daily transactions, it requires considerable computing power to detect such suspicious activities. The NYSE has a system with more than one million records on individuals who might have access to private information and therefore could be involved in a stock purchase or leveraged buyout. It also has a system for monitoring every transaction, which is first alerted by some unusual activity, the exact nature of which is not publicly available for obvious reasons. The second level is then triggered by analysis and comparison with normal behavior. The company is alerted and newspapers are consulted to uncover any information to explain the unusual occurrence. If no satisfactory explanation is discovered, a full investigation is initiated by the NYSE's surveillance staff.[95]

Black Monday and all the efforts to prevent a recurrence appear to have been successful, but now a another trend, the growing use of electronic networks to match buyers and sellers, may bypass all these security efforts and the exchanges as well. Fourth-market systems such as Reuters's Instinet can provide a "blackboard" for investors and buyers to post buying and selling prices. In some sense this represents a return to a precomputer period except that the walls have been removed and the players have been globally distributed. Such networks are not limited to the United States and truly global, 24 hour per day trading is now a reality. Regulation on a global scale offers interesting and difficult challenges.[96]

Not surprisingly, the Internet has become host to a variety of financial services including "virtual exchanges" and brokers that provide instantaneous stock buying and selling. Here are three different approaches:[97]

- PerfectData Corp. in Simi Valley, Calif., simply wants to match buyers and sellers over its electronic bulletin board system, PerfectTrade. The trades themselves, however, take place over the traditional stock exchanges.
- Direct IPO Corp. in Marina Del Rey, Calif., wants to help small Internet companies offer stock directly to investors via the World Wide Web.
- Wit Capital Corp. in New York hopes to create a system where multiple companies' stocks are traded directly on the net.

What is also attractive about online brokers is their fees. For example, Lombard Institutional Brokerage's Internet Trading and Research Information System offers trading fees as low as $36.50 a trade compared to $160 a trade for a typical standard broker. In addition, stock trades can be made 24 hours per day and the company offers a free service that permits customers to track a portfolio of stocks. Consider the following contrast in operating procedures to see why the Internet looms as a serious concern to traditional brokers:[98]

- *Major firms*   charge high commissions that support an array of services, sprawling networks of brokers, offices, and research staffs. To keep customers tied to their brokers, the firms equip brokers with computers to execute trades and access proprietary investment information for their clients.
- *Internet brokers*   keep their overhead low by having no brokers and few offices, with the Internet allowing customers to obtain everything from stock quotes to mutual-fund rankings.

Radio, Telephone, and TV on the Internet

These broadcast media and the telephone are available now on the Internet, the quality is improving, and the use of limited bandwidth is becoming more efficient. The long-distance telephone companies certainly feel threatened as their trade association, the America Carriers Telecommunication Association (ACTA), petitioned the Federal Communications Commission (FCC) on March 4, 1996 "to order the Respondents to immediately stop their unauthorized provisioning of telecommunications services . . ."[99] In somewhat more detail, ACTA expressed the following concerns:[100]

> This petition concerns a new technology: a computer software product that enables a computer with Internet access to be used as a long distance telephone, carrying voice transmissions, at virtually no charge for the call.
>
> ACTA submits that the providers of this software are telecommunications carriers and, as such, should be subject to FCC regulation like all telecommunications carriers. ACTA also submits that the FCC has the authority to regulate the Internet.
>
> ACTA submits that it is not in the public interest to permit long distance service to be given away, depriving those who must maintain the telecommunications infrastructure of the revenue to do so, and nor is it in the public interest for these select telecommunications carriers to operate outside the regulatory requirements applicable to all other carriers.

The Federation of American Research Networks (FARNET), representing a variety of both not-for-profit and for-profit organizations such as Internet Service Providers, Network Service Providers, Interexchange Companies, Regional Bell Operating Companies, Universities and Supercomputer Centers, urged the FCC to deny ACTA's petition. In part, it argued against singling out "for regulation one particular type of communication that is now taking place over the Internet. Besides being administratively burdensome, and perhaps even technically impossible, such an action would severely prohibit the future development of the Internet as a multi-media communications tool."[101] There are more arguments: "Regulation should not be used to inhibit the further development of technology" and "The commission has a clear mandate from the Telecommunications Act of 1996 to make pro-competitive, deregulatory decisions in the public interest."[102]

Similar arguments and counterarguments are being raised about radio and television on the Internet, and as technological developments squeeze more bandwidth out of existing hardware, the Internet may evolve more rapidly than expected into the Information Highway. Given that the Telecommunications Act of 1996 calls for less regulation and more competition, the government may be unwilling to restrict the use of the Internet for specific modes of communication previously carried elsewhere. The future seems to be wide open.

SUMMARY

Relations between government and business in the United States have been involved, torturous, occasionally acrimonious, sometimes beneficial, usually controversial, and always unpredictable. In this chapter, we have focused on certain industries—computers and communications—and certain problem areas—transborder data flows and technology transfer.

The development and significance of electronic banking has been discussed, with special emphasis on the dimensions of electronic banking and the potential problem areas. In somewhat more detail, the following points have been covered.

Although committed to the free enterprise system, the US government has at times found it necessary to challenge the activities of certain large companies. On January 8, 1982, the Justice Department dropped a 13-year antitrust suit against IBM. On the same day it also dropped an antitrust suit against AT&T, after AT&T agreed to divest itself of the local telephone companies.

IBM, freed of the antitrust suit, launched an aggressive challenge on all fronts to extend its domination of computer-related business. For example, within three years after the personal computer (the PC) was introduced in 1981, it held the lead in sales. AT&T's first steps after divestiture were somewhat more tentative. It was challenged in the profitable long-distance market by a number of companies and has yet to make its presence felt in the computer market.

In a major change fostered by technological innovation, the banking system is being transformed by the introduction of electronic banking. Examples of this process are the appearance of automatic teller machines, point-of-sales terminals, and electronic banking via home computers. Concerns about electronic banking include security of financial records, potential increased frequency of electronic crime, impact on competition, and impact on consumers.

Governments are extremely concerned about the competitiveness of their industries and prepared to provide support in a variety of ways. With the rise of Japan and Western Europe as the major economic competitors of the United States, some have called for the government to design a national policy to deal with the technological challenge. Some small steps have been taken but there is little support in Congress or the White House for a government-led approach. Nevertheless, the White House has been very active in promoting the rhetoric of the National Information Infrastructure.

Other areas in which the government must play a role with respect to business activities are the regulation of stock exchanges, especially problems arising from the use of computers and computer networks and the use of the Internet to carry telephone and broadcast transmissions.

NOTES

1. Figures taken from *Datamation's* rankings of the top 100 global computer companies for 1995 showed that in the Desktop category, IBM ranked first in sales with $12.95 billion, Compaq second with $9.18 billion, Fujitsu third with $8.84 billion, and Apple fourth with $8.53 billion. It should be noted that this category as defined by *Datamation*, combines "PCs and workstations into a single desktop category. Why? Because the fine line between them keeps getting fuzzier. And, as corporate users choosing their primary systems weigh the merits of desktop vs. laptop, the line between a system that doesn't move and one that goes with you is also getting fuzzier. We include in the desktop category all portable machines, including handhelds." "How We Put the DATAMATION 100 Together," *Datamation*, June 15, 1996. Accessed from the Web site with URL <http://www.datamation.com/PlugIn/issues/1996/june15/> on July 13,

1996. Of course in the PC market itself, IBM's share, in a fast growing market, has been sliding from about 12% in 1990 to less than 8% in 1994.

2. Charles E. Wilson, former president of General Motors, in testimony before the Senate Armed Forces Committee, 1952.

3. John Opel, president of IBM, as quoted in Bro Uttal, "Life After Litigation at IBM and AT&T," *Fortune*, February 8, 1982, p. 59.

4. Charles H. Ferguson and Charles R. Morris. *Computer Wars: The Fall of IBM and the Future of Global Technology.* (New York: Times Books, 1993).

5. *Ibid.*, p. xii.

6. David Kirkpatrick, "The Internet Saga Continues . . . IBM and Lotus: Not so Dumb After All," *Fortune*, July 8, 1996, pp. 62–64, 66, 68.

7. Information accessed from the Web site with URL: <http://www.ibm.com/> on August 18, 1996.

8. The world's largest software company is IBM. In 1995, IBM's software revenues were $12.95 billion compared to Microsoft's $7.42 billion. Of course, IBM's software is almost exclusively for its own systems and the gap has been narrowing over the years.

9. Stuart J. Johnston and Ed Scannell. "Microsoft Holds Steady under Probe," *Computerworld*, April 18, 1994, p. 30.

10. Stuart J. Johnston and Ed Scannell. "Users Hold Key to Antitrust Battle," *Computerworld*, April 18, 1994, pp. 1, 30. Accessed from the Web page with URL: <http://www.computerworld.com/search/AT-html/9404/940418SL15doj1.html> on August 19, 1996.

11. *Ibid.*, p. 30.

12. Mitch Betts. "A Step-by-Step Look at the Microsoft Case," *Computerworld*, July 25, 1994, p. 14. Accessed from the Web page with URL: <http://www.computerworld.com/search/AT-html/9407/940725SL29facts.html> on August 19, 1996.

13. *Ibid.*

14. *Ibid.*

15. "Antitrust, The Smart Way," Editorial, *Business Week*, August 1, 1994, p. 88.

16. *Ibid.*

17. Richard Brandt, Catherine Yang, and Amy Cortese. "Sorry, Bill, The Deal Is Off," *Business Week*, February 27, 1995, pp. 38–40.

18. Terence P. Paré. "Why the Banks Line Up Against Gates," *Fortune*, May 29, 1995, p. 18.

19. Mitch Betts, Ellis Booker, and Stuart J. Johnson. "Microsoft Opponents Go for Blood," *Computerworld*, May 29, 1995, p. 4.

20. Ted Smalley Brown. "DOJ's Flap with Microsoft over Winsock Continues," *PC Week*, December 5, 1995. Accessed from the Web page with URL: <http://www.pcweek.com/news/1204/05win.html> on August 19, 1996.

21. Kim S. Nash. "Netscape Takes Action against Microsoft's Web Practices," *Computerworld*, August 7, 1996. Accessed from the Web page with URL: <http://www.computerworld.com/search/AT-html/briefs/9608/960807net.html> on August 19, 1996.

22. Alexander Graham Bell, first complete sentence transmitted by telephone, March 10, 1876.

23. "Telecom Industry History," Blumenfeld & Cohen Law Company, 1992. Accessed from the Web page with URL: <http://www.technologylaw.com/techlaw/telephony.htm> on August 22, 1996.

24. Charles L. Brown, chairman of AT&T, as quoted in a full-page advertisement in *The New York Times*, January 10, 1982, p. 9.

25. Jeremy Main. "Waking up AT&T: There's Life after Culture Shock," *Fortune*, December 24, 1984, pp. 66–68, 70, 72, 74.

26. Frederic Withington. "Sizing Each Other Up," *Datamation*, July 20, 1982, p. 8.

27. Paul M. Eng. "Surfing's Biggest Splash," *Business Week*, March 11, 1996, p. 86.

28. "The Titans of Telecom," Special Report on Telecom's New Age, *Business Week*, April 8, 1996, insert after page 74.

29. "Overview of the Telecommunications Act of 1996," Blumenfeld & Cohen, 1996. Accessed from the Web page with URL: <http://www.technologylaw.com/techlaw/act_summary.html> on February 25, 1996.

30. Steven Levy. "Now for the Free-for-All," *Newsweek*, February 12, 1996, p. 42.

31. Andrew Kupfer. "AT&T: Ready to Run, Nowhere to Hide," *Fortune*, April 29, 1996, pp. 116–118, 122, 124, and 126.

32. Catherine Arnst and Amy Barrett. "AT&T Is Being Bitten on the Ankles," *Business Week*, August 5, 1996, pp. 26–27.

33. "How the New Telecommunications Law Will Affect You," *PC World*, May 1996. Accessed from the Web page with URL: <http://www.pcworld.com/workstyles/online/articles/may96/1405p058.html> on August 19, 1996.

34. Mark Landler. "Sigh of Relief Greets New Telephone Rules," *The New York Times*, August 2, 1996, pp. C 1, C 6.

35. "Washington's Wake-Up Call," *The Economist*, January 20, 1996, pp. 61–63.

36. Statistics taken from Chapter 2, Information Industry Convergence, *World Telecommunications Development Report*, International Telecommunications Union, 1995. Accessed from the Web page with URL: <http://www.itu.ch/WTDR95/c2.htm> on June 8, 1996.

37. *Information Technologies for Control of Money Laundering*. US Congress, Office of Technology Assessment, OTA-ITC-630. (Washington, DC: US Government Printing Office, September 1995), pp. 20–21. Available at the Web site with URL: <http://www.ota.nap.edu/>.

38. As quoted in Orin Kramer. "Winning Strategies for Interstate Banking," *Fortune*, September 19, 1983, p. 118.

39. Thomas D. Steiner and Diogo B. Teixeira. *Technology in Banking: Creating Value and Destroying Profits*. (Homewood, IL: Dow Jones-Irwin, 1990), p. 10.

40. Jane Bryant Quinn. "The Era of Debit Cards," *Newsweek*, January 2, 1989, p. 51.

41. "Future Belongs to Financial Service Organizations, Not Traditional Players, Says Fifth Annual Survey," Ernst & Young, May 2, 1996. Accessed from the Web page with URL: <http://www.ey.com/us/press/banksur.htm> on July 10, 1996.

42. "Why Security First National Bank?" Security First National Bank, 1996. Accessed from the Web page with URL: <http://www.sfnb.com/whyus/> on August 25, 1996.

43. Kim S. Nash and Thomas Hoffman. "Banks Hit Info Highway at Different Speeds," *Computerworld*, August 21, 1995, p. 52.

44. John Shoemaker. "Why Smart Cards?" Racom Systems, Inc., 1996. Accessed from the Web page with URL: <http://www.racom.com/page5.htm#Smart Card Market Growth> on July 26, 1996.

45. "Smart Cards," Electronic Payment Systems, March 18, 1996. Accessed from the Web page with URL: <http://www-sloan.mit.edu/15.967/group02/smart.htm> on July 26, 1996.

46. "Fact Sheet—About First Virtual," First Virtual Holdings Incorporated, January 1996. Accessed from the Web page with URL: <http://fv.com/ccdanger/facts.html> on August 1996.

47. Kelley Holland and Amy Cortese. "The Future of Money," cover story, *Business Week*, June 12, 1995, pp. 66–70, 72, 74, 78.

48. Joel Kurtzman. *The Death of Money: How the Electronic Economy Has Destabilized the World's Markets and Created Financial Chaos*. (Boston, MA: Back Bay Books, Little Brown and Company, 1993).

49. *Ibid.*, p. 16.

50. "US Policies Should Foster Broad Use of Encryption Technologies," press release, National Research Council, May 30, 1996. Accessed from the Web page with URL: <http://epic.org/crypto/reports/nrc_release.html> on June 16, 1996. The Overview and Recommendations of the National Research Council report are available from the Web page with URL: <http://www2.nas.edu/cstbweb/2646.html>.

51. Taken from a Statement by the Press Secretary, Office of the Press Secretary, The White House, April 16, 1993. Accessed from the Web page with URL: <http://www.scimitar.com/revolution/by_topic/express/techno/clipper/announce.html> on August 28, 1996.

52. *Answers to Frequently Asked Questions About Today's Cryptography, Version 3.0,* RSA Laboratories, 1996. Accessed from the Web page with URL: <http://www.rsa.com/PUBS/labs_faq.pdf> on June 7, 1996.

53. Susan Landau, Stephen Kent, Clint Brooks, Scott Charney, Dorothy Denning, Whitfield Diffie, Anthony Luck, Douglas Miller, Peter Neumann, and David Sobel. "Cryptography in Public: A Brief History," in Lance J. Hoffman (ed.), *Building in Big Brother: The Cryptographic Policy Debate.* (New York: Springer-Verlag, 1995), pp. 41–42.

54. Deborah Russell and G. T. Gangemi, Sr. "Encryption," in Hoffman (ed.), *Building in Big Brother,* pp. 19–20.

55. Lance J. Hoffman. "Key Escrow Systems, Keeping Secrets Secret Except When . . ." in Hoffman (ed.), *Building in Big Brother,* p. 109.

56. Steven Levy. "Battle of the Clipper Chip," *The New York Times Magazines,* June 12, 1994, p. 46.

57. *Ibid.*

58. "The Denning-Barlow Clipper Chip Debate," *Time* Online, March 10, 1994. Accessed from the Web page with URL: <http://ftp.eff.org/papers/barlow-denning.html> on August 28, 1996.

59. *Ibid.*

60. "Cryptographic Issue Statements: Letter to the Computer System Security and Privacy Advisory Board," American Civil Liberties Union, May 13, 1993. In Hoffman (ed.), *Building in Big Brother,* pp. 409–412.

61. *Ibid.*

62. *Op. cit.* "US Policies Should Foster Broad Use of Encryption Technologies."

63. David S. Bernstein. "Encryption's International Labyrinth," in Hoffman (ed.), *Building in Big Brother,* pp. 456–459.

64. *Op. cit.* "US Policies Should Foster Broad Use of Encryption Technologies."

65. "Letter to the President," 27 US Representatives, May 15, 1996. Accessed from the Web page with URL: <http://www.epic.org/crypto/key_escrow/house_letter_5_15_96.html> on June 1, 1996.

66. "Answers to Frequently Asked Questions About Cryptography Export Laws," RSA Data Security, Inc., 1996. Accessed from the Web page with URL: <http://www.rsa.com/PUBS/exp_faq.pdf> on June 7, 1996.

67. "Fact Sheet on Administration Anti-Terrorism Proposals," The White House, July 29, 1996. Accessed from the Web page with URL: <http://www.epic.org/privacy/terrorism/fact_sheet_july96.html> on August 28, 1996.

68. G7/P8 "Ministerial Conference on Terrorism," Paris, July 30, 1996. Accessed from the Web page with URL: <http://www.epic.org/privacy/terrorism/g7_resolutions.html> on August 28, 1996.

69. See reports of the first World Congress Against Sexual Exploitation of Children held in Stockholm, Sweden during August 1996. For example, Paul Knox, "Child Porn Flood Swells," *The Globe and Mail* (Toronto, Canada), August 27, 1996, pp. A 1, A 7.

70. As reported in Evan I. Schwartz, "Wanna Bet?" *Wired*, 3.10, October 1995, pp. 134–137, 190, 192.

71. *Ibid.*, p. 136.

72. *Ibid.*, p. 137.

73. Brian Bremner. "And Now for the Really Bad News," *Business Week*, July 10, 1995, pp. 50–51.

74. William J. Holstein and Laxmi Nakarmi. "Korea: Heads for High Tech's Top Tier," cover story, *Business Week*, July 31, 1995, pp. 56–59, 62–63.

75. "Endless Frontier, Limited Resources: US R&D Policy for Competitiveness," Council on Competitiveness, April 1966, Sector Study: Electronics Appendix. Accessed from the Web page with URL: <http://nii.nist.gov/pubs/coc_rd/apdx_elec.html> on August 30, 1996.

76. *Ibid.*

77. A visit to Al Gore's Web site on October 9, 1996, at <http://www.whitehouse.gov/WH/EOP/OVP/html/GORE_Home.html> reveals that "Vice President Gore, having first coined the term "information superhighway" 17 years ago, is the recognized public leader in the development of the National Information Infrastructure (NII)."

78. John S. Mayo. "The Evolution of Information Infrastructures: The Competitive Search for Solutions," in *Revolution in the US Information Infrastructure*. (Washington, DC: National Academy Press, 1995). Accessed from the Web page with URL: <http://www.nap.edu/readingroom/books/newpath/chap1.html> on August 31, 1996.

79. "A Nation of Opportunity," a final report of the United States Advisory Council on the National Information Infrastructure, February 1996. Accessed from the Web page with URL: <http://www.benton.org/KickStart/nation.keyroles.html> on August 31, 1996.

80. *Ibid.*

81. Gary H. Anthes. "NII Testbed Sounds Alarm," *Computerworld*, February 26, 1996, p. 57.

82. Robert Kuttner. "Industry Needs a Better Incubator Than the Pentagon," *Business Week*, April 30, 1990, p. 16.

83. Robert B. Reich. "Who Is Us?" *Harvard Business Review* **68** (1) January-February 1990, p. 53.

84. *Ibid.*, p. 54.

85. Gina Kolata. "Japanese Woo High-Tech Wizards," *The Globe and Mail* (Toronto, Canada), November 12, 1990, p. B 5. (Taken from the New York Times service.)

86. Gary H. Anthes. "Republican Ax-Wielding Blunts High-Tech Support," *Computerworld*, August 7, 1995, p. 32.

87. "RE: RM No. 8775, ACTA petition relating to 'Internet Phone' Software and Hardware," sent to the Federal Communications Commission by the Federation of American Research Networks, May 6, 1996. Accessed from the Web page with URL: <http://www.farnet.org/acta.htm> on July 13, 1996.

88. Franklin R. Edwards. "The Crash: A Report on the Reports," from Henry C. Lucas, Jr. and Robert A. Schwartz (eds.). *The Challenge of Information Technology for the Securities Markets: Liquidity, Volatility, and Global Trading.* (Homewood, IL: BUSINESS ONE IRWIN, 1989), p. 86.

89. *Ibid.*, p. 87.

90. As quoted in *ibid.*, pp. 87–88.

91. *Ibid.*, p. 88.

92. New York Stock Exchange Chairman John J. Phelan as quoted in Gary Weiss. "Two Key Questions: Was Program Trading to Blame . . . [?]" *Business Week*, November 2, 1987, p. 51.

93. M. Mitchell Waldorp. "Computers Amplify Black Monday," *Science*, October 30, 1987, pp. 602–604.

94. Edwards, *op. cit.*, pp. 98–99.

95. David Stamps. "The IS Eye on Insider Trading," *Datamation,* April 15, 1990, pp. 35–36, 38, 43.
96. David Zigas, et al. "A Trading Floor on Every Screen," *Business Week,* November 5, 1990, pp. 128–130.
97. Melissa Bane. "The Virtual Exchange," *Computerworld,* June 17, 1996, p. 125.
98. Leah Nathans Spiro and Linda Himelstein. "With the World Wide Web, Who Needs Wall Street?" *Business Week,* April 29, 1996, pp. 120–121.
99. "Before the Federal Communications Commission," Washington, DC, March 4, 1996. Accessed from the Web page with URL: <http://www.fcc.gov/Bureaus/Common_Carrier/Other/actapet.html> on July 13, 1996.
100. *Ibid.*
101. *Op. cit.* "RE: RM No. 8775, ACTA petition relating to 'Internet Phone' Software and Hardware."
102. *Ibid.*

ADDITIONAL READINGS

Industry Regulation

Anderson, Howard and Goetz, Martin A. "Sound Off! Is Microsoft Out of Control?" *Computerworld,* June 19, 1995, pp. 106–108.

Arnst, Catherine. "Ready, Set, Devour?" *Business Week,* July 8, 1996, pp. 118–120.

Arnst, Catherine and Coy, Peter. "AT&T: Will the Bad News Ever End?" *Business Week,* October 7, 1996, pp. 122–126, 128, 130.

Rebello, Kathy. "Inside Microsoft," *Business Week,* July 15, 1996, pp. 56–59, 62–63, 66–67.

Sager, Ira. "Serious Fun from IBM," *Business Week,* June 17, 1996, pp. 34–35.

Sager, Ira and Harris, Nicole. "The New I-Way Hog: IBM," *Business Week,* September 16, 1996, pp. 98–101.

Schlender, Brent. "Big Blue is Betting on Big Iron Again," *Fortune,* April 26, 1996, pp. 103–104, 108, 110, 112.

"A Survey of Telecommunications," *The Economist,* September 30, 1995. Accessed from the Web page with URL: <http://www.economist.com/surveys/distance/index.html> on June 8, 1996

The Telecommunications Act of 1996. Accessed from the Web page with URL: <http://www.technologylaw.com/techlaw/act.html> on February 24, 1996.

Wallace, James and Erickson, Jim. *Hard Drive: Bill Gates and the Making of the Microsoft Empire.* (New York: Harper Business, 1993).

World Telecommunication Development Report, International Telecommunication Union, 1995. Accessed from the Web page with URL: <http://www.itu.ch/WTDR95/> on June 8, 1996.

Zuckerman, Laurence. "I.B.M., in Its Dress Shoes, Chases Software Success," *The New York Times,* May 6, 1996, p. C 1, C 5.

Electronic Banking and Financial Transactions

Chaum, David. "Achieving Electronic Privacy," *Scientific American,* August 1992, pp. 96–101. Accessed from the Web page with URL: <http://www.digicash.com/publish/sciam.html> on May 26, 1996.

Fancher, Carol H. "Smart Cards," *Scientific American,* August 1996, pp. 40–45.

Gleick, James. "Dead as a Dollar." *The New York Times,* June 16, 1996, pp. 26 ff.

"An Introduction to Ecash." Digicash, date unknown. Accessed from the Web page with URL: <http://www.digicash.com/publish/ecash_intro/ecash_intro.html> on August 26, 1996.

Levy, Stephen. "The End of Money?" *Newsweek,* October 30, 1995, pp. 62–65.

Manasse, Mark. "The Millicent Protocols for Electronic Commerce," Digital Equipment, date unknown. Accessed from the Web page with URL: <http://www.research.digital.com/SRC/personal/Mark_Manasse/common/mcentny.htm> on August 25, 1996.

McWilliams, Brian. "Financial Insecurity," *Computerworld,* June 26, 1995, pp. 79–80, 84.

"The NetBill Overview." Carnegie Mellon University, May 15, 1995. Accessed from the Web page with URL: <http://www.ini.cmu.edu/NETBILL/publications/CompCon.html#RTFToC4> on August 25, 1996.

The Internet and Information Highway

Anthes, Gary H. "Dislike of Government Standard Isn't Cryptic," *Computerworld,* May 13, 1996, p. 28.

Anthes, Gary H. "Industry to Clinton: Drop Encryption Policy," *Computerworld,* June 3, 1996, p. 24.

Denning, Dorothy. "The Future of Cryptography," *Internet Security Review,* October 1995. A revised version, January 1996, was accessed at the Web page with URL: <http://www.cosc.georgetown.edu/~denning/crypto/Future.html> on August 28, 1996.

Denning, Dorothy. "A Taxonomy for Key Escrow Encryption Systems," *Communications of the ACM,* **39** (3), March 1996, pp. 34–40.

Greenberg, L. T. and Goodman, S. E. "Is Big Brother Hanging by His Bootstraps?" *Communications of the ACM,* **39** (7), July 1996, pp. 11–15.

King, Henry R. "Big Brother, The Holding Company: A Review of Key Escrow Encryption Technology," *Rutgers Computer & Technology Law Journal* **21** (1), 1995, pp. 224–262.

McConnell, Bruce W. and Appel, Edward J. Draft Paper: "Enabling Privacy, Commerce, Security and Public Safety in the Global Information Infrastructure," Executive Office of the President, Office of Management and Budget, May 20, 1996. Accessed from the Web page with URL: <http://www.epic.org/crypto/key_escrow/white_paper.html> on June 1, 1996.

Ramo, Joshua Cooper. "Winner Take All," *Time,* September 16, 1996, pp. 36–43.

Scheurer, Kirsten. "The Clipper Chip: Cryptography Technology and the Constitution—The Government's Answer to Encryption "Chips" Away at Constitutional Rights," *Rutgers Computer & Technology Law Journal* **21** (1), 1995, pp. 264–292.

Competitiveness

Brull, Stephen V. and Carey, John. "Japan's Blastoff in Science," *Business Week,* September 2, 1996, pp. 76, 78.

Corey, E. Raymond. *Technology Fountainheads: The Management Challenge of R&D Consortia.* (Boston, MA: Harvard Business School Press, 1997).

Creating the Superhighways of the Future: Developing Broadband Communications in the UK. Department of Trade and Industry, Government of the United Kingdom, November 1994. Accessed from the Web page with URL: <ftp://ftp.open.gov.uk/pub/docs/dti/broadband_comms.txt> on June 9, 1996.

Global Communication: Opportunities for Trade and Aid. US Congress, Office of Technology Assessment, OTA-ITC-642. (Washington, DC: US Government Printing Office, September 1995). Accessed from the Web page with URL: <http://www.ota.nap.edu/pdf/data/1995/9535.PDF> on May 30, 1996.

Gomory, Ralph E. "National Productivity and Computers," *IEEE Computer,* July 1995, pp. 66–72.

Innovation and Commercialization of Emerging Technology. US Congress, Office of Technology Assessment, OTA-BP-ITC-165. (Washington, DC: US Government Printing Office, September 1995). Accessed from the Web page with URL: <http://www.ota.nap.edu/pdf/data/1995/9539.PDF> on May 15, 1996.

Kalil, Thomas A. "Leveraging Cyberspace," National Economic Council, the White House, Draft April 17, 1996. Accessed from the Web page with URL: <http://nii.nist.gov/cyber/cyber.html> on June 29, 1996.

McKnight, Lee W. and Bailey, Joseph P. "An Introduction to Internet Economics," presented at MIT Workshop on Internet Economics, March 1995. Accessed from the Web page with URL: <http://www.press.umich.edu:80/jep/works/McKniIntro.html> on June 26, 1996.

Niosi, Jorge. *Technology and National Competitiveness.* (Montreal & Kingston, Canada: McGill-Queen's University Press, 1991).

Tennenhouse, David; Lampson, Butler; Gillett, Sharon Eisner; and Klein, Jennifer Steiner. "Virtual Infrastructure: Putting Information Infrastructure on the Technology Curve," Telemedia, Networks and Systems Group, Laboratory for Computer Science, Massachusetts Institute of Technology, October 13, 1995. Accessed from the Web page with URL: <http://www.tns.lcs.mit.edu/publications/VI/VI.html> on June 5, 1996.

The Unpredictable Certainty: Information Infrastructure Through 2000. NII Steering Committee, Computer Science and Telecommunications Board, National Research Council. (Washington, DC: National Academy Press, 1996). Accessed from the Web page with URL: <http://www.nap.edu/nap/online/unpredictable/> on April 22, 1996.

Wireless Technologies and the National Information Infrastructure. US Congress, Office of Technology Assessment, OTA-ITC-622. (Washington, DC: US Government Printing Office, July 1995). Accessed from the Web page with URL: <http://www.ota.nap.edu/pdf/data/1995/9547.PDF> on April 15, 1996.

Other Issues

Aley, James. "How Investors Can Use the Internet," *Fortune,* April 17, 1995, pp. 154–156, 158.

Arbel, Avner and Kaff, Albert E. Crash: *Ten Days in October . . . Will it Strike Again?* (Chicago: Longman Financial Services Publishing, 1989).

Greenwald, John. "The Secret Money Machine," *Time,* April 11, 1994, pp. 20–23.

Hof, Robert D. and Lesly, Elizabeth. "Don't Surf to Us, We'll Surf to You," *Business Week,* September 9, 1996, pp. 108–109.

Retkwa, Rosalyn. "Telephone Politics," *InternetWorld,* June 1996. Accessed from the Web site with URL: <http://www.internetworld.com/June96/politics.html> on July 3, 1996.

Vaughan-Nichols, Steven J. "Radio Comes to Cyberspace," *Byte,* October 1995, p. 46.

Venditto, Gus. "Intenet Phones—The Future Is Calling," *InternetWorld,* June 1996.

Verity, John. "Try Beating These Long-Distance Rates," *Business Week,* April 22, 1996, pp. 131–132.

"Video on the Internet, Webbed," *The Economist,* January 20, 1996, pp. 82–83. Accessed from the Web site with URL: <http://www.internetworld.com/June96/phones.html> on July 3, 1996.

12

THE INFORMATION SOCIETY

We must invest today to create the foundation for the networks of the 21st Century . . . This initiative will foster partnerships among academia, industry and government that will keep the U.S. at the cutting-edge of information and communications technologies. It will also accelerate the introduction of new multimedia services available in our homes, schools, and businesses.

The White House, Office of the Press Secretary, October 10, 1996. Available at the Web page with URL:<http://www.iitf.nist.gov/documents/press/internet.htm>.

INTRODUCTION

Time declared the computer "Machine of the Year" for 1982. In the form of the personal computer, it had truly arrived as a major factor in the national consciousness. On television and in magazines a Charlie Chaplin look-alike shows how a personal computer, the IBM PC, will save your small business. The once almost mystical mainframe has emerged from the cloistered computing center, transformed into a keyboard and a monitor. Other companies are also heavily engaged in trying to convince American families to purchase a computer. Such names as Apple, Compaq, Packard Bell, Digital Equipment, and Texas Instruments have become quite familiar. The competition is fierce, and there have been and will continue to be many casualties.

Some 15 years later, a similar story is being told, but now the theme is networks, the Internet, the Web, and the importance of being connected. The computer is seen by some as a means of getting online, of exploring a new frontier, making new (unseen) friends, playing new games (of all kinds), and generally cruising cyberspace. It sounds exciting and millions around the world have taken the plunge, as of course have the many thousands of companies that have established Web sites in hopes of doing business. This movement from a free-standing general-purpose computer to an active window on the world has come about remarkably quickly, with consequences that are difficult, if not impossible, to predict. We will briefly explore this transition and describe some of the features of online activities. For the present, note that a number of measures indicate that the creation, storage, and movement of information is becoming cheaper as befits the creation of an Information Society. Thus, the cost to perform one million instructions per second has fallen from about $90 in 1991 to about $25 in 1995; the cost to store a gigabyte of data has gone from over \$10 to about \$3; and the cost to send a megabyte of data from New York to Los Angeles over a modem has been reduced from just under \$1.00 to under 20 cents.[1]

The proponents of the revolutionary aspects of cyberspace have expressed extravagant claims that a new realm of experience has emerged, one in which the bounds of the physical world are no longer in force. It is possible to interact with others anonymously, currently with typed text, but spoken language is on the way. It is possible to create a persona that then interacts with other personae over the Internet in chat rooms, groups, or one-on-one. Such interactions are open-ended in that gender can be concealed or switched, appearance enhanced, experiences manufactured and altered to suit circumstances. You can become anything you desire and can reveal only what may serve current needs. If all the world's a stage, then cyberspace has become the stage of choice for many. Thus, it has become a *de facto* testbed for exploring gender switching, anonymity, role-playing, as well as the creation of communities for a number of purposes. Online communities, composed of people who will probably never meet, have been formed for political, sexual, religious, and many other purposes. These are certainly not communities in the traditional sense where people share ideas, engage in activities, and establish relations based on ongoing face-to-face encounters, which may or may not include family members and friends.

Enormous amounts of information are now available for free—after you pay for a computer, modem, software, and Internet Service Provider, of course. This information is provided on a growing number of Web sites set up by governments, libraries, companies, unions, consumer groups, universities, political organizations, religious groups, and individuals. In fact, the Web may be seen as a giant vanity press—anyone can publish and advertise, if willing to pay the costs of maintaining a Web site. And anyone can access this vast, diverse, distributed, and multiowned database, if they have the skills and resources. What about the large segments of the US population and elsewhere that do not have computers or even telephones? Will they again be marginalized? How can their interests be served in a society that is not inclined to use government to provide services that are not absolutely necessary? Will libraries, community centers, senior citizen centers, and of course the schools, be able to provide access services? There is an implicit assumption that information will continue to be free, or available at very low costs, but the future may be different. Governments may decide that for the large amounts of information they provide, the costs necessary to produce it should be recovered. Others providing free information may want users to subscribe formally and pay for what they use. The question of access to the Internet and the Information Highway to follow will not be answered soon, nor will the answers please everyone.

Given that the Internet was the sole preserve of a relatively small number of people just a few years ago and that the Web seems to have been born yesterday, it is almost impossible to predict future directions with any chance of accuracy. Nevertheless, business and governments must take steps to plan, to invest, to build infrastructures to take advantage of business opportunities and to better serve the public, respectively. Recognizing and anticipating technological limitations and developments is a necessary step. An overview of some of the expectations and goals of Information Highway proponents is therefore a useful exercise. In addition, the question of information as a commodity, to be produced, stored, and distributed must be addressed.

Finally, the increasing dependency on technology to provide a vast array of information and services may also mean an increased risk of harm both physically and financially. The more society depends on information, the more it is subject to the risks of inaccuracies, blunders, misuses, and criminal activities. Information must be protected against unauthorized use, which raises serious issues with respect to security. If the promise of the Information Society is increased wealth with less physical labor for many, then one of the costs is increased security for all and increased risk for some.

THE MAKING OF THE ONLINE WORLD

> The open society, the unrestricted access to knowledge, the unplanned and uninhibited association of men for its furtherance—these are what may make a vast, complex, ever growing, ever changing, ever more specialized and expert technological world, nevertheless a world of human community. (J. Robert Oppenheimer, 1953)

The Home/Personal Computer

Throughout the 1980s and 1990s, computers have been advertised in newspapers, magazines, and of course, on television. When the home computer first appeared, it was possible to distinguish it from the personal computer in the office, mainly by price, internal memory, and manufacturer. Although there was no clear dividing line, the home computer was generally under $1,000, usually under $500. In the early 1980s, the most popular of these computers were the enormously successful Commodore 20 and 64. The basic model was a keyboard with internal memory varying from 4K to 64K bytes and requiring a hookup to a television set, resulting in a picture less sharp than on a dedicated monitor. For all but the simplest tasks, peripheral devices are necessary—such as cassette recorders, floppy disk drives, and modems, as well as more memory. Printers varying in price from $200 to $1000 are usually necessary as well. Thus what begins as a rather modest investment quickly can accelerate to a substantial amount, to say nothing of open-ended expenditures for software.

The Home

For most of the 1980s, the selling of the home computer represented a triumph of American marketing ingenuity more than a fulfillment of a genuine need. The home computer was a machine in search of a purpose. Consumers were assaulted by advertisements that used the following strategies:

- *Induce guilt.* Parents will be denying their children "a piece of the future" if they do not immediately buy a computer.
- *Promise immediate solutions.* You can save your bakery or hat factory by organizing production with a personal computer.
- *Urge additional purchases.* The computer itself is only a small part of the story. It is also necessary to buy more software, a disk drive, a printer, and a modem.
- *Argue for the complete package.* For very little you can buy the whole thing.

• *Remind the customer of video games.* Although computers are useful, a wide range of exciting video games will be sure to please the whole family.

But in 1990, for a number of reasons IBM decided that the time was right to return to the home market, and a short time later Apple repackaged its Macintosh into a competitive product, the Macintosh Classic. IBM executives learned that 20% of its PS/2 computers were being used at home and that the home PC market had grown substantially, to 3.7 million units in 1989. At the end of June, IBM announced the PS/1, a specially tailored computer for the home market, designed to avoid the earlier mistakes.

As computer technology has advanced, including much more sophisticated software, the home computer became much more useful. In a 1990 survey of computer purchasers, the following reasons were given (with a percentage of respondents in parentheses): bringing work home from the office or running a home business (57); doing school work (47); and writing letters, budgeting, and other personal chores (19). (Some respondents bought a computer for more than one reason.) The first reason was obviously a major factor in IBM's decision to market the PS/1, especially since almost 35 million Americans operated a full- or part-time business at home in 1990. (This number increased to over 40 million in 1993.) Very few intend to use their PCs to play games—actually less than 3% compared with more than 30% in 1985—given the overwhelming popularity of Nintendo and other new generation video games. The current generation of improved software and faster hardware has greatly simplified computer use and has made it much easier for first-time users to feel comfortable with computers. The leader in this direction has been Apple with its graphics user interface (GUI) for the Macintosh. In 1990, Microsoft introduced its Windows software, with much success, to provide a GUI for IBM PCs and compatibles. If the early story of the home computer is more appearance than substance, the situation has been changing in the 1990s as witnessed by such success stories as Compaq, Dell, Gateway, and Acer to say nothing of IBM and Apple.

A comparison between the computer and the automobile in their early stages of development offers an interesting lesson: the car would never have become so popular had the consumer been required to acquire the skills of a mechanic to use it. The computer is being sold as a powerful device, immediately useful without much knowledge of its inner workings. However, the parallel between cars and computers breaks down in a fundamental way. A car has a straightforward, but narrowly defined purpose, and knowledge of how to operate it enables the driver to use it. A computer can do so many things that a knowledge of programming gives great power to the user. In its current state, however, programming is not particularly easy, and most likely never will be easy; so most users depend on others to program for them, hence the enormous market in such applications programs as spreadsheets, databases, word processors, and more recently Internet connect software and Internet browsers.

At Large

The computer has become a media star, in its ubiquitous personal form. The newsstands are becoming saturated with computer magazines—general interest ones such as Byte, Personal Computing, and Popular Computing, and others that appeal to owners of computers made by Compaq, IBM, Apple, Dell, and others. Everyone seems to be talking about home computers, either trying to decide which one to buy or justifying purchases already made. Much of this activity has the feel of a typical fad, but a substantial and important residue should remain after the initial novelty has worn off, for reasons given previously. Many people have become disillusioned because of the unexpected limitations of their home computers; for many others, though, a new world has been revealed. With a computer connected via a modem to the telephone, the user has access to a growing number of services and information sources. Now the excitement centers around being connected, having access, getting in touch, and maybe even making friends.

The Internet originated as a network to link researchers at universities, private institutions, and government laboratories, who carried out research funded by the Defense Advanced Research Project Agency of the US Department of Defense. This network encouraged researchers to exchange information prior to publication in journals and to reduce travel costs in the process. Thus although face-to-face interaction is invaluable, interaction over a network can also play an important role in facilitating the exchange of ideas and the writing of scientific papers. In the beginning, only text-based information was circulated, and it was of some importance that very few messages failed to reach their destination. It would have been impossible to guess that from such humble beginnings, such a worldwide phenomenon would have emerged. As the Internet was growing in the research environment, experiments were in progress in the private sector to create access for consumers to products over two-way television-like systems, called videotex.

From Videotex to the Internet

> . . . an interactive service which, through appropriate access by standardized procedures allows users of Videotex terminals to communicate with databases via telecommunication networks.[2]

What if a two-way communications network linked the homes of the nation via regional computer centers to a large number of businesses and services? From the comfort of home a vast array of transactions could be carried out, using a personal computer or a specially equipped television monitor with keyboard. This was the vision of the early 1980s as the first steps were taken towards interactive television. The following services were envisioned, some of which are currently commonplace:

- *Information retrieval.* Probably the most basic service, it includes electronic newspapers and specialized databases and directories, including stock market, entertainment, and sports, community, and health services information.
- *Commercial transactions.* Making reservations for entertainment, sporting events, and travel, paying bills and teleshopping.
- *Messaging.* A "switchboard" to store and forward messages from one user to another, electronic mail, electronic bulletin board (one-to-many communication), computer conferencing.
- *Computing.* Access to games and financial analysis programs, as well as more sophisticated software.

- *Telemonitoring.* Provision of home security by the remote sensing of fire or intruders with alarms triggered at security agencies; the control of systems within the home for energy management.
- *Working at home.* Accelerating current trends, stockbrokers, information systems professionals, designers, architects, real estate agents, travel agents, secretaries, editors, and so forth can do some or all of their work at home.
- *Services for the disabled.* Disabled people can be monitored at home and communication with them facilitated by the use of Bliss symbols, Braille printers, and voice synthesizers.
- *Education at home.* Extension of current television education courses can be carried out as part of the regular curricula and continuing education.

What is interesting about this list is how similar it is to current advertisements for the Internet. Thus, although the vision was realistic, the technology at the time was somewhat deficient; but there was a more serious problem. The real obstacles seemed to be twofold: sufficiently large numbers of interested information providers, and most importantly, a public convinced that videotex was something worth paying for. In fact there seemed to be something of a chicken-and-egg dilemma: many people were not interested in the few videotex services available, because they did not provide a sufficiently broad range of useful or interesting services; potential information providers were not interested because the number of current users was too small. A few commercial systems were actually marketed in the US although many previous experiments had failed. Of all countries in the world, France has had the most success although major investments have taken place in England, Germany, Canada, and Japan.

The Failure of Videotex

Three forms of information services marketed in the 1980s may be distinguished, as follows:

Information retrieval via online databases. Large databases storing many different kinds of information could be accessed on personal computers via telephone lines by paying a fee for services. Examples were newspaper indexes, financial information, and computer hardware and software specifications. The user must access a database, formulate a query, and interrogate the database.

Teletext. This system provided a continuous stream of information that was available over television channels. The information could be repeatedly broadcast in the "blanking interval" between frames on a television channel or the normal channel itself could be used. Using a special keypad, the viewer types a number to designate a teletext frame (i.e., a screen image) and the decoder freezes it for viewing. The amount of information available and the time needed to cycle through it determine how long the user must wait until the frames of interest appear.

Videotex. (The t is usually dropped at the end of this word, probably to lend it a high-tech gloss.) This term is used for a two-way information system. Typically, telephone lines are used to connect the central computer of the system to each individual user. The home user, by means of a special keypad or a home computer with appropriate software, requests information after viewing a menu of possibilities. The computer retrieves information from its own databases (or from others to which it has access) and transmits it. This information consists of text as well as graphics and can appear in color. Two national systems and US experiences will briefly be reviewed as a background to today's systems and those on the horizon.

Canada: Telidon

Canada's version of videotex was announced in 1978 after almost ten years of development. Telidon operated with menus and direct page numbers in the usual manner, but was more advanced than European systems in the quality of its graphics. The European systems— Oracle, Prestel, and Antiope, sometimes called first generation videotex—use a method of pictorial representation called alphamosaic. Pictures are built up from a pattern of blocks in which both color and intensity can be controlled. The resolution leaves much to be desired, as straight diagonal lines look like staircases.

Telidon is a more advanced, second generation system, employing a graphics method called alphageometric. A system of points, line, arcs, and polygons are used to produce a much more sophisticated image. Underlying the picture transmission is a communication protocol, the Picture Description Instructions (PDIs). For example, using PDIs, a line is described by its endpoints. A microprocessor in the Telidon terminal decodes the description of a picture, which has been transmitted in terms of PDIs, and then displays it on the screen. The description is independent of the display characteristics so that on a high resolution monitor, finer increments can be used and greater fidelity achieved. Telidon is well-suited to the representation of detailed graphics such as architectural plans, circuit diagrams, and weather maps, and cursive alphabets such as Arabic and Chinese.

Telidon was developed under the leadership of the Department of Communication and unlike the situation in the US considerable government financial support was made available. As in Britain, forecasts of market growth were wildly over-optimistic, with 3 to 4.3 million units predicted for 1990. By the end of 1981, 2,000 Telidon terminals were in use in several experimental projects such as an information system for farmers containing farm management information, market reports, weather reports, financial news, and crop data. US trials were undertaken, as well as one in Venezuela. The North American Presentation-level Protocol Standards incorporated a substantial portion of the Telidon specifications that seemed to indicate an important role for Telidon. By 1985, when its direct financial support ended, the Canadian government had spent $50 million (and the private sector $200 million) for research, development, and marketing.

France: Télétel

This system is more commonly known by the name Minitel, which is actually the name of the videotex terminal. In the late 1970s, a number of French laboratories were involved in the design of the representation of visual images for videotex (the Antiope standards), of the decentralized architecture of the computer system and databases, and of the videotex terminal. The French Telecommunications administration made a very important decision at this time to adopt a program to convert the telephone directory to an electronic form (the Electronic Directory) by distributing a free-of-charge terminal to all phone subscribers. Thus a potential market of up to 30 million terminals was possible in the 1990s and by the end of 1988, there were 3.6 million in use after only 12,000 had been installed by the end of 1982.[3] This captive market of users encouraged information providers to participate. The growth in the number of services was also quite rapid from 146 at the end of 1981, to some 9000 in 1987. The major uses, in terms of the number of hours connected to Minitel in 1987 was as follows (with percentage of total use in parentheses):[4] professional applications, like stock market reports (23%); messaging, chatting (22%); electronic telephone directory (18%); games (14%); practical services, like train reservations, home shopping (10%); banking, finance (9%); general information, like weather reports (4%).

One of the more popular services is known as Kiosque, a bulletin board, which provides "the user with anonymity as they [sic] can enter into date relationships with strangers."[5] Apparently such interactions have frequently been sexual in nature bringing considerable notoriety to Minitel as well as the government's attention, in the form of an increased sales tax. What does not seem to be happening is the use of the system as an electronic newspaper, that is, as a source of general and broad-based information. It is clear that users want customized services, appealing to special interests. France's Telecom expected to give away about 8 million terminals reaching about 25 million subscribers and hoped to pay off its investment by 1993. Surely the key step in this enormous venture has been the decision to give away the terminals to create a mass market for services. No other country has taken this step, or is likely to do so. Other reasons for the success of France's Minitel are as follows: a specially-designed portable video monitor without the inconveniences of ordinary television sets; the immediate availability of a service, the Electronic Book, lacking in other videotex programs; preliminary social experiments undertaken to test the service including the communication hardware and the information sources; and, the charging mechanism designed to encourage use.

The United States

During much of the early development of videotex, the United States was content to wait and watch as developments unfolded in Britain, Germany, Japan, France, and Canada. Meanwhile, commercial online information retrieval systems were being developed by such companies as Mead Data Central, Dow-Jones News/Retrieval, and Lockheed's Dialog Information Service, the world's largest electronic information retrieval company (sold to Knight-Ridder for some $353 million in 1988). With the appearance of the foreign videotex systems, a number of US companies began their own field trials. The earliest interactive system, QUBE, was implemented over cable by Warner Amex in 1977 in Columbus, Ohio. (See Chapter 7 for more detail.) Some 32,000 potential QUBE subscribers could have participated in a meeting of the town planning commission in 1978. No more than 2,500 actually tuned in and cast nonbinding votes. Although our concern here is not interactive participatory democracy, this application of two-way systems obviously has significant impact in the future. In January 1984, Warner Amex ended the interactive QUBE experiment because of its inability to attract larger audiences.

One of the most important videotex ventures was the Viewtron system launched in October 1983 by Knight-Ridder Newspapers. Their long-term aim was to sign up 150,000 subscribers in the Miami-Fort Lauderdale area. Prelaunch expenditures were $26 million. Customers were required to purchase a special terminal, manufactured by AT&T, for $600 (later to rise to $900), and pay a monthly fee of $12 along with an estimated telephone bill of $14 per month. The service sold no more than 1000 terminals, and even the introduction of a leasing arrangement did not help much, nor did the opening up of the system to personal computers, equipped with specialized software. The resolution of the monitor was quite poor compared to ordinary television, the color choices were limited, figures appeared to be constructed out of Lego blocks, and transmission rates were slow. Viewtron was terminated in 1986 after total expenditures of about $50 million. Other experiments also failed. Thus a *Business Week* article in January 1985 seemed to say it all: "For Videotex, The Big Time Is Still a Long Way Off."[6] Potential customers have not been willing to buy expensive terminals—or pay hefty monthly fees to lease them—because they did not see any services they particularly needed that they could not find elsewhere for less. And service providers with no ready audience have been slow to develop new offerings.

The Successful Private Networks?

Despite all the failures, much was expected, although reservations were voiced, when IBM and Sears, Roebuck teamed up in 1984 in a joint venture called Trintex. For example, in September 1987, Fortune asked, "Are IBM and Sears Crazy? Or Canny?"[7] By that time they had invested about $250 million in what came to be called Prodigy. Initial service began in the summer of 1988 in San Francisco, Atlanta, and Hartford and has since spread across the country. Prodigy began with news from USA Today and the Associated Press, business news and stock market quotes from Dow Jones, the ability to order merchandise from Neiman Marcus, J. C. Penney, and Levi Strauss, and to check airline schedules and make reservations. Near the end of 1990, Prodigy had 690,000 subscribers making it the most successful videotex system in the world, except for France's Minitel, but not for long. Users paid a fixed monthly fee of $12.95, with no additional time charges, and they also required a program to run on IBM-compatible computers. To encourage use, IBM included a 90-day subscription with every PS/1, its computer designed for the home market. The number of services expanded substantially:[8]

- *Travel*—Airlines and hotel reservations via EASY SABRE
- *Financial services*—Stock quotes, discount brokerage, and banking
- *Shopping*—Items from Sears, J. C. Penney, Spiegel, and others.[9]
- *Information*—Road & Traffic, Consumer Reports, PetCare Guide
- *Education*—Weekly Reader, Academic American Encyclopedia
- *Classified ads*—Listings from small businesses and individuals

Prodigy banked on a number of innovations to succeed where others failed. It planned on millions of subscribers, which means that instead of central mainframe computers to handle requests over long distance lines, the computing power will be distributed among minicomputers located in the cities being served as well as the personal computers of the subscribers themselves. Prodigy signed agreements with local telephone companies to manage the local minicomputer. Most information is handled by the local minicomputer that communicates with the mainframe in White Plains, NY, only when it needs information it does not already have. The program running on the user's home computer is able to interpret the messages from the minicomputer and display them appropriately. For example the request to display a weather map results in an overlay being sent to the user's computer and superimposed on a map supplied with the software.[10] Because of the large numbers of home computers currently in use, a videotex system based on their availability has a much better chance of succeeding than the earlier systems, which required a special-purpose terminal. Finally, both IBM and Sears, Roebuck have deep pockets (with expenditures as of 1990 exceeding $600 million) and a strong belief that Prodigy is the wave of the future for marketing and many other services. Others had this belief as well and acted upon it.

Currently, Prodigy, under new management, is running a poor third behind America Online (AOL) and CompuServe, the main competitors in the consumer online information services market. On May 12, 1996, IBM and Sears, Roebuck sold Prodigy for about $200 million, including real estate and the communications network, "a fraction of the estimated $1.2 billion that the International Business Machines Corporation and Sears, Roebuck had invested in prodigy over more than a decade."[11] It is difficult to determine with any accuracy the number of subscribers to the various systems, but Table 12.1 presents various estimates.

America OnLine is the clear leader and the margin is probably larger than that shown in Table 12.1. CompuServe, 80% of which is owned by H&R Block, has been struggling and may also be up for sale shortly, given that it has been losing subscribers and money, some $29.6 million for the quarter ending July 31, 1996.[12]

TABLE 12.1

ESTIMATES OF THE NUMBER OF WORLDWIDE SUBSCRIBERS TO THE MAJOR ON-LINE INFORMATION SERVICE PROVIDERS.

Online Service Providers	1995 Computerworld	1st Quarter 1996 New York Times	2nd Quarter 1996 Companies
America OnLine	4.5 Million	5.4 Million	6.2 Million
CompuServe	4.0 Million	3.2 Million*	5.2 Million
Prodigy	1.4 Million	1.0 Million	2.0 Million plus +

Sources: Mitch Wagner. "On-line Services Buzz with Deals and Debuts," Computerworld, March 25, 1996, p. 73.

Steve Lohr. "Prodigy Gets New Owners and Strategy," The New York Times, May 13, 1996, pp. C 1, C 3.

*Zachary Schiller and Paul M. Eng. "Plenty of Pain. Any Gain?" Business Week, June 17, 1996, pp. 127, 129. (Taken from company reports)

America OnLine Press Release, July 19, 1996. Accessed from the Web page with URL: <http://www.aol.com/about/press/1996/960719.txt on September 4, 1996.

CompuServe Press Release, August 20, 1996. Accessed from the Web page with URL: <http://www.compuserve.com/corp/pressbox/first.htm on September 4, 1996.

+ Prodigy Press Release, April 1, 1996. (First Quarter) Accessed from the Web page with URL: <http://www.prodigy.com/about/press/press3.html> on September 4, 1996.

The Internet and the World Wide Web

It was noted in Chapter 3 that as of January 1, 1997, there were over 16.1 million Internet hosts, but it is not clear that this number is meaningful. As the authors of the survey note, the definition of host is ambiguous: "A host used to be a single machine on the net. However, the definitions of a host has changed in recent years due to virtual hosting, where a single machine acts like multiple systems (and has multiple domain names and IP addresses). Ideally, a virtual host will act and look exactly like a regular host, so we count them equally."[13] The reason for the concern is that there is some correlation between the number of hosts and the number of users but it is not well defined. The Internet appears to be doubling in size every year or so. The final comment should be appreciated when reading about how many users there are. "In summary, it is not possible to determine the exact size of the Internet, where hosts are located, or how many users there are."[14] Thus, while commercial information service providers are having problems, the Internet is thriving, although it may be facing some technical limitations as the number of users grows and the volume of traffic increases because of the increased number of sound and image files. It is not surprising that one area of spectacular growth is in Web sites (hosts whose domain name is prefixed by www). In July 1993, the number of Web sites was minuscule but by July 1996, it was about 215,000.[15]

Although the terms are over-used, the wired world or *cyberspace* is becoming a reality to many, and the signs are clear. The number of Internet users in the US and Canada, defined as using the Internet at least once in the past year, was estimated by Nielsen/Commercenet in late 1995 as 23 million, probably too high compared to other surveys.[16] Even higher was the result produced by Adnet, which did a survey of surveys, and came up with a worldwide number of 50 million, of which 35 million were in the US as of mid-1996. (The term user was not defined, however.)[17] What is evident is that increasing numbers of businesses, schools, libraries, community centers, and homes are connected to the Internet by local Internet Service Providers (ISPs), long-distance telephone companies (AT&T), local telephone companies, online information service providers (America OnLine), and others.

Further evidence that the movement towards an Information Society is well under way is the following: capital spending for computers and communications equipment in 1992 was more than $130 billion (up from less than $50 billion in 1982), and spending for industrial equipment, machinery for services, mining, agriculture, etc. has hovered at about $100 billion for the same period.[18] Modem sales increased from about 500,000 in 1982 to almost 3.5 million in 1992, worldwide; and fiber-optic cable shipments increased from about 200,000 kilometers in 1983, in North America, to about 5.1 million kilometers in 1992. The number of ATM transactions per month in the US has gone from about 200 million in 1983 to about 650 million in 1993, and finally, the sum of the number of embedded controller chips in a typical home, office, and automobile has gone from six in 1980 to 101 in 1990, and is estimated to exceed 300 in 2000.[19] These numbers and many more are all indications of an inexorable trend, namely, the increasing dependency on information, especially in North America, as the foundation of the economy; furthermore, networks such as the Internet and whatever it evolves into will be the circulatory system.

In a survey of the Internet, *The Economist* referred to it as "The Accidental Superhighway," and contrasted its success with the failures of the giant telecommunications and cable companies to achieve similar results. "The Internet's builders laid no cables and dug no trenches; they simply leased existing telephone lines. When the Internet linked up with public and commercial networks in the mid-1980s, its growth accelerated."[20] It is *The Economist's* view that the wonders of the Internet occurred because it was "left to its own devices and filled unmet needs," not because large corporations thought that money could be made from certain technological advances or because governments made plans for systems that would benefit the general public. With the dawn of the World Wide Web, the stakes were raised substantially as the power of the Internet started to become clear. Again, The Economist's description is well worth considering:[21]

> Suddenly the light dawned. The Internet was not just a way to send e-mail and download the occasional file. It could be a place to visit, full of people and ideas: "cyberspace". It was a new medium, based on broadcasting and publishing but with another dimension added: interactivity. Internet veterans had known this for years; they could see the potential behind the screens of plain text and baffling computer commands. But thanks to the friendly, multimedia side of the Net, called the World Wide Web, a much broader audience started to catch on to it.

Communicating: Electronic Mail and Newsgroups

Two major functions spurred the early growth of the Internet: electronic mail and newsgroups. Electronic mail is the first technological step in connecting people asynchronously, independently of time. The Internet's reliability in completing transmissions successfully even though parts of the system were nonfunctioning encouraged the growth and confidence in this new technology. Messages, large or small, were separated into packets and routed by an incremental process and then reassembled at the destination. It worked so well that its use increased rapidly and other applications soon followed.

What seemed to trigger the metaphor and indeed the reality of cyberspace was the creation of discussion groups called newsgroups or bulletin boards that permitted the participation of anyone with an Internet account anywhere in the world. Whereas electronic mail is typically a one-to-one or a one-to-a-few process, newsgroups involve one-to-many; that is, one person posting a message that is accessible to anyone who subscribes to the newsgroup. The idea of a newsgroup arose from the use of small discussion groups in research environments, created for the purpose of sharing technical information. The topics then moved into less technically-oriented directions—political, social, religious, cultural, sexual, etc. In the process, a fiercely independent, vociferous, anarchic, and worldwide group of aficionados developed, for whom the Internet became a new way of life. This attitude has become endemic on the Internet, creating a clientele that is committed to defending a set of values it believes has been lost in the real world, namely independence, free speech, privacy, irreverence, and audacity.

Electronic Mail: New Ways of Keeping in Touch

One of the most important aspects of the office of the future described in Chapter 4 was electronic mail, the computer facility by which messages could be distributed simultaneously within an organization and to geographically remote points. In-house networks have been interconnected via telephone lines and satellite communication systems spanning countries and continents. The telephone conference call is a familiar event, but by using computers, conferences can be established over networks that operate independently of time and space. Another important use of networks is the electronic bulletin board, a system by which individuals can post messages, announcements, and opinions to make them available simultaneously to many other participants. Bulletin boards can be operated from homes and serve a small community of local users, or they can be nationwide and serve thousands. Over the past decade networks have spread across most countries, instantaneously linking interested people, eager to share information. During the terrible events in 1989 in Tiananmen Square, Beijing, electronic mail was used to keep people in the West informed.

For computer-generated documents, electronic mail has become an efficient means for distributing information. Within organizations, meetings can be announced by broadcasting time, place, and agenda to the relevant parties. Individuals can use electronic mail to avoid telephone tag; that is, a message is sent over a hardwired line, or by use of a modem over a telephone to a network and will be available whenever the receiving party signs on and checks the incoming mail. The number of networks linking the US and indeed the world is large and growing. There are gateways between many of these networks so that users can send messages to almost anyone on some network. Almost every company, large and small, has an in-house electronic mail system so that employees can easily exchange information and so that management can reach employees quickly and efficiently. Large, worldwide companies employ intercontinental networks to facilitate interaction among employees who are separated by long distances. The earliest users of electronic mail were universities and research institutions, who had developed the necessary software. It is now inconceivable to imagine a research environment or any business, large or small, for that matter, without electronic mail. Preliminary versions of papers, early research results, and tentative proposals are circulated among researchers for immediate comment and analysis.

A major report from Rand discussed the social implications of a universal system of e-mail. The report defines an electronic mail system as follows:[22]

1. Permits the asynchronous electronic interchange of information between persons, groups of persons, and functional units of an organization; and
2. Provides mechanisms supporting the creation, distribution, consumption, processing, and storage of this information . . .

By universal access, the authors assume that it is available "at modest individual effort and expense to (almost) everyone in the United States in a form that does not require highly specialized skills or, accessible in a manner analogous to the level, cost, and ease of use of telephone service or the US Postal Service."[23] This notion of a ubiquitous service has some very interesting consequences as the report makes clear. Efficiency is an important goal and one of the reasons for adopting universal e-mail is to replace the archaic postal service, which is so much slower than e-mail. But what is more interesting than the efficiency argument is the transforming argument: ". . . the hypothesis is made that electronic mail makes possible more egalitarian, deliberative, and reflective dialogs among individuals and groups . . . It might therefore lead to new social and political linkages within US society,

reduce the feelings of alienation that many individuals in the United States feel and give
them anew sense of 'community,' revitalize the involvement of the common citizen in the
political process, etc., and in general strengthen the cohesion of US society."[24]

An interesting coding system has arisen among users of electronic mail to replace the
missing vocal, facial, and body signals that usually accompany face-to-face conversations.
These symbols are scattered throughout the message to flesh-out the bare words appearing on the monitor. The following are a few of the more commonly used ones; they are
more easily appreciated if the head is tilted to the left:[25]

: -)	smile	; -)	wink	: - 0	bored	: - !	foot in the mouth
: -D	laughter	: - (	frown	: - x	angry		
: - /	skeptical	: - e	disappointed	: - 7	wry		

and some weird and obtuse ones:

: - F	buck-toothed vampire with one tooth missing		*: o)	clown
+-: -)	holds religious office	@= pro-nuclear	@: -)	wears a turban
: @)	Babe the pig	@@@@@@: -)		Marge Simpson

In addition to these symbols, documents are also filled with acronyms (to reduce the typing burden) such as the following: IMHO (In My Humble/Honest Opinion), BTW (By The
Way), TIA (Thanks In Anticipation), and ROTFL (Rolling On The Floor Laughing).

Another communication medium that has become popular is Fax, so popular that it has
challenged e-mail as a way of quickly distributing material, especially original hard copies,
over long distances. Fax is not really a new technology but it is an example of how the microprocessor has transformed and indeed created a vital new industry. Every office has a
Fax machine, as do many individuals, and an enormous amount of information is now
Faxed worldwide. Fax boards can be inserted into personal computers so that computer-
generated documents are immediately available for transmission and reception. The volume of information transmitted over the new electronic media continues to expand and
technological innovations contribute to more ways to transmit information, a direct reflection of the ever-increasing importance of information to advanced societies.

Newsgroups: Bulletin Boards

Near laundromats, supermarkets, and community centers, people post notices on public
bulletin boards advertising coming attractions, wanting to buy and sell furniture, rent
apartments, sell airline tickets, and meet new friends. Bulletin boards are a common feature of most communities, serving to reinforce community ties and indicative of community vitality. In 1977, the first electronic bulletin board in the US, the Community Memory Project, was founded in Berkeley, California. Terminals were placed in retail stores and
community centers in 1984 and people were encouraged "to speak [their] mind, check the
city council's agenda, find toxic hot spots in the neighborhood and locate used cars and
housing."[26] Other bulletin boards appeared all over the country organized by community
groups, clubs, and individuals. From the comfort of home a person could connect with

like-minded individuals to sell, buy, inform, advertise, commiserate, rejoice, and complain. Furthermore, distance is no obstacle as electronic bulletin boards are nationwide, and even worldwide.

Legal issues quickly arose as to the responsibility of the bulletin board operator, or systems operator (the *sysop*), with respect to the behavior of subscribers. If somebody posted an identification code and password for a proprietary computer system, is the sysop at fault? The law is not entirely clear but "people have been prosecuted for using the bulletin boards to post stolen credit card numbers, pirated software or, in one recent case, information traded among members of a pedophile ring."[27] These bulletin boards usually served local communities and had to respond to local or community values. When we turn to the newsgroups carried over USENET, different issues arise. As described previously, newsgroups began as discussion groups for technical issues. The move toward other topics created some dissension among the managers of the early Internet, but inevitably the range of topics covered, the organizational structure of USENET, and the number of newsgroups, grew rapidly and fostered an enormous number of regular users. It is almost impossible to determine how many generally accessible newsgroups exist, discounting the untold numbers of local ones, but well over 20,000 is the usual estimate. One of the problems is that newsgroups are created and disappear on a regular basis.

It is necessary to participate in a variety of newsgroups, or at least observe some of the interaction (as a *lurker*; a pejorative tag, used because your presence is known only by posting messages). The number of newsgroups reflects the incredibly diverse interests of contemporary society. It is necessary only to search, and in all likelihood an appropriate newsgroup for the moment will be found or created. Typically, discussions are interwoven with individual threads representing separate themes. Some threads go on for weeks as arguments and counter-arguments are posted. Then new threads appear and old ones finally die; the vitality of a newsgroup ebbs and flows as new members join and old ones move on. These newsgroups, especially the binary ones (or binaries), attracted the attention of Congress and its regulating zeal. A binary newsgroup is one that primarily carries postings in a coded form, and when decoded, these postings are frequently of a sexual nature, and occasionally are even obscene. However, in terms of the volume of information carried over the USENET, itself a small part of the total Internet traffic, probably very little actually violates criminal law. Nevertheless, the Internet is frequently characterized by the media as a cesspool, as a threat to common decency, and as having minimal useful content.

Some Problems

Flaming

Not all the postings to newsgroups are nice. Not all people are nice. The Internet can be an unfriendly place, a place for the thick-skinned or the thick-headed. If you are new to the Net (a *newbie*), any blunders you make will not be treated lightly by some and in fact asking for help or apologizing for mistakes will only inflame those who view their participation on the Internet as a license to be obnoxious, insulting, and downright crazy. The act of posting rude and outrageous messages directed at individuals or groups or whole countries for that matter, is known as *flaming*. Since quantifying flaming is not precise it is impossible to determine how common it is. Suffice it to say, that for the novice the tone of discourse is much higher pitched than in other media, although talk radio is no bed of roses for the timid. It is almost as if so much noise is on the Internet that to be heard, it is necessary to shout and shout and shout.

Jack Kapica, the writer of a weekly newspaper column on cyberspace, explored the issue of flaming and offered a number of interesting observations:[28]

- Cyberspace blurs notions of public and private.
- The Net does not transmit subtle emotions, hence the need for "emoticons"—smileys—to ensure those whose prose is weak that their comments are taken in the intended manner.
- Our culture abhors extreme emotional displays; flamers compose a message in which all the fury lies in the prose, and none in the physical presence.
- The very ephemerality of cyberspace is what starts so many flame wars.
- If they are in any way objectionable, people forget the public nature of these postings and take them personally.

In a paper written in 1985, the authors suggested a number of guidelines to deal with the problem of heightened emotions on the Internet as part of a program for electronic mail etiquette (later called netiquette when extended to the full range of Internet activities). Among these are the following helpful suggestions:[29]

- Sometimes just the annotation "Flame! Flame!" alerts the reader to the fact that the writer knows he or she is being emotional. The intent is that the reader should take that into account and not assume this is a careful reasoned statement . . .
- Resist the temptation to fire off a response. Go ahead and write the response, but file it away instead, and wait 24 hours. Reconsider the response later, in the light of a new day . . .
- Use alternative media to break the cycle of message-and-response. A telephone call or personal conversation can do wonders, when body language, eye contact, and all the other cues we've developed can take effect.

Although these are all reasonable and well-intentioned, therein lies the problem; those who would most benefit from adherence to them are least likely either to pay attention or to follow the advice.

Spamming

An Internet user has the freedom to send a message to any one of the more than 20,000 newsgroups in existence. Given that the message may be of interest to more than one newsgroup it can be cross-posted to as many newsgroups as appropriate by including the names of the newsgroups in the destination information. Although five, ten, or even twenty newsgroups may be appropriate, what about 2,000 or 5,000 newsgroups? Clearly enormous amounts of memory in hundreds of thousands of computers will be used to store all these messages, resulting in a possible degradation of service and inconvenience to many. Who would want to send the same message to thousands of newsgroups (or on occasion, the same message to the same newsgroup, many times)?

The first major incident occurred in January 1994, when "Clarence Thomas IV of Andrews University posted a message warning of Jesus' immanent return to all the newsgroups Andrews University receives—over six thousand."[30] The response of the USENET community was one of outrage as it had just experienced the full force of a major spam. Since then, there have been many occasions of spamming. The origin of this term is not clear but there are at least two possible sources: the word spam was used in a Monty Python skit in which it was repeated endlessly, and "the term may also have come from someone's low opinion of the food product with the same name, which is generally perceived as a generic content-free waste of resources."[31] If the USENET community values anything beyond a few basic freedoms, it is bandwidth because without available bandwidth, communication degrades and the *raison d'etre* of the Internet disappears.

Note that cross-posting a message is not wasteful of space because only a single copy exists at a host machine and newsreading software will not display the same message more than once to a given user. Spamming, however, can fill up hosts with multiple copies, especially if more than one incident occurs. It is seen as the worst violation of the understood principles governing acceptable Internet behavior. Probably no incident received as much publicity within the Internet community and among the public at large as the infamous Canter and Siegel spam on April 12, 1994. Lawrence A. Canter and Martha S. Siegel are lawyers, who sent out a message to more than 6,000 newsgroups: "Green Card Lottery 1994 May be the Last One!! Sign up now!!"[32] So many angry messages were sent to their Internet Service Provider that service was disrupted and their account was cancelled. Canter and Siegel wrote a book about their experience and advised others to ignore any inhibitions about ignoring netiquette if they were interested in making money. This event heightened the ongoing dichotomy on the Internet between the growing influence of the world of commerce and the purist attitude of the veteran user community.

VIRTUAL COMMUNITIES

I will close down the remailer for the time being because the legal issues governing the whole Internet in Finland are yet undefined. The legal protection of the users needs to be clarified. At the moment the privacy of Internet messages is judicially unclear. (Johan Helsingius, operator of anon.penet.fi, anonymous e-mail server)[33]

Mention has been made of the power of the Internet (or cyberspace, or the connected world) to foster the creation of relationships varying from intense one-on-one encounters to informal groups of people interested in gardening. Aside from the commercial applications currently being promoted heavily, what makes the Internet so exciting for so many people around the world is the possibility of establishing contact, exchanging views, presenting oneself in different ways to different people, recreating a persona on demand, or in a less glamorous mode, combining with others to form political, social, cultural, or sexual pressure groups. Underlying many of these relationships is the ability to assume whatever identity one wishes in order to hide one's true identity, namely, to maintain anonymity. If no one knows who you are you can be anything you wish. Obvious criticisms can be directed against those who employ anonymity. They must have something to hide, they are doing or saying things that they are ashamed of, or they want to deceive others maliciously or playfully. On the other hand, reasons are proposed for the use of anonymous postings: political suppression, whistle-blowing, recovering from abuse, or fear for their safety.

Therefore, it is not surprising that the Internet has provided means for individuals to maintain their anonymity, nor that some would feel that the use of these means permitted harassment, racism, and traffic in child pornography. The use of anonymous remailers has become a growth industry and many thousands of Internet regulars are clients. Anonymity supports the growth of many kinds of virtual communities that are described later in this chapter. The lobbying power of political, environmental, and social groups has become commonplace on the Internet. Whether protesting against the US government's attempts to implement the Clipper Chip technology or against the indecency provisions of the Telecommunications Act of 1996, a large core of Internet supporters can be counted on to stand up and have their messages counted. Supporters of environmental causes can be rallied instantaneously to confront threats directed against any forest or lake or river anywhere in the world. Political prisoners can have their cases placed on the world stage, requiring governments to answer for their actions rather than their preferred choice of hidden business as usual.

Anonymity

> Online, nobody knows if you're a dog. (Anonymous)

The purpose here is not to engage in a philosophical or psychological exploration into the nature of anonymity but rather how it is maintained on the Internet, to what degree, and most importantly to what end.

Anonymous Remailers

In the real world, it is very difficult to conceal your identity because proof is demanded for most commercial, educational, legal, and political transactions. To obtain a computer account, typically, you must provide proof of identity, and in using the account to send e-mail, your name is attached to the message or can be recovered relatively easily. Because of the perceived need to protect your identity on the Internet for a number of justified reasons (at least in the minds of some), the void was filled by the creation of anonymous remailers. An anonymous remailer is a computer service that privatizes your e-mail. A remailer allows you to send electronic mail to a USENET newsgroup or to a person without the recipient knowing your name or your e-mail address.[34] In response to the question "How does a remailer work?" the Anonymous Remailer FAQ responds by describing the operation of the most famous of all anonymous (or more precisely psuedo-anonymous) remailers, anon.penet.fi, maintained by Johan Helsingius in Finland:[35]

> His "an@anon.penet.fi" addresses are common in controversial news groups. Suppose you read a post from a battered woman <an123@anon.penet.fi> crying out for help. You can write her at <an123@anon.penet.fi>. Helsingius' computer will STRIP AWAY your real name and address (the header at the top of our e-mail), replace this data with a dummy address, and forward your message to the battered woman. Helsingius' computer will notify you of your new anonymous address; e.g., <an345@anon.penet.fi>. You can use

Helsingius' free service to forward letters to anyone, even to persons who do not use his service. His computer sends each user detailed instructions about his system.

More technically, this server is a psuedo-anonymous because although no one on the Internet knows the identity of an345@anon.penet.fi, Johan Helsingius does. However, there are anonymous remailers; one example is a Cypherpunk remailer:[36]

> If you want to mail messages without even an anonymized return address on it, then you should use a cypherpunk remailer. You can encrypt the messages sent to the remailer, and the remailer will decrypt them and send them on to the recipient, whose address is hidden inside the encrypted message. This means that someone who monitors your outgoing mail can't see who you are sending anonymous mail to. For even more security, you can also chain remailers, in other words use more than one remailer to send your message. Now not even the remailers you use know who is sending mail to who. Some remailers even allow you to post to USENET.

As of August 1996, Helsingius' anonymous server had more that 500,000 clients and was by far the most popular such server on the Internet. At the end of August, he shut down his system and therein lies an instructive tale.

anon.penet.fi and alt.religion.scientology

Here is a short version of this very complicated and unclear story. The Church of Scientology was engaged in a long term, vituperative debate about the operations of the church in the newsgroup alt.religion.scientology. Apparently, one or more ex-members downloaded secret documents from Church computers (no doubt a criminal act) and posted them on alt.scientology anonymously via anon.penet.fi. The Church protested that stolen and copyrighted material was being used without their permission. In addition, anti-Scientology messages began being cancelled mysteriously. Many newsreaders have cancellation software that can be used by posters who wish to cancel a message recently sent, but cancelling someone else's message is a serious violation of net etiquette and even of US law. A variety of dirty tricks followed, culminated by police raids at the homes of two prominent anti-Scientology activists, but the event of interest was a raid in Helsinki, Finland at Helsingius' office, in February 1995. Apparently, the Finnish police were willing to settle for the name of the anonymous poster to alt.religion.scientology or else they would confiscate the entire system. Helsingius agreed and subsequently posted a description of the events and offered to delete the name of any of his clients if asked to do so. Thus, an anonymous remailer had been breached and interestingly enough only a handful of people requested that their names be removed.

The Closing of anon.penet.fi

On Friday August 30, 1996 the following message was made available on the Internet:[37]

> Hello all,
>
> I just got off the phone with Johan Helsingius who runs the anon.penet.fi anonymous e-mail service.

1. He has decided to close the service.
2. This is not related to the article in The Observer. It is, in fact, due to a decision of a lower Finnish court on petition from the Church of Scientology. Penet went to court last week and made the decision today. The implication of the decision (rather than Penet's to shut the server) is that e-mail over the Internet is not protect by the usual Finnish privacy laws.
3. The server is currently down while Julf re-writes the software. Once it runs again, it will be phased out for private use, but groups such as the Samaritans and human rights agencies should be able to use it.
4. They are appealing against the decision.
5. Julf expects that revisions in Finnish law to provide a safe legal status for anonymous remailers will be in place at the earliest in Spring next year.
6. Once again: this is unrelated to The Observer's scandalous reporting.

Your faithful furry friend,

Azeem

An important institution was closing down, the victim of threats and lack of legal safeguards. The reference to "the article in The Observer" should be clarified. The Sunday, August 25, 1996 issue of the British newspaper, The Observer, had the following headline: "The peddlers of child abuse: We know who they are. Yet no one is stopping them."[38] The two people named and pictured are Clive Feather, a director of the Internet Service Provider, Demon Internet, and Johan Helsingius, described as follows: "Johan Helsingius is the man US police experts charge with being at the hub of 90 per cent of the child pornography on the Internet. Perverts can log on to and participate in 'live' and 'interactive' filmed sessions that involve the rape of infants."[39] This is the kind of outrageous, unsubstantiated charge that has created the image of the Internet as rife with pornography, child and otherwise. In a statement released by Helsingius, the following is included:[40]

> Police sergeant Kaj Malmberg from the Helsinki Police Crime Squad is specialized in investigating computer crimes. He confirms that already a year ago Johan Helsingius restricted the operations of his remailer so that it cannot transmit pictures.
>
> "The true amount of child pornography in Internet is difficult to assess, but one thing is clear: "We have not found any cases where child porn pictures were transmitted from Finland", Kaj Malmberg says.

Final Comments on Anonymity

The question remains: Is anonymity on the Internet a necessary evil or is there a basic right to be anonymous? As might be expected, there is considerable disagreement. The newsgroup alt.sexual.abuse.recovery (asar) provides a forum for people who have been sexually abused to share their experiences, including the events themselves and subsequent therapy and memories. Usually postings to this newsgroup contain warnings (SPOILER!!!) of unpleasant recountings to follow. Should people who find comfort in both telling their stories and hearing from others be required to use their real name or not post at all? How could such a community exist or provide support in the absence of anonymity? An organization in England, called the Samaritans, provides help to people in need and who ask for help by posting messages. Some of these are anonymous and some of the Samaritans offering help are anonymous. How else could it operate?

One of the major concerns about anonymity is its use in criminal activities. Fraudulent activities could become commonplace on the Internet in commercial transactions if money could be moved anonymously. What about raising money for political donations if donors of large sums can remain anonymous? How will the political process be affected? Although it was argued that many interactions on the Internet depend on anonymous participants, others would argue that communities built on deceit have little value and are in no way comparable to real world communities. Again in the real world, anonymous letters to newspapers and magazines are rarely printed; however, a letter writer may request that his or her name be withheld if the letter is published. Thus, responsibility is assured and public anonymity is guaranteed. Perhaps an equivalent model can be designed for the Internet.

Gender and Identity

This is one way of looking at the identity issue on the Internet or in cyberspace: "We are moving from modernist calculation toward post modernist simulation, where the self is a multiple, distributed system."[41] In the past few years, a number of writers and scholars from such diverse disciplines as architecture, literature, psychology, computer science, philosophy, sociology, anthropology, and visual arts have found in the Internet and cyberspace a metaphor for a disembodied world of minds and ideas, where self is a work in progress over time and space. In this section, an introduction will be made into some aspects of these concepts and in the next, a somewhat more mundane exploration of the notion of virtual communities as online versions of their real-world counterparts will be presented.

Mark Slouka, a lecturer in literature and culture at the University of California, San Diego, has written a book with the provocative and carefully chosen title *The War of the Worlds*[42] in recognition of the H. G. Wells classic novel. In that book, an alien invasion threatens the existence of Earth's people and in Slouka's book, an alien world, roughly comparable to virtual reality, threatens our world, the real reality. The threat is pervasive, increasing, and supported by several spokespersons, whose quoted remarks are simultaneously outrageous and ridiculous. Slouka leaves the impression that what is predicted is actually on the verge of being achieved, even though he warns that

> My quarrel is with a relatively small but disproportionately influential group of self-described 'Net religionists' and 'wannabe gods' who believe that the physical world can (and should) be 'downloaded' into a computer, who believe that the future of mankind is not in RL (real life) but in some form of VL (virtual reality); who are working very hard (and spending enormous amounts of both federal and private money) to engineer their very own version of the apocalypse.[43]

It is impossible to appreciate the large, tempting target confronting Slouka without a few choice quotations that make it difficult to believe that we are not being subjected to a colossal put-on. Consider the following representative remarks:

> In cyberspace, Nicole Stenger promised, multiplied versions of the self would 'blossom up everywhere.' These multiplied selves would be 'ideal, ironical, statistical.' It would be 'a springtime for schizophrenia!' "[44]

When virtual reality came on-line, Allucquere Rosanne Stone predicted, cyberspace would become 'a toolkit for reconfiguring consciousness'; it would make it possible for a man to be 'seen, and perhaps touched, as a women and vice versa—or as anything else.'[45]

"The only thing wrong with the universe is that it is currently running someone else's program." (Ken Karakotsios)[46]

"When the scales fall from our eyes, we will see that our 'origins are to be found in both the animal and the mechanical kingdoms, with the animal and the mechanical qualities together incorporated in the definition of human nature.' " (Bruce Mazlish)[47]

" 'As we wire ourselves up into a hivish network . . . many things will emerge that we, as mere neurons in the network, don't expect, don't understand, can't control, or don't even perceive.' But this, he explains patiently, is 'the price for any emergent hive mind.' " (Kevin Kelly)[48]

Slouka is not particularly concerned with the Information or Post-industrialist Society; rather it is the post-flesh, post-touching, post-human one that he fears. It is an easy vision to attack, and a frightening one for anyone with the slightest modicum of humanity. To trivialize human existence and its many thousands of years of development is to make mockery of everything that makes us human, and Slouka readily expresses his bewilderment and disgust at this unthinking and yes, unthinkable, vision of the future. Kelly's portrayal of the hive with its mass of worker bees creates images of the Nuremberg rallies in Slouka's mind, with their masses of humans as drones unthinkingly serving a single-minded goal.

We will describe briefly one well-known story of gender-switching and deceit. A number of users of a CompuServe chat service as far back as 1983 encountered a woman named Joan, a neuropsychologist, who apparently had been seriously injured in an automobile accident, confining her to a wheelchair and rendering her mute. Given a computer, modem, and a connection to CompuServe, she soon found her voice and began long-term relationships with women from the spring of 1983 to the spring of 1985. She was witty, sympathetic, and supportive in times of need. But as it turned out, she wasn't a woman either; Joan was a prominent New York psychiatrist in his early fifties "who was engaged in a bizarre, all-consuming experiment to see what it felt like to be female, and to experience the intimacy of female friendship."[49] In keeping with the electronic context, his activities have been called "mind rape." Indeed one women had a real affair with him, after he was introduced to her by Joan. All the women who had conversed with him felt betrayed, after having volunteered intimate details of their lives. Current online interactions are more sophisticated, in terms of the technology, but how many similar deceptions are being perpetrated and how many more people are being betrayed?

MUDS, MOOS, and . . .

One simple and early form of play for several players was invented in England in 1978 but soon spread around the world. It was called an MUD by its inventor, a "Multi-User Dungeon." The definition from the FAQ on MUDs and MUDding, provides the following definition:[50]

> A MUD (Multiple User Dimension, Multiple User Dungeon, or Multiple User Dialogue) is a computer program which users can log into and explore. Each user takes control of a computerized persona/avatar/incarnation/character. You can walk around, chat with other characters, explore dangerous monster-infested areas, solve puzzles, and even create your very own rooms, descriptions and items.

A MOO is an object-oriented MUD, that is, a MUD implemented in an object-oriented language that permits more, richer environments to be created. And the names roll on: LambdaMOO, "An offshoot of MOO. Added more functionality, many new features, and a great deal more stability, in a general rewrite of the code."[51] There has been an evolution of MUDs in many directions from their primarily wizard and warriors origins; one of these is into a class of MUDs called TinyMUDS, which are more social and provide an environment for individuals to meet and chat. Clearly, many varieties of MUDs are available on the Internet, and to become a player or participant it is necessary to telnet to the MUD's Internet protocol port. (This is as technical as the discussion will become.)

What is of interest in these online games or social groupings are the motivations of the players or participants, the group dynamics, and the benefits derived. One way to gain an understanding of MUDs is to examine the different classes of identities that players can assume. One information document describes three dimensions of this process:[52]

- *Name* [Y]ou could take the name of your favourite movie star and be a 007. You can take any word that is in your mind or create something new that either makes a good sound or makes it impossible for anyone to pronounce as a word. Unique to MUDs is the possibility to change your name as often as you want. [Of course changing your name means that others may or may not believe you are still the same person.]
- *Gender* Have you ever wanted to change to the other sex? Now there is a chance to do so and you may be surprised by the results. A lot of guys act as female characters to get special attention—female players are rare on MUDs. As a result the few real world females are male inside MUDs to avoid special attention! So you can never really be sure who your partner is.
- *Description* The two main areas to consider in the creation of a character, namely physical appearance and history/background. In terms of physical appearance some MUDs will issue a list of characteristics that have to be filled in, while others leave it up to the individual to pad out their character. Such aspect as 'what colour are your eyes?', 'how tall are you?' 'what colour hair do you have?' The history and background of the character should include such aspects as—where the characters was born, what the parents did for a living, and what kind of childhood they had.

Players can, of course, participate in more than one group and adopt more than one persona, with the attendant problems of keeping track of diverse characters. One point to ponder is why so many men adopt female identities. It has been argued that the point of playing is to be accepted into a group on the basis of one's creativity as manifested in an interesting, exciting, and dynamic character. As difficult as this process is in real life, in the virtual world it is a necessary requirement; but what are we to make of such communities, whose existence depends on the acceptance of deception as a fundamental basis upon which to explore relationships?

Why do males want to be females in virtual worlds? A few suggestions are given as follows:[53]

- Due to the pressure of cultural stereotypes, it may be difficult for some men to explore within themselves what society labels as "feminine" characteristics. These males may rely on the anonymity of cyberspace to express their "feminine" side which they feel they must otherwise hide Some of these males may strongly identify with women.
- Adopting a feminine role in cyberspace may be a way to draw more attention to themselves. Getting noticed and responded to in cyberspace is not always easy, especially in such distracting, "noisy" environments as the visual chat habitats.
- Some males may adopt a feminine identity to investigate male/female relationships. They may be testing out various ways of interacting with males in order to learn, first hand, what it's like being on the woman's side.
- Disguised as a female, a male looking for intimacy, romance, and/or cybersex from another male may be acting upon conscious or unconscious homosexual feelings.

What is cybersex? Is it like phone sex? "Virtual sex is a generic term for erotic interaction between individuals whose bodies may never touch, who may never even see each other's faces or exchange real names. This can include phone sex, exchanges of electronic e-mail encounters on chatlines, BBSs and other on-line virtual communities."[54] An informal survey reveals the following two not surprising views: "A lot of people find virtual sex to be a disembodied, alienating and ultimately meaningless experience. Others, however, have discovered that it can be as involving, intense and transformative as the best kinds of embodied erotic encounters, and that furthermore, its virtuosity enhances rather than detracts from the experience."[55]

One of the foremost commentators on these and other activities is Sherry Turkle. In an interview, she promotes the benefits of multiple personalities on the Internet, a matter of choice, as opposed to multiple personalities, in the real world: "people who assume online personas are aware of the lives they have created on the screen. They are playing different aspects of themselves and move fluidly and knowledgeably among them. They are having an experience that encourages them to challenge traditional ways of thinking about healthy selves as single and unitary."[56] The interviewer points out that Ms. Turkle has recounted the story of a young man "who tells you that for him, real life—RL, as he calls it—doesn't have any special status. It's just another window, along with the ones where he plays roles in a number of virtual communities." She agrees and comments that for this person, "RL is usually not even his best window." She goes on to note, "It's not uncommon. But for me, his case is important because it demonstrates how a bright young man who is doing well in school and who has real-life friends can easily go through a period when things are more interesting on the Net than off."[57]

If nothing else, virtual worlds will force us to rethink many of the ideas that we have long held about the unity of self, the notion of presentation, honesty, playfulness, and relationships. Ironically, this artificial medium, made possible only because of machinery—computers and telecommunications networks—has raised serious questions about what makes us human and how such social animals, as we are, form relationships and communities. Nevertheless, dangers do exist, in that dependency on artificial worlds for human relationships may be destructive of real relationship in the real world, which after all is not *just* another chat room, another MUD, or another window on a computer screen. Most striking is how the body is ignored as if it were an impediment in the way of really connecting. Some of the most vociferous virtual world or cyberspace proponents feel that freedom and perhaps even the next stage of evolution will free the mind, the true self, from the constraints of the body. How hundreds of thousands of years of evolution can be ignored, or swept aside, by virtue of a few years of rather primitive technology, is perhaps a tribute to the power of the human mind in projecting speculation into fact and ignoring history and biology, if necessary.

Social and Political Activity

The virtual communities just discussed seem to be characterized by individuals trying to understand themselves by entering environments in which they have some degree of control over what information about themselves is presented to others. By playing with different and even contrasting personae they hope to discover more about their interests, desires, and sexuality. But there are many other ways in which the Internet's global and asynchronous properties can be used to form communities, in which individuals reach out to others to form lobbying groups, to exchange information and support for a host of medical and psychological problems, to mount worldwide campaigns against political oppression, child exploitation, and looming environmental disasters. Some of these groups and their missions are listed in the Appendix. Many groups use a communication structure called a listserv, that can be viewed as either a newsgroup limited to formally subscribed members or an e-mail group in which every message posted immediately is made available to all group members. Joining and quitting usually is done automatically by posting an appropriate message, but some listservs have qualifications that prospective members must meet.

Online groups offer members a number of advantages including instantaneous delivery of announcements, a definite boon for organizational reasons; Web links to important information that is always available; accessibility from home and work, even for the disabled; a communication channel that is less inhibiting than face-to-face confrontations; and a never closing forum. The downside, even for these communities, is that posted material must be taken at face value and those seeking reliable information face a real dilemma, especially when medical conditions are at risk. Since both the source and quality of the information are generally unknown, the prevailing marketplace cautionary dictum continues to be appropriate, *caveat emptor*.[58] On the other hand, so many people of diverse backgrounds are part of help and self-help groups that errors and bad advice are usually noticed and corrected before any damage can be done.

Many of the online communities parallel their real world counterparts; others are unique to the Internet. Self-help, political, environmental, and religious organizations continue to exist with their efforts facilitated by computer networks. Thus, Greenpeace is able to mobilize opposition to a logging operation anywhere in the world, and Amnesty International can use the Internet to rally support for political prisoners at a moment's notice. Some groups such as the Electronic Privacy Information Center exist on the Internet, providing both archival and fast-breaking information for its supporters, encouraging them to lobby their members of Congress, mounting online petitions, and testifying before Congress on matters of vital interest. In May 1996, Human Rights Watch issued a report titled, "Silencing the Net: The Threat to Freedom of Expression On-line." Whereas in the US, extraordinary effort in defending free speech seems to be generated on behalf of those who create and post pornography that may be obscene, in many other parts of the world, the basic right to criticize and campaign against governments or ruling parties continues to be at risk. The report notes the following:[59]

> Governments around the world, claiming they want to protect children, thwart terrorists and silence racists and hate mongers, are rushing to eradicate freedom of expression on the Internet, the international "network of networks," touted as the Information Superhighway. . . . Authoritarian regimes are attempting to reconcile their eagerness to reap the economic benefits of Internet access with maintaining control over the flow of information inside their borders. Censorship efforts in the US and Germany lend support to those in China, Singapore, and Iran, where censors target not only sexually explicit material and hate speech but also pro-democracy discussions and human rights education. . . . Because the Internet knows no national boundaries, on-line censorship laws, in addition to trampling on the free expression rights of a nation's own citizens, threaten to chill expression globally and to impede the development of the Global Information Infrastructure (GII) before it becomes a truly global phenomenon.

Without freedom of expression guaranteed, the existence of activist social and legal groups is threatened, and as noted, the promise of a Global Information Infrastructure will not be realized, certainly not in a form that improves human existence worldwide.

ACCESS

The new universal service policy should:

- recognize the cost of not getting all citizens connected.
- allow users to control usage costs as available evidence suggests that usage costs are as important, if not more important, than access costs for achieving universal service goals.
- allow users to identify the set of services that enables the user to be served by a communication service with adequate facilities.
- provide citizens with affordable, quality customer premises equipment such as phones, modems and computers.
- provide ongoing consumer education so that individuals and organizations are aware of the options available to them, are able to make informed decisions about these options, understand the pricing of the services, and know how to get assistance if they have difficulties with service reliability, bills, privacy, marketing tactics, and/or other problems.[60]

In the Information Society, everyone can be a publisher as well as a consumer of information. The issues to be explored revolve around the questions of who will be able to gain access to the vast stores of information being made available over computer networks and at what costs. It is not a new question; the telephone, radio, television are all technologies whose introduction and growth raised questions of access. One model is the public library, an institution that is deemed so important that access is free and costs are borne by all citizens. The telephone has come to be accepted as virtually indispensable and for a long time, local rates were kept artificially low, subsidized in part by long-distance charges. With deregulation of this latter market, local rates rose, but a variety of charging strategies were introduced to enable low-income customers to have a basic, if typically inadequate, level of service. Television cable service is also structured to provide levels of service to accommodate different incomes and viewing habits, although access to television is not usually regarded as a right. The Internet is certainly not currently viewed as either a necessity or a right, but the Information Highway has been hailed as bringing a host of necessary services to all. And so we return to the questions raised previously: if access to the Information Highway is so important, how will it be provided, given that a certain amount of capital investment in technology must be in place and ongoing charges related to telephone use and connect time must also be provided? In addition, people will require adequate training and ongoing access to help facilities. Thus, one possibility is government subsidies to ensure a basic level of service, not likely in the current atmosphere of antipathy towards government involvement in the affairs of its citizens; another is industry willingness to provide an effective rate structure for different income levels, leaving the question of capital costs open. Other possibilities may exist.

Technological Factors

First, it is necessary to gain an appreciation of the shape and scope of digital information as it has been evolving over the past few years. Some of these features have been presented in bits and pieces so far and at this point we turn to what is currently available in the working environment, taking the World Wide Web as a model.

Digital Information

On Web sites around the world, enormous amounts of information are readily available for those with appropriate computers, modems, software, and Internet accounts or gateway access. What makes the Web so interesting is the ease with which it is possible to access, as well as to present information in a semistructured fashion and that the information exists as text, sound, and images, both single and multiple frame. Everything is stored digitally, that is accessible at the single-byte level. Thus, all forms of information are at root structured collections of bytes, many bytes. The Internet carried "US traffic equivalent to perhaps 1/1000 of the voice telephone network (20 trillion bytes per month in spring 1995)."[61] The Internet is currently doubling in size every year, and the Web traffic is growing even faster so that the Web is now the largest source of packets. All this information would be useless if it could not be searched and accessed readily, viewed and even downloaded.

Browsers and Search Engines

One of the success stories of the Web is that of Netscape, the most commonly used browser, in a heated competition with Microsoft's Internet Explorer. From rather humble beginnings, a browser has become an indispensable tool to the point that serious consideration is being given to a special-purpose Internet computer that is nothing more than a Web browser; that is, a device for linking Web sites and exploring the resources available. Browsers have been augmented to send and receive e-mail, to post and view messages on USENET newsgroups, and to play music and view videos. That is, in a real sense, browsers have become the operating systems for Web exploration; for many people this is all they require of their computers, and hence the impetus for a specialized $500 Internet computer.

Accessing Web sites, although the basic function of browsers, is not enough when faced with hundreds of thousands of Web sites and the problem of determining which ones contain information that might be useful at the moment. Almost immediately a class of programs called search engines appeared to meet the need of dealing with an enormous space of possibly useful information. Many of these names have become familiar to Web dwellers—Yahoo, Infoseek, Web Crawler, Lycos, Excite, Magellan, AltaVista, and HotBot. Many of these such as Lycos and AltaVista actually survey Web sites on a continuous basis, indexing keywords in new documents and adding this new information to the existing base. So we think of autonomous programs, intelligent agents, or web robots (webbots) scurrying about the Web, itself a biological metaphor, scrounging for information and bringing it home. Thus, AltaVista can be given a search query, consisting of a structured expression containing key words that characterize the topic of interest, and within a few seconds return with links to ten, a hundred, or thousands of potential "hits." "The Alta Vista search system has located 30 million pages found on 275,600 servers and four million articles from 14,000 Usenet newsgroups as of September 1996; the Lycos server claims to have found 19 million URLs with 2.3B words (32 GB)."[62] (A URL, Uniform Resource Locator, is the equivalent of an address for a Web site or page.)

Therefore, an infrastructure is in place for creating Web sites containing structured information, varying from advertisements, reports, studies, books, songs, pictures, videos, and arbitrary mixtures of these. In addition, and necessarily so, there is an array of relatively easy-to-use programs, for searching the space of Web documents, using rather simplistic key words for characterizing subjects of interest, and a means for displaying, playing, and viewing retrieved objects. Recent innovations include the downloading of small self-contained programs, written in Java, that run on the user's computer producing animated visual displays. We can expect improvements in search efficiency and accuracy, but the problem of intelligent searches will be challenging for years to come. Given the technology in place the discussion can turn to the fundamental question of access to information in a democratic society.

Telecommunications Technology

The last component of the current and anticipated technology is related to the speed by which information can circulate over the networks. The link between the computer and the network is the modem, which for most people operates between 14.4 and 33.6 Kbits per second. As multimedia formats are increasingly used, it becomes impractical to download large amounts of information, because of the lengthy waits to complete the process. Faster methods of transmission are available now and very fast ones are on the horizon. ISDN (Integrated Services Digital Network), which operates at speeds between 64K to 128K bits per second, is a welcome improvement in speed but unfortunately costs vary considerably from state to state. (For example, residential tariffed prices for 100 hours of 2B + D usage per month vary from $17.90 to $314.83.[63]) Trials are now in progress for cable modem technology in which cable systems are used to transmit data at very high rates, "officially, up to 10M bit/sec. in both directions, but bottlenecks may reduce that to 1.2M to 5.5M bit/sec. Speeds in some early trials have even been slower."[64] Not to be outdone, the telephone companies have been developing technologies to transmit at high speeds over twisted-pair lines that make up most of their installed base. In trials now is ADSL (Asymmetric Digital Subscriber Lines), that offer "1.5M bits/sec. to the user and 64K bit/sec. from the user . . . provides voice and data simultaneously."[65] There is more but the point is clear: much higher data transmission rates are necessary to realize the benefits of the Information Highway and industry is responding with the necessary technology. Whether competition will result in affordable rates for the average user is the open question.

Government Policies and Universal Access

The Telecommunications Act of 1996 was discussed in Chapter 8 with respect to one section, the Communications Decency Act and its attempt to limit free expression on the Internet. Other sections dealing with deregulation of the telephone and cable industries were reviewed in Chapter 11. For the present, the concern is with what role governments will play in ensuring that their citizens have access to the Internet and ultimately the Information Highway, and this where the Telecommunications Act comes into the picture. The Act places the following responsibilities on the Federal Communications Commission (FCC):[66]

- promote the availability of quality services at just, reasonable, and affordable rates;
- increase access to advanced telecommunications services throughout the Nation;
- advance the availability of such services to all consumers, including those in low income, rural, insular, and high cost areas at rates that are reasonably comparable to those charged in urban areas.

The private sector also has responsibilities with respect to universal service. In this regard, the Act states that:[67]

- all providers of telecommunications services should contribute to Federal universal service in some equitable and nondiscriminatory manner;
- there should be specific, predictable, and sufficient Federal and State mechanisms to preserve and advance universal service;
- all schools, classrooms, health care providers, and libraries should, generally, have access to advanced telecommunications services;
- and finally, that the Federal-State Joint Board and the Commission should determine those other principles that, consistent with the 1996 Act, are necessary to protect the pubic interest.

The FCC solicited comments from interested parties and apparently has received the views of more than 200. One organization that submitted comments on the Notice of Proposed Rulemaking regarding Universal Service was FARNET, whose membership consists of both not-for-profit and for-profit organizations including "Internet Service Providers, Network Service Providers, Interexchange Companies, Regional Bell Operating Companies, Universities and Supercomputer Centers."[68] FARNET was concerned about the following issues: rural access to the Internet (today, access to the Internet for most rural and many suburban Americans is available only over analog (POTS) telephone circuits); "the distinction between the access technologies necessary to deliver services and the enhanced services themselves" ("Yesterday the term universal service did not differentiate between access and the service itself, because for a phone call the phone and the service were essentially the same thing. Now, or in the future, we are talking about two different things"); and "adequate investment [be] made in a physical infrastructure (technologically neutral) capable of delivering high-performance access to the Internet."[69]

The Benton Foundation's Communications Policy Project is "a nonpartisan initiative to strengthen public interest efforts in shaping the emerging National Information Infrastructure (NII)."[70] It produced a document, one of many, which articulated the kinds of questions that public interest advocates should be addressing to themselves as well as the FCC. Among these are the following:[71]

- How should the discussion of Universal Service be framed? Is Universal Service about connecting phones? Connecting people with phones? Or connecting people with people?
- How is the value of a network—any network, phone or computer—diminished as fewer and fewer people have access to it? What can be done to identify the communities and individuals most at risk of falling off the networks that will make up the National Information Infrastructure?
- What telecommunications services should be "universal" in the information age? What flexibility should people have in picking the services they need?
- What role can nonprofit organizations and other community-based institutions play in delivering access to basic and advanced services?

Also submitting comments was TCI (Tele-Communications Incorporated), the nation's largest cable company. Not surprisingly, TCI is not enamored with providing subsidies, and would like them to be only narrowly used and controlled by the states. It believes that the marketplace will produce low competitive rates. Although it is eager to provide services to schools and libraries, they should not be too extensive or too heavily subsidized.[72] For another contrary position, consider the following: "New technologies and new networks require a shift toward regulation based not on universal service but on open access. The distinction is subtle, but crucial. Mandating universal service requires regulators to decide what services people should have and what prices they should pay. Regulation focused on open access, on the other hand, protects people's abilities to decide for themselves."[73] This argument is based on the belief that deregulating the telephone system will unleash a wave of competition, supported by continuing technological innovation that will result in lower rates and more services for consumers. Public interest groups do not have faith in this argument; they believe that government must continue to play an active role or many people, especially in rural areas, will continue to be disenfranchised.

Digital Libraries

One institution that is undergoing a major change, and not surprisingly so, is the library. Given that information is what libraries are really about, the movement towards digital information has fostered a parallel movement towards the digital library; that is, a library with networked access to worldwide information, and most important and frequently overlooked, the necessary expertise to search effectively for relevant information. Libraries face the dilemma of trying to maintain collections for the majority of their clientele that will require books for the foreseeable future while responding to the emerging needs of those who would like to connect to the Internet as well as the hundreds of specialized databases that are available on CD-ROMs, or by online subscriptions. Academic libraries have additional burdens because of the escalating costs of journals resulting from a spiral of fewer subscriptions driving increased costs. Experiments in online journals have shown that costs could be reduced and turnaround time improved, but the case is not closed yet. One other issue that demands attention is the problem of archiving frequently ephemeral electronic data. Should newsgroups be archived and if so who should do it and how? What about the archival media? While microfiche and microfilm have a very long lifetime, they are not a very convenient medium for search or retrieval purposes. Unfortunately magnetic tapes, magnetic disks, and videotapes have relatively short lifetimes and are also technologies that will soon be obsolete. Optical disks will physically degrade in fewer than 30 years. Shakespeare's first printed edition of Sonnet 18 dates from 1609 and is still quite readable.[74]

Libraries and Journals

One important experiment on the road to the digital library concluded at the end of 1995, after almost five years. The University Licensing Program (TULIP) involved the Netherlands publisher Elsevier Science and nine major US Universities: "Carnegie Mellon University, Cornell University, Georgia Institute of Technology, Massachusetts Institute of Technology, University of California (all campuses), University of Michigan, University of Tennessee, University of Washington and Virginia Polytechnic Institute and State University." This is the goal of the project:[75]

> . . . to jointly test systems for networked delivery to, and use of journals at, the user's desktop. In the TULIP project, the scanned page images plus bibliographic data and unedited, OCR generated, "raw" ASCII full text of 43 Elsevier and Pergamon materials science and engineering journals, were provided by Elsevier Science to the universities, which developed or adapted systems to deliver these journals in electronic form to the desktops of their end users. The focus of the research was on technical issues, on user behavior and on organizational and economic questions. The major focus of at least the first half of the project, was at the technical side of TULIP. When this project started, there were very few institutions willing or able to bring up large scale implementations, aimed at bringing primary information to the desktop on their entire campuses.

There are technical conclusions and organizational and management ones. From a technical standpoint, what is interesting is that for most universities the Web was the environment of choice, rather than X Windows or MS Windows; large-scale Internet ftp transfer is not feasible with the current transmission schemes and restricted bandwidth. Scalability of TULIP-like systems will also be hindered by the limits of current massive storage technology; speed is crucial for image viewing on the screen; printing page images is an important concern.[76] These results are sobering and suggest that technological infrastructure will be a dominant factor in the viability of working digital libraries. There are also notions of convenience for endusers: "ease to use: as intuitive as possible, and preferably using a familiar interface; access to all information from one source; effective search capabilities; high processing speed (downloading and printing); high publishing speed (timeliness of the information); good image text quality; sufficient journal and time coverage; linking of information."[77] Some final comments are also interesting and cautionary as they suggest that the revolution has not yet occurred: "There is enthusiasm about the concept of desktop access to electronic information, but the end of paper products seems to be far away still. Besides some practical benefits of paper products, there also seem to be "emotional" ties with paper and the library. [P]romotion does play an important and continuous role in the degree of success that can be achieved. [D]edicated project management, cooperation among the parties involved and having the right resources available at the right time,"[78] is crucial.

One of the leading proponents of the digital library is Michael Lesk of Bellcore, who has written a series of papers on many of the technical and social issues facing the development of digital libraries, the economics of digital information flow, and the problems of digitizing images. A summary of Lesk's position is given as follows:[79]

1. Digital libraries are now economically efficient, and the area is booming;
2. Digital technology offers great advantages for libraries;
3. The adoption of digital information will mean changes in the role of libraries, and in how we manage them.

Rather than an extensive treatment of Lesk's arguments (which after all are available at his Web site) the conclusion to this work is a succinct summary of a very persuasive point of view:[80]

> In summary, it is clear that digital libraries are coming, both in free and commercial versions, and in both image and ascii formats. This is an opportunity, not a threat. Digital information can be more effective for the users and cheaper for the librarians. Access will become more important than possession. But this must be used to encourage sharing, not competition. The real asset of a library is the people it has who know how to find information and how to evaluate it. It must emphasize its skills in training, not in acquisition. If we think of information as an ocean, the job of libraries is now to provide navigation. It is no longer to provide the water.

PROSPECTS FOR THE INTERNET AND THE INFORMATION HIGHWAY

> In another dimension, the effect of the Information Superhighway on communities is likely to be extraordinary—and highly beneficial. The Council believes that dispersed communities, such as those in rural areas, will be brought together; that distressed communities, such as those in the inner cities of many metropolitan areas, will be joined in helpful communication; that neighbors will be better able to help neighbors online; that family members will keep in touch via e-mail; and that many people will join "virtual communities" of like-minded individuals wherever they may be. Similarly, the Information Superhighway will invite disabled persons to reenter the workplace, to enjoy entertainment with others, and to become full-fledged members of the emerging electronic community.[81]

In Chapter 1, a brief description of the Information Highway (IH) was presented, as envisioned by both the US and Canadian governments, as they began their study of the implications of a broad-band network linking homes, schools, libraries, workplaces, and institutions of all kinds. Committees were formed, hearings held, reports commissioned, legislation proposed, and debates encouraged. Although the Internet is a work in progress, the IH is a vision in progress, and a great deal has been written and said that is pure speculation. The task at hand is to attempt a characterization of the current vision in terms of its scope, anticipated services, and its impact on commerce, education, health, and the operation of government. The Internet itself is under some strain as the number of users continues to grow rapidly and the volume of bytes transmitted grows even faster. Many feel threatened by well-publicized stories portraying the Internet as a haven for pornographers, racists, and terrorists. The Web has become so popular that it has become fashionable to have a URL in addition to an e-mail address. Change is so rapid that it is difficult to assimilate one innovation before a successor overtakes it.

Government Views

Canada

The final report of the Canadian Information Highway Advisory Council was issued on September 1995. It contained a large number of recommendations on fifteen different areas of vital concern. Some eight months later, the Canadian government responded with its commitment to the development of the IH. So many issues were covered that a brief review is bound to trivialize many important ones and ignore many others, but there are a few major concerns that have come to the fore. The Council was guided by three objectives and five principles:[82]

Objectives

- creating jobs through innovation and investment in Canada
- reinforcing Canadian sovereignty and cultural identity
- ensuring universal access at reasonable cost

Principles

- an interconnected and interoperable network of networks
- collaborative public and private sector development
- competition in facilities, products and services
- privacy protection and network security
- lifelong learning as a key design element of Canada's Information Highway.

Canada's objectives and principles are similar to the those of the US except for Canada's concern with its "sovereignty and cultural identity." As a close neighbor of a country with ten times its population and powerful international entertainment media, Canada has had a long-term concern with supporting its creative artists and providing ready access to its media. The IH could be seen as yet another powerful channel funneling US content into Canada and overwhelming indigenous culture. Of course Canada's concern is mirrored around the world as the global influence of US culture is pervasive and threatening to many countries. It should be noted that the US is not immune from these concerns as US law limits the degree to which its telecommunications companies can be owned by foreigners.

The Advisory Council expects the government to play a regulatory role and to provide policy, but it is the private sector that will build and manage the IH. It recommends that the government be involved in guaranteeing privacy for Canadians by passing appropriate legislation but does not recommend legislation to regulate content. It envisions the IH as an engine for job creation and growth, as a way to invigorate the educational system, and recommends that access be at least as readily available as telephone and television are today. In this regard, government should be the last resort if public/private sector collaboration does not do the job. The Canadian government's response was to issue a report in May 1996, in which it acknowledged its continuing commitment and responsibility for the development of the IH. It would support Canadian content in a variety of ways, make sure all Canadians benefit by supporting learning and social networks around the country, make government services and information dissemination easier and faster, and protect privacy: ". . . the ministers of Industry and Commerce, after consultation with the provinces and other stakeholders, will bring forward proposals for a legislative framework governing the protection of personal data in the private sector."[83]

United States

The United States Advisory Council on the National Information Infrastructure delivered its final report at the end of January 1996. It was only one of many committees and agencies charged with the responsibility of outlining and preparing detailed studies of the many dimensions of the IH, or the National Information Infrastructure (NII), from technical, commercial, social, and legal perspectives. The following are "five fundamental goals" the Council "urges the Nation [to] adopt:"[84]

> First, let us find ways to make information technology work for us, the people of this country, by ensuring that these wondrous new resources advance American constitutional precepts, our diverse cultural values, and our sense of equity.
>
> Second, let us ensure, too, that getting America online results in stronger communities, and a stronger sense of national community.
>
> Third, let us extend to every person in every community the opportunity to participate in building the Information Superhighway. The Information Superhighway must be a tool that is available to all individuals—people of all ages, those from a wide range of economic, social, and cultural backgrounds, and those with a wide range of functional abilities and limitations—not just a select few. It must be affordable, easy to use, and accessible from even the most disadvantaged or remote neighborhood.
>
> Fourth, let us ensure that we Americans take responsibility for the building of the Superhighway—private sector, government at all levels, and individuals.
>
> And, fifth, let us maintain our world leadership in developing the services, products, and an open and competitive market that lead to deployment of the Information Superhighway. Research and development will be an essential component of its sustained evolution.

In fulfilling these goals, the Federal government is urged to create initiatives and facilitate the development of electronic commerce, online educational access, telemedicine, and improvement in government services. It should ensure universal access, by acting when the private sector fails to do so: All individuals should have affordable, ubiquitous, convenient, and functional access to Information Superhighway services. All individuals should be able to be both consumers and producers of information. Design of its components should accommodate the needs of disabled individuals.[85] Contrary to the statements and actions of the White House, the Advisory Council recommends that existing laws and practices be reviewed "to implement the Council's privacy principles," and that "the government should not be in the business of regulating content on the Information Superhighway." Finally, the motto for developing the IH might be: the government should be the catalyst and the private sector should be the builder.

Another informed vision of the NII is a product of a quasi-government agency, the National Research Council. In attempting to characterize so elusive a target as the NII, especially when projected several years into the future, the NII 2000 Steering Committee deliberately chose a very broad and inclusive definition:[86]

> The national information infrastructure (NII) is the collection of all public and private information services both facilities- and content-based operating as a complex, dynamic system. It exists today but is and always will be in a state of flux.

This definition suggests that the NII is not a structure but rather a concept that can be used "to focus thinking about a very important set of resources whose value to society depends on their connectivity, accessibility, and functionality for many important purposes." Some of the tenets of the Information Society as compiled in this report are the following: broader and more user-oriented modes of information to be communicated, use of wireless systems for text or video communications, an erosion of the distinctions among home, work, and school because of the pervasiveness of communication networks, and the expansion of professional services over networks, as well as increased citizen participation in the political process in as yet unpredictable ways.

One last vision of the future and a critique of the past is a mandate prepared for the Progress and Freedom Foundation by four leading proponents of the Knowledge Age: Esther Dyson (president of the Electronic Frontier Foundation), George Gilder (writer and futurologist), Dr. George Keyworth (Science advisor to President Reagan), and Dr. Alvin Toffler (renowned futurologist). A more detailed discussion was presented in Chapter 3, but it is being partially reviewed here because it is also relevant in the present context. Their "Magna Carta" calls for a new vision and a discarding of old ideas tied to a materialist age. In this call to intellectual arms, the authors caution that[87]

> As humankind explores this new "electronic frontier" of knowledge, it must confront again the most profound questions of how to organize itself for the common good. The meaning of freedom, structures of self-government, definition of property, nature of competition, conditions for cooperation, sense of community and nature of progress will each be redefined for the Knowledge Age—just as they were redefined for a new age of industry some 250 years ago.

It might be noted again that for the most part, the Magna Carta secured rights for the barons under King John in 1215, not for the peasants. Hopefully ordinary citizens will do better in the Knowledge Age.

Limitations of the Internet

Is the Internet reaching any limits with respect to the volume of traffic it can accommodate without unacceptable delays? Will new applications such as video accelerate potential bandwidth problems and lead to crashes? Will the private sector carriers decide to reap greater profits by implementing a charging strategy for Internet communications? Does the increasing use of the Internet for commercial activities, especially the Web sites, signal the end of an old culture and the arrival of a new one more dedicated to money than community? Although there is some debate over the actual number and definition of users, the crucial number is growth rate, which does indicate that the Internet and other online services are on a steep growth curve. Can the Internet sustain such a growth rate and continue to provide adequate service? On August 7, America OnLine was down for 19 hours, depriving its six million customers of service. The faults were twofold: "a faulty roadmap of Internet addresses and a bug in the software of a powerful switching computer called a router."[88] In addition to these local problems, there may be some systemic problems that will soon plague the Internet. Consider the following:[89]

1. *It's Too Slow.* The Internet is a highway that stays congested no matter how many lanes are added. New Capacity is swallowed up by graphics—heavy Web pages, phone calls, video, and software "robots" that cruise for information.
2. *Good Stuff Is Hard To Find.* Few Web sites have found a recipe that keeps customers coming back.
3. *It's Not Built Right.* The Internet is struggling with missions it simply wasn't designed for. Security is weak. Important traffic gets stuck behind low-priority drivel. It's not well-suited for voice and video. There's no mechanism for counting usage—or charging for it.

This last point is quite important. As the Internet evolved from primarily a research-based network to a social, entertainment, and information medium, the backbone of the network in the US was sold to private companies. The only costs imposed on institutions connecting to the Internet was a monthly connect fee that was independent of the amount of traffic received or sent. One proposal to limit congestion is to charge users for the volume of traffic for which they are responsible. This would require a mechanism for measuring and charging that has yet to be agreed upon, although competing proposals are being discussed, especially by telecommunication companies such as MCI that carry a great deal of the Internet traffic. Not surprisingly, *Business Week* advocates such an approach: "It's time for Internet users to start paying for usage . . . Already, the largest Internet providers are beginning to bill smaller providers for handling their data. Soon, these fees will trickle down to individuals."[90]

The economist Hal Varian has written extensively on the economics of the Internet, on pricing, and on costing information. He cautions against the easy assumption that paying by the byte is the way to go:[91]

Many observers think that "by the byte"' pricing is likely to be a significant form of pricing. I expect the contrary: subscription-based pricing is likely to be the most significant way that information is sold. This is due to a fundamental property of information: you don't know if you want it until after you've seen it . . . and by then you've already paid for it. This means that there is a large ``reputation effect'' in information—I read the New York Times today because I liked what it said yesterday. The same things goes for most other forms of information I use: I tend to use the same sources since they have established a reputation (with me) for usefulness, reliability, and entertainment.

RISK AND SECURITY

Examples of coordination issues in security technology policy that the [Information Technology Security Policy Issues] Clearinghouse should be able to address are:

- Cryptographic Technology
- Public Key Infrastructure
- Access Control Systems
- Network Security
- Dual Use Technology
- Interoperability of Government and Industrial Systems
- Government Technology Transferable to Industry
- Export Controls for Technology
- International Security Technology Policy[92]

On September 17, 1991, AT&T long distance service in New York failed, resulting in five million blocked calls and a paralysis of the air traffic control systems. America OnLine's breakdown took place on August 7, 1996. These and many other smaller similar events are reminders that the Information Society is supported by a fragile infrastructure of computers and communication networks, or perhaps more precisely, by complex and fragile software, as hardware breakdowns are rarely the cause of system failure. As technology increases in complexity, the possibilities of accidents also increase and the results may be staggering. Witness such serious calamities as Bhopal, Challenger, and Chernobyl. Information systems underlie most of the present and future technologies at work, home, and play. As the requisite software increases in complexity, it becomes almost impossible to test it sufficiently to guarantee against failures, under a rare combination of circumstances. Furthermore, current software, subject to repeated "patches" is itself quite fragile and likely to crash. Systems may fail for a variety of reasons such as human mistakes, both in the design and operation of the system, rare acts of nature, hardware breakdowns, events unforeseen during the design phase, overload, or various combinations of these.

Given that humans are subject to lapses of memory, periods of inattention, and occasional physical disabilities, it is incumbent upon designers to foolproof systems as much as possible and to include clean, error-recovery procedures, because accidents will occur. The problems of developing strategies for risk management and reliability are difficult but obviously of growing importance if technological disasters are not to become a common occurrence. At times this emerging discipline tends to dwell on the unthinkable, namely, placing a monetary value on human life:[93]

> In any applied technology that touches human lives, the decision to accept some level of risk as inevitable calls on subjective judgment about the worth of those lives. The classic, if callous, tradeoff is a cost/benefit analysis of the expense of installing safety systems versus the value of the lives they may save and the political effectiveness of the move.

The major source on computer risks and security is the book, *Computer Related Risks,* by Peter G. Neumann, who is the moderator of the well-known Internet Risks Forum, a clearinghouse of tales of warnings, disasters, risks, and remedies. In discussing where to place the blame, Neumann notes that "most system problems are ultimately and legitimately attributable to people. However, human failings are often blamed on "the computer"—perhaps to protect the individuals. The attribution of blame seems to be common in computer affecting consumers, where human shortcomings are frequently attributed to "a computer glitch." Computer system malfunctions are often due to underlying causes attributable to people; if the technology is faulty, the faults frequently lie with people who create and use it."[94]

Neumann makes specific reference to the National Information Infrastructure (NII) and some of the associated risks to be incurred when virtually every computer in the US and subsequently the world is potentially linked. The dimensions of risk are overwhelming, multiplying the traditional concerns: ". . . it encompasses many now familiar risks and increasingly involves human safety and health, mental well-being, peace of mind, personal privacy, information confidentiality and integrity, proprietary rights, and financial stability, particularly as internetworking continues to grow."[95] Finally, taking the highway metaphor seriously, Neumann suggests a number analogies to computer network malfunctions:[96]

traffic jams	congestions
crashes	system wipeouts
roadkill	bystanders
drunken drivers	accidents waiting to happen
carjackers	malicious hackers
drag racers and joy riders switched vehicle identifiers	bogus E-mail
speed limits on the Autobahn	as well as the Infobahn
onramps and gateways	controlling access, authentication, and authorization
toll bridges	usage fees
designated drivers	authorized agents
drivers' licenses	system registration and inspections

As a conclusion to this section, the following advice of the social critic Jerry Mander as condensed in his "Ten Recommended Attitudes About Technology" is well worth considering:[97]

1. Since most of what we are told about new technology comes from its proponents, be deeply skeptical of all claims.
2. Assume all technology "guilty until proven innocent."
3. Eschew the idea that technology is neutral or "value free." Every technology has *inherent and identifiable* social, political, and environmental consequences.
4. The fact that technology has a natural flash and appeal is meaningless. Negative attributes are slow to emerge.
5. Never judge a technology by the way it benefits you personally. Seek a holistic view of its impacts. The operative question is not whether it benefits you, but who benefits most? And to what end?
6. Keep in mind that an individual technology is only one piece of a large web of technologies, "megatechnology." The operative question here is how the individual technology fits the larger one.
7. Make distinctions between technologies that primarily serve the individual or the small community (e.g., solar energy) and those that operate on a scale outside of community control (e.g., nuclear energy). The latter kind is the major problem of the day.
8. When it is argued that the benefits of the technological lifeway are worthwhile despite harmful outcome, recall that Lewis Mumford referred to these alleged benefits as "bribery." Cite the figures about crime, suicide, alienation, drug abuse, as well as environmental and cultural degradation.
9. Do not accept the homily that "once the genie is out of the bottle you cannot put it back," or that rejecting a technology is impossible. Such attitudes induce passivity and confirm victimization.
10. In thinking about technology within the present climate of technological worship, emphasize the negative. This brings balance. Negativity is positive.

What kind of technology is the NII, how should it be judged in these terms, and what actions, if any, are appropriate and necessary?

FINAL REMARKS

From the time of Gutenberg, and even before, information production has been controlled and has led to social stratification based on unequal access. What is of special significance about the current situation, is the centrality of information in all spheres of material production, as well as its increasing prominence throughout the economy. Today, information increasingly serves as a primary factor in production, distribution, administration, work, and leisure. For these reasons, how information itself is produced and made available become crucial determinants affecting the organization of the social system.[98]

That we, the US, Canada, Western Europe, and Japan, are moving towards an Information Society seems to be accepted dogma, even if the shape of that society is not well-defined. Throughout this book the various building blocks of the emerging information society have been discussed and associated societal implications described. It may be useful, at this point, to step back and attempt to assess some of the major overall features and large-scale impacts of that envisioned society.

Aspects of Information Society Research

One way to identify the important issues is to extract them from the body of research developed over the years. Consider the following characteristics so identified.[99]

Information Materialism, or Information as an Economic Commodity. From discussions throughout the book it is clear that services are gradually increasing their share of the economy and that throughout the economy the role of information is assuming a dominant position. But it is not just improved information processing as a means to increase productivity that is of interest here; rather, it is information as a commodity, as a product in its own right that is of importance. Various scholars have discussed this phenomenon, including Fritz Machlup, Daniel Bell, Marc Porat, and Andrew Oettinger.[100] A problem of definition exists in this area as information seems to be all-inclusive: information "goods" such as video cassette recorders, personal computers, and television sets; information gathered for one purpose reconfigured for another, for example, motor vehicle records used to identify potential purchasers for upscale products. Furthermore, although bought, sold, borrowed, or stolen, information is neither durable nor intrinsically valuable, but its commercial exchange does create a need to treat it as property.

Widely Diffused Information Technology. The development of global communication networks to transmit information instantaneously around the world holds enormous possibilities and is a major theme in any analysis of the information society. From McLuhan's global village to Ellul's technological society, computers and communications may well have eliminated geography as a factor in human society and perhaps real difference and choice as well.[101] Computers have become pervasive and virtually unchallenged as the leading edge of technological change. It seems almost impossible to think of the information society without the integral role played by computers.

Many Messages and Channels. An enormous number of devices that receive, send, and manipulate information have become ubiquitous in American homes: telephones, telephone answering machines, televisions, radios, VCRs, audio cassette recorders, compact disc players, home computers, modems, printers, and more recently Fax, copiers, and laser printers. In addition large and growing amounts of paper are flooding homes in the form of mail, newspapers, magazines, and advertisement circulars. They are indicative not only of the vast amounts of information available to Americans but also of the power of the media to shape and influence public opinion.

Interconnectedness. Because of the power and growth of the new information technologies, boundaries and distinctions among institutions have begun to disappear. The facilitation of information flow has created unlimited possibilities for companies to extend their activities beyond their original purpose. Thus overlapping financial services are available from an ever-increasing number of companies: banks offer credit cards and credit card companies offer banking services. Many of these possibilities have resulted from the growing number of interconnected channels for carrying information such as cable, satellites, direct broadcasting, personal computers for electronic mail, bulletin boards, and videotex.

A Large Information Workforce. Associated with the growth of information industries is an obvious growth in the associated workforce. Through a variety of approaches, it can be established that the largest percentage of the workforce is clearly involved in the manipulation of information, not in the manufacture of goods. This situation surely has some important implications for the structure of society.

The Special Status of Scientific Knowledge. Scientific knowledge describes the language that scientists employ in discussing their work and communicating ideas. Given the importance of science to the development of technology and hence societal change, science must be supported as a special and privileged domain of inquiry. Thus scientific knowledge represents in economic terms "intellectual capital," difficult to measure but obviously fundamental to growth and progress. Note that social scientists are included, as their activities support the direct relationship between product development and market acceptance.

Information as a Commodity

Of all of these issues, we wish to focus on the commoditization of information, or perhaps in a more felicitous description, information as a commodity. As mentioned elsewhere, the rapid growth of computers, telecommunications, and software have initiated a transformation in kind rather than degree; that is, it is not just that old things can be done faster but that new possibilities are created, that new markets are opened, and that new uses for old "products" are developed. Thus, information within companies is increasingly being used for purposes that transcend internal needs to external markets. Information as a commodity is not new but technology has accelerated the pace at which new markets are created and furthermore the existence of vast amounts of information in both private and public databases has provided additional motivation.

A long-time critic of the power and influence of the communication and information industries is Herbert Schiller, who has noted, ". . . the information sphere is becoming the pivotal point in the American economy. And, as the uses of information multiply exponentially by virtue of its greatly enhanced refinement and flexibility—through computer processing, storing, retrieving, and transmitting data—*information itself becomes a primary item for sale.*"[102] [original emphasis] The growing commercialization of information has some important effects on the role of public institutions, such as libraries, universities, and the government itself. As long as the costs of gathering, storing, and disseminating information were nonrecoverable, the public was expected to bear the expense, but as soon as it was possible to profit from the information as a product, demands were heard to remove government from the marketplace and to permit business to do its job. Thus the government is under pressure to privatize its information distributing agencies or at least limit their roles to bulk distribution, permitting private companies to provide customized services, usually electronically, over the Internet.

A Last (Polemical) Comment

The Information Society is not easily characterized but it is eagerly anticipated by technological enthusiasts. Futurologists can hardly wait for the wonders of technology to liberate everyone (read Americans) from work, hunger, and sickness. Inequities will diminish if not disappear. The Information Society is one of the streams of this bountiful future. The wonders of artificial intelligence, neurocomputers, and parallel processing are hailed as if they have already been realized rather than technologies with long-term potential. But this is the business of futurologists to allow their imaginations free reign and to extrapolate as if it were obvious that their vision is inevitable. And usually any negative events are minimized, if they are mentioned at all, and dismissed as minor irritations on the broad road to progress. Surely it is possible to explore the future, cognizant of the past and taking into account the complexity of social, political, economic, and cultural forces that shape the introduction and ultimate impact of technology. The impact of computers on work, both the nature of work and the distribution of jobs, on privacy, on education, on medicine, on the law, indeed on every aspect of life, is associated with a rich network of human values and concerns that must be considered in any study of technology.

SUMMARY

The gathering, processing, storage, and transmission of ever-increasing quantities of information is becoming the major activity of economically advanced societies. From home you can connect to a wide variety of computer networks (including, of course, the Internet and the World Wide Web) that provide services ranging from home banking to stock market quotations. Electronic mail and bulletin boards are becoming more popular beyond their early audience of researchers and computer buffs, for communicating over long distances.

With the exciting world of Web pages and their glitzy graphics, sounds, and video, it is sometimes overlooked that earlier experiments, many unsuccessful, laid the foundations for current systems. One such experiment, called videotex—or a two-way communication network—was intended to provide a wide range of information services, including shopping, banking, home security, education, and so forth. In many countries, especially France, but not the US, government-managed telephone companies assumed an active role in stimulating the growth of videotex. The most successful videotex system in the world is France's Minitel, whose growth was linked to the financial support of the telephone company. There was some concern that videotex would be controlled by a few large corporations and that its potential benefits would thus be compromised. A similar concern is held by some critics today.

The growth of such a global network as the Internet has fostered the parallel growth of virtual communities; that is, distributed networks of individuals who associate by communicating over the Internet to exchange information, support shared political, social, religious, ecological beliefs, and even to engage in make-believe games and relationships. Some have hailed these interactions as exciting ways to explore self (by assuming new personae), gender (by assuming the opposite), and any other variation on one's real-life situation. Many different selves can be projected to others, who are simultaneously exploring their repressed other personalities. These games are supposed to be liberating and to provide alternatives to difficult times in real life, but they could be seen as avoidance and escapism.

Since 1993, there has been considerable discussion and publicity about the Information (Super) Highway (IH) and the changes it will bring to society. Governments have invested considerable resources in committees, conferences, reports, and books to outline projected benefits of the (IH). It will connect the nation's homes, schools, libraries, community centers, and workplaces. New jobs will be created, new and unpredictable technologies will emerge, and those who traditionally have been silent will be given a voice. Such are the claims, but it will be necessary first to provide the necessary equipment and access or the silent will remain silent.

As the nation's economic infrastructure depends increasingly on computers and computer networks, the risk of breakdowns, with their associated costs, becomes a matter of serious concern. Much intellectual effort is being placed into improving techniques for building stable and fault-resistant systems, but it must be acknowledged that with complexity goes risk. The future is certainly exciting, but as societies prepare for such natural disasters as earthquakes, tornadoes, and floods, they must also prepare for disasters associated with the breakdowns of large, complex systems.

The information society has been a topic of study for many years. Concerns have arisen about the power of information and especially about those countries that control its flow. Information itself has become a commodity, to be bought and sold, beyond its importance within companies as a means to improve productivity. As systems become larger and society more dependent upon them the problems of failure become more serious. Whatever the future holds, the role of technology is crucial and the study of its impact must include the associated social effects.

NOTES

1. Thomas A. Stewart. "What Information Costs," *Fortune,* July 10, 1995, pp. 119–121.
2. The formal definition of videotex, adopted by the International Telecommunication Union, International Telegraph and Telephone Consultative Committee in 1984, in *New Telecommunication Services: Videotex Development Strategies,* ICCP, Information, Computer and Communication Policy Series. (Paris: OECD, 1988), p. 9.
3. Jean Devèze. "Minitel™ and Its Residential Services," in Felix van Rijn and Robin Williams, (eds.). *Concerning Home Telematics.* (New York: North-Holland, 1987), pp. 62–63.
4. James M. Markham. "France's Minitel Seeks a Niche," *The New York Times,* November 8, 1988, p. 29.
5. Riccardo Petrella. "Experiences in Home Telematics," in van Rijn and Williams. *Concerning Home Telematics,* p. 15.
6. Catherine L. Harris. "For Videotex, The Big Time Is Still a Long Way Off," *Business Week,* January 14, 1985, pp. 128, 132–133.
7. Bill Saporito. "Are IBM and Sears Crazy? Or Canny?" *Fortune,* September 28, 1987, p. 74.
8. Jeffrey Rothfeder and Mark Lewyn. "How Long Will Prodigy Be a Problem Child?" *Business Week,* September 10, 1990, p. 75.
9. In May 1991, Prodigy cancelled its supermarket shopping service, which had permitted users to order goods at participating stores. (*Computerworld,* May 27, 1991, p. 6.)

10. John Markoff. "Betting on a Different Videotex Idea," *The New York Times,* July 12, 1989, p. 27.

11. Steve Lohr. "Prodigy Gets New Owners and Strategy," *The New York Times,* May 13, 1996, p. C 1.

12. James P. Miller and Jared Sandberg. "H&R Block Postpones CompuServe Spinoff," reprinted in *The Globe and Mail* (Toronto, Canada), August 29, 1996, p. B 6.

13. "Domain Survey Notes," Net Wizards, July 1996. Accessed from the Web page with URL: <http://www.nw.com/zone/WWW/notes.html> on September 4, 1996.

14. *Ibid.*

15. Taken from a graph produced by General Magic, August 1996. Accessed from the Web page with URL: <http://www.genmagic.com/Internet/Trends/sld006.gif> on September 4, 1996.

16. "Internet Survey Companies and Constituencies," last updated June 17, 1996. Accessed from the Web page with URL: <http://www.nua.ie/choice/Surveys/SurveyLinks.html> on September 4, 1996.

17. *Ibid.*

18. Thomas A. Stewart. "The Information Age in Charts," *Fortune,* April 4, 1992, pp. 75–79.

19. *Ibid.*

20. "The Accidental Superhighway: A Survey of the Internet," *The Economist,* July 1, 1995. Accessed from the Web page with URL: <http://www.economist.com/surveys/internet/intro.html> on May 26, 1996.

21. *Ibid.*

22. Robert H. Anderson, Tora K. Bikson, Sally Ann Law, and Bridger M. Mitchell. "Universal Access to E-Mail: Feasibility and Societal Implications," RAND, MR-650-MF, 1995. Accessed from the Web site with URL: <http:www.rand.org/publications/MR/MR650/> on November 10, 1995.

23. *Ibid.*

24. *Ibid.*

25. "C=}>;())" The Economist, October 6, 1990, p. 104. Different cultures may use different symbols; for example, the Japanese use (^_^) for smile as compared with :-) in Europe and North America. Happy is (^o^) as compared with :-)) for very happy. Exciting is (*^o^*) and cold sweat is (^^;) . See Andrew Pollack, "Happy in the East (^_^) or Smiling :-) in the West," *The New York Times,* August 12, 1996, p. C 5.

26. J. A. Savage. "Nonprofit Firm Seeks to Create Low-Cost Networks," *Computerworld,* October 8, 1990, p. 60.

27. Felicity Barranger. "Electronic Bulletin Boards Need Editing. No They Don't," *The New York Times,* March 11, 1990, p. 4 E.

28. Jack Kapica. "Notes Toward a Theory of Flaming," *The Globe and Mail* (Toronto, Canada), August 2, 1996, p. A 5.

29. Norman Z. Shapiro and Robert H. Anderson. "Towards an Ethics and Etiquette for Electronic Mail," RAND, July 1985. Accessed from the Web page with URL: <http://www.rand.org/areas/r3283.html> on November 22, 1995.

30. Ed Korthof. "Spamming and USENET Culture," *Bad Subjects,* Issue #18, January 1995. Accessed from the Web page with URL: <http://english-www.hss.cmu.edu/bs/18/Korthof.html> on September 5, 1996.

31. Definition for "Spam (or Spamming)" taken from The Full Glossary. Accessed from the Web page with URL: <http://www.matisse.net/webgen/glossary/pages/Definition.87.htm> on September 5, 1996.

32. A. Michael Froomkin. "An Introduction to the 'Governance' of the Internet," University of

Miami Law School, 1995. Accessed from the Web page with URL: <http://www.law.miami.edu/~froomkin/seminar/ilsx.htm> on September 5, 1996.

33. "The Closing of anon.penet.fi," August 30, 1996. Accessed from the Web page with URL: <http://epic.org/privacy/internet/anon_closure.html> on September 6, 1996.

34. Andre Bacard. "Anonymous Remailer FAQ," September 4, 1996. Accessed from the Web page with URL: <http://www.well.com/user/abacard/remail.html> on September 6, 1996. A FAQ (Frequently Asked Questions) is a guide to some arcane Internet topic usually structured in the form of a series of questions and answers, and maintained by a knowledgeable Net regular.

35. *Ibid.*

36. Arnoud "Galactus" Engelfriet. "Anonymity: Remailers: Cypherpunk remailers," September 4, 1996. Accessed from the Web page with URL: <http://www.stack.urc.tue.nl/~galactus/remailers/index-cpunk.html> on September 6, 1996.

37. *Op. cit.,* "The Closing of anon.penet.fi," August 30, 1996.

38. Front page of *The Observer,* August 25, 1996. Accessed from the Web page with URL: <http://scallywag.com/obsfront.jpg> on August 30, 1996. Note that this item is a photograph of the actual front page. The stories, on page 16, can be accessed from the Web page with URL: <http://scallywag.com/obsin.gif>.

39. *Ibid.*

40. "Johan Helsingius Closes His Internet Remailer," press release, August 30, 1996. Accessed from the Web page with URL: <http://epic.org/privacy/internet/anon_closure.html> on September 6, 1996.

41. Sherry Turkle. "Who Am We?" *Wired,* 4.01, January 1996, pp. 148–152, 194, 196–199.

42. Mark Slouka. *War of the Worlds: Cyberspace and the High-Tech Assault on Reality.* (New York: BasicBooks, A Division of HarperCollins Publishers, 1995).

43. *Ibid.,* p. 10.

44. *Ibid.,* pp. 61–62.

45. *Ibid.,* p. 63.

46. *Ibid.,* p. 66.

47. *Ibid.,* p. 68.

48. *Ibid.,* p. 97.

49. Lindsay Van Gelder. "The Strange Case of the Electronic Lover," *Ms. Magazine,* October 1985. Reprinted in Rob Kling (ed.). *Computerization and Controversy: Value Conflicts and Social Choices.* 2nd Edition (San Diego, CA: Academic Press, 1996), pp. 533–546.

50. "Frequently Asked Questions (FAQs): Basic Information about MUDs and MUDding," posted in the newsgroup, rec.games.mud.announce, on August 31, 1996

51. *Ibid.*

52. "The Characters in MUDding," Sheffield University, United Kingdom, date unknown. Accessed from the Web page with URL: <http://www.shef.ac.uk/uni/academic/I-M/is/studwork/groupe/chara.html> on September 9, 1996.

53. John Suler. "Do Boys Just Want to Have Fun? Male Gender-Switching in Cyberspace (and How to Detect it)." Part of an unpublished manuscript, "Psychology of Cyberspace," Rider University, May 1996. Accessed from the Web page with URL: <http://www1.rider.edu/~suler/psycyber/genderswap.html> on September 6, 1996.

54. Shannon McRae. "Coming Apart at the Seams: Sex, Text and the Virtual Body," 1995. Accessed from the Web page with URL: <http://dhalgren.english.washington.edu/~shannon/vseams.html> on September 6, 1996.

55. *Ibid.*

56. Herb Brody. "Session with the Cybershrink: an Interview with Sherry Turkle," *Technology Re-*

view, November 1995. Accessed from the Web page with URL: <http://orca.csudh.edu/~jjef-fers/courses/hci-turkle.html> on September 6, 1996.

57. *Ibid.*
58. Let the buyer beware.
59. "Silencing the Net: The Threat to Freedom of Expression On-line," *Human Rights Watch,* 8 (2 G), May 1996. Accessed from the Web page with URL: <gopher://gopher.igc.apc.org:5000/00/int/hrw/general/27> on May 11, 1996.
60. "Reply Comments of Benton Foundation Before the Federal Communications Commission in the Matter of FCC 96-93, CC Docket No. 96-45, Federal-State Joint Board on Universal Service," April 12, 1996. Accessed from the Web page with URL: <http://www.benton.org/Goin-gon/uniserv-replycomments.html> on August 28, 1996.
61. Michael Lesk. "Libraries and the Web," 1995. (To appear in *Libraries and Information World Wide,* 1996.) Accessed from the Web page with URL: <http://community.bellcore.com:80/lesk/liww/liww.html> on September 4, 1996.
62. *Ibid.*
63. "Selected ISDN Tariffs, Consumer Project on Technology, version 1.0b," March 8, 1996. Accessed from the Web page with URL: <http://www.essential.org/cpt/isdn/survey.txt> on May 10, 1996.
64. Steve Alexander. "Wired to Wire," *Computerworld,* August 26, 1996, pp. 90–91.
65. *Ibid.*
66. "Report No. DC 96-21, Commission Establishes Joint Board and Initiates Rulemaking for Consideration of Universal Service Issues Pursuant to Telecommunications Act of 1996," Federal Communications Commission, March 8, 1996. Accessed from the Web page with URL: <http://www.fcc.gov/Bureaus/Common_Carrier/News_Releases/nrcc6019.txt> on August 28, 1996.
67. *Ibid.*
68. "In the Matter of Federal-State Joint Board on Universal Service, Reference: CC Docket No. 96-45, Federal Communications Commission," Federation of American Research Networks (FARNET), April 11, 1996. Accessed from the Web page with URL: <http://www.farnet.org/universalservice.html> on July 13, 1996.
69. *Ibid.*
70. "Public Interest Advocates, Universal Service and the Telecommunications Act of 1996," the Benton Foundation, 1996. Accessed from the Web page with URL: <http://www.benton.org/Goingon/advocates.htm> on August 28, 1996.
71. *Ibid.*
72. "Comments of Tele-Communications, Inc. in the Matter of Federal-State Joint Board on CC Docket No. 96-45, Universal Service," before the Federal Communications Commission, April 12, 1996. Accessed from the FCC Web site with URL: <http://www.fcc.org/>.
73. John Browning. "Universal Service (An Idea Whose Time Is Past)," *Wired,* 2.09, September 1994. Accessed from the Web page with URL: <http://nswt.tuwien.ac.at:8000/cs/papers/univ-service.html> on August 28, 1996.
74. Jeff Rothenberg. "Ensuring the Longevity of Digital Documents," *Scientific American,* January 1995, pp. 42–47.
75. "[TULIP] The University Licensing Program," Final Report, July 18, 1996. Accessed from the Web page with URL: <http://www.elsevier.nl:80/homepage/about/resproj/trmenu.htm> on September 10, 1996.
76. *Ibid.*
77. *Ibid.*
78. *Ibid.*

79. Michael Lesk. "The Future Value of Digital Information and Digital Libraries," a lecture given November 9, 1995 at the Kanazawa Institute of Technology Roundtable on Libraries and Information Systems, Kanazawa, Japan. Accessed from the Web page with URL: <http://community.bellcore.com/lesk/kanazawa/kanazawa.html> on September 11, 1996.

80. *Ibid.*

81. *A Nation of Opportunity: A Final Report of the United States Advisory Council on the National Information Infrastructure,* Key Roles Section, January 1996. Accessed from the Web page with URL: <http://www.benton.org/KickStart/nation.home.html> on September 12, 1996.

82. *The Challenge of the Information Highway: Final Report of the Information Highway Advisory Council,* Industry Canada, Ottawa, Ontario, September 1995. Available from the Web site with URL: <http://info.ic.gc.ca/info-highway/ih.html>.

83. *Building the Information Society: Moving Canada into the 21st Century,* Industry Canada, Ottawa Ontario, May 1996. Available from the Web site with URL: <http://info.ic.gc.ca/info-highway/ih.html>.

84. *A Nation of Opportunity,* a final report of the United States Advisory Council on the National Information Infrastructure, January 1996. Accessed from the Web page with URL: <http://www.benton.org/KickStart/nation.home.html> on September 12, 1996.

85. *Ibid.*

86. *The Unpredictable Certainty: Information Infrastructure Through 2000.* NII Steering Committee, Computer Science and Telecommunications Board, National Research Council. (Washington, DC: National Academy Press, 1996). Also available from the Web page with URL: <http://www.nap.edu/nap/online/unpredictable/>.

87. Esther Dyson, George Gilder, George Keyworth, and Alvi Toffler. "Cyberspace and the American Dream: A Magna Carta for the Knowledge Age," Progress & Freedom Foundation, Release 1.2, August 22, 1994. Accessed from the Web page with URL: <http://www.pff.org/pff/position.html> on February 20, 1996.

88. Peter Coy, Robert D. Hof, and Paul C. Judge. "Has the Net Finally Reached the Wall?" *Business Week,* August 26, 1996, pp. 62–64, 66.

89. *Ibid.*

90. "Needed: Toll Plazas on the I-Way," editorial, *Business Week,* August 26, 1996, p. 80.

91. Hal R. Varian. "Economic Issues Facing the Internet," draft, University of California, Berkeley, September 7, 1996. Accessed from the Web page with URL: <ftp://alfred.sims.berkeley.edu/pub/Papers/econ-issues-internet.html> on September 13, 1996.

92. "Security Task Report," Technology Policy Working Group, Committee on Applications and Technology, Information Infrastructure Task Force, July 29, 1996. Accessed from the Web page with URL: <http://nii.nist.gov/pubs/sec_task_rpt.html> on August 14, 1996.

93. Trudy Bell. "Managing Risk in Large Complex Systems," special report, *IEEE Spectrum,* June 1990, p. 22.

94. Peter G. Neumann. *Computer Related Risks.* (New York: ACM Press; Reading, MA: Addison-Wesley, 1995), p. 286.

95. *Ibid.,* p. 299.

96. *Ibid.,* p. 301.

97. Jerry Mander. *In the Absence of the Sacred: The Failure of Technology & the Survival of the Indian Nations.* (San Francisco: Sierra Club Books paperback edition, 1992).

98. Herbert I. Schiller. "Paradoxes of the Information Age," an address to a conference on microelectronics, Santa Cruz, California, May 1983, as quoted in George Gerbner. "The Challenge Before Us," in Jorg Becker, Goran Hedebro, and Leena Paldan (eds.), *Communication and Domination: Essays to Honor Herbert I. Schiller.* (Norwood, NJ: Ablex Publishing, 1986), p. 233.

99. Jorge Reina Schement and Leah A. Lievrouw (eds.). *Competing Visions, Complex Realities: Social Aspects of the Information Society.* (Norwood, NJ: Ablex Publishing, 1987), pp. 3–9.

100. Fritz Machlup. *The Production and Distribution of Knowledge in the United States.* (Princeton, NJ: Princeton University Press, 1962). Daniel Bell. *The Coming of the Post-Industrial Society: A Venture in Social Forecasting.* (New York: Basic Books, 1973). Marc U. Porat. *The Information Economy, Volume 1: Definition and Measurement.* (Washington, DC: US Department of Commerce, 1977). Anthony Oettinger. "Information Resources: Knowledge and Power in the 21st Century," *Science,* July 4, 1980, pp. 191–209.

101. Marshall McLuhan. *Understanding Media: The Extensions of Man.* (New York: McGraw-Hill, 1964). Jacques Ellul. *The Technological Society.* (New York: Alfred A. Knopf, 1964).

102. Herbert I. Schiller. *Information and the Crisis Economy.* (Norwood, NJ: Ablex Publishing, 1984), p. 33.

ADDITIONAL READINGS

Introduction

Birkerts, Sven. *The Gutenberg Elegies: The Fate of Reading in an Electronic Age.* (Winchester, MA: Faber and Faber, Inc., 1994).

Krantz, Michael. "Cashing in on Tomorrow," *Time,* July 15, 1996, pp. 36–37, 40.

Rushikoff, Douglas. *Cyberia: Life in the Trenches of Hyperspace.* (New York: HarperCollins Publishers, 1994).

The Making of the Online World

Anthes, Gary H. and Nash, Kim S. "Internet Wizards Keep Chaos at Bay," *Computerworld,* February 1, 1996. Accessed from the Web page with URL: <http://www.computerworld.com/search/data/cw_951106-960108/960102SL52net3.html> on September 4, 1996.

Bezold, Clement; Olson, Robert; Dighe, Atul; and Mayer, Erica. "The Changing Role of Electronic Messaging: Snapshots of the Future," Institute of the Future, Electronic Messaging Association Conference, EMA '96. Accessed from the Web page with URL: <http://www.ema.org/html/ema96/vision/change.htm> on September 4, 1996.

"Blacklist of Internet Advertisers," June 26, 1996. Accessed from the Web page with URL: <http://math-www.uni-paderborn.de/~axel/BL/> on September 5, 1996.

Dibbell, Julian. "A Rape in Cyberspace or How an Evil Clown, a Haitian Trickster Spirit, Two Wizards, and a Cast of Dozens Turned a Database Into a Society," *The Village Voice,* December 21, 1993, pp. 36–42. Accessed from the Web page with URL: <gopher://jefferson.village.virginia.edu/00/related/NVR/VillageVoice> on August 9, 1996.

Garfinkel, Simon. "Spam King! Your Source for Spams Netwide!" *Wired,* 4.02, February 1996, pp. 84, 88, 90, 92.

Godfrey, David and Chang, Ernest (eds.), *The Telidon Books.* (Victoria, Canada: Press Porcepic, 1981).

Hughes, Kathleen A. "IBM-Sears Computer-Services Venture Shows Promise, But a Lot of Kinks Remain," *The Wall Street Journal,* February 8, 1989, pp. B 1, B 2.

Morris, Mary E. S. "How to Make a Fortune," Finesse Liveware, date unknown. Accessed from the Web page with URL: <http://arganet.tenagra.com/morris/realities.html> on September 5, 1996.

Sigal, Efram et al. *The Future of Videotext*. (White Plains, NY: Knowledge Industry Publications, 1983).

"The Web Maestro: An Interview with Tim Berners-Lee," *Technology Review*, July 1996. Accessed from the Web page with URL: <http://web.mit.edu/afs/athena/org/t/techreview/www/articles/july96/bernerslee.html> on July 26, 1996.

Virtual Communities

Benedikt, Michael. *Cyberspace: First Steps*. (Cambridge, MA: The MIT Press, 1991).

Bruckman, Amy. "Finding One's Own in Cyberspace," *Technology Review*, January 1996. Accessed from the Web page with URL: <http://web.mit.edu/afs/athena/org/t/techreview/www/articles/jan96/Bruckman.html> on September 9, 1996.

Frankel, Alison. "Making Law, Making Enemies," *The American Lawyer*, March 1996. Accessed from the Web page with URL: <http://www.counsel.com/spotlight/scien2.html> on August 10, 1996.

Froomkin, A. Michael. "Anonymity and its Enmities," *Journal of Online Law*, 1995. Accessed from the Web page with URL: <http://warthog.cc.wm.edu/law/publications/jol/froomkin.html on May 15, 1996.

Godwin, Mike. "Who Was That Masked Man? *Internet World*, January 1995. Accessed from the Web page with URL: <http://pubs.iworld.com/plweb-cgi/idoc.pl?27+unix+_free_user_+pubs.iworld.com..80+Publications+Publications+Internet_World+Internet_World++spamming> on January 12, 1996.

Grassmuck, Volker. " 'Don't Try to Control the Network Because It's Impossible Anyway,' interview with Johan Helsingius on Internet Remailers," *IC Magazine*, December 1994. Accessed from the Web page with URL: <http://www.race.u-tokyo.ac.jp/RACE/TGM/Texts/remailer.html> on September 7, 1996.

Grossman, Wendy M. "alt.scientology.war," *Wired*, 3.12, December 1995. Accessed from the Web page with URL: <http://www.hotwired.com/wired/3.12/features/alt.scientology.war.html> on September 6, 1996.

Heim, Michael. *The Metaphysics of Virtual Reality*. (New York: Oxford University Press, 1993).

Hertz, J. C. *Surfing on the Internet: A Nethead's Adventures On-Line*. (Boston, MA: Little, Brown and Company, 1995).

Lewis, Peter H. "Computer Jokes and Threats Ignite Debate on Anonymity," *The New York Times*, December 31, 1994, pp. 1, 29.

Rheingold, Howard. *The Virtual Community: Homesteading on the Electronic Frontier*. (Reading, MA: Addison-Wesley, 1993).

"The Rise of Electronic Communities," accessed from the *Information Week* Web site at the Web page with URL: <http://techweb.cmp.com/iwk/583/csc.htm> on July 6, 1996.

Rossney, Robert. "Metworlds," *Wired*, 4.06, June 1996. Accessed from the Web page with URL: <http://www.hotwired.com/wired/4.06/features/avatar.html> on July 3, 1996.

Turkle, Sherry. *Life on the Screen: Identity in the Age of the Internet*. (New York: Simon & Schuster, 1995).

Access

Bush, Vannevar. "As We May Think," *The Atlantic Monthly*, July 1945. Accessed from the Web page with URL: <http://www.isg.sfu.ca/~duchier/misc/vbush/> on September 11, 1995.

Dibbell, Julian. "Smart Magic," *Time Digital*, July 1, 1996, pp. TD 16–TD 21.

"Digital Libraries," special issue, *Communications of the ACM,* 38 (4), April 1995.

KickStart Initiative: Connecting America's Communities to the Information Superhighway. National Information Infrastructure Advisory Council, 1996. Accessed from the Web page with URL: <http://www.benton.org/KickStart/kick.home.html> on February 14, 1996.

Lesk, Michael. "Why Digital Libraries," Follett lecture on electronic libraries, given 19 June 1995, BBC Conference Center, London, England. Accessed from the Web page with URL: <http://community.bellcore.com:80/lesk/follett/follett.html> on September 10, 1996.

Schatz, Bruce and Chen, Hsinchun. "Building Large-Scale Digital Libraries," *IEEE Computer,* May 1996. Accessed from the Web page with URL: <http://www.computer.org:80/pubs/computer/dli/> on September 9, 1996.

Schement, Jorge Reina; Pressman, Rebecca R.; and Povich, Laurance. "Transcending Access Toward a New Universal Service," conference on Universal Service in Context: A Multidisciplinary Perspective, New York Law School, December 6, 1996. Accessed from the Web page with URL: <http://www.benton.org/Uniserv/transcend.html> on August 28, 1996.

Stix, Gary. "The Speed of Write," *Scientific American,* December 1994, pp. 106–111.

Prospects for the Internet and the Information Highway

"America in the Age of Information: A Forum," Committee on Informational Communications, National Science and Technology Council, July 1995. Accessible from the Web page with URL: <http://www.hpcc.gov/cic/forum/CIC_Cover.html>.

"Breaking the Barriers to the National Information Infrastructure," a conference report by the Council on Competitiveness, December 1994. Available at the Web page with URL: <http://nii.nist.gov/pubs/barriers/cover1.html>.

Brody, Herb. "<Internet@Crossroads.$$$>" *Technology Review,* May/June 1995, pp. 24–31.

"Information Superhighway: An Overview of Technology Challenges." US General Accounting Office, GAO/AIMD-95-23. (Gaithersburg, MD: US General Accounting Office, January 1995). Available at the Web page with URL: <http://nii.nist.gov/pubs/gao.txt>.

MacKie-Mason, Jeffrey K. and Varian, Hal R. "Some FAQs about Usage-based Pricing." Accessed from the Web page with URL: <ftp://gopher.econ.lsa.umich.edu/pub/Papers/useFAQs.html> on September 2, 1996.

Realizing the Information Future: The Internet and Beyond. Computer Science and Telecommunications Board, National Research Council. (Washington, DC: National Academy Press, 1994).

Sprout, Alison L. "Waiting to Download," *Fortune,* August 5, 1996, pp. 64–67, 70.

The Technological Reshaping of Metropolitan America. US Congress, Office of Technology Assessment, OTA-ETI-643. (Washington, DC: US Government Printing Office, September 1995). Accessible from the Web page with URL: <http://www.ota.nap.edu/pdf/data/1995/9508.PDF>.

Risk and Security

Anthes, Gary H. "Hackers Step Up Attacks," *Computerworld,* June 10, 1996, pp. 65–66.

Denning, Peter. *Computers Under Attack: Intruders, Worms, and Viruses.* (New York: ACM Press; Reading, MA: Addison-Wesley, 1990).

Hoffman, Thomas. "Risk Mounts for Mission-Critical Data," *Computerworld,* March 27, 1996, p. 82.

Molander, Roger C., Riddile, Andrew S., and Wilson, Peter A. *Strategic Information Warfare: A*

New Face of War. (Santa Monica, CA: RAND, 1996). Accessed from the Web page with URL: <http://www.rand.org/publications/MR/MR661/MR661.pdf> on May 29, 1996.

Wagner, Mitch. "AOL Unplugged," *Computerworld*, August 12, 1996, pp. 1–16.

Final Remarks

Berleur, Jacques; Clement, Andrew; Sizer, Richard; and Whitehouse, Dianne. *The Information Society: Evolving Landscapes.* (New York: Springer-Verlag, 1990).

de Sola Pool, Ithiel. *Technologies of Freedom.* (Cambridge, MA: Harvard University Press/Belknap, 1983).

Katz, Raul Luciano. *The Information Society: An International Perspective.* (New York: Praeger, 1988).

"Key Technologies for the 21st Centuries," *Scientific American* (150th Anniversary Issue), September 1995.

Miller, Stephen E. *Civilizing Cyberspace: Policy, Power, and the Information Superhighway.* (New York: ACM Press; Reading, MA: Addison-Wesley, 1996).

Mosco, Vincent and Wasko, Janet (eds.). *The Political Economy of Information.* (Madison, WI: University of Wisconsin, 1988).

—13—

ETHICS AND PROFESSIONALISM

Why be moral?	*Socrates*
Do the right thing!	*Spike Lee*
You know what's right!	*My mother*

INTRODUCTION

Throughout this book we have discussed a wide range of issues associated with the use of computers in contemporary society. Many of the examples have pointed to applications that might have detrimental effects on some segment of society. Among these examples are the following:

- The introduction of computers into the office with the immediate result that some employees, usually women, may lose their jobs or discover that their working conditions have changed for the worse: monitoring of their work patterns, reduced social interaction, fear of harmful effects from their terminals, or restricted upward mobility options.
- Computer-aided instruction causes some teachers to feel threatened because they know very little about the subject, have not been properly instructed themselves, and are concerned about the impact on their students.
- Enormous expenditures on high technology medicine—CAT, PET, and MRI scanners, for example—has limited the amounts of money available for preventative medicine, which has a significant impact among poorer people.
- Governments maintain large numbers of databases, with information of all kinds about their citizens and this information may or may not be strictly controlled. Either carelessness or maliciousness may result in the disclosure of personal information damaging to individuals or groups.

- Someone breaks into a computer system via a telephone connection and just "looks around," copies some information into his or her own computer, destroys one or more files immediately, or inserts a program, a virus or worm, to destroy files later in both this system and in others with which it communicates.
- A company purchases a new spreadsheet program and several employees make copies to take home so that they can do some of their work there. Some spouses and children discover this new program and decide it will be useful for their clubs, or other purposes, and also make copies to share with their friends.
- A credit bureau releases information to a reporter on one of the consumers in its database, which causes considerable embarrassment and possible financial loss to that consumer.
- A worker is refused a new job for which he or she is well-qualified because the prospective employer discovers, via a commercial database to which he subscribes, that he or she has been involved, in a previous job, with a group attempting to limit daily exposure to video display terminals.
- A group concerned about racist Web sites urges an Internet service provider to terminate the account of a client that it believes manages one. The provider refuses, claiming no responsibility for the content of Web pages on his system.

In all of these examples, to a lesser or greater degree, individuals or organizations have had to make decisions that affect the lives of other individuals. How these decisions are made, what the essential ingredients are, and to what principles, if any, appeals are made, form part of the subject of this chapter, namely ethics and professionalism.

In the last few years, the concern with ethical behavior has moved from academia and religious institutions into the public consciousness, propelled by a number of events, some of which have been conditioned by recent technological innovations. Probably no area has had a greater impact, nor received more publicity, than the investment industry and big business in general. The spate of insider trading and stock and bond violations have given the impression that honesty and ethical behavior are in short supply when big money is concerned. Consider the following remarks taken from those who either comment on, or who are intimately involved in, the business.

- What is this—the business news or the crime report? Turn over one stone and out crawls Boesky's tipster, investment banker Dennis Levine, dirt clinging to his $12.6 million insider-trading profits. Turn over another and there's a wriggling tangle of the same slimy creatures, from minute grubs like the Yuppie Gang to plump granddads like jailed former Deputy Defense Secretary Paul Thayer.[1]
- As the revelations of illegality and excesses in the financial community begin to be exposed, those of us who are part of this community have to face a hard truth: a cancer has been spreading in our industry . . . The cancer is called greed.[2]
- Not since the reckless 1920s has the business world seen such searing scandals. White-collar scams abound: insider trading, money laundering, greenmail. Greed combined with technology has made stealing more tempting than ever. Result: what began as the decade of the entrepreneur is becoming the age of the pin-striped outlaw.[3]
- The Justice Department is considering almost doubling the office's securities fraud staff . . . there is enough business there to support doubling the current effort.[4]

The public also had some strong feelings about insider trading, the trading of stocks based upon information not available to stockholders or the general public. When given a selection of reasons why some brokers engaged in illegal activities, even though many were legitimately making hundreds of thousand of dollars a year, those surveyed in a *Business Week*/Harris Poll taken during August 1986 answered as follows:[5] pure greed (56%), many others on Wall Street were doing it (21%), they made too much money too early in age (11%), they were criminal by nature (6%). Most were not surprised by the revelations; when asked how common insider trading was, 63% said very common or somewhat common, 21% said only occasionally, and 5% said not common at all. Finally, 80% said that the news about insider trading had not made much difference in their opinion about people who work on Wall Street. This last result indicates either a surprising degree of cynicism by the general public or a level of sophistication and realism beyond that revealed by breast-beating market analysts who seem considerably more surprised than warranted, given their supposed expertise. One of the highest profile cases of the 1980s was Michael Milken of Drexel Burnham Lambert, who practically invented junk bond trading. He was convicted, heavily fined (although he managed to hold on to about $500 million), served a jail sentence, was barred from returning to his previous activities upon release, and was on the cover of *Fortune* to celebrate his return to an active and financially advantageous lifestyle.[6] It may be difficult to mount a convincing ethical argument to aspiring business school graduates that activities such as those engaged in by Milken should be avoided.

Some ten years later, enough stories of financial misbehavior are reported so that it does not seem that much has changed, although greater amounts of money must be involved to make the story newsworthy. For example, John Jett, head government bond trader at Kidder Peabody, was fired in April 1994, after having "concocted $350 million of phony profits over a 29-month period. He claims to have been acting with the knowledge of his superiors. The scandal led Welch [General Electric's CEO] to sack the Kidder [GE-owned brokerage unit] Chairman, Michael Carpenter."[7] On the international scene, several cases of sufficient magnitude have made the headlines. Nick Leeson, the former general manager of Barings Futures in Singapore was sentenced to a six and a half year jail term, on December 12, 1995, for covering up losses of about $1.3 billion that precipitated the demise of the 233-year-old merchant bank. About the same time, a "$1.1 billion [loss was] racked up by a rogue trader at Japan's Daiwa Bank, but the largest unauthorized trading loss in history was suffered by the giant Sumitomo Corp. with worldwide assets of $50 billion." The president of Sumitomo, Tomiichi Akiyama, announced on June 13, 1996 that, "Sumitomo had just fired its former chief copper trader, Yasuo Hamanaka, for engaging in unauthorized transactions over an entire decade. Piling mistake on mistake, Hamanaka had lost a staggering $1.8 billion."[8]

Another area of growing concern for applied ethics is the impact of recent developments in reproductive medicine, including in vitro fertilization, surrogate motherhood, frozen embryos, the use of fetal tissue in the treatment of Parkinson's disease, control of genetic defects by gene insertion, and planned pregnancies to obtain compatible bone marrow for older siblings. All of these technologies, as well as those on the horizon, challenge traditional views of parenthood and raise serious ethical issues for prospective parents, physicians, and of course the judicial system. The courts have already dealt with cases in which the surrogate mother whose egg was fertilized by the husband of the couple wanting the child, changed her mind about giving up the infant. More recently, a surrogate mother, whose uterus was, in some sense, rented to carry an externally fertilized egg to term, petitioned for joint parenthood and was denied.

What if we knew more about into what kind of person a fertilized human egg would eventually develop? Which gender? What size? How high or low the IQ? Which illnesses would necessarily, or with known probability, plague this person? Gender can be determined *in utero* and it is not uncommon in some cultures for females to be aborted. Consider the following possibility of genetic testing:[9]

> New genetic tests are moving rapidly from research laboratories into doctors' offices, where they are being marketed as a way to predict people's chances of getting common diseases such as colon cancer, breast cancer and Alzheimer's disease.
>
> But instead of offering clear views of the future and strategies for altering it, genetic tests have raised the specters of DNA-based discrimination and loss of health insurance, and the prospect of people learning just enough to scare them but not enough to cure them.

Clearly there are serious ethical questions to be resolved, such as what is the responsibility of the physician to tell a patient that there is a 70% chance of certain illness developing, when this may have a devastating effect on that person's siblings or children. There is more:[10]

> The stakes are high on both sides of the issue. The fledgling genetic testing industry, which foresees soaring profits in the next few years, is pushing hard to get its tests to market, arguing that patients have the right to learn about their own genes even if the information is incomplete or inconclusive. Similarly, health insurers desperately want the right to peek at their clients' genes to help predict their medical fates—and to set their insurance rates accordingly—in part because they are afraid that people who discover they have faulty genes may try to take out large policies.

Such cases in medicine and in business, and others in government, law, and science, have heightened the concern about ethics and professional conduct and raised such questions as whether there has been a decline in ethical conduct, if so what are the contributing factors, how can the situation be improved, and what responsibility do the professional schools bear. In the wake of the insider trading scandals, several major corporations donated large amounts of money to Business Schools to endow chairs in applied ethics, presumably to raise the consciousness of future business leaders. Special commissions and panels were formed by government and professional societies to hold hearings, articulate the relevant issues, and form policies to help professionals deal with difficult problems. Many of the professions have codes of ethics, or codes of professional conduct to provide guidance and to serve as standards against which charges of inappropriate or unethical behavior can be evaluated. Even such a young discipline as computer science has developed such codes both for academic practitioners and information processing professionals. The form and purpose of these codes will be examined later in this chapter, as will some of the issues associated with professionalism.

Professionals have a responsibility to their clients, or patients, to their profession, to themselves, and to society at large. In some cases these responsibilities clash and it is often difficult to resolve the competing interests. In the public's perception, professional societies tend to protect their members rather than to censure them and bring their actions to the public's attention. On those rare occasions when professionals cannot persuade their superiors that current practices violate ethical or professional standards and feel compelled to blow the whistle, their societies are not always eager to defend their interests. Such an image has lessened the regard in which many professional societies are held.

How are professionals to acquire knowledge of what constitutes ethical behavior or proper standards of conduct? How can they recognize that they are confronted with an ethical problem and then do the right thing? Are the ethical decisions that a professional must make fundamentally different than those facing the ordinary citizen? The questions are numerous and relatively concise but the answers are long, involved, and often ambiguous. That is, there is rarely a situation in which the right thing to do is obvious.

ETHICS

> Whatsoever things I see or hear concerning the life of men,
> in my attendance on the sick or even apart therefrom, which
> ought not be noised abroad, I will keep silence thereon,
> counting such things to be as sacred secrets. (Oath of Hippocrates, 4th Century, B.C.E.)

It is obviously not possible to include an introductory course on applied ethics with a special emphasis on computer-related problems in the limited space available, but some important issues can be introduced, discussed, and pointers provided to more detailed and comprehensive treatments. In its most simplistic form, ethics deals with right and wrong. Among the earliest questions considered by philosophers were: How should one know what is good? How should one act to achieve it? The task has gotten no easier over the centuries. For the doctor, lawyer, and engineer, the ethical responsibilities of the ordinary citizen are compounded by professional responsibilities. Or are they? A brief overview of approaches to ethical behavior may be helpful.

Approaches to Ethical Behavior

> There can be no question of holding forth on ethics. I have seen people behave badly with great morality and I note every day that integrity has no need of rules.[11]

Most ethical theories are normative in character; that is, they attempt to define, by a variety of methods, what people should do in given situations. The breadth of such theories is determined by how comprehensive and principled they are. Other approaches are descriptive; that is, they describe what actually happens in the world and are supposed to be evaluated by appeal to the real world. A statement that describes a situation as true or false could be answered presumably by looking for empirical evidence. Throughout this book many examples have been given of how individuals and institutions use computers, accompanied by comments that certain instances may be problematic whereas others seem to be socially useful. In the absence of an ethical framework, all such comments may be seen as gratuitous, as emerging from an unknown author, with questionable consistency. As Deborah Johnson notes, "ethical theories provide a framework for (1) getting at the underlying rationale of moral arguments, (2) classifying and understanding various arguments, and (3) most importantly, defending a conclusion about what is right and what is wrong."[12] A brief overview of three important ethical approaches follows.

Ethical Relativism

When philosophers wish to disparage an opposing ethical theory they occasionally describe it as ethical relativism. Simply put, this doctrine claims that there are fundamental differences between the ethical principles of individuals, in the sense that even if agreement could be achieved on all the properties of the concepts being defined, there would still be disagreement on the principles. For example, in anthropology, a version of ethical relativism called cultural relativism holds that all disagreements follow cultural lines, although some may also derive from the differing constitutions and personal history of individuals. From this position it follows that there are no universal principles of what is right or wrong, that each individual's behavior must be viewed as relative to his or her own culture. One argument against this approach is that just because people behave in accordance with their culture's normative principles does not automatically mean that they should. For example, suppose at some university called Comp U. it is common practice for computer science students to attempt to gain entry into the files of all their costudents and leave behind a message indicating their success. At the end of the year, the student with the maximum number of verifiable coups is given an award. A graduate of Comp U. attends another university and upon being discovered attempting to enter a student's files, offers the explanation that at Comp U. it is accepted, and even encouraged behavior.

Utilitarianism

This term is most often associated with the English philosopher of the late eighteenth and early nineteenth century, Jeremy Bentham. The short-hand version of utilitarianism is that one must always act to achieve the greatest good for the greatest number. This definition obviously requires the definition of good, the computation of the greatest good, and the greatest number for that good, not an easy task under the best of conditions. Bentham proposed a psychological theory involving pain and pleasure, from which a definition of happiness as the excess of pleasure over pain emerged. Then maximizing happiness is equivalent to achieving the greatest good, or in Bentham's own words, the general principle of utility: "approves or disapproves of every action whatsoever, according to the tendency which it appears to have to augment or diminish the happiness of the party whose interest is in question." There are problems with the definition of happiness, as well as the calculus to compute overall good, but nevertheless the political consequences of the movement inspired by utilitarianism were positive in bringing about legislative reforms in England. The theory also places public good over private good without justifying this preference.

Deontological Theories

In utilitarianism, it is the consequence of acts, not the acts themselves that are right or wrong. Deontologists, however, take the act itself to be prime and to carry moral weight. Thus, although under a utilitarian approach the happiness of some people may have to be sacrificed to achieve a greater good, for deontologists acts of this sort, as well as others, will have to be rejected. Deontological theories derive in part from the philosophy of Immanuel Kant (1724–1804), whose ethical theory is the most important rival of utilitarianism. His theory is built on three principles: the examination of the facts of moral experience, the analysis of the logic of ethical judgment, and the formulation of the metaphysical principles presupposed by ethical judgments, as distinct from scientific generalizations.[13] What has come to be thought of as most lasting about Kant's theory are his moral or categorical imperatives. A moral, or genuinely categorical imperative, is a rule that commands a type of action independently of any desired end, including happiness. Kant's greatest contribution is the criterion of universality, "that is, the logical possibility of requiring universal obedience to a rule of action (logical for 'strict' duties and psychological for 'meritorious' duties). It expresses more precisely and unambiguously the 'golden rule' to be found in all the great religions . . ."[14] Johnson expresses it as "Never treat another human being merely as a means but always as an end in himself or herself."[15]

The obvious objection to Kant is that surely no one would agree that any one rule should always be followed, without exception. Sissela Bok, in discussing Kant's arguments in support of the maxim "Do what is right though the world should perish," notes that in Kant's time no one took such a maxim literally because no action of any individual could bring the end of the world. However, now such an act is a real possibility and certainly sheds a new light on the absolutist position.[16] Given an order to fire his nuclear missiles, should a submarine commander have second thoughts if he believes that the order is ill-advised under current circumstances? "If we accept the need for exceptions to moral principles in emergency conditions, it becomes necessary to take every precaution to avoid the dangers that Kant rightly stressed—of self-delusion, misunderstanding, lack of moral concern, shortsightedness, and ignorance on the part of government leaders and advisors."[17]

PROFESSIONALISM

The emergence of professionalism—at first through associations, or guilds, of individuals in the clergy, law, and medicine in eleventh century Europe—has bestowed special privileges and special duties on their members. In North America, the movement towards professionalism seems to be a necessary step to legitimize practitioners of a given skill. Along with doctors, lawyers, dentists, engineers, and others, computer professionals have seen the need to establish standards for membership in their community.

The major distinguishing (and controversial) feature of professionalism is the self-regulatory function of professional societies or organizations. Such societies define a separate group with membership determined by standards they set, and expulsion solely determined by them as well. By maintaining high standards, societies hope to assure the public that all practitioners can be relied upon to serve the public responsibly and competently. For the most part the public is well served, and in fact places considerable confidence in most of its professionals—especially doctors, dentists, teachers, and engineers. However, there is some sense that the major functions of professional societies include the maintenance of high income levels and the protection of members accused of improper actions. Societies attempt to proclaim their responsibility by disciplining wayward members, however infrequently, and by publicizing their stringent membership requirements. However, keep in mind that the professional's allegiance is frequently divided: "Now the engineer's professional obligation to protect the well-being of the community, as well as to shun participation in deceptions, conflicts with another obligation: to serve as a faithful agent of his clients."[18] Another step taken in recognition of having achieved a professional status is to design a code of ethics or standard of conduct.

The philosopher, James Moor, argues for computer ethics as a special branch of applied ethics. He proposes the following definition: "*Computer ethics* is the analysis of the nature and social impact of computer technology and the corresponding formulation and justification of policies for the ethical use of such technology."[19] The term computer technology is meant to be quite comprehensive and includes hardware, software, and communication networks. This definition clearly focuses on the study and analysis of social impact, not overtly on responsibility and ethical behavior, although in his immediately subsequent discussion Moor does include behavior: "A central task of computer ethics is to determine what we should do in such cases, i.e., to formulate policies to guide our actions." One question that immediately comes to mind concerns the actual need for a special branch of ethics related to computers. Why not automobile ethics, or camera ethics, or telephone ethics? Each of these technologies certainly raises a variety of social concerns and particular ethical problems, but those associated with the computer seem to have a special and far-reaching quality.

Those who are involved in developing the discipline of computer ethics are really attempting to respond to the concerns, within and without the field, about a class of ethical problems that seem to be tightly linked to computers, large and small, as well as computer networks, such as the Internet. Also of prime importance is the process of diffusing the accepted results into the educational system to inform both teachers and students about their power and responsibility.

Professional Codes of Ethics

> As an ACM computing professional I will . . . Give comprehensive and thorough evaluations of computer systems and their impacts, including analysis of possible risks.[20]

Probably the best known and oldest code governing professional behavior is the Hippocratic oath, for the medical profession, attributed to the Greek physician Hippocrates (460?–370? B.C.) For the computing profession, scarcely 50 years old, a code of ethics may be somewhat premature, as relevant issues are still emerging. Nevertheless, many concerns specifically related to computers exist—such as the responsibility for gathering, verifying, storing, protecting, and distributing information—that seem to argue for the establishment of a code of ethics. Some applications of computers are sufficiently controversial that an ethics code seems to have intrinsic merit. Motivated by engineering concerns, Stephen Unger has suggested a number of features of such a code, as follows:[21]

- a recognition of the responsibilities of individuals.
- an attempt to create a general recognition and acceptance of ethical behavior.
- the establishment of readily accessible guidelines.
- justification for actions taken in opposition to directives by superiors.
- useful in lawsuits that may follow certain actions.
- a statement to the public at large that the profession is concerned about the actions of its members.

A major problem in enacting codes is how to restrict them to matters of professional concern without being influenced by political, economic, or religious opinions. For example, the US Army Corps of Engineers used computer models to formulate economic policy with respect to the construction of large dam projects. The Department of Defense runs computer war simulations as a fundamental part of its planning requirements. Computer Professionals for Social Responsibility (CPSR) has focused on the role of computers and automated decision-making by the military in determining a rapid response to a possible attack by strategic missiles. CPSR has acted to make their colleagues aware of how their research might be used, to serve as a pressure group to influence public opinion, and to lobby the government. Our response to working on these projects certainly depends on our political and social beliefs. Thus drafting a code of ethics requires extreme care, treading a line between professional responsibility and personal belief among many issues that must be considered. More on this topic later.

Mark Frankel identifies three types of codes of ethics: aspirational, a statement of lofty principles towards which members should aspire; educational, a pedagogical approach to explanation and guidance; and regulatory, with enforceable rules to govern behavior and determine compliance.[22] He also provides a list of eight functions that codes of professional ethics may perform:[23]

1. Enabling document. So that professionals may make informed choices.
2. Source of public evaluation. So that the public knows what to expect of professionals.
3. Professional socialization. To reinforce solidarity and collective purpose.
4. Enhance profession's reputation and public trust.
5. Preserve entrenched professional biases. It may be difficult to introduce innovations.
6. Deterrent to unethical behavior. Code may provide sanctions and monitoring provisions.
7. Support system. Against debatable claims by clients or intrusions by government.
8. Adjudication. To deal with disputes among members or between members and others.

Codes of Ethics for Computer Professionals

Codes of ethics and standards for professional conduct have been adopted by the following major organizations that represent computer professionals.

Association for Computing Professionals (ACM). The oldest association for computer professionals, with considerable representation among academics, has a new Code of Ethics and Professional Conduct for computer scientists that was adopted by the ACM Council on October 16, 1992.

Institute for Electrical and Electronic Engineers (IEEE). Although it is primarily an organization for engineers, the proportion of the membership involved with computers has increased dramatically in recent years. The IEEE Board of Directors endorsed a simplified Code of Ethics that includes coverage for computer engineers, in August 1990, which took effect on January 1, 1991. The new Code is shorter, clearer, and more attuned to a worldwide membership, according to a past president of the IEEE, Emerson Pugh, who initiated the revision.

Data Processing Managers Association (DPMA). The DPMA has adopted a Code of Ethics and Standard of Conduct for the managers of computer systems and projects.

Institute for Certification of Computer Professionals (ICCP). The ICCP offers a voluntary certification program for computer professionals and has a Code of Ethics and Codes of Conduct and Good Practice for certified computer professionals.

Canadian Information Processing Society (CIPS). CIPS adopted a brief Code of Ethics in 1975 and a more comprehensive version in 1984.

Other organizations related to information processing, which either have codes or are in the process of adopting or revising them include International Federation for Information Processing (IFIP), American Society for Information Science (ASIS), and Information Systems Security Association (ISSA).

The ACM code is given in its entirety in Figure 13.1 (but without the associated guidelines), the IEEE Code of Ethics in Figure 13.2, the DPMA Code of Ethics in Figure 13.3, and the ICCP Code of Ethics in Figure 13.4. Not included here is the forward to the DPMA code, the associated standards of conduct and the extensive standards of conduct enforcement procedures, or the ICCP codes of conduct and good practice. Martin and Martin identify a number of common themes in these codes,[24] of which the first six appear in all four codes: personal integrity/claim of competence; responsibility to employer/client; responsibility to profession; confidentiality of information/privacy; public safety, health and welfare; increase public knowledge about technology. These four appear in at least two codes: personal accountability for work; conflict of interest; dignity/worth of people; participation in professional societies.

A cautionary note about all these codes is that they lack procedures to deal with emerging issues resulting from technological advances. They vary in their success in integrating ethical behavior into daily activities and this must be an important concern, as computers continue to play a growing role in our lives. Other critics question the effectiveness of ethical codes and even the reasons for adopting them. Among the most prominent is Samuel Florman, engineer and author of the best-selling book, *Blaming Technology*. His opinion is expressed forcefully as follows:[25]

Preamble. Commitment to ethical professional conduct is expected of every member (voting members, associate members, and student members) of the Association for Computing Machinery (ACM).

This Code, consisting of 24 imperatives formulated as statements of personal responsibility, identifies the elements of such a commitment. It contains many, but not all, issues professionals are likely to face. Section 1 outlines fundamental ethical considerations, while Section 2 addresses additional, more specific considerations of professional conduct. Statements in Section 3 pertain more specifically to individuals who have a leadership role, whether in the workplace or in a volunteer capacity such as with organizations like ACM. Principles involving compliance with this Code are given in Section 4.

The Code shall be supplemented by a set of Guidelines, which provide explanation to assist members in dealing with the various issues contained in the Code. It is expected that the Guidelines will be changed more frequently than the Code.

The Code and its supplemented Guidelines are intended to serve as a basis for ethical decision making in the conduct of professional work. Secondarily, they may serve as a basis for judging the merit of a formal complaint pertaining to violation of professional ethical standards.

It should be noted that although computing is not mentioned in the imperatives of section 1.0, the Code is concerned with how these fundamental imperatives apply to one's conduct as a computing professional. These imperatives are expressed in a general form to emphasize that ethical principles which apply to computer ethics are derived from more general ethical principles.

It is understood that some words and phrases in a code of ethics are subject to varying interpretations, and that any ethical principle may conflict with other ethical principles in specific situations. Questions related to ethical conflicts can best be answered by thoughtful consideration of fundamental principles, rather than reliance on detailed regulations.

1. GENERAL MORAL IMPERATIVES.

As an ACM member I will . . .

1.1 Contribute to society and human well-being.
1.2 Avoid harm to others.
1.3 Be honest and trustworthy.
1.4 Be fair and take action not to discriminate.
1.5 Honor property rights including copyrights and patents.
1.6 Give proper credit for intellectual property
1.7 Respect the privacy of others.
1.8 Honor confidentiality.

2. MORE SPECIFIC PROFESSIONAL RESPONSIBILITIES.

As an ACM computing professional I will . . .

2.1 Strive to achieve the highest quality, effectiveness and dignity in both the process and products of professional work.
2.2 Acquire and maintain professional competence.
2.3 Know and respect existing laws pertaining to professional work
2.4 Accept and provide appropriate professional review.
2.5 Give comprehensive and thorough evaluations of computer systems and their impacts, including analysis of possible risks.
2.6 Honor contracts, agreements, and assigned responsibilities.
2.7 Improve public understanding of computing and its consequences
2.8 Access computing and communication resources only when authorized to do so.

FIGURE 13.1 ACM Code of Ethics and Professional Conduct.*

3. ORGANIZATIONAL LEADERSHIP
IMPERATIVES.

As an ACM member and an organizational leader, I will . . .

3.1   Articulate social responsibilities of members of an organizational unit and encourage full acceptance of those responsibilities.

3.2   Manage personnel and resources to design and build information systems that enhance the quality of working life.

3.3   Acknowledge and support proper and authorized uses of an organization's computing and communication resources.

3.4   Ensure that users and those who will be affected by a system have their needs clearly articulated during the assessment and design of requirements; later the system must be validated to meet requirements.

3.5   Articulate and support policies that protect the dignity of users and others affected by a computing system.

3.6   Create opportunities for members of the organization to learn the principles and limitations of computer systems.

4. COMPLIANCE WITH THE CODE.

As an ACM member, I will . . .

4.1   Uphold and promote the principles of this Code.

4.2   Treat violations of this code as inconsistent with membership in the ACM.

*Bylaw 17 of the Constitution of the Association for Computing Machinery. © Association for Computing Machinery. Reprinted by permission.

FIGURE 13.1   *Continued*

Engineers must be honorable and competent. Agreed. But engineering ethics cannot solve technical problems or resolve political conflicts. It cannot determine which tradeoffs should be made between safety or economy or between growth and environmental protection. It cannot provide consistent guidelines for individuals who are troubled by conflicting loyalties. In sum, engineering ethics cannot cover up differences of opinion that are deep and heartfelt . . . Engineers owe honesty and competence to society. The rest of engineering ethics is a matter of taste—which is to say, political choice.

Whistleblowing

One response to a situation involving an ethical dilemma may be the need to appeal to the public at large, because all avenues available internally seem to be blocked and there is no prospect that any change will be forthcoming. It is not an action taken lightly, for a great deal is at risk—personal reputation, career, professional status. Why do some people blow the whistle? Perhaps the situation they find themselves in is so intolerable, so offensive to their ethical standards that they cannot remain silent, they cannot walk away, they must inform the world:[26]

"Whistle-blower" is a recent label for those who . . . make revelations meant to call attention to negligence, abuses, or dangers that threaten the public interest. They sound an alarm based on their experience or inside knowledge, often from within the very organization in which they work. . . . Most know that their alarms pose a threat to anyone who benefits from the ongoing practice and that their own careers and livelihood may be at risk.

We the members of the IEEE, in recognition of the importance of our technologies in affecting the quality of life throughout the world, and in accepting a personal obligation to our profession, its members and the communities we serve, do hereby commit ourselves to the highest ethical and professional conduct and agree:

1. to accept the responsibility in making engineering decisions consistent with the safety, health, and welfare of the public, and to disclose promptly factors that might endanger the public or the environment;

2. to avoid real or perceived conflicts of interest whenever possible, and to disclose them to affected parties when they do exist;

3. to be honest and realistic in stating claims or estimates based on available data;

4. to reject bribery in all its forms;

5. to improve the understanding of technology, its appropriate application, and potential consequences;

6. to maintain and improve our technical competence and to undertake technological tasks for others only if qualified by training or experience, or after full disclosure of pertinent limitations;

7. to seek, accept, and offer honest criticism of technical work, to acknowledge and correct errors, and to credit properly the contribution of others;

8. to treat fairly all persons regardless of such factors as race, religion, gender, disability, age, or national origin;

9. to avoid injuring others, their property, reputation, or employment by false or malicious action;

10. to assist colleagues in their professional development and to support them in following this code of ethics.

*The Institute, A News Supplement to IEEE Spectrum, October 1990, p. 2.

© 1990 IEEE. Reprinted with permission, from The Institute of Electrical and Electronics Engineers.

FIGURE 13.2 IEEE Code of Ethics.*

As Sissela Bok further notes, three factors make whistle blowing a particularly unsettling act for everyone concerned:[27]

Dissent. By whistleblowing private dissent becomes public

Breach of Loyalty. The whistleblower acts against his or her own associates, or team. What about implicit or explicit oaths of loyalty and the sense of betrayal that their violation arouses?

Accusation. It is the charge of impropriety itself that most upsets people. Individuals or groups are singled out as having behaved badly, as having violated the public trust, as having turned their back on responsible behavior.

In spite of the terrible costs involved, whistleblowing is not a rare event. It happens in government bureaucracies, in large companies, and in other institutions. Motives may be po-

I acknowledge:

That I have an obligation to management, therefore, I shall promote the understanding of information processing methods and procedures to management using every resource at my command.

That I have an obligation to my fellow members, therefore, I shall uphold the high ideals of DPMA as outlined in its International Bylaws. Further, I shall cooperate with my fellow members and shall treat them with honesty and respect at all times.

That I have an obligation to society and will participate to the best of my ability in the dissemination of knowledge pertaining to the general development and understanding of information processing. Further, I shall not use knowledge of a confidential nature to further my personal interest, nor shall I violate the privacy and confidentiality of information entrusted to me or to which I may gain access.

That I have an obligation to my employer whose trust I hold, therefore, I shall endeavor to discharge this obligation to the best of my ability, to guard my employer's interests, and to advise him or her wisely and honesty.

That I have an obligation to my country, therefore, in my personal, business, and social contacts, I shall uphold my nation and shall honor the chosen way of life of my fellow citizens.

I accept these obligations as a personal responsibility and as a member of this association. I shall actively discharge these obligations and I dedicate myself to that end.

Data Management, October 1981, p. 58. © 1981 Data Processing Management Association. All Rights Reserved.

FIGURE 13.3 DPMA Code of Ethics.*

litical—to expose hidden government policy as in the case of Daniel Ellsberg and the Pentagon Papers—or because of a perceived violation of accepted professional standards. A 1993 report by the US General Accounting Office (GAO) noted that "A survey of federal workers who have sought whistleblower reprisal protection from the Office of Special Counsel (OSC) found that the vast majority were frustrated with the complaint process and did not believe that investigators gathered all of the information needed to examine their claims."[28] GAO called for an education program for federal workers to improve their awareness of "their right to protection from whistleblower reprisals." The very existence of the government's whistleblowing program is encouraging but somewhat paradoxical given that the government is setting rules for its employees to inform against it and be protected as well.

If any institution demands complete loyalty in the chain of command, it is the military, and breaches of this central and hallowed injunction are neither taken lightly nor treated lightly when discovered. Hence, the 1988 Military Whistleblower Protection Act, if seriously intended to protect those with sufficient courage to reveal serious problems, must also prove to be effective in its execution. Not surprisingly, all was not smooth and the GAO was called in to review the quality of protection provided by the Act.[29] One of the interesting features of the Act is that only those whistleblowers who complain to the Department of Defense's Inspector General fall under its protection. Of particular interest to this study is that allegations existed that some whistleblowers had been subject to mental

Certified computer professionals, consistent with their obligation to the public at large, should promote the understanding of data processing methods and procedures using every resource at their command.

Certified computer professionals have an obligation to their profession to uphold the high ideals and the level of personal knowledge as evidenced by the Certificate held. They should also encourage the dissemination of knowledge pertaining to the development of the computer profession.

Certified computer professionals have an obligation to serve the interests of their employers and clients loyally, diligently and honestly.

Certified computer professionals must not engage in any conduct or commit any act which is discreditable to the reputation or integrity of the data processing profession.

Certified computer professionals must not imply that the Certificates which they hold are their sole claim to professional competence.

*Your Guide to Certification as a Computer Professional, Institute for Certification of Computer Professionals, © 1973 ICCP.

FIGURE 13.4 ICCP Code of Ethics.*

health evaluations. Very few cases were available for investigation but the GAO concluded that reprisals for whistleblowing did occur. The use of mental health examinations is interesting because in the heyday of the Soviet Union, dissenters were frequently placed in mental institutions to undergo evaluations. Queries from the West were met with responses that no, they were not being punished for their political beliefs, but were merely undergoing standard psychiatric evaluations that required considerable time and effort. These examples reinforce the widely held belief that, in the case of whistleblowing, doing the right thing can be dangerous.

Some Thoughts on Ethical Codes for Computer Professionals

The previous discussion suggests a number of features that ethical codes for professionals should contain, with special emphasis on computer-related issues. The following list is illustrative rather than exhaustive but it does indicate a variety of concerns that an effective code must address.

Readability, elegance, and generality. The code should be easily understood or it will not be useful. Elegance is a bonus but generality is a necessity; otherwise, the code will be extremely lengthy and unwieldy. In this regard, the IEEE Code is a model. The ACM code, however, is considerably longer especially if the associated guidelines are included, but the explanatory sections (not included in Figure 13.1) are very helpful in understanding the intentions of the various imperatives and responsibilities.

"Living" code. It must be the original intention of the society that the code is written to be used and therefore its use must be regularly monitored and it must be regularly updated.

Responsibility of the society for the ethical behavior of its members. Enunciating a code is just a first step. The society must respond to questions and problems raised by its members, quickly and effectively. It must use its good offices with employers and act as an ombudsman for its members.

Legal liability of the society for the actions of its members and for the enforcement of its code. Some important issues must be settled with respect to what, if any, legal liability the society has for the actions of its members.

Responsibility of the society to educate, train, and inform its members of their rights and responsibilities. The society must provide regular training and educational sessions to upgrade the professional qualifications of its members, to assure that they meet minimal standards of performance, and to guarantee that they are fully aware of their rights and responsibilities under the Code of Ethics.

Problems specific to computer professionals must be addressed. A number of issues are of special interest to computer professionals, and should be addressed at the risk of violating the injunctions about elegance and generality. Among these are ethical behavior with respect to intellectual property (when software should be copied), privacy (awareness of issues associated with databases, their development, maintenance and use, electronic mail, and electronic monitoring), computer crime (viruses, worms, and hackers), and computer risks (system security and breakdowns).

Political Actions by Professional Societies

Professional societies are supposed to represent the best interests of their members. Of course, what is best usually is determined by the executive committee of the organization and may involve appeals to the general public to explain recent actions by members or to drum up support for actions to be taken. The government may be petitioned to implement certain procedures and regulations that affect the working lives of the professionals or it may be lobbied with respect to procedures and regulations that affect society at large and about which the professional society has some expertise. This latter situation brings to the fore a pivotal question about the role of professional societies: What responsibility, if any, do they have in engaging in political activity that is not directly related to the professional lives of their members? Of course some organizations have been formed by professionals to carry out political lobbying and public education and obviously people join because they believe in these activities. The question is directed only at traditional professional societies. A few examples might help in answering it.

In March 1991, the ACM issued a statement on privacy urging its members to observe the privacy provisions of its Code of Professional Conduct, affirming its support for the Code of Fair Information Practices, and supporting "the establishment of a proactive governmental privacy protection mechanism in those countries that do not currently have such mechanisms, including the United States, that would ensure individual privacy safeguards."[30] Four years later, the presidents of five leading US computer organizations, American Association for Artificial Intelligence, ACM, Computer Professionals for Social

Responsibility, IEEE Computer Society, and Society for Industrial and Applied Mathematics, wrote a letter to Senator James Exon expressing their concern about the proposed Communications Decency Act. In part they noted "this legislation would impose unreasonable technical and financial burdens on the increasing number of institutions, large and small, that rely on the Internet for communication. We believe that these burdens will significantly harm the technological and communications opportunities now emerging from the Internet."[31] Of course, a year later this Act, as part of the Telecommunications Act of 1996, was enacted.

That the lobbying efforts failed is not the issue. What is important is that professional societies engaged in vigorous lobbying efforts to influence the shape of legislation that would affect all Americans. Presumably individual members of these societies had differing opinions about the merits of the Communications Decency Act as well as the actions of their societies. But many members must have felt that their professional society was acting in accordance with its code of professional conduct, or its equivalent, and were encouraged to see what many had felt to be abstract principles being put into practice. Such actions could not help but reinforce a sense of professional responsibility in the minds of the members of these societies and further encourage them to act responsibly in their own individual professional lives. Note that the ACM and other societies also took actions with respect to the government's proposals on copyright (Information Infrastructure Copyright Act, H.R. 2441) and encryption, by supporting the legislation introduced by Senator Conrad Burns (Encrypted Communications Privacy Act) against the Clinton administration's proposals.[32]

PEDAGOGY AND ETHICS

> A man's ethical behavior should be based effectually on sympathy, education, and social ties; no religious basis is necessary. Man would indeed be in a poor way if he had to be restrained by fear of punishment and hope of reward after death. (Albert Einstein [1879–1955])[33]

What is the expected outcome of a program to instruct soon-to-be computer professionals in ethics and professionalism? To answer this question, we must acknowledge that computer scientists (as do other professionals) face situations that require coming to terms with conflicting goals that may seem equally worthwhile. It is impossible to make an informed decision without first understanding, as well as we practically can, the issues involved, their interrelationships, and their impacts, no matter how convoluted these may be. This section may therefore serve as an introductory "Guide to the Perplexed,"[34] by suggesting some ways in which difficult decisions can be made, given the prior requirement, of course, that the existence of one or more problems is perceived and acknowledged. Assuming responsibility for your actions is at the heart of the matter and clearly beyond the scope of pedagogy. Exploration, identification, discussion, analysis, and appeal to social, legal, historical, philosophical, and yes, religious principles, are all part of the process of growing and nurturing ethical antennae, but the translation to action depends ultimately on personal choice, and that is as it should be.

Recent proposals for teaching applied ethics to computer science and information systems students will be presented in the context of the kinds of issues that arise in computing environments such as the office, the school, and the Internet. A series of representative case studies will be introduced and analyzed as part of the process of developing abilities to recognize situations that do require ethical analysis and how to proceed in that endeavor. Two important concerns must be kept in mind: The discussion is not to be viewed as a handbook and it is not and cannot be exhaustive. If you are left feeling uncomfortable it should not be surprising. Knowing when to do the right thing is difficult and doing it is even more difficult.

Teaching Ethical Behavior in Computing

Project ImpactCS

An attempt to create a meaningful ethical component in the computer science curriculum, Project ImpactCS was undertaken under the leadership of C. Dianne Martin (George Washington University) and Chuck Huff (St. Olaf's College) and involved a steering committee of prominent computer scientists and applied ethicists, in 1994. Since then it has produced a series of reports that include a particular strategy in presenting the social issues that arise in computer projects and implementations and the ethical and social principles and skills necessary to deal with them. The issues that motivate the development of the ethics curriculum are similar to those discussed previously. For example, consider the following questions:[35]

- Who is accountable when bugs in medical software result in patient deaths?
- Is being an imposter on a bulletin board system, creating violations of trust mitigated by the fact that some positive result is also achieved?
- When a multimillion-dollar software project is behind schedule, should technical staffers who doubt it can be rescheduled and completed as promised inform the client organization?
- Should there be limits to how managers and owners of private firms examine the movements of their employees?
- Are computer scientists morally responsible for anticipating and publicizing the problems that could result from the systems they designed?

A general framework for organizing the relationship between topics in ethical analysis and levels of social analysis can be thought of as a chart, in which the columns are divided into classes, namely Responsibility (individual and professional) and Ethical Issues (quality of life, use of power, risks and reliability, property rights, privacy, equity and access, and honesty and deception), and the rows are categorized as individuals, communities and groups, organizations, cultures, institutional sectors, nations, and global. Thus the entire framework could be represented as a series of charts, each one headed by a particular technology, such as medical, computer-aided manufacturing, or electronic communications, with individual relevant intersections identified where appropriate.[36] Identifying which levels of social analysis are relevant to which topics of ethical analysis for a given computer-related technology is an important exercise in understanding the complexities of social impact and ethical responsibility. Obviously, there is much more, but for the present it is useful to list the important ethical and social principles and skills that the Steering Committee highlighted:[37]

Ethical Principles
- Ethical claims can be discussed rationally.
- Ethical claims must be defended with reason.
- Ethical choices cannot be avoided.
- Some easy ethical approaches are questionable.

Ethical Skills
- Arguing from example, analogy, and counter-example.
- Identifying ethical principles and stakeholders in concrete situations.
- Identifying and evaluating alternative courses of action.
- Applying ethical codes to concrete situations.

Social Principles
- Social context influences the design and use of technology.
- Power relations are central to all social interactions.
- Technology embodies value decisions made by designers.
- Empirical data is crucial to the design process.

Social Skills
- Identifying and interpreting the social context of a particular implementation.
- Identifying assumptions and values embedded in a particular design.
- Evaluating, by use of empirical data, a particular implementation of a technology.

Learning about ethics and professional codes and standards provides a rich library of acknowledged principles that can subsequently be employed in these tasks. As noted, the professional lives of many computer scientists will not be empty of ethical challenges and it is hoped that by providing a deep and integrated program of instruction they will be equipped to undertake a useful examination of these challenges and discover approaches to confront them.

Teaching Business Ethics

Business Schools have been involved in the attempt to make ethics a meaningful part of the curriculum for quite a while, with mixed empirical results. Consider the problem facing instructors of ethics courses in business schools as described by the authors of a recent paper:[38]

> For long-term survival, any economic system requires a moral component. This assumption leads to the call for teaching ethics courses in our business schools . . . However, because America's free-enterprise economic ideology assumes no vocabulary of ethics, students come to our classes without categories for ethical reasoning in the context of business. Given the importance of teaching business ethics, it is incumbent on business school professors to devise effective pedagogical methods for stimulating the moral imagination of their students who enter business ethics courses without a vocabulary permitting them to discuss business decisions and dilemmas in moral terms.

At the risk of quibbling about the assumptions underlying this enterprise, we question the first sentence of this quotation and the necessary inference that "teaching business ethics is important." Some would argue that the only moral imperative of business is to succeed, that is, to be profitable, and from this, good things will follow. To be fair, the authors note later in the paper that "Because the amoral theory of business holds sway today, business students enter our courses without a vocabulary of ethics for economic relations." One version of this "amoral theory" is that obedience to the law is all that is required of a business; another is that since no universal ethical theory exists, individuals can decide for themselves what is ethical or can assume that narrow selfish interests are sufficient. The authors believe that more is necessary and propose ways in which ethics and morality, admittedly used interchangeably, can be made significant and useful in the lives of business students. Their use of the term vocabulary is somewhat confusing as they intend it to be much more inclusive than its usual interpretation as a collection of words and phrases.

They employ the method of the cautionary tale or the morality play as found in literary works from all historical periods. This method assumes that a carefully constructed exposure to important literary works can influence ethical behavior in the lives of business professionals. Examples presented in this paper are the television play and later the 1957 movie, "Twelve Angry Men," the novel "The Great Gatsby" by F. Scott Fitzgerald, the play by Friedrich Durenmatt, "The Visit," and the classical Greek play, "The Clouds" by Aristophanes. Many more example are presented and each literary work is discussed in terms of the lessons that it teaches with respect to ethical dilemmas and their solutions. The authors are quite realistic in terms of their aims and expectations:[39]

> Of course, exposure to this vocabulary of ethics—including the minimum conception of morality, the barriers to morality, and the three dominant moral theories of our day—does not ensure that students will think or behave ethically. A grasp of this vocabulary, however, does provide students: the opportunity to develop an ethical perspective they can apply to business life; the ability to recognize an ethical business dilemma when they are confronted with one; the capability of discerning ethical (or unethical) styles of others within and between organizations; an awareness when consciously choosing to behave ethically or unethically in a business situation; a conceptual line of defense against immoral business decisions made unwittingly; and finally, an understanding that the amoral paradigm, which assumes economic relations to be a morally neutral part of social life, provides a mental and emotional cover for immoral decision making.

This an admirable statement; all those involved in the enterprise to teach and understand ethical responsibility would be well advised to adopt it. Of course, the real measure of success cannot be effectively determined, no matter how high the grades that are achieved. So the basic article of faith is that such a course makes a difference in the world, a difference that improves rather than harms the lives of people and their environment.

Case Studies

Another method of teaching professional ethical behavior, after an introduction to ethical principles, is to explore a variety of supposed real-life situations, or scenarios, to isolate potential ethical dilemmas, then to determine various approaches to deal with them, and finally to select the most appropriate, if possible. If enough different situations are studied in a principled fashion, it is held, students will acquire skills to identify ethical problems, and tools to deal with them. There are obviously no guarantees that a case-based approach will be successful but then it is virtually impossible to measure success. The general public, as shown previously, has no illusions about the ethical standards of Wall Street traders. As calls for improvements in the education of future business leaders have grown in volume, the usual response has been to establish applied ethics courses, a bonanza for philosophy professors. Will they result in a decrease in business crimes, in a reduction in sudden plant closures, in a reduction in privacy violations of employees, in a practical recognition of the worth of employees, in the termination of bribes to foreign governments, in a limitation on significant cost overruns on government contracts, in a reduction in special deals with government agencies, and so on?

In any case, the examination of a few scenarios in engineering and information processing will at the very least highlight some of the ethical problems likely to confront practicing computer professionals.

Case 1[40]

> In an effort to keep track of your classmates after graduation, you have developed a database with everyone's name, home address and phone number, job title, work address, work phone number, and FAX number. You have printed out a directory which was mailed to everyone listed. In addition to the normal records it keeps, the alumni office also has a copy of this database.
>
> Recently, the alumni office was purchased by a direct marketing firm, which wishes to purchase this database and use it for direct mail campaigns. These campaigns would be for high quality organizations whose products and services are targeted at recent graduates of prestigious universities. For example, people in the directory could receive "two-for-one" coupons for restaurants, discounts on cruises, and other vacation packages.
>
> Should your university sell the database to the direct marketing firm? What responsibility do you have about the uses to which your database is put?

The various agents in this story are you, your classmates, the alumni office, and the university. The direct marketing firm's activities are business as usual and do not fall within the ethical concerns of interest. Your classmates are passive agents and part of the problem is to protect their interests, which include the control of the circulation of personal information, however worthy the supposed benefits. It would be helpful to know how the alumni office acquired the database and under what terms. The people directly affected by your actions should have an opportunity to be consulted *before* that action takes place. In fact it is an accepted standard of collecting personal information for databases that information collected for one purpose not be used for another. (Actually this applies for federal government databases that are covered by the 1974 Privacy Act and not private databases that are more or less unregulated; nevertheless, this principle is rooted in common sense and furthermore can easily be subsumed under Kant's categorical imperative.) None of the agents who hold this database, in trust, have a right to sell it to the direct marketing firm without obtaining prior permission from each individual who may choose to have his or her name removed. You collected the information and built the database; you somehow permitted the alumni office to obtain a copy; you have a special responsibility to your classmates not to permit the sale of the database. The university must have general, well-publicized guidelines on how it treats the various databases that it controls. Students, faculty, and staff should be given the opportunity to request that their names not be included in any commercial arrangements made between the university and interested companies.

Case 2[41]

A computer programmer worked for a business enterprise that was highly dependent on its own computer system. He was the sole author of a computer program he used as an aid in his own programming work. Nobody else used the program, and his manager was only nominally aware of its existence. He had written it and debugged it on a weekend, but had used his employer's materials, facilities, and computer services.

The programmer terminated his employment, giving due notice, and with no malice on his or his manager's part. He immediately went to work for a competitor of his former employer.

Without his former employer's permission, he took the only copy of the program with him to his new employer and used it in his work. He did not share it with any others. The new employer was not aware of the program or its use, but it enhanced the programmer's performance.

This scenario was presented to a panel, who were asked the following questions: Is an ethics issue involved? Was the programmer's action unethical or not unethical? What general principles apply? Perhaps you might want to think about this scenario before continuing.

The panel was split, with 13 considering his action unethical, 11 not unethical, and 3 finding no ethics issue. In the comments of the participants the following issues were raised. It was generally agreed that the first employer acquired an interest in the program because it was developed using his resources. The program's value depended solely on its use by the programmer. The analogy of a workman's tools was used to justify the program moving with the programmer even though there is some question about whether the programmer owns the program in the same way the workman owns the tools he or she has purchased. The fact that the program was developed on personal time convinced some that the programmer's act was not unethical, but perhaps there was fault in making unauthorized use of company resources. Although the program enhanced the programmer's skills, for the benefit of the company, some panelists did not feel that the programmer was morally required to turn the program over to the company so that other programmers could benefit from its use. Most agreed with the following two statements: The property of one company, a program, was taken and used to benefit a competitor. It is not the case that "as long as the programmer uses his program for his own work and does not sell it, there is nothing wrong with his action."

The general principles identified by the panel are the following:[42]

Items developed with company resources belong, at least partly, to the company.
A programmer possesses the tools of his trade.
Current use of a product owned in whole or in part by one's employer should not be the sole criterion for determining who has a right to it.

The foregoing discussion has a certain self-serving flavor, as if computer professionals want to ensure that their creative activities are protected from their employers if not explicitly developed as part of the job. Suppose the programmer, realizing how helpful the program could be to others decides to market it after leaving the first employer and does not feel that this employer is owed anything. Is this an ethical act? Surely after having used the employer's facilities without direct permission, the developer owes the employer some share of any profits earned.

What is the difference between this situation and the one described previously? Does the answer depend on the fact that in the first instance the program was used only to improve personal productivity whereas in the second it was marketed for personal financial gain? If so, what is the critical difference?

Case 3 [43]

> The information security manager in a large company was also the access control administrator of a large electronic mail system operated for company business among its employees. The security manager routinely monitored the contents of electronic correspondence among employees. He discovered that a number of employees were using the system for personal purposes; the correspondence included love letters, disagreements between married partners, plans for homosexual relations, and a football betting pool. The security manager routinely informed the human resources department director and the corporate security officer about these communications and gave them printed listings of them. In some cases, managers punished employees on the basis of the contents of the electronic mail messages. Employees objected to the monitoring of their electronic mail, claiming that they had the same right of privacy as they had using the company's telephone system or internal paper interoffice mail system.

Again this scenario was presented to a panel who were asked the following question, in addition to the first and last questions mentioned previously: Were the information security manager's, the employees', and the top management's actions unethical or not unethical?

Six ethical situations were identified: (1) the information security manager monitoring the electronic mail of employees; (2) informing the management of abuse; (3) not asking for rules on the use of personal e-mail from management; (4) employees using e-mail for personal communication; (5) top management for not setting up company rules for e-mail use and informing employees; and (6) for punishing some of the employees on the basis of the contents of the collected e-mail. A number of questions must be clarified before these situations can be evaluated, including the nature of e-mail, the prerogatives of management, and the rights of employees. Does e-mail within a company enjoy the same protection that a private telephone conversation does? Because an employer provides the e-mail system, interoffice mail, and interoffice telephone service, does management have the right to examine all such communications, without prior warnings? Do employees surrender their rights as citizens during the eight hours per day they are at work? Worker rights are under assault, as companies employ a variety of tests under the mantle of management exercising its legitimate responsibilities. These include drug tests, psychological tests, and even genetic tests as well as surprise searches. Given this environment, it will be difficult for employees to claim privacy for their communications whether by telephone, mail, or e-mail.

The panel's responses to these situations are somewhat mixed. For situation (1), a bare majority (14 to 11) found the monitoring itself unethical, but by a 22 to 2 margin, they found the reporting of the actual messages to management (2) unethical. For situation (3), the use by the employees of the e-mail system for private messages, 10 considered it unethical and 11 thought it was not unethical. For (4), 4 members thought there was no ethics issue, 10 agreed that the information security manager's behavior in not asking for rules of use for the e-mail system was unethical, and 11 disagreed. But top management was almost unanimously condemned for its behavior: 20 to 2 for failing to set rules and 23 to 0 for using the messages to punish employees. The root of all the problems seems to be the lack of a clearly stated and well-publicized policy. The lack of such a policy created a moral vacuum, in which management, both junior and senior, acted irresponsibly and unethically, while employees treated the system as a common resource, similar to the telephone, a rather mild misuse of a company-supported resource. To be sure, in the context of traditional management-employee relations in the US, the actions taken by management would not seem unusual or particularly subject to criticism, but they are wrong and are indicative of a complete lack of respect for workers as people with feelings and rights.

Case 4[44]

> A large state university serves as a network "hub" for the state's high schools. The university itself is networked with every faculty member, staff member, and student having a network computer on his or her desk. The university also is connected to the Internet. A student electronically scans pictures of men and women in various sexual poses.

Presumably one of the issues raised is that of free speech and its limitations when the content of that speech may be legally obscene. A complicating factor is the legal position of a state university with respect to the behavior of its students because the operation of the university is supported by state funds. There is also the responsibility of the university to articulate clearly a use policy that includes the downloading and public display of sexually explicit images. Such a policy must also provide for counseling and education programs. Whatever else is involved in a discussion of rights or obligations, it should start from the acknowledgment that the law is the ultimate authority, that it provides a set of limits with effective enforcement procedures, and that to ignore its existence is futile. As one of the participants in the February 1993 forum, which furnished the material for the discussion of this case, lawyer Allan Adler notes that "The university needs to consider how its policies are consistent with the law, because a state university exists in a jurisdiction that probably has indecency and obscenity laws . . . We do not voluntarily submit ourselves to the law. It is the reality in which we live."[45]

What if anything should be done to the student? If the university does not have in place a policy for acceptable use, it is in no position either to define offenses on the fly or to mete out punishment if the student is found responsible for violating this newly defined one. What about First Amendment rights? Most universities regulate free speech and indeed it seems unarguably right within the classroom or the office but there are some open questions about electronic networks.[46] Furthermore, a well-publicized use policy that conforms with the university's role as a defender of free and open inquiry could be seen as a justification for the expenditure of public funds for electronic discussion forums. The moderator of this discussion, law professor Henry Perritt, summed up the discussion as follows: "panel members generally agreed on the importance of establishing rules under which electronic forums operate. Rules need not be the same from forum to forum, as Perry [George Perry, vice president and general counsel for the Prodigy Services Company] pointed out, but they need to be explicit and give important consideration to the views of stakeholders-operators and users . . . the disagreements were over the extent (if any) to which other mechanisms were needed to enforce those rules."[47]

Case 5[48]

> While dropping a memo on your boss's desk, you happen to notice her computer password listed on a stray Post-it note. You know that layoffs are scheduled and you might use the password to search her private files for information on who's going to get the axe. But you were raised to respect the privacy of others. What do you do now?

This situation seems very straightforward—do nothing or even tell your boss that she should be more careful about concealing her password. It may be interesting, however, to spell out in some detail the possible justifications for three different options.[49]

    (a) You think about it, then decide you've got no problem dipping into your own file. It's not really an invasion of privacy if the information concerns you—and your future's at stake.

    (b) You've always been taught that snooping is wrong, and now it's time to put that precept into action. You decide to tell your boss that the password is out, and that she would be wise to change it.

    (c) This is a tough one. You stand to gain, sure, but so do your co-workers. Do you have the right to deny them that information? Is it fair to think only of your own dilemma? You decide to snoop on your own behalf—and theirs.

The three choices, simply put, are protect yourself by accessing the system without authorization, be honest and report a compromised password, or help your fellow workers and yourself. A brief examination of the ACM Code of Ethics reveals the following relevant imperatives:

    1.3 Be honest and trustworthy
    1.7 Respect the privacy of others
    2.8 Access computing and communications resources only when authorized to do so.

On the basis of these, option (b) must be selected. Appeals to class solidarity are stirring and perhaps appropriate in undemocratic societies, but in a democratic society they do not justify inappropriate, and possibly illegal, behavior. Acting only in your self interest is surely suspect and the attempted justification doesn't work. Information about a person does not necessarily belong to that person unless you subscribe to the hacker's rallying cry that all information is or should be open.

Case 6 [50]

A computer company is writing the first stage of a more efficient accounting system that will be used by the government. This system will save the taxpayer a considerable amount of money every year. A computer professional who is asked to design the accounting system, assigns different parts of the system to her staff. One person is responsible for developing the reports; another is responsible for the internal processing; and a third for the user interface. The manager is shown the system and agrees that it can do everything in the requirements. The system is installed, but the staff finds the interface so difficult to use that their complaints are heard by upper-level management. Because of these complaints, upper-level management will not invest any more money in the development of the new accounting system and they go back to their original, more expensive system.

What is the issue raised in this case? A quality product, contracted for with public funds has not been produced, and "the failure . . . becomes a clear violation of ethical behavior." In support of this position, consider the following appropriate imperatives from the ACM Code:

2.1 Strive to achieve the highest quality, effectiveness and dignity in both the process and products of professional work.

3.4 Ensure that users and those who will be affected by a system have their needs articulated during the assessment and design of requirements. later the system must be validated to meet requirements.

2.4 Accept and provide appropriate professional review.

It appears from the description that the entire process lacked basic consultation and professional review procedures and hence failure was inevitable. Thus the computer company is clearly culpable of violating professional standards as are the government managers. This is not a matter of management's prerogatives in treating its employees as it wishes; it is a failure to recognize that an omission of an important and necessary part of the development and implementation process has seriously compromised the project and ultimately caused its failure. Professional and ethical standards have been violated.

Other Guidelines to Appropriate Behavior

The codes and standards of professional societies are binding only on their members. In some environments, such as the Internet, long-time users have developed behavioral norms that users, old and new alike, are expected to follow. The term netiquette is commonly used to describe the Internet's acceptable etiquette. Violations are usually met with rapid and typically unsympathetic responses, as newcomers (or newbies) are severely chastised for their "stupid" mistakes. However, various organizations concerned with both the rights and the responsibilities of Internet users and with an eye to the future, have formulated policies to create equitable online environments. Clearly these are not binding on anyone because they are intended to apply to the diverse Internet community, but since such policies are usually formulated by groups of committed users, they do represent operating norms reflecting years of experience. They generally differ in the emphasis placed on particular activities and perceived rights.

EDUCOM's Bill of Rights and Responsibilities for Electronic Learners

"EDUCOM, founded in 1964, is a nonprofit consortium of higher education institutions which facilitates the introduction, use, access to, and management of information resources in teaching, learning, scholarship, and research."[51] Given this statement of purpose, it is not surprising that EDUCOM proposed this "Bill of Rights" to articulate in some detail what users can expect and what is to be expected of them while using the Internet for educational purposes. The Bill has four major divisions or articles: Individual Rights, Individual Responsibilities, Rights of Educational Institutions, and Institutional Responsibilities. To get a flavor of this document, samples of the sections of each division follow:[52]

Article I: Individual Rights
- **Section 1.** A citizen's access to computing and information resources shall not be denied or removed without just cause.
- **Section 4.** The constitutional concept of freedom of speech applies to citizens of electronic communities.
- **Section 5.** All citizens of the electronic community of learners have ownership rights over their own intellectual works.

Article 2: Individual Responsibilities
- **Section 1.** It shall be each citizen's personal responsibility to actively pursue needed resources: to recognize when information is needed, and to be able to find, evaluate, and effectively use information.
- **Section 2.** It shall be each citizen's personal responsibility to recognize (attribute) and honor the intellectual property of others.

Article 3: Rights of Educational Institutions
- **Section 1.** The access of an educational institutions to computing and information resources shall not be denied or removed without just cause.
- **Section 3.** Each educational institution has the authority to allocate resources in accordance with its unique institutional mission.

Article 4: Institutional Responsibilities
- **Section 3.** The institution shall treat electronically stored information as confidential. The institution shall treat all personal files as confidential, examining or disclosing the contents only when authorized by the owner of the information, approved by the appropriate institutional official, or required by local, state or federal law.
- **Section 4.** Institutions in the electronic community of learners shall train and support faculty, staff, and students to effectively use information technology. Training includes skills to use the resources, to be aware of the existence of data repositories and techniques for using them, and to understand the ethical and legal uses of the resources.

This document is interesting and important in that it is intended to apply to both users and the institutions that supply them with services. The access to information is a two-way process, and the associated rights and responsibilities should reflect this reality. Of course, the Bill is purely voluntary and no one is bound by it; however, its existence establishes certain expectations about what are reasonable rights and under what conditions such rights are to be exercised.

Ten Commandments of Computer Ethics

Since ten is such a congenial number, it is not surprising that a fairly well-known code for promoting ethical behavior should be cast as ten injunctions, or rather in keeping with a Judeo-Christian perspective, ten commandments. The Computer Ethics Institute, located in Washington, D.C., proposed the following pithy commandments in 1992:[53]

1. Thou shalt not use a computer to harm other people.
2. Thou shalt not interfere with other people's computer work.
3. Thou shalt not snoop around in other people's computer files.
4. Thou shalt not use a computer to steal.
5. Thou shalt not use a computer to bear false witness.
6. Thou shalt not copy or use proprietary software for which you have not paid (or been given authority to do so).
7. Thou shalt not use other people's computer resources without authorization or proper compensation (includes using computers or telephones for personal business, or printing nonacademic materials with university-owned printers).
8. Thou shalt not appropriate other people's intellectual output.
9. Thou shalt think about the social consequences of the program you are writing or the system you are designing.
10. Thou shalt always use a computer in ways that insure consideration and respect for your fellow humans.

Allowing for the failure to be consistent in the use of the Biblical thou, this code does express moral principles that have been extended to the computer world. Its limitation is that it has very little to say about the Internet and its host of special concerns.

FINAL COMMENTS

> Silence is the language of complicity. (Anonymous)

Hacker Ethics

Hackers were discussed in Chapter 8 with respect to their violations of computer system security and their strong belief in their inalienable right to access information anywhere and any time. In his book, *Hackers,* Steven Levy outlined what he called the "hacker ethic," an approach to computers and information at odds, apparently, with much of the foregoing discussion on ethics. Consider the following statement of this "hacker ethic" and some of the additional features:[54]

> *The Hacker Ethic.* Access to computers—and anything which might teach you something about the way the world works—should be unlimited and total. Always yield to the Hands-On-Imperative!
>
> *Implications:*
> - All information should be free.
> - Mistrust authority—promote decentralization.
> - Hackers should be judged by their hacking, not bogus criteria such as degrees, age, race, or position.
> - You can create art and beauty on a computer.
> - Computers can change your life for the better.

Adherents of the hacker ethic increasingly have come into conflict with the law and most of the other people associated with computers. Abrogating to themselves the right to enter systems at will and to freely distribute information discovered there, places them beyond the pale. As an embattled minority, possessing advanced computer skills, their self-righteousness borders on the hysterical at times. Their facile dismissal of privacy rights and property rights has obviously not won them many friends. Many hackers do not recognize software ownership and believe all software should be available freely. The hacker ethic seems to constitute an anti-ethic to most established ethical codes, and hackers themselves are usually viewed as anarchists, if not outlaws. In their concern with the individual against the establishment, hackers do strike a responsive cord among many who feel isolated and occasionally oppressed by the power of large institutions.

The distinguished computer scientist Dorothy Denning has written at length about hackers and has characterized their motives and activities in ways that differ substantially from the typical media portrayals. For example, in reporting on the initial findings of a study on hackers, Denning suggests that[55]

> hackers are learners and explorers who want to help rather than cause damage, and who often have very high standards of behavior. My findings also suggest that the discourse surrounding hacking belongs at the very least to the gray areas between larger conflicts that we are experiencing at every level of society and business in an information age where many are not computer literate. These conflicts are between the idea that information cannot be owned and the idea that it can, and between law enforcement and the First and Fourth Amendments.

She claims that all the hackers she encountered "said that malicious hacking was morally wrong . . . , and that they themselves are concerned about causing accidental damage." Furthermore, although they believe that information should be shared, it is not personal information that they have in mind, but rather corporate and government information. Some five years later, after more interviews, especially with law enforcement officials, Denning's views altered somewhat.[56] Hackers cause more disruptions than they are willing to acknowledge, even if you accept their protestations of nonmalicious intent. By providing detailed knowledge about how to crack systems, they encourage novices to engage in activities with little understanding of the impact of their actions. She is far less inclined to take their views at face value, especially that victims are responsible for being victimized and no longer recommends working with hackers to find solutions to the hacker problem.

Computer Scientists and Society

The most sophisticated and well-meaning of ethical codes will have very little influence on individual behavior if society at large is unsympathetic, nonsupportive, or actually hostile. In the midst of large bureaucracies, individual responsibility can sometimes fade and disappear. History is rich with examples of individuals either standing up for their principles at great risk, or immersing themselves in the whole and abrogating any sense of personal responsibility. Large computer systems, in their regular use, provide a bureaucratic excuse that can relieve the individual of any reason to accept blame or to provide explanations. Responsibility is diffused and individuals become mere cogs in a great machine. This response is precisely that which Adolf Eichmann's defense argued in his 1961 trial in Jerusalem. Eichmann's responsibility was to ensure that the trains carrying victims to the extermination camps during World War II ran efficiently in the context of the larger transportation system. What happened to the "passengers" was not his concern. Hannah Arendt, the esteemed social critic has noted: "As for the base motives, he was perfectly sure that he was not what he called an *innerer Schweinehund,* a dirty bastard, in the depths of his heart; and as for his conscience, he remembered perfectly well that he would have had a bad conscience only if he had not done what he had been ordered to do—to ship millions of men, women, and children to their deaths with great zeal and the most meticulous care."[57]

Langdon Winner, in commenting on the impact of large systems on traditional concepts of ethical behavior, writes: "What is interesting about the new ethical context offered by highly complex systems is that their very architecture constitutes vast webs of extenuating circumstances. Seemingly valid excuses can be manufactured wholesale for anyone situated in the network. Thus the very notion of moral agency begins to dissolve."[58] And this is the great fear that in large systems of all kinds, no one person either takes or receives responsibility. Unless ethics codes can combat this tendency they will become mere window dressing, if they are not so already. One example of personal integrity may stand as a beacon for computer professionals everywhere.

David Parnas, a distinguished software engineer with a long history of consultation to the US Department of Defense, was asked in 1985 to serve on a $1000/day advisory panel, on Computing in Support of Battle Management, a "Star Wars" project. Two months later he resigned publicly, although he had previously expressed support for any approach that would remove nuclear weapons as a deterrent factor. It is important to note that Parnas believes that people with a strong sense of social responsibility should work on military projects. A statement of his position on professional responsibility follows:[59]

Some have held that a professional is a 'team player' and should never blow the whistle on his colleagues and employer. I disagree. As the Challenger incident demonstrates, such action is sometimes necessary. One's obligations as a professional precede other obligations. One must not enter into contracts that conflict with one's professional obligations.

The basic question is how did work on this project violate Parnas's sense of his professional obligations. Is there a general principle in force that will be helpful to others in similar circumstances or is this an instance of idiosyncratic behavior? Again Parnas's own words are necessary and instructive: [60]

> . . . I solicited comments from other scientists and found none that disagreed with my technical conclusions. Instead, they told me that the program should be continued, not because it would free us from the fear of nuclear weapons, but because the research money would advance the state of computer science! I disagree with that statement, but I also consider it irrelevant. Taking money allocated for developing a shield against nuclear missiles, while knowing that such a shield was impossible, seemed like fraud to me.
>
> When I observed that the SDIO [Strategic Defense Initiative Organization] was engaged in "damage control," rather than a serious consideration of my arguments, I felt that I should inform the public and its representatives of my own view. I want the public to understand that no trustworthy shield will result from the SDIO-sponsored work. I want them to understand that technology offers no magic that will eliminate the fear of nuclear weapons. I consider this part of my personal professional responsibility as a scientist and educator.

This statement conveys a strong sense of honesty, responsibility, and commitment, both personal and professional, especially given his past record of involvement in military research and development. Parnas's negative evaluation of the prospects of success of Star Wars has been challenged but for the present purposes, it is his strong action and public statement that are important.

The final words of this section will be given by Joseph Weizenbaum, viewed by some as the conscience of computer science and by others as just a cranky nuisance. Weizenbaum makes it clear that he is not arguing against technology itself, which can be used for good or ill, but rather for responsible, informed decision making:[61]

> Today it is virtually certain that every scientific and technical result will, if at all possible, be incorporated in military systems. In these circumstances, scientific and technical workers have a responsibility to inquire about the end uses of their work. They must attempt to know to what ends it will be put. Would they serve these ends directly? Would they personally steer missiles to their targets and watch people die?
>
> Many . . . scientists say that the systems on which they work can help take astronauts to the moon and bring them back as well as guarantee that missiles aimed at a city will actually hit it if fired. How then can they be held responsible for their work's consequences? . . . But the attitude, "If I don't do it, someone else will," a thinly disguised version of this disorder, cannot serve as a basis of moral behavior, or else every crime imaginable is so justifiable.

The Social Cost of Technology

We live in age of serious contradictions. Technological development is accelerating, and without doubt the benefits to society have been massive and persuasive. To list some of them is to stand in awe of human ingenuity; electrical power, airplanes, space exploration, television, communication networks, microelectronics, genetic engineering, and computers. Surely, the improvements in health, food supply, longevity, living standards, safety, working conditions, and so forth are real and largely attributable to discoveries in science and technology. This fact applies to the industrial and burgeoning post-industrial countries of the world. Many other countries, to a greater or lesser degree, are facing such basic issues of survival that the debate over the benefits and dangers of technology is largely irrelevant.

Most attempts to describe and analyze the impact of technology on society inevitably produce a list of putative good effects, a shorter list of obvious bad effects, and an assurance that we can ultimately control how the actual technology will be used. Perhaps the choice is ours, although in many cases, the reverse is true, but in certain areas control seems elusive at best. Nuclear power is an example, in both its peaceful and military contexts. Compared to the potential holocaust of nuclear war or serious power-plant accidents, all other issues fade into insignificance. The use of the technology of nuclear or thermonuclear weapons could result in the destruction of most of the planet. Up to fairly recently, control has rested on a delicate balance of mutual threats and assured destruction. With the dissolution of the Soviet Union, part of this threat has dissipated; unfortunately, as a byproduct there is some uncertainty that Russia, the Ukraine, and other former republics still exert effective control over the weapons in their possession. Thus the apparent lessening in tension is not a result of a reasoned decision to "bury the bombs."

Having created such weapons of mass destruction, humanity still lives under a shadow that affects every person's life, albeit a reduced one and one not particularly a matter of concern to most people. Here is an example of a technology that seems to control us. A study of the history of the atomic bomb reveals that many of the scientists involved in its original development assumed that they would be consulted about its uses. Such was not the case. Decision making was assumed by the executive branch and the military, surely an obvious step, and the bomb became an instrument of national policy. Although some of the scientific team had opposed its initial use at Hiroshima, preferring a demonstration blast to convince Japan to surrender, most were certainly opposed to a second explosion, at Nagasaki, believing that not enough time had been allotted to permit the full implications of the first blast to sink in. But as noted, it was not up to them; they had built the weapons and their job was over. It is a fact that technological innovators rarely continue to exercise authority over their invention or discovery, after it leaves the laboratory. If technology can be controlled for the benefit of society, we must therefore ask, controlled how and by whom?

Even the peaceful uses of nuclear energy have not met the initial optimistic expectations of very low-cost safe power. Plant costs have escalated, and the environmental protection movement has rallied public support to limit the growth of the nuclear industry. Anxiety about the safety of nuclear reactors for power generation has been translated, in North America, into a marked reduction of plant construction. In this regard events at Three Mile Island in the US and Chernobyl in the Ukraine have been decisive. The impact of aroused public opinion has been effective in this area and demonstrates the possibility of an aware public exercising its political power. Other technological concerns currently reaching public awareness include global warming, reproductive technologies, and genetic engineering. In each of these cases, growing political activity may result in the enactment of controls to protect health and safety or not, if the consequences seem remote and the costs of enforcement and affected economic activities are deemed too severe.

Meeting the Challenge

It is a formidable undertaking to evaluate the effect of technological change on social, political, and economic institutions. A study of the past is informative and necessary, but predictions of the future have not been particularly accurate, notwithstanding the emergence of a forecasting industry and powerful tools such as large computers and refined simulation techniques.

In a book on computers and culture, J. David Bolter makes the following forceful statement:[62]

> Until recently, however, our technical skills were so feeble in comparison with the natural forces of climate and chemistry that we could not seriously affect our environment for good or ill, except over the millenia. High technology promises to give us a new power over nature, both our own nature and that of our planet, so that the very future of civilization depends upon our intelligent use of high technology.

He further notes that the crucial element in high technology is the computer. Clearly, the attempt to locate the computer in the history of technology to survey its applications is to probe associated benefits and problems, and to assess the future impact is a worthwhile and in fact necessary exercise.

As with most technological innovations, the choice of when and how to proceed is not usually left up to the individual members of society. Governments and companies, both large and small, multinational and local, have the power and resources to make the important decisions. As ordinary citizens, we live in a world that for the most part is not of our making. Nevertheless, an informed and sufficiently aroused public can make a difference. In discussing the nature of a liberal democracy, the Canadian political scientist C. B. Macpherson analyzed the opinions of the American scholar, John Dewey as follows:[63]

> He has few illusions about the actual democratic system, or about the democratic quality of a society dominated by motives of individual and corporate gain. The root difficulty lay not in any defects in the machinery of government but in the fact that the democratic public was "still largely inchoate and unorganized," and unable to see what forces of economic and technological organizations it was up against. There was no tinkering with the political machinery: the prior problem was "that of discovering the means by which a scattered, mobile, and manifold public may so recognize itself as to define and express its interests." The public's present incompetence to do this was traced to its failure to understand the technological and scientific forces which had made it so helpless.

SUMMARY

Many of the decisions taken by computer professionals have serious social repercussions and affect the well-being of many individuals. The past few years have witnessed serious ethical dilemmas in reproductive biology, including in vitro fertilization and surrogate motherhood, and ethical breakdowns among major players in the financial markets, mainly associated with insider trading. All of these issues have awakened an interest in ethical behavior and have stimulated the academic field of applied ethics.

Three major approaches, with of course many subdivisions, have emerged. These are ethical relativism, utilitarianism, and the class of deontological theories. They all attempt to characterize ethical behavior for individuals but additional questions are raised when the behavior of doctors, lawyers, and other professionals is included. There is some debate about how a professional's responsibility to self, client, and society at large can be reconciled. Examples are given of how computer professional societies have entered the political arena to defend positions or to oppose proposals, that they feel do a disservice to their members as well as society at large.

Most professional organizations have adopted codes of ethics or standards of behavior to guide their members and to announce to the public the level of conduct that can be expected of their members. Such codes attempt to resolve the potential conflict between social and professional responsibility. Six case studies explore a variety of situations that may arise when engineers and information systems specialists encounter ethical problems. These may serve to illustrate the distance between theory and practice. Under some circumstances, it may be necessary for individuals to go public, however painful that may be, because institutions are unresponsive to genuine misdeeds.

Computer science departments have long been concerned that their students enter the workplace with adaptable skills that will serve them and their employers well both immediately and down the road. They are gradually becoming convinced that among such technical skills, there must be the ability to identify potentially problematic situations as well as the skills to deal with them appropriately.

That group of computer addicts, sometimes called hackers, seem to operate under a set of "principles" at considerable odds with those held by the vast majority of the information processing community. Computer scientists, in general, may be faced with difficult choices about the immediate and long-term implications of computers.

Especially troublesome are military applications; cautionary remarks have been addressed to computer scientists by Joseph Weizenbaum, a critic of the technological imperative and David Parnas, a vigorous proponent of professional responsibility.

NOTES

1. Myron Magnet. "The Decline & Fall of Business Ethics," *Fortune*, December 8, 1986, p. 65.
2. Felix Rohatyn. "The Blight on Wall Street," *The New York Review of Books*, March 12, 1987, p. 21.
3. Stephen Koepp, Harry Kelly, and Raji Samghabadi. "Having it All, Then Throwing it All Away," *Time*, May 25, 1987, p. 26.
4. Robert Taylor. "US May Boost New York Office Staff to Pursue Mounting Securities Fraud," *The Wall Street Journal*, January 19, 1988, p. 12.
5. The *Business Week/* Harris Poll, August 1986. *World Opinions Update*, September 1986, p. 108.
6. Jeanie Russell Kasindorf. "What to Make of Mike," *Fortune*, September 30, 1996, pp. 86–88, 90, 94, 96.

7. John Greenwald. "Jack in the Box," *Time*, October 3, 1994. Accessed from the Web page with URL: <http://pathfinder.com/@@cmfBwAQA1h49I53p/time/magazine/domestic/1994/941003/941003.business.html> on September 16, 1996.

8. Michael S. Serrill. "Billion Dollar Losers," *Time*, June 24, 1996. Accessed from the Web page with URL: <http://pathfinder.com/time/international/1996/960624/japan.html> on September 16, 1996. Subsequent reports have increased the size of the loss to $2.6 billion. See Norihiko Shirouzu. "Sumimoto Plans to Sue Copper Trader," *The Globe and Mail*, September 20, 1996, B 5. (Reprinted from *The Wall Street Journal*.)

9. Rick Weiss. "Tests' Availability Tangles Ethical and Genetic Codes," *The Washington Post*, May 26, 1996, p. A 1. Accessed from the Web page with URL: <http://wp2.washingtonpost.com/cgi-bin/displaySearch?WPlate+3629+%28ethics%29%3Aheadline> on September 16, 1996.

10. *Ibid.*

11. Albert Camus. *The Myth of Sisyphus*. (New York: Knopf, 1957), p. 65.

12. Deborah Johnson. *Computer Ethics*. (Englewood Cliffs, NJ: Prentice-Hall, 1985), p. 6.

13. Raziel Abelson. "History of Ethics," in Paul Edwards (ed.). *The Encyclopedia of Philosophy, Volume Three*. (New York: Macmillan, 1967), p. 95.

14. *Ibid.*

15. *Op. cit.,* Johnson. *Computer Ethics,* p. 17.

16. Sissela Bok. "Kant's Arguments in Support of the Maxim 'Do What Is Right Though the World Should Perish'," in David M. Rosenthal and Fadlou Shehadi (eds.). *Applied Ethics and Ethical Theory*. (Salt Lake City: University of Utah Press, 1988), pp. 191–193.

17. *Ibid.,* p. 210.

18. Stephen Unger. *Controlling Technology: Ethics and the Responsible Engineer*. (New York: Holt, Rinehart and Winston, Inc., 1982).

19. James H. Moor. "What Is Computer Ethics?" *Metaphilosophy*, **16** (4), October 1985, p. 266.

20. Rule 2.5 of the Association for Computing Machinery Code of Ethics and Professional Conduct. Available from the Web page with URL: <http://www.acm.org/constitution/bylaw17.txt>.

21. *Op. cit.,* Unger. *Controlling Technology,* pp. 32–55.

22. Mark S. Frankel. "Professional Codes: Why, How, and with What Impact?" *Journal of Business Ethics*, 8 (2&3), February-March 1989, pp. 110–111.

23. *Ibid.,* pp. 111–112.

24. C. Dianne Martin and David H. Martin. "Comparison of Ethics Codes of Computer Professionals," presented at an Ethics Symposium organized by the Special Interest group on Computers and Society of the Association of Computing Machinery, Washington, DC, September 1990. An earlier version appeared in *Social Science Computer Review*, **9** (1), 1990 and *Computers and Society*, **20** (2), June 1990, pp. 18–29. Note that the ACM Code of Ethics and Professional Conduct and the IEEE Code of Ethics used in this paper have been superseded by the ones in Figure 13.1 and Figure 13.2, respectively.

25. Samuel C. Florman. "A Skeptic Views Ethics in Engineering," *IEEE Spectrum*, August 1982, p. 57.

26. Sissela Bok. *Secrets: On the Ethics of Concealment and Revelation*. (New York: Pantheon Books, a Division of Random House, source; Vintage Books paperback), p. 211.

27. *Ibid.,* pp. 214–215.

28. "Whistleblower Protection: Reasons for Whistleblower Complainants' Dissatisfaction Need to Be Explored," US General Accounting Office, GGD-94-21, December 15, 1993. Accessed from the Web page with URL: <http://www.access.gpo.gov/cgi-bin/waisgate.cgi?WAISdocID=193859675+72+0+0&WAISaction=retrieve> on June 25, 1996.

29. "Whistleblower Protection: Continuing Impediments to Protection of Military Members," US General Accounting Office, GAO/NSIAD-95-23, February 1995. Accessed from the Web page with URL: <http://thorplus.lib.purdue.edu:8100/gpo/GPOAccess.cgi?gao/PDF/33476/3=0%20-33476%20/diskb/wais/data/gao/ns95023.txt;7=%00;> on September 16, 1996.

30. "ACM Statement on Privacy," Association for Computing Machinery, March 1991. Accessed from the Web page with URL: <http://www.acm.org/usacm/privacy.html> on September 14, 1996.

31. "Computer Society Professionals Oppose Internet Censorship," ACM Press Release, March 22, 1995. Accessed from the Web page with URL: <http://www.acm.org/usacm/EXON.HTML> on September 14, 1996.

32. Letter to Carlos J. Moorehead, Chairman, Subcommittee on Courts and Intellectual Property, House Judiciary Committee, ACM, February 15, 1996. Accessed from the Web page with URL: <http://www.acm.org/usacm/hr2441_statement.html> on September 14, 1996. Letter to Conrad Burns, Chairman, Subcommittee on Science, Technology and Space, Senate Commerce, Science and Transportation Committee, ACM and IEEE, April 2, 1996. Accessed from the Web page with URL: <http://www.acm.org/usacm/burns_letter.html> on September 14, 1996.

33. From an online collection. Copyright: Kevin Harris 1995.

34. *Guide to the Perplexed* is a three volume work completed in 1190 by the Jewish physician and philosopher, Maimonides, as an explanation of the philosophy and theology of Judaism.

35. Chuck Huff and C. Dianne Martin. "Computing Consequences: A Framework for Teaching Ethical Computing," *Communications of the ACM,* December 1995, pp. 75–84.

36. In some sense, this approach is both a generalization and an extension to ethical issues of the representation given in Figure 1.1, Chapter 1 of this book. The author was a member of the ImpactCS Steering Committee.

37. *Op. cit.,* Huff and Martin.

38. Jon M. Shepard, Michael G. Goldsby, and Virginia W. Gerde. "Teaching Business Ethics Through Literature," *The Online Journal of Ethics,* **1** (3), Article 1, 1995. Accessed from the Web page with URL: <http://condor.depaul.edu/ethics/gerde.html> on March 27, 1996.

39. *Ibid.*

40. Thanks to Mary Culnan, School of Business Administration, Georgetown University, Washington, DC, for the original version.

41. Eric Weiss. "A Self-Assessment Procedure Dealing with Ethics in Computing," *Communications of the ACM,* **25** (3), March 1982, pp. 185–191. The material was edited by Mr. Weiss from Donn Parker, *Ethical Conflicts in Computer Science and Technology.* (New York: AFIPS Press, 1981).

42. *Ibid.,* p. 191.

43. Eric Weiss. "The XXII Self-Assessment: The Ethics in Computing," *Communications of the ACM,* **33** (11), November 1990, pp. 119, 127–130. The material was edited from Donn R. Parker, Susan Swope, and Bruce N. Baker, "Ethical Conflicts in Information and Computer Science, Technology and Business," final report, August 1988, SRI International Project 2609.

44. *Rights and Responsibilities of Participants in Networked Communities,* Steering Committee on Rights and Responsibilities of Participants in Networked Communities, Computer Science and Telecommunications Board, National Research Council. (Washington, DC: National Academy Press, 1994). Available at the Web page with URL: <http://www.nap.edu/readingroom/books/right>. This report is based on workshops and a forum held between November 1992 and December 1993. This scenario is taken from Chapter 4, Free Speech.

45. *Ibid.*

46. The reader is reminded that the discussion in Chapter 8 on "Sexual Harassment and Electronic Networks," is particularly relevant here.

47. *Ibid.*

48. Rosa Harris-Adler. "Modern Daze: Right vs. Wrong in the '90s," *The Globe and Mail West,* May 1991, p. 33.

49. *Ibid.*

50. This case is Case 4: Quality in Professional Work Taken from Ronald E. Anderson, Deborah G. Johnson, Donald Gotterbarn, and Judith Perolle. "Using the New ACM Code of Ethics in Decision Making," *Communications of the ACM,* **36** (2), February 1993, p. 102.

51. EDUCOM Programs as presented in every issue of the EDUCOM *review.*

52. "Bill of Rights and Responsibilities for Electronic Learners," EDUCOM *review,* May/June 1993, pp. 24–27. Available at the Web page with URL: <http://www.luc.edu/infotech/sae/bill-of-rights.html>.

53. "Ten Commandments of Computer Ethics," The Computer Ethics Institute, Washington, DC. It appeared in *Computerworld,* June 7, 1993, p. 84. An annotated version was accessed from the Web page with URL: <http://spigot.princeton.edu/net/ethics.html> on August 30, 1996.

54. Stephen Levy. *Hackers: Heroes of the Computer Revolution.* (New York: Doubleday, a division of Bantam, Dell Publishing Group, Inc.). (Source: Dell paperback, 1985, pp. 39–49.)

55. Dorothy E. Denning. "Concerning Hackers Who Break into Computer Systems," *13th National Computer Security Conference,* Washington, DC, October 1–4, 1990. Accessed from the Web page with URL: <http://www-swiss.ai.mit.edu/6095/articles/denning_defense_hackers.txt> on September 14, 1996.

56. Dorothy E. Denning. "Postscript to 'Concerning Hackers Who Break into Computer Systems'." Accessed from the Web page with URL: <http://guru.cosc.georgetown.edu/~denning/hackers/Hackers-Postscript.tx> on September 25, 1996.

57. Hannah Arendt. *Eichmann in Jerusalem: A Report on the Banality of Evil, Revised and Enlarged.* (New York: The Viking Press, 1964), p. 25.

58. Langdon Winner. *Autonomous Technology: Technics-out-of-control as a Theme in Political Thought.* (Cambridge, MA: The MIT Press, 1978), pp. 303–304.

59. David Lorge Parnas. "Professional Responsibility to Blow the Whistle on SDI," in M. David Ermann, Mary B. Williams, and Claudio Gutierrez (eds.). *Computers, Ethics & Society.* (New York: Oxford University Press, 1990), p. 360.

60. *Ibid.,* pp. 364–365.

61. Joseph Weizenbaum. "Facing Reality: Computer Scientists Aid War Efforts," *Technology Review,* January 1987, pp. 22–23.

62. J. David Bolter. *Turing's Man: Western Culture in the Computer Age.* (Chapel Hill, NC: The University of North Carolina Press, 1984), pp. 3–4.

63. C. B. Macpherson. *The Life and Times of Liberal Democracy.* (Oxford, England: Oxford University Press, 1980), p. 73.

ADDITIONAL READINGS

Introduction

Davis, Joel. *Mapping the Code: The Human Genome Project and the Choices of Modern Science.* (New York: John Wiley & Sons, 1990).

Ermann, M. David; Williams, Mary B., and Gutierrez, Claudio. Computers (eds.). *Ethics & Society.* (New York: Oxford University Press, 1990).

Johnson, Deborah G. and Nissenbaum (eds.). *Computers, Ethics & Social Values.* (Englewood Cliffs, NJ: Prentice Hall, 1995).

Teitelman, Robert. *Gene Dreams: Wall Street, Academia, and the Rise of Biotechnology.* (New York: BasicBooks, 1989).

Ethics

Dejoie, Roy; Fowler, George; and Paradice, David (eds.). *Ethical Issues in Information Systems.* (Boston, MA: Boyd & Fraser Publishing Company, 1991).

Edwards, Paul (ed.). *The Encyclopedia of Philosophy, Vol. Three.* (New York: Macmillan, 1967), pp. 69–134.

Fitzgerald, Karen. "Whistle-Blowing: Not Always a Losing Game," *IEEE Spectrum,* December 1990, pp. 49–52.

Iannone, A. Pablo. (ed.). *Contemporary Moral Controversies in Technology.* (New York: Oxford University Press, 1987).

Rosenthal, David M. and Shehadi, Fadlou (eds.). *Applied Ethics and Ethical Theory.* (Salt Lake City: University of Utah Press, 1988).

Williams, Oliver F., Reilly, Frank K., and Houck, John W. (eds.). *Ethics and the Investment Industry.* (Savage, MD: Rowman & Littlefield, 1989).

Professionalism

Andrews, Kenneth R. (ed.). *Ethics in Practice: Managing the Moral Corporation.* (Boston, MA: Harvard Business School Press, 1989).

Benson, George C. S. "Codes of Ethics," *Journal of Business Ethics,* 8 (5), May 1989, pp. 305–319.

Hoffman, W. Michael and Moore, Jennifer Mills (eds.). *Business Ethics: Readings and Cases in Corporate Morality, Second Edition.* (New York: McGraw-Hill, 1990).

Johnson, Deborah G. and Snapper, John W. (eds.). *Ethical Issues in the Use of Computers.* (Belmont, CA: Wadsworth Publishing, 1985).

Lewis, Philip V. "Ethical Principles for Decision Makers: A Longitudinal Survey," *Journal of Business Ethics,* 8 (4), April 1989, pp. 271–278.

Neumann, Peter G. "Certifying Professionals," *Communications of the ACM,* **34** (2), February 1991, p. 130.

On Being a Scientist: Responsible Conduct in Research. Committee on Science, Engineering, and Public Policy, National Academy of Sciences, National Academy of Engineering, Institute of Medicine (Washington, DC: National Academy Press, 1995). Available from the National Academy of Sciences Web site with URL: <http://www.nas.edu>.

Pedagogy and Ethics

"An Information Bill of Rights," The Aspen Institute, Communications and Society Program, July 1995. Accessed from the Web page with URL: <http://www.aspeninst.org/dir./current/Infobill.html> on September 24, 1996.

Dahlbom, Bo and Mathiassen, Lars. *Computers in Context: The Philosophy and Practice of Systems Design.* (Cambridge, MA: NCC Blackwell, 1993).

"Ethics and Computer Use," special section of the *Communications of the ACM*, 38 (12), December 1995.

Loch, Karen D. and Conger, Sue. "Evaluating Ethical Decision Making and Computer Use," *Communications of the ACM*, 39 (7), July 1996, pp. 74–83.

Rinaldi, Arlene H. "The Net User Guidelines and Netiquette," Academic/Institutional Support Services, Florida Atlantic University, July 1994. Accessed from the Web page with URL: <http://www.toyama-u.ac.jp/tya/library/netiquee.html> on September 25, 1996.

Riser, Robert and Gotterbarn, Don. "Ethics Activities in Computer Science Courses," *ACM Computers and Society*, 26 (3), September 1996, pp. 13–17.

Wood-Harper, A. T., Corder, Steve, Wood, J.R.G. "How We Profess: The Ethical Systems Analyst," *Communications of the ACM*, 39 (3), March 1996, pp. 69–77.

Final Remarks

DeMarco, Joseph P. and Fox, Richard M. (eds.). *New Directions in Ethics: The Challenge of Applied Ethics*. (New York: Routledge & Kegan Paul, 1986).

Forester, Tom and Morrison, Perry. *Computer Ethics: Cautionary Tales and Ethical Dilemmas*. (Cambridge, MA: MIT Press, 1990).

Lackey, Douglas P.(ed.). *Ethics and Strategic Defense: American Philosophers Debate Star Wars and the Future of Nuclear Deterrence*. (Belmont, CA: Wadsworth Publishing, 1989).

─────Appendix─────

MAGAZINES, JOURNALS, ASSOCIATIONS, AND WEB SITES

POPULAR MAGAZINES

Computer

- *Byte.* For computer professionals and home users. Reviews of new products and occasional articles on social issues. (http://www.byte.com/)
- *Computerworld.* Tabloid format. For business users. Reviews of major trends, government policies, and frequent discussion of many social issues, including privacy and free speech. (http://www.computerworld.com/)
- *Datamation.* Sold primarily by subscription. For business professionals. Wide coverage of the industry. Primarily devoted to technical issues with occasional articles on social issues. Renowned for its annual list of the world's top 100 information processing companies. (http://www.datamation.com/)
- *Information Week.* (http://techweb.cmp.com/iwk/current/)
- *Internet World.* (http://www.internetworld.com/) (http://home.zdnet.com/home/filters/main.html)
- ZD group of magazines: *PC Week, PC Computing, MacWeek, MacUser, InternetUser, Family Computing, PC.* (http://home.zdnet.com/home/filters/main.html)

Technology

- *Discover.* A Time Warner Publication with a wide coverage of scientific and technological developments, including a section on computers. (http://pathfinder.com/@@CjLaQgUAUysYoTSo/welcome/?navbar)

- *New Scientist.* A British publication with wide coverage of scientific and technological innovations. Somewhat oriented to British issues.
- *Scientific American.* The most prestigious popular science magazine in the US. Articles written by prominent scientists, with excellent graphics. Computers and related technologies are treated infrequently but very well. (http://www.sciam.com/)
- *Technology Review.* Published by the Massachusetts Institute of Technology. Well-written and interesting articles on a wide variety of issues. High level of social concern. (http://anxiety-closet.mit.edu:8001/activities/techreview/tr.html)
- *Wired.* The most trendy and glitzy magazine appealing to Internet users. Interviews and articles on all the major technical and social issues related to the Internet and the Web. (http://www.hotwired.com/wired/)

Business

- *Business Week.* Regular, extensive coverage of technological developments and associated business, labor, and economic issues. Frequent in-depth studies of the Internet, the Web, IBM, and AT&T. (http://www.businessweek.com/)
- *Fortune.* Well known for the *Fortune* 500 list of leading US companies. Excellent coverage of technology. Good records of spotting trends and anticipating problems. (http://pathfinder.com/@@CjLaQgUAUysYoTSo/welcome/?navbar)
- *Wall Street Journal.* Primarily business-oriented but with frequent in-depth articles on computers and applications. (http://www.wsj.com/)

General

- *The Economist.* British magazine similar to *Time* and *Newsweek,* but much deeper analyses and regular special surveys of finance, telecommunications, and computers. (http://www.economist.com/)
- *Time.* Regular, limited coverage of developments in computers. (http://pathfinder. com/@@CjLaQgUAUysYoTSo/welcome/?navbar)
- *The New York Times.* Excellent treatment of information users in the Monday "The Information Industries" section. Extensive coverage of business and social problems. Requires Acrobat reader to view a daily eight-page online version. (http://nytimesfax. com:80/cgi-bin/tmp/timesfax)
- Times Newspapers: *The Times, The Sunday Times, The Times Higher Education Supplement* (United Kingdom). (http://www.the-times.co.uk/news/pages/home.html? 1159109)
- *USA Today.* Very popular, brief treatment of many issues. (http://www.usatoday. com/)
- *The Washington Post.* Similar to *The New York Times* in the depth of its treatment on many business, government, and social issues. (http://www.washingtonpost.com/)

Technical Journals

- *Computer.* A publication of the Institute of Electrical and Electronics Engineers. Covers technical issues in papers written by academics. Special issues on such topics as security and CAD/CAM.
- *Communications of the ACM.* A publication of the Association of Computing Machinery (ACM). Includes state-of-the-art articles by leading figures in computer science. In-depth analysis of many social issues. (http://www.acm.org/cacam/)
- *Science.* A publication of the American Association for the Advancement of Science. Most of the articles deal with advanced research topics in biology, chemistry, physics, and so forth. Periodic serious coverage of technological innovations and their social impact. (http://www.sciencemag.org/)
- *IEEE Spectrum.* Important technical journal that treats serious topics at a nonspecialist level. Special issues on social impact of technology. (http://www.spectrum. ieee.org/)
- *Harvard Business Review.* Coverage of important issues associated with computers in business. Regular treatment of management information systems, impact on labor, and Japanese management techniques. (http://www.hbsp.harvard.edu/groups/hbr/)
- *Sloan Management Review.* Similar to the *Harvard Business Review* but with the MIT perspective. (http://web.mit.edu/smr-online/)
- *Privacy Journal.* Not really a journal, in spite of its title, but rather a newsletter with up-to-date information about privacy issues, legislation, and trends. (5101719 @mcimail.com, P.O. Box 28577, Providence, R.I. 02908)

PROFESSIONAL SOCIETIES AND ORGANIZATIONS

- *Professional Societies*

  ACM Special Interest Group on Computers and Society (SIGCAS) (http://www. acm.org/)

  IEEE Society on Social Implications of Technology (SSIT) (http://www.ieee.org/)

- *Privacy and Free Speech Organizations*

  ACLU Freedom Network (http://www.aclu.org/)

  American Communication Assoc. (http://cavern.uark.edu/comminfo/www/ACA.html) Anonymous Surfing (the Anonymizer) (http://www.anonymizer.com/)

  CCSR (Centre for Computing and Social Responsibility) (http://www.cms.dmu.ac. uk/CCSR/)

  The Center for Democracy and Technology (http://www.cdt.org/)

  Citizen's Guide (to Internet Resources) (http://asa.ugl.lib.umich.edu/chdocs/rights/ Citizen.html)

Citizens Internet Empowerment Coalition (http://www.cdt.org/ciec/index.html)

Computer Professionals for Social Responsibility (CPSR) (http://www.cpsr.org/dox/home.html)

Consumer Project on Technology (http://www.essential.org/cpt/)

CyberWatch (http://www.wiesenthal.com/watch/index.html)

EFF—The Electronic Frontier Foundation (http://www.essential.org/cpt/)

Electronic Frontier Canada (http://insight.mcmaster.ca:80/org/efc/)

Electronic Privacy Information Center Home Page (http://epic.org/)

Encryption Policy Resource Page (http://www.crypto.com/)

GILC—Global Internet Liberty Campaign (http://www.privacy.org/gilc/)

Global Internet Liberty Campaign (http://www.privacy.org/gilc/ GILC)

Internet Privacy Coalition (http://www.privacy.org/ipc/)

Plague of Freedom (Declan McCullagh) (http://www.eff.org/~declan/global/)

Privacy International Home Page (http://www.privacy.org/pi/)

Reporters Committee for Freedom of the Press (http://www.rcfp.org/rcfp/)

Sex, Censorship, and the Internet (Carl Kadie's HP) (http://www.eff.org?CAF/cafuiuc.html)

Voters Telecommunications Watch (http://www.vtw.org/)

- *Family Values*

  Christian Coalition Interactive (http://www.cc.org/)

  The Family Research Council (http://www.frc.org/)

- *Intellectual Property*

  Copyright Resources Online (http://www.library.yale.edu/%7Eokerson/copyproj.html)

- *Online Access*

  Alliance for Public Technology (http://apt.org/apt/)

  Benton Foundation Projects (http://www.benton.org/)

  The FARNET WWW Server (http://www.farnet.org/)

- *US Government*

  Bureau of Labor Statistics (http://stats.bls.gov/blshome.html)

  GAO Home Page (http://www.gao.gov/)

  Office of Technology Assessment Archives (http://www.ota.nap.edu/)

  Welcome to the White House (http://www.whitehouse.gov/WH/Welcome.html)

- *NII/Information Highway*

  Industry Canada—Information Highway (http://info.ic.gc.ca/info-highway/ih.html)

  Information Infrastructure Task Force (http://www.iitf.nist.gov/)

International Telecommunication Union (http://www.itu.ch/index.html)

National Telicommunications and Information Administration (http://www.ntia.doc.gov/)

Telecom Information Resources on Internet (http://www.spp.umich.edu/telecom/telecom-info.htm)

US National Information Infrastructure Virtual Library (http://nii.nist.gov/nii.html)

- *Women*

  The National Organization for Women (NOW) (http://now.org/now/home.html)

  TAP: The Ada Project (http://www.cs.yale.edu/HTML/YALE/CS/HyPlans/tap/)

  WITI Campus Women in Technology International (http://www.witi.com/)

  Women and Computers (http://www.sacbee.com/news/projects/women/index.html)

- *Labor*

  AFL-CIO Home Page (http://www.aflcio.org/)

  International Labour Organization (http://www.ilo.org/)

  UAW Home Page (http://www.UAW.Org/)

- *Department of Computer Science, University of British Columbia*

  CPSC 430 Computers and Society Course Home Page (http://www.ugrad.cs.ubc.ca/spider/z4e192/cs430/cs430.html)

INDEX

INDEX